Organized Crime

To Ulrich Eisenberg

SAGE was founded in 1965 by Sara Miller McCune to support
the dissemination of usable knowledge by publishing innovative
and high-quality research and teaching content. Today, we
publish more than 850 journals, including those of more than
300 learned societies, more than 800 new books per year, and
a growing range of library products including archives, data,
case studies, reports, and video. SAGE remains majority-owned
by our founder, and after Sara's lifetime will become owned by
a charitable trust that secures our continued independence.

Los Angeles | London | New Delhi | Singapore | Washington DC

Organized Crime

Analyzing Illegal Activities, Criminal Structures, and Extra-legal Governance

Klaus von Lampe

*John Jay College of Criminal Justice,
City University of New York*

Los Angeles | London | New Delhi
Singapore | Washington DC

Los Angeles | London | New Delhi
Singapore | Washington DC

FOR INFORMATION:

SAGE Publications, Inc.
2455 Teller Road
Thousand Oaks, California 91320
E-mail: order@sagepub.com

SAGE Publications Ltd.
1 Oliver's Yard
55 City Road
London EC1Y 1SP
United Kingdom

SAGE Publications India Pvt. Ltd.
B 1/I 1 Mohan Cooperative Industrial Area
Mathura Road, New Delhi 110 044
India

SAGE Publications Asia-Pacific Pte. Ltd.
3 Church Street
#10-04 Samsung Hub
Singapore 049483

Acquisitions Editor: Jerry Westby
Editorial Assistant: Laura Kirkhuff
Production Editor: Libby Larson
Copy Editor: Karin Rathert
Typesetter: C&M Digitals (P) Ltd.
Proofreader: Dennis W. Webb
Cover Designer: Anupama Krishnan
Marketing Manager: Terra Schultz

Printed in the United States of America

Library of Congress Cataloging-in-Publication Data

Lampe, Klaus von, 1961-
Organized crime : analyzing illegal activities, criminal structures, and extra-legal governance / Klaus von Lampe.

Cover image: El Lissitzky, Proun 6, 1919/20, oil on canvas (original: Kunstmuseum Moritzburg, Halle/Saale, Germany)

pages cm
Includes bibliographical references and index.

ISBN 978-1-4522-0350-8 (pbk. : alk. paper)

1. Organized crime. I. Title.

HV6441.L36 2016
364.106—dc23   2015006464

This book is printed on acid-free paper.

15 16 17 18 19 10 9 8 7 6 5 4 3 2 1

Contents

Preface

This book provides a systematic overview of the processes and structures commonly labeled organized crime, drawing on the empirical and theoretical literature on the subject from a broad range of academic disciplines, including criminology, sociology, economics, and political science. The book is global in scope in that the discussion is not limited to any specific country or region in the world, although it incorporates insights and findings mainly from scholars based in North America, Europe, and Australia.

This book is not supposed to be just another text on organized crime. Conventional textbooks on organized crime are primarily descriptive. They are structured along the lines of particular criminal groups and areas of crime, and they incorporate theory primarily in terms of established criminological theories. Classifications tend to be based on superficial criteria, such as the ethnic make-up or the geography of criminal groups, while neglecting underlying similarities and differences. In so doing, these texts fail to take account of the increasing level of sophistication the study of organized crime has attained globally as a serious scientific, multidisciplinary endeavor in terms of conceptualization, theorizing, and empirical research.

In contrast to the existing textbook literature, this book adopts a more analytical approach by placing the main emphasis on underlying patterns and dynamics that transcend any specific historical manifestations of organized crime. It seeks to lay out a general conceptual and analytical framework that captures the multifaceted and dynamic nature of the organization of crime and criminals across different social, economic, and political contexts.

Throughout the book, notorious and less well-known cases are examined in detail to provide concrete empirical reference points for the discussion. No attempt is made to comprehensively and exhaustively describe all past or current organized crime phenomena. Empirical manifestations of organized crime are described in detail only selectively and only insofar as they represent prototypical or ideal-typical examples that serve to illustrate particular dimensions and categories. However, readers will find references to further academic literature that deals with aspects that are given only scant attention in this book.

The structure of the book is such that the complexities of the phenomena labeled organized crime are broken down into key dimensions and categories. The book follows a distinction of three basic dimensions: (a) illegal activities,

(b) patterns of interpersonal relations that are directly or indirectly support-ing these illegal activities, and (c) overarching illegal power structures that regulate and control illegal activities and the individuals and groups involved in these activities. Organized crime phenomena are examined along these lines, first in their own right and then in a broader societal and transnational context, particularly with a view to the relation between underworld and upper-world, a relation that may take on the form of confrontation, accommodation, or integration.

The Purpose of the Book

This book is intended as the core text for courses on organized crime and transnational crime on the undergraduate, graduate, and post-graduate levels. Beyond classroom use, this book is meant to serve as a reference and guide to the academic literature on organized crime for academics, intelligence analysts, law enforcement officials, policymakers, and the general public.

The starting point for this book is the assumption that organized crime is not something that lends itself easily to scientific scrutiny. It is not a coherent empirical phenomenon but first and foremost a construct, reflecting social reality as much as the emotions, prejudices, and ideologies of those involved in the construction process. Scholarly efforts have aimed at disentangling the web of imagery associ-ated with organized crime. They have contributed to a better understanding of the underlying phenomena and have shed light on some intricate links that justify placing these diverse phenomena in a broader theoretical context. While there is little overall consistency in the research conducted within this broad field, there are certain clusters of research that have contributed to a cumulative body of knowledge around certain themes, such as illegal enterprise, certain historical phenomena, such as the Sicilian and American Cosa Nostra, or certain method-ological approaches, such as criminal network analysis.

The book presents this research within a coherent framework to help readers achieve three goals:

- To understand the categorical differences and similarities between the various phenomena associated with the term organized crime in order to avoid comparing apples and oranges
- To understand the way these phenomena manifest themselves empirically in order to separate myth from reality
- To understand the various theoretical propositions that on different levels of abstraction and within different frames of reference explain key aspects of organized crime in order to gain a sense of what matters more and what matters less in the organization of crime and criminals

The ultimate goal of the book is to provide readers with an analytical toolkit that enables them to critically assess and to put into perspective any organized crime phenomena or any depictions thereof and to formulate meaningful ques-tions for further inquiry.

The Content of the Book

Any endeavor intended to contribute to a better understanding of organized crime is faced with two considerable challenges. The first challenge is to emancipate the audience from stereotypical and mythical imagery created and promoted in the media and—unfortunately—also in some of the academic literature. The second challenge is to overcome the confusion that stems in part from the diversity of conceptualizations in the public and scholarly debate on organized crime and in part from the diversity of the empirical phenomena that are associated with organized crime.

The book addresses these challenges with its emphasis on a comprehensive classificatory scheme and consistent terminology, which encompasses aspects that otherwise might be addressed only in an unsystematic, anecdotal way, only in passing or not at all. These issues include individually and in context the following:

- The modus operandi and logistics of criminal activities
- The individual offender characteristics
- The structure and dynamics of the organization of offenders
- The structure and dynamics of the organization of criminal milieus
- The interrelations between criminal activities and criminal structures and the broader social, cultural, political, and economic environment

The book is divided into 14 chapters grouped into four parts. Part I lays the foundation with an introduction (Chapter 1), an examination of the conceptual history and definition of organized crime (Chapter 2), and an overview of the history and the main currents of the scholarly study of organized crime (Chapter 3). Part II examines empirical manifestations of organized crime in terms of illegal activities, criminal structures, and extra-legal governance (Chapters 4–8). Chapter 4, against the backcloth of two case studies (cocaine trafficking and the trafficking in stolen motor vehicles), examines categorical differences between market-based, predatory, and illegal governance crimes and presents frameworks for the in-depth analysis of specific criminal endeavors. Chapter 5 gives an introduction to the analysis of criminal structures. Taking pedophile networks as an empirical point of reference, it discusses for what purposes and under what circumstances criminals establish and maintain ties to other criminals. Key points that are addressed include the differentiation of criminal structures by function (entrepreneurial, associational, and quasi-governmental structures) and by form (markets, networks, and hierarchies) and the role that trust and violence play in interactions between criminals. Chapter 6 continues the examination of fundamental questions about the organization of criminals, with a focus on illegal entrepreneurial structures. Starting with a case study of a cocaine distribution enterprise, the chapter discusses how and why structures that are geared toward obtaining material benefits vary and to what extent illegality imposes restraints on the organization of criminals. Chapter 7 deals with a central element of the popular imagery of organized crime, associations of criminals like the Italian mafia-type organizations. Case studies of the Sicilian Mafia, of the Chinese triads, the post-Soviet Thieves in Law, and as an example of outlaw motorcycle gangs, the Hell's Angels illustrate the various social, noneconomic functions that these structures perform for their members. Chapter 8 examines two essential forms of the concentration of power within the sphere of illegality that are often confused: illegal market monopolies and illegal monopolies of violence. The chapter discusses similarities and differences between legal and illegal markets with respect to the processes and consequences of monopolization. It also provides an overview of illegal governance structures that regulate and control illegal entrepreneurial activities in a territory or market. American Cosa Nostra families are presented as a prime example for elaborate quasi-governmental structures within the underworld. Part III places the various empirical manifestations of organized crime in a broader context. Chapter 9 explores the social embeddedness of criminals, criminal activities, and criminal structures with respect to two main questions, to what extent organized crime can be explained by the public demand for illegal goods and services, and to what extent organized crime is rooted in particular segments of society. Chapter 10 focuses on the relationship between organized crime and the legal economy with a view to criminal influence on individual businesses as well as on entire business sectors. Chapter 11 deals with the relationship between organized crime and the state. It presents historical examples of alliances as well as of violent confrontations between underworld and upperworld in the United States, Mexico, Colombia, Russia, and Italy. Chapter 12 investigates how crimes and criminals are organized on an international level and in cyberspace. Part IV of the book brings all the various aspects together that are discussed in the preceding chapters, first by sketching a "big picture" of organized crime (Chapter 13) and then by reviewing the various countermeasures that have been adopted to combat and prevent organized crime (Chapter 14).

It goes without saying that a subject as complex as that of organized crime cannot be exhaustively addressed in one book. Even the aspects that are covered in this book would lend themselves to more in-depth examination. Placing the main focus on the academic literature means that little use is made of the vast body of journalistic and official reports on organized crime. But even the coverage of the scholarly research and writing is far from complete. First of all, the book does not follow the study of organized crime in all of its ramifications. For example, with a wide audience in mind, the more sophisticated levels of criminal network analysis and the kind of abstract modeling of organized crime to be found on and off in economics journals have been consciously excluded from discussion. Second, there are practical and intellectual limits to the volume of literature that can be identified and meaningfully processed for presentation within one coherent framework. While it is true that not everything that has been published is worth citing, the author's own limitations are the main reason why some academic work does not find proper mention. In this sense, the book is no substitute for an independent exploration of the ever-growing body of literature on organized crime. The ambition behind the book is that it can serve as a key to the study of organized crime as a serious scientific endeavor.

Acknowledgments

With *Organized Crime: Analyzing Illegal Activities, Criminal Structures, and Extra-legal Governance*, I have tried to write the kind of book I would have liked to read when I started getting interested in the topic of organized crime more than 20 years ago. I am deeply indebted to a number of great scholars who have supported and encouraged me along the way and who have willingly shared their knowledge and wisdom, namely James O. Finckenauer, Henner Hess, Per Ole Johansen, Ulrich Eisenberg, Marcus Felson, Michael Levi, Alan Block, Dick Hobbs, James B. Jacobs and, last but not least, Petrus C. van Duyne. In the past two decades I have also been influenced by many of the organized crime scholars of my own generation, namely Peter Klerks, Edward Kleemans, Arthur Hartmann, Carlo Morselli, Letizia Paoli, Tom Vander Beken, Jeff McIllwain, Dina Siegel, and Federico Varese.

Most of the literature used for writing this book was accessed through the Lloyd Sealy Library at John Jay College of Criminal Justice in New York and through the Don M. Gottfredson Library at Rutgers University in Newark, New Jersey, with the notable help of Phyllis Schultze.

The work on this book began in 2010 after Patrick "Pat" Collins, then interim chair of the Department of Law, Police Science and Criminal Justice Administration at John Jay College, introduced me to SAGE's Jerry Westby, who would guide me through the publication process with a gentle yet firm hand.

The writing of the book manuscript extended from July 2011 until February 2015, and during this time I profited greatly from the support I have received throughout the years from my colleagues and from the administration at John Jay College. I would like to thank in particular Serguei Cheloukhine and Lior Gideon as well as Maria "Maki" Haberfeld, all of whom were central to my decision to relocate to the United States and to find a new academic home at John Jay College.

I also owe a great deal to the John Jay students in my organized crime, comparative criminal justice, international criminal justice, and criminology classes, in particular Magdalena Rysiejko, who helped me with an initial review of the literature on countermeasures against organized crime (Chapter 14), and Kathryn Kikendall, who reviewed the literature on the Chinese triads (Chapter 7).

Valuable feedback was received from James B. Jacobs, Kathryn Kikendall, and Marin Kurti, who read parts of the manuscript, and from Edward Kleemans and Carlo Morselli, who gave me insightful comments on the first complete draft of the book. I am also grateful for the advice received from the official reviewers of the prospectus and of various batches of draft chapters of this book. The following scholars have served as reviewers:

Dennis Anderson (St. Cloud State)

G.S. Bajpai (National Law Institute University, Bhopal, India)

Thomas Baker (University of Scranton)

Kevin Cannon (Southern Illinois University)

Joseph Carlson (University of Nebraska at Kearney)

William Cleveland (San Jose State University)

William Daddio (Georgetown University)

Patrick Dunworth (Central New Mexico Community College)

Lisa Eargle (Francis Marion University)

Rob Hornsby (University of Northumbria)

Richard Inscore (Charleston Southern University)

Joseph Jaska (Saginaw Valley State University)

S. Kris Kawucha (University of North Texas)

Andrea Lange (Washington College)

Robert Lombardo (Loyola University Chicago)

David MacDonald (Eastfield College)

Richard Mangan (Florida Atlantic University)

Paul Margo (Ball State University)

Abu Mboka (California State University at Stanislaus)

Mark Mills (Glenville State College)

Jerome Randall (University of Central Florida)

Paddy Rawlinson (London School of Economics & Political Science)

Tim Robicheaux (Penn State)

Gary Smith (University of Nebraska at Kearney)

Simon Sneddon (University of Northampton)

Federico Varese (Oxford University)

Gennaro Vito (University of Louisville)

Richard Wiebe (Fitchburg State University)

Robert Wright (Lewis University)

While the book primarily draws on the existing scholarly literature, I have also profited greatly from conversations I have had over the years with many experts from the ranks of the police, customs services, prosecutor's offices, and intelligence services in Europe and North America and also from the numerous conversations with "organized criminals" whom I have met under different circumstances and in different capacities, as political activist, attorney, and researcher. Florian Chaghomy and Manuel Weber navigated me through many encounters with members of the German underworld and discussed with me the organization of crime and criminals.

Marin Kurti deserves particular mention as the one who shouldered many of the burdens that have come with the research projects on the illegal cigarette trade that we have pursued parallel to me writing this book.

Finally, I owe immeasurable gratitude to my wife Claudia and my children Caroline and Richard, who had to share the precious little time we have had together with the project of writing this book.

Klaus von Lampe
New York City, March 2015

About the Author

Klaus von Lampe is an associate professor in the Department of Law, Police Science and Criminal Justice Administration at John Jay College of Criminal Justice in New York City. He teaches courses in the areas of criminology, comparative criminal justice, and international criminal justice. Prior to coming to John Jay College in 2008, he has directed the Organized Crime Research Project at Free University Berlin, Germany, and practiced law as an attorney with a specialization in representing victims of investment fraud. Dr. von Lampe is the author, co-author, and co-editor of numerous books, book chapters, and journal articles on crime, crime prevention, and corruption with a special focus on the illegal cigarette trade, illegal power structures, and transnational crime. He is editor-in-chief of the peer-reviewed journal *Trends in Organized Crime* (since 2007) and a past President (2012–2013) of the International Association for the Study of Organized Crime.

PART I

*Organized Crime as
a Construct and as
an Object of Study*

CHAPTER 1

Introduction—The Study of Organized Crime

The study of organized crime encompasses the examination of a broad range of phenomena. In a nutshell, researchers try to find out three things:

- How and why crimes such as, for example, drug trafficking or serial burglary are committed
- How and why criminals are connected and organized in networks, gangs, syndicates, cartels, and mafias
- How and why criminals acquire power and use this power to control other criminals and to gain influence over aspects of legitimate society, namely business and politics

This book discusses answers to these questions within a general conceptual framework that is not tied to any particular case, country, or historical period. The ambition is to provide readers with the analytical tools necessary to come to a sound assessment of phenomena irrespective of when or where they may manifest themselves. While the book is global in scope, most of the referenced literature has been published in English by European, North American, and Australian authors. Accordingly, the discussion is somewhat narrowed to the phenomena that these authors have examined, which unfortunately leaves some parts of the world not receiving the level of attention that they deserve.

PHENOMENA ASSOCIATED WITH ORGANIZED CRIME

The term *organized crime* is not used consistently. When people speak of organized crime they have different things in mind. And even when they think of the same phenomena, they may have different ideas about what it is that makes organized crime distinct: Is it the organization of crime, the organization of criminals, or the exercise of power by criminals?

The Organization of Crime

Much of what is commonly associated with the term *organized crime* has to do with the provision of illegal goods and services. Certain goods and services are prohibited (e.g., child pornography), so strictly regulated (e.g., drugs), or so highly taxed (e.g., cigarettes) that suppliers and consumers seek ways to circumvent the law. Arguably the drug trade is currently the main problem of this kind globally. There are few if any countries in the world today that are not in some way or other affected by the production, smuggling, and distribution of substances, such as cocaine, heroin, and methamphetamine. Other crime problems of a global dimension are, for example, the trafficking in humans for sexual exploitation and for labor exploitation, illegal arms trafficking, and the trafficking in counterfeit luxury goods and pharmaceuticals. All of these illegal markets change over time. Some laws that criminalize certain products or behaviors are repealed while new products and behaviors are outlawed. Famously, the production and sale of alcohol, including beer and wine, was illegal in the United States during the Prohibition Era, from 1920 until 1933. Gambling, considered the main line of business of organized criminals in the United States in the 1940s through the 1970s, has likewise seen a shift from criminalization toward legalization. The urban poor, who once placed bets on daily numbers with an illegal lottery in their neighborhood, now buy tickets from state-run lotteries. Prostitution, a crime in most of the United States, has only recently been decriminalized in some countries (e.g., Germany) while new criminal laws against prostitution, targeting customers rather than prostitutes, have been passed at about the same time in other countries (e.g., Sweden). Consumer preferences follow the ebbs and flows of fashion, shifting, for example, between different kinds of illegal drugs. The successes and failures of law enforcement shape illegal markets in their own way. For example, the successful interception of marijuana smuggled from Colombia to the United States in the 1970s promoted a shift to the smuggling of a far less bulky illegal substance: cocaine.

Organized crime is not only associated with the supply of illegal goods and services but also with predatory crimes, such as theft, robbery, and fraud. In fact, when the term organized crime first came in use in the mid-1800s in colonial India, it referred primarily to gangs of highway robbers. Likewise, the first consistent use of the term organized crime in the United States around the year 1920 was linked to theft and robbery much more than to illegal gambling or, for that matter, the illegal sale of alcohol (see Chapter 2).

All of these illegal activities, be they centered on supplying willing customers or harming innocent victims, have in common that they can be carried out in a more or less "organized" fashion. Organized in this context means that crimes are committed on a continuous basis involving planning and preparation as opposed to impulsive, spur-of-the moment criminal acts. Organized can also mean that a crime is not a simple, one-dimensional act, like the snatching of a purse, but an endeavor that requires the coordinated completion of interlocking tasks. For example, the trafficking in stolen motor vehicles may involve the combination of such tasks as overriding the car-door lock with a special tool, manipulating the board computer of the car using illegally obtained servicing

Image 1.1   A large clandestine laboratory for the production of methamphetamine discovered at a ranch near Guadalajara in Mexico in May 2011. Authorities found 1,000 kg of crystal meth and hundreds of bags of sodium hydroxide, a chemical used for the production of methamphetamine.

Photo: ©STRINGER/MEXICO/Reuters/Corbis

software, replacing identifying marks on the car, and forging the accompanying documents (see Chapter 5).

The organization of crime does not necessarily imply that more than one offender is involved. But the cooperation of several criminals will tend to make the commission of crimes easier as the scale and complexity of an operation increases. Simply put, four or five persons can rework a stolen car or unload contraband from a 40-foot container much quicker than a single person. Likewise, a group of four or five criminals is more likely than any individual criminal to combine the skills, expertise, and capital necessary to steal a car and to change it into a seemingly legitimate car or to set up an investment-fraud business or an illegal drug laboratory. This is one of the reasons why not only crimes but also criminals are organized.

The Organization of Criminals

A law-abiding citizen who fantasizes about committing a crime will likely envision him- or herself acting alone in complete secrecy, without letting anyone in on the crime and, accordingly, without being able to draw on the help and support of anyone. The world of crime that the term organized crime relates to is quite different from this image of a lone offender. The world of organized crime is populated by criminals who know other criminals, who socialize with other criminals, who commit crimes with other criminals, and who quarrel with other criminals. Above and beyond that, these criminals may well be known as such in their communities. The term organized crime conjures up images of gangsters like Al Capone, who are public figures, who hold respect because of the wealth and power they have accumulated from crime. Often the problem for law enforcement is not to find out who the organized criminals are but to link them to specific, indictable offenses.

One of the main challenges in the study of organized crime is to sort through the myriad social relations of criminals and to understand how these relations influence and shape criminal behavior. What may be most readily associated with the organization of criminals are criminal groups that are centered on the commission of particular crimes. A classic example is that of the "working groups" of pickpockets and con artists described by criminologist Edwin Sutherland (1937) in his book *The Professional Thief*. A working group of, for exam-

Image 1.2 Two pickpockets in action in early 19th century London. After C. Williams, scene in St. Paul's Churchyard.

Photo: © Heritage Images/Corbis

ple, pickpockets, comprises perhaps two to four members who collaborate according to their individual abilities. Some of these groups disband quickly; others continue to exist for many years. And there may be some fluctuation in membership, with some criminals constantly moving from one group to the next.

Another now classic example of working groups of criminals is that of the Colombian drug trafficking organizations that dominated the global cocaine trade in the 1980s and early 1990s. A handful of organizations, each with about 100 to 200 full-time employees, managed much of the processing of cocaine in clandestine laboratories and the smuggling of the cocaine from Latin America to markets in the United States, Europe, and elsewhere. Some organizations had set up "cells" within destination countries, namely, in the United States, to also handle the wholesale distribution of the cocaine. Under the leadership of notorious kingpins like Carlos Lehder and Pablo Escobar in Medellin and the Rodriguez Orejuela brothers in Cali, these organizations had quite elaborate internal structures with separate branches for handling specialized tasks apart from the core functions of drug trafficking, including security, counterintelligence on state anti-drug efforts, and the laundering of drug profits. In many instances, the large drug trafficking organizations drew on a host of smaller groups and freelancers on a regular or ad hoc basis to transport precursor chemicals and drugs, launder money, or to carry out contract killings (Kenney, 1999a; Zabludoff, 1997).

Professional thieves, drug traffickers, as well as other criminals form and join working groups essentially to make money, and, as Sutherland (1937, p. 28) points out, they may not even speak socially to one another. Apart from these businesslike, crime-focused criminal groups, criminals are connected in other ways that have more to do with social aspects, with crime as a lifestyle, and less with crime as a profession. There is, first of all, what is commonly referred to as the *underworld*, an often idealized criminal subculture with its own rules and its own slang, a community of criminals separated from mainstream society, although many links to the *upperworld* may exist. The underworld is a historical phenomenon that is closely linked to urbanization and to the lower-class quarters of large cities like Berlin, London, or Shanghai (Hobbs, 2013). The underworld materializes in the bars, clubs, and other hangouts where criminals meet, socialize, and gossip. It is here that criminals receive advice, recognition, and support, and it is here that they find accomplices and hatch their plots (McIntosh, 1975,

Image 1.3   Yakuza is a generic term for an assortment of Japanese criminal associations that are independent but share the same subcultural norms and values. In this 1993 picture a Yakuza member shows his hands with two fingers cut off. The practice of amputating fingers, called *yubitsume*, can be a form of punishment or a way to show atonement for wrongdoing in hope of avoiding more severe punishment. *Yubitsume* may also serve as a demonstration of one's sincerity in settling a dispute (Hill, 2003, pp. 74–75).

Photo: TWPhoto/Corbis

p. 24). Not just anyone who commits crimes is automatically part of the under-world. One has to be accepted as a more or less capable and trustworthy criminal (Fordham, 1972, p. 23). The underworld as a subculture of hundreds, thousands, or even tens of thousands of criminals has no formal structure, yet what has often been described is an informal status hierarchy. Some criminals garner more respect than others because of their personality, skills, or wealth; because of their notoriety in the media; or because of their connections to even more influential persons in the underworld and in the upperworld. Lower-status criminals tend to cluster around these higher-status criminals for support and protection and to increase their own standing within the underworld (see, e.g., Albini, 1971; McIntosh, 1975; Rebscher & Vahlenkamp, 1988).

There are other, much more cohesive and more formalized amalgamations of criminals than the rather amorphous urban underworlds: the clannish criminal fraternities that are at the very center of the mythology surrounding the subject of organized crime, organizations like the Sicilian Mafia, the Calabrese 'Ndrangheta, the Neapolitan Camorra, the North American Cosa Nostra, the Chinese triads, the Japanese yakuza groups, or the post-Soviet Thieves in Law. All of these groups have their own rituals, symbols, and ideologies, and they have been in existence over many generations. Some trace their history back to medieval times. Sicilian mafiosi, for example, see their origins in an uprising against foreign oppressors in the 13th century (Arlacchi, 1993), and the yakuza place themselves in the tradition of Japan's ancient warrior class of the samurai (Hill, 2003). By their own accounts and in the perception of others, these organizations constitute criminal elites. Being accepted into their ranks is what many criminals strive for and what may carry with it an enormous boost in prestige and power. That the myth and reality of these criminal organizations do not always match is a different matter.

The Exercise of Power by Criminals

Criminal fraternities like the Sicilian Mafia or the North American Cosa Nostra can be found in a role other than that of just inwardly looking clannish, secretive combinations of criminals. One meaning of the term organized crime is that crime in a specific area is under the control of a particular group of criminals, such as a branch of the Sicilian Mafia or of the North American Cosa Nostra. In a situation like this, criminals are not free to commit any crime. They need permission from the ruling criminal group. Certain crimes may not be tolerated because they go against the moral convictions of those in power or because these crimes may attract unwanted attention by the police—for example, street robberies or dealing hard drugs like heroin. As a result, neighborhoods under the control of a criminal group, ironically, can have relatively low crime rates (Marshall, 2013). The criminals who are allowed to operate in a controlled area may have to share some of their profits in the form of what in the U.S. underworld is called a "street tax" (Lombardo, 2013, p. 161). One of the facets of organized crime, then, is to bring a level of order to crime and criminals in some form of an underworld government. At the same time, the power that criminals exert may well extend into the upperworld.

Image 1.4   In the 1931 German film classic "M," directed by Fritz Lang and said to be based on a true story, criminals impart their form of justice to another criminal. A child murderer (Peter Lorre, left) stands trial before a panel of the most powerful members of the underworld. Some of the extras in the film reportedly were real criminals who had been hired under the threat that otherwise the filming would be sabotaged (Hartmann & von Lampe, 2008, p. 108).

Photo: © Photos 12 / Alamy

Of course, there are many organized crimes that target law-abiding citizens, and corruption and intimidation are ways in which organized criminals can influence government officials, from the cop on the beat, to prosecutors, judges, and mayors and, in some cases, all the way to members of parliament and the highest representatives of the state. Yet, arguably the most far-reaching criminal advance into the upperworld is of a different nature, when criminal groups take the place of legitimate government. This can happen on a small scale—for example, when in a marginalized urban neighborhood problems are not taken to the police or the courts but to the local gang. The same can occur on a grand scale, when, for example, legitimate businesses routinely turn to criminals to solve a dispute over a contract or to collect an outstanding debt because there is no faith in the efficient functioning of the legal system. This could be observed in former Soviet Bloc countries during the 1990s when it was a normal aspect of conducting a legitimate business to draw on the protection and assistance of criminal groups in exchange for a share of the profits (Skoblikov, 2007; Varese, 2001; Volkov, 2002).

When criminals exercise power, they do not necessarily do so on their own account. A scenario that finds frequent mention in descriptions of organized crime is that of underworld-upperworld alliances. In these alliances, the gangster element is often in a subservient role and tasked with doing the dirty work for political and business elites. Namely, in the United States there has been a long tradition of politicians recruiting criminal gangs to stuff ballot boxes and to intimidate the voters of opposing candidates and a similarly long tradition of businesses employing criminals to counter efforts of unionizing workers (Asbury, 1927; Block & Chambliss, 1981; Whyte, 1943/1981).

Myth and Reality: The Case of "Scarface" Al Capone

A recurring theme in the debate on organized crime is how powerful criminal organizations and individual organized criminals truly are. Journalists are quick to award the title of "most powerful" to a host of gangs or gangsters. One stands out among the many who have been glorified and mystified: Al Capone. To put things into perspective, it appears useful to take a closer look early in this book at this particular individual, arguably the most notorious organized criminal of all times. His name continues to conjure up images of the wealth and power of the underworld.

Alphonse "Al" Capone was born in New York City in 1899. His parents had immigrated to the United States a few years earlier from a town near Naples, Italy. Capone's father made his living as a barber while his mother cared for the children, nine in all, at home. At age 19, Al married his life-long wife Mae following the birth of their only child. The young family moved to Baltimore, where Al worked as a bookkeeper for a legitimate construction firm for the next two years. In 1920, however, Al Capone left the path of a law-abiding life and returned to a career of vice and crime that he had already begun at an earlier age on the streets of Brooklyn, New York (Bergreen, 1994).

Al reportedly had dropped out of school at the age of 14 following a violent confrontation with his teacher. He was involved in fights between Irish and Italian youths and before long ran errands for a local underworld figure, John Torrio, who had a stake in the illegal lottery business and also managed a number of brothels. Torrio would later become Capone's mentor in Chicago. But before that happened, Capone entered the service of another New York gangster. Al Capone became a bouncer and bartender in a Coney Island bar and dance hall owned by Frank Yale. It was there that Capone got in a brawl with a knife-toting customer and received the famous scar on his left cheek that earned him the nickname "Scarface." In the meantime, John Torrio had left for Chicago to join his uncle "Big Jim" Colosimo, a politically well-connected restaurateur, loan-shark, and brothel owner (Kobler, 1971).

In 1920, shortly after the onset of Prohibition, Colosimo was murdered and his gambling and prostitution businesses were taken over by Torrio, who enlisted Al Capone to be his right-hand man. Torrio recognized the opportunities presented to illegal entrepreneurs by the prohibition of the manufacture and sale of alcohol. He assumed control over a number of legitimate breweries that supplied a burgeoning black market with beer while officially only producing "near beer," real beer de-alcoholized to .5 percent (Allsop, 1968; Kobler, 1971, 1973).

Like gambling and prostitution, the illegal alcohol business thrived under the protection of corrupt politicians. When in 1923 a reform mayor took office in

Chicago to replace the corrupt "Big Bill" Thompson, Torrio lost his high-level protection and was forced to move his center of operations to the suburb of Cicero where, one year later, massive voter intimidation organized by Al Capone assured the election of a gangster-friendly local government. With the ousting of mayor Thompson in Chicago in 1923, an era of centralized protection of vice and crime had come to an end, resulting in the collapse of a system of peaceful coexistence between the leading gangs of the city, a system that Torrio had carefully crafted. What followed was a series of violent confrontations over alcohol shipments and territories, dubbed the "beer war," that claimed the lives of hundreds of gangsters. Al Capone assumed a leading role in this conflict, reputedly commanding whole troops of gunmen (Kobler, 1971; Landesco, 1929).

In 1925, John Torrio only narrowly escaped an attempt on his life and decided to return to New York City. With Torrio gone, Capone assumed the leadership role and increasingly received public attention. In fact, unlike other underworld figures, he courted the press. One crime reporter for the *Chicago Tribune* newspaper, quoted by Al Capone biographer Laurence Bergreen, even suggested in hindsight that Capone's dominating position had been a media fabrication: "We built him up as the big shot in the gang world" (Bergreen, 1994, p. 211).

From what is known about the inner workings of the so-called "Capone Syndicate," Al Capone shared interests in a number of illegal and legal businesses with different partners, namely his older brother Ralph Capone, their cousin Frank Nitti, and Al Capone's trusted friend Jack Guzik, the oldest of three Russian-born brothers with a background in prostitution and human trafficking. From other businesses, Capone exacted a share of the profits in return for political and physical protection. During its heyday in the late 1920s and early 1930s, the "Capone Syndicate" is believed to have had a total of 181 members, although it is not clear on what basis the membership was defined (Lombardo, 2013, p. 920.) Among the top echelon, Al Capone stood out insofar as he commanded the "military arm" of the organization, a small standing army of bodyguards who drew regular salaries (Haller, 1990; Papachristos & Smith, 2014).

Image 1.5 Al Capone was at the height of his power at age 32 when this picture was taken in 1931.

Photo: uncredited/ /AP/Corbis

Despite his growing notoriety as "gangster overlord," efforts to put Al Capone out of business and behind bars failed, until in 1931 he was sentenced in federal court to 11 years in prison for tax evasion. There are two myths surrounding this case: One myth is that Al Capone was the first criminal ever to be prosecuted for failing to report his illegal income, the other that he would otherwise have remained "untouchable." The truth is that a similar case had been brought against a South Carolina bootlegger as early as 1921, upheld by the U.S. Supreme Court in 1927, and a number of Chicago gangsters, including his brother Ralph, had been charged with tax evasion before Al Capone. Had this prosecution strategy failed, Al Capone would most likely have been convicted for violating the alcohol prohibition laws. An indictment listing more than 5,000 such transgressions had been filed against Capone one week after the indictment for tax evasion, and Capone had pleaded guilty to all of those charges in hope of a mild sentence of two and a half years. Only because the judge rejected the plea and opted for a trial did the tax indictment take precedence (Hoffman, 1993).

Al Capone served his time in the infamous Alcatraz federal penitentiary before receiving an early release on medical grounds in 1939. He showed symptoms suggesting damage to the central nervous system characteristic of advanced syphilis, a disease he had contracted at a young age. Al Capone died in his retirement home in Florida in 1947, shortly after his 48th birthday (Bergreen, 1994).

CONCEPTUAL CONFUSION

The issues that are being addressed under the rubric of organized crime, many of which appear in the life story of Al Capone, can be approached from different angles. The purpose of this book is not to advocate one particular perspective or to replace existing interpretations with a novel conception of the nature of organized crime. This would only add to the confusion. Instead the aim is to put things into perspective within one overarching conceptual framework.

The problem that everyone faces who is drawn to this subject is the diversity of views of what organized crime constitutes. This diversity has led to a great deal of talking at cross-purposes. Usually, the more one hears and reads about a subject, the clearer things become. In the case of organized crime the opposite may be true.

Organized Crime and the Social Construction of Reality

Before taking a closer look at the various phenomena associated with organized crime in later chapters of this book, it is important to understand why it is so difficult to come to terms with this subject and why there is still such a great deal of confusion. Contrary to what one might expect, this has not so much to do with the sinister and clandestine ways of gangsters and mafiosi. Instead it has to do with a general problem of how people perceive and make sense of the world they live in. First of all, people cannot possibly grasp reality in all of its complexity. Their perception is inevitably selective, which means they focus on certain aspects while neglecting others. Secondly, what they see they tend to frame and rearrange into categories that are in line with their pre-existing views, attitudes, and values. Thirdly, people make sense of the world not as individuals but as social beings. They come to shared understandings of how to view and interpret reality in a process that has been called the *social construction of reality* (Berger & Luckmann, 1966). It is important to realize that the social construction of reality is a dynamic process, influenced by numerous factors, with many possible outcomes. This also applies to the notion of organized crime.

The central thesis on which this book is based and which will be further elaborated below is that organized crime is not something that exists clearly discernible out in the real world, such as the Egyptian pyramids. This does not mean that what the concept of organized crime refers to is a figment of someone's imagination without any link to reality. The diverse phenomena which are variously labeled organized crime are quite real—some exaggerations, misinterpretations, and mystifications notwithstanding. However, in order to be able to speak of organized crime, certain aspects of the social universe first have to be separated out from a dense web of individuals, actions, and structures and brought into a unifying context on the conceptual level. Organized crime, in this sense, is a construct, an attempt to make sense of a complex social reality. Strictly speaking, organized crime as something that is clear-cut and self-evident only exists on paper, in the combination of the two words *organized* and *crime*. At the same time, the meaning of these two words is loose, flexible, and contradictory. For example, some associate organized crime essentially with the organization of criminal *activities*, while for others the term organized crime refers primarily to the organization of *criminals*. As will be discussed in Chapter 2, there are similarly divergent views on the meaning of the term organized crime in several other respects as well, and there is no firm basis on which to say that one view is right and the other is wrong.

Is a Definition of Organized Crime Needed to Study Organized Crime?

Scholars have dealt with the existing conceptual confusion in different ways. Perhaps the most common and also most obvious approach is the attempt to increase clarity by defining organized crime.

Attempts to Arrive at an Authoritative Definition of Organized Crime

There are some who have not simply formulated working definitions of organized crime for specific purposes but have tried to come up with an authoritative definition that would end the debate over the meaning of the term once and for all. Given the continuous stream of new definitions that are being proposed, this approach has not been successful. Others acknowledge that it is difficult to arrive at a generally accepted definition of organized crime, yet they believe that there are some attributes that provide a basis for determining if something constitutes organized crime or not. For example, Howard Abadinsky (2013, p. 3) has proposed a list of eight attributes that he believes help in deciding "if a particular group of criminals constitutes organized crime." Note that Abadinsky assumes that organized crime is a particular class of *groups* of criminals. His list of attributes includes, for example, a hierarchical group structure, the willingness to use violence, and the absence of political goals.

What all attempts to delineate the meaning of the term organized crime have in common is that the line they draw between organized crime and non-organized crime in the end is arbitrary. For example, confining organized crime to criminal *groups* and only to those groups with a *hierarchical* structure, "a vertical power structure," as Howard Abadinsky (2013, p. 3) advocates, means ignoring a large class of serious crime phenomena that for many others are at the center of the study of organized crime. Many include in their definition sets of individual criminals that are connected through social ties and who collaborate in criminal activities as equals without any hierarchy and with only a rudimentary division of labor (see, e.g., Fijnaut, Bovenkerk, Bruinsma, & Van de Bunt, 1998, p. 27; Godson, 2003c, p. 274).

Arguments for and Against the Need for a Definition

Despite the intricate problems that have become apparent in defining organized crime, some argue that a definition is nonetheless needed, not only for legal and policy purposes (Lebeya, 2012, p. 1) but also for research purposes (Finckenauer, 2005; Schneider, 1993, p. 130). The argument, in essence, is that in order to be able to study organized crime one first has to be clear about what to study. At first glance this seems to be a logical and, in fact, irrefutable proposition. However, things are more complicated when dealing with a subject that is first and foremost a construct rather than a coherent empirical phenomenon. In a case like this, social science research is confronted with a subject that is encapsulated in preexisting lay perceptions and assumptions (Hagan, 1983). Organized crime is not a scientific discovery. The notion of organized crime was first promoted by civic leaders, politicians, and journalists and only later adopted by social scientists (von Lampe, 2001a). How social scientists should deal with prescientific, lay notions, such as that of organized crime, has first been discussed by one of the founding fathers of sociology, Emile Durkheim. He declared it the first rule of social science to eradicate such lay notions that, he said, are "confused and unorganized" products of human experience, reflecting social reality as much as emotions, prejudices, and ideologies (Durkheim, 1895/1964, p. 33). Sociological research, Durkheim maintains, cannot take as an object of study the reality as it is framed in lay perceptions. Rather, sociological research has to go deeper. Sociologists first have to define and categorize the underlying phenomena: In the case of organized crime this would include phenomena like drug trafficking, illegal markets, criminal organizations, and underworld governments. Then they need to explore to what extent these diverse phenomena are indeed connected in a way that would justify subsuming them under one unifying concept.

From this line of reasoning follows that research on organized crime cannot have a definition of organized crime, the notion of a clear and coherent object of study, as its starting point. On the contrary, the very purpose of the study of organized crime is to determine to what extent such a coherent phenomenon indeed exists. A definition, therefore, is a possible *outcome* of rather than a precondition for the study of organized crime (Kelly, 1986, p. 28; von Lampe, 2009b, p. 165–166). And, it must be added, in this respect the study of organized crime still has a long ways to go. Strictly speaking, as later chapters in this book will highlight, the study of organized crime is still in its infant stages.

Where the research efforts within this field will eventually lead is uncertain, provided the research process is open and unbiased. While it is possible that organized crime will at some point in time be translated from a heterogeneous construct into a scientific concept informed by empirical data and theory, the research process may also lead, in the other extreme, to a complete "evaporation" of the concept of organized crime (Van Duyne, 2003, p. 28).

WHAT IS THE OBJECT OF
STUDY IN THE STUDY OF ORGANIZED CRIME?

So, if for the time being there is no useful definition of organized crime, what then exactly is the object of study in the study of organized crime? The short answer is, there is not one object of study but many different objects of study, comprising, for a lack of discriminating criteria, everything that in some way or other has been associated with organized crime. Chapter 2 will specify what this entails. For now it is important to clarify how on such an abstract level the boundaries of the study of organized crime can be defined without defining the term organized crime. There are, in fact, two ways to do this. *Nominally*, the study of organized crime comprises all research and theorizing explicitly designated by the respective scholars as relating to organized crime, regardless of how the term may be interpreted.

However, the same subject matter may be explored by different scholars with some using the concept of organized crime and others avoiding it. For example, the structure of drug trafficking groups, the logistics of investment fraud, or the use of violence within the Sicilian Mafia are issues that are not necessarily studied under the rubric organized crime. Therefore, a more inclusive way is to delineate the study of organized crime in substantive terms so that it comprises all research and theorizing relating to phenomena that have been labeled organized crime, regardless of whether or not in a particular instance the concept actually comes into play. In both cases, of course, the study is in the end simply marked off by the range of meanings attached to the term organized crime. In other words, the study of organized crime is the study of whatever is labeled organized crime, in line with the only definition of organized crime that is based on a clear-cut common denominator and is comprehensive at the same time: Organized crime is what people so label (von Lampe, 2001a, p. 113). It is in this sense that the term is used throughout this book as a vague denominator of a mixed basket of phenomena that have variously been labeled organized crime.

CHAPTER 2

The Concept of Organized Crime

This chapter examines how the label organized crime has been applied historically and in systematic terms. In so doing, the first aim is to show the haphazard use of the concept and to highlight the uncertainties inherent in the social construction of reality. The second aim is to demonstrate the extent of the existing conceptual confusion surrounding the term and to undermine any notion of a consensus about the nature of organized crime. Finally, by pointing out the different empirical phenomena associated with the term, this chapter lays a foundation for identifying the major themes in the study of organized crime that will be addressed in the later chapters of this book.

THE CONCEPTUAL HISTORY OF ORGANIZED CRIME

The concept of organized crime as it is used today is essentially a U.S. invention. While its origins go back to at least the 19th century, it was not until the early 20th century, in the United States, that a more or less consistent meaning was attached to the combination of the words *organized* and *crime*. Inspired by the debate on organized crime in the United States, the term has then come to be used more or less consistently in other parts of the world, namely in Europe, since the 1960s and 1970s, and on a global scale since at least the 1990s in the run-up to the UN Convention against Transnational Organized Crime, the so-called Palermo Convention, which was adopted in the year 2000.

Organized crime is a good example of how, in modern societies, problems are identified and placed on the political agenda. This alone makes the conceptual history of organized crime an interesting subject for social scientists to study. However, it is also important for those interested in the underlying empirical phenomena to understand how the concept has evolved. First of all, as indicated before, the use of the concept is what at the moment best delineates the scope of the study of organized crime. Secondly, the conceptual history reveals how volatile assumptions about the nature of organized crime have been and how much

Image 2.2   In the mid 1800s, groups accused by the British colonial administration in India of engaging in highway robbery and other crimes, were among the first to be labeled organized crime.

Photo: Science & Society Picture Library/Contributor/Getty Images

Organized Crime and Mafia

In the United States, isolated instances of the connection between organized crime and criminal organizations can be found throughout the 19th century (K. H. R., 1835). Early on, the term appeared in connection with mafia organizations rooted in Italy that, of course, would later be regarded by many as the epitome of organized crime (Appleton, 1868). Interestingly, however, while the existence of these criminal organizations was present in the public conscience since the late 1800s, not least in the United States, it was not until the 1950s that Mafia and organized crime came to be seen as largely synonymous (see von Lampe, 2001a).

On two occasions in particular, public attention in the United States was directed to Italian criminal organizations. The first incident was the murder of the popular chief of police in New Orleans, David Hennessey, in 1890. According to one interpretation, Hennessey had been shot to death by members of one of two rivalling groups of Italian American criminals. Following a verdict of not guilty, allegedly as a result of jury tampering, eleven suspects of Italian decent were killed by a lynch mob (Lombardo, 2010, p. 168). The Hennessey case triggered a hysteria about Italian criminal organizations allegedly gaining a

CHAPTER 2

The Concept of Organized Crime

This chapter examines how the label organized crime has been applied historically and in systematic terms. In so doing, the first aim is to show the haphazard use of the concept and to highlight the uncertainties inherent in the social construction of reality. The second aim is to demonstrate the extent of the existing conceptual confusion surrounding the term and to undermine any notion of a consensus about the nature of organized crime. Finally, by pointing out the different empirical phenomena associated with the term, this chapter lays a foundation for identifying the major themes in the study of organized crime that will be addressed in the later chapters of this book.

THE CONCEPTUAL HISTORY OF ORGANIZED CRIME

The concept of organized crime as it is used today is essentially a U.S. invention. While its origins go back to at least the 19th century, it was not until the early 20th century, in the United States, that a more or less consistent meaning was attached to the combination of the words *organized* and *crime*. Inspired by the debate on organized crime in the United States, the term has then come to be used more or less consistently in other parts of the world, namely in Europe, since the 1960s and 1970s, and on a global scale since at least the 1990s in the run-up to the UN Convention against Transnational Organized Crime, the so-called Palermo Convention, which was adopted in the year 2000.

Organized crime is a good example of how, in modern societies, problems are identified and placed on the political agenda. This alone makes the conceptual history of organized crime an interesting subject for social scientists to study. However, it is also important for those interested in the underlying empirical phenomena to understand how the concept has evolved. First of all, as indicated before, the use of the concept is what at the moment best delineates the scope of the study of organized crime. Secondly, the conceptual history reveals how volatile assumptions about the nature of organized crime have been and how much

Image 2.2 In the mid 1800s, groups accused by the British colonial administration in India of engaging in highway robbery and other crimes, were among the first to be labeled organized crime.

Photo: Science & Society Picture Library/Contributor/Getty Images

Organized Crime and Mafia

In the United States, isolated instances of the connection between organized crime and criminal organizations can be found throughout the 19th century (K. H. R., 1835). Early on, the term appeared in connection with mafia organizations rooted in Italy that, of course, would later be regarded by many as the epitome of organized crime (Appleton, 1868). Interestingly, however, while the existence of these criminal organizations was present in the public conscience since the late 1800s, not least in the United States, it was not until the 1950s that Mafia and organized crime came to be seen as largely synonymous (see von Lampe, 2001a).

On two occasions in particular, public attention in the United States was directed to Italian criminal organizations. The first incident was the murder of the popular chief of police in New Orleans, David Hennessey, in 1890. According to one interpretation, Hennessey had been shot to death by members of one of two rivalling groups of Italian American criminals. Following a verdict of not guilty, allegedly as a result of jury tampering, eleven suspects of Italian decent were killed by a lynch mob (Lombardo, 2010, p. 168). The Hennessey case triggered a hysteria about Italian criminal organizations allegedly gaining a

CHAPTER 2

The Concept of Organized Crime

This chapter examines how the label organized crime has been applied historically and in systematic terms. In so doing, the first aim is to show the haphazard use of the concept and to highlight the uncertainties inherent in the social construction of reality. The second aim is to demonstrate the extent of the existing conceptual confusion surrounding the term and to undermine any notion of a consensus about the nature of organized crime. Finally, by pointing out the different empirical phenomena associated with the term, this chapter lays a foundation for identifying the major themes in the study of organized crime that will be addressed in the later chapters of this book.

THE CONCEPTUAL HISTORY OF ORGANIZED CRIME

The concept of organized crime as it is used today is essentially a U.S. invention. While its origins go back to at least the 19th century, it was not until the early 20th century, in the United States, that a more or less consistent meaning was attached to the combination of the words *organized* and *crime*. Inspired by the debate on organized crime in the United States, the term has then come to be used more or less consistently in other parts of the world, namely in Europe, since the 1960s and 1970s, and on a global scale since at least the 1990s in the run-up to the UN Convention against Transnational Organized Crime, the so-called Palermo Convention, which was adopted in the year 2000.

Organized crime is a good example of how, in modern societies, problems are identified and placed on the political agenda. This alone makes the conceptual history of organized crime an interesting subject for social scientists to study. However, it is also important for those interested in the underlying empirical phenomena to understand how the concept has evolved. First of all, as indicated before, the use of the concept is what at the moment best delineates the scope of the study of organized crime. Secondly, the conceptual history reveals how volatile assumptions about the nature of organized crime have been and how much

Image 2.1   The adoption of the UN Convention against Transnational Organized Crime in Palermo in the year 2000 marked the acceptance of organized crime as a key criminal policy concept on the global level. Austrian President Thomas Klestil's signature is witnessed (from left to right) by Kofi Annan, UN General Secretary; Pino Arlacchi, head of the UN Office for Drugs and Crime (UNODC); and Leoluca Orlando, mayor of Palermo and anti-Mafia activist.

Photo: Reuters/Corbis

they have been influenced by external factors that have little or nothing to do with the reality of crime. This induces a healthy sense of scepticism, which is a good mind-set for studying organized crime. Nothing that has been said or written about the subject should be accepted at face value.

The Origins of the Concept of Organized Crime

As far as can be seen, the combination of the two words *organized* and *crime* appeared sporadically but with increasing frequency in the English language since about the 1830s, both in the United States and in the British Empire. The meaning of the term varied greatly up until the years following World War I when one can speak, for the first time, of a coinage of the term in the sense of a regular usage with roughly the same content.

Two clusters of context and meaning of the term can be discerned in the period from the early 1800s until about 1920: organized crime referring to the political realm and organized crime referring to more conventional crime phenomena.

War and Political Violence as Organized Crime

War or civil war was repeatedly branded as being organized crime in the decades before 1920 (see, e.g., Spencer, 1881, p. 23). The same is true for atrocities committed in the context of military conflict, including tactics ascribed to the South in the U.S. Civil War (Boutwell, 1865), Germany during World War I ("A Woman's Dread," 1915), and the Bolsheviks during the Russian civil war following the October Revolution of 1917 ("Germans Lost Riga," 1919). In the aftermath of the U.S. Civil War, organized crime was also repeatedly employed as a label for the practices of the Ku Klux Klan (see, e.g., "Senator Morton's Committee," 1871). Another political context in which the term appeared were struggles against political and economic oppression, either referring to the oppressors, such as the British colonial regime in India (St. John, 1852, p. 232), or the oppressed, for example, Irish peasants revolting against British rule (Lewis, 1836, p. iii) and U.S. workers fighting for their rights ("Otis Sees," 1912). In fact, the term in some instances has been a play of words to denounce labor unions. In one *New York Times* editorial, for example, a militant miners' union was attacked as "a labor organization so lawless and abhorrent to the primary ideas of civilization that it might fairly be described not as organized labor, but as organized crime" ("Undesirable Citizens," 1907). In this context it should be noted that the term *organized* was a popular prefix in the 19th century, appearing in creations such as *organized society*, *organized government*, *organized capital*, *organized industry*, and *organized business*.

Criminals, Criminal Groups, and Criminal Activities as Organized Crime

Apart from the context of political conflict, the term organized crime appeared in reference to crime as conventionally understood, particularly predatory crime, such as theft, robbery, and burglary. In some instances, organized crime referred to criminal activities in a generic sense, implying, for example, that crimes were "systematized on a commercial scale" ("Attacks on Gaynor," 1912). In other instances, the term referred more to criminals and criminal groups. There is the notion, first of all, that organized crime pertains to the community of professional criminals, of "accomplished villains, . . . men of talents, mind, and genius" (Todd, 1837, p. 25), who are more capable and more sophisticated than other criminals. Then there is the notion that organized crime has to do with criminal organizations.

The British colonial administration in India, where the term seems to have been used with some regularity in the mid-1800s, found itself confronted with indigenous seminomadic bands of traders and plunderers engaged in highway robbery and other predatory crimes (Brown, 2002). These groups, under the heading organized crime, were described in official documents as "dangerous fraternities" (Arnold, 1862, p. 264) and "criminal tribes . . . whose members for generations have been and are addicted to criminal pursuits" (Hutchinson, 1870, p. 412). Probably because of the specific nature of the underlying phenomena, there has been no traceable continuity in the use of the term from the British colonial rule in India of the 1800s until today.

Image 2.2   In the mid 1800s, groups accused by the British colonial administration in India of engaging in highway robbery and other crimes, were among the first to be labeled organized crime.

Photo: Science & Society Picture Library/Contributor/Getty Images

Organized Crime and Mafia

In the United States, isolated instances of the connection between organized crime and criminal organizations can be found throughout the 19th century (K. H. R., 1835). Early on, the term appeared in connection with mafia organizations rooted in Italy that, of course, would later be regarded by many as the epitome of organized crime (Appleton, 1868). Interestingly, however, while the existence of these criminal organizations was present in the public conscience since the late 1800s, not least in the United States, it was not until the 1950s that Mafia and organized crime came to be seen as largely synonymous (see von Lampe, 2001a).

On two occasions in particular, public attention in the United States was directed to Italian criminal organizations. The first incident was the murder of the popular chief of police in New Orleans, David Hennessey, in 1890. According to one interpretation, Hennessey had been shot to death by members of one of two rivalling groups of Italian American criminals. Following a verdict of not guilty, allegedly as a result of jury tampering, eleven suspects of Italian decent were killed by a lynch mob (Lombardo, 2010, p. 168). The Hennessey case triggered a hysteria about Italian criminal organizations allegedly gaining a

foothold in the United States, namely the Sicilian Mafia and the Camorra from Naples. An editorial in the *New York Times* raised the question "whether 300,000 or 400,000 Italian immigrants have imported with themselves their characteristic methods of banding themselves into secret, oath-bound societies which reach private ends by murder" ("The Mafia in the United States," 1890). Interestingly, however, in the flurry of articles and editorials about mafia organizations that were published in the aftermath of the Hennessey murder, hardly any contained the term organized crime (see Lombardo, 2010, p. 174).

A few years later, the notion of Italian criminal organizations operating on U.S. soil returned to center stage with the "Black Hand." Some view the Black Hand as the predecessor to the Italian American Mafia, Cosa Nostra, which took shape in the 1920s and 1930s. In fact, many contemporary observers believed that the Black Hand was nothing but an offspring of the Sicilian Mafia. Others, then and now, see it more as a method of extortion employed by individuals and small groups primarily within the Italian immigrant communities of cities such as Chicago and New York. The scheme, first documented in 1903, involved the sending of extortion letters bearing the symbol of a black hand, or signed Black Hand, respectively "La Mano Nera" (Lombardo, 2010; Pitkin & Cordasco, 1977). Again, while reports on the Black Hand were numerous, the term organized crime was rarely used; once, for example, to describe black hand extortion as "organized crime among the low-class Italians" ("Topics of the *Times*," 1906).

The sporadic and volatile appearance of the combination of the words organized and crime in the English language since the early 19th century did not have a lasting effect on language usage. It was not until the years after World War I that the concept of organized crime was first coined and ceased to merely represent a play of words. For the first time it served as a conceptual reference point for political and academic debates, although this reference point remained vague and shifted over time.

The First Coinage of the Concept of Organized Crime in the United States

As far as can be seen, the first coinage of the term organized crime occurred in the deliberations of the Chicago Crime Commission, a civic organization created in 1919 by businessmen, bankers, and lawyers concerned about rampant crime, primarily predatory crime, in the city of Chicago (von Lampe, 1999; von Lampe, 2001a). In the pronouncements of the Chicago Crime Commission, organized crime referred not to criminal organizations but in a much broader sense to the orderly fashion in which the so-called "criminal class" of an estimated "10,000 professional criminals" allegedly pursued "crime as a business" (Chamberlin, 1919, 1920, 1921; Holden, 1920; Sims, 1920). The debate centered on the perceived ineffectiveness and corruption of the criminal justice system, while also criticizing widespread indifference and even open sympathy on the part of the general public toward criminals. This characterization of organized crime as part of the fabric of society reflected the perspective of the old-established protestant middle class on Chicago as a city that, after years of rapid growth and cultural change, seemed to be drowning in crime and moral decay (von Lampe, 2001a, p. 104).

During the Prohibition Era, the period from 1920 until 1933, when the production and selling of alcoholic beverages was illegal in the United States, the understanding of organized crime changed significantly. By the late 1920s, organized crime no longer referred to an amorphous "criminal class" but to "gangsters and racketeers" who were organized in "gangs," "syndicates," and "criminal organizations," following "big master criminals" who functioned as "powerful leaders of organized crime" (Lashly, 1930; Smith, 1926; "Pershing Asks Repeal," 1932). Some of these leaders moved into the limelight and gained celebrity status, most notably Al Capone.

While the picture of the criminal class became more and more differentiated, the understanding of the relation between organized crime and society took a decisive turn. Organized crime was no longer seen as a product of conditions that could be remedied by means of social and political reform. Instead, the emphasis was on vigorous law enforcement in a "war on organized crime" ("Mulrooney Wants Criminals," 1933).

The Merging of the Concepts of Organized Crime and Mafia

It should be noted that throughout the Prohibition Era, which in hindsight constitutes the classical era of gangsters in the United States, the term organized crime was still only used rather sparingly, sometimes superseded by the term *racketeering*. More importantly, the term still had no ethnic connotation. This changed dramatically in the 1950s and 1960s with the resurgence of the imagery of Italian mafia groups having taken root in the United States.

This shift in perception was brought about to no small degree by nationally televised hearings held by a U.S. Senate committee chaired by Estes Kefauver (Special Committee to Investigate Organized Crime in Interstate Commerce). The so-called Kefauver Committee focused its attention on a group of underworld figures from Chicago and New York suspected of controlling illegal gambling operations in various parts of the country. Guided by information provided by the Federal Bureau of Narcotics (FBN), the Kefauver Committee concluded that numerous criminal groups throughout the United States were tied together by "a sinister criminal organization known as the Mafia" (S. Rep. No. 307, 1951, p. 2).

The Kefauver Committee marked a significant turning point in the conceptual history of organized crime in three respects. First, organized crime no longer appeared to be primarily a local problem but instead one that existed on a national scale and threatened local communities from the outside. Second, the notion of the Mafia as an organization of Italian Americans added an ethnic component to the concept of organized crime. Third, for the first time the law enforcement community, namely the FBN, not to be confused with the FBI, was assuming an active role in the conceptualization of organized crime, which previously had been the domain of journalists, civic leaders, and politicians. The FBI for its part rejected the notion of organized crime in the United States until 1963. FBI Director J. Edgar Hoover not only ruled out the existence of an Italian American Mafia, he also criticized more general conceptions of criminal organization

Image 2.3   Televised hearings held in 1950 and 1951 before a U.S. Senate committee chaired by Estes Kefauver promoted the view that Italian-American gangsters epitomize organized crime. Shown is the March 1951 testimony of Frank Costello whose position as boss of one of New York City's five Mafia families was not known at the time. Costello tried to downplay his ties to politicians and to a number of notorious underworld figures including Al Capone, Meyer Lansky, and Lucky Luciano.

Photo: © Bettmann/CORBIS

(Powers, 1987). In an article on women trafficking published in 1933, for example, Hoover voiced his disapproval of "considerable misconceptions by the public of the extent of so-called vice rings." The occasional discovery of such an organization, he maintained, cannot be taken as an indication of their prevalence (Hoover, 1933, p. 479).

The interest in organized crime and in the Italian American Mafia that the Kefauver Committee had stirred was reinforced by a series of events that, by the late 1960s, culminated in the merging of the two concepts of organized crime and Mafia. In 1957, Senate hearings on the influence of Italian American criminals on legitimate businesses coincided with the discovery of a national meeting of Italian American criminals near Apalachin in New York State. In 1963, a Mafia-turncoat from New York City, Joe Valachi, testified before a Senate committee about the inner workings of what he called Cosa Nostra, which forced the FBI to acknowledge the existence of a nationwide organization of Italian American criminals. In 1967, a Presidential commission on crime in essence declared this organization to be the embodiment of organized crime in the United States, arguing that Cosa Nostra largely controlled the provision of illegal goods and services in the country. Finally, in 1969, Mario Puzo's hugely successful novel *The Godfather* presented the mafia imagery in a consumer-friendly form while the release of transcripts of secretly taped conversations of a Cosa Nostra boss, Simone Rizzo (Sam the Plumber) de Cavalcante (De Cavalcante tapes), provided additional credibility to the official depiction of the Cosa Nostra as a formal organization with defined membership (von Lampe, 2001a).

Challenges to the Mafia Paradigm

In a nutshell, the view on organized crime that had emerged by the late 1960s saw practically all gambling, loan sharking, drug trafficking, and other crimes in the United States directly or indirectly controlled by one organization of some

Image 2.4   A chart prepared for a U.S. Senate hearing in 1964 by the New York Police Department depicting the formal (hierarchical) structure of a Cosa Nostra family, then designated as the Magliocco Family but better known otherwise as the Profaci or Colombo family. The chart distinguishes three levels of authority, the leadership with a boss and an underboss, the middle-ranking caporegime, and the ordinary members ("soldiers"/"buttons"). It also indicates what criminal activities the members have been involved in. Most commonly they are known for involvement in gambling, loan sharking, and extortion.

5,000 men of Italian descent. The organization was believed to function under the protection of corrupt officials as an underworld government and as an illegal business, with local branches, so-called families, structured along the lines of military units, each with a "boss" at the top of the hierarchy and some of these bosses, in turn, forming a governing body for the entire organization, the so-called commission (Cressey, 1969). This image reduced the confusing reality of crime to one very simple model that could easily be conveyed to the law enforcement community and the general public. To no small degree, however, the image of a nationwide Mafia had been the result of a focus on New York City, a Mafia stronghold with five Cosa Nostra families. Despite its tremendous impact on public perception, this image soon proved inadequate for capturing the crime situation in other parts of the country.

The U.S. Congress refrained from outlawing membership in Cosa Nostra and instead, in 1970, passed legislation with a far broader scope, the Racketeer Influenced and Corrupt Organizations Act (RICO), which does not require involvement in a criminal organization such as Cosa Nostra but merely an "association in fact" (Chapter 14). Likewise, many state-level commissions on organized crime that had been established in response to the national debate at best paid lip service to the characterization of Cosa Nostra as an all-encompassing criminal organization. Instead, they defined organized crime in much broader terms to include less structured gangs and illicit enterprises (Governor's Organized Crime Prevention Commission, 1973; Hawaii Crime Commission, 1978; Missouri Task Force on Organized Crime, n.d.). A similar uneasiness with the Mafia paradigm became evident among law enforcement officials at the state and local levels (National Advisory Committee, 1976) and even among members of the Federal Organized Crime Strike Forces that had been established since 1967 in a number of cities with assumed Cosa Nostra presence. While some Strike Force members equated organized crime with Cosa Nostra, others included any group of two or more persons formed to commit a criminal act (U.S. Comptroller General, 1977).

In the long run, the notion that there is more to organized crime in the United States than Cosa Nostra did not lead to a profound revision of the concept. In the late 1970s and early 1980s, the concept of *nontraditional organized crime* emerged that merely transferred the Mafia model to other groupings similarly defined along ethnic lines and with allegedly a similar structure and purpose, such as East Asian, Latin American, and Russian groups, outlaw motorcycle gangs, and so-called prison gangs (President's Commission on Organized Crime, 1983).

Since the 1990s, the term organized crime has once again been primarily applied to Cosa Nostra as far as the situation within the United States is concerned, while with regard to other countries a wide array of phenomena has come to be labeled organized crime, irrespective of their resemblance to Cosa Nostra—for example, maritime piracy ("Piracy and Terrorism," 2004).

Two developments are significant for the current understanding of organized crime in the United States. The first is the series of successful prosecutions against members and associates of Cosa Nostra since the early 1980s that have continuously reinforced a narrow use of the term (Jacobs, 1994, 1999). The law enforcement campaign against Cosa Nostra also had another notable effect: a shift in perception from organized crime constituting an imminent threat to internal security to organized crime becoming an element of American folklore celebrated in TV shows such as the *Sopranos* and in movie comedies such as *Analyze This* and *Mickey Blue Eyes*.

The second important development in the current understanding is the internationalization of the concept of organized crime. The use of the term in other countries and on the international level, originally inspired by the United States, has increasingly become detached from the U.S. context, and in turn has come to influence the use of the term in the United States.

THE RECEPTION OF THE AMERICAN CONCEPT OF ORGANIZED CRIME IN OTHER COUNTRIES

The U.S. debate on organized crime, as it gained momentum in the 1950s, 1960s, and 1970s, did not go unnoticed elsewhere in the world, especially not in western countries that invariably saw the United States as a model for their own societal developments. What had come to light about the organization and influence of criminals in the United States appeared like a premonition of things to come. Even in Italy, with its very own entrenched organized crime problems, renewed public interest in the Mafia was partly inspired by events like the Kefauver hearings (Dickie, 2004, p. 319). Most countries, however, found themselves in essentially the same position as those parts of the United States that did not have a Cosa Nostra presence. The typical response to the Mafia-centered notion of organized crime was to either reject the concept altogether or to redefine it. Western Europe is a case in point.

Beginning in the 1960s, the official usage of the term organized crime in Western Europe has been vacillating between, on the one hand, the desire to depart from U.S. imagery in order to accommodate the specifics of the European crime situation and, on the other hand, the temptation to hold on to the concept of organized crime in order not to relinquish the "emotional kick" (Levi, 1998b, p. 336) that comes with it exactly because of the connotation of sinister criminal organizations.

At first, the notion prevailed that organized crime was an ill-fitting term

Image 2.5   In the 1999 movie comedy *Analyze This*, a psychologist (Billy Crystal, r.) has to fill in for his client, a Mafia boss (Robert De Niro, l.), at a Cosa Nostra meeting.

Photo: Ronald Siemoneit/Sygma/Corbis

in the (Western) European context. A study sponsored by the Council of Europe in 1970, for example, found that police forces across Western Europe had little use for this concept. The researchers noted a general agreement that U.S.-style organized crime (in the sense of the provision of illegal goods and services by well-organized and politically entrenched crime syndicates) was almost nonexistent. Instead, developments in the area of predatory crime were believed to pose a much greater and far more immediate threat. One perceived trend pertained to a weakening of traditional localized underworld milieus and the emergence of a more anonymous, nonterritorial network of criminals. Clusters of individual criminals from different social and regional backgrounds were seen to cooperate and pool resources for the commission of specific crimes. This network of criminals, it was stressed, did not have "any elaborate collective organisation," nor was there a "Mr. Big" (Mack & Kerner, 1975, p. 54). Accordingly, the organized crime label was at first only very hesitantly and sparingly used in Western Europe. Over time, however, the networks of criminals that seemed to bear so little resemblance to the imagery of mafia syndicates came to be viewed as the specifically European manifestation of organized crime. This development coincided and, in fact, may be explained at least in part by the formation of law enforcement units and agencies with a specialization in the use of investigative tools, such as electronic surveillance and undercover agents. The concept of organized crime helped to legitimize these innovations and it also facilitated the delineation of jurisdictional boundaries within law enforcement (Pütter, 1998).

A major shift in the public perception of organized crime did not occur until the late 1980s. The inclusion of so-called nontraditional, that is, non-Italian organized crime in the official U.S. parlance at the time, the growing migration problem in Western Europe, the discussion of new police powers in the fight against drug trafficking, and finally the profound changes following the fall of the Iron Curtain in 1989 and the demise of the Soviet Union can be seen as some of the factors that contributed to a revitalization of the threat image of mafia organizations. In contrast to the original perception of the 1960s, however, according to which these organizations were not present in Western Europe, journalistic depictions and official reports now saw Europe as a hotbed of transnational, mostly ethnically defined "mafias" (Europol, 2002; Freemantle, 1996; Sterling, 1994). Ironically, official definitions and the day-to-day police work in Europe have remained oriented at a very broad conception of organized crime that encompasses in essence all crime for profit involving the continuous cooperation of three or more individuals (Symeonidou-Kastanidou, 2007).

To put it in a nutshell, the conceptual history of organized crime has been characterized by two competing views, a narrow one centered on clear-cut criminal organizations and a broad one encompassing myriad forms of criminal structures and criminal activities. The narrow perspective on organized crime clearly dominates public perceptions. In fact, it was only after the emergence of a narrow understanding with a focus on the Italian American Mafia that the concept of organized crime gained wide acceptance. In criminal statutes and in the practice of law enforcement, however, a broad conception prevails. This ambiguity provides politicians and law enforcement officials with convenient opportunities for a flexible use of the concept of organized crime (von Lampe, 2001a).

LESSONS TO BE LEARNED FROM
THE CONCEPTUAL HISTORY OF ORGANIZED CRIME

When one looks at the conceptual history of organized crime, it is important to note that the use of the term as such and the way it is used are not inherently and inadvertently linked to the reality of crime. First of all, the phenomena that eventually came to be labeled organized crime had existed long before the concept of organized crime first emerged, dating back centuries (Egmond, 1993; Fijnaut, 2014b; Mansour, 2008; Newton, 2011; Sharpe, 1984; Van Wees, 1998). Secondly, the disconnect between concept and reality is not just a matter of perception lagging behind the actual development of crime. While crime phenomena may at times be difficult to detect because of their clandestine nature, in the case of mafia organizations this does not explain why it took more than 60 years, from the hysteria following the murder of police chief Hennessey in New Orleans by alleged mafiosi in 1890 until the 1950s and 1960s, that organized crime and Mafia came to be treated as synonymous. Thirdly, those views that are most prevalent at a given point in time are not necessarily the views that are most accurately reflecting reality. Namely, the Cosa Nostra-centered conception of organized crime in the United States has been criticized for overemphasizing the role of Italian American criminals. Historians have argued that, perhaps with the exception of New York City, Cosa Nostra never had such a dominating position within the underworld and that there were other important groups actually profiting from a tunnel vision on the Mafia (Jenkins & Potter, 1987). Criminologist also have pointed out, as will be examined more closely in later chapters, that Cosa Nostra as an organization has relatively little to do with the day-to-day commission of crimes and that its influence within the underworld, even under favorable conditions, has remained limited (Reuter, 1983). Finally, there is a persistent argument that conceptions of organized crime tend to center on powerless, marginalized social groups, such as Italian immigrants in the United States, while ignoring the harm done by crimes of the powerful (Pearce, 1976; Rawlinson, 2002; Woodiwiss, 2001).

There is an entire literature that seeks to explain why certain views on organized crime have become prevalent while others failed to gain broad acceptance. This literature has highlighted a number of institutional and political interests and cultural influences that have come to shape perceptions of organized crime (Hobbs & Antonopoulos, 2013; Kelly, 1978; Sheptycki, 2003; Smith, 1975, 1976, 1991; Van Duyne, 2004; Van Duyne & Nelemans, 2012; von Lampe, 2001a; Woodiwiss, 1990, 2001, 2003; Woodiwiss & Hobbs, 2009). At this point it must suffice to note that the way organized crime has been conceptualized since the early 1800s has always been a matter of choice and a matter of convenience.

OVERVIEW OF DEFINITIONS OF ORGANIZED CRIME

The meanings that have been attached to the term organized crime are more diverse, of course, than could be highlighted in the brief account of the conceptual history presented in the previous section. There is not just a narrow,

Mafia-centered conception competing against a broad one pertaining to a wide array of crime phenomena. To clarify the complexity of views, it helps to systematically look at the various definitions of organized crime that have been proposed. Scholars, law enforcement officials, journalists, and politicians "have turned defining organized crime into an industry" (Beare, 2003b, p. 159), and the number of definitions is continuously growing.

As others have pointed out before, most of these definitions are not definitions in the strict sense of the word but mere descriptions (Reuter, 1994; Van Duyne, 2003). Definitions are supposed to precisely delineate the boundaries of something by providing clear rules for deciding where something begins and ends. Many definitions of organized crime are too vague and ambiguous to meet this requirement (Van Duyne, 2003) and are therefore of only very limited value in the context of research, legislation, and policymaking. However, for the present purpose of analyzing the scope of different meanings attached to the term organized crime, these shortcomings do not pose a fundamental problem.

Three Notions of the "Nature" of Organized Crime: Activity, Structure, Governance

There are at least three different notions of the core nature of organized crime: one centered on criminal *activity*, one centered on criminal *organization*, and one centered on illegal *governance*. According to one view, organized crime is primarily about crime. Many definitions in essence state that organized crime is crime. Organized crime, therefore, is seen as a specific type of criminal activity. What makes crime organized is either the nature of these activities or the criminals behind them. Criminal activities are regarded as being organized, for example, because of a certain level of sophistication, continuity, and rationality, or by a certain level of harm. Take, for example, this definition by Samuel Porteous in a study prepared for the Canadian government: "Organized crime encompasses any organized *profit-motivated criminal activities* [emphasis added] that have a *serious impact* [emphasis added]" (Porteous, 1998, pp. 1–2, 10).

Another view holds that it is not so important what offenders do or how they do it but how offenders are linked to and associated with each other. Organized crime, then, is about some form of organization of criminals in contrast to lone, independently operating offenders. The FBI, for example "defines organized crime as any *group having some manner of a formalized structure* [emphasis added] and whose primary objective is to obtain money through illegal activities" (Federal Bureau of Investigation, n.d.).

Finally, there is a view that organized crime does not have to do primarily with specific forms of criminal activities or specific forms of criminal organization but with the concentration of illegitimate power in the hands of criminals. In one scenario, criminals create an underworld government that controls, regulates, and taxes illegal activities. In another scenario, criminals gain influence in legitimate society by either replacing legitimate government or by entering into alliances with corrupt members of political and business elites for the purpose of manipulating the constitutional order in their favor. From this perspective, the term organized crime denotes primarily a systemic condition.

Alan Block has argued that organized crime can be understood as "a *social system* [emphasis added] . . . composed of relationships binding professional criminals, politicians, law enforcers, and various entrepreneurs" (Block, 1983, p. vii; see also Albini, 1971, pp. 63, 77; Ianni & Reuss-Ianni, 1976, p. xvi).

Notions About Criminal Organization

Apart from these fundamental categorizations of organized crime (activity, structure, governance), there are a number of other definitional controversies on a smaller scale. Those who regard the organization of criminals as a key aspect, including those who define organized crime as crime committed by members of criminal organizations, do not agree on the defining criteria for these criminal organizations. This controversy mainly runs along the lines of structure and size.

Some definitions do not contain any qualifying criteria for the organization of criminals. Political scientist Roy Godson, for example, in his definition of organized crime accepts a broad range of structural forms:

> Organized crime refers to *individuals and groups* [emphasis added] with ongoing working relationships who make their living primarily through activities that one or more states deem illegal and criminal. Organized crime can take a *variety of institutional or organizational forms* [emphasis added]. This includes tight vertical hierarchies with lifelong commitments, as well as looser, more ephemeral, nonhierarchical relationships. (Godson, 2003c, p. 274)

Other definitions establish certain minimum standards that criminal organizations have to meet in order to be classified as organized crime. Criminologist John Conklin, for example, emphasizes enduring, formal structures:

> Organized crime has the characteristics of a formal organization: a *division of labor, coordination* [emphasis added] of activities through *rules* and *codes* [emphasis added], and an *allocation of tasks* [emphasis added] in order to achieve certain *goals* [emphasis added]. (Conklin, 2010, p. 73)

As far as size is concerned, most definitions that address this aspect set the minimum limit at three participants. There are, however, also definitions according to which two criminals are sufficient to constitute organized crime. In Australia, for example, the Queensland Crime and Misconduct Act 2001 defines organized crime in essence as criminal activity that involves two or more persons (see also Chapter 14).

Violence and Corruption

There are also differences in opinion regarding the use of violence and corruption. For some, these are defining features of organized crime. In fact, one of the very first definitions of organized crime stated that it "is a technique of violence, intimidation and corruption" (Special Crime Study Commission on Organized Crime, 1953, p. 11). In other definitions, violence and corruption appear only as possible attributes of organized crime, while in yet others these two aspects are not mentioned at all.

Profit and Politics

Finally, an important controversy surrounds the question what aims criminals and criminal organizations, respectively, have to pursue in order to qualify as organized crime. Some definitions emphasize material gain as the central motif of organized crime and implicitly or explicitly exclude political goals (Abadinsky, 2013, p. 3; Lebeya, 2007, p. 17; Valencic & Mozetic, 2006, p. 130); others add power and political influence, though mostly as a means to economic ends (Finckenauer, 2005, p. 81; Rhodes, 1984, p. 4; Winslow & Zhang, 2008, p. 430). Yet, there are also definitions of organized crime that include political or ideological agendas (Chibelushi, Sharp, & Shah, 2006, p. 156; Clark, 2005, p. 105; Swain, 2009, p. 5), which leads to an overlap of the concepts of organized crime and terrorism.

Accounting for the Diversity of Definitions of Organized Crime

The lack of consensus in the definition of organized crime, as has already been pointed out, should not come as a surprise. This is a reflection of the different ways in which reality can be constructed and the different factors that influence the social construction of reality. It is not something, of course, that is unique to organized crime. Similar conceptual confusion also surrounds related issues such as gangs, corruption, or terrorism as well as more general sociological concepts such as society, family, group, and organization.

All definitions of organized crime, including those proposed by scholars, are in the last instance shaped by practical and political considerations or simply by individual preferences. After all, there is not the one imperative conception of organized crime dictated by reality that would effectively rule out any such external influences. In some respects, it appears to be a political decision how organized crime is defined. For example, there are different rationales for arguing that the use of violence is a defining characteristic of organized crime. One rationale, arguably, is the desire to protect social elites, who tend to be involved in nonviolent rather than violent criminal activity, from the stigmatizing label of organized crime. Similarly, the decision on whether or not to include politically motivated crime in the definition of organized crime can be influenced by considerations of whether or not the same law enforcement unit or agency should have jurisdiction over profit-oriented crime as well as cases of terrorism. In fact, that is the reason why, for example, the official German definition of organized crime explicitly excludes terrorist acts (Kinzig, 2004, p. 57).

In other cases, attempts to define organized crime rest on the notion that somehow a level of certainty exists about what organized crime is. This certainty, however, rests on shaky grounds. Three lines of argument can be discerned. Ideas about the nature of organized crime are often derived from the analysis of specific empirical phenomena. For example, when in 1967 a Presidential commission in the United States famously defined organized crime along the lines of its perception of the Italian American Mafia or Cosa Nostra, this meant that everything not closely resembling the Cosa Nostra would not be considered organized crime. Apart from the fact that the commission's interpretation of Cosa Nostra has been highly controversial, the tunnel vision on Cosa Nostra can be viewed as having been arbitrary and misguided to begin with. Sometimes, a notion of certainty about the nature of organized crime is also derived from what "most observers agree" on (Maltz, 1994, p. 25). This means that organized crime is what a majority, for whatever diverse reasons, believes organized crime to be (see, e.g., Abadinsky, 2013, p. 2; Albanese, 2011, p. 4; Hagan, 2006; Finckenauer, 2005).

Finally, a notion of the nature of organized crime is sometimes deduced from the words organized and crime themselves (Kollmar, 1974, p. 2). At times, what is taken as the literal meaning of organized crime, for example "crime that is organized," is then narrowed down to something believed to be "true organized crime" (Finckenauer, 2005, p. 76). In any case, taking the literal meaning as the basis for a definition leads to the peculiar consequence that the meanings each of these two words, organized and crime, have separately acquired in common language usage determine what empirical phenomena are being viewed within one conceptual framework of organized crime.

OUTLINE OF A CONCEPTUAL FRAMEWORK FOR THE STUDY OF ORGANIZED CRIME

The review of the various definitions of organized crime leads back to the question of how to deal with the existing conceptual confusion from a social science perspective. As has been argued in Chapter 1, a definition is a possible outcome of the study of organized crime, but there is no definition that could meaningfully delineate the study of organized crime as a field of research. At least, this is true for the time being as long as there exists no profound understanding of the interplay between the various phenomena that have been labeled organized crime. To clarify this point, it may help to talk about the weather for a moment. Defining the concept of "weather" is facilitated by the insights that meteorologists have gained into how factors, such as temperature, clouds, precipitation, wind, and barometric pressure, influence and depend on each other. Comparable insights have not yet been produced in the study of organized crime about the interplay of such factors as the individual characteristics of organized criminals, the logistical requirements of particular criminal activities, or the structural features of criminal organizations.

The alternative to a field of study delineated by an all-encompassing definition is, as already indicated, to depart from the concept of organized crime as an analytical category and to shift attention to the underlying phenomena that according to one view or the other have been associated with organized crime. It is on the level of these underlying phenomena, such as illegal markets and criminal organizations, that definitions make much more sense.

This line of reasoning follows a number of scholars who are skeptical of the scientific value of the concept of organized crime because it is "too vague and too contradictory" (Van Duyne, 2000, p. 370). Dwight C. Smith formulated his fundamental critique of the concept of organized crime as early as 1971:

How should the problem of defining organized crime be approached? Very simply: by not looking for organized crime itself. As a contrived concept, at least in contemporary usage, it does not possess its own logic, but requires interpretation from a variety of viewpoints. The question is not: "What is organized crime?" Rather, the question is: "What insights may be obtained from history, economics, sociology, psychology—even philosophy and theology—that would facilitate efforts to understand why the phenomena we categorize as organized crime occur, and what forces trigger their occurrence?" (Smith, 1971, p. 63)

From a similar angle, the German criminologists Ulrich Eisenberg and Claudius Ohder have suggested that it might be appropriate to avoid the category organized crime altogether and, instead, to break it down into a larger number of concrete research questions and aspects (Eisenberg & Ohder, 1990, p. 578). However, this view neglects the function of the term organized crime as a somewhat fuzzy yet useful conceptual "rallying point" for scholars with similar, intersecting, or overlapping research interests.

Basic Dimensions of Organized Crime

In order to come to a clearer, less ambiguous conceptual framework, the concept of organized crime can be broken down, in a first step, into the three basic dimensions that have already been highlighted in this and the previous chapter: criminal activities, offender structures, and illegal governance. Within these dimensions, further meaningful differentiations can be made.

Activity

The first basic dimension of the concept of organized crime pertains to the way criminal activities are carried out. The study of organized crime is concerned with phenomena that fall somewhere on a continuum ranging from spontaneous, impulsive, isolated acts in one extreme to, in the other extreme, criminal endeavors that follow a rational plan, involve the combination of different tasks, and extend over long periods of time. Where exactly organized crime should be positioned on this continuum is not as important as to understand how under conditions of illegality, in an essentially hostile environment, fairly sophisticated, continuous activities are possible. Any kind of illegal activity is of interest for the study of organized crime as long as its examination helps in answering this question. Three main types of illegal activity are at the center of attention in the study of organized crime: (a) market-based crimes involving the provision of illegal goods (e.g. child pornography) and services (e.g., illicit debt collection) to willing customers, (b) predatory crimes such as theft, robbery, and fraud characterized by offender-victim relations, and (c) what could be termed "control-oriented" or "regulatory" or "governance" crimes involving the setting and enforcing of rules of conduct and the settling of disputes in the absence of effective government regulation and, in turn, the taxation of illegal profit-making activities.

Structure

The second basic dimension of the concept of organized crime has to do with the ways criminals are connected to other criminals. These structures can take on various forms with various degrees of complexity and formalization. Again for the study of organized crime, it is not important where a dividing line should be drawn between organized crime and "non-organized crime." The main concern is to understand how it is possible that criminals willingly disclose to others the fact that they are criminals and that they are willing to associate and cooperate with other criminals, even though at first glance this increases the risk of arrest and conviction, given that every confidant and every accomplice is a potential informant and witness. In essence, every case involving offenders that do not strictly operate on their own, in complete social isolation, can offer insights into the organization of criminals, and these cases should not be excluded by an inevitably arbitrary definition of organized crime. There are a number of crucial classifications of offender structures that will be highlighted in later chapters. One key classification pertains to the forms of these structures. There are essentially three forms of relations between offenders: (a) market-based interactions between independent suppliers and customers, (b) interactions between members of one organization who basically follow the same directives, and (c) network-based interactions where both sides make decisions independently but they are bound by underlying social ties.

Governance

The third basic dimension of the study of organized crime, illegal governance, has to do with the amassing and use of power in a way that is more akin to government and politics than to market-based or predatory crime. There are two spheres of society where the power amassed and exercised by criminals may come to bear: underworld and upperworld. In the underworld, that sphere of society where the state has no ambition to regulate behavior other than to suppress it because it is illegal, forms of self-regulation may develop that can take on the form of an underworld government. Individuals or groups may emerge that, as indicated before, set and enforce rules of conduct and settle disputes among criminals and in turn demand a share of illegal profits. Such influence can also extend into the legal spheres of society, especially where the state is weak. This typically occurs in the form of an alliance of criminal, business, and political elites. The overriding question in both cases is how it is possible that crime, the quintessential violation of commonly shared norms and values, can create order, sometimes even enjoying a high degree of legitimacy, as ethically twisted as this order may be.

Other Basic Dimensions

There are other fundamental issues not fully captured by the three basic dimensions of activities, structures, and governance. On the one hand, there is the question of the embeddedness of the activities and structures associated with organized crime in the broader context of society. On the other hand, the question is what role the individual, and individual characteristics, play in shaping these activities and structures. While the embeddedness of organized crime will be specifically addressed in later chapters (Chapters 9, 10, and 11), the individual organized criminal, although a recurring theme throughout the book, will receive only relatively little attention, given the scarcity of pertinent research (Chapter 13).

Links Between Basic Dimensions

Each of these basic dimensions can be examined separately. For example, there is plenty to study about the logistics of criminal activities, such as drug trafficking or investment fraud, without having to be overly concerned with offender structures. Likewise, there is plenty to study about the way criminals are organized in "networks" and "mafias" without having to be overly concerned with the particulars of the criminal activities they engage in. Yet, against the background of the debate on organized crime, questions should also be raised about the extent to which these dimensions are interdependent. For example, one may wonder if there is a connection between the way criminal activities are carried out and the way offender structures are shaped. As will be discussed later in this book (Chapters 5 and 6) an argument can indeed be made that how offenders organize themselves is influenced by the activities they engage in. Similarly, it has been argued that illegal governance structures depend on the prevalence of particular types of crime, namely criminal activities such as illegal gambling that are carried out on a continuous basis and are highly visible and therefore easy for an underworld government to monitor. Of course, more complex interconnections can also be explored. Interrelations potentially exist between individual offender characteristics, the form of offender structures, the nature of criminal activities, the form and extent of illegal governance structures, and environmental variables, such as community support for criminals, demand for illegal goods and services, and the intensity and direction of law enforcement pressure. This entails exploring, in as many social and historical settings as possible, how the phenomena in question vary in time and space and in what combinations they appear (von Lampe, 2003a, p. 43). With this kind of approach to the study of organized crime, the focus shifts from the question, What is organized crime? to the question, How organized is crime, and how organized are criminals under specific circumstances?

THE CONCEPT OF ORGANIZED CRIME: SUMMARY AND CONCLUSION

In the introductory chapter and in this chapter an important distinction has been made between social reality and the construction of social reality. While the term organized crime is often used in the public debate and in the scholarly literature as if it denoted a clear and coherent phenomenon, it is in fact an ever-changing, contradictory, and diffuse construct. As Michael Levi has observed: "Like the psychiatrist's Rorschach blot, its attraction as well as its weakness is that one can read almost anything into it" (Levi, 2002b, p. 887). Myriad aspects of the social universe are lumped together in varying combinations within different frames of reference depending on the respective point of view of the observer. While these various phenomena by themselves may be perfectly real, it is only on the conceptual level that they are brought into one unifying context (von Lampe, 2001a; von Lampe, 2008c).

Accordingly, when the debate on organized crime is boiled down, there is not one core understanding of the nature of organized crime to be found. A lot of the confusion in the debate can be explained by the failure to realize that there are different ways to conceptualize organized crime and that each approach can lead to different understandings and assessments of the very same situation. For example, drugs may be trafficked through a chain of independent sellers and buyers. From one point of view this may not seem to amount to much since there is no organization, while from another angle the smooth and efficient way in which the drugs are moved from hand to hand may look like a prime example of organized crime.

It is also important to acknowledge that the various facets of the overall picture are not static. Whereas definitions of organized crime have a tendency to focus on one specific constellation of these facets, for example, criminal organizations using violence and corruption, it seems far more adequate to place the emphasis on the fluidity and diversity of the constellations in which the various attributes ascribed to organized crime manifest themselves—for example, under what circumstances criminal organizations emerge and under what circumstances these criminal organizations resort to violence and corruption. Rather than opting for one particular perspective, therefore, it is much more appropriate to break down the concept into a number of smaller-scale categories. On the most abstract level the discussion in this book will follow the distinction of the three basic dimensions pertaining to how crimes are committed, how criminals associate and interact with other criminals, and how power is amassed and used by criminals to control other criminals and to gain influence in legitimate society.

Discussion Questions

1. What element in definitions of organized crime is politically the most controversial?

2. What consequences does it have to include terrorism in a definition of organized crime?

3. Imagine no one would ever have come up with the concept of organized crime, would this make a difference for law enforcement?

4. Imagine no one would ever have come up with the concept of organized crime, would this make a difference for social science research?

Research Projects

1. Find a recent report on organized crime and determine with what meaning(s) and how consistently the term organized crime is used.

2. Do a full-text search of a newspaper for a period of six months or a year and determine with what meaning(s) and how consistently the term organized crime is used.

Further Reading

The Conceptual History of Organized Crime

Albanese, J. S. (1988). Government perceptions of organized crime: The Presidential commissions, 1967 and 1987. *Federal Probation, 52*(1), 58–63.

Bersten, M. (1990). Defining organised crime in Australia and the USA. *Australian and New Zealand Journal of Criminology, 23*(1), 39–59.

Levi, M. (1998). Perspectives on organised crime: An overview. *The Howard Journal, 37*(4), 335–345.

Moore, W. H. (1974). *The Kefauver Committee and the politics of crime 1950–1952.* Columbia, MO: University of Missouri Press.

Paoli, L., & Vander Beken, T. (2014). Organized crime: A contested concept. In L. Paoli (Ed.), *The Oxford handbook of organized crime* (pp. 13–31). Oxford, UK: Oxford University Press.

Smith, D. C. (1991). Wickersham to Sutherland to Katzenbach: Evolving an official definition for organized crime. *Crime, Law and Social Change, 16*(2), 135–154.

van Duyne, P. C. (2004). The creation of a threat image: Media policy making and organised crime. In P. C. van Duyne, M. Jager, K. von Lampe, & J. L. Newell (Eds.), *Threats and phantoms of organised crime corruption and terrorism* (pp. 21–50). Nijmegen, Netherlands: Wolf Legal.

The Emergence of the Mafia Paradigm and the Focus on Italian Americans

Bernstein, L. (2002). *The greatest menace: Organized crime in cold war America.* Amherst, MA: University of Massachusetts Press.

Gambino, R. (1994). Italian Americans, today's immigrants. *Italian Americana, 12*(2), 226–234.

Smith, D. C. (1975). *The Mafia mystique.* New York: Lanham.

Defining Organized Crime

Varese, F. (2010). What is organized crime? In F. Varese (Ed.), *Organized crime: Critical concepts in criminology* (pp. 1–33). London: Routledge.

von Lampe, K. (2015). *Definitions of organized crime.* http://www.organized-crime.de/organizedcrimedefinitions.htm

von Lampe, K., van Dijck, M., Hornsby, R., & Markina, A. (2006). Organised crime is. . . . Findings from a cross-national review of literature. In P. C. van Duyne, A. Maljevic, M. van Dijck, K. von Lampe, & J. L. Newell (Eds.), *The organisation of crime for profit: Conduct, law and measurement* (pp. 17–42). Nijmegen, Netherlands: Wolf Legal.

CHAPTER 3

Organized
Crime Research

THE STUDY OF ORGANIZED
CRIME AS AN ACADEMIC SUBDISCIPLINE

The study of organized crime is not the exclusive domain of scholars. Investigative journalists as well as crime analysts embedded in law enforcement agencies have made important contributions to the understanding of the organization of crimes and criminals. Still, it is only with the establishment of the study of organized crime as a systematic academic endeavor that a coherent body of knowledge has begun to take shape.

An academic discipline is constituted by a self-referential system comprising elements such as specialized journals, professional associations, university courses, and textbooks. By this measure, the study of organized crime has emerged, since the 1960s, as at least a separate subdiscipline within the broad field of criminology and the social sciences.

There are three established academic (peer-reviewed) journals with an exclusive or major focus on organized crime: *Crime, Law and Social Change*, which has the longest tradition and highest prestige among the three journals; *Global Crime*, which has previously been published under the name *Transnational Organized Crime*; and *Trends in Organized Crime*, the journal which is affiliated with the International Association for the Study of Organized Crime (IASOC) and the only one of the three currently with an exclusive focus on organized crime. The editorial boards of these journals have partially overlapping membership, indicating the density of the overall network of scholars in this field. Two professional associations provide additional structure, IASOC and the Standing Group Organised Crime of the European Consortium for Political Research (ECPR). Finally, there are regular meeting places for scholars interested in organized crime, either at larger conferences, such as those of the American and European societies of criminology (ASC and ESC), or at thematically focused conferences and workshops, such as the Cross-Border Crime Colloquia held annually at changing locations throughout Europe since 1999.

Courses on organized crime have been regularly taught in criminology and criminal justice programs in the United States for decades, with universities in other parts of the world, especially Australia and Europe, now following suit. A number of textbooks focusing specifically on organized crime have been published since the mid-1970s. The two current textbooks with the longest tradition, authored by Howard Abadinsky and Jay Albanese, respectively, saw their first editions in the 1980s.

While scholars interested in organized crime are scattered all across the globe, certain centers of research activity have emerged since the 1990s. Some of these research centers are institutionally independent, like the Centre for the Study of Democracy (CSD) in Sofia, Bulgaria, or the Institute for Security Studies (ISS) in South Africa. Some are integrated into governmental structures, such as the Research and Documentation Center (WODC) of the Ministry of Security and Justice in the Netherlands and the Council for Crime Prevention (Brå) in Sweden. Some are affiliated with universities, such as CIROC in the Netherlands, Transcrime in Italy, Ghent University's Institute for International Research on Criminal Policy (IRCP), and the Terrorism, Transnational Crime and Corruption Center (TraCCC), a research institute with headquarters at George Mason University in Virginia and various branches in Russia, Ukraine, and the former Soviet Republic of Georgia. Some universities have become centers of organized crime research, not by virtue of formal structures but because of continuous research by scholars, including PhD students, with a specialization in organized crime studies, for example San Diego State University in California, Rutgers University in New Jersey, John Jay College of Criminal Justice in New York, the University of Montreal in Quebec, Cardiff University in Wales, Tilburg University in the Netherlands, and the University of Leuven in Belgium. Several supranational research and documentation centers, finally, like the European Monitoring Centre for Drugs and Drug Addiction (EMCDDA) in Lisbon, the United Nations Office on Drugs and Crime (UNODC) in Vienna, or the Geneva-based International Organization for Migration (IOM) have made significant contributions to the study of organized crime in specific areas, namely drug trafficking, human trafficking, and human smuggling.

THE HISTORY OF THE STUDY OF ORGANIZED CRIME

Research on organized crime predates by several decades the development of a distinct subdiscipline. The history of the study of organized crime in many ways reflects the conceptual history of organized crime with science repeatedly taking cues from the public debate. The development can be roughly divided into five phases, a classical period in the 1920s, followed by what might best be termed a "journalistic period" from the 1930s through the 1960s. The late 1960s saw the emergence of an academic literature critical of the mafia paradigm that had come to dominate official and public perceptions of organized crime. Since the 1980s a gradual shift has been taking place away from the heavy emphasis on disputing the mafia paradigm to a more bottom-up analysis of the phenomena labeled organized crime.

Scientific interest in organized crime dates back to at least the second half of the 19th century, when Italian scholars such as criminologist Cesare Lombroso and ethnologist Guiseppe Pitrè began to look at the phenomena of Mafia and

Camorra in southern Italy. But as far as can be discerned, it was not until the 1920s that the term organized crime entered the scientific vocabulary.

The Pioneers: Frederic Thrasher and John Landesco

The first scientific studies that applied the concept of organized crime were conducted in the United States: Frederic Thrasher's *The Gang*, originally completed as a doctoral dissertation in 1926, and John Landesco's *Organized Crime in Chicago*, published in 1929. Given the history of the concept of organized crime, it is not surprising that these studies came out of Chicago, where the term was first coined (see Chapter 2).

In *The Gang*, Frederic Thrasher attempted to present a systematic analysis of the juvenile gang phenomenon in Chicago. In one chapter, "The Gang and Organized Crime," however, he also examined adult gangs. Similar to the discussions of the Chicago Crime Commission that Thrasher repeatedly cited, organized crime to him was not so much a matter of particular criminal organizations but of the underworld as a whole in the sense of a criminal community within which gangs were only one, albeit an important, element. Gangs, Thrasher observed, provide criminals fellowship, status, excitement, security, and the chance to better profit from crime. At the same time, he saw gangs being enlisted by businesses, labor unions and politicians in violent confrontations over economic and political interests, thereby constituting an important link between underworld and upperworld (Thrasher, 1927/1963).

John Landesco's study of organized crime in Chicago similarly looked at the "social world" (Landesco, 1929, p. 1087) of criminals and the broader societal context, although his focus was specifically on the prominent gangs and gangsters of his day and their respective historical predecessors. Landesco argued that gangsters were the product of social conditions that had existed long before Prohibition. The only significant change he noted was that the relations between gangsters and between underworld and upperworld had become more business-like and less reliant on close social ties, such as a "neighborhood play group."

Thrasher and Landesco did not immediately inspire any other researchers to conduct similar studies. While organized crime appeared as a theme in some theoretical and empirical publications in the 1930s, 1940s, and 1950s, for example, Frank Tannenbaum's *Crime and the Community* (1951) and William F. Whyte's *Street Corner Society* (1943/1981), no coherent scientific debate developed for the next forty years.

The Journalistic Period

Research on organized crime during the 1930s through 1950s was primarily the domain of journalists. Herbert Asbury, for example, wrote a number of books on the underworlds of major U.S. cities of which his early work *Gangs of New York* (Asbury, 1927) is the best known to this day (see also Asbury, 1933, 1942). In contrast to Asbury's ambitious writings, which have received some recognition by scholars, many journalistic accounts of organized crime of that era have

Image 3.1 Gangster funerals such as that of Angelo Genna, a major player in the illegal alcohol business and Capone ally who had been slain in May of 1925, served John Landesco to elicit the position Chicago underworld figures occupied in society. Genna's high standing was evidenced by the front ranks of the mourners, among them a State Senator, several other politicians as well as leading members of the underworld. Three hundred cars followed the coffin, including thirty cars containing flowers (Landesco, 1929, p. 1035).

Photo: Bettmann/Corbis

been dismissed as sensationalist and outright bizarre. These books promoted imagery of all-powerful nationwide or even global criminal organizations. As early as 1935, newspaper reporter Martin Mooney described a "super-racketeering organization of Crime, Incorporated" in which criminals were the junior partners of politicians and businessmen (Mooney, 1935, p. 8). Others saw the Sicilian Mafia at work in the United States. The Mafia, they claimed, constituted a global "super-government of crime" (Reid, 1952, p. 25) with influence in the White House and connections reaching as far as Russia and China (Lait & Mortimer, 1950, p. 176).

Donald Cressey

As indicated in Chapter 2, the notion that organized crime manifested itself in one all-encompassing criminal organization increasingly dominated the public

Image 3.2 Donald R. Cressey, a criminologist at the University of California, was asked to serve on a Task Force on Organized Crime as part of President Johnson's Commission on Law Enforcement and Administration of Justice. Based on this experience he wrote his controversial book *Theft of the Nation* which appeared in 1969, the same year Mario Puzo's bestselling novel *The Godfather* was first published.

Photo: University of California

perception in the United States during the 1950s and 1960s, although not necessarily with the connotation of high-level conspiracy or worldwide expansion. It was this notion that criminologist Donald Cressey, arguably the founding father of the modern study of organized crime, cast in a scientific mold with his 1969 book *Theft of the Nation: The Structure and Operations of Organized Crime in America.* Cressey had been asked to analyze organized crime for a Presidential Commission (Cressey, 1967a). In this capacity he was able to gain unprecedented access to law enforcement data, and he was given the opportunity to talk to Mafia-turncoat Joe Valachi (Rogovin & Martens, 1992). The analysis presented in *Theft of the Nation* comprised four dimensions: the range of forms of criminal organization, the relationship between Cosa Nostra and other criminal organizations, the functions of Cosa Nostra, and its formal and informal structures. Cressey saw Cosa Nostra at the upper end of organizational sophistication among criminals and, in fact, similar in many ways to a legitimate organization. Cosa Nostra, he argued, is a confederation of local organizations, called "families," unified under a ruling body, the "commission," and with an initiation rite that clearly distinguishes members from nonmembers. There is, as Cressey further explained, a hierarchical structure of different levels of authority and a division of labor between a number of specialized tasks that are carried out either on a permanent or on a temporary basis. This organization, according to Cressey, fulfills a dual function, that of a business involved in a range of illegal activities and that of an underworld government that regulates and controls the behavior of individuals involved in illegal activities (Cressey, 1969).

All of these claims have been contested more or less vigorously. Arguably the most controversial notion conveyed in Cressey's book, however, is that "while Cosa Nostra still tolerates some major operations by criminals of ethnic backgrounds which are not Sicilian or Italian, if one understands Cosa Nostra he understands organized crime in the United States" (Cressey, 1969, p. 21). It is this position to which Cressey's views on organized crime are commonly reduced, the claim that the phenomenon of organized crime can largely be explained by reference to one bureaucratic organization of criminals with a particular ethnic background. This is in essence what critics of Cressey have dubbed the "mafia model" or "bureaucratic model of organized crime," or respectively the "alien conspiracy theory." The fact that *Theft of the Nation* as well as a later book, *Criminal Organizations* (Cressey, 1972) contains a much more cautious and differentiated analysis has for the most part been ignored.

Cressey's ambition clearly was to show that a scientific approach is necessary to overcome the sensationalist imagery of organized crime created and promoted by the media (Cressey, 1969, p. 59). Indeed, reminiscing about his work on organized crime several years later he could rightfully take credit for making "the study of organized crime a respectable academic pursuit" (as cited in Laub, 1983, p. 162). Yet, tragically, his importance lies not so much in the breadth and depth of his analysis but in serving as a sort of "punching bag" for an entire generation of scholars who gave contour to their findings by seeking to contradict Cressey. While critical comments about the sensationalist depictions of organized crime had occasionally been made by academics before (Bell, 1953), it was only after Cressey had presented the mafia model within a scientific framework that a scholarly debate on organized crime developed.

The Post-Cressey Era

The academic literature that followed the publication of *Theft of the Nation* can be classified according to the various points of attack against the mafia model. Some critics questioned the accuracy of historical claims Cressey had made, others disputed Cressey's analysis of the function and purpose of Cosa Nostra.

Historical Research

A number of studies sought to disprove certain elements of the factual basis on which the mafia model in the United States rested. Cressey and others assumed that Cosa Nostra had been created in the aftermath of a violent underworld conflict, the so-called "Castellammarese War" that pitted traditionalist Sicilian-born criminals against a faction of young "Americanized" gangsters. The conflict allegedly culminated in September 1931 in the murder of some forty Italian gang leaders across the United States (Cressey, 1969, p. 44). A systematic analysis of contemporary newspapers, however, found no evidence of these events except for reports on four murders in the New York City area (Block, 1980; see also Nelli, 1976, p. 183; and the critique by Rogovin & Martens, 1992, of Block's methodology).

Another historical study characteristic of the post-Cressey era examined the alleged dominance of Italian American criminals in the city of Philadelphia, home to a major Cosa Nostra family. Drawing on court files and other archival material as well as information obtained from a reputed high-ranking underworld figure, the study found that up until the 1950s, criminal activities in

Philadelphia were controlled by an alliance of gangsters, politicians, and police officials. It was only toward the late 1950s, according to this study, that a separate Italian American group took shape and eventually, in the 1960s, gained notoriety as the Cosa Nostra family of Philadelphia, even though there existed several other at least equally powerful criminal groups in that city. The authors concluded that the authorities in Philadelphia, in an effort to meet public expectations, focused their attention on Cosa Nostra:

> The supposed rise of the Mafia after 1960 did not represent a real change in power. Rather, it reflected the use of a new perspective by official agencies responding to urgent bureaucratic needs. The Italians were not more powerful than before; it was simply that their rivals had ceased to be noticed. (Jenkins & Potter, 1987, p. 483)

Corresponding to the argument made by Jenkins and Potter (1987), there is an important body of primarily historical literature highlighting the existence of organized crime phenomena in the United States prior to and independent from any individuals or groups originating in southern Italy (Block & Chambliss, 1981; Chambliss, 1978; Dickson-Gilmore & Woodiwiss, 2008; McIllwain, 2004; Potter & Gaines, 1995; Woodiwiss, 2001).

Economic Analyses

Other researchers critical of Cressey aimed at revisions of the mafia model by examining Cosa Nostra within more comprehensive frameworks. Two important studies by economists who had access to extensive law enforcement data shed light on the inner workings of Cosa Nostra and its position within the underworld: Annelise Anderson's study of the business activities of the Philadelphia Cosa Nostra family published in 1979 (Anderson, 1979) and Peter Reuter's study of gambling and loan sharking in New York City published in 1983 (Reuter, 1983). Both studies found that Cosa Nostra families do not function as business enterprises. Instead, individual members and associates in varying combinations run illegal enterprises, something that Donald Cressey, in fact, had already noted in *Theft of the Nation*. However, in contrast to Cressey's assessment, both studies also found that businesses linked to Cosa Nostra did not hold a monopoly position and did not use violence to eliminate competition. Still, Cosa Nostra appeared to occupy a preeminent position within the underworld in certain respects. In Philadelphia, according to Anderson, the leading Cosa Nostra members owned a so-called layoff bank where illegal gambling businesses could buy insurance against heavy losses. The layoff bank provided a tool for controlling the illegal gambling market by economic means to the extent gambling businesses, because of a lack of sufficient funds, relied on layoff services.

Reuter emphasized the role of Cosa Nostra in New York City as a provider of nonviolent conflict resolution services for illegal entrepreneurs who, in effect, could buy security and protection by subscribing to these services. In this respect, the New York Cosa Nostra families appeared to hold a monopoly position of sorts in that no one outside of Cosa Nostra was allowed to offer similar arbitration services. However, the resulting influence seemed to be limited to certain illegal markets and, because of a lack of consistency and coordination within Cosa Nostra, did not translate into an ability to systematically control and extort illegal businesses.

*Field Research on
Italian American Crime*

Whereas scholars such as Anderson and Reuter did not dispute the existence of Cosa Nostra as a formalized, hierarchically structured organization, other scholars fundamentally questioned the validity of this assumption. Soon after the publication of Cressey's *Theft of the Nation*, anthropologists Francis Ianni and Elizabeth Reuss-Ianni presented an influential study of what they called an "Italian-American crime family," a family clan of Sicilian decent residing in New York that had been involved in both legitimate and illegitimate businesses for two generations. The study was based on observations and informal interviews Francis Ianni had conducted while socializing with members of this family over a period of several years. Ianni and Reuss-Ianni argued that organized crime cannot be explained by reference to a formal organization alone.

Image 3.3   Economist Peter Reuter used material seized by the police, interviews with law enforcement officials and interviews with informants to explore the role of the Mafia in illegal gambling and loan sharking in New York City. In his seminal book *Disorganized Crime: The Economics of the Visible Hand* he concluded that by the late 1970s the Mafia had less control over illegal markets than was commonly assumed and that it "may be a paper tiger" living off a reputation it no longer deserved (Reuter, 1983, p. xi).

Photo: University of Maryland

While they acknowledged formalization in the organization of the legal and illegal businesses a crime family runs, the crime families themselves they saw as "traditional social systems" that had not been rationally constructed for particular purposes (Ianni & Reuss-Ianni, 1972, p. 108). Ianni and Reuss-Ianni, given their limited access to relevant information, left open the question whether the members of the family clan they studied belonged to some larger mafia organization.

Sociologist Joseph Albini in his 1971 book *American Mafia: Genesis of a Legend*, which heralded in the post-Cressey era of the study of organized crime, went much further in his critique of the mafia model. He explicitly dismissed the notion of Cosa Nostra being a nationwide, formal organization, arguing that this claim was based on unfounded and contradictory assumptions (Albini, 1971, p. 254). Albini drew on informants from among law enforcement and the underworld to present an alternative view, pertaining primarily to the case of Detroit and centering on the concept of "syndicated crime." Syndicated crime in Albini's terminology is the provision of illegal goods and services by criminals who are flexibly organized in ways that depend upon the specific type of activity and the specific societal context. In essence, however, these structures, according to Albini, are best "understood in terms of patron-client relationships within and between syndicates" (Albini, 1971, p. 223). Patrons are those who can offer protection or business opportunities while they, in turn, may be the clients of other patrons themselves. Such a system, Albini argued, is adaptable to the fluidity of syndicated crime, whereas "a rigidly structured organization would only serve as a detriment to efficient syndicate activity" (Albini, 1971, p. 284).

Albini's work shows some interesting parallels to an award winning study of the Sicilian Mafia which German sociologist Henner Hess had completed at about the same time (Hess, 1970/1996). Hess maintained that the Sicilian Mafia did not constitute a coherent, clearly structured organization and that the individual Mafia groups, the equivalent to the Cosa Nostra families in the United States, are best understood in terms of networks of patron-client relationships.

Research on Non-Italian Crime

The studies cited here as representative of the immediate post-Cressey era provided blueprints for research that focused on phenomena other than Italian American criminals. In variations of the critique of the mafia model, they examined crime phenomena commonly framed in ways similar to Cosa Nostra, or they looked at certain areas of crime or certain geographical areas to demonstrate that conventional conceptions of organized crime failed to adequately capture reality. For example, a number of studies have taken issue with media portrayals of the "Russian Mafia" as a dominant force in the criminal world. These studies include one conducted by James Finckenauer and Elin Waring who, drawing on extensive law enforcement data, rejected claims that a sophisticated criminal organization made up of emigrants from the former Soviet Union existed in the United States (Finckenauer & Waring, 1998). A study of crime in the Netherlands likewise found no evidence of a "Russian Mafia" (Weenink & van der Laan, 2006), just as a study of drug trafficking in Russia concluded that there are no large criminal organizations controlling this illegal market (Paoli, 2002).

THE MAIN LINES OF CONTEMPORARY RESEARCH

The conflict between Cressey and his early critics has remained an undercurrent in the study of organized crime. Not all of the literature, however, is necessarily critical of the conventional view on organized crime that had emerged in the United States during the 1950s and 1960s. An echo of the alarmist voices that had alerted the public to the threat posed by mafias and crime syndicates can still be found in some academic writings today.

Regardless of where scholars stand in this dispute, much of contemporary research on organized crime is primarily descriptive and can be grouped by the phenomena under investigation. There is, for example, a body of research on particular mafia organizations such as Cosa Nostra, on specific countries or regions or ethnic groups, and on certain areas of crime. At the same time, there are clusters of research that, respectively, share a more or less coherent conceptual framework (von Lampe, 2002a, 2008c, 2009b).

Out of scholarly efforts to undermine sensationalist imagery of organized crime developed several lines of research that went beyond the busting of myths and going in the direction of devising novel conceptualizations and theories to better understand the phenomena variously labeled organized crime. It is this body of conceptually and theoretically ambitious research that is the focal point of the following chapters rather than the numerous descriptive studies that address the situation in a particular region, for a particular ethnic group, or for a particular type of crime. The main lines of research that are of interest here are centered on four themes: (a) illegal enterprises and illegal markets, (b) illegal governance, (c) criminal networks, and (d) the logistics and modus operandi of illegal activities.

Illegal Enterprises and Illegal Markets

Perhaps the most influential and most widely adopted view among scholars has been to look at organized crime in terms of business. This is reflected in the use of concepts such as *crime trade* (van Duyne, 1996, p. 342), *illegal trade* (Larsson, 2009, p. 64), *crime industry* (Mack & Kerner, 1975) or *enterprise crime* (Kirby & Penna, 2010, p. 195), which are often used synonymously with or as an alternative to the term organized crime. While the notion of organized crime as business has been a recurring theme in the academic literature since the 1920s (Conboy, 1929; Landesco, 1929; Tannenbaum, 1951; Sellin, 1963), it was not until the 1970s that coherent theoretical frameworks were first developed.

Looking at organized crime in business terms implies three basic assumptions: (a) that organized crimes are a form of economic activity, aimed at generating profits, (b) that the individuals and groups involved in these activities resemble enterprises that are in many ways similar to their legitimate counterparts, and (c) that these enterprises sell their illegal products to customers in a market setting dictated by the laws of supply and demand.

The most sweeping attempt to reconceptualize organized crime in terms of business is the Spectrum-Based Theory of Enterprise developed by Dwight C. Smith in a number of publications in the 1970s and 1980s (Smith, 1975, pp. 335–347; Smith, 1978, 1980, 1982). Drawing on organization theory (Thompson, 1967) and echoing an argument previously made by Joseph Albini, Smith's theory posits that organized crime is best understood by looking not at criminals or criminal organizations but at the criminal activities they are engaged in. Smith argued that the nature of a particular type of illegal activity, along with the specific social context, determines to a large extent what criminals do and how they organize themselves. In this respect, Smith assumed, offenders face many of the same challenges and imperatives that entrepreneurs at the other end of the spectrum of legitimacy face. The fence who sells stolen goods, for example, has a lot in common with a legitimate retail dealer but less so, for example, with a loan-shark, a criminal who hands out usurious loans. The loan-shark, according to Smith, has more in common with a bank.

Interestingly, Smith proposed not only to examine conventional profit-making crimes through the enterprise lens but also activities of a quasi-governmental nature, such as the provision of security and what he called the "power brokering" between underworld and upperworld, for example, in the form of bribing officials (Smith, 1978, pp. 173–174). Smith's lasting accomplishment has been to introduce insights from the field of organizations studies and economic sociology to the study of organized crime in order to explain variations in the structure of criminal organizations (Smith, 1994).

Peter Reuter in his study of illegal gambling and loan sharking in New York raised some of the same questions. In his theory of the constraints of illegality, however, he placed the main emphasis on the factors that prevent illegal entrepreneurs from creating business structures similar to those of legal enterprises. Reuter concluded that because illegal entrepreneurs are threatened by police intervention and cannot seek the assistance of the courts in enforcing contracts, illegal markets tend to be populated "by localized, fragmented, ephemeral, and undiversified enterprises" (Reuter, 1983, p. 131; Chapter 6). Reuter's work has been highly influential, sometimes to the point that it seems to have been misconstrued to represent a natural law according to which large, complex criminal organizations do not and cannot exist.

Similar to the study of illegal enterprises, the study of illegal markets has partly been driven by attempts to contradict popular notions of organized crime. While imagery of bureaucratic criminal organizations has been the central reference point for studying illegal enterprise structures, the study of illegal markets has been concerned with the question to what extent there is a natural tendency toward monopolization. From this rather narrow focus, research has moved to a more comprehensive analysis of illegal markets, especially with regard to drug markets. Issues that have been addressed include the size of illegal markets, trends in price levels, and the characteristics of commodities and distribution channels (Bouchard & Wilkins, 2010).

Illegal (Extra-legal) Governance

The second major line of research within the study of organized crime, apart from the study of illegal enterprises and illegal markets, is to study organized crime in terms of the provision of "extralegal governance" (Varese, 2011, p. 6). This perspective rests on the distinction alluded to earlier between illegal enterprises on one hand and criminal organizations that exert control over illegal enterprises, on the other. A number of scholars have made this distinction using different wording, including Mark H. Haller and some of those already mentioned, namely Annelise Anderson and Peter Reuter. Following a terminology proposed by Alan Block, one can usefully distinguish *enterprise syndicates* and *power syndicates* (Block, 1983, p. 13).

Thomas C. Schelling, an economist who would later receive the Nobel Prize, suggested in a paper published in 1971 that the business of organized crime is not the provision of illegal goods and services, as others had argued, but the extortion of those who provide illegal goods and services. Schelling assumed that power syndicates typically prey on illegal enterprises that are easy to locate and to monitor, such as gambling and prostitution businesses. While Schelling acknowledged that power syndicates may sometimes offer something in return, such as protection against competition, in the end he viewed these services merely as schemes devised to facilitate the extraction of payments. In contrast, sociologist Diego Gambetta contended that in many cases criminal organizations respond to an existing demand for protection. Gambetta developed his ideas in an examination of the Sicilian Mafia, while others have applied his analytical framework to crime phenomena in other countries, including China (Chu, 2000), Japan (Hill, 2003), and Russia (Varese, 2001). The Sicilian Mafia, in Gambetta's interpretation, is "an industry which produces, promotes, and sells private protection" (Gambetta, 1993, p. 1). A demand for protection, according to Gambetta, typically arises in a market where there is a lack of trust between market participants and where their interests are not sufficiently safeguarded by the state. This applies to illegal markets, where the state, by definition, does not assume a regulatory function but also to legal markets if and when the state fails to provide effective protection. Criminal organizations then step in, for example, to enforce contracts or to keep new competitors out of a market in exchange for a share of the profits.

The "extralegal governance" perspective has been developed within an economic framework. Gambetta explicitly speaks of the business of selling private protection and only cautiously draws parallels between mafia organizations and the state. Still, its primary focus is on the political functions of criminal organizations in terms of "underground governments" (Naylor, 2003, p. 96) or "primitive states" (Skaperdas & Syropoulos, 1995).

Criminal Network Analysis

The third main line of research in the study of organized crime, criminal network analysis, follows a specific methodological approach rather than a particular conception of organized crime. Criminal network analysis is an extension of social network analysis, which examines social reality in terms of webs of direct and indirect relations. The basic unit of analysis is a dyadic tie, that is, a tie that connects two individuals. The underlying assumption is that individual behavior and the behavior of groups is significantly influenced by the structure of social relations and by the position individuals occupy within social networks (Boissevain, 1974; Scott, 2000).

Criminal network analysis in essence entails observing if and how offenders are connected to each other, for example, by communicating over the phone or by committing a crime together. Collecting and analyzing information of this nature is fairly straightforward and less prone to misinterpretations than attempts to frame criminal structures as organizations in the narrow sense of the word.

One of the pioneers of criminal network analysis has been Francis Ianni, the anthropologist who had observed an "Italian-American crime family" and who, in the early 1970s, turned to studying criminal structures among African Americans, Puerto Ricans, and Cubans. For this latter research, Ianni adopted a network approach that social anthropologists had previously utilized in studying legitimate society and which does not presuppose the existence of any formalized structures. Similarly, Ianni did not expect to find clear-cut criminal organizations among African American, Puerto Rican, or Cuban criminals and therefore needed a conceptual framework capable of capturing less elaborate group structures (Ianni, Fisher, & Lewis, 1973). Ianni found two types of networks relevant for understanding organized crime: associational networks that provide a basis of trust among offenders and entrepreneurial networks that organize the relations of offenders around particular criminal activities (Ianni, 1974).

A common misunderstanding is to assume that criminal networks and criminal organizations are mutually exclusive, that one only exists where the other does not. It is important to note, however, that networks and organizations are distinct analytical categories, while empirically they may overlap. In fact, an organization can be examined through the lens of network analysis with a view to how the members of that organization are linked to each other. Mangai Natarajan (2006), for example, used a network analysis framework to study a heroin-trafficking operation involving 294 individuals. Her aim was to discern whether these individuals were part of a distinct organization or rather represented a segment of the heroin market. Natarajan, drawing on extensive wiretap data, identified a small core group and a large number of peripheral network members with many overlapping cliques and individuals frequently switching their roles, suggesting fluid and ambiguous structures that defy easy categorizations along organizational lines.

Another example for the analysis of criminal structures through the network lens is provided by Carlo Morselli (2009a), who compared the formal ranks within an outlaw motorcycle gang with the positions the same individuals occupied in a drug distribution network. Like Natarajan, Morselli drew on surveillance data to conclude that those highest in the biker hierarchy were not the most important players in the drug business, a finding that underscores the importance of differentiating various types of criminal structures, namely entrepreneurial and non-entrepreneurial structures. Carlo Morselli, arguably the leading scholar in the area of criminal network analysis, has demonstrated the versatility of this approach in a number of studies. For example, he studied how the trajectories of criminal careers are influenced by networking (Morselli, 2001, 2003), how criminal structures are shaped (Morselli & Savoie-Gargiso, 2014) and adapt to variations in risk (Morselli, Giguere, & Petit 2007), what importance particular individuals have within criminal networks, and what impact the removal of these individuals has, namely as a result of law enforcement intervention (Morselli & Giguere, 2006; Morselli & Petit, 2007; Morselli & Roy, 2008).

Crime-Specific Analyses

The fourth main line of research is concerned with understanding the mechanisms of organized criminal activities. The underlying rationale is, for the most part,

Image 3.4   Carlo Morselli, professor of criminology at the University of Montreal, Canada, explains the importance of non-redundant connections within criminal networks. In cliques where everyone knows everyone else, no relationship is special. In contrast, someone who can broker between individuals and cliques that would otherwise not be connected is in an influential position. Morselli has argued that the most successful criminals are those with many non-redundant ties.

Photo: Centre international de criminologie comparée

to identify points of intervention for preventive or repressive measures. For this purpose, an organized criminal endeavor is broken down into its component parts.

One popular approach is "script analysis," which assumes that criminal endeavors are best viewed as a series of interconnected events (Cornish, 1994; see also Chapter 3). However, while originally the script concept implied a strict sequential order of tasks that offenders have to accomplish in the course of a criminal endeavor, there is now a tendency to think of complex crimes more in terms of webs of interconnected criminal events (Cornish & Clarke, 2002, p. 51; Levi, 2008, p. 390). Script analysis has been applied to a number of crime types, for example, the trafficking in stolen motor vehicles (Tremblay, Talon, & Hurley, 2001), drug trafficking (Chiu, Leclerc, & Townsley, 2011; Jacques & Bernasco, 2013; Lavorgna, 2014), child sex trafficking (Brayley, Cockbain, & Laycock, 2011), human trafficking (Savona & Giommoni, 2013), the illegal trade in endangered species (Moreto & Clarke, 2013), and illegal waste disposal (Tompson & Chainey, 2011).

Threat Assessments

Apart from the research highlighted here and the numerous empirical and theoretical studies that are difficult to group in similarly broad categories, there is a body of applied research that should be mentioned, although it lies outside the scope of this book. In particular, there is a body of applied research that aims at assessing threat levels emanating from organized crime phenomena through the use, for example, of risk and harm analysis methods (Black, Vander Beken, Frans, & Paternotte, 2000; Levi, Innes, Reuter, & Gundur, 2013; Paoli, Greenfield, & Zoutendijk, 2013; Tusikov, 2012). The intended purpose is to give guidance to policymakers and law enforcement officials in devising strategies for combating organized crime and allocating scarce resources. However, the necessary insights into the functioning of criminal activities and criminal structures are not always available, given the current state of empirical research and theorizing (von Lampe, 2004a, 2004b).

CHALLENGES TO THE STUDY OF ORGANIZED CRIME

Despite the growing body of research, the study of organized crime, in many ways, is still in its infant stages. Some blame the very nature of the subject matter for the somewhat slow progress. It has been argued, for example, that data on organized crime are difficult to access and that research is hampered because it is dangerous for scientists to study organized crime. Without denying the existence of specific challenges and risks, it is important to point out from past research that there are no insurmountable obstacles for examining the phenomena labeled organized crime.

Data Collection

The study of organized crime is not fundamentally different from any other area of the social sciences in that it is confronted with the same problems of finding good data and meaningfully describing, systematizing, and explaining the social phenomena under investigation. All principal means of data collection common in social science research (see Atteslander, 2003) have been utilized: observation, interviews, and analysis of written and electronic records.

Observation

Direct observations of organized criminals have admittedly been rare, and most of these studies pertain more to the social life of criminals rather than to their illegal activities. This is true for Francis Ianni's previously mentioned ethnographic research on an Italian American crime family; it is also true for Anton Blok's *The Mafia of a Sicilian Village* (1974) based on 30 months spent in the field, and Patricia Adler's *Wheeling and Dealing* (1985), an account of socializing with and interviewing upper-level drug dealers in California.

Others spent extended periods of time in areas notorious for organized criminal activity, gradually gaining access to insiders, such as gamblers, pimps, and prostitutes, who would then provide background information on observable crime and the protection of crime by corrupt law enforcement and government officials. Three intriguing examples for this kind of fieldwork are William F. Whyte's *Street*

Corner Society, a study of an Italian American neighborhood in Boston (Whyte, 1943/1981), William Chambliss's *On the Take*, an examination of the situation in Seattle, Washington (Chambliss, 1978), and Gary Potter's *Criminal Organization*, a study of Morrisburg, an industrial town in the northeastern United States (Potter, 1994). The more recent study of Sudhir Venkatesh of a drug dealing and extortion gang in a Chicago housing project, published in the book *Gang Leader for a Day*, also falls into this category (Venkatesh, 2008).

A different approach was taken by Georgian researchers who investigated smuggling and corruption by posing as smugglers themselves and covertly interviewing members of a criminal group and a corrupt police officer (Kukhianidze, Kupatadze, & Gotsiridze, 2004).

Interviews

An increasing number of studies on organized crime draw on interviews, including interviews with experts, namely police investigators, interviews with victims, and interviews with incarcerated or non-incarcerated offenders. Surveys with large randomized samples of respondents, however, the methodology of choice for many branches of the social sciences, is largely absent from the study of organized crime, except for occasional surveys of victims of organized crimes or customers of illegal goods and services (see, e.g., Luk, Cohen, Ferrence, & McDonald, 2009). This has to do with difficulties in generating representative samples and achieving satisfactory response rates. With regard to organized criminals, there even used to be a widespread belief that they are generally inaccessible for researchers (Mack & Kerner, 1975, p. 152) and that scholars who try can expect to either find uncooperative sources or "to be shot" (Gambetta, 1993, p. 9). This view has been proven wrong. There are, for example, various studies on mid- and upper-level drug trafficking that draw on information provided by large numbers of incarcerated offenders, including one conducted by the Matrix Knowledge Group (2007) in the United Kingdom involving 222 respondents (see also Decker & Townsend Chapman, 2008; Desroches, 2005; Pearson & Hobbs, 2001; Reuter & Haaga, 1989). Incarcerated mafiosi and those in witness protection programs have also been interviewed by scholars (Arlacchi, 1993; Cressey, 1969; Paoli, 2003a). In addition, researchers have been able to seek out and interview non-incarcerated, organized criminals. There are different ways to accomplish this, depending on a researcher's social network and networking skills. Some researchers have been able to mobilize existing direct and indirect ties for conducting interviews, which means that they themselves or friends, or "friends of friends" already knew potential interview partners (Albini, 1971; Jacques & Wright, 2008; Rawlinson, 2008; Siegel, 2008; Zhang & Chin, 2004). Alternatively, researchers have purposefully entered social milieus in efforts to meet potential interview partners. Damian Zaitch, for example, an Argentinean living in the Netherlands, frequented settings favored by Colombian immigrants, such as salsa bars, churches, and private parties, in order to meet and eventually interview Colombian drug traffickers (Zaitch, 2002; see also Chambliss, 1978; Potter, 1994; Rawlinson, 2008; Troshynski & Blank, 2008).

In some cases, researchers have contacted potential interview partners they had identified through media reports and information provided by law enforcement agencies. Mika Junninen (2006), in an effort to study the Finnish underworld, selected his eventual respondents from a list of reputed top criminals. Jana Arsovska, as part of her research on Albanian criminals, read about an alleged boss of the so-called Albanian Mafia she later successfully recruited for an interview through a number of intermediaries (Arsovska, 2008). Similarly, Potter and Jenkins (1985) mobilized a number of contacts to gain access to a leading member of the Philadelphia Cosa Nostra family.

Apart from these active strategies to access interview partners, researchers have also taken advantage of chance encounters. For example, a casual chat with an employee of a neighborhood minimarket in the United Kingdom unexpectedly opened up the opportunity for criminologist Georgios Antonopoulos to interview former cigarette traffickers in Greece (Antonopoulos, 2008b). Another example is Patricia Adler's study of upper-level drug traffickers (Adler, 1985). She gained entrance to the community of drug traffickers in Southern California because she became friends with her next-door neighbor, who turned out to be a major drug smuggler.

Finally, it has happened that organized criminals themselves have taken the initiative. Per Ole Johansen, a criminologist who for many years has studied the illegal alcohol market in Norway, interviewed some offenders who had learned about his research and contacted him, eager to share their views and experiences (Johansen, 2008, p. 6).

Analysis of Written and Electronic Records

The third basic method of data collection is the analysis of texts and, more broadly speaking, of recorded information. There are two main types of sources that students of organized crime have been drawing on: open sources, namely media reports and published official reports, and internal law-enforcement data in the form of investigative files, intelligence files, court files, and electronic databases. For example, researchers affiliated with WODC in the Netherlands have examined the social background and career trajectories of organized criminals (Kleemans, 2013; Kleemans & De Poot, 2008; Kleemans & Van de Bunt, 2008; Van Koppen, De Poot, Kleemans, & Nieuwbeerta, 2009). Similarly, criminal network analysis, as already indicated, typically utilizes law enforcement surveillance transcripts to establish the web of links between co-offenders (Natarajan, 2000, 2006; Morselli, 2009a). Researchers have also fruitfully analyzed documents seized as evidence by police, for example, the records of illegal gambling and loan-sharking operations (Reuter, 1983; Soudijn & Zhang, 2013), or documents voluntarily shared by criminals, for example, the records of a drug distribution business (Levitt & Venkatesh, 2000).

Limitations

All of these methods (observation, interviews, and analysis of recorded information) have their specific advantages and drawbacks. Generally speaking, organized crime researchers tend to tap into different sources, as any one source usually only provides incomplete data and data of questionable validity and reliability. For example, offenders who have agreed to an interview may exaggerate their involvement in criminal activities and their position in a criminal organization, and they may present hearsay as first-hand knowledge, all in an attempt to impress the researcher. Similarly, the content of investigative files cannot be accepted at face value. Information may be inaccurate for various reasons, for example, because of errors in translation in the case of intercepted communication between foreign criminals. Likewise, the absence of information is not necessarily an indication that something does not exist or an event has not occurred. It may simply be that this information was not deemed relevant for the purpose of a criminal investigation or that this information was not available to investigators in the first place. While the combination of different data sources promises a more complete and more accurate picture, it is not always easy to triangulate evidence. For example, cross-checking information obtained from offender interviews with information contained in investigative files may conflict with the need to protect one's sources, as the request to access particular files would provide clues about the identity of interview partners.

Risks for Researchers

Studying organized crime means studying potentially dangerous and influential people. Researchers, therefore, face certain risks, and these risks are greater and more immediate the closer one comes to investigating ongoing events and existing structures. The fact of the matter is that numerous journalists who have done just that have faced ruinous libel suits or have paid with their lives. According to the organization Reporters Without Borders, "141 journalists and media workers were killed during the decade of the 2000s in attacks and reprisals blamed on criminal groups" (Hervieu, 2011, p. 2). It does not seem, however, that scholars, who are generally less interested than journalists in reporting specific names and dates, face similar risks. According to Louise Shelley, intimidation of scholars "is rare but not unknown" (Shelley, 1999b, p. 39). In a paper published in 1999, she listed three examples from Russia, Italy, and Israel. In the latter case, the country's leading organized crime researcher, Menachem Amir, was forced to temporarily seek refuge abroad after being threatened by members of a criminal group he had studied.

Bill Chambliss, when exploring the alliance of underworld and upperworld in Seattle, experienced pressure of a different nature. His telephone was bugged and he was put under surveillance from time to time, the Internal Revenue Service received a false "tip" about unreported income, and two attractive women were used in what appeared to be an attempt to take compromising photos of Chambliss, presumably in an effort to pressure him into giving up his research (Chambliss, 1978, p. 111).

Problems of Research

There are other reasons for the slow progress in the study of organized crime. There is relatively little continuity in research on the individual and institutional level. Many studies are one-time-only excursions into the field of organized crime by researchers, namely PhD students, who then move on to other areas, while only very few scholars consistently work on organized crime for extended periods of time. This is in part because of the lack of funding. What Kenney and Finckenauer have noted in 1995 is still true today: Funding for organized crime research is limited and sporadic (Kenney & Finckenauer, 1995, p. 356). It may also be that because of the interdisciplinary nature of the study of organized crime, it is not a field that is appealing to young scholars who usually feel the need to establish themselves firmly within their own discipline. The "quantitative bent of modern criminology" creates an additional disincentive for researchers, as statistical data on organized crime are difficult to develop (Reuter, 1994, p. 91).

The lack of continuity in organized crime research, in turn, hampers continuous communication and the emergence of a common terminology among scholars that would help overcome talking at cross purposes. While there are fairly established conceptual frameworks in some areas of research, namely in the analysis of illegal markets and in the area of criminal network analysis, overall there is not much of a common language that scholars of organized crime share.

A lack of continuity also works against the coordination of research and cooperation between researchers nationally and internationally. Given the importance of comparisons for the development of social science theories in general and the value of comparative research for the study of organized crime in particular, this is highly problematic. Finally, continuity is important for developing trustful relationships between researchers on one hand and data owners, including law enforcement agencies, private sector entities, offenders and victims, on the other. It may take years until organized crime researchers gain access to information they need. Few have the resources and the patience to be that persistent.

So although there are no fundamental obstacles in studying the phenomena labeled organized crime, there are a number of factors that have hampered the emergence of a coherent, cumulative body of knowledge about these phenomena. Accordingly, what will be presented in the following chapters are clusters of knowledge that are often fragmented and inconsistent and lack overall coherence.

RESEARCH ON ORGANIZED CRIME: SUMMARY AND CONCLUSION

The study of organized crime is characterized by separate, only loosely connected lines of research. The largest clusters of research are centered on illegal enterprises and illegal markets, illegal governance structures, criminal networks, and analyses of specific criminal activities. While challenges do exist, research on organized crime has not encountered insurmountable obstacles. In particular, researchers have been able to gain direct access to organized criminals and have conducted interviews relating to their activities and to the organizational structures they are or have been a part of.

Arguably, the main challenge for the study of organized crime comes from a lack of institutional support. Research on organized crime tends to be multidisciplinary and interdisciplinary and is therefore difficult to fit in an academic system built on the distinction of disciplines. Obtaining funding for studies on organized crime also faces specific difficulties in that access to data tends to be more time consuming and plagued with more uncertainties than is the case for other areas of criminological and social science research. This means that research on organized crime cannot as easily be conducted within the rigid time frames commonly set by grant-giving institutions. The solution would be the creation of independent research centers with long-term secured funding.

Discussion Questions

1. What is the best way to collect data on organized crime?
2. Should researchers be allowed to infiltrate a criminal gang in order to study it?
3. Who do you think is better to talk to for a researcher, an incarcerated gangster serving a life prison sentence or a gangster who is still in the business?
4. What dangers do researchers face who study organized crime?

Research Projects

1. Interview someone you know personally who is or has been involved in organized criminal activity.
2. Examine discarded cigarette packs in your neighborhood to estimate the prevalence of contraband cigarettes.

Further Reading

The History of the Study of Organized Crime

Albini, J. L. (1988). Donald Cressey's contributions to the study of organized crime: An evaluation. *Crime and Delinquency, 34*(3), 338–354.

Chambliss, W. J. (1975). On the paucity of original research on organized crime: A footnote to Galliher and Cain. *American Sociologist, 10*(1), 36–39.

Fijnaut, C. (1990). Organized crime: A comparison between the United States and Western Europe. *British Journal of Criminology, 30*(3), 321–340.

Reynolds, M. (1995). *From gangs to gangsters: How American sociology organized crime 1918 to 1994.* Guilderland, NY: Harrow and Heston.

Rogovin, C. H., & Martens, F. T. (1992). The evil that men do. *Journal of Contemporary Criminal Justice, 8*(1–2), 62–79.

The Study of Organized Crime

Arsovska, J. (2012). Researching difficult populations: Interviewing techniques and methodological issues in face-to-face interviews in the study of organized crime. In L. Gideon (Ed.), *Handbook of survey methodology for the social sciences* (pp. 397–415). New York: Springer.

Berlusconi, G. (2013). Do all the pieces matter? Assessing the reliability of law enforcement data sources for the network analysis of wire taps. *Global Crime, 14*(1), 61–81.

Cornish, D. B., & Clarke, R. V. (2002). Analyzing organized crimes. In A. R. Piquero and S. G. Tibbetts (Eds.), *Rational choice and criminal behavior: Recent research and future challenges* (pp. 41–62). New York: Routledge.

Cressey, D. R. (1967). Methodological problems in the study of organized crime as a social problem. *Annals of the American Academy of Political and Social Science, 374*(1), 101–112.

Edwards, A., & Levi, M. (2008). Researching the organization of serious crimes. *Criminology and Criminal Justice, 8*(4), 363–388.

Fijnaut, C. (1990a). Researching organised crime. In R. Morgan (Ed.), *Policing organised crime and crime prevention* (pp. 75–86). Bristol, UK: Bristol and Bath Centre for Criminal Justice.

Hobbs, D., & Antonopoulos, G. A. (2014). How to research organized crime. In L. Paoli (Ed.), *The Oxford handbook of organized crime* (pp. 96–117). Oxford: Oxford University Press.

Kleemans, Edward R. (2015). Organized crime research: Challenging assumptions and informing policy. In E. Cockbain & J. Knutsson (Eds.) *Applied police research: Challenges and opportunities* (pp. 57–67). New York: Routledge.

Ritter, A. (2006). Studying illicit drug markets: Disciplinary contributions. *International Journal of Drug Policy, 17*(6), 453–463.

Sandberg, S., & Copes, H. (2013). Speaking with ethnographers: The challenges of researching drug dealers and offenders. *Journal of Drug Issues, 43*(2), 176–197.

von Lampe, K. (2006). The interdisciplinary dimensions of the study of organized crime. *Trends in Organized Crime, 9*(3), 77–95.

von Lampe, K. (2012b). Transnational organized crime challenges for future research. *Crime, Law and Social Change, 58*(2), 179–194.

PART II

Empirical Manifestations of Organized Crime

The previous three chapters have dealt with the debates surrounding the concept of organized crime and how the social sciences have responded to these debates. Beginning with the following chapter on organized criminal activities (Chapter 4), the focus shifts to the underlying empirical phenomena. For much of the remainder of the book, the discussion is centered on the actions and structures that, according to one view or other, are associated with organized crime.

The approach taken here differs from conventional treatises of the subject that commonly attempt to cover all or at least the most notorious manifestations of organized crime one by one. Organized criminal activities, for example, are typically discussed in terms of a set of crimes, such as drug trafficking, human trafficking, and illegal gambling, that are believed to be committed in an organized fashion or committed by criminal organizations. For each crime category, then, information is presented in greater or lesser detail pertaining to, for example, the volume of crime and illicit profits and the criminal groups involved in these activities. Sometimes, select high-profile cases are at the center of attention.

While these descriptive accounts are interesting, their value is limited from an analytical perspective, when it comes to answering the questions researchers of organized crime are concerned about. In the following chapters, descriptions of particular organized crime phenomena will only be presented in an exemplary fashion in the form of case studies and illustrative examples. The main emphasis is placed on more general underlying patterns.

The study of organized crime as a scientific endeavor strives to gain deeper insights that go beyond a particular case. Researchers seek to arrive at generalizations that help to understand broader classes of cases. For example, when researchers look at a local drug market they do so with a view to a bigger picture. They either try to come up with general statements about how under given circumstances local drug markets emerge, how they are structured, how they function, how they react to outside influences, and so forth. This is done by comparison between different local drug markets and between different phases in the development of a local drug market. Or, in the opposite direction, researchers apply general statements derived from previous research to understand why a particular local drug market is shaped and structured and functions in a particular way. Such a scientific approach, as opposed to a journalistic approach, entails the development of clear and coherent conceptual frameworks that can be systematically applied to different cases. Conceptual frameworks are sets of interrelated concepts with which to organize research and theorizing. They establish for a particular subject matter what aspects of reality are important to look at and from what perspective and what possible relations between these aspects need to be explored in order to solve a problem or answer a particular question. It is primarily through the lens of such general conceptual frameworks that organized criminal activities and organized criminal structures will be examined in the following chapters.

CHAPTER 4

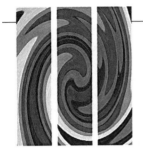

Organized Criminal Activities

WHY STUDY ORGANIZED CRIMINAL ACTIVITIES SEPARATE FROM CRIMINAL ORGANIZATIONS?

Drug trafficking, human trafficking, arms trafficking, illegal gambling, extortion, and the like are part and parcel of the imagery surrounding organized crime. Yet, it is not a given to start an empirical and theoretical discussion of organized crime with a discussion of criminal activities. As noted before, there is a long-lasting controversy over whether organized crime should be conceptualized primarily in terms of activities in the sense of crimes that are organized, or primarily in terms of structures in the sense of the organization of criminals (see Cohen, 1977, p. 98; Finckenauer, 2005, p. 76). If one equates organized crime with criminal structures, one tends to define organized criminal activities as those that are committed by criminal organizations (see, e.g., Abadinsky, 2013). From this vantage point, criminal activities may not even deserve attention separate from the examination of criminal organizations.

The approach taken here follows a different rationale, one that assumes that criminal activities are important to study in their own right and are usefully examined *prior* to examining criminal organizations. There are several considerations that come into play here. First, in a lot of what criminals do they act in a particular way not because someone, say a "mafia boss," told them to but because a particular kind of behavior is inherent in the nature of the specific criminal activity they are engaged in. In order to successfully commit a particular crime, certain routines may have to be followed and certain techniques may have to be employed. For example, in the processing of cocaine, certain raw and intermediate products have to be mixed with certain chemicals in certain ways (see the case study of cocaine production and trafficking below) irrespective of who does it. The variation and complexity of these criminal activities makes them an interesting subject to study in their own right, and a better understanding of their nature is a necessary precondition for devising successful counter-measures (Clarke & Brown, 2003, p. 206). For example, the monitoring and control of the sale of precursor chemicals may help in curbing the production of illegal drugs (see, e.g., Cunningham, Liu, & Callaghan, 2009).

Second, as already indicated, the nature of criminal activities can help answer important questions with regard to other aspects of organized crime, namely, why criminal organizations emerge in the first place and how they are shaped and structured. A key question in the study of organizations in general and in the study of criminal organizations in particular is, "Does an organization determine its actions, or do actions determine an organization?" (Smith, 1994, p. 121). Many scholars believe that to a large extent the latter is the case. Joseph Albini, for example, has argued that "criminal groups are dynamic entities, not static ones," and that "they change with the nature of the criminal acts they commit" (Albini, 1971, p. 49; see also Potter, 1994, p. 120). According to this view, organizational structures need to be viewed primarily as "emergent properties" of criminal behavior (Cornish & Clarke, 2002, p. 52), as an "outcome" rather than a precondition for organized criminal activities (van Duyne, 1997, p. 203).

Third, looking separately at the nature of criminal activities helps to explain the emergence of power syndicates. As mentioned before, the term *power syndicates*, following a classification proposed by Alan Block, refers to criminal groups that extort illegal businesses or *enterprise syndicates*, in Block's terminology (Block, 1983, p. 13). It has been argued that the type of criminal activity enterprise syndicates engage in determines how prone they are to falling under the control of power syndicates. For example, activities that are carried out on a more regular basis and are more visible, such as the operation of an illegal gambling casino, are believed to make enterprise syndicates more vulnerable to extortion than activities of a more clandestine nature, such as the theft of cars (see Schelling, 1971).

Finally, the nature of criminal activities potentially influences the relationship between (organized) crime and society. Crimes that create victims, such as the theft of cars, will entail a more hostile environment for criminals than the provision of illegal goods and services to a demanding public, such as the sale of alcohol during Prohibition (see Potter, 1994).

OUTLINE OF THIS CHAPTER

The discussion of organized criminal activities in this chapter begins with two case studies, (a) cocaine trafficking and (b) the trafficking in stolen motor vehicles. Both types of crime are widely regarded as constituting manifestations of organized crime, and they will serve as reference points in this and later chapters in the book. It is important to understand what offenders are doing and what skills, tools, and other resources they need to employ in the process of committing these crimes.

Against the backdrop of the two case studies, organized criminal activities will then be more generally examined from three distinct angles. One angle is to ask to what extent there is a difference between organized and non-organized criminal behavior. It is argued that there are differences in degree, while it is futile to have a debate about where exactly a dividing line should be drawn. Another angle is to classify those crimes that are more organized than others. The question is by what criteria one can meaningfully group the various kinds of organized crimes into different categories for the purpose of scientific analysis, that is, to avoid comparing apples and oranges. One clarification that will be advocated is the distinction between market-based crimes, predatory crimes, and illegal-governance crimes. The third angle, finally, is to look at a specific organized criminal activity and its component parts. There are two approaches that are of relevance in this respect, script analysis and the so-called Logistics of Organized Crime approach. The script and logistics approaches help break down specific kinds of complex criminal endeavors into their component parts, so that one gets a better understanding of what exactly criminals do, how they do it, and ultimately, what can be done about it. The level of detail that can be found in script and logistical analyses is only hinted at in the following descriptions of cocaine trafficking and the trafficking in stolen motor vehicles.

CASE STUDY: COCAINE TRAFFICKING

Cocaine trafficking is an example for an illegal trade with global ramifications. It is notorious for the involvement of so-called drug cartels, such as the Cali Cartel and the Medellin Cartel under the leadership of infamous drug barons, such as Pablo Escobar. These phenomena will be addressed in later chapters. Here, the focus is on the criminal activities making up the trafficking of cocaine as such, irrespective of the involvement of criminal organizations.

Coca and Cocaine

Cocaine is a psychoactive alkaloid, a chemical compound containing nitrogen, which is extracted from the leaves of certain varieties of the coca plant, a small to medium-size evergreen shrub. Most cocaine is produced from the *Erythroxylum coca var. Coca* (ECVC) variety that grows naturally at altitudes between approximately 500 and 1,500 m (1,500–4,500 ft) along the moist tropical eastern slopes of the Andes mountains in Bolivia and Peru. Coca plants have been cultivated here since precolonial times, and its leaves mixed with lime are traditionally chewed by the indigenous population to help relieve altitude sickness, hunger, and fatigue (Casale & Klein, 1993; Freye & Levy, 2009; Rottman, 1997). Although coca plants can be cultivated under different climatic and soil conditions (Casale & Klein, 1993), coca cultivation for the illegal production of cocaine has remained concentrated in the Andes region, namely in the traditional coca-growing countries Bolivia and Peru and, more recently in Colombia (UNODC, 2014b).

The Harvesting of Coca Leaves

Coca bushes can first be harvested about six months after planting and thereafter several times a year. About 700 kg (1,500 lb) of coca leaves, stripped off the bushes by hand, are needed to produce one kilogram of cocaine. If a laboratory is nearby, the fresh leaves may be immediately processed. Otherwise they need to be dried to prevent rotting and also to reduce their weight for transportation. To facilitate the drying, the leaves are placed in the open and raked and turned frequently. The dried leaves are then either transported to a market for sale or delivered directly to a laboratory (Casale & Klein, 1993; Mejia & Posada, 2008, pp. 3–4).

The Production of Cocaine

The production of cocaine from coca leaves involves three main steps: (a) the extraction of crude coca paste, (b) the purification of the coca paste to cocaine base, and (c) the conversion of cocaine base into the final product cocaine hydrochloride (cocaine HCl), the salt form of cocaine. There are, however, variations in the procedures and in the chemicals used (Casale & Klein, 1993; Mejia & Posada, 2008, p. 4).

The Production of Coca Paste

One method for the production of coca paste, the first intermediate product, is the so-called solvent extraction technique. The dried coca leaves are chopped up into little pieces, put in an open container, a barrel or a pit lined with a heavy-duty plastic sheet, and dusted with lime. After a while, a solvent such as kerosene, diesel

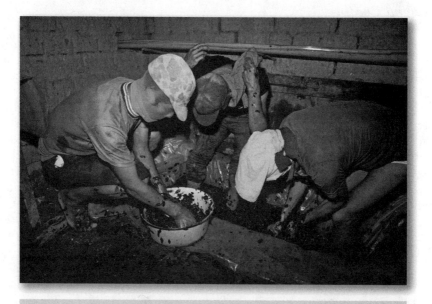

Image 4.1   Workers in the process of producing coca paste are stomping coca leaves in a lab hidden in the jungle near the Yungas Mountains in Bolivia.

Photo: Jeffrey L. Rotman/Corbis

fuel, or gasoline is added. Two to three days later, the solvent that now contains the cocaine alkaloids is separated from the leaves. This is done, for example, by pressing or filtering. The next step is to remove the cocaine from the solvent. For this purpose, the solvent and water with diluted sulfuric acid are mixed and then allowed to sit until the solvent and water re-separate. The kerosene can then be poured off for re-use, leaving a yellowish-brown solution containing the cocaine, called *agua rica*. The final step in the production of coca paste is to slowly add a substance, such as lime, which neutralizes the sulfuric acid and causes a yellowish-solid substance, the coca paste, to precipitate out of the solution. After filtering and drying, the coca paste is ready for the next stage, the production of cocaine base (Casale & Klein, 1993; Freye & Levy, 2009, pp. 29–30).

In an alternative procedure, called the acid extraction technique, the coca leaves are initially treated with dilute sulfuric acid instead of a solvent, such as kerosene, and then typically stomped by workers for one to two hours. The acidic liquid is removed while the leaves are soaked in fresh, dilute sulfuric acid and stomped another two to four times. After the acidic liquid is removed, it is filtered and mixed with lime or carbonate, causing a very crude coca paste to precipitate, which is then back-extracted with a small amount of kerosene. After allowing the solution and the kerosene containing the cocaine to re-separate, the kerosene is separated and treated with fresh dilute sulfuric acid, generating *agua rica*, which is treated exactly as in the solvent extraction technique to obtain coca paste (Casale & Klein, 1993).

The Production of Cocaine Base

The production of cocaine base from coca paste is a purification process. Coca paste contains between 30% and 80% cocaine, depending on the extraction technique, the type of coca plant, and the amount of time and care invested in the procedure. The first step in the conversion of coca paste into cocaine base is dissolving the paste in dilute sulfuric acid to obtain a new *agua rica* solution. Potassium permanganate is added until the solution, originally with a yellowish-brown color, has turned colorless. Adding potassium permanganate too quickly or adding too much of it would result in decomposition and loss of cocaine. The solution is then filtered and treated with a solution of base, such as dilute ammonia. The ammonia causes purified cocaine base to precipitate, which is filtered and dried (Casale & Klein, 1993).

The conversion of coca paste into cocaine base may be skipped in a process called leaf-to-base technique, where coca paste is never isolated. Instead, the original *agua rica* solution is filtered, mixed with carbonate or bicarbonate salt, and then directly treated with potassium permanganate (Casale & Klein, 1993; Freye & Levy, 2009, p. 31).

The Production of Cocaine Hydrochloride

The procedures used for the production of cocaine hydrochloride out of cocaine base vary greatly, especially with regard to the solvent used. One method involves dissolving the cocaine base in diethyl ether. This solution is added to a solution of hydrochloric acid and acetone, and the resulting solution is thoroughly mixed and let sit for three to six hours or for 30 minutes in a hot bath. The cocaine hydrochloride precipitates, and then it is filtered and dried under a heat lamp or in a microwave oven while the solvents are usually recycled. The final product may be pressed into standardized blocks, for example, one kilogram bricks, and then packaged (Casale & Klein, 1993).

While the production of coca paste and cocaine base only requires common chemicals and simple equipment, such as barrels and buckets, the final step of producing cocaine hydrochloride requires rather expensive chemicals, more sophisticated laboratory equipment, and more extensive expertise (Casale & Klein, 1993).

Transportation of Intermediate Products

Like the initial drying of the harvested coca leaves, the conversion of coca paste into cocaine base results in a weight reduction that greatly facilitates transportation. The weight loss from fresh to sun-dried leaves is over 50%, while about 2.5 kg of coca paste are turned into 1 kg of cocaine base, which then is turned into 1 kg of cocaine hydrochloride (Casale & Klein, 1993). Cocaine hydrochloride, while having similar purity levels as cocaine base, is the desired end product because it is soluble in water, which means it can be consumed by snorting or injecting. It is also more stable and therefore better suited for storage than cocaine base (Freye & Levy, 2009, p. 32).

The production of cocaine may involve the transportation of all intermediate products, coca leaves, coca paste, and cocaine base, over some distances. It appears that most coca paste and cocaine base production takes place near the centers of cultivation of coca plants in the Andes region, whereas laboratories producing cocaine hydrochloride have been found farther away. For many years, coca cultivation was concentrated in Bolivia and Peru, later also in Colombia, while most cocaine processing during that entire time period took place in Colombia. In recent years, a still small but increasing number of laboratories producing cocaine hydrochloride has been detected in other Latin American countries, such as Argentina and Venezuela. This means that some cocaine base is smuggled across international borders. For the most part, however, smuggling operations involve the final product, cocaine hydrochloride, with the main trafficking routes connecting the Andes region with drug markets in North America and West and Central Europe (UNODC, 2014b, pp. 35–39).

Cocaine Smuggling

Cocaine is illegally transported across borders using four basic schemes: (a) smuggling embedded in legal cross-border travel, (b) smuggling embedded in legal cross-border trade, (c) smuggling by mail or parcel service, and (d) smuggling outside of regular cross-border travel or trade (Caulkins, Burnett, & Leslie, 2009; Decker & Townsend Chapman, 2008; Desroches, 2005; see also von Lampe, 2011c, and Chapter 12).

In the case of smuggling embedded in legal cross-border travel, the cocaine is hidden in the luggage, in the clothes, on the body, or inside the body of an individual. Smuggling embedded in legal cross-border trade entails cocaine hidden among or inside legally traded goods. Similarly, cocaine sent by mail or parcel service is shipped under the guise of private or legitimate commercial content. In the case of cocaine smuggled by way of the irregular crossing of borders, for example, using tunnels, semi-submersible, sea-going vessels or airplanes, smugglers try to prevent customs and border control from detecting any kind of cross-border movement.

The smuggling of cocaine may involve the use of different means of transportation as well as storage and repackaging along the way. Depending on the type of smuggling scheme, special preparations of the cocaine itself or the means of transportation and corresponding activities to recover the cocaine at the point of destination, may be necessary (Decker & Townsend Chapman, 2008). For example, to avoid detection by customs, cocaine may be dissolved in other substances, which then requires reverting that process once the border has been crossed (UNODC, 2011b, pp. 104–105).

Wholesale and Retail Distribution

Once a cocaine shipment has arrived in the country of destination, it may be stored, repacked, diluted, and broken up into smaller consignments before it is sold to individual consumers. Cocaine is diluted by adding substances that simply add weight, for example, flour or plaster, by adding less costly psychoactive drugs, like

Image 4.2 600 kilograms of cocaine were found on board this sailing-boat off the coast of Portugal in October 2014.

Photo: EPA/Louis Forra

amphetamine or caffeine that may augment the effects of cocaine, and by adding local anesthetics, such as lidocaine, to imitate the anesthetic effect of cocaine (Freye & Levy, 2009, pp. 36–37). While transactions of cocaine above the level of retail selling are typically arranged and carried out under conspiratorial circumstances, the selling to consumers may take place in private settings, such as apartments, in semipublic settings, such as bars, or in public settings, such as street corners or parks (Curtis & Wendel, 2000, pp. 128–130; Gruter & Van de Mheen, 2005, p. 27).

CASE STUDY: THE TRAFFICKING IN STOLEN MOTOR VEHICLES

The trafficking in stolen motor vehicles is chosen as the second case study of an organized criminal activity because, like cocaine trafficking, it is often referred to in the literature on organized crime. It is also instructive because it highlights the importance of technological developments, in this case antitheft technology, for the shaping of criminal behavior. It is also interesting because it is a crime that is closely linked to the legal spheres of society in various ways. There is some overlap with legal businesses, namely car dealerships and car repair shops, and the framework for the registration of motor vehicles defines much of what offenders need to accomplish in order to be successful.

The trafficking in stolen motor vehicles involves three main elements: the taking of the car, the altering of the identity of the car to give it the appearance of a legitimate car, and the transportation of the car to a location where it is eventually sold in the same way a legitimate car would be sold.

Phase 1: Obtaining a Car

While cars may be stolen as opportunities arise, it is more common that offenders target specific makes and models. A particular kind of car may have been ordered in advance by a customer, it may generally be in high demand and therefore expected to yield the highest profit, or it may be targeted because it best matches the know-how and modus operandi of offenders. This is namely the case where the identity of a legitimate car is transferred to the stolen car. The make and model of that legitimate car, then, determines the make and model of the car that is to be stolen. Cars are typically targeted in places where large numbers of vehicles are left unattended, such as the parking lots of shopping malls and airports, or in places where a particular kind of car is more likely to be found. For example, offenders would search for luxury cars in upscale neighborhoods or directly in car dealerships.

Once a suitable car is located, the next challenge for offenders is to gain entry into the car and then to start the engine. Up until around the 1980s, this was a fairly simple thing to do. A car could quickly be opened with a "slim jack," a flat piece of metal, and "hotwired" by connecting the two ignition wires pulled out from under the dashboard (Cook, 1987). Since then, continuous technological advances in crime-proofing vehicles have placed increasing demands on the resourcefulness of car thieves (Longman, 2006). Today cars feature a variety of anti-theft devices that either make it more difficult to open and set in motion a vehicle (e.g., steering wheel locks, motion and impact alarms, immobilizers blocking ignition), or make it easier to trace and identify a vehicle once it is stolen (e.g., vehicle identification number, GPS-based tracking devices) (Mangine, 2006; Terp, 2006). Offenders cope with these devices in different ways, depending on their expertise and the tools at their disposal.

Obtaining the Original Car Key

A number of schemes involve obtaining the original key to the car that is to be stolen. Owners may be tricked into surrendering the key, for example, by someone pretending to be a potential buyer who wants to take the car for a test drive. Car keys may also be obtained through burglarizing private homes or businesses (Copes & Cherbonneau, 2006, p. 923).

Certain schemes involve obtaining both the key and the car from the owner by fraud or force. A common method is to lease or rent cars under a false identity, through a front company or through an economically disadvantaged individual recruited for this purpose (Gounev & Bezlov, 2008, p. 426). The use of violence occurs in cases of "carjacking," where the driver is forced out of the car. This method is widespread only in certain countries (Clarke & Brown, 2003, p. 207, Copes & Cherbonneau, 2006, p. 924; Ratzel & Lippert, 2001, pp. 709–710). There are also instances where owners collude with traffickers. The car is handed over voluntarily, perhaps in exchange for a relatively small amount of money, and then brought to another country, where it is registered and sold. The original owner then reports the car stolen and collects insurance compensation. In these cases the crime committed is insurance fraud (Gerber & Killias, 2003, pp. 220–221; Ratzel & Lippert, 2001, p. 710).

Entry Without the Original Car Key

If offenders cannot use the original key and the doors are not left unlocked, offenders need to find a different way to gain entry into the car and then to start the engine. One way is to duplicate the original key, for example, from the lock of a fuel tank cap or directly from the original key. For instance, a parking attendant may hand over car keys in his care to a locksmith who is able, within minutes, to cut duplicates. The same, reportedly, can be done with the keys that deactivate immobilizers (Antonopoulos & Papanicolaou, 2009, p. 151). Other tools, some professionally manufactured for legitimate or illegitimate purposes, have made it possible in the past to open the door of a car and also to start the engine without knowledge of the specific characteristics of the original key (von der Lage, 2003, p. 361). Finally, car thieves may simply break a window and reach into the car to unlock the door from the inside. This method, however, like other more brute techniques, is likely to set off alarm systems equipped with impact sensors.

Starting the Engine

Once entry into the car has been gained, the engine needs to be started and the car driven away to a safe location. In order to do this, a number of protections

Image 4.3   Members of the New Jersey State Police stand near cars that were recovered from an auto theft ring, February 2014. Twenty-seven of more than 160 cars recovered in the investigation were carjacked, according to the attorney general's office. The rest were stolen off car carriers, at airports, or at car washes or by thieves targeting wealthy neighborhoods where people left cars unlocked, sometimes with keys inside.

Photo: ASSOCIATED PRESS/Amy Newman

may have to be overcome, including steering wheel locks and immobilizers. This may require a laptop computer that has manufacturer-issued maintenance software installed. Such a laptop computer hooked up to the board computer makes it possible to quickly and easily disable the security system of a car (CSD, 2007, pp. 163–164). Obtaining this special software, of course, is a task in itself.

Before the car is moved to a safe location, it may be scanned for GPS-tracking devices that may be hidden in a number of places inside the car. Once found, GPS devices are removed and discarded or placed on other cars (CSD, 2007, p. 163).

Phase II: Changing the Identity of a Car

A stolen car has little commercial value if it is identifiable as such. Unless it is taken apart and sold in parts, which is one common scheme (Tremblay et al., 2001, p. 569; Antonopoulos & Papanicolaou, 2009, p. 157), efforts have to be made to disguise the fact that the car has been stolen. In more sophisticated operations, this entails giving it the identity of an existing legitimate car or to create a false identity, which requires a considerable level of technical expertise and the availability of tools and machinery. Less sophisticated operations simply involve the repainting of the car and exchanging license plates (CSD, 2007, p. 165).

A common method for giving a stolen car the identity of a legitimate car is called "body switching." A wrecked car is legally purchased, which puts offenders in possession not only of a set of identifying data, including the vehicle identification number (VIN), but also the accompanying documents. A car similar in make, model, and color to the wrecked car is then stolen. Subsequently, the identifying marks are removed from the stolen car and replaced by those of the wrecked car. This may entail, for example, cutting out parts of the chassis with the VIN of the wrecked car and exchanging them with parts of the chassis of the stolen car or welding plates with the VIN of the wrecked car over the VIN of the stolen car (Antonopoulos & Papanicolaou, 2009, pp. 153–154). In other cases, the identifying data of an existing car are obtained under the pretense of an intended purchase. This information is then used to alter the identifiers on the stolen car and to forge the accompanying documents (Gounev & Bezlov, 2008, p. 425). In both cases, the stolen car can be officially registered under the cloned identity and offered on the legal market domestically or abroad. Most commonly, it seems, stolen cars are exported with trade routes typically connecting richer source countries with poorer destination countries (Clarke & Brown, 2003, p. 198).

Phase III: Transportation and Marketing

Once a stolen car is transformed into a seemingly legitimate car it can fairly safely be moved across borders. In some cases, however, stolen cars are moved abroad without any alterations. For example, in the southern United States, cars are sometimes driven across the border into Mexico before they are reported stolen (Clarke & Brown, 2003, p. 207), and cars stolen in Canada have been directly shipped to Russia without any prior alterations (Tremblay et al., 2001, p. 575).

As is true for all crimes involving the smuggling of illicit goods, there are different schemes that offenders may employ to bring stolen cars across borders: transportation embedded in legal tourist travel, which entails couriers driving the cars over land or using ferries, transportation across the "green border," where regular border crossings are avoided, and transportation embedded in legal cross-border commerce, typically in sealed containers, where either false or forged documents are used to disguise the nature of the shipped goods or the stolen cars are falsely declared as legitimately exported cars (Antonopoulos & Papanicolaou, 2009, pp. 155–156; Clarke & Brown, 2003, p. 203; Tremblay et al., 2001, p. 574; von der Lage, 2003, pp. 361–362). In the country of destination, the stolen cars are then introduced to the legal market and eventually sold to customers who may well be ignorant of the car's origin (Gerber & Kilias, 2003, p. 224).

CONCEPTUALIZATIONS OF ORGANIZED CRIMINAL ACTIVITIES

The trafficking in cocaine and the trafficking in stolen motor vehicles have in common that they entail a number of interlocking criminal acts that are carried out repetitively and in a sequential order. This alone sets these two types of illegal activities apart from the mass of ordinary crimes that are typically committed in a hit-and-run fashion. Moreover, the interlocking acts that characterize cocaine trafficking and the trafficking in stolen motor vehicles, respectively, differ greatly.

The cultivation of coca is different from the production of coca paste, cocaine base, and cocaine and different from the smuggling and distribution of cocaine just as the stealing of a car is not the same as altering the identity of a car or smuggling and selling a stolen car. These differences have consequences not only for the routines that offenders have to follow but also for the resources they have to have at their disposal in terms of know-how, tools, and material. The resulting complex interplay of distinct tasks further removes illegal activities such as the trafficking in cocaine and stolen motor vehicles from the class of ordinary violent and property crimes. However, not all elements of the trafficking in cocaine and stolen motor vehicles are equally complex and sophisticated. For example, the production of coca paste places much less demand on chemicals, equipment, and skills than the production of cocaine hydrochloride; and the hijacking of a car at a traffic light is more primitive than fraudulently obtaining a car from a rental car business or stealing a parked car with a cloned key and through the manipulation of the on-board computer.

While the level of complexity and variability in cocaine trafficking and the trafficking in stolen motor vehicles are roughly similar, there are also principal differences between the two types of illegal activities apart from the fact that cocaine and cars are different kinds of commodities. The major difference, arguably, is that the trafficking in cocaine is characterized by a series of production processes connected by voluntary transactions between sellers and buyers, beginning with the coca farmers who market their harvested coca leaves. The trafficking in stolen motor vehicles, in contrast, is centered on the predatory act of taking away someone's car.

Given the complexities inherent in cocaine trafficking and the trafficking in stolen motor vehicles it may seem obvious why these crimes are commonly associated with organized crime. However, it is not necessarily clear in what respect exactly they are supposed to be organized and how representative they are of organized criminal activities in general. In fact, the study of organized crime is concerned with a broad spectrum of criminal activity. This even includes activity one may be hesitant to call organized at all, such as the opportunistic stealing of a car that ends up being trafficked. Likewise, what criminal organizations or organized criminals do does not always fit the organized label. Take, for example, the robbing of parking meters that, according to FBI undercover agent Joseph Pistone, used to be one of the money making activities that members of the New York Mafia engaged in (Pistone, 1989, p. 138).

Organized Criminal Activities and Non-organized Criminal Activities

The degree to which criminal activities are organized can be conceptualized in different ways, for example with regard to (a) the amount of planning, (b) the coordination of different tasks, and (c) the period of time involved in the execution of a crime (see, e.g., Albanese, 2011, p. 26; Lupsha, 1986, p. 33; Spapens, 2010, p. 191; see also Turvey, 2011, pp. 83–87, on the (contested) "organized/disorganized" distinction made in the profiling of serial offenders). In essence, the term organized refers to deviations from an assumed normal case of criminal behavior where the decision to commit a crime and the execution of the crime occur on the spot, at the same time and at the same place. This means, roughly speaking, that criminal activities vary along a spectrum of organization ranging from spontaneous, impulsive, erratic, isolated acts, in one extreme, to criminal endeavors that follow a rational plan, involve the combination of interlocking tasks, and are carried out on a continuous basis, in the other extreme.

Where along this broad spectrum criminal activities change from being non-organized to organized is not clearly delineated, and it is not really a question that matters much from a social science perspective. With tongue in cheek, one could say, it is not the job of scholars to award the label "organized" as if it was an honorary title. As indicated before, the principal question in the study of organized crime in general and in the study of organized criminal activities in particular is not, is it organized, but how organized is it?

An Overview of Different Classifications of Criminal Activities

In the academic literature, a number of rather different classificatory schemes can be found by which criminal activities are systematized (Table 4.1). Some classifications place narrow conceptions of organized crime in a broader context and therefore might be viewed as somewhat off topic for the present discussion. Yet, they should not be ignored when thinking about meaningful conceptualizations of organized criminal activity. Three classificatory schemes in particular are noteworthy in this respect, which can be found in influential works authored by Joseph Albini (1971), Mary McIntosh (1975), and Joel Best and David Luckenbill (1994). Each of these conceptualizations is centered on a different aspect: the criminal activity itself, the relationship between those involved in the criminal activities, or the specific goals that offenders pursue with a particular criminal activity.

Table 4.1   Classifications of (Organized) Criminal Activities

Authors	Focal Point	Categories
McIntosh	Criminal act	Craft crimes Project crimes Continuing criminal enterprises
Best & Luckenbill	Underlying relationships	Individual deviance Deviant exploitation Deviant exchanges
Albini	Pursued goals	Political-social organized crime Mercenary/predatory organized crime Group-oriented organized crime Syndicated crime
Naylor	Economic effects	Predatory offenses Market-based offenses Commercial offenses
von Lampe	Underlying relationships	Market-based crimes Predatory crimes Illegal-governance crimes

Mary McIntosh: Craft Crimes, Project Crimes, and Continuing Criminal Enterprises

Mary McIntosh, in a treatise on *The Organisation of Crime*, discusses modern day organized crime with a view to historical continuities and discontinuities of criminal behavior (McIntosh, 1975). She comes up with a threefold typology based primarily on variations in frequency, expenditure of time, and volume of proceeds per criminal act. McIntosh distinguishes craft crimes, project crimes, and continuing criminal enterprises. Craft crimes, such as picking pockets, comprise '"highly skilled routines for taking small amounts from a large number of victims" (McIntosh, 1975, p. 35). Project crimes are one-off predatory crimes and compared to craft crimes "larger in scale, greater in risk, more complicated and technically advanced, and less routinized." Typical examples of project crimes, according to McIntosh, are large-scale frauds and robberies, such as the Great Train Robbery in England in 1963 (McIntosh, 1975, p. 45). Continuing criminal enterprises, finally, include extortion and the provision of illegal goods and services and involve criminal conduct on a continuous basis (McIntosh, 1975, pp. 50, 53). Both case studies (cocaine trafficking and the trafficking in stolen motor vehicles) would fall into this latter category. However, large shipments of cocaine that may require smugglers months to prepare and carry out (Decker & Townsend Chapman, 2008, p. 46) are more akin to project crimes.

Best & Luckenbill: Deviant Transactions

While Mary McIntosh focuses on characteristics of criminal acts, Joel Best and David Luckenbill, in their book *Organizing Deviance,* distinguish criminal activities with regard to the patterns of relationships underlying what they call "deviant transactions." They distinguish "individual deviance" involving one actor performing a deviant role (e.g., snorting cocaine) from "deviant exchanges" involving two cooperating actors (e.g., a coca farmer selling leaves to a lab) and "deviant exploitation" involving two actors in conflict (e.g., a thief stealing a car from its owner) (Best & Luckenbill, 1994, p. 94).

Joseph Albini's Four-Fold Typology of Organized Crime

Joseph Albini, in turn, distinguishes four main types of organized crime by the goals that criminals pursue. His typology, presented in his now classical work *The American Mafia,* includes (a) "political-social organized crime" directed at "changing or maintaining the existing social or political structure" (Albini, 1971, p. 38), which would encompass, in today's terminology, politically and religiously motivated terrorism, (b) "mercenary crime" ("predatory crime"), including theft and fraud, aimed at direct financial profit (Albini, 1971, pp. 45–46), (c) "in-group-oriented organized crime," consisting of "adventurous activities" of motorcycle gangs and adolescent gangs (Albini, 1971, p. 46), and (d) "syndicated crime," the provision of illegal goods and services on a continuous basis (Albini, 1971, pp. 47–48). Interestingly, Albini does not see these four types as exhaustive. He also mentions "violence-oriented, white collar, and many other forms" as falling within the scope of organized crime (Albini, 1971, p. 48).

Image 4.4 Police officers inspecting the scene of the Great Train Robbery of 8 August 1963 where a group of professional criminals removed mail bags from the Glasgow to London night train with contents estimated to be worth more than £2.5 million (Morton, 1992, p. 187).

Photo: Bettmann/Corbis

Primary and Secondary Criminal Activities

While the typologies proposed by McIntosh, Best and Luckenbill, and Albini are based on the notion of a spectrum of organized criminal activity, there is also the notion of a hierarchy between primary and secondary criminal activities (Naylor, 2003). Primary activities are geared toward profit making, in contrast to "enabling" (Wright, 2006, p. 49) or "facilitating" (Europol, 2006, p. 5) activities, such as corruption, document forgery, and money laundering, which aid in the commission of profit-making crimes and in the safeguarding of offenders and illicit proceeds (see also Australian Crime Commission, 2011).

Provision of Illegal Goods and Services and Other Crimes

Most contemporary scholarly classifications of organized criminal activities, however, center on the provision of illegal goods and services in contrast to other types of crime. Donald Liddick distinguishes between the provision of goods and services, on one hand, and extortion on the other (Liddick, 1999b, pp. 52–53). Jay Albanese juxtaposes the provision of illicit goods and services with what he calls "the infiltration of legitimate business or government," defined as the "coercive use of legal businesses or government agencies (from the inside or from the outside) for purposes of exploitation" (Albanese, 2011, pp. 7–8). Inherent in these classifications is the same distinction of consensual and predatory crimes that can also be found in the typologies by Albini and by Best and Luckenbill presented above.

A more complex classification, a threefold typology of profit-making crime, has been proposed by R.T. Naylor. His main concern is with the different economic effects of criminal activities where profit is at least partially the motive (Naylor, 2003, p. 83). Naylor distinguishes three categories of offenses: predatory, market based, and commercial (see also van Duyne, 1996, p. 342). Predatory crimes, according to Naylor, are characterized by the coercive or deceptive "redistribution of existing legally owned wealth" (Naylor, 2003, p. 84). Market-based crimes, in contrast, involve the voluntary transfer of illegal goods and services based on some notion of a fair market value (Naylor, 2003, p. 85). Commercial offenses, finally, are defined by Naylor as crimes committed "by otherwise legitimate entre-preneurs, investors or corporations" involving the production or distribution of inherently legal goods and services by illegal means to the detriment of workers, suppliers, customers, and the general public (Naylor, 2003, p. 88).

THE MAIN TYPES OF ORGANIZED CRIMINAL ACTIVITIES

The distinction between market-based crimes and predatory crimes is a useful starting point for a comprehensive classification of organized criminal activities. Naylor's typology is particularly valuable because it pertains to two important dimensions: the properties of criminal activities and the social impact of these activities. However, by focusing on profit-making crime, it is too narrow to capture the full range of criminal activities variously associated with organized crime. For different reasons this is also true for the other classifications reviewed above. None fully incorporates predatory crimes and those criminal activities that are linked to illegal governance, the exercise of power by criminals to con-trol, regulate, and tax illegal and also legal activities.

The classificatory scheme proposed here is more encompassing and places a stronger emphasis on the sociological dimensions of criminal behavior by focus-ing primarily on relational patterns between those committing crimes and those directly affected by these crimes. This classificatory scheme comprises three main categories of organized criminal activities while also considering various subcategories and hybrid forms: (a) market-based crimes, (b) predatory crimes, and (c) illegal-governance crimes.

Market-Based Crimes

Market-based crimes, following Naylor's conceptualization, are those pertaining to the provision of illegal goods and services. Market-based crimes are character-ized by cooperative relationships, typically between suppliers and customers, respectively sellers and buyers. In these cases an illegal good such as cocaine or an illegal service such as a contract killing are provided in exchange for money. However, at times, illegal goods and services may also be provided in the form of nonmonetary exchanges. For example, illegal drugs may be bartered for illegal arms, a phenomenon typically reported for insurgent groups such as the FARC in Colombia or the Taliban in Afghanistan, who have control over territories where drugs are produced and who at the same time have a need for military equipment (Makarenko, 2004, pp. 131–132; UNODC, 2009, p. 112). At times, the same type of illegal commodity is exchanged, namely in the case of child pornography where pedophiles share photos and videos, for example, through newsgroups on the Internet or peer-to-peer file sharing software (Beech, Elliott, Birgden, & Findlater, 2008; Fortin, 2014; Jenkins, 2001).

As R. T. Naylor has pointed out, it is not only the offenders providing illicit goods and services who seek to gain something from market-based crimes but also the partners in these illegal exchanges. Illegal market exchanges tend to be mutually beneficial for suppliers and customers (Naylor, 2003, p. 84). That is why market-based crimes are often called "victimless crimes." This label, however, is problematic. There may well be victims even though those exchanging illicit goods and services are willing participants in the transaction. More remote victims include abused children in the case of child pornography, copyright owners in the case of the trade in counterfeit brand products, and the rightful owners in the case of the trade in stolen goods. But there are also victims of crime directly involved in an illegal transaction, for example in the case of human trafficking when a person is sold into slave labor or a forced prostitute in a brothel is made to provide sexual services to customers (see Shelley, 2010). The slave seller and slave buyer are voluntary participants in a market-based transaction, as are the brothel owner and the customer, while the slave laborer and the forced prostitute, respectively, are directly victimized by the transaction.

Still, the fact that market-based crimes are centered on voluntary transactions will tend to contribute to an environment for offenders that is less hostile than in the case of predatory crimes. Customers of illicit goods and services, it is fair to assume, are on average far less inclined to report to law enforcement authorities than victims of predatory crime. This, in turn, implies that the traditional approach of *reactive policing*, acting upon reported incidents of crime, is less relevant against market-based crime. The policing of market-based crime, instead, depends much more on *proactive policing*. This means that law enforcement agencies have to allocate scarce resources and mobilize community support for actively seeking out illegal market places and illegal market participants (see Abadinsky, 2013, p. 378; Albanese, 2011, p. 255; Chapter 14). Such efforts may not be deemed worthwhile, especially when they do not lead to significant criminal sanctions. Illegal gambling in the United States is a case in point. Law enforcement agencies have reportedly been reluctant to build cases against gamblers because of a concern that "a jury may be predisposed to the attitude that gambling is 'okay, everyone does it so why should this defendant be hammered for it'" (Edelhertz & Overcast, 1993, p. 27).

Predatory Crimes

Predatory crimes, in a broad sense, are crimes through which perpetrators obtain a benefit at someone else's expense. Most notably this includes, following the conceptualizations by Albini and Naylor, profit-making crimes involving the involuntary transfer of wealth, such as theft and fraud. However, there is no reason why other forms of exploitative and harmful criminal behavior should not also be included in the category of predatory crimes, even though they do not produce an immediate monetary gain. Criminal activities such as, for example, sexual abuse or the use of slave labor are similarly relevant for the study of organized crime because they may just as well be carried out in an organized way by organized offenders. For example, groups of pedophiles may jointly bring children under their control for the purpose of sexual exploitation (Karremann, 2007; see the case study in Chapter 5). Such cases are potentially as suitable for answering key questions raised in the debate on organized crime as cases of profit-oriented predatory crimes, such as serial burglary or investment fraud.

Predatory crimes are characterized by a conflict, an antagonistic relationship between offender and victim. The confrontational nature of this relationship may manifest itself openly with the use or threat of force in the case of such crimes as robbery and extortion. But there are also less visible forms of predatory crime, for example, where the victimization occurs by use of stealth, as in the case of pick pocketing and many forms of predatory cybercrime, or by deception, as in the case of fraud. In any case, predatory criminals are essentially facing a hostile environment. They have to assume, under normal circumstances, that once their behavior is detected, it will be reported to law enforcement authorities and that their behavior will not be condoned or tolerated by any significant elements of the community (see Naylor, 2003, pp. 84–85). The situation is different, of course, where police-community relations are strained and where, accordingly, there is little willingness to report crimes of any nature (Van Dijk, 2011, pp. 466–468) or where criminal groups are so firmly in control that they can successfully discourage victims and witnesses from cooperating with the police (Felson, 2006a, p. 91).

Hybrid Forms of Market-Based and Predatory Crimes

The distinction between market-based and predatory crimes is often difficult to draw in reality. The provision of illegal goods and services and predatory acts may constitute elements of one and the same type of criminal activity (Naylor, 2003, p. 87). This is namely the case where stolen goods are marketed, be it tangible items such as cars or intangible items such as credit card information and associated customer data. In a stolen motor vehicle scheme, the initial act, the stealing of a car, is a predatory crime. The altering of the appearance and identity of the car, along with the forgery of the accompanying documents, may be done as an illegal service provided to a car trafficker. The car may then be smuggled to a market abroad, possibly again with the help of illegal service providers, such as courier drivers and professional smugglers. If the car is then sold to someone who is fully aware of the fact that it is stolen, there is, once again, an illegal market transaction. Yet, when the car is finally sold to an unsuspecting customer, this sale constitutes a predatory crime, more specifically a fraud, because the customer will have paid more than the car is worth, since it may have to be returned to the rightful owner.

In the case of the theft of credit card information, the intrusion into a database and the illegal copying of credit card information is a predatory crime.

Selling this information (e.g., through online forums) is a market-based crime, while the use of the stolen credit card information to defraud banks and retailers, once again, falls into the category of predatory crimes (Holt & Lampke, 2010). This means that the social context may change in the course of a criminal activity, shifting between more confrontational and more cooperative patterns of relations that offenders find themselves involved in.

The Special Cases of Business and Labor Racketeering

There are two forms of criminal activity commonly associated with organized crime that do not neatly fit into the categories of predatory and market-based crimes: business racketeering and labor racketeering. At their core, there is a strong element of extortion, yet the schemes are more complex than that, as will be explored in greater detail in Chapter 10. The term *business racketeering* refers to the creation or infiltration of business associations for the purpose of extracting payments from legal businesses in the form of membership fees and for the purpose of creating cartels in legal markets. *Labor racketeering* means the creation or infiltration of labor unions and labor union locals for the purpose of diverting union funds and also for using labor union power to extort legal businesses and to help enforce cartel agreements in legal markets. In the United States, business racketeering has typically gone hand-in-hand with labor racketeering (Jacobs, 2006). While both types of crime are predominantly predatory in nature, there are also elements of market-based and illegal-governance crimes. Business and labor racketeering may involve the provision of services to legal businesses willing to engage in illegal practices. For example, legal businesses may invite racketeers to help them create a cartel to increase profits and ward off competition. Legal businesses may also collude with racketeer-controlled labor unions to sign so-called sweetheart contracts that permit paying substandard wages (Jacobs, 1999, 2006; Reuter, 1985, 1987).

In extreme cases, business and labor racketeering becomes tantamount to the regulation of a legal market where criminals have control over who may do business and under what terms (Gambetta, 1993; Jacobs, 1999). In these cases, business and labor racketeering are, in fact, a form of illegal governance, and they might be more appropriately subsumed to the category of illegal-governance crimes.

Illegal-Governance Crimes

The concept of illegal-governance crimes refers to activities that are inherently linked to the exercise of power within criminal organizations, within criminal milieus and beyond. The phenomenon of illegal governance, in the sense of "power syndicates" constituting quasi-governmental structures, has already been briefly addressed in the first two chapters and will be discussed in greater detail in Chapter 8. More narrowly it also involves the self-governance of criminal associations that will be examined in Chapter 7. At this point, it should be

Image 4.5   The Fulton Fish Market in New York has been under the influence of racketeers since the 1920s. Control over a local of the United Seafood Workers, Smoked Fish and Cannery Union and over various business associations gave Cosa Nostra members the power to extract direct and indirect payments from businesses. For example, suppliers of fish were forced to pay tribute in order to have their goods unloaded without delay (Jacobs, 1999).

Photo: © Bettmann/CORBIS

sufficient to emphasize that illegal-governance activities are similar in function to what a government does in legitimate society. This includes the regulation of behavior of subordinates, the resolution of conflicts between subordinates, the protection against external threats, and the generation of revenues through some form of taxation. Accordingly, illegal-governance crimes may comprise activities such as the enforcing of rules through some form of *underworld policing* or *disciplinary procedure* within a criminal group, the settlement of disputes between criminals through some form of *underworld justice*, the use of force against rival criminal groups in *underworld wars*, negotiations of agreements with rival criminal groups and with (corrupt) officials in some form of *underworld diplomacy*, and the collection of taxes, or protection payments.

Some of these activities may occur with some regularity—namely, the collection of protection payments—while other illegal-governance crimes, such as meting out punishment against police informants, tend to be more sporadic in nature. When those holding power are firmly entrenched and the rules they seek to enforce are well established, there is little need for continuous action. For example, if a power syndicate has prohibited the selling of drugs to minors in order to avoid unwanted police attention in its territory, it will only have to act when this rule is violated. If the mere threat of reprisal is a sufficient deterrent, this will rarely or never be the case (Reuter, 1994).

Illegal-governance crimes have similarities with both market-based crimes and predatory crimes regarding the underlying relational patterns. Illegal governance, just like legal governance, has an element of coercion. Power is exercised with or without the consent of the subordinates. To the extent there is no consent, illegal-governance crimes are similar to predatory crimes. In fact, the collection of underworld taxes comes close to extortion. However, by definition, illegal governance begins where pure extortion ends. Illegal governance provides benefits for subordinates by reducing uncertainty. Illegal governance implies that there is a concentration of power, an illegal monopoly of violence, and that protection payments have to be made to only one entity. Should someone else attempt to extort money, those in power would step in to protect their position, thereby also protecting their subordinates.

To the degree certain rules are enforced, the behavior among subordinates also becomes more predictable, which in turn, facilitates illegal business and reduces the level of risk for the individual criminal. For example, if in a neighborhood the ruling gang severely punishes those who collaborate with the police, a criminal has less reason to assume that another criminal will act as a police informant. Illegal-governance crimes, then, such as collecting protection payments and punishing police informants, are similar to market-based crimes in that they are beneficial not only to the perpetrators but also to others, in this case the subordinates of a power syndicate. In fact, inherent in illegal-governance crimes is that they tend to acquire some degree of legitimacy over time. This means that subordinates accept illegal-governance crimes as justified and useful in the furtherance of individual and common interests (Gambetta, 1993).

Implications of the Three Main Types of Organized Criminal Activities

Three main types of crime have been distinguished here with regard to the relational patterns between those committing crimes and those directly affected by these crimes: (a) market-based crimes, (b) predatory crimes, and (c) illegal-governance crimes. Market-based crimes are characterized by voluntary transactions of illegal goods and services; predatory crimes involve offender-victim relations; illegal-governance crimes involve the exercise of power to regulate the behavior of subordinates. The three categories of crime differ in the levels of hostility that offenders are likely to encounter. Offenders committing market-based crimes will tend to operate in relatively less hostile environments than predatory criminals, while the level of hostility for offenders of illegal-governance crimes will tend to decrease the more benefits subordinates derive from the exercise of illegal power.

The three types of crime may also differ with regard to the expenditure of time. Market-based crimes tend to be committed on a continuous basis, although the intervals of illegal transactions may vary across different illegal markets and across different levels of the same illegal market. For example, the retail selling of illegal drugs may occur on a daily basis, while the smuggling of large shipments of illegal drugs may have the character of project crimes that require weeks or months of preparation. Predatory crimes tend to be committed as opportunities arise rather than in a rhythm set by the offender. Illegal-governance crimes, in contrast, will tend to be committed only sporadically, with the exception of the collection of protection payments that, however, primarily reflects the regularity of the market-based activities that are being taxed by a power syndicate.

Finally, the explanations for the prevalence of organized criminal activities differ across the three categories. Market-based crimes can be explained as a result of the matching of supply of and demand for illegal goods and services and, more fundamentally, as a result of the legal restrictions imposed on the production and exchange of certain goods and services (Arlacchi, 1998; Chapter 9). Predatory crimes, in turn, exploit opportunities arising from the vulnerabilities of potential victims (Cohen & Felson, 1979; Hindelang, Gottfredson, & Garofalo, 1978). Illegal-governance crimes are committed because the government is unwilling or unable to regulate behavior in certain areas, thereby creating a vacuum that may be filled by illegal power structures. In illegal markets, for example, the government, as a matter of principle, does not intend to regulate but instead only to prevent behavior (Skaperdas, 2001; Chapter 8).

ILLEGAL MARKETS

The differences between market-based, predatory, and illegal-governance crimes have implications for the way crimes are committed, which in turn, may have implications for how offenders are organized and how crimes and offenders fit in the broader social context. A similarly useful classification can be made with regard to different kinds of market-based crimes and therefore different kinds of illegal markets (Table 4.2).

Table 4.2   Classifications of Organized Criminal Activities and Illegal Markets

Predatory Crimes	Market-Based Crimes	Illegal-Governance Crimes
Offenders and victims	Suppliers and customers	Government and subordinates

Illegal Markets

For prohibited goods and services:
Absolute contraband

For regulated goods and services:
Relative contraband
Fiscal contraband

Source: Further elaboration of a classification proposed by R. T. Naylor (2003).

An illegal market can be defined as an arena for the regular voluntary exchange of goods and services for money where the goods and services themselves, their production, selling, and/or consumption violates the law (Arlacchi, 1998, p. 7; Beckert & Wehinger, 2011, p. 2). Of course, the legal framework that defines illegal markets varies across time and across jurisdictions. The history of the criminalization and decriminalization of, for example, alcohol, drugs, gambling, prostitution, and pornography provides illustrative examples for the relativity of illegality (see, e.g., MacCoun & Reuter, 2001).

Different Types of Illegal Markets

Illegal markets can be divided into two basic categories: (a) markets for goods and services where the commodity itself is illegal under all circumstances and (b) markets for goods and services where the commodity or its exchange are regulated to some extent. The regulation may center on restrictions on who can sell and buy a commodity and under what circumstances, or it may center on the payment of taxes and customs duties (Table 4.2).

Absolute Contraband

There are relatively few goods and services that are prohibited without any exceptions and for which, accordingly, no parallel legal markets exist. At least this is true for most countries. Goods that cannot be sold legally include humans, child pornography, and counterfeit currency. Services that cannot be provided legally under any circumstances (at least one would hope so) include sexual services by children (child prostitution) and contract killings. In these cases R. T. Naylor (2003, p. 86) speaks of "absolute contraband."

Relative Contraband

For most goods and services, legal and illegal markets coexist. This means that while the provision of these goods and services may be illegal under some or even most circumstances, it is possible, at least for some under certain circumstances, to sell and buy these goods and services without breaking the law. This category includes goods such as drugs and weapons and services such as debt collection and waste disposal. They constitute "relative contraband" in Naylor's terminology (Naylor, 2003, p. 86).

The legal restrictions that define illegal markets vary in degree and with regard to what, specifically, is affected by these legal restrictions. Apart from absolute prohibitions that rule out the existence of any legal market, there are prohibitions of goods and services that allow exceptions. For example, drugs like cocaine and hazardous substances like nuclear material may be legally produced and traded for medical and scientific purposes. In other cases, the goods and services as such are legal, although the production and/or selling are restricted in certain respects. Some markets are illegal because the commodities traded have been produced in violation of the law. This is true, for example, for poached animals, stolen goods, and counterfeit brand products

Image 4.6   Counterfeit U.S. dollars on display at a press conference in Lima, Peru, in April 2013. Counterfeit currency is absolute contraband because there is no parallel legal market for the sale, for example, of fake dollar bills.

Photo: © ENRIQUE CASTRO-MENDIVIL/Reuters/Corbis

(product piracy). Some markets are illegal because the selling of a good or service is against the law. For example, in countries where extramarital sex is legal but prostitution illegal, the commercialization of sexual services is outlawed, not the sexual services as such. Similarly, where the trade in organs has been made illegal, the commercialization of the provision of donor organs is criminalized, not the transplanting of organs as such (Beckert & Wehinger, 2011). In many cases, restrictions are imposed on who may provide and who may buy certain goods and services. Prescription drugs, for example, may only be sold in licensed outlets to someone with a medical prescription. Likewise, the legal sale of a gun commonly requires permits for both the seller and the buyer.

Fiscal Contraband

Finally, there are markets that are illegal because some or all of the taxes and duties imposed on a particular commodity are evaded. Naylor (2003, p. 86) calls these commodities "fiscal contraband." This includes highly taxed goods, such as alcohol, gasoline, and diesel fuel, and cigarettes and other tobacco products. Common schemes include the legal export (not subject to taxation) and illegal reimport, that is, smuggling of goods without paying any taxes and customs duties, and the smuggling of goods purchased in low-tax jurisdictions with taxes being paid in the country of purchase but not in the country of sale (von Lampe, 2011b). There are also services that may fall into this category of illegal markets—for example, illegal labor brokerage, which allows businesses to save on social insurance payments (Heber, 2009b; Van Duyne & Houtzager, 2005).

Implications of Differences Between Illegal Markets

The differences in the types of illegal markets have some noteworthy implications. First of all, variations in the degree to which goods and services are restricted are likely to translate into variations in the levels of law enforcement pressure exerted on an illegal market. Generally speaking, illegal markets for prohibited goods (e.g., child pornography) are more likely to be targeted than illegal markets for regulated goods (e.g., cigarettes).

Secondly, the differences in the types of illegal markets can be expected to influence their relationship to legal markets. R. T. Naylor, for example, has argued that there is a link between price levels in legal and parallel illegal markets. He suggests that while there is no reference point for the pricing of goods and services that are subject to absolute prohibitions, the prices for restricted goods and services will in most cases be higher on illegal markets than on the parallel legal markets. In contrast, according to Naylor, where the production of a good or service violates the law or where taxes and duties are evaded, illegal prices will be lower than the legal prices for the same commodity (Naylor, 2003, p. 86). This is plausible because in most cases of restricted goods and services, such as prescription drugs, illegal markets will attract those buyers who cannot easily access the same goods legally. These buyers can be expected to willingly pay a higher price to obtain the desired commodity. However, where only the modalities of production determine the illegality of a commodity, the price for an illegal product will be lower than for its legal counterpart for two reasons. First,

Table 4.3   Typology of Illegal Markets

Type of Illegal Market	Examples: Goods	Examples: Services
Prohibited goods (absolute contraband)	Child pornography Humans Counterfeit currency	Child prostitution Contract murder
Regulated goods (relative contraband)	Drugs Weapons Nuclear material Protected wildlife	Illegal debt collection Illegal waste disposal
Regulated goods (fiscal contraband)	Alcohol Gasoline Cigarettes Loose tobacco	Illegal labor Illegal labor brokerage

Source: Further elaboration of a classification proposed by Naylor (2003).

the illegal production will tend to cut costs, as it will be cheaper, for example, to steal rather than to produce a product and cheaper to counterfeit a brand product rather than to pay license fees to the brand owner. Second, a lower price will tend to be the only incentive for a buyer to prefer an illegal over a legal product. The same is true in the case of illegal markets for highly taxed goods and services. By evading taxes, suppliers can undercut legal retail prices and still make a profit.

There are also important variations with regard to the overlap between illegal and legal markets. Illegal markets for prohibited commodities will tend to be more clearly separated from legal markets than illegal markets for regulated commodities. In fact, illegal goods that are indistinguishable from legal goods— such as, for example, stolen merchandise—can fairly easily be introduced into legal distribution channels (Beckert & Wehinger, 2011, p. 17).

THE CONCEPTUALIZATION OF PARTICULAR ORGANIZED CRIMINAL ACTIVITIES

The classificatory schemes that have been presented in this chapter so far identify and group different types of organized criminal activities in broad categories with a view to a few salient features. With the two conceptual frameworks discussed in the section below, in contrast, the focus shifts to a microscopic view of organized criminal activities, be they market-based, predatory, or illegal-governance crimes. The two frameworks, script analysis and the Logistics of Organized Crime approach, break specific criminal endeavors down into smaller component parts.

Crime Scripts

One way to examine and better understand the degree of organization of a given criminal activity is to develop a step-by-step account of the procedures that offenders use in committing a crime. This approach is known as *procedural analysis* or *script analysis*. It has been introduced to the study of (organized) crime by Derek Cornish, a representative of the rational choice school of thought in criminology (Cornish, 1994). The rational choice school views "offending as relatively skilled instrumental action guided by choices and decisions made in the light of situational circumstances" (Cornish & Clarke, 2002, p. 45).

The underlying assumption of the crime script approach, borrowed from cognitive science, is that individuals engaged in commonplace routines are guided by structured conceptions, called scripts, about how to understand and how to carry out these routines, similar to theatrical scripts that break down plots into acts and scenes that are incorporated in a sequential order (Cornish, 1994, p. 158).

Cornish proposes that many crimes, likewise, can meaningfully be viewed as "scripted" events. Subjectively, script analysis aims at understanding offender accounts of crime commission, while objectively, it is a tool to organize all available information about the "procedural aspects and procedural requirements of crime commission," primarily in an effort to identify possible points of intervention (Cornish, 1994, p. 160).

Script analysis goes beyond the mere description of the modus operandi of offenders—for example, how the VIN on a stolen car is exchanged in a "body switching" operation or punishment is meted out by an underworld government. It is concerned with a comprehensive examination of the essential elements of a criminal event, including the individuals (cast) involved, their decisions and actions, the tools (props) they use, and the settings (locations) they operate in (Cornish & Clarke, 2002, p. 59).

There are no commonly accepted rules on how to construct crime scripts as an analytical device (Brayley, Cockbain, & Laycock, 2011, p. 133). Cornish, in his seminal paper on crime script analysis, illustrated his approach with an analysis of the trafficking in stolen motor vehicles, presenting the typical commission of this crime as a sequence of six stages or "scenes": preparation, theft, concealment, disguise, marketing, and disposal (Cornish, 1994, p. 173). Each of these scenes, as Cornish pointed out, can be played in different ways—for example, cars can be stolen from a parking lot or they can be rented from a rental car business, and the disguise of the true identity of a stolen car can be accomplished in different ways, requiring different levels of sophistication. For example, transferring the VIN from a wrecked car is more sophisticated than just exchanging the license plate. The availability of alternative options for each scene means that a script offers different pathways or tracks to its completion (Cornish, 1994, p. 175).

In a more recent paper, Tompson and Chainey (2011) developed a framework for the script analysis of illegal waste disposal, taking electronic waste as a case study. Deviating from Cornish's terminology, they refer to the key stages of a crime script as "acts," and they distinguish six such acts in the illegal disposal of electronic waste: creation, storage, collection, transport, treatment, and disposal. The first two acts, creation and storage, constitute essentially legal activities. Electronic waste is created—for example, when a business upgrades its computers, making the old equipment redundant. The sequence of illegal acts begins with the transfer of the electronic waste to an unauthorized waste carrier (collection), who may refurbish those parts that are not beyond repair (treatment), before shipping everything to a country with a demand for refurbished electronic devices (transportation), where an importer eventually abandons the electronic waste (disposal) (Tompson & Chainey, 2011, p. 195).

In line with theatrical terminology, Tompson and Chainey propose to break down each of these "acts" into four "scenes", preparation, pre-activity, activity, and post-activity:

I. Preparation. This requires the analyst to consider what opportunities exist for committing illegal waste activity (i.e., by "thinking thief"). This can help to identify the opportunity structure for illegal waste activity.

II. Pre-activity. This relates to the logistical or transactional steps that need to be carried out prior to the activity.

III. Activity. This relates to the illegal waste activity itself and can take the form of various offences or noncompliance.

IV. Post-activity. This refers to logistical or transactional steps necessary to exit from the illegal activity.

(Tompson & Chainey, 2011, pp. 188–189)

It is largely a matter of the specific crime in question that determines into how many layers a crime script is best broken down. It may also be appropriate to distinguish different interconnected crime scripts in the case of more complex criminal events that would follow an overarching "master script" (Cornish & Clarke, 2002, p. 50). In the case of the trafficking in stolen motor vehicles, this would mean that there is a separate script for obtaining a car and a separate script for altering the identity of the car.

Finally, Cornish and Clarke suggest examining the links between crime scripts within a given geographical area. The emphasis then is not on a strict sequential order of acts and scenes but on "webs of interconnected offending," where certain elements of different crimes converge (Cornish & Clarke, 2002, p. 51). This is the case, for example, where the same smuggling channels are used for different kinds of contraband (Cornish & Clarke, 2002, p. 59), as has been reported for mixed shipments of cocaine from Latin America and Moroccan hashish going from North Africa to illegal drug markets in Europe (Gamella & Jimenez Rodrigo, 2008, p. 272).

The Logistics of Organized Crime Approach

The Logistics of Organized Crime approach shares many similarities with the crime script approach. It is also an analytical tool with which complex criminal events can be broken down into component parts, and historically, it likewise has primarily been developed as a device to identify points of intervention for preventive and repressive measures. The main difference between the two approaches is that the logistics approach places the main emphasis not so much on a sequential order of decisions and actions, as the crime script approach does. Rather, the focus is on a comprehensive system of tasks, some of which have to be accomplished in a sequential order, some of which have to be accomplished concurrently, possibly over the entire course of a criminal endeavor.

While the notion of criminal logistics appears quite frequently in the organized crime literature on a rhetorical level, the Logistics of Organized Crime approach has remained the only elaborate analytical framework of its kind to date. It was formulated by Ulrich Sieber and Marion Bögel in a study commissioned by the German police agency Bundeskriminalamt (BKA) (Sieber & Bögel, 1993; see also Sieber, 1995) following up on earlier discussions within the BKA (Kube, 1990). Sieber and Bögel developed and applied their conceptual framework in an empirical analysis of four areas of crime: trafficking in stolen motor vehicles, exploitative prostitution, human trafficking, and illegal gambling.

The concept of logistics has its origins in military thinking and has only more recently been introduced to the area of business administration. In essence it pertains to the effective procurement and use of resources—such as materials, tools, personnel, and information—by an organization, be it an army or a business (Gudehus & Kotzab, 2012, p. 4).

Sieber and Bögel (1993) derived their framework primarily from the logistics of legal businesses while also taking aspects into account that are more typical for military organizations. The starting point for the Logistics of Organized Crime approach is the assumption that there are considerable similarities between legal and illegal businesses. In both cases, goods or services are created and marketed through the coordinated use of required resources. At the same time, there are specific challenges that illegal businesses face, namely with respect to the threat of arrest and incarceration and the threat of the seizure and forfeiture of assets.

Sieber and Bögel differentiate two broad categories of logistics: core business logistics that can also be found in the case of legal businesses and which largely follow a sequential order, and "overarching logistics elements," which are typical for illegal businesses and which transcend the sequential order of the core logistics (Sieber & Bögel, 1993, p. 115). The core business logistics involve three stages: the procurement of required resources, the production of commodities using these resources, and the marketing of the produced commodities (Sieber & Bögel, 1993, pp. 42–44). Applied to the trafficking in stolen motor vehicles, they differentiate procurement logistics (locating and obtaining a car by various means), production logistics (altering the identity), marketing logistics (transportation and sale abroad), and additionally the logistics of money laundering (use of illicit proceeds) (Sieber & Bögel, 1993, pp. 87–115). The "overarching logistics elements" include the flow of information (e.g., use of coded language), camouflage (e.g., use of legal businesses as fronts), the use of violence and corruption (e.g., to influence accomplices), and legal defense against criminal prosecution (Sieber & Bögel, 1993, pp. 115–124).

Although there are some differences in detail, the classification proposed by Sieber and Bögel is a variation of the crime script approach with regard to the core logistics, but it presents an added dimension with regard to the overarching logistical elements. The question, however, is what extent the logistics of the flow of information, the logistics of camouflage, the logistics of the use of violence and corruption, and the logistics of the legal defense against criminal prosecution are indeed overarching aspects that pertain to a complex criminal event as a whole. The crime script approach proposed by Cornish and others suggests that it is better to consider these aspects separately within the context of each stage (act, scene) in the process of crime commission. Which approach is preferable, of course, is ultimately determined by the specific circumstances of a given criminal event and by the purpose of analysis.

ORGANIZED CRIMINAL ACTIVITIES: SUMMARY AND CONCLUSION

This chapter has discussed organized criminal activities as a separate object of study but with a view to how it relates to the study of organized crime in general. It has been argued that there are reasons to look at criminal activities separately, especially separate from the existence of criminal organizations, while at the same time emphasizing that the nature of criminal activities may well influence how criminals are organized, how criminals acquire and exercise power, and how crime fits into the broader context of society. The starting point for this discussion has been the assumption that there are differences in degree between organized and non-organized criminal activities and that these differences potentially matter with regard to a number of themes addressed in the study of organized crime.

Against the backcloth of various typologies proposed in the academic literature, a classificatory scheme has been outlined that centers on three-fold typologies of criminal activities and of illegal markets. Three main types of organized criminal activity were identified: (a) market-based crimes, (b) predatory crimes, and (c) illegal-governance crimes. This typology focuses on the relations between those committing crimes and those directly affected by these crimes. Market-based crimes connect sellers and buyers in illegal markets, while predatory crimes are defined by a confrontational relationship between offender and victim. Illegal-governance crimes, finally, have to do with the exercise of power where relationships resemble those between government and the governed.

The distinction between these three types of criminal activities, like the distinction between different types of illegal markets, has implications for the degree to which crime is embedded in society and enjoys some level of acceptance. Most obviously, predatory crimes will tend to be confronted with a more hostile environment than market-based crimes, although illegal markets for prohibited goods such as child pornography can be expected to face a more hostile environment than illegal markets for goods that are not illegal per se, such as cigarettes. There are also differences in the way criminal activities are carried out. For example, market-based crimes tend to be committed on a continuous basis in fairly regular intervals, as is the case for the distribution of cocaine. Predatory crimes, in contrast, tend to be more dependent on the availability of opportunities, while illegal-governance crimes, for the most part, are committed rather sporadically once a criminal group has successfully established its position of power.

In order to better understand the variations in the level of organization of criminal activities, however, one has to go beyond general classifications and take a close-up look at specific criminal endeavors. Two analytical frameworks for such an in-depth examination have been presented: script analysis and the Logistics of Organized Crime approach. In essence, these are tools for breaking down complex events—such as cocaine trafficking or the trafficking in stolen motor vehicles—into meaningful component parts that can then be examined separately and also with a view to how these components are interconnected. Script analysis and logistics analysis draw attention to what exactly offenders do, what resources and settings they use, and what risks they face when committing a crime. It is important to note, taking cocaine trafficking and the trafficking in stolen motor vehicles as examples that the characteristics of organized criminal activities tend to change from one step to the next in the overall process of crime commission. There are, for example, different demands on the skills, equipment, and materials and different time requirements for the cultivation of coca and the production of coca paste, cocaine base, and cocaine hydrochloride. Roughly speaking, the amount of time required for each step decreases while the level of sophistication of the operation increases from coca cultivation to the production of cocaine. The smuggling of cocaine, in turn, can be carried out in more or less sophisticated and time-consuming ways while the distribution of cocaine places comparatively minor demands on offenders in terms of time and expertise.

Differences in the degree to which the components of a criminal activity are interconnected can be highlighted by way of a comparison between cocaine trafficking and the trafficking in stolen motor vehicles. In the case of cocaine, each individual step in the sequence of events involves the production of a marketable intermediate or final product (coca leaves, coca paste, cocaine base, and cocaine hydrochloride), followed by a sequence of steps where the final product is moved in the direction of final consumers in increasingly smaller batches. The order of events, of course, follows an inherent logic that cannot be changed. But beyond that, the individual steps are only rather loosely interconnected. For example, by whom and how coca paste is produced, whether using the solvent extraction or the acid extraction method, is not predetermined by the way the coca leaves have been harvested, and it likewise does not determine by whom and how the coca paste is processed and converted into cocaine in subsequent phases of the crime script.

Such a lack of connectedness is not necessarily characteristic of the trafficking in stolen motor vehicles, where an order placed by a customer further down the distribution chain or the availability of a wrecked car may determine what kind of car is being stolen. In turn, how a car is obtained has an impact on what needs to be done to alter its appearance. There are, for example, methods for opening a car that result in the destruction of the door locks that then have to be replaced in order to disguise the fact that the car has been stolen. It should be obvious that such a level of interdependence between the phases in a car trafficking script necessitates a higher degree of coordination across phases than is true for the stages in the process of producing cocaine. The need for coordination, in turn, has potential implications for the way the offenders involved in these activities are linked to each other. However, one needs to be careful not to jump to conclusions. As will be clarified later in this book, the greater need for coordination does not necessarily mean that offenders involved in the trafficking of stolen motor vehicles are more organized than offenders involved in cocaine trafficking. The possible interrelations between the characteristics of a criminal activity and aspects such as the organization of offenders are too complex to permit a definitive statement, at least at this point. The purpose of the discussion in this chapter can only be to highlight variations in organized *crimes* and to illustrate why these variations may be important to consider in the overall study of organized crime.

The following chapters will revisit these issues from other perspectives in order to arrive at a denser picture. At this point, the various categories of organized criminal activities that have been presented in this chapter are best viewed as pieces of a puzzle that reveal some insights but will reveal much more when assembled with other pieces into a larger picture.

Discussion Questions

1. Which activity is more organized, cocaine trafficking or trafficking in stolen motor vehicles?

2. Which type of crime (market based, predatory, illegal governance) is the most desirable for offenders to be engaged in?

3. Which type of criminal activity poses a greater threat: project crimes or continuing criminal enterprises?

Research Projects

1. Conduct a script analysis of cocaine trafficking.

2. Examine the production of methamphetamine. Identify the different phases in the production and determine the skills and resources required for each and compare this to the production of cocaine.

3. Examine the anti-theft features of a new model luxury car and make an assessment of how offenders involved in the stolen car business might cope.

4. Pick an endangered species, find out to what extent the trade in that species is illegal and how widespread this illegal trade is.

5. Find out the various commercial uses of cocaine before it was made illegal.

Further Reading

Script Analysis and the Logistics of Organized Crime

Ekblom, P. (2003). Organised crime and the conjunction of criminal opportunity framework. In A. Edwards & P. Gill (Eds.), *Transnational organised crime* (pp. 241–263). London: Routledge.

Hancock, G., & Laycock, G. (2010). Organised crime and crime scripts: Prospects for disruption. In K. Bullock, R. V. Clarke, & N. Tilley (Eds.), *Situational prevention of organised crimes* (pp. 172–192). Cullompton, UK: Willan.

Korsell, L., Vesterhav, D., & Skinnari, J. (2011). Human trafficking and drug distribution in Sweden from a market perspective-similarities and differences. *Trends in Organized Crime, 14*(2-3), 100-124.

Motor Vehicle Theft

Heitmann, J. A., & Morales, R. H. (2014). *Stealing cars: Technology and society from the Model T to the Grand Torino*. Baltimore, MD: Johns Hopkins University Press.

Mullins, C.W., & Cherbonneau, M.G. (2011). Establishing Connections: Gender, motor vehicle theft, and disposal networks. *Justice Quarterly, 28*(2), 278–302.

Drug Trafficking

McKetin, R., McLaren, J., Kelly, E., & Chalmers, J. (2009). The market for crystalline methamphetamine in Sydney, Australia. *Global Crime, 10*(1–2), 113–123.

Pietschmann, T. (2004). Price-setting behaviour in the heroin market. *Bulletin on Narcotics, 56*(1–2), 105–139.

Reuter, P. (2014). Drug markets and organized crime. In L. Paoli (Ed.), *The Oxford handbook of organized crime* (pp. 359–380.). Oxford: Oxford University Press.

Human Trafficking

Dragiewicz, M. (Ed.). (2015). *Global human trafficking: Critical issues and contexts*. New York: Routledge.

Hepburn, S., & Simon, R. J. (2013). *Human trafficking around the world: Hidden in plain sight*. New York: Columbia University Press.

Kleemans, E. R., & Smit, M. (2014). Human smuggling, human trafficking, and exploitation in the sex industry. In L. Paoli (Ed.), *The Oxford handbook of organized crime* (pp. 381–401). Oxford: Oxford University Press.

Palmiotto, M. J. (Ed.). (2015). *Combating human trafficking: A multidisciplinary approach*. Boca Raton, FL: CRC Press.

Pennington, J. R., Ball, A. Dwayne, H., Ronald, D., & Soulakova, J. N. (2009). The cross-national market in human beings. *Journal of Macromarketing, 29*(2), 119–134.

Shelley, L. (2010). *Human trafficking: A global perspective*. Cambridge, UK: Cambridge University Press.

Siddharth, K. (2010). *Sex trafficking: Inside the business of modern slavery*. New York: Columbia University Press.

Viuhko, M. (2010). Human trafficking for sexual exploitation and organized procuring in Finland. *European Journal of Criminology, 7*(1), 61–75.

The Illegal Cigarette Trade

L'Hoiry, X. D. (2013). "Shifting the stuff wasn't any bother": Illicit enterprise, tobacco bootlegging and deconstructing the British government's cigarette smuggling discourse. *Trends in Organized Crime, 16*(4), 413–434.

Shen, A., Antonopoulos, G. A., & von Lampe, K. (2010). "The dragon breathes smoke": Cigarette counterfeiting in the People's Republic of China. *British Journal of Criminology, 50*(2), 239–258.

von Lampe, K. (2006). The cigarette black market in Germany and in the United Kingdom. *Journal of Financial Crime, 13*(2), 235–254.

von Lampe, K., Kurti, M., & Bae, J. (2014). Land of opportunities: The illicit trade in cigarettes in the United States. In P. C. van Duyne, J. Harvey, G. A. Antonopoulos, K. von Lampe, A. Maljevic, & A. Markovska (Eds.), *Corruption, greed and crime money: Sleaze and shady economy in Europe and beyond* (pp. 267–289). Nijmegen, the Netherlands: Wolf Legal Publishers.

von Lampe, K., Kurti, M., Shen, A., & Antonopoulos, G. A. (2012). The changing role of China in the global illegal cigarette trade. *International Criminal Justice Review, 22*(1), 43–67.

Illegal Gambling

Liddick, D. (1998). *The Mob's daily number: Organized crime and the numbers gambling industry*. Lanham, MD: University Press of America.

Spapens, T. (2014). Illegal gambling. In L. Paoli (Ed.), *The Oxford handbook of organized crime* (pp. 402–418). Oxford: Oxford University Press.

White, S., Garton, S., Robertson, S., & White, G. (2010). *Playing the numbers: Gambling in Harlem between the wars*. Cambridge, MA: Harvard University Press.

Environmental Crime

Bisschop, L. (2012). Is it all going to waste? Illegal transports of e-waste in a European trade hub, *Crime, Law and Social Change, 58*(3), 221–249.

Boekhout van Solinge, T. (2014). The illegal exploitation of natural resources. In L. Paoli (Ed.), *The Oxford handbook of organized crime* (pp. 500–526). Oxford: Oxford University Press.

Gossmann, A. (2009). Tusks and trinkets: An overview of illicit ivory trafficking in Africa. *African Security Review, 18*(4), 50–69.

Lemieux, A. M., & Clarke, R. V. (2009). The international ban on ivory sales and its effects on elephant poaching in Africa. *British Journal of Criminology, 49*(4), 451–471.

Massari, M., & Monzini, P. (2004). Dirty businesses in Italy: A case-study of illegal trafficking in hazardous waste. *Global Crime, 6*(3–4), 285–304.

Wyatt, T. (2013). From the Cardamom Mountains of Southwest Cambodia to the forests of the world: An exploration of the illegal charcoal trade. *International Journal of Comparative and Applied Criminal Justice, 37*(1), 15–29.

Wyatt, T. (2014). The Russian Far East's illegal timber trade: An organized crime? *Crime, Law and Social Change, 61*(1), 15–35.

Fraud

Levi, M. (2014). Organized fraud. In L. Paoli (Ed.), *The Oxford handbook of organized crime* (pp. 460–481). Oxford: Oxford University Press.

Pashev, K. (2008). Cross-border VAT fraud in an enlarged Europe. In P. C. van Duyne, J. Harvey, A. Maljevic, M. Scheinost, & K. von Lampe (Eds.), *European crime-markets at cross-roads: Extended and extending criminal Europe* (pp. 237–259). Nijmegen, the Netherlands: Wolf Legal.

van Gestel, B. (2010). Mortgage fraud and facilitating circumstances. In K. Bullock, R. V. Clarke, & N. Tilley (Eds.), *Situational prevention of organised crimes* (pp. 111–129). Cullompton, UK: Willan.

CHAPTER 5

Criminal Structures— An Overview

The life story of famous underworld figure Al Capone, briefly summarized in Chapter 1, sheds some light on the many ways in which criminals can be connected to other criminals. Capone led a personal army of paid gunmen as part of a larger alliance of about 180 criminals from various ethnic backgrounds. He was a close associate of his brother Ralph, his cousin Frank Nitti, and his friend Jack Guzik, who shared in the leadership of what became known as the "Capone Syndicate." The four men were also partners, jointly or separately, in a number of illicit and licit business ventures. It is not possible to capture all of these various types of connections with one notion of "organization." The purpose of this chapter is to provide an overview of the different forms in which criminals are organized. Most criminal structures do not have a moniker like the "Capone Syndicate" or a formalized structure with membership defined by an initiation ritual like the American Cosa Nostra. Most are more fluid and less easily discernible (Bouchard & Morselli, 2014). However, as will be shown in this and later chapters, they are no less important for understanding what criminals do and how they do it. In fact, the importance of criminal organizations, such as the Italian American Cosa Nostra, for the day-to-day activities of criminals tends to be overrated.

The term *criminal structure* is used here as a generic concept that encompasses terms such as *criminal group, criminal organization, illegal enterprise, illegal firm, mafia, crime syndicate,* and *criminal network,* which are frequently but inconsistently used in the organized crime literature. A criminal structure, as understood here, is an arrangement of relationships between criminals that have an impact—directly or indirectly—on the commission of crime. Such a broad concept is necessary to account for the variations and dynamics of the patterns of interaction and association that can be observed in the world of crime. It is important to understand and to meaningfully systematize these differences. Just like the differentiation of types of criminal activity discussed in the previous chapter, this is a matter of trying to avoid comparing apples and oranges. It is important to differentiate criminal structures in a way that helps formulate and answer research questions and aids in devising and implementing sound policy.

There are a variety of classifications of criminal structures that will be reviewed in this chapter. One approach that appears particularly suitable for capturing the variations in the organization of criminals is to classify criminal structures based on the different functions they serve. Some structures help criminals successfully commit crimes, some structures foster social bonds between criminals, and yet other structures regulate and control the behavior of criminals. Another important classification pertains to the degree to which criminals are integrated into delineable organizational structures. In one extreme, criminals interact as autonomous actors in one-off transactions. In the other extreme, they are integral, permanent parts of an overarching organization.

To illustrate the diversity of relational structures that may connect criminals, this chapter begins with a case study of pedophile networks. At first glance, this may appear peculiar because pedophiles hardly fit the cliché imagery of organized crime. But the very fact that pedophiles do not resemble stereotypical gangsters like Al Capone is advantageous in that it provides for an unobstructed view on criminal structures.

CASE STUDY: PEDOPHILE NETWORKS

Pedophiles are individuals, mostly but not exclusively men, who have a "persistent sexual interest in prepubescent children" (Seto, 2008, p. 164). Similar to heterosexuality or homosexuality, this sexual preference emerges early in life and is stable across the lifespan (Seto, 2008, p. 165). Having this preference as such is not a crime, but when pedophiles are acting out their sexual preference, namely by consuming child pornography or by engaging in sexual contact with children, they violate criminal statutes.

The violation of criminal law alone does not warrant any attention in the context of the study of organized crime. What deserves attention is the existence of networks of pedophiles. It can be argued that these networks are prototypical criminal structures as they promote, directly or indirectly, the commission of crimes. At the same time, they do not fit the stereotypical image of criminal gangs or syndicates made up of socially marginalized career criminals. Pedophile networks, as far as can be seen, tend to represent a cross-section of society. Networks of pedophiles have existed in different forms. A political movement aiming at the legalization of pedophile acts emerged in the 1950s and gained some prominence in the course of the sexual revolution of the 1960s and 1970s. Since then, whatever public tolerance for pedophiles might have existed has largely disappeared.

The advent of the Internet has greatly simplified the networking of pedophiles, especially among those that do not want their sexual preference to be known publicly. Online forums permit pedophiles, under the protection of relative anonymity, to come into contact with each other, to communicate, and to exchange child pornography (Holt, Blevins, & Burkert, 2010; Jenkins, 2001). In turn, communication via the Internet has facilitated the establishing of face-to-face contacts within close-knit circles of pedophiles at the local and global levels (Tremblay, 2002).

Manfred Karremann, an investigative journalist, infiltrated the "pedo-scene" in Germany in the early 2000s. The following is a summary of his findings (Karremann, 2007). Karremann presented himself as a pedophile who is financially independent because of a large inheritance and who does not like computers and therefore does not exchange child pornography. With this cover story, Karremann gained access to pedophile self-help groups in Cologne, Munich, and Berlin. These self-help groups met once or twice each month. Some meetings were "official" and open to novices, while to other meetings only "tested" members were admitted. However, even novices first had to undergo a screening procedure and may have needed a member to vouch for them in order to keep unwanted individuals out, namely undercover police officers. At meetings, as well as in online chatrooms, pedophiles discussed how to best cope with being pedophilic without getting depressed and ending up in prison. As Karremann explains, this communication, first of all, meets the individual needs of pedophiles. The feeling of being alone with oneself and one's thoughts would be difficult to bear for many of these men. The silence that they impose on the children they abuse they themselves have to maintain throughout their live, except with like-minded people (Karremann, 2007, p. 50). In addition, the communication among pedophiles helps to create a specific subculture centered on the notion that it is okay to be pedophilic. In some groups and especially in closed meetings restricted to tested members, which Karremann was able to attend, pedophiles also talked explicitly, and exchanged know-how about their abusive relationships with children. This included discussing tactics about how to approach a child and how to build up and maintain a relationship of material and emotional dependency. Participants also shared information about sex tourism and prices on the child prostitution market. These kinds of meetings, Karremann (2007) concluded, not only strengthen the self-image of pedophiles as being "normal," but they also provide a basis for further communication, interaction, and cooperation in furtherance of pedophile crimes. For example, addresses of parents who "rent out" their children for sexual abuse are passed on under the seal of confidentiality. Most notably, however, some pedophiles team up to find child victims and to organize the continued abuse of these children. For this purpose, pedophiles may operate in pairs or small groups in places where children typically congregate, such as public swimming pools or playgrounds, to try to identify and contact suitable targets. Sometimes they employ other children or juveniles to initiate these contacts. In one case described by Karremann involving members of a Berlin self-help group, two pedophiles rented an apartment where five boys were enticed to spend their time and play in exchange for the granting of sexual favors. The boys were abused by several pedophiles over the course of a year.

After the police raided the apartment and arrested four men, the head of the Berlin self-help group summoned Karremann to a meeting to confront him with suspicions that he was a police informant. Karremann had to answer questions on his background and was eventually able to dispel doubts in his trustworthiness. It is not clear what would have happened otherwise, but Karremann did not deem his interrogators to be violence prone. One may speculate that the group would simply have severed all ties to Karremann.

Table 5.1   Classifications of (Organized) Criminal Structures

Authors	Focal Point	Categories
Best & Luckenbill	Structure (sophistication)	Loner Colleagues Peers Mob Formal organization
UNODC	Structure (hierarchy)	Standard hierarchy Regional hierarchy Clustered hierarchy Core group Network
McIntosh	Criminal activity	Picaresque organizations Craft organizations Project organizations Business organizations
Beare	Sociopolitical position	Predatory groups Parasitical groups Symbiotic groups
Ianni	Function	Associational networks Entrepreneurial networks
Anderson	Function	Illegal enterprise Quasi government
Block	Function	Enterprise syndicate Power syndicate
von Lampe	Function	Entrepreneurial structures Associational structures Quasi-governmental structures

EXISTING CLASSIFICATIONS OF CRIMINAL ORGANIZATIONS

The case study of pedophile networks, even though it does not pertain to stereotypical criminal organizations, captures many, if not all of the kinds of structures that are addressed in the study of organized crime. Before going into detail and discussing the case study within the conceptual framework adopted in this book, other classifications of criminal structures proposed in the academic literature have to be reviewed. Many of these classifications, to be found in conventional treatises of the subject, are largely descriptive in that they focus on certain observable features, namely the nationality or ethnic background of criminals (Abadinsky, 2013; Lyman & Potter, 2011; Mallory, 2012; Roth,

2010). Other classifications have some theoretical underpinning. There is a wide range of categories by which criminal organizations (in a broad sense) can potentially be grouped—for example, by size and structure, by the type of their activities, by the geographical scope of their activities, and by the relationship to and level of integration into the existing political and economic system (Shelley, 1999a; Table 5.1).

Categorization by Structure

One of the earliest classifications of criminal structures was presented by Donald Cressey (1972). He emphasized varying degrees of formalization or rationality of criminal organizations, marked by the existence of certain positions in a division of labor. According to his classification, criminal organizations can be placed on a continuum. At one end of the spectrum are groups with no internal role differentiation. At the other end Cressey saw formal criminal organizations, best represented, he believed, by Cosa Nostra, with assigned roles for members in charge of obtaining protection through corruption and assigned roles for members tasked with maintaining internal discipline. Joel Best and David Luckenbill (1994) follow a somewhat similar route by proposing to array deviant structures along a continuum of "sophistication" from loner, colleagues, peers, and mobs to formal organizations.

A more recent attempt to arrive at a typology of organized crime groups based on their structure has been undertaken by researchers at the United Nations Office on Drugs and Crime (UNODC). Select U.N. member states were asked to provide information on "the three most prominent organized criminal groups in their country" (UNODC, 2002, p. 11). In comparing the reported phenomena, the UNODC researchers came up with a fivefold typology that differentiates criminal groups primarily by the degree to which they have developed a hierarchical structure, that is, an internal line of command. The five types include the following:

(1) Standard hierarchy. A group with a centralized authority structure and "strong internal systems of discipline."

(2) Regional hierarchy. Like standard hierarchies except that the group consists of regional subunits that enjoy some degree of autonomy.

(3) Clustered hierarchy. A set of interconnected groups under a common system of coordination and control that encompasses all illegal activities these groups engage in.

(4) Core group. An unstructured group surrounded by a network of individuals engaged in criminal activities.

(5) Criminal network. Individuals loosely and fluidly connected "who constitute themselves around a series of criminal projects." (UNODC, 2002, p. 34)

This typology is the detailed elaboration of a notion that is often found in the debate on organized crime, namely, that criminal structures can be placed on a continuum ranging from bureaucratic, hierarchical organizations to loose and fluid criminal networks (see, e.g., Shaw, 2006, p. 191). Sometimes the notion is simplified to a dichotomy that means organized criminals are believed to belong to either bureaucratic organizations or to loose and fluid networks. There is also the claim that there is a trend away from criminal organizations to criminal networks—for example, with regard to the Colombian drug cartels of the 1980s and early 1990s compared to the organization of cocaine trafficking in later years (Decker & Townsend Chapman, 2008). This claim, however, may be based more on changing perceptions of drug trafficking structures—and criminal structures more generally—rather than on actual changes in the way drug traffickers are organized (Kenney, 2007).

Categorization by Activity

Mary McIntosh developed a typology of criminal organizations that is closely linked to her classification of criminal activities (see Chapter 4). She distinguished four varieties of criminal organization that she called "picaresque," "craft," "project," and "business" organizations (McIntosh, 1975).

Picaresque organizations, according to McIntosh, are represented by pirates and brigands. These full-time criminals, in order to escape justice, stay in places that are uninhabited and unpoliced. They form gangs under the leadership of a single individual and share the profits from their crimes according to rank (McIntosh, 1975, pp. 29–31). Craft organizations are fairly permanent teams of thieves and confidence men, each performing specific tasks in the routinized commission of skilled but small-scale (craft) crimes (McIntosh, 1975, pp. 35–38). Project organizations are ad-hoc teams of specialists formed for the commission of large-scale crimes, such as burglaries, robberies, frauds, or smuggling operations, involving complicated techniques and advance planning. Sometimes these teams are mustered by an entrepreneur for a specific job (McIntosh, 1975, pp. 42–48). Business organizations, finally, are involved in extortion or the supply of illegal goods and services on a continuous basis. They are, according to McIntosh, the largest in scale and have the most elaborate division of tasks and the most permanent organizational structures. In order to survive, McIntosh surmised, they also need to obtain protection by corrupting public officials (McIntosh, 1975, pp. 50–54).

Categorization by Sociopolitical Position

While McIntosh focused on types of criminal activity to differentiate criminal organizations, she also considered variations in the sociopolitical position of these organizations. Picaresque organizations operate from sanctuaries in remote areas, unless they receive protection from the local population in conflicts with a despised central government (McIntosh, 1975, p. 31). In contrast, craft, project, and business organizations by nature operate in the midst of society, using either stealth or corruption to evade prosecution.

A more recent typology is centered on the relations of criminal organizations to the existing political system. This typology has been proposed by Margaret

Beare (1996). Her typology encompasses two dimensions, the interconnectedness with the state and the legality of the organization as such. Beare argues that criminal organizations vary along a continuum from legitimate groups that engage in criminal activities on the side to groups "that exist for no other reason than to commit crimes" (Beare, 1996, p. 45). In her classification of the different levels of interconnectedness to the state, Beare draws on an evolutionary model of criminal organizations developed by Peter Lupsha (1988, 1996). According to this model, criminal groups may go through three subsequent stages: from a predatory stage where they rely on the use of physical violence to a parasitical stage where risks of prosecution are reduced by corruption and contributions to political parties. In the

Image 5.1   Angelo Bruno was the boss of the Cosa Nostra in Philadelphia during the 1960s and 1970s. From studying the Cosa Nostra family under Bruno's reign, Annelise Anderson (1979) and Mark H. Haller (1991) concluded that a distinction has to be made between criminal structures that serve economic purposes and those, like Cosa Nostra, that serve non-economic purposes.

Photo: Associated Press

symbiotic stage, finally, criminal organizations have become an integral part of the political system. The political regime relies for its survival on the collusion with criminals (Beare, 1996, p. 46; see also Chapter 13).

Categorizations by Function

All of the typologies reviewed so far treat variations among criminal structures more or less as a matter of degree rather than pointing to categorical differences. All criminal organizations are conceptualized essentially as enterprises engaged in either the supply of illegal goods and services or in the commission of predatory crimes. However, there are also classifications that emphasize fundamental differences in the purpose and function of criminal organizations. These classifications suggest that there are criminal structures other than illegal businesses and that typologies based merely on organizational design boil down to comparing apples and oranges.

As indicated in the first three chapters, various conceptualizations of organized crime have been proposed that, respectively, distinguish illegal businesses from other kinds of criminal structures. Francis Ianni, in his analysis of the organization of criminals in the Puerto Rican, Cuban, and African American communities in New York City and Paterson, New Jersey, found that cooperation in illegal activities tends to be rooted in "associational networks" that are held together by close personal ties. Such close bonds may be created, according to Ianni, by familial ties but also, for example, through membership in a youth gang. As a result, there are two kinds of structures that constitute an organizational framework for crimes and criminals: "entrepreneurial networks" that are centered on the commission of crimes, and "associational networks" that provide a basis of trust for those involved in the commission of crimes (Ianni, 1974, pp. 290–293, 307).

Mark H. Haller arrived at a somewhat similar differentiation with regard to the Cosa Nostra family in Philadelphia. Arguing against the claim that Cosa Nostra families are businesses, Haller drew a dividing line between the illegal activities that the individual Cosa Nostra members are engaged in and the functions the Cosa Nostra as an organization performs. According to Haller, there are three functions in particular that Cosa Nostra serves for the benefit of its members. It is a fraternal organization that provides male bonding and social prestige. It is a businessmen's association that provides contacts and mutual assistance. And it is an institution of self-governance that enforces certain rules of behavior and settles disputes among members and associates (Haller, 1992, pp. 2–4).

The juxtaposition of enterprise structures and governance structures can also be found in other classifications. Anneliese Anderson (1979), in her study of the Philadelphia Cosa Nostra family, distinguished between illegal enterprises run by members or nonmembers and the Cosa Nostra family as a quasi government. Alan Block's (1983) distinction of "enterprise syndicates" and "power syndicates" refers to the same functional difference; although his emphasis is less on governance and more on the systematic extortion of illegal enterprises in a given territory (see also Schelling, 1971).

When one distinguishes criminal organizations by function, then one arrives at three basic types, adopting the terminology of Ianni (1974) and Anderson (1979): entrepreneurial, associational, and quasi-governmental criminal structures (Table 5.2). Note that these are "ideal types" (Weber, 1968, p. 20) representing phenomena in their "pure" form, while in reality there may be criminal structures where the three functions partially or fully overlap. It is this threefold typology that provides the basis for the discussion of criminal structures throughout this book.

Table 5.2   Classifications of Criminal Structures by Function

Function	Purpose	Example
Entrepreneurial	Material gain	Burglary gang
Associational	Status Support Ideology	Outlaw motorcycle gang
Quasi governmental	Protection (conflict avoidance, conflict resolution) Material gain (taxation)	Cosa Nostra family

THE THREE BASIC TYPES OF CRIMINAL STRUCTURES

The assumption that the most basic categorization of criminal structures is one that pertains to different functions rests on the notion that criminals organize themselves to respond to specific needs. It can be argued that all else being equal, criminals face increased risks of apprehension and prosecution and also an increased risk of predatory exploitation when they reveal themselves to and interact with other criminals. Every coconspirator and every co-offender are potential police informants and witnesses in court. Likewise, every coconspirator and every co-offender are potential fraudsters or thieves (Gambetta, 2009; Reuter, 1983). Only if these risks are outweighed by benefits that criminal structures provide is it likely that criminals will organize in the first place.

There are a number of needs that criminals may have and that may be met by criminal organizations (Best & Luckenbill, 1994, pp. 73–74). These needs include

- access to resources that enable or facilitate the commission of crimes,
- an ideology to justify criminal behavior,
- social status (in the underworld and beyond),
- security from prosecution, and
- security from other criminals.

Entrepreneurial, associational and quasi-governmental structures, respectively, address these needs in specific ways.

Entrepreneurial Criminal Structures

Entrepreneurial criminal structures serve economic functions in a broad sense in that they are geared toward generating financial or other material benefits (Chapter 6). Criminals are connected in such a way that compared to a lone offender, the commission of predatory or market-based crimes is made possible, easier, more profitable, or less risky. This includes obtaining and coordinating necessary resources such as skills, know-how, finances, raw materials, and equipment.

Entrepreneurial criminal structures can appear in many different guises, including the types of criminal organizations identified by Mary McIntosh (picaresque, craft, project, and business organizations), such as the crew of a pirate ship, a troupe of pickpockets, a team assembled for a bank heist, or the management and staff of an illegal gambling casino. Another example is provided in the case study of pedophile networks presented above. The pedophiles who collaborated in the maintenance and use of the apartment in Berlin for the purpose of regularly abusing children were part of an entrepreneurial criminal structure. Their relations were shaped and structured in certain ways—for example, in the form of pooling financial resources and in the form of influencing their victims in a coordinated fashion—so that the abuse of children was made easier and less risky.

Associational Criminal Structures

Entrepreneurial criminal structures have to be distinguished, analytically, from associational criminal structures that support entrepreneurial activities only indirectly by serving functions of a social nature (see Chapter 7). Internally, associational structures establish and reinforce bonds between their respective members and create a sense of belonging. Externally, they delineate a group of criminals as possessing certain qualities that other criminals or others in society more broadly, supposedly, do not possess.

Belonging to such an associational structure—for example, a mafia organization or an outlaw motorcycle gang—conveys some degree of exclusivity and may translate into an enhanced social status within criminal subcultures or social milieus. To the extent associational structures select members according to their worth as criminals, membership conveys a sense of reliability and trustworthiness. This facilitates contacts among potential co-offenders and provides a relatively safe forum for the exchange of information and the pooling of resources conducive to the commission of crimes. The communication within associational structures will also tend to reinforce deviant values and promote a positive self-image as criminal. In this respect, associational structures meet the need of criminals for an ideology that frames criminal behavior as tolerable or even desirable, thereby neutralizing any notions of wrongdoing (see Sykes & Matza, 1957).

Associational criminal structures may also improve the security of criminals. This is the case, for example, when members are obligated to provide mutual aid in conflicts with nonmembers. Associational structures may also protect members against other members by establishing and enforcing internal rules of conduct—for example, to the effect that members should not cheat each other. In this respect, associational structures can serve a governance function vis-à-vis their membership similar to underworld governments with regard to an entire criminal milieu (see below).

There are numerous examples of associational structures, first and foremost secret societies and fraternal associations with a defined membership, such as the Italian American and the Sicilian Mafia, Chinese triads, or outlaw motorcycle gangs. But less clearly discernible structures such as the friendship networks among drug traffickers and the entire community of dealers and smugglers in Southern California described by Patricia Adler (1985) also fall into this category (see also Huisman & Jansen, 2012; Larsson, 2009, p. 72). A similar example is provided by the self-help groups of pedophiles mentioned in the case study above. These self-help groups do not organize the abuse of children, but to the extent they provide a forum for discussing the abuse of children and for mutually reinforcing the idea that pedophilic activities are normal, they fulfill the need of pedophile criminals for an ideology justifying their behavior.

Quasi-Governmental Criminal Structures

Quasi-governmental criminal structures serve governance functions (Chapter 8). Three essential governance functions can be distinguished, irrespective of whether the context is legal or illegal. The first function is to define and enforce *property rights*. Governance determines who has control over a given object. The second governance function is to protect and enforce *contractual agreements*. Governance ensures that both sides abide by the terms of the contract they have entered into. The third governance function is to promote the common good through *collective action*. Governance helps to pool resources to attain collective goals (Skarbek, 2014, pp. 4–6).

Quasi-governmental structures, namely criminal groups like the "Capone Syndicate" that control a particular area, support illegal entrepreneurial activities by creating a more predictable and more secure environment in a sphere that the legitimate government is unwilling or unable to regulate. Quasi-governmental structures can define and protect property rights of criminals, such as a pimp's right of exclusive control over a prostitute or a bookmaker's right to his book-making operation. When, for example, a prostitute is wooed away by another pimp or a criminal muscles into a bookmaking operation, then the aggrieved party has a chance to take recourse to whoever has assumed a governance function. Quasi-governmental structures can likewise enforce "contracts" between criminals—for example, the contract between a seller and a buyer of illegal drugs. Finally, quasi-governmental structures can attain collective goals like avoiding police attention through, for example, a mechanism of nonviolent dispute resolution that reduces overall levels of violence. Underworld governments, by pooling resources, may also facilitate the corruption of officials and thereby reduce the risk of law enforcement intervention. For these and other reasons, illegal governance structures are not only beneficial for those exercising power but also for their subordinates (Reuter, 1983). In return, illegal entrepreneurial activities may be "taxed," which means that those forming governance structures share in the proceeds from those (predatory and market-based) crimes that are committed under their control (Abadinsky, 1981; Anderson, 1979; Lombardo, 2013).

At times, quasi-governmental structures are misconstrued as constituting the executive level of a large-scale, diversified criminal corporation. The assumption is that all the different criminal activities that are under the control of and taxed by an underworld government constitute specialized divisions centrally directed by a common management. Based on this assumption, notorious gangster Lucky Luciano was convicted on charges of "running" prostitution in New York City (Stolberg, 1995). However, underworld governments, such as the one represented by Lucky Luciano, tend not to interfere with the day-to-day affairs of illegal enterprises. Accordingly, the removal of an underworld government will not influence the way illegal businesses are run. What may change is the level of security illegal enterprises enjoy with respect to competitors, predatory criminals, and law enforcement.

A typical example for quasi-governmental structures is provided by territorially based criminal groups such as Cosa Nostra families or street gangs that control and "license" illegal activities in their respective neighborhoods. But quasi-governmental structures can also appear in more ephemeral forms, as can be seen in the case study on pedophile networks. When the police raided the apartment in Berlin where children had been abused for over a year, suspicions among pedophiles emerged that they had been infiltrated by a police informant and the suspicions were directed at undercover reporter Manfred Karremann.

The head of the Berlin pedophile self-help group, which as such was not directly involved in the abuse of children, acted as an investigator and convened an ad-hoc tribunal to determine whether Manfred Karremann was in fact a police informant. The purpose of this tribunal, it seems, was to collectively enforce an implicit rule in the pedophile community, that one pedophile should not inform on another pedophile. The self-help group as an associational structure, thus, assumed for a moment the role of a judicial institution and thereby fulfilled a governance function within the "pedo-scene" of Berlin.

THE BASIC FORMS OF CRIMINAL STRUCTURES: MARKETS, NETWORKS, AND HIERARCHIES

Entrepreneurial, associational and quasi-governmental structures, as already indicated, are not necessarily mutually exclusive. The same group of criminals may serve different functions. Mafia families, for example, constitute fraternal associations and may at the same time have locally acquired the position of an underworld government (see Chapters 7 and 8). A second classification has to be made with respect to the *forms* in which criminal structures appear. Entrepreneurial, associational, and quasi-governmental structures are not linked to any particular organizational format. In fact, as has already been shown with the examples of friendship-networks among drug traffickers and the case study of pedophile networks, economic, social, and governance functions can be performed by structures that lack any degree of integration into a cohesive organizational entity.

Following a classification from the areas of economic sociology and organization theory, three ideal-typical forms can be distinguished in which criminal structures may appear: *markets*, *networks*, and *hierarchies* (Powell, 1990). While the analogy best fits entrepreneurial structures (see Chapter 6), this classificatory scheme can also be applied more or less well to associational and quasi-governmental structures. The distinction between markets, networks, and hierarchies refers to different mechanisms of interaction and coordination marked by different levels of commitment and interdependence between participants (see Figure 5.1).

Markets

In an ideal-typical market setting, individuals interact as independent, autonomous parties of one-off exchanges. Between the two parties there is no obligation other than that of the fulfillment of the terms stipulated in the (formal or informal) agreement underlying the exchange. The participants of market exchanges engage in "individually self-interested, non-cooperative, unconstrained social interaction" and are "free of any future commitments" beyond the exchange at hand (Powell, 1990, p. 302).

Pure market exchanges are rare under conditions of illegality just as in legitimate society because exchanges tend to take place between individuals who already know each other. This means that a transaction is commonly embedded in the preexisting relations that make up an individual's social network (see Flap, 2002, pp. 30–31; Granovetter, 1992). In the context of criminal activities,

Figure 5.1 Basic Forms of Criminal Structures

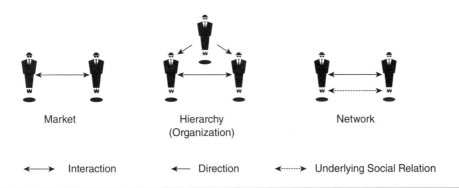

Market	Hierarchy (Organization)	Network

⟷ Interaction   ⟵ Direction   ⟵----⟶ Underlying Social Relation

This graph depicts three basic types of relationships between criminals: market relations between independent actors; hierarchies, where criminals are integrated into a line of command; and networks where criminals cooperate as independent partners but where the continued existence of an underlying long-term relationship is at stake.

exchanges between truly independent partners appear to be prevalent only in the street vending of illegal goods—such as drugs, counterfeit products, or contraband cigarettes—although even here longer-term relations between sellers and buyers may evolve (Antonopoulos, Hornsby, & Hobbs, 2011, p. 8; Gruter & Van de Mheen, 2005, p. 27; Sandberg, 2012, p. 1144; see also Dwyer & Moore, 2010, p. 94).

Hierarchies (Organizations)

In terms of the interdependence of actors, the opposite of markets are hierarchies. Those who interact as component parts of a hierarchy perform tasks in a coordinated way under the direction of a common management (Powell, 1990). Hierarchies typically have defined boundaries and internal divisions and a centralized chain of command. However, there are also organizational structures, mostly small in size, where members subordinate themselves not to a central authority but to a collective decision-making process that defines roles and tasks that are then assumed by members jointly or individually (Ahrne, 1994, p. 89). Hierarchies understood in this way are delineable organizations with structures that guide and coordinate the interaction of their members. They can be found in the case of entrepreneurial, associational, as well as quasi-governmental illegal structures.

Networks

The third basic type of mechanism of interaction and coordination, networks, is similar to pure market settings in that those involved in an exchange make independent decisions as autonomous actors. At the same time, there is a mutual commitment beyond any single exchange. What is at stake are underlying longer-term relationships. In order not to jeopardize these relationships, network members are inclined "'to forego the right to pursue their own interests at the expense of others" (Powell, 1990, p. 303).

The Relationship Between the Concepts of Network and Organization

There is some confusion about how the two key concepts of network and organization relate to each other. Some use both concepts interchangeably, typically with a meaning that is closer to organization than to network; others treat networks and organizations as the two endpoints of a continuum of structural sophistication, ranging from simple, loose networks to elaborate, tightly structured organizations. Sometimes it is assumed that criminals are organized either in networks or in organizations. In all cases there is a tendency to narrow the scope of analysis to readily observable structures. Whenever a delineable group of criminals becomes discernible, this is what the attention is focused on with little consideration of the broader web of relations in which the criminals in question may be embedded.

A more encompassing approach is to treat networks and organizations as two distinct *analytical* categories, representing different dimensions of relational structures (see Powell, 1990). A network is a web of ties connecting two or more individuals directly or indirectly. An organization likewise consists of a combination of individuals. But in contrast to a network, an organization is more than just the sum of its parts, as it entails a certain degree of integration. An organization takes on an existence of its own by establishing a system of norms and expectations that members follow regardless of individual interests or properties (Hall, 1982, pp. 37–38). It is important to note, however, that networks and organizations are not empirically independent. Organizations may evolve out of and may be transcended by networks, just as every organization can be defined as a network because its members are by definition connected through specific ties (Nohria, 1992). The question, then, is not whether in a given situation there is a criminal network *or* a criminal organization. Instead, the question is whether criminal organizations in the narrow sense of the word have evolved out of and are shaped and transcended by a given criminal network.

THE CONCEPTUALIZATION OF CRIMINAL NETWORKS

Treating networks and organizations as two distinct analytical categories implies a bottom-up, two-step approach in the analysis of criminal structures. The first step is to ascertain in a very general sense the existence of criminal networks. The second step is then to examine the nature of the network ties and to determine the level of integration of these ties into delineable organizational entities. The following three chapters will discuss in some detail how the level of integration can vary with respect to entrepreneurial structures (Chapter 6), associational structures (Chapter 7), and quasi-governmental structures (Chapter 8). In contrast, the remainder of this chapter will be devoted to questions about the existence of criminal structures as such. One question is how conceptually to ascertain the existence of criminal networks. Another, empirical question is how criminal networks emerge and persist over time in what can generally be considered a hostile environment.

Constitutive Elements and Boundaries of Criminal Networks

The question of how to ascertain the existence of a criminal network is not as straightforward as it may seem. One problem is that connections between criminals are not necessarily easy to observe. Another problem is that it is not self-evident what kinds of connections between what kinds of individuals should be taken into consideration. Conventional academic and law enforcement analyses tend to limit the analysis of criminal networks to the most tangible links between criminals, those links that can be inferred from the joint commission of a crime, from communication, or from shared membership in a criminal association. But this likely produces only a very incomplete picture of the patterns of relations that matter for understanding the organization of

Figure 5.2 Criminally Exploitable Ties

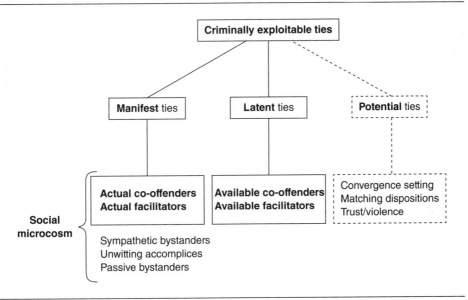

This graph depicts criminally exploitable ties as consisting of two components: manifest ties that are activated in a given criminal endeavor and latent ties that could be activated for criminal purposes when the need arises. In addition, the graph includes potential ties that reflect existing opportunities for the formation of new criminally exploitable ties. These opportunities are created by convergence settings where individuals with matching criminal dispositions can meet and manage to cope with the mutual risk of betrayal. Finally, the graph positions the concept of the "social microcosm of illegal entrepreneurs" in the overall conceptual framework, highlighting that in a given crime event there tend to be individuals who to varying degrees are in a position to influence the success or failure of the criminal endeavor.

crime, namely, those webs of relations that enable or facilitate criminal conduct. For every co-offender in a given criminal venture, there may be many others who would have been willing and able to participate, and every new criminal venture may see a different set of co-offenders from a larger pool of criminals who know each other. Empirical research suggests that most areas of crime are characterized by individual offenders, partnerships, and small clusters of criminals linked up by more or less temporary cooperative arrangements (Bruinsma & Bernasco, 2004; Englund, 2008; Kostakos & Antonopoulos, 2010; Leman & Janssens, 2008; Matrix Knowledge Group, 2007; Ruggiero & Khan, 2007; Soudijn & Kleemans, 2009). Criminal associations, in turn, primarily fulfill social functions and only indirectly influence criminal behavior. Therefore, the shared membership in a criminal association may reveal little about the actual interaction between criminals. It is not a given that any two members of the same criminal association—for example, a mafia group or an outlaw motorcycle gang—commit crimes together at all. Instead members may individually engage in criminal activities or in cooperation with nonmembers (Tenti & Morselli, 2014; Chapter 7).

When one assumes that organized crime has to do with criminals benefiting from the connections they have to others, then the scope of analysis has to be expanded beyond tangible co-offending networks and membership-based criminal associations. There are two directions in particular in which the scope of analysis can be broadened. One is to shift the frame of analysis from the narrow group of co-offenders to the wider circle of individuals who have an impact on a given criminal venture. This is captured by the concept of the *social microcosm of illegal entrepreneurs* (von Lampe, 2007; Figure 5.3). The other direction is to move from the criminal relations that manifest themselves in the commission of a particular crime to the full range of relations that a criminal could draw on at a given point in time. This is captured by the concept of *networks of criminally exploitable ties* and the distinction of *manifest* and *latent* criminal ties (von Lampe, 2001b, 2003a, 2009a).

The Social Microcosm of Illegal Entrepreneurs

Conceptions of criminal networks typically focus on those individuals who are directly involved in the commission of crimes. Sometimes a distinction is made between core members and peripheral actors (see, e.g., Lemieux, 2003, pp. 12–13), but overall, the term criminal network is commonly confined to the narrow circle of coconspirators (Tremblay, 1993, p. 20; Weerman, 2003, p. 398). This perspective, however, neglects other individuals who in various ways may influence a criminal endeavor. There may be individuals (facilitators) who, while not participating in a specific crime, wittingly lend general support to criminals—for example, by sharing know-how, by providing legal advice or money-laundering services, or simply by endorsing a criminal lifestyle. Then there are *unwitting* accomplices who directly contribute to the successful execution of a criminal endeavor without becoming aware of the role they play. Criminals may, for example, draw on the services of hauling companies and banks under the guise of legal business activities to smuggle contraband and launder money (see, e.g., Desroches, 2005, p. 123; Vander Beken, Defruytier, Bucquoye, & Verpoest, 2005; von Lampe, 2009c).

Figure 5.3   The Social Microcosm of an Illegal Entrepreneur

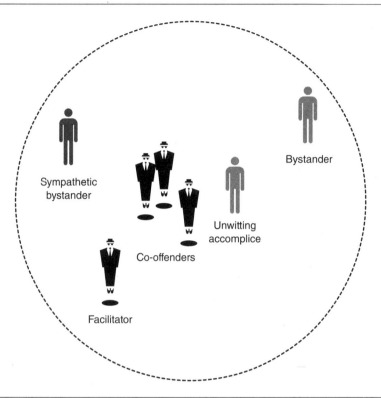

The social microcosm of criminals encompasses all individuals who are in a position to influence, negatively or positively, the outcome of a criminal endeavor, from the circle of co-offenders who are directly involved in the commission of a given crime to passive bystanders who decide not to intervene.

One could even go further and also take those individuals into consideration that contribute to criminal activities merely by passively standing by without interfering. Noninterference of bystanders can have different reasons (see Levine, 1999). They may not realize the illegality of the activities they observe, they may find intervention inconvenient or burdensome or risky, or they may tolerate or even be sympathetic to these illegal activities because they adhere to some subcultural value system or because they feel a personal allegiance to the perpetrators.

All of these individuals, from accomplice to passive bystander, make up what can be called the *social microcosm of a criminal entrepreneur*. The social microcosm encompasses all individuals an offender encounters in the course of a criminal endeavor and who are in a position to influence the success or failure of that endeavor, if only by not alerting the police (von Lampe, 2007, p. 132). Thus, the social microcosm demarcates the outer reaches of the interpersonal relations that criminals count on for the successful commission of a given crime.

The concept of social microcosm adds considerable complexity to the analysis of organized crime. It highlights the fuzzy and fleeting nature of the boundaries between criminal structures and noncriminal social structures, and it emphasizes the diversity of roles that individuals can play in the furtherance of criminal ventures.

Networks of Criminally Exploitable Ties

Criminally exploitable ties are interpersonal relations that enable an individual to interact with other individuals in the furtherance of criminal activities whenever the need or opportunity arises (von Lampe, 2003a). This may be the case on a continuous basis or only sporadically or not at all. The concept of criminally exploitable ties rests on a distinction between manifest and latent criminal structures. Manifest structures are those patterns of relationships that are activated and become evident in the interaction of criminals. Latent structures consist of ties to those who at a given point in time would be available to lend support in a criminal endeavor. These ties are dormant but could be activated. Manifest and latent criminal ties combine to form a network of criminally exploitable ties (von Lampe, 2003a; von Lampe, 2009a, p. 95).

Irrespective of the actual frequency with which they are activated, criminally exploitable ties are important because they provide what Bill McCarthy and John Hagan (2001, p. 1038) have called "criminal social capital." Criminally exploitable ties demarcate the social space within which a criminal can operate and cooperate with others without having to invest in the establishing of new relationships. And this social space will tend to be larger than any manifest co-offending network or any membership-based association might suggest (Bouchard & Ouellet, 2011, p. 76). Networks of criminally exploitable ties can also differ from manifest criminal networks in the way they are structured. For example, a central figure in a co-offending network, say the leader of a gang of car thieves, might occupy only a rather marginal position in the overall context of his or her web of criminally exploitable ties by being at the beck and call of more influential members of the underworld.

In order to be criminally exploitable, a relation between two individuals will tend to show both of the following characteristics: corresponding criminal *dispositions* and some common basis of *trust*. It appears plausible that someone engaged in criminal activities can draw on others only to the extent they have similar interests and preferences. This may not be the case, for instance, when a heroin trafficker and a distributor of child pornography meet. Each might vehemently object to the other's line of business. Once two individuals with corresponding criminal dispositions have met, it is unlikely, although not impossible, that they will cooperate simply based on the mutual interest in the successful completion of a given endeavor. Instead, cooperation will tend to be founded on some basis of trust (von Lampe, 2001b, 2003a; von Lampe & Johansen, 2004b). This assumption, which will be discussed in more depth further below, rests on two general notions, that social interaction tends to be embedded in existing social networks (Granovetter, 1992) and that criminals need to minimize the risks inherent in illegal interaction emanating from law enforcement, from disloyal accomplices, and from predatory criminals (Gambetta, 2009; Reuter, 1983).

THE EMERGENCE AND
PERSISTENCE OF CRIMINAL NETWORK TIES

The discussion so far has focused on two key dimensions in the analysis of criminal structures: (a) the different types of criminal structures by *function* (economic, social, and quasi governmental) and by *form* (markets, networks, hierarchies), and (b) the scope of criminal structures with a view to the gradation of relations from the links between co-offenders to the relations between offenders and unwitting accomplices and passive bystanders within the social microcosm of a criminal and with a view to manifest and latent criminal relations. One important question has been touched upon only briefly: How do the relations that constitute criminal structures emerge in the first place? And by extension one can ask, How easy or difficult is it for criminal structures to grow and to recover from disruptions, such as the death or arrest of a member?

Potential Network Ties and Offender Convergence Settings

One way to approach the question of the emergence of criminal structures is to frame it in terms of the *formation* of criminally exploitable ties. This is a matter of determining how easy it is for criminals with similar dispositions to become aware of each other and to meet and how easy it is for them to form a bond of trust. An important aspect that comes into play here are locations where criminals encounter other criminals. Marcus Felson has argued that offender networks tend to be "amorphous, unbounded and unstable" and that, in order to account for the recurrence of co-offending, one must look not at network structures but at the locations (offender convergence settings) where offenders meet and socialize (Felson, 2003, p. 156). What Felson describes, in a sense, are socio-ecological conditions defining neither manifest nor latent, but *potential* ties (von Lampe, 2009a, p. 97). These potential network ties are constituted by a given pair of compatible criminals who have access to the same convergence setting at the same time. The assumption is that potential network ties, under favorable conditions, make future cooperation between criminals as likely as criminally exploitable ties within a latent or manifest criminal network. From this angle, a comprehensive analysis of criminal structures needs to encompass manifest relations, latent relations, and potential relations linked, namely, to offender convergence settings.

From what is known about offender networking (see, for example, Adler, 1985; Desroches, 2005; Zaitch, 2002) it appears that there is a wide range of constellations of how organized criminals meet and form relationships: relationships that lead, directly or indirectly, to the commission of crime, respectively to the more effective, more widespread, and more continuous commission of crime. First, the context within which relationships are formed may be more or less detached from illicit activities. It can range from purely legitimate settings such as neighborhood, school, or workplace to deviant or criminal subcultures and outright congregations of criminals. Second, a particular contact may result from a chance encounter, or it may have been purposefully brought about by one or both parties searching for suitable co-offenders. Third, a link may initially have no illicit connotation—for example, when a childhood friendship or a legitimate business contact eventually transforms into a criminal partnership— or it may be of an illegal nature from the start, as in the case of the relationship between a street peddler of drugs and his or her customers.

The ideal-typical offender convergence setting as described by Felson (2003, 2006b) covers only some of these constellations. It is a place where potential co-offenders have a high likelihood of meeting even though the location itself— for example, a restaurant—may serve exclusively legitimate purposes and even though potential offenders may converge without the intent of finding a partner in crime. Yet, partnerships are assumed to form quickly, setting "the stage for criminal acts in nearby times and places" (Felson, 2003, p. 151). The convergence settings described in the organized crime literature go beyond and partly deviate from this picture. Offender convergence settings do not only give rise to short-term but also to longer-term endeavors. It is also important to note that offender convergence settings are not only relevant for co-offending networks. They appear to provide the basis for the emergence and continued existence of criminal structures in general, including fraternal associations and illicit governance structures. In fact, places where criminals meet and interact seem to be an important factor for underworld structures and short-term co-offending networks alike. Mary McIntosh, for example, has emphasized the importance of

Image 5.2   Amsterdam Central Station is reportedly a convergence setting for buyers and suppliers of drugs. Those who come to the city known for its role as a major hub for drug trafficking in Europe are met by individuals who sell drugs or arrange contacts to drug dealers.

Photo: Douglas Schwartz/Corbis

"haunts," such as unlicensed drinking and gambling clubs or public houses, as places where criminals "learn their trade, find colleagues to work with, and be warned of impending danger" (McIntosh, 1975, p. 23; see also Best & Luckenbill, 1994, p. 52). A similar function is played by prisons, which are commonly regarded as meeting places and "academies" of criminals (Desroches, 2005, p. 55; McIntosh, 1975, p. 24; Pearson & Hobbs, 2001, p. 30; Ruggiero & South, 1995, pp. 181–184). Several notorious criminal associations owe their existence to the congregation of criminals in prison, namely the Sicilian Mafia (Lupo, 2009, p. 49; see also Chapter 7), and some organizations that have first existed as prison gangs before they expanded their influence to the outside world, such as the Thieves in Law in the former Soviet Union (Varese, 2001, p. 164; see also Chapter 7), the so-called Mexican Mafia in the United States (Abadinsky, 2013, p. 164), or the Primeiro Comando da Capital (PCC) in Brazil (Pedra & Dal Ri, 2011, p. 68).

Other permanent convergence settings are less secluded and less closely linked to illicit contexts. For example, businesses of logistical relevance for certain illicit activities, such as transport companies and banks, may set the stage for bringing together potential coconspirators, typically across the divide between the licit and illicit spheres of society (Kleemans & Van de Bunt, 2008; Tilley & Hopkins, 2008). Even the most public places can apparently function as meeting places for prospective partners in crime. The central railway station in Amsterdam, for example, is reported to be for drug dealers "one of the best places for new contacts" because suppliers of drugs and contact brokers already await incoming trains (Junninen, 2006, p. 157).

Not all convergence settings for organized criminals are permanent in nature and attached to one specific location. Interprovincial meetings among members of the different branches of the Sicilian Mafia, for example, have reportedly taken place during cattle fairs held periodically at various locations in southern Italy (Paoli, 2003a, p. 41). Likewise in the subculture of upper-level drug dealers observed by Patricia Adler, social interaction was centered not only on certain bars, stores, restaurants, and recreational areas frequented by drug market insiders but was also created at private gatherings, such as weddings or parties, the larger ones being described as "dealers' conventions" (Adler, 1985, p. 77).

The Role of Trust for Criminal Networking

To say that criminals have many opportunities to establish new contacts only partially explains the formation of criminal structures. It is also important to understand how these contacts, be they long-term relations or chance encounters, turn from social network ties into criminally exploitable ties. The question is what brings a criminal to interact with others in furtherance of criminal endeavors despite the inherent risks of betrayal. These risks as well as the benefits of criminal cooperation have already been pointed out. For example, offenders can draw on others to obtain the know-how and tools necessary for committing a crime. Yet, this does not explain why offenders believe that they can enjoy these benefits while escaping the risks. One answer to this question has become a truism in the organized crime literature, the claim that what brings and holds criminal structures together are bonds of trust (see, e.g., Ayling, 2009; Campana & Varese, 2013; Kleemans, 2013).

Trust, like organized crime, is a "very imprecise and confusing notion" (Misztal, 1996, p. 9; see also Seligman, 1997, p. 7). It has to do with how people cope with risks and uncertainty. One person trusts another person where effective means to control the other's behavior are unavailable and where the other's behavior is potentially harmful in a broad sense of the word, and still the trusting person is confident that no harm will be done (Figure 5.4).

There are two dimensions along which the concept of trust and the emergence of trust are discussed. One dimension refers to the level of rationality or irrationality in the decision of a trusting person to trust. The other dimension refers to the foundation or point of reference of trust (von Lampe & Johansen, 2004b, p. 166). In the spectrum from rationality to irrationality, trust takes up a space somewhere between purely rational calculation of probabilities and irrational blind faith. The point of reference for both rational calculation and blind faith may be the trusted person or some institution or social group that the person belongs to. In the latter cases, trust is based on generalizations about how a particular type of person behaves. Depending on whether or not the trusting person (trustor) and the trusted person (trustee) belong to the same social group, this kind of trust can have different roots. An outsider may be guided by stereotypes while within the same social group there may be a sense of shared habits, norms, and values that bind members. Belonging to the same social group may also create moral obligations to place trust in others. Trust in these cases, then, "is a moral commandment to treat people as if they were trustworthy" (Uslaner, 2002, p. 3).

The Emergence of Trust Under Conditions of Illegality

There are numerous trust-producing situations that may come into play in the formation of criminal structures. On the individual level, trust can be expected to result, for example, from the continuous interaction in delinquent peer groups or in prison settings, out of which affectionate bonds and a sense of predictability of each other's behavior may develop (see, e.g., Ianni, 1974).

Figure 5.4   Trust

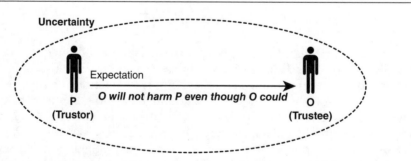

This graph depicts the notion that trust is an expectation of a person P, under conditions of uncertainty, that (a) another person O will not harm P, even though (b) O could harm P (von Lampe & Johansen, 2004a, p. 104).

Various personal characteristics can be expected to foster trust, including reliability in keeping appointments and deadlines, providing support, maintaining self-control under stress, and of course, not cooperating with authorities (Zaitch, 2002, p. 279).

Another aspect that needs to be taken into account is that trust may be mediated. In this case, no direct bond of trust exists between trustor and trustee, but an intermediary convinces the trustor that the trustee is trustworthy. This can happen in different ways. The trustor may have faith in the intermediary's judgment that the trustee is trustworthy, or the intermediary may guarantee that the trustee will not harm the trustor. In the language of the street, the intermediary "vouches" for the trustee, which means that if anything goes wrong, the intermediary will be held liable by the trustor (Desroches, 2005, p. 122).

A similar triangular constellation exists where the trustor relies not on a specific intermediary but on the reputation the trustee has acquired among a larger group of people. This type of trust hinges first and foremost on the flow of information through the underworld "grapevine system" first described by Frederic Thrasher (1927/1963, p. 285), or in the case of cybercrime (see Chapter 12) through electronic communication channels (Lusthaus, 2012). But one can also think of a criminally relevant reputation being created by the media, possibly in concert with law enforcement agencies, as has been surmised in the case of Al Capone, who allegedly owed much of his reputation of being a powerful underworld leader not to his actual position but to the attention he received in the press (Bergreen, 1994, p. 211; Chapter 1).

Trust based on generalizations can be linked, for example, to members of a delinquent subculture or a mafia-like fraternal association when they are perceived to uniformly adhere to particular codes of conduct, namely mutual support and non-cooperation with law enforcement (Reuter, 1983, p. 158). Such a belief can be quite rational, especially in the case of fraternal associations like Cosa Nostra that, at least in former times, have only admitted new members after an extensive period of testing and schooling (Haller, 1992, pp. 3–4; Jacobs, 1994, p. 102; Chapter 7). But the same may also be true for a deviant subculture where, by definition, members share a set of norms and values and are likely to harbor feelings of solidarity in view of what is perceived to be a hostile outside world. This has been noted, for example, in the case of the community of professional thieves in the United States in the early 20th century described by Edwin Sutherland (1937, pp. 202–206) and in the case of the Western European drug culture of the 1960s and 1970s (Ruggiero & South, 1995, p. 134).

The Emergence of Criminally Relevant Trust From Licit Social Relations

Criminally relevant trust does not only emerge under conditions of illegality. Licit social relations may also provide a basis of trust for criminal structures. In fact, in the organized crime literature the focus has been first and foremost on criminal structures rooted in licit social relations, namely kinship, friendship, and ethnic ties. Other kinds of social relations that may play a role in the formation of criminal structures include local communities and business networks (Adler, 1985; Denton, 2001; Desroches, 2005; Hobbs, 2001; Kleemans & Van de Bunt, 2008).

Familial Ties as Sources of Trust. The notion that family ties can shape criminal structures is in line with general assumptions about a close link between family and trust. Anthony Giddens (1990, p. 101), for example, suggests that "kinspeople can usually be relied upon to meet a range of obligations more or less regardless of whether they feel personally sympathetic towards specific individuals involved." Trust among members of the same family, it is argued, grows out of continuous interaction and rests on a sense of similarity and shared norms and values (Misztal, 1996).

There are, in fact, a number of examples for the partial or complete overlap of criminal structures and kinship structures. There are cases where illegal enterprises are run as "family businesses" (Curtis & Wendel, 2000; Hobbs, 2001, 2013; Ianni & Reuss-Ianni, 1972), and there is evidence that criminals prefer to collaborate with members of their own family. Decker and Townsend Chapman (2008, p. 98), for example, report that many of the drug traffickers they interviewed "expressed the belief that they were less likely to be 'snitched out' by relatives" (see also Adler, 1985, p. 66; Denton, 2001, pp. 68, 73; Zaitch, 2002, p. 277).

Apart from entrepreneurial structures, there are also some fraternal associations that are largely made up of members of the same blood family, as is true, for example, for the local branches of the Calabrian mafia, the 'Ndrangheta, and the Neapolitan mafia, the Camorra (Campana & Varese, 2013; Paoli, 2003a). At the same time, associational structures—such as mafia organizations, through

Image 5.3 The twin brothers Ronald and Reginald Kray, having tea at home in 1966, were dominant figures in the London underworld in the 1950s and 1960s. Familial ties often serve as a binding force within criminal structures.

Photo: Hulton-Deutsch Collection/Corbis

initiation rites—may also create ritual kinship ties, artificial bonds likened to the relationship between brothers or between father and son (Paoli, 2003a). However, the binding force of kinship is not ubiquitous. In the words of Damian Zaitch (2002, p. 278), who summarizes the accounts of cocaine traffickers, "betrayal between blood relatives is infrequent, though not rare." Likewise, Pino Arlacchi (1986, p. 135) has pointed out in his analysis of Italian mafia groups, that "often relations between families of brothers are marked less by co-operation and solidarity than by disagreement and impulses towards mutual conflict." This, according to Arlacchi, has led to structural arrangements centered on shared control within mafia organizations that are specifically designed to minimize conflict in the absence of sufficient trust between blood relatives (Arlacchi, 1986, p. 136).

Local Communities and Ethnicity as Sources of Trust. Similar to families, local communities may produce trust through familiarity and conformity (Giddens, 1990, p. 101; Luhmann, 1988, p. 94). For example, close-knit, local communities in rural Norway provide a safe context for the illegal alcohol business that is centered on illegal distilleries. Disloyal behavior toward a business partner would be perceived as being directed against the entire community (von Lampe & Johansen, 2004b, p. 173). Community ties also become apparent in criminal structures that are formed among migrants. In some cases, the origin from the same village best explains the collaboration of a particular set of criminals abroad (Kleemans & van de Bunt, 1999, p. 25).

The notion of trust created by familiarity and conformity would seem to apply not only to family and community ties but to a certain extent to ethnicity as well. In fact, many depictions of organized crime rely heavily on categorizations along ethnic lines, implying that ethnicity is an important binding factor. Others have argued that this is a misconception and that in many instances where bonds of trust are attributed to ethnic cohesion, trust is rooted in kinship and community ties (Ianni, 1974; Kleemans & van de Bunt, 1999, p. 25; Lupsha, 1986, p. 34; Potter, 1994, p. 121; von Lampe & Johansen, 2004b, p. 173).

However, ethnicity seems to play a role not only in the minds of the public but also in the minds of criminals, so that it cannot be completely discounted as a factor influencing the emergence of criminal structures. For example, according to the interview-based study of drug traffickers conducted by Decker and Townsend Chapman, Colombians "are more likely to trust another individual of Colombian ethnicity than to trust members of other ethnic groups." Likewise, they found that "Cubans were much more likely to recruit and trust other Cubans" (Decker & Townsend Chapman, 2008, p. 96; see also Arsovska, 2015, p. 135; Desroches, 2005, pp. 63–64).

Contrary to the notion of ethnically cohesive criminal groups, ethnicity can also foster the formation of criminal structures in a different way, across ethnic lines. At least some criminals are influenced by ethnic stereotypes that make it more or less likely that they will trust criminals of a particular ethnic background other than their own (Junninen, 2006, pp. 159–160; Ruggiero & South, 1995, p. 118). Damian Zaitch, in his interview-based study of Colombian drug traffickers in the Netherlands, found that they tended to prefer to do business with Italians and Spaniards because they viewed them as the most professional, true to their word and bound by honor compared to, for example, native Dutch, Russian, Yugoslavian, or Surinamese criminals. Interestingly, these stereotypes were fairly consistent irrespective of personal experiences with members of these ethnic groups (Zaitch, 2002, p. 281; see also Bovenkerk, Siegel, & Zaitch, 2003). Ethnic stereotypes that foster trust may be shaped by personal experiences, gossip, or the media, but they may also arise from rational considerations. For example, if an ethnic minority group is marginalized in society it will be less likely to have police informants or undercover police officers in its midst (von Lampe, 2003b, p. 58; von Lampe & Johansen, 2004b, pp. 174–175).

Business Relations as Sources of Trust. While ethnicity cannot be ruled out as a trust-building factor, at least under certain circumstances, there is another social context that possibly has a much greater significance for the trust-based emergence of criminal structures: legal business. Business relations, to the extent they are characterized by frequent interactions embedded in broader social networks, can be expected to create trust as a result of a combination of factors, including affectionate bonds, observations of personal conduct, reputation, and the reliance on shared norms and values. There is some evidence not only from the literature on corporate crime but also from the organized crime literature in the narrow sense, that the world of legal business can be the breeding ground for criminally exploitable ties (Kleemans & van de Bunt, 2008; von Lampe & Johansen, 2004b; Waring, 1993). In one case reported by Kleemans and Van de Bunt (2008, pp. 191–192), a group of tax advisers, lawyers, asset managers, and directors of companies had met regularly at international tax conferences and eventually colluded in devising and carrying out elaborate tax fraud schemes.

Trust Building in the Absence of Trust

Trust facilitates the formation of criminal structures, but it is not always a necessary precondition. A relationship may start with little or no trust in the other, or there may be outright mistrust (von Lampe & Johansen, 2004b). This is not an unusual situation given that social networks that provide a basis of trust, namely kinship and friendship ties, are limited in size and reach (Morselli, 2005, p. 22).

One approach taken by criminals in the absence of trust is to interact in such a way that trust can be built over time. For example, in an effort to gain trust criminals may reveal compromising information about themselves that the other can use to retaliate in case of disloyal behavior. The information serves as collateral. At the same time, the one who provides the information signals that he or she is willing to trust the other, which may provide the other individual with an additional motivation to enter into a criminal relationship. Diego Gambetta argues that this is a widespread bonding strategy (Gambetta, 2009, p. 66). In turn, criminals may adopt strategies to ascertain someone else's trustworthiness. Strategies of this nature include test deals and trial periods (Decker & Townsend Chapman, 2008, p. 104; Denton, 2001, p. 76; Zaitch, 2002, p. 278). Al Capone, according to biographer Laurence Bergreen, was put to a test at a young age by his future mentor Johnny Torrio. Torrio reportedly ordered Capone to show up at his place of business "at a certain time, and when Al showed up, Torrio made a point to be absent, but he had left behind a tempting sum of money where it could be easily taken." Capone withstood the temptation and thus gained Torrio's trust (Bergreen, 1994, p. 38). Apart from more or less elaborate testing procedures, some criminals also pride themselves with being able to quickly size up a person and to determine more or less on the spot if this person is trustworthy (Adler, 1985, p. 73; Gambetta, 2009, p. 8).

How successful these various strategies for establishing a basis of trust are in the medium and long run is a matter of debate. Some see trust growing over time as a result of successful, mutually beneficial interaction (Morselli, 2005, p. 35), while others are more skeptical. They argue that only "highly fragile" trust relationships exist between criminals irrespective of the time period over which these relations have evolved (Williams, 2002, p. 79). According to Diego Gambetta, because of "their propensities, criminals have little hope of finding 'thick' trust in each other: they stand hardly any chance of finding people of good character in their line of business and can aspire, at best, to find ways to sustain the 'thin' or 'calculative' version of trust" (Gambetta, 2009, p. 37).

There is some anecdotal evidence in support of this assumption. There are at least some criminals who have told researchers that they live by the rule that they trust no one, or they just fatalistically hope that other criminals will be honest (Zaitch, 2002, pp. 278, 280; see also Adler, 1985, p. 69; Desroches, 2005, p. 62; von Lampe & Johansen, 2004b, p. 179). Even mafia organizations, which are often depicted as cohesive, trust-bound structures, appear in a different light in many insider accounts (see, e.g., Arlacchi, 1993). Notorious underworld figure Meyer Lansky sarcastically said, "they were so honorable that no one in the Mafia ever trusted anyone else" (Lacey, 1991, p. 75). From this perspective, criminal structures can only be fully understood when taking into account not only how criminals find a basis of trust—for example, in preexisting social network ties—but also how they cope with a chronic lack of trust.

Coping With a Lack of Trust and Mistrust

There are a number of plausible explanations why criminals interact without a sufficient basis of trust. For example, criminals may feel that the benefits of cooperation outweigh the risk of betrayal, especially when they are under economic pressure, or as already indicated, they may fatalistically accept the possibility of betrayal (von Lampe & Johansen, 2004b, p. 179). However, in the organized crime literature the discussion is primarily centered on two strategies with which criminals cope with a lack of trust and mistrust and attempt to reduce the risks of betrayal: (a) information management and (b) incentives and disincentives for loyal and, respectively, disloyal behavior.

Information Management

The information management of criminals aims at maintaining secrecy. But it is more than keeping one's mouth shut. It pertains to procedural and struct arrangements that criminals adopt with regard to other criminals in an effo reduce opportunities for betrayal and to minimize the impact from disl behavior should it occur. The general assumption is that criminals will seek to monitor the dealings of their accomplices and business partners as best as possible while trying to limit the spread of information pertaining to themselves as much as possible (Desroches, 2005; Reuter, 1983).

Given the clandestine nature of most illegal activities, monitoring among criminals tends to be difficult, although, as anecdotal evidence suggests, it is not impossible (Reuter & Haaga, 1989, pp. 41–45). For example, drug "mules"—individuals recruited to smuggle drugs hidden inside their body or in their luggage—may be secretly monitored by a representative of the smuggling enterprise who unbeknownst to the mules travels with them on the same plane (Molano, 2004, pp. 8–9).

More common seem to be schemes designed to reduce the amount of potentially damaging information available to other criminals. For example, criminals may keep their true identity a secret. This is typical in the relationship between criminal entrepreneurs and individuals that are hired for specific tasks, for example the transportation of drugs. But even where collaboration extends over long periods of time, criminals may not know the other's name and address (Desroches, 2005, pp. 126–127; Reuter, 1983, p. 115; Reuter & Haaga, 1989, p. 44).

Generally speaking, concerns for secrecy lead to the segmentation of criminal structures. In the case of illegal enterprises, this means that responsibilities are divided and tasks are being delegated so that no individual member has complete knowledge about who is involved and what specific activities are being carried out (Reuter, 1983). A criminal who ran several drug labs together with a long-time business partner explains how segmentation is achieved as follows:

> When you become a laboratory man, everything is done to ensure the utmost secrecy. Here's me and my partner of 12 years. We've done multimillion-dollar deals together, yet he doesn't even know where the dope is kept or where the cash is kept. Only me. He doesn't need to know. He dealt with other customers that I never met. There was no need for me to meet them or to know who they were. You divide up the division of labour and everything is so segmented and secret. Everything is compartmentalized. (as cited in Desroches, 2005, p. 125)

The effect of this kind of information management is that in the case of disloyal behavior—for example, when someone becomes a police informant—the consequences are limited, as the information that can be passed on may not be sufficient for an arrest or a conviction.

Incentives and Disincentives

In addition to strategies designed to diminish opportunities for and the consequences of disloyal behavior, there are also strategies aiming at the decision-making of accomplices. These strategies involve giving incentives for loyal behavior and disincentives for disloyal behavior in order to reduce the likelihood of betrayal. Incentives, most obviously, may come in the form of monetary rewards—for example, when an illegal entrepreneur pays his or her employees disproportionately high wages (Reuter, 1983, p. 116). Similarly, nonmaterial rewards in the form of, for example, attention, respect, and affection, may induce loyal behavior (Desroches, 2005, p. 156).

In the opposite direction, accomplices may be discouraged from disloyal behavior by the threat of punishment. There are some forms of punishment among criminals that are nonviolent in nature. For example, monetary compensation may be demanded before collaboration is resumed, a drug dealer may no longer supply drugs on credit, or the individual who has been disloyal may be excluded from future interaction altogether (Adler, 1985, p. 70). However, violence is the focal point in many discussions of how criminal structures are held together.

Violence as a Functional Alternative to Trust

Violence is viewed by some as a defining characteristic of organized crime. While this may be an overly narrow conception, it is safe to assume that the actual or potential use of violence has some relevance for many if not all aspects of organized crime. That is why violence is a recurring theme throughout this book. In the present context, the question is to what extent and in what way the threat or use of violence accounts for the existence of criminal structures as a functional alternative to trust (Arlacchi, 1998, p. 211).

Violence can be the basis for the formation of criminal structures in the very direct sense that individuals are coerced into participating in criminal activities and into joining a criminal organization. Reuter and Haaga (1989, p. 43), for example, report a case where South American drug traffickers kidnapped a woman to force her husband to do business with them. Apart from these rather rare occurrences, violence is widely regarded as an explicit or implicit option for responding to disloyal behavior. This constant threat of violent retribution for wrongdoing may promote a sense that disloyal behavior is unlikely and that therefore the risk of cooperating with other criminals is minimized (see, e.g., Denton & O'Malley, 1999; Desroches, 2005, p. 120; Junninen, 2006, p. 70). At the same time, violence can also be a means for minimizing the consequences of disloyal behavior. For example, buyers of illicit goods who are delinquent on their payments may be coerced into paying up. Kidnappings are reportedly used by some drug traffickers to collect outstanding debts (Zaitch, 2002, p. 269). Likewise, violence can be used to neutralize the threat from informants. They or close relatives may be threatened or killed, although witness protection programs may reduce the effectiveness of such strategies (Desroches, 2005, pp. 120–121; Chapter 14).

There is some debate on the actual level of violence among criminals. While there are cases of high levels of violence, for example in the Mexican "drug war" (Beittel, 2011), most studies that have looked at this issue, it seems, have found that the avoidance of violence rather than the use of violence is characteristic of criminal structures. Damian Zaitch, for example, in talking to Colombian drug traffickers, was "amazed about the number of conflicts that did not lead to physical violence" (Zaitch, 2002, p. 262; see also Desroches, 2005, p. 120; Junninen, 2006, p. 68–70; Schlegel, 1987).

The secondary importance of violence has been explained by the costs of the use of violence and the costs of a reputation of being violence prone (Reuter,

Image 5.4   The decomposing body of William "Action" Jackson is found in the trunk of his Cadillac in downtown Chicago in August 1961. Jackson collected debts on usurious loans for members of the Chicago "Outfit" and had come under false suspicion of being an FBI informant. He was tortured to death in a meat rendering plant with the use of a meat hook, a cattle prod, a hammer and ice picks (Roemer, 1989, p. 280). Violent acts like these are meant to become public. They send a message that violations of the underworld code will not go unpunished.

Photo: Bettmann/Corbis

1983; Gambetta, 2009, p. 36). Violence may attract unwanted attention from the public and from law enforcement. And "too much violence can discourage potential business partners to deal with a reputed violent entrepreneur" (Zaitch, 2002, 264; see also Desroches, 2005, p. 150; Reuter, 1983, p. 151).

The level of violence may vary with the circumstances and with the individuals involved. For example, it has been noted that an increase in violence occurred in the illegal drugs market in the United Kingdom in the 1970s following a transition from dealers with mostly a middle-class background to dealers from the ranks of professional lower-class criminals (Dorn, Murji, & South, 1992, p. 39). Still, it seems that even where violence is less prevalent it remains "a matter of last resort" for dealing with conflicts within criminal structures (Edelhertz & Overcast, 1993, p. 128; see also Denton & O'Malley, 1999, p. 524; Junninen, 2006, p. 70; von Lampe, 2006b).

CRIMINAL STRUCTURES: SUMMARY AND CONCLUSION

This chapter has discussed criminal structures, defined as arrangements of inter-personal relationships that have an impact on the commission of crime. Two main issues have been addressed: how criminal structures can best be classified and how criminal structures emerge and persist.

Following a review of classifications that can be found in the organized crime literature, a three-fold typology has been proposed based on the functions that criminal structures perform. According to this typology, one needs to differentiate entrepreneurial, associational, and quasi-governmental structures. Entrepreneurial structures enable criminals to pool resources and to coordinate their activities to achieve material gain through market-based or predatory crimes. Associational structures provide status, cohesion, and mutual support, and they provide a forum for communication, thereby strengthening deviant values. Quasi-governmental structures regulate the behavior of criminals in the areas under their control. They enforce certain rules and settle disputes, and they may neutralize law enforcement through centralized corruption, thereby reducing the risks and uncertainty that criminals face in committing crimes and interacting with other criminals.

There are inherent risks in interacting with other criminals, as these may turn out to be police informants or fraudsters or thieves. A key challenge for organized criminals, therefore, is to reduce the risk of betrayal. A number of risk-minimizing strategies that criminals use have been discussed. These include the selection of trustworthy accomplices and measures to reduce the opportunities for and benefits from betrayal. Much of this discussion has centered on the importance of trust and violence. Trust rooted, for example, in kinship, friend-ship, and legal business relations is highly relevant but not always present in criminal structures. Violence can be a functional alternative to trust, and it is a latent option for criminals as a means of coping with the risk of betrayal. However, it may be more appropriate to assume that avoidance of violence rather than the use of violence characterizes criminal structures.

Criminal structures, be they entrepreneurial, associational, or quasi-governmental, can take on different forms. The classification of markets, networks, and hierar-chies highlights different levels of interdependence between interacting criminals. Pure market relations between fully independent actors are rare in illegal as well as legal contexts as interaction tends to be embedded in preexisting relations. In most cases, criminals interact within network structures where individuals make auton-omous decisions, but they are bound by underlying ties that would be jeopardized by disloyal behavior. Out of networks more integrated structures can emerge that guide and coordinate the interaction of individual participants.

Criminal investigations tend to produce only snapshot images of more far-reaching and more complex webs of relations that link criminals in a variety of ways. It is important to look beyond tangible relations in the form of co-offending networks or in the form of shared membership in formal criminal associations. A more complete picture is obtained when one looks at the underlying networks of criminally exploitable ties, of which manifest criminal structures tend to represent only a smaller part. In addition, one needs to take into account how new criminally exploitable ties are formed to understand the level of resilience of criminal structures.

In the end, what follows from this general discussion of criminal structures is that criminal behavior can be shaped and influenced by various partly overlapping and interdependent patterns of interaction and association. As Figure 5.5 depicts, a given organized criminal endeavor (criminal activity) is the product of the interaction of a specific set of co-offenders that are linked to each other in some form of entrepreneurial criminal structure. This entrepreneurial structure may be embedded in a broader network of criminally exploitable ties, which means that the co-offenders are part of a larger pool of individuals willing and able to assist each other in criminal endeavors. This willingness may be derived from underlying bonds of trust rooted in and reinforced by previous interaction in entrepreneurial criminal structures and derived from preexisting social networks. Confidence in accomplices may also be the result of shared norms and values stemming from joint membership in an associational criminal structure, such as a mafia organization or an outlaw motorcycle gang. It is likely that a criminal association, in turn, also relies on criminally exploitable ties for recruiting

Figure 5.5   Interplay of Different Kinds of Structures in Influencing Criminal Activities

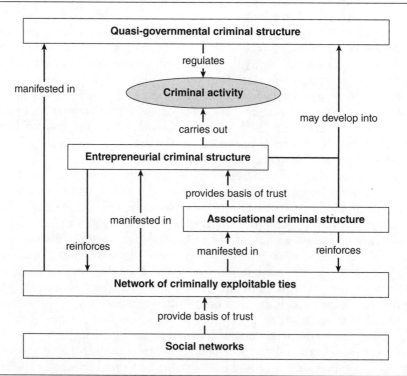

This graph depicts how different types of relations between criminals may influence a given criminal activity. It highlights the interrelations between the three basic types of criminal structures (entrepreneurial, associational, and quasi governmental) and their embeddedness in broader networks of criminally exploitable ties, which in turn may grow out of normal social networks.

new members; at the same time, a criminal association will reinforce and create networks of criminally exploitable ties by creating fraternal bonds between its members. Finally, the criminal endeavor may be influenced by a quasi-governmental criminal structure that may, for example, restrict or tax certain criminal activities and may offer a mechanism for nonviolent conflict resolution. Such a quasi-governmental structure, like the other types of criminal structures, is a manifestation of criminally exploitable ties. In some cases, quasi-governmental criminal structures grow out of associational or entrepreneurial structures.

Against the backdrop of the various overlapping and interdependent structures that may influence organized criminal activity, it should be obvious that in most cases one cannot expect an easy and straightforward answer to the question: How organized is it? What is required is a differentiated analysis. In the following chapters, entrepreneurial, associational, and quasi-governmental structures will be discussed in greater depth. This provides the opportunity for adding more detail to the many facets of the organization of criminals.

Discussion Questions

1. Imagine you are visiting a country under a dictatorship and you need to escape prosecution because you have publicly made a derogatory remark about the dictator. Who would you trust to help you? An aunt who is a member of the ruling party? A long-time business partner of yours who has a branch office in the country? A pickpocket you observe in a public square?

2. As a criminal, would you rather be feared or loved?

3. Is it possible for criminals to collaborate over an extended period of time without a common basis of trust?

Research Projects

1. Analyze the autobiography of an organized criminal with a view to the importance and basis of trust in the interaction with other criminals.

2. Analyze the autobiography of an organized criminal with a view to the importance of the threat and use of violence.

3. Analyze the autobiography of an organized criminal and examine for one specific event that is described in some detail for the importance of entrepreneurial, associational, and quasi-governmental structures.

Further Reading

Violence in the Context of Organized Crime

Amir, M. (1995). Organized crime and violence. *Studies on Crime and Crime Prevention*, 4(1), 86–104.

Geis, G. (1963). Violence and organized crime. *Annals of the American Academy of Political and Social Science, 365*, 86–95.

Hopkins, M., Tilley, N., & Gibson, K. (2013). Homicide and organized crime in England. *Homicide Studies, 17*(3), 291–313.

Taylor, A. (2007). *How drug dealers settle disputes: Violent and nonviolent outcomes.* Monsey, NY: Criminal Justice Press.

Criminal Network Analysis

Bright, D. A., Hughes, C. E., & Chalmers, J. (2012). Illuminating dark networks: A social network analysis of an Australian trafficking syndicate. *Crime, Law and Social Change, 57*(2), 151–176.

Carrington, P. J. (2011). Crime and social network analysis. In J. Scott, & P. J. Carrington (Eds.), *Sage handbook of social network analysis* (pp. 236–255). London: Sage.

Schwartz, D. M. & Rousselle, T. (2009). Using social network analysis to target criminal networks. *Trends in Organized Crime, 12*(2), 188–207.

Van der Hulst, R. C. (2009). Introduction to social network analysis (SNA) as an investigative tool. *Trends in Organized Crime 12*(2), 101–121.

The Organization of Criminals

Alach, Z. J. (2011). An incipient taxonomy of organised crime. *Trends in Organized Crime, 14*(1), 56–72.

Ayling, J. (2009). Criminal organizations and resilience. *International Journal of Law, Crime and Justice, 37*(4), 182–196.

Southerland, M., & Potter, G. W. (1993). Applying organization theory to organized crime, *Journal of Contemporary Criminal Justice, 9*(3), 251–267.

Windle, J. (2013). Tuckers firm: A case study of British organised crime. *Trends in Organized Crime, 16*(4), 382–396.

CHAPTER 6

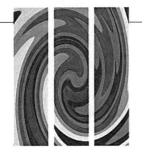

Illegal Entrepreneurial Structures

INTRODUCTION

The previous chapter has introduced three basic types of structures that connect criminals: entrepreneurial, associational, and quasi governmental. These structures differ with regard to the functions they perform, and they each represent unique responses to the specific challenges that criminals face. In this and the two following chapters, these three functional types will be examined one by one, beginning with illegal entrepreneurial structures in this chapter, followed by illegal associational structures in Chapter 7 and illegal quasi-governmental structures in Chapter 8.

The three chapters are similar in that they investigate the specific nature and main characteristics of each type of structure. At the same time, there are important differences between this chapter and the following two chapters reflecting differences in the underlying phenomena and differences in the way these phenomena have been studied. Illegal associational and especially illegal quasi-governmental structures are somewhat limited in number, and research tends to concern itself with just a few notorious cases. In contrast, there are countless illegal entrepreneurial structures, and research tends to be less interested in the specifics of individual cases in their own right and more oriented toward answering general questions about the organization of criminals. In fact, many of these studies are of relevance not only for understanding entrepreneurial structures, but insights from analyzing how criminals organize around illegal economic activities can also be applied to associational and quasi-governmental structures. That is why this chapter serves in part as a further, more in-depth introduction to the study of criminal structures in general.

Entrepreneurial criminal structures as defined here are patterns of relationships centered on economic activity in a broad sense. Criminals are connected in ways that help in obtaining financial or other material benefits, mainly by producing, buying, and selling illegal commodities (goods or services). Typical entrepreneurial criminal structures include such phenomena as drug trafficking groups, illegal gambling casinos, and illegal brothels, all of which cater to willing customers. However, the category of illegal entrepreneurial structures also includes structures centered on predatory crime such as theft and fraud or collective sexual abuse. This broad conception of illegal entrepreneurial structures is not particularly exotic. It is in line with the conception of organized criminal group of the UN Convention against Transnational Organized Crime (see Schloenhardt, 2012, p. 155).

Entrepreneurial criminal structures can take on different forms. Following the classification of markets, networks, and hierarchies introduced in the previous chapter, three ideal types of illegal entrepreneurial structures can be distinguished: illegal *markets*, illegal entrepreneurial *networks* and illegal firms (*hierarchies/organizations*).

Illegal firms are delineable organizational entities that are roughly similar in function to organizations in the legal economy, commonly referred to as businesses, business enterprises, enterprises, corporations, or firms (see Moore, 1986, p. 55). Apart from one-person operations of individual entrepreneurs, they consist of a number of individuals who are integrated into an overarching structure that directs and coordinates their actions in pursuit of a common purpose—for example, the distribution of drugs. It should be noted that the term *firm*, as it is used here, is borrowed from economics. It is different from the more associational, family-based structures Dick Hobbs (2001; Hobbs, 2013) and other British authors commonly refer to as firms in their research of the underworld in England.

Illegal entrepreneurial *networks*, like illegal firms, are centered on a specific economic activity, such as the distribution of drugs, but with a lower level of integration and coordination. As discussed in the previous chapter, network relations as an ideal-type are connecting autonomous parties who make independent decisions. At the same time, there are underlying longer-term relationships at stake. The underlying bonds that connect the network members reduce the likelihood of the pursuit of self-interest by one at the expense of the other. As also indicated in the previous chapter, networks and firms are not necessarily mutually exclusive. While there are entrepreneurial networks that are just that, that is, networks, the transition to the more integrated structure of an illegal firm is fleeting, and it may be a matter of perspective whether a particular set of individuals is analyzed in terms of a network or in terms of an organization.

Illegal *markets* are arenas of regular voluntary exchange of illegal goods or services under conditions of competition (Beckert & Wehinger, 2011, p. 2). As an ideal typical coordinating mechanism, illegal markets are defined by transactions between independent, autonomous parties of one-off exchanges. The interaction between fully independent individuals, however, is a rather rare occurrence, given that the exchange of illegal goods and services tends to be embedded in preexisting social relations (see Chapter 5).

Illegal firms are typically not self-sufficient, isolated entities. They are commonly part of larger entrepreneurial criminal structures through which they can obtain required resources and distribute illegal goods and services. This means that illegal firms (including individual entrepreneurs) are usually connected to other illegal firms and ultimately to consumers by market relations or, more likely, by network relations. The only exception would be self-sufficient groups of predatory criminals who keep their ill-gotten gains for their own consumption.

The conception of markets, networks, and hierarchies rests on the assumption that economic activity is not necessarily linked to one specific structural form. In other words, the same kind of task in the production and distribution of legal or illegal goods and services can be accomplished through market exchanges, through cooperation within a network, through the joint efforts of the members of one firm, or through a combination of these patterns of interaction. This means that in a given area of crime, it depends on the circumstances whether criminals interact in a market setting, within network structures, or as members of an illegal firm. This also means that the organizing mechanism for a given criminal activity may change over time. For example, market-based relations may transform into network relations and network relations into hierarchical relations, just like individuals may leave a hierarchical structure only to continue to contribute to the illegal firm on a "freelance" (network) basis.

Southerland and Potter (1993), in reviewing the pertinent empirical research, summed up this notion of the fluidity of criminal entrepreneurial structures as follows:

> Organized crime consists of a large number of actors coming together in an organization, leaving that organization, forming and re-forming new organizations, and entering into a series of partnerships. All of this occurs in a constantly shifting panorama of criminal activity and organizational configurations. There is no single criminal organization. There are overlapping roles and relationships in a continually changing census of crime enterprises. (Southerland & Potter, 1993, p. 262)

The fluidity of criminal structures poses considerable challenges for researchers (and intelligence analysts) when they set out to define and identify units of analysis. They have to separate out discernible structures from at times confusing webs of relations and interactions. The task of identifying coherent criminal structures, namely illegal firms, is particularly problematic because written contracts, constitutions, and bylaws that define and shape organizations in the legal spheres of society are largely absent in the illegal spheres of society.

In addition, illegal firms as understood here commonly lack formalized procedures and symbols to mark their boundaries, unlike associational structures such as outlaw motorcycle gangs or Japanese yakuza organizations that use initiation rites, tattoos, and distinct clothing to distinguish their members from outsiders (see Chapter 7).

Another key challenge apart from delineating specific illegal entrepreneurial structures for analysis is to determine under what circumstances particular organizing mechanisms (markets, networks, or hierarchies) come into play. This question is discussed in the academic literature primarily with respect to the factors that account for the emergence of illegal firms from more diffuse entrepreneurial structures.

Another question is how illegal entrepreneurial structures, once they have come into existence, are shaped and what factors account for the variations that can be observed. This is a question that is raised with regard to illegal markets, networks, and firms. In this chapter, however, only the characteristic features of illegal entrepreneurial networks and illegal firms will be examined. The structure of an illegal market is primarily a matter of the relations between large numbers of illegal firms and entrepreneurs and therefore is an issue situated on a higher level of observation and is best discussed in a later chapter (Chapter 8).

The discussion of the structural characteristics of illegal networks and firms encompasses two main issues. The first issue is how to conceptualize networks and organizations beyond the vague and ambiguous language of "loosely structured" versus "tightly organized" that is annoyingly pervasive in the organized crime literature. The second issue is how to account for the differences in structure that can be observed across illegal entrepreneurial networks and across illegal firms. One fundamental question from organization studies that is also relevant here is whether an organization determines its actions or whether actions determine an organization (Smith, 1994, p. 121). Another key question is to what degree illegal businesses can be organized similar to legal businesses and to what degree illegality imposes constraints on the organization of criminals.

Before these questions are addressed, a case study of a drug trafficking operation is presented. This case study is meant to illustrate some salient features of illegal entrepreneurial structures and to provide a concrete empirical reference point for the subsequent discussion.

CASE STUDY: THE LAVIN ENTERPRISE

The following is a brief description of perhaps the best-documented case of a drug distribution enterprise operating within the United States. Two detail-rich books, written by journalists Carol Saline (1989) and Mark Bowden (2001), trace the story of a Philadelphia-based wholesale business that sold marijuana and then cocaine on an increasing scale between the mid-1970s and mid-1980s. By 1983 the business reportedly had a monthly turnover of between 60 and 80 kilos of 95 to 98 percent pure cocaine, which was distributed locally and to customers in different parts of the United States. The mastermind behind this drug enterprise was Larry Lavin. He attended college and dental school at the University of Pennsylvania and later worked as a dentist in Philadelphia until he was arrested in September of 1984 at the age of 29. While the accounts of Saline and Bowden are not always consistent, a fairly clear picture of the structure of this drug operation emerges from a careful reading of both books.

The Lavin enterprise went through distinct phases in the roughly ten years of its existence, marked by a gradual shift from the distribution of marijuana to the distribution of cocaine in the late 1970s and a series of changes in management starting in 1980. At that time, Larry Lavin handed over the day-to-day business to a dental school classmate who was the first in a string of managers who, for different reasons, gave up this position after relatively short periods of time. In the course of the first half of 1984, Larry sold his business by gradually transferring his customers to another Philadelphia drug dealer, Frannie, who had previously been a competitor.

Larry became a drug dealer in 1974, in his sophomore year in college. Through his "big brother" in the fraternity, he had gained access to suppliers who were willing to front him ten pounds of marijuana, which he was able to sell to friends within a week. The volume of his sales grew quickly, and soon he purchased marijuana in bulk from different sources, mainly in Florida. The expansion of his business seems to have been attributable to a marketing strategy based on two principles: (a) the packaging of the drugs by weight and quality according to customer preferences, and (b) the willingness to front drugs and to wait for payment until after Larry's customers had sold the drugs on to their respective customers. This strategy required detailed records of purchases, sales, and debts, which Larry initially kept in the form of tiny handwritten notes (Bowden, 2001, pp. 37–38). Early on Larry drew on the help of fellow students to procure, package, and deliver drugs. He closely collaborated with two students in particular, L. A. and Andy, who were in their junior and freshman year, respectively, when Larry started dealing marijuana as a sophomore. By early 1975, Larry and L.A. had formed a partnership and evenly split the profits from their drug dealing, with L.A. handling the procurement of drugs and Lavin focusing on the distribution. After L. A. got arrested on a purchasing trip to Florida in 1976, Lavin offered Andy to become a full partner (Bowden, 2001, p. 36). Andy made trips to Florida from then on until he himself was arrested while returning by train with about sixty-five pounds of marijuana hidden in two suitcases. Andy, who later had the charges against him dropped on legal grounds, remained a partner in the business; however, the runs to Florida were assigned to three other students recruited for this purpose (Bowden, 2001, pp. 58–59). This meant that at this point in time the Lavin drug enterprise was made up of at least five co-offenders who collaborated on a continuous basis.

With the increasing size of shipments, the transportation of marijuana from Florida to Philadelphia became more and more of a challenge. At the same time, consumer preferences gradually began to shift from marijuana to cocaine, which was easier to transport and to conceal. In addition, cocaine provided for much higher profit margins per weight unit. It is not surprising, therefore, that before long Larry began dealing cocaine. The initial purchases, half kilos and soon two kilos at a time,

Image 6.1   Larry Lavin after his arrest in 1986. He had been a fugitive for a year and a half, living with his family under an assumed name in Virginia Beach, Virginia.

Photo: http://cdn2-b.examiner.com/sites/default/files/styles/image_content_width/hash/e1/ce/e1ce0e792604ad54dcdf7033595bab02.jpg?itok=21tRL_74

were joint investments by Larry and several of his long-time friends (Bowden, 2001, p. 79).

Larry distributed the cocaine through his marijuana customers. This created tensions with his partner Andy, who was also upset about Larry's decision to expand the customer base beyond the campus to include drug dealers in the African American and Italian American neighborhoods of Philadelphia. Andy believed that these changes were too risky, and in 1979 he took the consequences and withdrew from the business (Bowden, 2001, p. 75).

By that time, Larry had entered dental school and had become friends with two of his classmates, Ken and David. In early 1978, Ken had agreed to have his apartment used for breaking down and repackaging drug shipments, and Ken also started selling marijuana and cocaine supplied by Lavin (Bowden, 2001, p. 68; Saline, 1989, p. 67).

Ken became further integrated into the business when he began making purchasing trips to Florida. When one day in 1979 Ken was unable to go to Florida to buy cocaine, Larry asked David to make the trip. David had become Ken's customer, and he was also involved in purchasing inositol for Ken and Larry, a B-vitamin compound used for cutting cocaine to maximize profits (Saline, 1989, p. 67). On his trip to Florida, David handled the dealings with the cocaine supplier, Miguel, so well that Lavin started to employ David for a number of different tasks (Bowden, 2001, p. 84). While working for Larry, David and Ken formed a partnership of their own for distributing cocaine. They bought the drugs from Larry until, in early 1980, Larry allowed David and Ken to make their own buys in Florida (Bowden, 2001, p. 121).

In the fall of 1980, Larry, David, and Ken decided to merge their drug businesses. The idea was for Larry to hand over his customers and the day-to-day management to David and Ken. Soon, however, Ken stepped back from the business, leaving David in the position of chief operating officer (Saline, 1989, p. 107). This allowed Larry and Ken to concentrate on finishing dental school without pulling out of the drug business entirely. Larry continued to receive a percentage of the profits from his old customers and any new customers, and Ken a percentage of the profits from the customers he and David had supplied, while the rest of the profits stayed with David (Bowden, 2001, p. 185). As a result of this arrangement, Ken's involvement changed to that of a silent partner whereas Larry, although withdrawn from the day-to-day business, stayed in contact with customers and regularly consulted with David (Bowden, 2001, pp. 151–152; Saline, 1989, pp. 106–107).

In 1981, the Lavin enterprise experienced a substantial expansion in terms of volume and geographical reach. Monthly turnover of cocaine increased from 2 to 3 kilos to 10 to 15 kilos, which was mailed or hand-delivered to customers in places like Chicago, Los Angeles, New York City, Phoenix, Arizona, and Tampa Bay, Florida. The geographical expansion came primarily as a result of customers graduating from the University of Pennsylvania and moving to other parts of the country (Saline, 1989, p. 110). Cocaine also went to a brother and a sister and a childhood friend of Larry's for distribution in New England, where Larry had grown up (Bowden, 2001, pp. 136–137).

Along with the expansion in volume and geographical reach, the Lavin enterprise under the management of David also expanded in size with regard to the number of individuals involved. In January 1981, David asked his former girlfriend Suzanne to assist him in running the business. He provided her with an apartment and paid her $1,500 per week in exchange for keeping the books and meeting customers in the apartment (Bowden, 2001, pp. 148–149). Within weeks, David also hired Christine who had worked together with Suzanne as a waitress. Christine was likewise given an apartment rent free in addition to receiving $500 per week for running errands, counting money and filling cocaine orders (Saline, 1989, p. 348). Later, Suzanne earned a commission of $500 on every kilo that was sold, which by the end of 1981 amounted to $100,000, and Christine's salary rose to $1,500 a week (Bowden, 2001, p. 149; Saline, 1989, p. 122).

The management comprising David, Suzanne, and Christine, under the oversight of Larry, employed a number of runners for transporting cash to Miami and cocaine back to Philadelphia, and delivering it to customers. Runners were paid up to $2,000 per trip to or from Miami (Saline, 1989, pp. 105, 120). The main person in charge of this part of the operation during 1981 was Willie, a college dropout and bartender, who had initially been recruited by David as a part-time courier to pay off a drug debt, delivering cocaine to customers on the West Coast for between $150 and $1,000 per trip (Saline, 1989, p. 120). Willie recruited three other young men, Gary, Daniel, and Roger, to help him with regularly bringing consignments of 10 kilos of cocaine or more to Philadelphia (Bowden, 2001, p. 165). Yet another person, Mark, had been recruited by David in early 1981 to help in various phases of the drug business (Bowden, 2001, p. 150). This brought the number of individuals directly and continuously involved in the Lavin enterprise in 1981 to nine (see Fig. 6.1).

Figure 6.1   The Lavin Enterprise in 1981

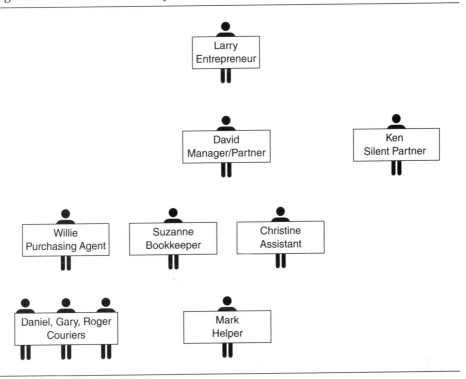

Source: Bowden (2001), Saline (1989).

Of course, there were also suppliers and customers who regularly interacted with the Lavin enterprise over extended periods of time. Namely, the main source of cocaine remained the same from 1979 until 1982. The first supplier, Miguel, as well as another source in Miami, Vivian, were backed by the same person, a Cuban named Rene, who in turn was a middleman for a group of Colombians. As the volume of transactions increased, the Lavin enterprise was passed up the chain of suppliers to deal directly with Rene and eventually with the Colombians, represented by two men, Pepe and Paco. The relationship between the Colombians and the Lavin enterprise ended in the summer of 1982, when Paco refused to lower the price of $56,000 per kilo even though there were others who charged less than $35,000 for a kilo of cocaine of equal quality (Bowden, 2001, pp. 194–195).

On the distribution side, the Lavin enterprise maintained long-term relationships to a number of customers. The single most important customer was Billy, who distributed marijuana and later also cocaine locally in lower-class neighborhoods of Philadelphia. At first, starting in 1976, Billy obtained the drugs through a middleman, Hank, but began dealing directly with Larry in 1979 after Hank got shot in an argument with other drug dealers (Bowden, 2001, pp. 79–80). In 1981 Larry convinced Billy to expand and professionalize his operation. Billy was taught by David and Suzanne how to keep books and how to cut the cocaine according to his customers' preferences (Bowden, 2001, p. 163; Saline, 1989, p. 134).

Eventually, Billy was granted the privilege of obtaining large quantities of uncut cocaine at just $2,000 over cost. Only one other buyer was enjoying the same preferential treatment, Larry's old college roommate and close friend Paul (Saline, 1989, p. 116).

The relations between the Lavin enterprise on the one hand and its suppliers and customers on the other, while extending over long periods of time, were vulnerable. As the break-up of the relationship with Paco and Pepe demonstrates, neither side could force the other to continue collaborating. The Lavin enterprise had no leverage to successfully renegotiate prices, and when subsequently it switched to other suppliers, Paco and Pepe tried in vain to reestablish the relationship (Bowden, 2001, p. 194).

The same was true when Billy stopped buying from the Lavin enterprise in 1982. Billy had grown increasingly discontent with David, who had developed a severe cocaine habit and had become unreliable. It was only months later, after Larry transferred the day-to-day management to Willie, that Billy resumed his purchases (Saline, 1989, p. 192).

Inside the Lavin enterprise, relationships were of a somewhat different nature. Larry seems to have been able to make all the important decisions, even against outspoken opposition from his partners—for example, when he expanded the customer base beyond the campus and moved from marijuana to cocaine. His power apparently resulted from the dependencies that he created between himself and the individuals he brought into the business. They were either in debt or had investments tied up in the business. David, for example, was reportedly constantly worried that Larry would object to the way he managed the business and would simply "take it all back" (Bowden, 2001, p. 153). David in turn kept members of the staff in line with similar threats. In one incident in 1981, Willie had driven up from Florida with 18 kilos of cocaine and at first refused to help with the repackaging. But when David threatened to fire him, Willie gave in (Bowden, 2001, pp. 168–169). When in the following year Larry decided that David had to leave the business, he did not take it all back. Instead he calculated the share of the business David held and paid him out (Saline, 1989, p. 195).

At no time in the lifespan of the Lavin enterprise was violence used to maintain internal discipline. Larry resorted to coercive measures only once, when a woman who had been hired to exchange small denomination bills into larger bills was suspected of having embezzled $80,000. Larry confronted her together with a menacing "big black man who trained fighters" and a friend who wielded an unloaded pistol. The woman confessed and Larry allowed her to keep some of the money (Bowden, 2001, pp. 108–109).

THE ILLEGAL FIRM

The Lavin case can serve as an example for illegal entrepreneurial structures on two levels of observation, (a) the overall web of participants at the various stages of the drug distribution chain and (b) the set of individuals centered on Larry Lavin.

All of the individuals mentioned in the description of the Lavin case can be considered part of one illegal entrepreneurial structure. This includes Lavin and those around him as well as suppliers and customers and even those individuals further up and down the distribution chain, from coca farmers in Latin America to retail dealers in North America who, for understandable reasons, received little to no attention in the accounts presented by Bowden (2001) and Saline (1989). All of these individuals who may well number in the hundreds were directly or indirectly connected to each other in ways that made the distribution of drugs easier, more efficient, and more profitable compared to an individual acting alone.

It is not clear to what extent relations within this overall structure constituted pure market relations. It is probably safest to assume that it was a large illegal entrepreneurial network interspersed with illegal firms. The set of individuals closely connected to Larry Lavin, collectively referred to in the above case study as the "Lavin enterprise," formed one such firm. It can be considered a fairly typical example of the patterns of cooperation at this level of the illegal drug trade. Mangai Natarajan has summed up the empirical research as follows:

> [Most entrepreneurial structures] involved in upper and middle market drug distribution are small, led by one or two individuals, who control the money and who have contacts with a small number of producers or wholesalers. These individuals employ small teams of runners, sometimes on a casual basis, who collect and deliver batches of drugs to customers. (Natarajan, 2006, p. 172)

Operations of this kind can be conceptualized as illegal firms. In economic terms, an illegal firm is "some person or institution with the ability to commit a particular set of assets to specific purposes" (Moore, 1986, p. 55), namely the production and distribution of illegal goods and services. Assets are tangible and intangible resources that can be mobilized in order to exploit an opportunity for material gain (Dean, Fahsing & Gottschalk, 2010, p. 8; Edelhertz & Overcast, 1993, p. 122).

Assets

The assets of illegal firms tend to be primarily intangible rather than tangible resources (Moore, 1986; Potter, 1994; Reuter, 1983). Tangible assets include cash and technology such as laboratory equipment and tableting machines used for the production of synthetic drugs (see, e.g., Gruppo Abele, 2003). The Lavin enterprise, it seems, had made relatively large investments in technology in the form of cars for the transportation of drugs and the furnishings of various rented apartments, particularly those used by Suzanne and Christine, which included safes to store cash and drugs (Bowden, 2001, p. 149, 166; Saline, 1989, p. 151).

The most important resources of an illegal firm appear to be intangible assets that for the most part are linked to particular individuals, namely skills, relationships, and reputations (Edelhertz & Overcast, 1993, p. 125; Moore, 1986, pp. 55–58; Reuter, 1983, p. 25). Personal skills of the members of an illegal firm are assets to the extent they help in attaining the firm's goals, which in turn depends on the specifics of a firm's line of business and its logistics (see Chapter 4). Required skills may include general and crime-specific know-how. The core skill set that was required in the operation of the Lavin enterprise included dealing with suppliers and customers, bookkeeping, and elaborate techniques for cutting cocaine and hand-producing "rocks," chunks of cocaine erroneously valued by customers as an indicator of high purity levels (Saline, 1989, p. 112). These skills were passed on whenever there was a change in key personnel (Bowden, 2001, p. 214)

Apart from technical skills, the capacity to use violence is regarded by some as a key asset of illegal firms (Moore, 1986, p. 56), although in cases like the Lavin enterprise, violence is of secondary importance for maintaining internal discipline as well as for responding to outside threats. This is different in the case of quasi-governmental structures, where the capacity for the effective use of violence tends to be of central importance (see Chapter 8).

A variety of relationships can constitute important assets for an illegal firm, namely, relationships to suppliers and to customers but also to providers of support services, such as financial agents who aid in laundering illicit proceeds, and to corrupt law enforcement officials who may be in a position to reduce the risk of prosecution (Moore, 1986, p. 56). The Lavin enterprise did not actively seek to corrupt officials. However, in 1980 through a customer's wife who worked in the district attorney's office, they were warned of an impending raid on Larry's home where at the time he kept all of his cocaine (Saline, 1989, p. 100).

A particular reputation can be a valuable asset in that it can attract business and reduce costs (Bovenkerk, Siegel & Zaitch, 2003). For example, firms with

Image 6.2   An investigator of the German customs service inspects the equipment of a clandestine factory for the production of counterfeit cigarettes discovered in a warehouse in Oberhausen, Germany, in 2003. Illegal firms do not commonly have fixed assets such as industrial machines.

Photo: Associated Press

a reputation for reliably supplying illegal goods and services of high quality will be in an advantageous position for maintaining and expanding their customer base. Likewise, a reputation for the use of violence may facilitate the collection of debts (Reuter, 1983, p. 41), whereas a reputation for being unreliable in making payments on time may result in a firm being cut off from supply or having to pay higher prices (Adler, 1985, p. 70).

It seems that the Lavin enterprise was able to establish a reputation for reliability and quality that, however, was primarily tied to Larry Lavin personally. Whenever problems arose or a change in management took place, Larry got in contact with customers to assure them that he would resolve these problems. In the end, it was Larry's relations to his customers that were the only assets that were transferred when he sold his business (Saline, 1989, p. 28).

Boundaries

When one thinks of an illegal firm as an entity with "the ability to commit a particular set of assets to specific purposes" (Moore, 1986, p. 55), this does not necessarily mean that these assets are directly held by that firm, respectively by the individuals who make up the firm. An illegal firm, just like a legal firm, may draw on resources from someone from the outside, someone who is not integrated into the organizational structure of the firm and instead provides specialized services on a contractual basis (see, e.g., Dorn, Levi, & King, 2005, p. 16; Zaitch, 2002, pp. 253–254). Such arrangements of contracting out certain tasks transcend and blur the boundaries of a firm. They are one of the reasons why it may be difficult to separate out illegal firms from broader illegal entrepreneurial structures (see Natarajan, 2006). Peter Reuter has proposed two criteria by which to make a distinction between the member of a firm and what he calls "an independent supplier to" the firm: nonexclusivity and lack of control by the entrepreneur over the actions of a given individual. If a person simultaneously works for more than one firm and if that person is paid on the basis of results not on the basis of input, then, Reuter suggests, it is an independent supplier (Reuter, 1985, p. 11).

It is not uncommon to see individuals being involved in two or more illegal firms at the same time. For example, they may be employees of one firm while also running their own business on the side (see, e.g., Reuter, 1983, p. 49). In the case of the Lavin enterprise, some of those who were partners of Larry Lavin or functioned as managers, such as David, Ken, and Willie, where selling drugs to their personal customers on the side (Bowden, 2001, p. 164). Most strikingly, prior to merging their customer list with Larry's in 1980, David and Ken ran a drug business parallel to the Lavin enterprise and procured cocaine in Florida simultaneously for Larry as well as for their own business (Bowden, 2001, p. 121).

To complicate matters further, individuals may be integrated into a firm to different degrees depending on their position within the organization. The positions that are commonly observed in illegal firms can be roughly grouped into four categories: entrepreneurs, managers, permanent employees, and temporary employees. Individual entrepreneurs and entrepreneurs operating as partners reap the profits and bear the risk of financial loss. They are the ones who have the highest level of commitment to a firm. Entrepreneurs may manage the firm themselves or may lay the direction of the day-to-day operations of a firm in to the hand of one or more managers. Managers have some level of influence over the firm, and they may receive a percentage of the profits or a commission based on the volume of the business (von der Lage, 2003, pp. 359–360). Managers, like entrepreneurs, can be expected to have a high level of commitment to the firm. Permanent employees work for the firm on a continuous basis and either draw a fixed salary or receive a commission for repetitive tasks that they complete in fairly regular intervals (Caulkins et al., 2009, p. 79). Permanent employees will have some degree of commitment to the firm, although they may not have a good understanding of the nature of the firm they work for. Temporary employees finally are recruited for specific tasks, and their understanding of the firm they work for may be highly limited. In some cases—for example, in the case of couriers, temporary employees may not even be aware of the specific nature of the illegal activity they are involved in. One could argue that because of their limited involvement, temporary employees, similar to subcontractors, are not really part of the firm.

Another reason why it is difficult to discern and delineate illegal firms is the fluidity of relations. From the available empirical research, it seems that illegal entrepreneurial structures can show a considerable fluctuation in the individuals who are involved and in the specific roles these individuals play (Kleemans & van de Bunt, 1999). This is particularly true for drug trafficking (Bright & Delaney, 2013; Dorn, Levi, & King, 2005) but also for crimes such as the trafficking in stolen motor vehicles (Gounev & Bezlov, 2008, p. 420). As regards the Lavin enterprise, it should be noted that Larry Lavin himself was the only person who was continuously involved in the drug operation over the entire period of some ten years. His first partners, L. A. and Andy, and his later partners, Ken and David as well as Willie, who succeeded David as manager, participated in the business for periods of only three to four years. The last two managers of the Lavin enterprise, Brian and Bruce, were involved for only one or two years. Many others participated in the operations of the Lavin enterprise for far shorter periods of time, down to those temporary employees who were hired for making just one or two runs to Florida (Saline, 1989, p. 72). The example of Ken and David is also illustrative of the changes in the roles played by many of those involved in the Lavin enterprise. They both moved through different positions, from customer, gofer and courier to manager and finally to silent partner. Others moved between the roles of customer and employee—for example, Paul, who started as courier and later became a major customer (Bowden, 2001, p. 59), while many customers who fell behind with payments were made to transport drugs to reduce their debts (Saline, 1989, p. 71).

The Lavin enterprise, thus, vividly illustrates that while illegal firms may be discernible organizational entities, their internal structure and their boundaries to the broader illegal entrepreneurial structures within which they are embedded tend to be fuzzy and fleeting. This leaves illegal firms, on one hand, and less integrated structures in the form of illegal entrepreneurial networks and illegal markets, on the other, as valid frames of reference for analysis.

CONCEPTUALIZING ILLEGAL ENTREPRENEURIAL STRUCTURES

The question of how to delineate entrepreneurial structures leads to the question of how to best describe and characterize them. The following section will focus on the structural variations of illegal entrepreneurial networks and illegal firms, while leaving aside the structure of illegal markets, which will be addressed in Chapter 8. The main emphasis is on basic concepts from the fields of social network analysis and organization theory, which are frequently though inconsistently applied in the organized crime literature.

As already pointed out, the discussion of the characteristics of networks and organizations is relevant for all functional types of criminal structures, which will be discussed separately in this and the following two chapters. Entrepreneurial, associational, and quasi-governmental structures are not linked to a specific organizational form. There are, for example, entrepreneurial *networks*, associational *networks* and *networks* that fulfill quasi-governmental functions. Likewise, there are not only illegal firms but also criminal associations, such as outlaw motorcycle gangs, and quasi-governmental structures, such as territorially based Mafia families, that qualify as *organizations* in the narrow sense of the word. The concepts of network and organization, thus, are both potentially applicable to a large number of criminal structures. And, as was emphasized before, these structures may be usefully analyzed in terms of networks as well as in terms of organizations, because both concepts represent different ways in which patterns of interaction and association can be framed.

Following the bottom-up approach outlined in the previous chapter, the following section will first present conceptual frameworks for the analysis of networks as the more elementary form of entrepreneurial structures. Then the discussion will proceed to the structural characteristics of illegal firms.

Table 6.1   Key Concepts for Criminal Network Analysis

Concept	Meaning
Size	Number of members (= number of individuals connected by a defined type of tie)
Density	Number of actual ties in relation to the number of possible ties between network members
Centrality	Degree to which a network member is part of the (direct or indirect) links between all other network members
Broker	Individual through whom two or more parts of a network are connected

Source: Knoke & Kuklinski (1982), Scott (2000).

Basic Concepts for Analyzing Criminal Networks

A network is commonly defined as a web of dyadic ties, links that, respectively, connect two individuals. Different types of ties identify different networks—for example, friendship networks, communication networks, or collaborative networks. Irrespective of the nature of the relations in question, the framework of network analysis always remains the same (Knoke & Kuklinski, 1982, p. 12). The concepts that are being highlighted here (Table 6.1), therefore, apply to illegal entrepreneurial networks in terms of manifest co-offending networks as well as to the broader networks of criminally exploitable ties within which they are embedded (see Chapter 5). Likewise, the concepts are applicable to associational networks and networks that function as quasi-governmental structures. The aim is always to understand the overall size and structure of a network and the strategic positions of particular individuals within the network.

Network Size

The size of a network depends on the number of individuals who are linked through the type of dyadic ties that define the network. For example, all individuals who participate in the trafficking of a given batch of cocaine, from production to the smuggling and eventually to wholesale and retail selling, are all connected through co-offending ties and therefore constitute one illegal entrepreneurial (co-of-fending) network. Criminal networks, thus, can be fairly large, as a case examined by Carlo Morselli indicates. He analyzed data from an extensive investigation into a hashish and cocaine importation network in Montreal, Canada, and was able to identify 110 participants implicated in the trafficking (Morselli, 2009b, p. 30). In a similar way, Mangai Natarajan analyzed a heroin trafficking network centered in New York City that comprised 294 individuals identified by name during an extensive police investigation (Natarajan, 2006).

A Swedish study of convicted drug offenders gives an idea of the size of networks of criminally exploitable ties. Starting from a set of 95 drug offenders who were convicted in Stockholm (the capital city of Sweden) in 2003, law-enforcement data spanning the years 1995 through 2003 were analyzed to determine the number of other offenders they had committed crimes with and with how many additional offenders these accomplices in turn had committed crimes. The study found that each of the 95 Stockholm drug offenders was connected through direct or indirect co-offending links to on average 108 other offenders who had been suspected of crimes in various parts of Sweden. Since the data were confined to cases of suspected co-offending in Sweden, it is likely that the actual networks of criminally exploitable ties were much larger and, given the nature of drug trafficking, that they extended into other countries (Heber, 2009a).

Network Density

Size is an important parameter, but it tells relatively little about the structure of a criminal network because it does not reveal to what extent and in what specific ways network members are linked to each other. One key concept with which to capture the structure of a network is density. Density refers to the number of *existing* direct links compared to the number of *possible* direct links within a network. A network is denser the more network members are directly linked to other network members (Knoke & Kuklinski, 1982, p. 45).

Figure 6.2 shows a hypothetical network with low density. Out of a total of 45 possible dyadic ties directly connecting the 10 network members, only 10 dyadic ties exist. However, there are parts of the network that have a high density. H, I, and J form a cluster (or "clique") where everyone is directly linked to everyone else. An important part of the analysis of criminal networks is to determine to what extent a network is fragmented into such clusters and how these clusters, then, are connected to each other. In reality, these clusters may be anything from illegal firms to friendship-based groups of criminals and territorially based mafia groups. The network in Figure 6.2 could represent, for example, a car trafficking operation where A and B are car thieves who sell the cars they have stolen to C, who works together with E to alter the identity of the cars. D might be someone who helps E in exchanging VIN plates, while F provides false documents. The altered cars might then be sold on to G, who delivers them to H, who runs a used-car dealership together with I and J, where the cars are sold to unwitting customers. Such a network that is subdivided into

Figure 6.2   A Hypothetical Network

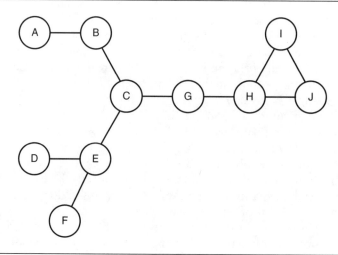

This graph depicts a hypothetical social network where each circle represents an individual and the connecting lines represent a specific kind of relationship (e.g., work together or know each other) by which the overall network is defined.

individuals, partnerships (A and B; C and E) and small groups of co-offenders (H, I, J), as already indicated, is regarded as typical for many areas of crime (see, e.g., Bruinsma & Bernasco, 2004).

Strategic Positions

In a dense network the members are connected to each other through numerous direct and indirect ties. The ties are redundant in that they lead to the same people. The lower the density of a network, the more important the existing ties become and the more important it is where in the network an individual is positioned (Morsell, 2005, p. 24). There are different parameters that identify different kinds of strategic positions that imply that the individuals occupying these positions have some degree of power and influence. One important parameter is centrality. In its simplest form, it determines to what degree an individual is involved in all of the (direct and indirect) relations within a network (Knoke & Kuklinski, 1982, p. 52). In Figure 6.2, C is the most central individual because most relations between any two-network members go through C.

G also occupies a crucial position in the network by connecting C and H and, through them, the two main components of the overall network. G serves as what is commonly called a *bridge* or *broker*. In the reality of crime, a broker can play a crucial role in bridging cultural and language barriers between different criminal groups and milieus, facilitating the flow of information and bringing together complementary resources (Morselli, 2005; see also Zaitch, 2002, p. 252). Networks can be highly efficient, yet this does not preclude the formation of more integrated structures that resemble organizations in the narrow sense of the word.

Table 6.2 Key Concepts for Analyzing Criminal Organizations

Concept	Meaning	Application
Complexity	Vertical differentiation (hierarchy) Horizontal differentiation (division of labor) Spatial dispersion	All types of criminal organizations (illegal firms, criminal associations, underground governments)
Formalization	Degree to which roles and positions are explicitly defined independent from any particular individuals	All types of criminal organizations (illegal firms, criminal associations, underground governments)
Centralization	Degree of concentration of authority	All types of criminal organizations (illegal firms, criminal associations, underground governments)
Vertical integration	Incorporating segments up-stream and down-stream in the supply chain into a single organization (firm)	Illegal firms
Diversification	Expanding into different kinds of activities (markets)	All types of criminal organizations but best applicable to illegal firms

Source: Bedeian & Zamuto (1991), Hall (1982), Scott (1981)

Basic Categories for Analyzing Criminal Organizations

Organizations are social entities with some permanency resulting from the continuous commitment of individuals who yield to some form of control (Ahrne, 1990, p. 33). Organizations in general and criminal organizations in particular can be classified along different dimensions. The categories that are most often referred to in the organized crime literature include complexity, formalization, centralization, vertical integration, and diversification. These concepts can also be more or less usefully applied to the other two types of criminal structures: criminal associations and illegal quasi-governmental structures.

Complexity

The concept of complexity is used with broader and narrower meanings (see Southerland & Potter, 1993, pp. 253–254). Drawing on a conceptualization from the field of organization studies, three main parameters of complexity can be identified: vertical differentiation, horizontal differentiation, and spatial dispersion (Hall, 1982, p. 78).

Vertical differentiation refers to the number of hierarchical levels within an organization in terms of a chain of command (Hall, 1982, p. 81). A good example for a vertically differentiated criminal organization is provided by the families of the American Cosa Nostra, who in the past have had four levels of hierarchy with a boss at the top, followed by an underboss, several capos or lieutenants, and finally, subordinate to each capo, a number of ordinary members, also called soldiers or buttons (Cressey, 1969, pp. 113–115; Image 2.4, Chapter 2). From the boss down, the individuals on the higher level can give orders to those on the lower level (see Chapter 7).

Horizontal differentiation, also referred to as division of labor, is the degree to which tasks are divided among the members of an organization. The more tasks are performed by specialized individuals, the higher the horizontal differentiation. This is typical for illegal firms engaged in technically relative sophisticated activities—for example, the processing of cocaine or the altering of the identity of stolen cars—where the division of labor may be imposed by the technologies and procedures that are being employed or where the division of labor can at least result in significant increases in efficiency. The Lavin enterprise provides an example for a moderate level of division of labor. In 1981 it consisted of two main segments, a group of individuals led by Willie in charge of procuring the cocaine and a group including David, Suzanne, and Christine who handled the repackaging and selling of the cocaine. However, Willie was also involved in the repackaging. Within these two segments, there was a further division of labor—namely, between Suzanne, who kept the books, and Christine, who ran errands, while they both handled specific tasks jointly, including repackaging of cocaine and counting money (Bowden, 2001; Saline, 1989). In contrast, mafia groups such as the American Cosa Nostra families display *no* horizontal differentiation because their military-like structure is not differentiated into specialized tasks. Specific roles such as that of "enforcer," someone who enforces discipline and commits acts of violence on behalf of the organization, are not connected to a specific position and can be played by different members depending on the circumstances (Cressey, 1969, p. 165).

Spatial dispersion, the third main element of the concept of complexity, refers to the degree to which the members of an organization operate across geographical distances (Hall, 1982, p. 82). A high degree of spatial dispersion can be found in the case of some drug trafficking enterprises, which station representatives abroad (Soudijn & Huisman, 2011). In the Lavin case, something similar occurred with the rental of apartments in Florida that were used by drug couriers and to hide drugs (Bowden, 2001, p. 142; Saline, 1989, p. 73). Some mafia associations, such as the Calabrian 'Ndrangheta with units existing in different parts of Italy and in other countries, also show a high degree of spatial dispersion (Varese, 2011; see also Chapter 12).

Formalization

Formalization refers to the degree to which the behavior and the relations between the members of an organization are explicitly specified and defined independently of the individual characteristics of those occupying positions within the organization (Scott, 1981, p. 15). Illegal firms, it seems, usually have little or no formalized structures, as the roles individuals play tend to constantly shift (see, e.g., Zaitch, 2002). However, in the case of the Lavin enterprise, there were two positions defined by sets of tasks that remained largely unchanged irrespective of the individuals who occupied these positions. One was that of the main person in charge of bringing cocaine from Florida. The other position was that of day-to-day manager (Bowden, 2001; Saline, 1989). In contrast, associational structures can be highly formalized—for example, in the case of mafia organizations and outlaw motorcycle gangs. They not only have a formalized membership with standardized procedures for inducting new members but also defined positions within their hierarchical structure that have the same function and the same inherent authority irrespective of who holds that position. These issues will be reexamined in greater detail in the next chapter (Chapter 7).

Centralization

The concepts of complexity and formalization capture much of the structure of an organization, but they reveal little about the distribution of power. Vertical differentiation only refers to the number of levels of authority without specifying the degree to which authority is concentrated at the top or delegated from higher to lower levels down the chain of command. This is what the concepts of *centralization* and decentralization refer to. A highly centralized organization is characterized by a concentration of the decision-making authority in the hands of one person, whereas in a decentralized organization decisions are made independently by numerous individuals (Bedeian & Zamuto, 1991, p. 137; Hall, 1982, p. 114). Just as in the case of legal organizations (Bedeian & Zamuto, 1991, p. 137), most illegal organizations seem to fall somewhere between these two extremes.

An example for a highly centralized illegal firm is the Cali Cartel, a cocaine trafficking enterprise that was based in the Colombian city of Cali and headed by brothers Gilberto and Miguel Rodriguez Orejuela and their childhood friend Jose Santacruz Londono. All important decisions where reportedly made by the leadership in Cali and then transmitted via phone to front-line operatives. Miguel Rodriguez Orejuela in particular is said to have micromanaged the smuggling operations and the distribution within the United States

Image 6.3   Gilberto Rodriguez Orejuela, shortly before being extradited to the United States in December 2004. The older of the two brothers heading the Cali Cartel, Gilberto is said to have been responsible for the strategic planning while Miguel Rodriguez Orejuela micromanaged the drug trafficking business.

Photo: © Reuters/Corbis

and to have sent supervisors to the United States to monitor the performance of cartel operatives there (Chepesiuk, 2005, pp. 26, 88; Kenney, 2007, p. 248; Rempel, 2012, p. 24). While the organization had a number of specialized divisions dealing with the logistics of drug trafficking, money laundering, security, and corruption, these subunits had no authority to make their own decisions. All they were allowed to do was to make recommendations to the cartel leaders (Kenney, 1999a, p. 124). This management model required a level of communication and record keeping that made the organization vulnerable to law enforcement intervention. An intercepted telephone conversation on a one-ton shipment of cocaine led to the indictment of the two Rodriguez-Orejuela brothers in the United States and in Colombia and the seizure of extensive written and electronic records provided a wealth of additional evidence (Chepesiuk, 2005; Kenney, 1999a; Rempel, 2012)

In the case of the Lavin enterprise, strategic decisions seem to have been made solely by Larry Lavin. However, from 1980 onwards he delegated the day-to-day decisions to a manager, and it also seems that for some time the decision from what source to buy the cocaine was left to the respective individual who made the purchasing trips to Florida (Bowden, 2001, pp. 141, 194).

Vertical Integration

All of the categories discussed so far describe the structure of an organization irrespective of what the organization does. The concepts are universally applicable beyond the realm of business. An important concept that pertains specifically to business organizations and therefore also to illegal firms, is the concept of *vertical integration*. It refers to the segments of a production and distribution process that are handled by a single organization. Organizations may be integrating backwards to the acquisition of raw materials and forward into retail distribution (Bedeian & Zamuto, 1991, p. 233; Reuter, 1983, p. 117; Scott, 1981, p. 196).

The so-called Cali Cartel can once again serve as an example. Reportedly, the organization headed by the Rodriguez brothers and Santacruz incorporated all activities from the processing of cocaine to the wholesale distribution of two to three kilo consignments (Chepesiuk, 2005), which constitutes an extraordinarily high level of vertical integration. The Lavin enterprise, in contrast, displayed a low degree of vertical integration. It started out as a retail business for marijuana and in later years was confined to the wholesale distribution of cocaine (Bowden, 2001; Saline, 1989).

Diversification

Just like firms may incorporate different phases of a production and distribution process, they may also diversify to operate in numerous product and geographic markets at the same time (Reuter, 1983, p. 107). *Diversification* can serve to reduce the dependency on specific environmental conditions, and it can be a strategy for organizational growth (Bedeian & Zammuto, 1991). Some diversification on a limited scale can be observed among illegal firms, namely in the case of drug trafficking operations that handle different types of drugs

(Pearson & Hobbs, 2001, p. 9; Reuter, 1983, p. 129). The Lavin enterprise handled different types of drugs for some period of time but eventually specialized in cocaine (Bowden, 2001; Saline, 1989).

EXPLAINING THE STRUCTURE OF ILLEGAL FIRMS

This chapter so far has presented a conceptual framework for describing illegal entrepreneurial networks and illegal firms. It is now necessary to turn from description to *explanation* with regard to the ways in which criminals organize themselves around specific economic activities. Two issues are of main concern: (a) the circumstances under which criminals come to create illegal firms in the first place, and (b) the factors that account for specific structural features of illegal firms once they have come into existence.

The Emergence of Illegal Firms

Illegal firms are the most highly integrated forms of illegal entrepreneurial structures (compared to markets and mere networks). In an illegal firm, criminals commit themselves to a mechanism of coordination that, in comparison to market and network relations, limits individual autonomy and flexibility. It is not a given that illegal firms come into being at all, and where they appear it is not necessarily the result of conscious decisions (Van Duyne, 1997, p. 203).

Transaction Cost Economics

One explanation for the emergence of illegal firms comes from the field of economics and is tied to the notion of *transaction costs*. According to *transaction cost economics*, it is a matter of the relative costs whether transactions occur within a market setting or within a hierarchical business organization (Williamson, 1975; Williamson, 1985; Williamson, 1989). Drawing on this idea, Dwight C. Smith (1994) argues that illegal firms emerge over time when the benefits of organization outweigh the costs of organization. In other words, illegal firms only come into being and expand when this helps in reducing the costs of doing business compared to transactions that occur in a market or network setting (Smith, 1994, p. 133). For example, a drug trafficker who brings cocaine into the country via overseas containers may seek out accomplices for the handling of every new shipment. Each time the drug trafficker would have to find people for such tasks as clearing the container with customs, unloading the container, storing and repackaging the cocaine, and for handing the cocaine over to customers. The terms under which these accomplices participate would have to be negotiated anew with every incoming shipment. Alternatively, the drug trafficker may enter into permanent agreements with others to continuously carry out these tasks, either on a partnership basis or as employees. The result would be some form of an illegal firm.

In the case of repeated, complex transactions, Smith assumes that three factors determine whether these transactions are negotiated and carried out by autonomous entrepreneurs or within the confines of a firm: (a) bounded rationality, (b) opportunism, and (c) asset specificity (Smith, 1994, pp. 134–135).

The concept of *bounded rationality* refers to the limited capacity of individuals to consider all present and future circumstances that are relevant for a transaction. Organizations help in coping with bounded rationality—for example, in that they allow tackling problems in the sequence in which they arise rather than having to anticipate all potential problems at the time the terms of a transaction are negotiated (Williamson, 1975, pp. 25, 255).

Opportunism refers to "self-interest seeking with guile," manifested in "efforts to mislead, disguise, obfuscate, and confuse" (Smith, 1994, p. 135; Williamson, 1989, p. 139). An organization limits opportunism by subordinating both parties of a transaction to an overarching structure and restricting opportunities for acting in self-interest at the expense of others (Williamson, 1975, pp. 29–30).

Asset specificity means that certain resources such as specialized skills and machinery cannot be flexibly used for a variety of purposes (Williamson, 1989, pp. 142–143). Organizations respond to the asset specificity problem primarily in two ways. Necessary skills and other assets that are not readily available because they are so specific will tend to be incorporated into the organizational framework of a firm—for example, by hiring skilled laborers rather than relying on daily spot hiring. Once investments into specific resources have been made, an organization may protect these investments through backward and forward vertical integration (see above) to ensure the supply of raw materials and the distribution of goods and services (Smith, 1994, p. 135).

Transferred to the realm of illegal enterprise, transaction cost economics suggest that illegal firms may be a response to two key problems criminals face in interactions with other criminals: the problem of trust, respectively the lack of trust (opportunism) and the problem of obtaining information in a sphere characterized by secrecy (bounded rationality). Indeed, it appears plausible that as trust between criminals is built and reinforced over time with every successful joint endeavor, the interest in continuous collaboration will increase. This then gives rise to permanent forms of organization that provide a more efficient framework for dealing with unforeseen circumstances than one-time agreements. Take, for example, a drug shipment hidden in an overseas container that is delayed because of bad weather. When a vertically integrated drug trafficking organization handles both smuggling and wholesale distribution, this would be an internal problem. In contrast, where smugglers and wholesale dealers are independent parties (supplier and customer) in a contractual agreement, such a situation can lead to a conflict that may easily get out of hand. If supplier and customer have not agreed beforehand on how to cope with a delay in delivery because of bad weather, they would have to negotiate after the fact what the consequences should be. For example, is the buyer still obliged to take the drugs and pay the originally negotiated price? What if the buyer was forced to seek out an alternative source of supply in the meantime, possibly at a higher price?

In the case of the Lavin enterprise, asset specificity seems to have been the main driving force toward organizational cohesion. The key tasks of negotiating with suppliers and distributing the drugs were respectively handled by individuals who were taught specialized skills and were bound to the business as partners or as highly paid permanent employees (Bowden, 2001; Saline, 1989). However, there were no investments in specific assets that would have required backward or forward vertical integration. To the contrary, over the years the Lavin enterprise increasingly distanced itself from the retail level by ceasing to sell less than one kilo of cocaine at a time, while making no efforts to extend the activities of the firm to the importation of drugs (Saline, 1989, p. 118).

The Cali Cartel may be an example for vertical integration in response to asset specificity. The drug laboratories and the smuggling schemes it had set up constituted considerable investments (Chepesiuk, 2005) that called for a continuous flow of cocaine to customers. Integrating the processing of cocaine, the smuggling and wholesaling into one organization can be interpreted as a strategy to protect these investments.

Core and Periphery

Transaction cost economics suggest that illegal firms can be a rational response to certain challenges that crime entrepreneurs face. Some of these challenges seem to exist in the same way in the legal as well as in the illegal economy, namely, asset specificity. Others seem to be more prevalent in the illegal economy, namely, opportunism and bounded rationality. There is another factor unique to the illegal economy that may account for the emergence of illegal firms, the need for security from law enforcement. A pattern frequently observed, especially in the area of drug trafficking, is that entrepreneurs insulate themselves by recruiting others to carry out the most exposed tasks, such as transporting and storing drugs (Desroches, 2005, p. 123; Pearson & Hobbs, 2001, p. 33).

Dorn, Oette, and White (1998) describe this pattern as follows:

> A fully capitalized and risk-adverse smuggling organization has one or more number 1s, who interact only with one or more number 2s who are trusted and/or too fearful to give evidence against the number 1. The number 2s carry out at least that part of the organizing that involves hiring services from other, potentially less reliable number 3s, who may be considered expendable. The number 3s may be required simply to put distance between hazardous parts of the work and the number 1, the role of the courier being an obvious example, or because their legitimate role establishes useful cover, for example lorry drivers, or because they have specialist skills such as the ability to construct concealments. (Dorn, Oette, & White, 1998, p. 548)

Dorn et al. (1998, p. 552) argue that the peripheral participants, the number 3s, increase security because they have only limited knowledge of the organization and therefore have little information to offer to authorities should they be apprehended. At the same time, they point out that this strategy is costly and characteristic only for well-funded entrepreneurs. Carlo Morselli, drawing on his analyses of criminal networks, likewise suggests that seeking insulation through peripheral individuals "is typically a luxury" (Morselli, 2009b, p. 159).

This appears to be even truer for illegal entrepreneurs who draw on a number of peripheral participants and task them separately with carrying out the same

Figure 6.3   Factors Believed to Influence the Size and Complexity of Illegal Firms

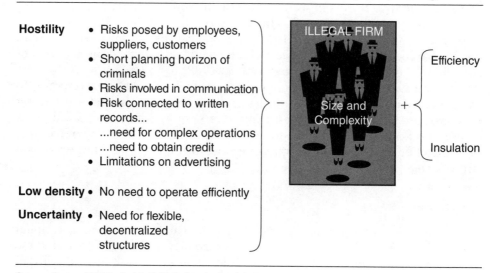

Hostility
- Risks posed by employees, suppliers, customers
- Short planning horizon of criminals
- Risks involved in communication
- Risk connected to written records...
  ...need for complex operations
  ...need to obtain credit
- Limitations on advertising

Low density • No need to operate efficiently

Uncertainty • Need for flexible, decentralized structures

Efficiency

Insulation

Source: Reuter (1983), Smith (1994), Southerland & Potter (1993)

kind of activity, for example operating labs for the production of synthetic drugs (Chiu, Leclerc, & Townsley, 2011, p. 366). These redundancies reduce the impact of law enforcement intervention because the discovery of individual labs will not stop the operation of the enterprise as a whole (Williams, 2001, pp. 80–81). At the same time, the duplication of tasks creates additional costs.

The Consequences of Illegality for the Structure of Illegal Firms

The discussion of the factors that may contribute to the emergence of illegal firms is part of a broader discussion of the consequences of illegality for how economic relations are shaped and structured. Much of the discussion pertains specifically to illegal firms, but the implications for the most part also extend to illegal entrepreneurial structures (including networks and markets) more generally.

Cliché imagery of organized crime is centered on large, hierarchical criminal organizations with close resemblance to corporate, governmental or military structures. In the academic literature, in contrast, there is a strong assumption that illegal structures tend to be smaller, less complex, and to have a shorter life span than legal structures. Illegal firms in particular are believed to "have relatively simple structures" (Southerland & Potter, 1993, p. 254) and are "localized, fragmented, ephemeral, and undiversified" (Reuter, 1983, p. 131). R. T. Naylor even goes so far as to say that illegal firms do not exist separate from individual entrepreneurs, who in turn are embedded in broader illegal networks and markets (Naylor, 2002, p. 20). However, the empirical evidence is somewhat ambiguous (Bouchard & Ouellet, 2011). Some scholars acknowledge the fluid and ephemeral nature of many entrepreneurial structures while also pointing to the existence of organizational entities with some coherence and permanency in structure (Fijnaut, Bovenkerk, Bruinsma, &

Van de Bunt, 1998; Larsson, 2009; Mackenzie & Davis, 2014; Van Duyne, 1996; von Lampe, 2003b; Zaitch, 2002). In fact, there is some evidence that contrary to the notion of small, ephemeral illegal enterprises, there is a tendency for illegal firms to emerge, to grow, and to become more heterogeneous in makeup the larger the volume of its business. This means that, as more is at stake and the risks increase—for example, along with the size of contraband shipments, illegal firms increase in size and in complexity as well as in the diversity of their membership (Gamella & Jimenez Rodrigo, 2008; von Lampe, 2007; see also Arlacchi, 1986, p. 202; Van Duyne, 1997, p. 206; Van Duyne, 2006, p. 185).

Of central importance in this discussion is the work of Peter Reuter, arguably the main proponent of an economic analysis of organized crime. The consequences of illegality for participants in illicit economic activities, according to Reuter (1983, pp. 109, 114), are twofold:

- Participants face the threat of police intervention, which may entail the seizing of assets and arrest and imprisonment or other forms of punishment.
- Agreements cannot be enforced in a court of law. More generally, participants cannot have recourse to the police or courts in cases of conflict.

These fundamental consequences of illegality may influence illegal entrepreneurial structures in different ways as illegal entrepreneurs negotiate between security and efficiency (Morselli, Giguere, & Petit, 2007).

Restrictions on Employment

The most immediate consequence of illegality, as Reuter argues, "is the need to control the flow of information about participation in the illegal activity" (Reuter, 1983, p. 114). This pertains to the number of individuals who share information as well as to the amount of information that is being shared. For an illegal firm, it means that every supplier and customer and every employee poses a risk. This risk can be reduced by limiting the number of individuals an entrepreneur interacts with and by using incentives (financial rewards) or disincentives (threat or use of violence) to induce loyal behavior (see Chapter 5). An entrepreneur can also try to "create positive noneconomic ties with employees" or draw on preexisting ties of this nature, namely by recruiting friends and relatives (Reuter, 1983, p. 116). However, these strategies are costly, or they are restricted to a limited pool of recruits who may not have the necessary skills, so that in the end, Reuter (1983, p. 117) assumes, illegal firms tend to be small (see also Hammersvik, Sandberg, & Pedersen, 2012).

Reuter also argues that with the number of employees in an illegal enterprise the risk of factionalism and internal conflict increases (Reuter, 1983, p. 146). Yet another consequence of illegality that restrains employment, according to Reuter, is that the planning time horizons of illegal entrepreneurs tend to be shorter than those of legal entrepreneurs in light of the threat of arrest and punishment but also the threat of a violent death. This reduces the incentives for entering into long-term employment relationships and to invest in the development of specific skills (Reuter, 1983, p. 119).

Restrictions on Written Records

The need to control the flow of information not only influences the extent to which an entrepreneur communicates with suppliers, customers, partners, and employees, but it also influences the form in which information is passed on and stored. Written records present an obvious risk. They may reveal the nature and extent of illegal activities and the identity of those involved and thereby can constitute damning evidence in criminal investigations (Reuter, 1983, p. 120).

Despite these risks, a variety of illegal firms have been found to use extensive written (or electronic) records of their activities. There seems to be a tendency to keep records where activities are voluminous and complex. It may be difficult to keep track of customers and customer-specific arrangements, or records may be required to determine payouts among partners and to employees who work on a commission basis.

A typical example for illegal firms relying on written records is presented by the traditional illegal lotteries, so-called numbers lotteries, in the United States. Numbers lotteries accept bets on a three-digit number with payout rates typically between 500 to 1 and 600 to 1. Bets are taken by collectors and recorded on betting slips, which are passed on to a "bank," the logistical center of a numbers operation. The bank determines the winners and amounts of payout and passes this information on to the collectors who pay out winnings. In regular intervals, typically every week, accounts between the bank and the collectors are settled, so that each collector ends up with no more and no less than the agreed-upon share of earnings. The written records of a numbers lottery are used not only to determine winners and to settle accounts with collectors but also as proof in the case of conflict, especially when customers claim that they have bet on the winning number (Liddick, 1999a; Reuter, 1983).

Other examples of extensive record keeping include the Cali Cartel. Each of its four wholesale branches in the United States had to keep identical sets of records, which later allowed authorities to determine the volume of their business (Chepesiuk, 2005, p. 47). Additional business records were kept by an accountant in Cali (Rempel, 2012, p. 75). The Lavin enterprise likewise relied on extensive bookkeeping to calculate payouts linked to profit and turnover, and detailed records were kept about customer preferences for the cutting and packaging of cocaine. In addition, Lavin stored the names and telephone numbers of his customers on a handheld computer (Saline, 1989, p. 229).

Restrictions on the Expansion of Business

Where entrepreneurs are more risk averse and avoid written records, it is assumed that illegal firms are limited in the scale and complexity of the activities they can engage in, which in turn is expected to result in illegal firms being small and simple in structure (Potter, 1994, pp. 165, 167).

The absence of written records, according to Reuter, also curtails the growth of illegal firms because it prevents the development of an external capital market. In order to obtain credit or to attract investors, an illegal firm cannot present audited books. Instead, creditors and investors have to rely on assurances about the profitability of the business or they have to become directly involved in the management in order to be able to effectively monitor its performance (Reuter, 1983, p. 120).

The growth of illegal firms may also be impeded because they cannot expand their customer base in the same way legal firms can. With every customer, illegal firms face risks similar to those posed by business partners and employees, because every customer is likewise a potential informant and witness (Reuter, 1983, p. 149). In addition, illegal firms, even if they are willing to accept these risks, are limited in their ability to attract customers. Illegal firms cannot readily advertise their products or establish brand loyalty. Advertising would attract law enforcement attention. At the same time, illegal firms have no recourse to the laws that protect brand property rights in the legal economy. This means that where illegal entrepreneurs try to establish a brand—for example, in the area of synthetic drugs—they are vulnerable to counterfeiting by other illegal entrepreneurs (Duterte, Jacinto, Sales & Murphy, 2009).

Restrictions on the Complexity of Illegal Firms

The risks emanating from the flow of information increase with the number of individuals an illegal entrepreneur interacts with but also with the complexity of an organization. Complex organizations require extensive internal communication to monitor the performance of subunits (Reuter, 1983, p. 127), especially in light of the pervasiveness of cheating by employees (Reuter, 1983, p. 147). In addition, communication channels have to exist up and down the chain of command to provide the management with the up-to-date information needed to make sound decisions and then to transmit these decisions to subunits. This problem can be illustrated with an anecdote about the Cali Cartel. A truckload of cocaine was supposed to be delivered to a warehouse in Texas. When the individuals making the delivery realized that the warehouse was staked out by law enforcement agents, they tried in vain to contact their Cartel superiors to get new instructions. Fearing that they might be killed if they did not follow their orders, they delivered the cocaine to the warehouse only, of course, to be promptly arrested (Chepesiuk, 2005, p. 153).

The alternative to such a centralized business model would be a decentralized structure where rules and formalized procedures define acceptable behavior that does not require the explicit approval of supervisors. In the extreme, decentralization leads to a segmented structure within which subunits are given broad autonomy, bordering on the dissolution of the organization as a coherent entity (Potter, 1994, p. 167).

Environmental Factors

So far, illegal firms have been discussed with regard to two aspects, the conditions under which illegal firms emerge in the first place and the constraints that are imposed on the size and complexity of illegal firms. This still leaves some questions unanswered about how illegal firms, to the extent they exist at all, are shaped and structured.

The Spectrum-Based Theory of Enterprise

One answer to the question why illegal firms are organized in particular ways is provided by Dwight C. Smith's spectrum-based theory of enterprise (Smith, 1975, pp. 335–347; Smith, 1978; Smith, 1980; Smith, 1982), which has already been highlighted in Chapter 3. The spectrum-based theory is a sophisticated variation of the popular notion that there are fundamental similarities between criminal organizations and legitimate businesses. Smith ties these assumed similarities to core technologies, a concept that he borrowed from organization theorist James Thompson (1967).

Core technologies are the processes by which a business generates and markets its products (Smith, 1975, p. 337). According to Smith, illegal businesses may vary greatly in the ways they are organized—for example, when one compares loansharking with the sale of illegal alcohol. At the same time, greater similarities may exist between certain illegal and legal businesses. A loansharking business has greater similarities with a bank than with a speakeasy serving illegal liquor, because loan-sharks and banks share the core technology of lending money. Simply because of the external criterion of legality, Smith argues, loan-sharks and banks are positioned on opposite ends of the "spectrum of legitimacy" (Smith, 1978, pp. 172–173). In other words, just like the logistics of loansharking mirrors to some extent the logistics of money lending by a legitimate bank, illegal firms generally are largely shaped by what they do.

A second factor that is considered in the spectrum-based theory of enterprise is the specific context within which an illegal firm operates. Again drawing on Thompson (1967), Smith argues that the structure of an illicit enterprise is not determined by the core technology alone. A business is also influenced by its task environment. The *task environment* comprises external conditions that enable a business to function and, at the same time, offer hazards to its continuance (Smith, 1975; Smith, 1978; Smith, 1980).

Later, Smith reemphasized this point with a reference to multiple-constituencies theory (MCT) according to which organizations are not the initiators but the result of action. Organizations, MCT theory argues, are continuously shaped and reshaped in exchanges between various stakeholders, namely suppliers and customers (Smith, 1994, pp. 132–133; see also Halstead, 1998).

Uncertainty, Density and Hostility of the Environment

Another example of the adoption of conceptual frameworks from organization theory to the study of organized crime is provided by Southerland and Potter (1993) and Potter (1994). They discuss how the structure of illegal firms is potentially affected by the broader environment within which they operate. Gary Potter (1994) has identified three dimensions of the environment in particular which may potentially account for how illegal firms are shaped and structured: uncertainty, density, and hostility.

Uncertainty exists to the degree the environment is too complex to be fully understood and future developments cannot be anticipated (Bedeian & Zammuto, 1991, p. 522; Thompson, 1967, pp. 69–70; Williamson, 1975,

p. 23). Under conditions of uncertainty, organizations tend to develop specialized, decentralized structures that can quickly process information and respond to any sudden changes in the environment. In a stable, simple environment, a centralized structure is appropriate (see Thompson, 1967, pp. 70–73).

Potter assumes that the uncertainty of the environment varies with the type of activity an illegal firm is engaged in. While a numbers lottery faces a relatively certain, predictable environment, a drug dealer is confronted with constant changes in products, suppliers, customers, and prices. The structure of a numbers lottery, according to Potter, is therefore fairly centralized and displays a low level of complexity. In contrast, Potter assumes that heroin-trafficking organizations need to be informal and decentralized (Potter, 1994, pp. 168–170). This also seems to be true in the case of the Lavin enterprise where Larry Lavin delegated authority, for example, to those in charge of procuring drugs in Florida (Bowden, 2001, pp. 141, 194).

Density, according to Potter's conceptualization, "is a combination of two factors: the number of organizations that seek to exploit a given environmental niche and the availability of resources in that niche" (Potter, 1994, p. 170). A high-density environment exists either in a resource-poor environment with few organizations or in a resource-rich environment with a large number of organizations. Potter argues that for various reasons illegal firms tend to operate in environments with low density and are under little pressure to increase efficiency by investing in complex technologies and by developing complex structures with, for example, an elaborate division of labor. One factor cited by Potter is the so-called *crime tariff,* the risk premium illegal entrepreneurs can add to the price of illegal goods and services to compensate for the risk of apprehension (Packer, 1964; Potter, 1994, pp. 125, 170; Wisotsky, 1990, pp. 34–35). Another factor is that through law enforcement efforts, a certain number of illegal firms are culled out (Potter, 1994, p. 170). The Lavin enterprise seems to confirm this view. It existed parallel to other, less complex and less efficiently run operations, namely, that of Frannie who eventually took over Lavin's business (Bowden, 2001, p 222). There is no indication that any of these businesses was under pressure to increase efficiency in order to survive.

The third and most important environmental factor influencing the structure of illegal firms, according to Potter, is *hostility.* It refers on one hand, to the intensity with which the laws are enforced that illegal firms break, and on the other hand, to the degree to which communities are willing to support law enforcement (Potter, 1994, pp. 163–164). The assumption is that illegal firms in a hostile environment are severely restrained in their development while in a more tolerant or even supportive environment large, more durable and more complex structures may develop (Bouchard & Ouellet, 2011).

The hostility of the environment, it is assumed, varies with the type of criminal activity. In the United States, for example, illegal gambling has traditionally been tolerated more than drug trafficking in terms of the resources invested in law enforcement, the severity of punishment, and public attitudes (Morris & Hawkins, 1970; Potter, 1994; Reuter, 1983). This provides an additional explanation for why, at least in the United States, illegal lotteries have tended to be larger and more complex structures than drug trafficking operations.

ILLEGAL ENTREPRENEURIAL STRUCTURES: SUMMARY AND CONCLUSION

This chapter has discussed how criminals organize themselves around illegal economic activities and how the patterns of relations between these criminals are predicated by the particular activity engaged in. Under the general category of illegal entrepreneurial structures, three ideal types of coordinating mechanisms have been distinguished: illegal markets, illegal entrepreneurial networks, and illegal firms—the latter in the sense of coherent organizational entities. Focusing specifically on networks and organizations, it has been pointed out that because of the fluidity of illegal entrepreneurial structures the boundaries of illegal firms may be fleeting and that it may be a matter of perspective whether to analyze a given structure in terms of networks or organizations.

The main emphasis of this chapter has been on the factors that potentially influence how illegal entrepreneurial structures are shaped. A number of structural features of networks and organizations were highlighted as well as a number of ways in which illegality imposes constraints on the organization of criminals. However, it must be cautioned that it would be an oversimplification to assume that illegal firms are always and inevitably small and ephemeral. Under favorable circumstances, illegal firms can grow to be quite large, complex, and durable, and sometimes organizational growth is a means to cope with a hostile environment, namely, by adding layers of peripheral employees to insulate a core group of criminal entrepreneurs. What is most remarkable about illegal entrepreneurial structures, then, is the great variety in the patterns of relations connecting criminals engaged in illegal economic activity.

Discussion Questions

1. Is it possible to run and organize an illegal business just like a legal business?

2. What difference does it make if a particular illegal economic activity—for example, the distribution of drugs—is carried out by an illegal firm rather than within a less integrated illegal entrepreneurial network?

3. Is it wise for an illegal entrepreneur to insulate him- or herself from the actual commission of crimes through the use of "expendable" employees?

Research Projects

1. Analyze the autobiography of an organized criminal with a view to the way illegal economic activities are structured in terms of markets, networks, and hierarchies.

2. Analyze the autobiography of an organized criminal with a view to how much effort is placed on increasing security versus increasing the efficiency of illegal economic activities.

Further Reading

Illegal Enterprises

Andersson, H. (2003). Illegal entrepreneurs: A comparative study of the liquor trade in Stockholm and New Orleans 1920–1940. *Journal of Scandinavian Studies in Criminology and Crime Prevention, 3*(2), 114–134.

Levi, M. (1998). Organising plastic fraud: Enterprise criminals and the side-stepping of fraud prevention. *Howard Journal, 37*(4), 423–438.

Malm, A., & Bichler, G. (2011). Networks of collaborating criminals: Assessing the structural vulnerability of drug markets. *Journal of Research in Crime and Delinquency, 48*(2), 271–297.

Ruggiero, V., & Khan, K. (2007). The organisation of drug supply: South Asian criminal enterprise in the UK. *Asian Journal of Criminology, 2*(2), 163–177.

Zabludoff, S. J. (1997). Colombian narcotics organizations as business enterprises. *Transnational Organized Crime, 3*(2), 20–49.

Transaction Cost Economics and Illegal Entrepreneurial Structures

Dick, A. R. (1995). When does organized crime pay? A transaction analysis. *International Review of Law and Economics, 15*(1), 25–46.

Moeller, K. (2012). Costs and revenues in street-level cannabis dealing. *Trends in Organized Crime, 15*(1), 31-46.

Moyle, B. (2009). The black market in China for tiger products. *Global Crime, 10*(1–2), 124–143.

CHAPTER 7

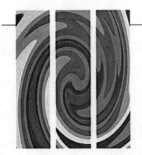

Associational Structures

INTRODUCTION

This chapter continues the examination of the three basic types of structures that define the organization of criminals: entrepreneurial structures, associational structures, and quasi-governmental structures. The previous chapter discussed entrepreneurial structures that link criminals who interact in the commission of one or a number of crimes. Entrepreneurial structures, by definition, are centered on economic activities in a broad sense. They are geared toward attaining financial or other material benefits through market-based crime (e.g., drug dealing) or predatory crime (e.g., burglary). In contrast to illegal *entrepreneurial* structures, this chapter examines *associational* structures, which support illegal economic activities only indirectly, by serving functions of a social nature. For example, associational structures facilitate contacts between criminals; they give status, reinforce deviant values, and provide a forum for the exchange of criminally relevant information (Haller, 1992).

In accordance with the terminology of the previous chapters, *structure* is used as a generic term. The term *associational structure* refers to a wide range of patterns of relations. In contrast, the term *association* as used here pertains more narrowly to organizational entities with a coherent structure and some degree of formalization, especially with regard to the definition of membership.

CASE STUDIES OF ASSOCIATIONS OF CRIMINALS

Before systematically examining the structure and functions of associational structures, case studies of four notorious associations of criminals are presented. These associations have received considerable attention in the debate on organized crime: the Sicilian Mafia (Cosa Nostra), Chinese triads, focusing primarily on Hong Kong-based triads, the criminal fraternity Vory v Zakone (Thieves in Law), which originated in the Soviet Union, and the Hell's Angels, as one manifestation of the phenomenon of so-called outlaw motorcycle gangs. The term *illegal* associational structures is intentionally avoided here because outlaw motorcycle gangs are not necessarily illegal organizations per se.

Case Study: The Sicilian Mafia (Cosa Nostra)

The Sicilian Mafia, also known as Cosa Nostra, has been at the center of a fierce academic debate for decades. Scholars have held fundamentally different views about the nature and purpose of the Sicilian Mafia and have disagreed on whether or not it constitutes an organizational entity at all. Some have argued that the Mafia is simply a method in a power play or a cultural trait, a way of life inextricably linked to Sicilian culture (see Hess, 1996, pp. 10–13). This view is no longer tenable, however. Based on the testimony of numerous mafiosi who have become state witnesses, it can now be considered an established fact that the Sicilian Mafia is indeed a coherent organization made up exclusively of men—to the exclusion of women and children—who belong to one of about one hundred local units, so-called families or *cosche* (Paoli, 2003a, p. 5). The Mafia is "a formal, secret association, with rigorous rules of conduct, decision-making bodies, specific functions, plans of action, and clearly defined admissions procedures" (Arlacchi, 1993, p. 6). What is still in dispute is the exact purpose and structure of this secret association and how important the overall organization is compared to the individual families and individual members.

One key aspect that will be discussed further in later chapters (Chapter 8 and Chapter 10) is the role of individual families of the Sicilian Mafia in controlling and regulating illicit and licit economic activities in certain parts of Sicily and beyond. According to one study, an estimated 70 percent of shops in Sicily and 80 percent of all businesses in the city of Palermo pay protection money to the Sicilian Mafia (as cited in Partridge, 2012, p. 345). It is with reference to this quasi-governmental function that Diego Gambetta speaks of the Sicilian Mafia as "a specific economic enterprise, an industry which produces, promotes, and sells private protection" (Gambetta, 1993, p. 1).

In the present context of associational criminal structures, the focus is on the Sicilian Mafia in terms of a "secret society," a "criminal fraternity" (Paoli, 2003a, p. 87). As such it is said to serve two main functions: (a) protection of its members' interests—namely, those interests that are linked to illegal activities, through mutual aid and support—and (b) avoidance and resolution of conflicts among its members through a system of rules and procedures (Arlacchi, 1993, p. 8; Lupo, 2009, p. 27).

The origins of the Mafia go back to the 1800s. At that time, a power vacuum existed in Sicily in the wake of the abolition of feudalism and the struggles of the newly formed state of Italy to establish its authority (Paoli, 2003a, p. 179). In the western parts of Sicily, the area of the port city of Palermo where agriculture and commerce prospered, the power vacuum was filled by groups who offered private protection services to landowners, farmers, and merchants (Catanzaro, 1992; Gambetta, 1993). A number of these groups came to share the same freemasonic rituals and oaths. Why these groups took cues from freemasons and arrived at a standardized form of organization is not clear. Salvatore

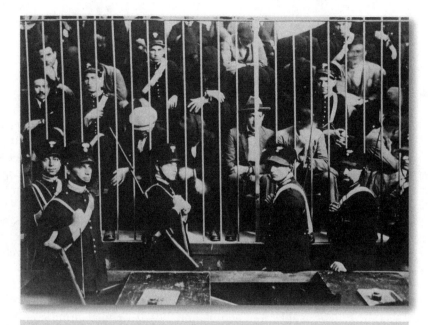

Image 7.1   Suspected Mafiosi stand trial in Palermo, Sicily, in 1928, the year that marked the conclusion of a massive campaign of suppression launched in 1925 by the fascist Italian government. Thousands were rounded up and sent to prison under suspicion of being connected to the Mafia. The campaign directed by prefect Cesare Mori is believed to also have prompted several Mafiosi to leave Italy, mostly for the United States (Lupo, 2009, p. 174; Varese, 2011, p. 105).

Photo: Bettmann/Corbis

Lupo suggests that this process is an outgrowth of a "far broader phenomenon of popular associationism" and reflects the popularity of freemasonry in Sicily during the second half of the 19th Century. Lupo also assumes that the standardization was facilitated by members of different groups being confined together, particularly in Palermo's Ucciardone prison (Lupo, 2009, p. 49; see also Paoli, 2003a, pp. 40, 101–104). It seems that the sharing of initiation rituals, codes of behavior, and a sense of quasi-religious unity facilitated the mutual recognition of potentially competing groups (see Gambetta, 1993, p. 154).

The external boundaries of Cosa Nostra are clearly defined through formalized membership. Before novices are formally inducted into Cosa Nostra, more specifically a particular Cosa Nostra family, they go through a period of observation and training by older members to assure that they adhere to the Mafia "subuniverse of meaning" (Paoli, 2003a, p. 91). They also have to commit a murder or other violent act to demonstrate their strength and courage (Paoli, 2003a, p. 74).

The initiation ceremony, in which the novice is introduced to the members of the family and is advised of a set of conduct rules, culminates in the swearing of a solemn oath. The index finger of the candidate's right hand is cut or pricked so that blood drips on the image of a saint, usually Our Lady of the Annunciation. The image of the saint is then set on fire in the hand of the candidate who has to declare: "I burn you as a paper, I adore you as a saint; as this paper burns, so my flesh must burn if I betray the Cosa Nostra" (as cited in Paoli, 2003a, p. 68; see also Gambetta, 1993, pp. 146, 268).

According to Letizia Paoli (2003, p. 5) the Sicilian Mafia counts "at least thirty-five hundred full members." They come from all layers of society, including doctors, lawyers, and priests, with the notable exception of judges and police officers, although the majority of mafiosi are said to be businessmen (Arlacchi, 1993, pp. 38–39).

The Mafia initiation is a "rite of passage," a "symbolic representation of death and resurrection" (Paoli, 2003a, p. 67). It creates a sense of belonging to an elite community of "men of honor," and it establishes ritual kinship ties that promote trust and entail obligations of correctness and solidarity vis-à-vis the other members. These ties provide the basis for collaboration between members on a wide range of endeavors, even between members from different families who have never met before (Paoli, 2003a, pp. 81, 89, 150). This does not mean, however, that the relationships between Mafia members have always been harmonious. On the contrary, growing tensions between mafiosi adhering to traditional values of humility and honor and mafiosi engaging in the profitable drug trade have been blamed for violent internal conflicts and widespread distrust within the Sicilian Mafia (Catanzaro, 1992, p. 107; Paoli, 2003a, p. 93).

The basic unit of the Cosa Nostra is the family or *cosca*, which may range in size from a handful to more than a hundred members (Gambetta, 1993, p. 111–112). Each family is headed by a *capo* (boss), also known as *rappresentante*, who is normally elected by the members on a yearly basis (Gambetta, 1993, p. 111; Paoli, 2003a, p. 42), even though in a number of cases individual men of honor have come to power through violence (Paoli, 2003a, p. 43). To counterbalance the authority of the *capo*, families have one or more elected *consiglieri* (counselors) who participate in important decisions (Arlacchi, 1993, pp. 34–35; Paoli, 2003a, p. 40). In larger families, members are organized in subunits under so-called *capidecina* (Arlacchi, 1993, p. 33; Gambetta, 1993, p. 111).

The head of a family and the *capidecina* constitute a hierarchical structure subjecting individual members to strict obedience (Paoli, 2003a, p. 83). However, the exercise of power is constrained by tradition and the need to legitimize decisions. As Letizia Paoli argues: "Even in areas that are left to his discretion, the leader is supposed to rule in the interest of all members and is largely dependent on their willingness to comply with his orders, since he has no means to enforce them" (Paoli, 2003a, p. 44). A different picture emerges in cases where individuals have assumed control over a family by means of violence and can rely on an "administrative staff" of loyal followers to impose their will (Paoli, 2003a, p. 45).

Initially, beginning in the mid-1800s, Cosa Nostra constituted an organizational entity through standardized rituals and the mutual recognition of individual families and of the status of their members as men of honor. Tattoos and other signs of recognition such as ritual sentences and gestures were used for some time to identify each other but have since been replaced by the strict rule that members must be introduced by a third member who knows the status of both (Gambetta, 1993, p. 123; Paoli, 2003a, p. 113).

It was not until the mid-1900s that efforts were made to create an overarching organizational structure in the form of coordinating bodies on the provincial level and beyond. These bodies, called *commissione* or *cupola*, were established to regulate conflicts between families and also within families. For example, members have not been allowed to kill another member without approval by the respective provincial commission (Gambetta, 1993, p. 113; Paoli, 2003a, p. 128). The *commissione*, to protect common interests, also imposed prohibitions on certain illegal activities, namely, kidnapping for ransom (Lupo, 2009, p. 238), and it has restricted the killing of representatives of legitimate society, such as politicians and judges (Paoli, 2003a, pp. 53–54).

Mafia groups are not economic enterprises aimed at the maximization of profits. Profit-making activities are not systematically planned or coordinated by each *cosca* or by the Cosa Nostra as a whole, although, illicit activities are sometimes run by the heads of single families and the profits divided more or less equally between the affiliates (Paoli, 2003a, p. 144). The only illegal activity run by a Mafia family as a whole is extortion, respectively the provision of protection, within the territory under its control (Gambetta, 1993, p. 227; Paoli, 2003a, p. 170). In this respect, Mafia families function as neither an illegal enterprise nor as an associational structure but as a quasi-governmental entity, as will be discussed in Chapter 8.

Case Study: The Hong Kong Triads

Triads are fraternal organizations originating in China. They are most prevalent in Hong Kong and Taiwan but are believed to also have established a presence within overseas Chinese communities and, more recently, in mainland China (Chu, 2000, p. 13; Lo, 2010, p. 857). The term *triad* is an English designation referring to the symbol of the triad societies, a triangle representing the union of heaven, earth, and man (Ip, 1999, p. 3).

The origins of the triads are traced back to a secret society called Hung Mun or Tiandihui (Heaven and Earth Society), which is shrouded in mystery. According to a widely held assumption, the Hung Mun dates back to the time following the Manchurian conquest of China in the mid-1600s and was formed to overthrow the Manchurians and to reestablish the ancient Ming Dynasty (Kwok & Lo, 2013, p. 74). Another view holds that the Hung Mun was a mutual-aid society created in 1761 or 1762 "to resolve the conflict among various migratory dialect groups in the southern regions of Fujian province in mid-eighteenth century China" (Chu, 2000, p. 3). The primary purpose of the Hung Mun or Tiandihui, Chu (2000, p. 12) explains, "was to form pseudo-familial networks among unacquainted people through the rituals of sworn brotherhood for mutual protection." Various means of recognition, such as passwords, poems, signs, and secret gestures, allowed members to identify each other. This organization, according to Chu, was involved in various crimes early on, especially "the selling of private protection to those who needed to travel frequently," and it was declared illegal in 1786 (Chu, 2000, p. 12). Since then, numerous triad societies have been formed in the tradition of the Hung Mun. Their original purpose may not necessarily have been criminal, but it is commonly believed that over the past decades crime has become central to their existence (Chu, 2000, pp. 11, 20; Kwok & Lo, 2013, p. 74). The 14K triad, for example, was originally a pro-Nationalist organization formed in Guangdong province in the mid-1940s. After the Communist Party assumed power, 14K members escaped to Hong Kong, where they regrouped to protect each other against triad extortion and eventually emerged as a notorious triad society themselves (Chu, 2000, p. 134).

Triad members consider themselves "part of the universal triad brother-hood," and members of different triad societies socialize and collaborate with each other and feel an obligation for mutual protection (Chu, 2000, pp. 19, 36, 137; see also Ip, 1999, p. 5; Lo, 2010, p. 852). Triad societies are supposed to respect each other's spheres of influence (Chu, 2000, p. 38). Since the 1990s, however, competition over territory as well as internal conflicts have increased (Chu, 2000, p. 30; Lo, 2010, p. 852).

There are 50 known triad societies in Hong Kong, of which 15 to 20 "regularly come to the attention of the police by their involvement in crime," including the 14K (Chu, 2000, pp. 135–136; Ip, 1999, p. 3). The largest, most influential and most cohesive triad society, however, is said to be Sun Yee On, with tens of thousands of members, while others may have only about 100 members (Chu, 2000, p. 136; Lo, 2010, p. 855).

The structure of triad societies varies. In essence they are rather loose combi-nations of individual gangs. Some triads "may exist in name only because their triad gangs cooperate only on an ad hoc basis" (Chu, 2000, p. 29). Most triad societies have a "central committee" composed of influential and senior mem-bers that elect a chairperson and treasurer at an annual or biannual meeting (Chu, 2000, p. 27; Ip, 1999, p. 3). In the case of the Sun Yee On, the leading members reportedly come from the same family (Chu, 2000, p. 137). The cen-tral committee's power is limited. It controls promotions, supervises internal discipline, and settles internal and external disputes. But triad leaders "are not likely to dictate to their members in which criminal activities they should get involved," and apart from payments on special occasions, such as initiation ceremonies, promotions, and the Chinese New Year, they do not generally receive any shares of the profits from the members' activities (Chu, 2000, p. 27; see also Ip, 1999, p. 4; Kwok & Lo, 2013, p. 85).

In contrast, the gangs that belong to a given triad society are hierarchically structured organizational units. The gangs are often territorially based. They are headed by a boss and may comprise a group of fifteen or twenty core members who in turn may have street gangs and youth gangs at their disposal (Chu, 2000, pp. 28–29). It is at the level of these street gangs and youth gangs that triads most often come to the attention of the police (Ip, 1999, p. 5).

Triad members are divided into mainly three rank categories: office bearer (426 or *red pole*), ordinary member (49), and affiliated member (*hanging the blue lantern*) (Chu, 2000, p. 39; Kwok & Lo, 2013, p. 75). Affiliated members are verbally accepted to join a triad without going through the formal initiation ceremony. Allegiance may have been shown by having paid a *red packet* (sum of money) or having verbally pledged loyalty to a triad member (Kwok & Lo, 2013, p. 82). Full membership depends on the passing of an initiation ritual. Recruits have to be sponsored by a triad official, and names of prospective recruits have to be submitted to the society for approval (Chu, 2000, p. 31). A typical ceremony is described by Chu as follows:

> The recruit, accompanied by his sponsor, is first informed of the history of the triads and reminded that his initiation must be completely voluntary. He takes an oath before an altar which is decorated to represent the mythical triad capital of Muk Yeung. He is then warned of the fate of traitors, swears loyalty to his brothers which may include drinking a mixture of his own blood and that of other initiates, and pays a symbolic sum of lucky money as a form of joining fee. At the end of the ceremony the recruit is taught some recognition signals and triad poems so that he can recognise fellow members. (Chu, 2000, p. 33)

The obligations of loyalty and secrecy as well as mutual aid are core elements of the triad code of conduct (Chu, 2000, pp. 3, 19). In this respect, triads are similar to other illegal associations. One element that sets them apart is their apparent openness to female members. While triads are predominantly male organizations, there are a small number of women who are full (49) triad members (Chu, 2000, p. 139; T. Wing Lo, personal communication, 2 February 2013). Since the 1990s, triads have also expanded their membership to nonethnic Chinese to recruit locally born Indian and Pakistani youth as junior members (Chu, 2000, p. 137).

Triad membership, according to Ip, is "a lubricant which facilitates personal contacts and co-operation between different triad groups or individuals" (Ip, 1999, p. 4) and it gives individuals a level of security non-member criminals do not possess (Chu, 2000, p. 93). Triad members are involved in a wide range of activities individually or jointly with members and non-members (Lo, 2010, p. 852). They are most prominent in the illegal provision of protection services, extortion, and certain aspects of the prostitution business (Chu, 2000), while in other areas of crime, such as drug trafficking and human smuggling, their role appears to be limited (Ip, 1999; Zhang & Chin, 2002).

Case Study: Vory v Zakone (Thieves in Law)

The Vory v Zakone are a secret criminal fraternity originating in the prison system of the Soviet Union. "*Vory v zakone*" is Russian for "thieves in law" where *vor* is the singular and *vory* the plural form. *Vory v zakone* has also been translated more loosely as "thieves professing the code" (Serio & Razinkin, 1995) or "thieves-with-a-code-of-honor" (Varese, 2001, p. 8).

The *vory* see themselves as the elite of the underworld, the highest caste in the hierarchy of professional criminals (Gilinskiy & Kostjukovsky, 2004, p. 193; Serio, 2008, p. 157). The role of a *vor* is to provide patronage to lower-level criminals, to arbitrate disputes and to manage a communal fund (*obshchak*). The *obshchak* is maintained through contributions from the *vory* themselves and the criminals under their influence and is used to bribe prison officials, support members, and to finance criminal activities (Serio, 2008, p. 160; Volkov, 2002, p. 58)

The cultural roots of the Vory v Zakone have been traced back to organizations of thieves in Tsarist Russia and the traditional Russian village community, stressing solidarity, a sense of equality, and defiance for state authority (Cheloukhine, 2008; Sobolev, Rushchenko, & Volobuev, 2002, pp. 37, 40). Some influence is also attributed to political dissidents who were sent to prison camps in large numbers during Soviet times (Serio, 2008, pp. 151–152).

There may have been thousands of *vory* in the Soviet prison system in the 1930s, before their numbers were decimated by mass executions in the late 1930s, by World War II, and by internecine war in the 1940s and 1950s, which had purposefully been fueled by the Soviet prison authorities (Gilinskiy & Kostjukovsky, 2004, pp. 195–197).

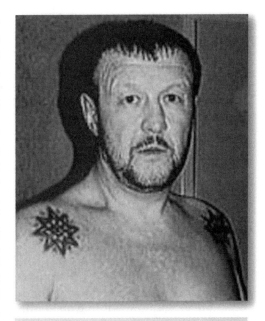

Image 7.2 Vyacheslav Ivankov (1940–2009), a.k.a. Yaponchik (little Japanese), was a famous thief in law who served time in the Soviet Union and the United States. His status as a vor is discernible from the tattoos on his shoulders.

Photo: http://news.bbc.co.uk/2/hi/special_report/1998/03/98/russian_mafia/70485.stm

In 1989, shortly before the demise of the Soviet Union, authorities placed the approximate number of *vory* at 512, of which 240 were incarcerated. In 2005, an estimated 200 *vory* were based in Russia (Serio, 2008, p. 168). The total number of members is likely to be significantly higher, given that the organization extends beyond the borders of Russia (Pullat, 2009; Siegel, 2012, p. 40). It is also noteworthy that the Vory v Zakone is an ethnically diverse association, reflecting the ethnic diversity of the Soviet Union. According to data from the mid-1990s, 33.1 percent of members are Russians, 31.6 percent Georgians, 8.2 percent Armenians, 5.2 percent Azerbaijanis, with Uzbeks, Ukrainians, Kazakhs, Abkhazi, and other ethnic groups accounting for the remaining 21.9 percent (Serio & Razinkin, 1995, p. 100).

Traditionally, new members were only admitted after a lengthy selection process and based on the recommendation of two or three other *vory*, confirming that the novice strictly adhered to the *vory* code. Similar to the initiation rites of Cosa Nostra, the induction into the Vory v Zakone takes place as part of a ceremony during which the novice has to swear an oath before his peers, promising never to cooperate with the authorities (Serio, 2008, p. 165).

The code of the *vory* is more rigid and encompasses more aspects of life than the rules spelled out to new members of Cosa Nostra. The *vory* code is also more reflective of the situation within prison and places high value on defying the prison administration. According to an English translation provided by Joseph Serio (2008, pp. 155–156; see also Serio & Razinkin, 1995, pp. 96-97; Cheloukhine, 2012, p. 112; Gilinskiy & Kostjukovsky, 2004, pp. 193–194) the *vory* code contains the following rules:

1. A thief must turn his back on his family—mother, father, brothers, and sisters. The criminal community is family.

2. It is forbidden to have a family—wife, children.

3. It is forbidden to work. A thief must live off the fruits of criminal activity only.

4. A thief must give moral and material assistance to other thieves using the *obshchak* (money fund).

5. A thief must give information about accomplices and their whereabouts (e.g., locations of hideouts) only in the strictest confidentiality.

6. If a thief is under investigation, a petty thief must take responsibility upon himself to give the suspected thief time to flee.

7. When a conflict arises in a criminal group or among thieves, there must be a meeting *(skhodka)* to resolve the issue.

8. When necessary, a thief must attend a meeting *(skhodka)* to judge another thief if his conduct or behavior comes into question.

9. Punishment for a thief decided by the meeting must be carried out.

10. A thief must be proficient in criminals' jargon *(fenia, blatnaya muzyka)*.

11. A thief must not enter a card game if he does not have the money to pay.

12. A thief must teach his craft to novice thieves.

13. A thief should keep a gofer *(shestiorka)* under his influence.

14. A thief must not lose his sense when drinking alcohol.

15. A thief must not in any way become involved with the authorities. A thief must not participate in social activities. A thief must not join social organizations.

16. A thief must not take up weapons from the hands of state authority. A thief must not serve in the army.

17. A thief must fulfill all promises made to other thieves.

While the *vory* see themselves as the underworld elite, the internal structure of the Vory v Zakone, unlike Cosa Nostra, is nonhierarchical. *Vory* regard themselves as equals, although older members reportedly wield greater moral authority (Serio, 2008, p. 165; Varese, 2001, p. 157).

As a reflection of the embeddedness in a larger prison subculture, tattoos play an important role in signaling the status of a *vor v zakone*. Tattoos in general have been used by inmates of Soviet and Russian prisons to document their personal history and status. In the same way, *vory* are recognizable by distinct tattoos that are not tolerated on nonmembers (Cheloukhine & Haberfeld, 2012, p. 33; Schmelz, 2010, p. 108).

In the post-Soviet era, *vory* have less of a prison background. Long incarceration is no longer a precondition for being inducted into the fraternity. Many young criminals are simply buying membership, whereas in other instances the title *vor v zakone* is bestowed on deserving criminals, and obtaining the title signals a promotion within the underworld (Varese, 2001, p. 175).

From this description follows that *vory v zakone* do not have a power base of their own. In fact, the *vory* code of conduct, unlike mafia culture in Sicily, does not particularly emphasize the use of violence. Rather, the *vory*'s position of power seems to depend on their individual role within criminal gangs and on the high reputation they enjoy in criminal circles (Volkov, 2002, pp. 57, 75–76). From this also follows that the Vory v Zakone as an organization are not "organizing" criminal activities. Each *vor* is free, within the limits established by the *vory* code, to engage in criminal activities with other *vory* and with non-thieves (Gilinskiy & Kostjukovsky, 2004, p. 195). The most influential position ascribed to *vory* is the "supreme council" of the Solntsevskaya organization. The Solntsevskaya emerged from a gang that engaged in protection racketeering

Image 7.3 The estimated 2,000 members of the Hell's Angels are easily recognizable to outsiders. They are organized in about 100 charters, most of them in North America and Europe. Pictured are members from different chapters who are attending a funeral in Germany in August 2013.

Photo: ASSOCIATED PRESS/Thomas Frey/picture-alliance/dpa

in the Solntsevo neighborhood on the outskirts of Moscow during the 1980s. By the 1990s it was described as "Russia's most powerful and most international organised criminal grouping" (Galeotti, 2004, p. 63). While much about its structure is shrouded in mystery, it is believed to serve as an umbrella organization for a number of semiautonomous or independent groups that are licensed to use the name Solntsevskaya (Serio, 2008, pp. 216–217; Varese, 2011, pp. 66–68). Members of the group are said to be active in over 30 countries, including the United States and China (Galeotti, 2004, p. 68). The organization is allegedly overseen by a group of *vory v zakone*, who regularly meet in different parts of the world (Varese, 2001, p. 171; Varese, 2011, p. 67).

Case Study: Hell's Angels

The Hell's Angels are the prototypical outlaw motorcycle gang (OMG). Originating in California in the late 1940s, they now have branches (chapters, charters) virtually all over the world, including North and South America, South Africa, Europe, Turkey, Thailand, Australia and New Zealand (http://www. hells-angels.com/?HA=charters).

The term outlaw initially had no criminal connotation and referred to motorcycle clubs who were not part of the American Motorcyclists' Association (Veno, 2009, p. 21). Since the 1970s, outlaw motorcycle gangs are increasingly depicted by law enforcement agencies and in the media as a manifestation of organized crime (California Bureau of Organized Crime and Criminal Intelligence, 1979; Hill, 1980; U.S. Senate, 1983). Apart from the Hell's Angels, this includes a number of other internationally dispersed clubs, including the Bandidos, Mongols, Outlaws, and Pagans, which are part of a larger outlaw biker subculture (Barker, 2007; Quinn & Koch, 2003).

Clubs like the Hell's Angels occupy much of their members' social life, through regular meetings and events centered on motorcycling. Beyond shared leisure time activities, the Hell's Angels see themselves as "a very select brotherhood of men who will fight and die for each other, no matter what the cause" (Barger, 2001, p. 67). The mutual support extends from barroom brawls to disputes over drug deals and from posting bail to helping fugitive members (Barger, 2001; Marsden & Sher, 2007; Veno, 2009).

The first Hell's Angels motorcycle club had been formed in San Bernardino, California, in 1948. Other clubs using the same name sprang up in the following years, including one created in Oakland in 1957. A year later, Ralph "Sonny" Barger became president of the Oakland club. Barger is credited with changing the Hell's Angels from a loose assortment of independent clubs into a more coherent organization with strict rules under which new chapters would be permitted to join (Barker, 2007, p. 36). In 1966 the Hell's Angels Motorcycle Corporation was incorporated, which owns the rights to the club symbol (death head with wings) and has registered the name "Hell's Angels" as a trademark. The corporation licenses symbol and name to the individual chapters (Barger, 2001, pp. 36–37; Veno, 2009, p. 58).

It is not clear how many charters and how many individual members the Hell's Angels have. Exact figures are not published. According to one estimate, there are 2,000 Hell's Angels organized in about 100 chapters, compared to 900 individual members of the Outlaws and 500 Pagans. The number given for individual Bandidos members ranges from 900 to 3,850 because of the "volatility of the club" (Veno, 2009, pp. 56, 58).

The membership of the Hell's Angels is limited to men 21 years and older, predominantly with a lower-class social background (Barker, 2007, pp. 46, 55–56). However, members from the middle class, including an airline pilot and a stockbroker, have also been reported (Marsden & Sher, 2007, p. 153). Likewise, while traditionally Hell's Angels have been perceived as being ethnically homogeneous to the exclusion of non-whites, reportedly leading Hell's Angels in New Zealand are Maori, and several chapters in Europe have accepted members of sub-Sahara African descent (Veno, 2009, pp. 116–117).

Before someone becomes a Hell's Angel, he has to go through an extensive trial period, which may extend over several years and which comprises two distinct phases, the phase of being a so-called hang-around and the phase of being a probationary member or prospect. In the phase of hang-around, the club members have a chance to get to know and thoroughly check the background of a person interested in joining the club. As a prospect the novice has to demonstrate his loyalty to the club. He is bound by the same rules as full-members and is integrated into the club activities as a "gopher" for the club (Barger, 2001, pp. 42, 44; Barker, 2007, pp. 66–68). The initiation is marked by handing over the "colors," a vest with the club insignia on the back, including a patch of the club symbol and the so-called top and bottom rockers, patches indicating the club (*Hells Angels* without the hyphen) and the location of the chapter (Barker, 2007, pp. 71–72). The colors as well as tattoos that only members are allowed to have, make a member of the Hell's Angels immediately visible to outsiders (Barker, 2007, p. 93; Marsden & Sher, 2007, p. 289). The claim that new members are obliged to kill someone (Lavigne, 1989, p. 72) appears to be a myth (Marsden & Sher, 2007, p. 6). However, most members of the Hell's Angels, just like the members of other outlaw motorcycle clubs, seem to engage in criminal activities of some kind or other, and one purpose of the extensive trial phase is apparently to prevent police informants and undercover agents from infiltrating the club (Barker, 2007, p. 123; Marsden & Sher, 2007, p. 196). A study in Sweden, for example, found that of 100 members of the Hell's Angels and Bandidos in that country, 75 had been formally charged with a criminal offence and nine more were suspected of crimes "on good grounds" (Sundberg, 1999, p. 51).

The members of the Hell's Angels are bound by rules that have not been made public in their entirety and may differ among chapters (Detrois, 2012, p. 223; Lavigne, 1989, p. 82). There is a strong emphasis on participation in club activities, on not harming other members, on providing mutual aid, and on refraining from actions that may harm or bring disgrace to the club. For example, Hell's Angels must regularly attend club meetings and, similar to the rules of Cosa Nostra, Hell's Angels must not get involved with another member's wife or girlfriend (Barger, 2001, pp. 42–45).

Membership pertains to the chapter in the area where the member lives. The exception to this rule is constituted by the so-called Nomad chapters, which are not restricted to a specific geographical location (Marsden & Sher, 2007, p. 3).

Each chapter has a hierarchical structure with distinct leadership positions, comprising a president and vice-president, a treasurer, and a sergeant-at-arms, who is responsible for maintaining order during club meetings. Another position with relevance only for club trips and outings is the road captain, who is responsible for the logistics and security during these events (Barker, 2007, p. 90).

Above the individual chapters there is no permanent overarching structure. Unlike other outlaw motorcycle gangs the Hell's Angels do not have a president or officers to govern the club as a whole, although Ralph Barger seems to have wielded considerable influence in an informal way (Lavigne, 1989, p. 66). Important decisions are made by chapter presidents collectively or even by the entire membership (Barger, 2001, p. 35; Detrois, 2012, p. 235; Lavigne, 1989, pp. 67–68)

A continuing controversy surrounds the question to what extent the Hell's Angels are an association of criminals and to what extent they constitute a criminal organization directly involved in illegal activities (Barker, 2007, p. 12). Some argue that there is a continuum and that certain Hell's Angels chapters "operate as gangs oriented toward criminal profit rather than motorcycle clubs" (Barker & Human, 2009, p. 178). This would imply that the chapters as organizational entities, through their formal structure, carry out profit-oriented crime. However, it seems that the Hell's Angels, in an effort to protect their organization from law enforcement intervention, try to separate club activities and illegal activities. This means that members engage in criminal activities individually or jointly outside of the organizational structure of the Hell's Angels. At the same time, they profit from the protection and mutual support they enjoy as members, and in turn, they share their profits with the organization (Abadinsky, 2013, p. 231; Barker, 2007, p. 90; Quinn & Koch, 2003; see also Morselli, 2009a).

Some observers see a trend in that the Hell's Angels are progressing from a motorcycle club to an organization centered on criminal activity and that the ability to generate proceeds from criminal activity is becoming more important for admission into the club than adherence to the outlaw biker subculture (Detrois, 2012; Veno, 2009, pp. 246–247). It is from this angle that the violence between outlaw motorcycle gangs, such as the Scandinavian "biker war" between Hell's Angels and Bandidos during the 1990s, has been interpreted as a struggle for dominance in the illegal drugs market (Barker, 2007, p. 10). However, the violent confrontations seem to have largely been confined to the realm of the outlaw biker subculture. These confrontations can be traced back to the conflict between the Hell's Angels and Mongols that started in the 1970s. The Hell's Angels insisted that only they were allowed to wear the bottom rocker "California." The conflict quickly escalated to shootings and car bombings (Marsden & Sher, 2007, pp. 66–67).

VARIATIONS ACROSS ILLEGAL ASSOCIATIONAL STRUCTURES

There are various other associational structures that could be presented here in detail. Apart from the Sicilian Mafia, there are a number of other mafia-type associations in Italy that include the Calabrian 'Ndrangheta, the Camorra in

Naples, and the Sacra Corona Unita in Apulia, and there is the Italian American Cosa Nostra in the United States and Canada. Criminal fraternities with some similarities to Italian mafia-type organizations and Chinese triads also exist in Japan in the form of yakuza organizations, such as the Yamaguchi-gumi (Hill, 2003). The Vory v Zakone share their origins in prison with the various so-called prison gangs in the United States, such as the Mexican Mafia and La Nuestra Familia, which are likewise fraternal associations of criminals (Koehler, 2000; Skarbek, 2014). The Hell's Angels belong to a larger category of outlaw motorcycle gangs, which also includes, as indicated, other internationally dispersed clubs, such as the Bandidos, Outlaws, and Mongols, and numerous other outlaw biker clubs with only regional or local significance (Barker, 2007). Prison gangs and outlaw motorcycle gangs share some similarities, namely, their expressive nature, with so-called criminal street gangs (Decker, Bynum, & Weisel, 1998), some of which have attained an international presence, such as the Mara Salvatrucha, also known as MS 13 (Cruz, 2010).

Although associational structures share similar core functions (see below), they vary across some key dimensions. Some, like the various Italian mafia-type associations, have always been criminal in nature. Others have a noncriminal origin, such as those Chinese triads, namely 14K, which began as political organizations. Yet others, namely, outlaw motorcycle gangs, have been formed as legal associations and have retained this status while also developing features of criminal associations.

Significant variations likewise exist with regard to the vertical and horizontal differentiation and the degree of formalization of associational structures. Mafia-type organizations, prison gangs, as well as biker gangs and street gangs have in common that usually their boundaries are clearly defined by formal membership, which entails

Image 7.4 Cosa Nostra boss Joseph Bonanno (1905–2002) explained in his 1983 autobiography what membership in a Mafia family entails: "Obviously, obedience to one's superiors was one of the duties of a Family member. Silence was another cardinal duty. One had to learn to keep a secret and not betray one's friends. Also, for young men especially, one had to learn to curb one's desire toward the wives and women relatives of friends. Becoming a Family member, therefore, made one strictly accountable for one's actions, and it also required that one be ready, if necessary, to bear arms to protect the Family's interests" (Bonanno, 1983, p. 77).

Photo: Bettmann/Corbis

some form of initiation rites and, in some cases, visible symbols, such as distinct clothing (e.g., the patches of biker gangs) or tattoos. Other associational structures that provide a sense of belonging, cohesion, and a code of conduct for criminals have less formally defined boundaries. These include family clans, friendship networks, and also entire deviant subcultures (see, e.g., Brymer, 1991; Huisman & Jansen, 2012).

Some associational structures have multilevel hierarchies, such as the Sicilian Mafia with its ranks of member, *capodecina* and *capo*. Some have fairly elaborated horizontal divisions of tasks, such as outlaw motorcycle gangs with their positions of president, treasurer, sergeant-at-arms, and road captain. An institutionalized division of labor of this kind, it should be noted, does not typically exist in mafia-type associations, where arguably the only standard horizontal role differentiation can be found at the top of the hierarchy, between *capo* and *consigliere*.

THE CORE FUNCTIONS OF ASSOCIATIONAL STRUCTURES

Criminals benefit from belonging to an associational structure in essentially four different ways. Associational structures (a) create and reinforce social bonds, they (b) facilitate communication, they (c) promote mutual aid, and they (d) establish and enforce codes of conduct among their members.

Bonding

Associational structures, by definition, are patterns of social relations that connect individuals, in our case criminals, over extended periods of time. They instill a sense of belonging resting either positively on shared characteristics, interests, or values or negatively on the opposition to something or on a combination of the two. The latter is probably true—for example, for outlaw motorcycle gangs who defy mainstream society and at the same time adhere to a certain notion of brotherhood and a hedonistic lifestyle centered on motorcycling (Quinn & Koch, 2003).

Sense of Belonging

Internally, associational structures establish bonds or they reinforce preexisting bonds between their members. Mafia-type associations such as the Sicilian and American Cosa Nostra and especially the Calabrian 'Ndrangheta show significant overlap with blood families, yet the obligations from the ritual bonds they create go above and beyond kinship ties (Cressey, 1969, p. 152; Paoli, 2003a, pp. 30–31). Externally, associational structures imply a distinction between members and nonmembers, suggesting that members possess certain qualities which nonmembers lack. In other words, belonging to an associational structure tends to convey some degree of exclusivity. This may be the case even where a formal sense of membership is absent—for example, where criminals belong to friendship networks or where individual criminals group themselves around a charismatic underworld figure. But the notion of exclusivity is especially salient in the case of associations with formal membership, such as the Sicilian Mafia, Vory v Zakone, and Hell's Angels, which at least by their own standards, are highly selective in their recruitment and admit new members only after an extended period of testing and schooling. Accordingly, all three associations portray themselves as elites in their respective sphere. Being accepted into such an association means a personal achievement for the individual member and may translate into an enhanced social status within a criminal subculture or a larger subsection of society (Haller, 1992, p. 2; Lombardo, 1994, p. 300; Paoli, 2003a, p. 152).

The sense of belonging that comes with membership is amplified by initiation ceremonies and by secrecy, which are defining characteristics of secret societies including, first and foremost, the Italian mafia-type organizations and the Chinese triads. The rite of initiation and the shared secret of the inner workings of the association demarcate a world separate from and in opposition to the larger society (Paoli, 2003a, p. 18; Simmel, 1950, p. 359). At the same time, relationships within this separate world are modeled after structures from the larger society—namely, kinship ties. Criminal associations typically frame the relationships among members in quasi-familial terms as those between brothers, between younger brother and older brother, between nephew and uncle, or between son and father (Chu, 2000, p. 19; Hill, 2003, pp. 67–68). The underlying rationale appears to be that these artificial or ritual kinship ties create the most cohesive bonds possible and that as a result, members can rely on and trust each other, even though they may not know each other personally (Cressey, 1969, p. 159). This means that becoming a member of a criminal association can be expected to lead to a sudden increase in the number of criminally exploitable ties (Morselli, 2003).

Promotion of Trust

Associational structures promote bonds of trust in a variety of ways. Assuming that associational structures are characterized by a relatively high level of homogeneity, solidarity and trust may emerge from a sense of likeness (Paoli, 2003a, p. 52). The continuous interaction between criminals within associational structures can also be expected to generate trust, namely, through the formation of affectionate bonds and a growing sense of predictability of the others' behavior. Members of criminal associations such as mafia-type organizations typically spend considerable time socializing with other members (Arlacchi, 1993, p. 146; Ulrich, 2005, p. 78). The same is true for informal friendship networks of criminals such as those described by Adler (1985), with regard to drug traffickers, and by Ianni (1974), with regard to a variety of neighborhood-based networks of illegal entrepreneurs.

To the extent associational structures select members according to their worth as criminals, trust can be based on the rational expectation that these individuals have proven their reliability and trustworthiness. This expectation may not only be shared among members but also by outsiders. In these instances, trust is based on the assumption that the members of a particular associational structure can generally be trusted (Skarbek, 2014, p. 77; von Lampe & Johansen, 2004b, p. 170).

Linked to their role in facilitating communication between criminals (see below), associational structures can also play an important role in spreading information about the trustworthiness of individual criminals. Desroches (2005, pp. 127–131), for example, reports on how drug dealers exchange information about potential customers and business partners through what he calls "information networks" that connect members of the drug scene. Another example is provided in the memoirs of London underworld figure Ron Kray. He once met with a member of the New York Cosa Nostra to discuss joint ventures. Before the negotiations could start, the New York mafioso called the boss of the Philadelphia branch of Cosa Nostra, who was known to be familiar with the London underworld, to verify that Kray was indeed the kind of gangster he claimed to be (Kray & Kray, 1989, p. 50).

Communication

An associational structure can provide a forum for the relatively safe communication between criminals to the extent that members can have confidence in the reticence of the other members. This is a matter of mutual trust and of the adherence to and enforcement of a code of conduct that emphasizes secrecy (see below). By facilitating communication, associational structures play an important role in two respects. First, they support the illegal entrepreneurial activities of their members, and second, they contribute to the strengthening of a criminal ideology (see Quinn & Koch, 2003, pp. 287–288).

Members of associational structures can be said to possess privileged communication channels for sharing information relevant for the successful commission of crimes. This includes, as indicated, information about potential co-offenders but also information about, for example, opportunities for crime, know-how for carrying out criminal endeavors, and information on how to elude law enforcement. Chapter 5 provided an example with the groups of pedophiles who regularly meet behind closed doors to share their experiences gained from approaching and abusing children.

The communication between criminals within associational structures will also strengthen, directly or indirectly, a positive self-image and an ideology that justifies or even glorifies criminal activities and a life-style of crime. This is what investigative Journalist Manfred Karremann (2007) observed in his investigation of pedophile networks. The promotion of a deviant ideology can be assumed to neutralize feelings of guilt (Sykes & Matza, 1957) and, along with peer pressure and pressure exerted in hierarchically organized associations of criminals, the promotion of deviant norms and values will tend to increase the willingness of individuals to commit crimes, be they on behalf of the criminal association, for example, meting out punishment, or for personal profit (see Quinn & Koch, 2003, pp. 287–288).

Mutual Aid and Mutual Protection

By virtue of the bonds they create and foster and of the rules they establish and enforce, associational structures tend to promote solidarity and mutual aid among their members. In the case of mafia-type associations, according to Letizia Paoli, who draws on sociologist Max Weber and anthropologist Marshall Sahlins, the initiation ceremony marks a "status contract" and a "contract of fraternization" that subject members to a "regime of generalized reciprocity." Members are obliged to help other members "with no expectation of short-term rewards" (Paoli, 2003a, p. 17). In less formalized structures similar expectations may exist, although they may not be as extensive.

Various forms of mutual aid and support can be observed among members of associational structures of criminals, and criminals can benefit from this aid and support in different contexts. This does not mean, however, that belonging to an associational structure translates into an obligation to participate in or support particular criminal endeavors. Associational structures, it seems, merely provide a framework for the voluntary formation of entrepreneurial structures. Members of associational structures, even mafia-type associations, are generally free in their choice of co-offenders: "They are in no way obliged to select their partners from within the mafia community" (Paoli, 2003a, p. 5; see also Chu, 2000, p. 87).

Mutual aid and solidarity primarily come into play in the protection against law enforcement and against other criminals (Paoli, 2003a, p. 81). Protection against law enforcement can take on different forms. This includes, for example, the corruption of law enforcement officials, the intimidation of witnesses, support for fugitive and incarcerated criminals and their families, and financial aid to cover legal costs. Aid may be provided directly by one individual criminal to another or in an organized way where the associational structure constitutes a framework for the pooling of resources. It needs to be stressed that not all criminal associations actually provide these services. For example, in the case of the American Cosa Nostra, a study found that "there is little evidence that spouses and families of organized crime members or associates are taken care of in any systematic way if husbands are imprisoned" (Edelhertz & Overcast, 1993, p. 135). At the same time, mutual support does not require a formal organization. Informal networks, such as friendship groups or entire underworld milieus, may serve a similar function by raising funds on an ad hoc basis (Fordham, 1972, p. 115; Kerner, 1973, p. 214).

In some cases, financial aid is institutionalized in the form of a communal fund to which members and sometimes also nonmembers have to contribute— for example, through entry fees and regular membership dues or on special occasions. The example of the Vory v Zakone has already been presented where a communal fund, the *obshtchak*, is a central element of the organization. Other criminal associations have likewise created centralized funds. This includes the 'Ndrangheta and the Catania family of the Sicilian Mafia, and historically, other Sicilian Mafia families and certain families of the American Cosa Nostra (Paoli, 2003a, pp. 48, 86; Anderson, 1979, p. 35). Also worth mentioning in this respect are outlaw motorcycle clubs and the German Ringvereine of the 1890s through 1930s. The Ringvereine were explicitly created as mutual aid societies of ex-convicts and eventually transformed into criminal associations (Hartmann & von Lampe, 2008). Commonly, it seems, centralized funds serve to provide aid on a case-by-case basis to individual members in need. In some instances, however, centralized funds are a means for continuously redistributing income among members to the point that members receive regular salaries, which reportedly is true for most 'Ndrangheta families and some larger groups of the Sicilian Mafia (Paoli, 2003a, p. 85).

There are also cases where the corruption of public officials is a centralized function of a criminal association, for example, in the Cosa Nostra family of Philadelphia in the 1960s and 1970s (Anderson, 1979, p. 37; see also Paoli, 2003a, p. 86). In other Cosa Nostra families, any individual member with contacts to corrupt officials is expected to use this influence on behalf of other members (Cressey, 1969, p. 251; see also Iannuzzi, 1995, pp. 229–313).

Apart from support in coping with the threats and consequences of law enforcement, criminals who are part of an associational structure may receive aid in conflicts with other criminals. As has been pointed out before, criminals are vulnerable because they have no recourse to the protection provided by the legal system (see Chapter 5). By forming and joining associational structures, criminals can achieve strength in numbers in confrontations with predatory criminals as well as with disloyal partners in illegal business dealings.

Former mafia boss Joseph Bonanno, in his memoirs, gives an illustrative example of the principle that an attack against one is regarded as an attack against all. This example involves the family of another boss of the New York Cosa Nostra, Joe Profaci:

> I remember an instance when robbers broke into the house of Joe Profaci's nephew and stole a safe containing jewelry and money. Profaci's men found out that the thieves, although Italian, were not associated in any way with the Families. An attempt was made to negotiate with the thieves for the return of the valuables. However, intermediaries reported that the robbers scoffed at the gesture and held themselves independent from the sanctions of our world. Thereafter, the identity of the thieves was passed on to all the Families in New York. It was each member's responsibility to take action if he spotted any of them. No incentive, monetary or otherwise, was offered to bring the thieves to justice. Justice was done. (Bonanno, 1983, p. 155)

Finally, mutual aid may extend to the private sphere. For example, members of outlaw motorcycle clubs are said to feel obliged to assist each other in conflicts irrespective of their nature and of who is at fault, starting with the most mundane barroom brawls (Barger, 2001, pp. 39–40; Queen, 2006, p. 195).

Codes of Conduct

The behavior of the members of illegal associational structures is guided by certain rules that, according to Letizia Paoli (2003, p. 120), may "constitute a separate legal order." The setting of rules and the enforcement of rules, generally speaking, increase the predictability of individual behavior, thereby reducing the complexity that criminals face in interacting with other criminals (Haller, 1992). Some of the rules, which may be written or unwritten, are specific to a particular associational structure or subcultural context; some are widely shared and represent something of a universal code of conduct for individuals associating under conditions of illegality. Various authors have pointed out how similar the rules are that govern, for example, the Sicilian Mafia, Chinese triads, and Japanese yakuza groups but also underground movements like the French Resistance during World War II (Chu, 2000, p. 3; Cressey, 1969, p. 171; Hill, 2003, p. 73). All of these groups, according to Donald Cressey (1969, p. 171), "stress (1) extreme loyalty to the organization and its governing elite, (2) honesty in relationships with members, (3) secrecy regarding the organization's structure and activities, and (4) honorable behavior which sets members off as morally superior to those outsiders who would govern them." These concerns protect, first of all, the existence of the associational structure as such, and where a hierarchical structure exists, they protect in particular the interests of the leadership. Directly or indirectly, however, rules also benefit the individual members and respond to the needs and interests that motivate individuals to become a part of an associational structure in the first place.

General Conduct Rules

The main purpose of some rules, it seems, is to define the associational structure as a separate entity with distinct qualities. The Vory v Zakone, the 'Ndrangheta, and also some of the German Ringvereine forbade members to earn their income from legal employment (Hartmann & von Lampe, 2008, p. 112; Paoli, 2003a, p. 125; Serio, 2008, p. 152), which perhaps is the most extreme way of establishing and safeguarding the character of an association of criminals. Similarly, for members of illegal associational structures, it is usually forbidden to seek assistance from the government, especially in matters of security and justice. For example, in the Sicilian Mafia, according to turncoat Salvatore Contorno, "it is a fundamental rule for every man of honor never to report a theft or crime to the police" (as cited in Gambetta, 1993, p. 119; see also Paoli, 2003a, p. 109).

Numerous rules stipulate how members should behave in order to be honorable, and by implication, how they should strengthen and uphold the reputation of the associational structure they belong to (Decker et al., 1998, p. 408; Gambetta, 1993, p. 120). Some of these general conduct rules are context specific. In the case of Italian mafia-type associations, rules are closely linked to conservative norms and values centered on masculine honor and sexuality and family morality (Travaglino, Abrams, Randsley de Moura, & Russo, 2014). Mafiosi are expected "to lead an irreproachable family life" (Gambetta, 1993, p. 120; see also Paoli, 2003a, p. 74). Mafiosi are also required to "live an outwardly modest life" (Cressey, 1969, p. 216) and are supposed to "conceal their own importance, and to minimize any signs of their power" (Paoli, 2003a, p. 111). In the case of outlaw motorcycle gangs, fundamentally different general conduct rules apply that emphasize promiscuity and aggressive machoism as well as the obligation to ride a motorcycle regularly (Barker, 2007; Quinn & Koch, 2003).

There are other rules designed to ensure the continued existence especially of criminal associations. These rules pertain to the continuous participation of members in the activities of the association—for example, by paying regular membership dues and attending regular meetings (Barger, 2001, p. 42; Hartmann & von Lampe, 2008, p. 117).

Code of Silence

Central to the sets of rules governing associational structures are norms intended to enhance security and to reduce the threat of outside interference, namely, from law enforcement. First and foremost, members are bound by rules of secrecy. A code of silence generally prohibits the sharing of information with outsiders. However, there are some significant variations. In one extreme, it is forbidden to acknowledge the very existence of the associational structure—for example, in the case of the Sicilian Mafia (Gambetta, 1993, p. 121; Paoli, 2003a, p. 108). In the other extreme, for example, in the case of officially chartered organizations such as outlaw motorcycle gangs and, historically, the German Ringvereine, their existence and also the identity of their membership is public knowledge and merely the inner workings of the association must be kept secret (Barker, 2007, p. 19; Hartmann & von Lampe, 2008, p. 118).

The code of silence overlaps with the prohibition of cooperation with the authorities. Criminals must not inform on other criminals. Journalistic accounts sometimes give the impression that this is something specific to the Sicilian and American Mafia and their code of omertà. Omertà is a concept that is linked to "the idea of a true man" in Sicilian culture. A man is supposed to protect his honor, his property, and his family through his own efforts (Hess, 1996, p. 109). In this respect, it is indeed somewhat specific to the Mafia. However, understood in a narrow sense, essentially prescribing silence and non-cooperation with the government (Paoli, 2003a, p. 109), it is a principle that is widely propagated in criminal circles, including underworld milieus and inside prisons and more broadly in marginalized segments of society (Albini, 1971, pp. 267–269; Cressey, 1969, p. 176; Ianni, 1974, pp. 306–307; Sutherland, 1937, p. 10; Taylor, 1984, p. 149). For example, London gangster Ron Kray, in his memoirs, speaks about "that old East End wall of silence, that code of conduct which says you never grass to the law" (Kray & Kray, 1989, p. 98).

Secrecy rules may be flanked by rules of behavior that minimize the risk of disclosing information. In the Sicilian Mafia, for example, members are obliged to exercise "stringent self-control and self-discipline" and must refrain "from getting drunk or using drugs" (Paoli, 2003a, p. 111). Likewise, mafiosi are forbidden to put in writing any information concerning the mafia group (Paoli, 2003a, p. 112). In a similar vein, in some associational structures the commission of certain crimes is prohibited, partly because they are deemed dishonorable, partly because they may attract increased law enforcement attention (Haller, 1992, p. 4). In the case of mafia-type associations, for example, more or less strictly enforced prohibitions have existed against direct involvement in drug trafficking and kidnapping for ransom (Anderson, 1979, p. 37; Haller, 1991, p. 6; Paoli, 2003a, p. 125) and against violence directed at law enforcement officials and ordinary citizens (Lombardo, 2013, p. 164).

The code of silence is a specific expression of a more general obligation of unequivocal loyalty toward the associational structure and its members. Another manifestation of this principle of loyalty is absolute obedience to the

Image 7.5 Members of the Bandidos outlaw motorcycle gang mourn the death of a comrade who had been shot in Sydney, Australia, in 2006. Bandidos rules promote cohesion, trust, and conflict avoidance: "You don't lie. You don't steal. This includes OL' Ladies as well" (Barker, 2007, p. 172).

Photo: ASSOCIATED PRESS/Marius Becker/picture-alliance/dpa/AP Images

leadership in the case of hierarchically structured criminal associations, such as the Sicilian Mafia and Japanese yakuza groups (Cressey, 1969, 168; Hill, 2003, p. 72). A core function of the leadership is to settle disputes among members and to enforce internal discipline; in this context, obedience to the leadership may require using violence against close associates and also submitting oneself to punishment even if it means death (Pistone, 1989).

Obligations Toward Other Members

Apart from the rules that primarily protect associational structures as such, there are also some rules that protect first and foremost the interests of individual members. Two basic rules need to be mentioned here: the obligation toward mutual aid, which has been discussed in some detail already, and the obligation not to bring harm to other members. This latter principle is translated into a number of rules that apply to most if not all-associational structures of criminals. A general rule prescribes honesty in dealings with other members. A mafioso, for example, must not lie to another mafioso. "The rule of truth," Gambetta (1993, p. 122) explains, "is said to be even more important than the notorious rule of silence."

More specific rules address typical conflict scenarios and are designed to avoid or resolve disputes between members of an associational structure. A member is usually not allowed to physically assault another member (Abadinsky, 2013, p. 59; Hill, 2003, p. 72; Decker et al., 1998, p. 407), or in the case of the Hell's Angels, only according to rules that limit injuries: "Any fights between members will be STRICTLY one onto one, no rings are to be worn, no weapons to be used, no kicking when a guy is down" (as cited in Detrois, 2012, p. 234). Personal property also must be respected (Decker et al., 1998, p. 407). Likewise, a member is not allowed to get involved with the wife or girlfriend of another member (Barker, 2007, p. 48; Chu, 2000, p. 3; Hill, 2003, p. 73; Skarbek, 2014, p. 118). There is also commonly an obligation to respect (and further) the business interests of individual members and not to enter into direct competition with each other (Anderson, 1979, p. 71; Edelhertz & Overcast, 1993, p. 113; Haller, 1991, pp. 6–7; Sutherland, 1937, p. 12).

Persistence and Change of the Code of Conduct

It seems that within most illegal associational structures there are no formalized procedures for establishing and changing rules of behavior. There is usually no separate legislative branch and decisions may be made by the leadership or by the membership as a whole. In many cases, rules are merely implicitly adopted from the surrounding social context, for example, traditional norms from Sicilian culture in the case of the Sicilian Mafia (Paoli, 2003a) or "common sense" underworld rules in the case of street gangs (Decker et al., 1998, p. 407).

Although there seems to be some continuity in the normative system of illegal associational structures, there are numerous cases of the setting of new rules and the altering of existing rules for pragmatic reasons, typically in response to specific events or threats or in order to cope with the changing of broader social conditions. For example, in the Sicilian Mafia the rule forbidding mafiosi to report crimes to the police was altered by the *commissione* in the 1970s, so that cars could be reported stolen. The underlying rationale for this controversial amendment allegedly was the concern that members would otherwise be in danger of being held accountable for crimes committed with the use of the stolen vehicle (Gambetta, 1993, p. 120; Paoli, 2003a, p. 125). The Vory v Zakone softened their prohibition of legitimate work within the prison system in response to increased pressure from the prison administration. New rules that were adopted after fierce debate, permitted *vory* to take on certain tasks "in case of extreme need" (Serio, 2008, p. 153). The Hell's Angels dropped the rule that members may not commit "drug burns," ripping-off drug dealers, because this rule was used by prosecutors to argue that the Hell's Angels were involved in drug dealing (Barger, 2001, pp. 46–47). This kind of flexibility in the normative system is also observable in the enforcement of behavioral codes.

Enforcement of Rules

The rules that guide the behavior within associational structures can be enforced in different ways. In their most developed forms, associational structures—for example, the Sicilian and the American Cosa Nostra, have an established quasi-judicial system for responding to rule violations with formalized responsibilities and regulations for the adjudication process (Cressey, 1969, pp. 207–211). In less developed associational structures, for example, friendship networks, responses to rule violations are more informal, involving members on an ad hoc basis.

Irrespective of the degree to which the enforcement of rules is institutionalized within an associational structure, four types of norms need to be distinguished with regard to the way in which they are enforced: customs, conventions, norms enforced by reprisal, and laws. Some norms are followed merely out of tradition, and deviations from these customs have no consequences. At the same time, adhering to these norms, "being old school," may enhance the status of an individual. Some norms, Max Weber (1968, p. 34) has called them "conventions," are enforced through reactions of disapproval. Then there are norms that are enforced through reprisal by an injured party in accordance with rules that allow for or even mandate revenge. In the Sicilian Mafia as well as in the 'Ndrangheta, for example, "the punishment for some rule violations is, according to the code of honor, directly entrusted to the aggrieved individuals" (Paoli, 2003a, p. 127; see also Bonanno, 1983, p. 154), although in an effort to reduce internal feuds, these rights and obligations have been limited in recent years (Paolia, 2003, p. 128). Finally, there are norms that are protected by individuals designated to enforce these norms according to a set of procedural rules. In these cases, Weber (1968, p. 34) speaks of "laws."

The responsibility for the enforcement of rules may fall to various individuals and collectives. In the case of mafia-type associations, for example, depending on the nature and gravity of wrongdoing, individual ranking members, representatives of different branches of the organization, or the commission as an overarching body can be involved (Cressey, 1969, pp. 207–211; Paoli, 2003a, p. 75). In other cases, for example the Vory v Zakone's *skhodka* (meeting), judicial functions are exercised collectively by the membership (Varese, 2001, p. 157; see also Paolia, 2003, pp. 128–129).

Depending on whether the violated norms primarily protect the associational structure as a whole or the interests of individual members, the internal judicial system can take on the form of criminal justice or civil justice or a combination of both. Criminal justice means that punishment is meted out for a wrongdoing against common interests, while civil justice aims at the resolution of conflicts between two parties of equals. Typical punishments that associational structures use include fines, temporary suspension of membership, expulsion, humiliation, corporal punishment, and death (see, e.g., Paoli, 2003a, pp. 128–129). Typical outcomes of civil justice are orders to desist from an inappropriate action, to financially compensate a victim of wrongdoing, or to show gestures of reconciliation (Cressey, 1969, p. 210; see also Maas, 1997, pp. 172–173).

Rule Breaking and Arbitrary Adjudication

The fact that illegal associational structures are governed by codes of conduct and may even possess an institutionalized system of rule enforcement does not mean that members always adhere to the code of conduct and that the enforcement of rules occurs only in an altruistic way. Such a romanticized view would be misguided.

Rule violations appear to be widespread—for example, in the Siclian Mafia (see, e.g., Arlacchi, 1993). At the same time, the enforcement of rules often seems to be handled flexibly and selectively. Particularly valuable members may be spared punishment even for severe transgressions (Gambetta, 1993, pp. 120–121). Finally, it should be noted that the internal judicial system, where it is linked to specific individuals, may be abused. Cressey, for example, has argued that the entire code of honor of the Mafia, because it is unwritten, serves as an instrument of power in the hands of the bosses. The code of honor "can be said by the rulers to provide for whatever the rulers want, and to prohibit whatever the rulers do not want" (Cressey, 1969, p. 204).

DELINEATING ASSOCIATIONAL STRUCTURES FROM ENTREPRENEURIAL STRUCTURES AND FROM QUASI-GOVERNMENTAL STRUCTURES

Associational structures do not always appear in pure form. Sometimes there is an overlap with entrepreneurial structures, respectively with quasi-governmental structures, or both. It may be that an associational structure is at the same time an entrepreneurial structure. This would be the case when the members of an associational structure jointly engage in criminal activity. However, this seems to be an exception rather than the rule because it is unlikely that the position occupied by a member in relation to the other members is identical irrespective of whether the group engages in social or in economic activities (see Morselli, 2009a; Tenti & Morselli, 2014). The greatest approximation to an overlap of associational and entrepreneurial structures can perhaps be seen in "corporate street gangs" (Levitt and Venkatesh, 2000; see also Venkatesh, 2008), where features of mutual protection societies coincide with features of drug dealing organizations. For example, those higher in the gang hierarchy may provide lower-level members with drugs (Densley, 2012, 2014). The often made claim, however, that street gangs function as business enterprises, should be met with caution, as this claim may well be a misconception resulting from a failure to distinguish between what members do and what the gang as an organizational entity does. Decker, Bynum, and Weisel (1998), for example, note that in their interview-based study of four street gangs in the United States, there was a great disparity between general statements by gang members "that their gang organizes drug sales (between 63 percent and 80 percent)" and the responses to specific questions that revealed that members sold drugs independently. As Decker et al. (1998, p. 412) explain, "gangs play a role in these sales, largely through contacts that exist within the gang and in cliques or subgroups of friends in the gang," and the degree of organization "is primitive at best, and at worst non-existent." Likewise, James Densley concludes from interviews with members of several street gangs in London, England, that even though drugs are supplied through the internal gang hierarchy, "drug sales are fundamentally an individual or small-group activity, not coordinated by the collective gang. The gang instead provides the reputational and criminogenic resources to sustain the enterprise" (Densley, 2014, p. 533).

What may distinguish the case of street gangs from that of other criminal associations is that street gang members, especially lower-ranking members, are less likely to cooperate with outsiders in profit-making criminal activities given the divisive nature of gang affiliations in gang-dominated areas. It may be for this reason that illegal enterprises appear to be encapsulated within street gangs.

Rather than hybrids of criminal associations and illegal enterprises, it seems more likely to see an overlap between associational and quasi-governmental structures (see Chapter 8). For example, in the case of the Sicilian and the American Cosa Nostra, the internal governance function is extended to nonmembers who operate in the territory controlled by a given Mafia family (Gambetta, 1993). Under these circumstances, associational and quasi-governmental structures merge into one pyramidal edifice. Protection and conflict-resolution services are provided to the respective lower levels, from the mafia boss down, all the way through the senior, mid-level and lower ranks within the mafia hierarchy to protected, that is, connected nonmembers (associates). In the opposite direction, tribute payments are passed upwards through the mafia hierarchy. These payments are often fixed percentages of the illicit income of the respective next lower level. For example, a mafia associate who runs a gambling casino might give a 50 percent share of his profits to the mafia member he is associated with. This mafia member, in turn, will pass on part of this sum, along with a share of the profits from other illicit activities, to the person above him in the mafia hierarchy. This ranking member likewise will share a percentage of the money with his respective superior, and so on, depending on the number of hierarchical levels in a given mafia association (Pistone, 1989, p. 78). The pattern of overlapping associational and quasi-governmental structures is by no means unique to the Cosa Nostra organizations in Italy and the United States. It can also be observed in other criminal associations, for example, Japanese yakuza groups (Hill, 2003, p. 90).

The overlap of mafia-type criminal fraternities and underworld governments should not come as a surprise because the structure of the organization, a hierarchy with centralized authority, is compatible with both functions (associational and quasi governmental). An overlap of different functions may also occur where within an associational structure a parallel structure exists that is more entrepreneurial in nature. For example, in the case of the German Ringvereine, reportedly an inner circle existed parallel to the official executive committee of each club. The inner circle consisted of the most outstanding criminals who directed the illegal side of club business, such as the planning of crimes, the retaliation against delinquent members and outsiders, and the distribution of loot (Hartmann & von Lampe, 2008, p. 118). In any case, the challenge for researchers and crime analysts is to discern the exact nature of the relations that link a given set of criminals and to avoid premature judgments and oversimplifications.

ASSOCIATIONAL STRUCTURES: SUMMARY AND CONCLUSION

This chapter has examined associational structures of criminals. Following the presentation of four case studies (Sicilian Mafia, Hong Kong triads, Vory v Zakone, Hell's Angels), similarities and differences have been discussed across the broad range of associational structures that can be found in different countries and in different historical periods.

Associational structures have in common that they serve social functions rather than economic or quasi-governmental functions. Associational structures foster bonds of trust between criminals and provide status, and they constitute a forum for relatively safe communication, thereby facilitating the dissemination of crime-relevant information and promoting deviant norms and values. They promote mutual aid and mutual protection against law enforcement and against predatory or competing criminals. Finally, by setting and enforcing conduct rules, they create a fairly predictable social environment for their members.

Associational structures vary with regard to the degree of formalization, the level of secrecy, and the legal status. Some associational structures, such as friendship networks of criminals, have a low degree of formalization, whereas in the other extreme, there are highly formalized organizations, such as mafia-type associations and those organizations with a legal status, such as outlaw motorcycle clubs that, in addition to being highly formalized, are also highly visible to the general public.

Discussion Questions

1. Does it make a difference whether an individual criminal keeps to him- or herself or is part of a criminal association?

2. Does it make a difference whether or not a criminal association uses elaborate initiation ceremonies?

3. Does it make a difference if a criminal association is organized as a secret society, such as a Chinese triad, or as a legally registered organization, where members are publicly recognizable as such through openly worn symbols, such as in the case of an outlaw motorcycle club?

Research Projects

1. Collect information on a street gang and determine to what extent it is an associational structure.

2. Analyze the autobiography of an organized criminal with a view to the importance of associational structures.

3. Analyze a case of white-collar crime with a view to the existence and importance of associational structures of business criminals.

Further Reading

Chin, K.-L. (1996). *Chinatown gangs: Extortion, enterprise, and ethnicity*. New York: Oxford University Press.

Chin, K.-L. (2014). Chinese organized crime. In L. Paoli (Ed.), *The Oxford handbook of organized crime* (pp. 219–233). Oxford: Oxford University Press.

Katz, K. (2011). The enemy within: The outlaw motorcycle gang moral panic. *American Journal of Criminal Justice, 36*(3), 231–249.

Massari, M. (2014). The Sacra Corona Unita: Origins, characteristics, and strategies. In N. Serenata (Ed.), *The 'Ndrangheta and Sacra Corona Unita: The history, organization and operation of two unknown Mafia groups* (101–116). Cham: Springer.

Massari, M., & Motta, C. (2007). Women in the Sacra Corona Unita. In G. Fiandaca (Ed.), *Women and the Mafia: Female roles in organized crime structures* (53–66). New York: Springer.

Quinn, J. F., & Forsyth, C. J. (2011). The tools, tactics, and mentality of outlaw biker wars. *American Journal of Criminal Justice, 36*(3), 216–230.

Paoli, L. (2008). The decline of the Italian Mafia. In D. Siegel & H. Nelen (Eds.), *Organized crime: Culture, markets and Policies* (15–28). New York: Springer.

Paoli, L. (2014). The Italian Mafia. In L. Paoli (Ed.), *The Oxford handbook of organized crime* (121–141). Oxford: Oxford University Press.

Roberti, F. (2008). Organized crime in Italy: The Neapolitan Camorra today. *Policing, 2*(1), 43–49.

Thompson, H. (1967). *Hell's Angels: A strange and terrible saga.* New York: Ballantine Books.

Thompson, T. (2013). *Outlaws: One man's rise through the savage world of renegade Bikers, Hell's Angels and global crime.* New York: Penguin.

Van den Eynde, J., & Veno, A. (2007). Depicting outlaw motorcycle club women using anchored and unanchored research methodologies. *The Australian Community Psychologist, 19*(1), 96–111.

CHAPTER 8

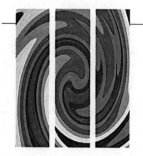

Illegal-Market Monopolies and Quasi-Governmental Structures

INTRODUCTION

The previous two chapters have examined illegal structures that are centered on either economic or social functions for which the terms *entrepreneurial structures* and *associational structures* have been used. This chapter is devoted to describing and explaining a third category, one that encompasses illegal structures that are political in nature because they are centered on the exercise of power. These phenomena fall into the category of quasi-governmental structures because in their purest, ideal-typical form they do indeed represent some form of underworld government.

Quasi-governmental structures enable certain criminals to control other criminals who operate in a particular illegal market or in a particular geographical area. Quasi-governmental structures regulate behavior, they protect contractual and property rights in the context of illegal business, they provide protection against predatory criminals and against law enforcement, they offer dispute resolution services, and in return, they tax illegal income.

In some cases the influence of quasi-governmental structures reaches beyond the confines of the underworld. Mafia groups in Italy, for example, provide protection to illegal as well as legal businesses, and by protecting legal businesses they enter into direct competition with the state. This will be discussed in greater detail in later chapters (Chapter 10 and 11) as it pertains to the relationship between organized crime on one hand and the legal economy and the state on the other. The present chapter is focused on the governance of criminal milieus and illegal markets.

Quasi-governmental structures are sometimes confused with and have to be distinguished from monopolies in illegal markets. The latter are illegal firms, that is, entrepreneurial structures (see Chapter 6), which face no competition in their respective markets. These illegal-market monopolies are similar to underworld governments in that they exert power. However, this power is economic in nature and is used for economic purposes. Economists speak of "market power." Simply put, a monopoly allows an illegal firm to impose higher prices because customers do not have the option of switching to a cheaper supplier.

Both illegal market monopolies and quasi-governmental structures and the differences between the two will be discussed in this chapter in some detail. First, however, a case study of perhaps the most notorious quasi-governmental structure in the history of crime is presented: the American Cosa Nostra. At this point it needs to be reemphasized what has repeatedly been pointed out in previous chapters: the three basic types of illegal structures (entrepreneurial, associational and quasi-governmental) are not necessarily mutually exclusive. The American Cosa Nostra, just like other mafia-type organizations, is an example of the overlap of associational and quasi-governmental structures. That is why the case study of the American Cosa Nostra presented below could have been included in the previous chapter on associational structures, just like the case study of the Sicilian Mafia featured in the previous chapter could have been included here. However, while Chapter 7 has highlighted the characteristics that make the Sicilian Mafia an associational structure, this chapter highlights the features of the American Cosa Nostra, which make it—or rather the individual Cosa Nostra families—a prime example of an illegal quasi-governmental structure. What is important to bear in mind is that the distinction between associational and quasi-governmental structures is made for analytical purposes and to avoid comparing apples and oranges where associational and quasi-governmental structures manifest themselves in separate entities.

CASE STUDY: THE AMERICAN COSA NOSTRA

The American Cosa Nostra, also referred to as American Mafia or—in FBI jargon—La Cosa Nostra or simply LCN, is a mafia-type organization with great similarities to its southern Italian counterparts, namely the Sicilian Mafia, the Neapolitan Camorra, and the Calabrian 'Ndrangheta. It is a criminal association centered on mutual aid and mutual protection and at the same time it has functioned in some places as a form of underworld government (Anderson, 1979; Haller, 1992).

The origins of the American Cosa Nostra can be traced back to the immigration of Italians to North America in the late 1800s and early 1900s. Although there is no indication that Italian mafia-type organizations made a conscious attempt to expand to the New Continent, mafiosi and camorristi were among those immigrants and became involved in organized criminal activities in the United States. While the exact circumstances of the formation of the American Cosa Nostra as a distinct organization are in dispute, it can be considered an established fact that by the early 1930s Italian criminals in New York had organized themselves in a number of similarly structured and mutually recognized units called families, each under the leadership of an influential underworld figure (see Critchley, 2009; Dash, 2009; Lombardo, 2010; Varese, 2011). By the 1960s, a total of 24 such families were believed to exist in various parts of the United States, with a clear concentration in New York City with five coexisting families. A second important center of Cosa Nostra presence has been Chicago, where the local branch, a successor to the "Capone Syndicate," is called "the Outfit" (Cressey, 1969; Lombardo, 2013). The American Cosa Nostra became synonymous with organized crime in the public conscience during the 1950s and 1960s as a result of a number of congressional and journalistic inquiries (see Chapter 2). Since at least the mid-1980s, in the course of sweeping prosecutions and as a result of demographic changes, the American Cosa Nostra has been in decline (Haller, 1991; Lombardo, 2013; Reuter, 1995).

Given variations between and within Cosa Nostra families and changes over time, it is difficult to make definitive statements about the American Cosa Nostra. Historically membership has been restricted to adult males of southern Italian descent who have undergone an extensive period of testing and schooling. New members are inducted in a ceremony that seems to have been adopted from the Sicilian Mafia and that includes the swearing of an oath and the burning of the image of a saint (Haller, 1992, p. 4; Jacobs, 1994, p. 4). Only some units of the Chicago Outfit apparently have not used this traditional initiation rite (Abadinsky, 2013, p. 73; Lombardo, 2013, p. 156).

The individual families have a three-tiered hierarchical structure. Under the leadership of a boss, who is assisted by an underboss and a consigliere (adviser and arbitrator), mid-ranking captains or capos supervise groups of ordinary members called soldiers or buttons (Cressey, 1969). Each member of the Cosa Nostra may be tied to numerous nonmember associates, who have the formal status of being "connected" (Abadinsky, 2013, p. 51).

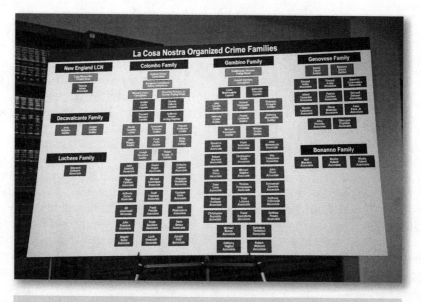

Image 8.1 A chart presented at a press conference by U.S. Attorney General Eric Holder in New York in January 2011 lists Cosa Nostra members and associates who had been arrested by the FBI in a massive roundup. Holder announced that this was the biggest crackdown ever on the New York area's Cosa Nostra.

Photo: EMMANUEL DUNAND/Staff

Above the individual families, a body called commission has provided a forum for the most influential bosses to come to agreements on matters of general importance, such as the admission of new members and the resolution of conflicts within and between the families. Commission meetings have been held on the national level and, in New York, on the local level (Abadinsky, 2013, p. 59).

Cosa Nostra members are engaged in a variety of legal and illegal activities individually or in cooperation with members and nonmembers (Anderson, 1979, p. 2; Cressey, 1969, p. 118). Members and associates have to seek approval from their direct superior before engaging in a criminal activity, and a percentage of the profits from illegal activities has to be passed up to those higher in the hierarchy. In turn, members and associates are entitled to draw on the Cosa Nostra for protection and conflict resolution (Abadinsky, 2013, p. 51; Pistone, 1989, p. 77).

It is not uncommon for illegal entrepreneurs to voluntarily associate with Cosa Nostra members, as this promises protection and status (Lombardo, 1994, p. 301). At the same time, Cosa Nostra families have tried to establish control over territories and illegal markets by coercive means to the effect that only connected illegal entrepreneurs are permitted to operate. However, certain groups have reportedly remained untouched, such as ethnic minorities and outlaw bikers (Edelhertz & Overcast, 1993, p. 138; Haller, 1991, pp. 5, 23; Lombardo, 1994, p. 306). Robert Lombardo quotes one Chicago bookmaker (a professional gambler who takes bets on sports events) describing the system of Outfit control:

> In order to book, you have to get the O.K. It is accepted that you have to pay in order to book. I have to split 50/50. For that I get the right to book. It is a tax. If you make money legitimate, you pay taxes. If you make money illegally, you pay the Outfit. (Lombardo, 1994, p. 303)

Cosa Nostra members draw on a wide network of underworld contacts to identify rogue illegal entrepreneurs and use a variety of means to stop unauthorized operations. These means include violence and more subtle methods, such as informing the police (Lombardo, 1994, p. 304; see also Rudolph, 1992, pp. 310–311). The system of control has typically centered on illegal gambling and prostitution, but in some cases, even more-difficult-to-monitor ordinary professional criminals, such as burglars, have been forced to pay a street tax to the local Cosa Nostra family (Abadinsky, 1981, pp. 30, 104; Lombardo, 2013, pp. 160–161). The taxing of criminals, it seems, goes beyond mere extortion to include protection and dispute resolution services similar to the benefits accorded ordinary members. In one example, presented by Peter Reuter (1983, p. 163), a group of thieves who had gotten into an argument over how to divide the loot from a burglary, submitted to the ruling of a panel of Cosa Nostra members. After a hearing, the mafiosi rejected the claim made by one of the thieves that he had been wrongfully deprived of his share.

Apart from taxation and adjudication, Cosa Nostra families may regulate criminal activities in yet another way: by outright banning certain crimes in the neighborhoods they control, namely, predatory street crimes and drug selling. In these cases, Cosa Nostra assumes a policing function similar to legitimate government (Abadinsky, 2013, p. 84).

In a neighborhood or market controlled by a Cosa Nostra family, it appears that typically illegal entrepreneurs who are Cosa Nostra members and illegal entrepreneurs who are nonmembers operate side by side. In other words, Cosa Nostra control is usually not geared toward eliminating competition for mafiosi-run illegal businesses, although the latter may be allowed to operate under more favorable conditions (Anderson, 1979, p. 52; Edelhertz & Overcast, 1993, pp. 28, 152; Lombardo, 1994, p. 303). Protection against competition is only provided in the sense that the overall number of enterprises allowed to operate in the territory of a Cosa Nostra family may be limited, and exclusive areas of operation may be assigned within the territory (Anderson, 1979, pp. 44, 52–53).

ILLEGAL-MARKET MONOPOLIES AND QUASI-GOVERNMENTAL STRUCTURES

Examining the case of the American Cosa Nostra is important because it has been at the center of two of the main controversies in the scholarly organized crime literature. One controversy, alluded to in the previous chapter, is over whether the American Cosa Nostra is a business (Cressey, 1969; Haller, 1992). As has been pointed out in the case study above, it is not an entrepreneurial structure but rather, as Mark H. Haller (1992) has argued, an association of illegal entrepreneurs. The other, related controversy pertains to the role the American Cosa Nostra plays in illegal markets. According to one view, it tries—and has partly succeeded—to monopolize illegal markets by effectively removing competition to mafia-owned illegal enterprises. According to another view supported by empirical research and presented in the case study above, the American Cosa Nostra seeks to regulate illegal markets populated by members and nonmembers. To understand the role of the American Cosa Nostra and the exercise of power under conditions of illegality more generally, it is important to understand the differences between the underlying notions of market monopoly and the kind of illegal market regulation the Cosa Nostra has achieved in the past. There are two basic forms of centralized control over an illegal market (see Figure 8.1).

One form of market control is a market monopoly. Market monopolies exist where there is only one firm present selling a particular good or service and new sellers are effectively prevented from entering the market. A market monopoly also exists where all firms are combined in a cartel that acts as a single seller (Welch & Welch, 2010, p. 387). It should be noted here that the term *cartel* as used by economists is different from the term cartel used by the media and law enforcement officials to describe cooperative arrangements and power alliances between criminals in Latin American countries, namely Colombia and Mexico, and elsewhere (see Grillo, 2011, pp. 60–62).

The monopolist firm (or cartel) can set prices and can determine how much of the commodity is sold without concern that consumers might switch to competitors, because by definition and for a variety of possible reasons, other sellers have no access to the market. As a result, the monopoly position generates

Figure 8.1 Basic Forms of Centralized Control Over Illegal Markets

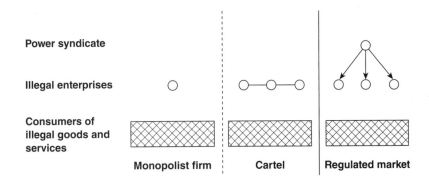

This graph depicts three different constellations where power is concentrated with regard to an illegal market: a monopoly, with a single (monopolist) firm providing an illegal good or service to numerous consumers; a cartel, where a combination of several firms operate as a single seller of an illegal good or service; and a number of competing firms under the control of a power syndicate, which taxes and regulates the behavior of these competing firms.

Source: von Lampe (2001b, p. 468).

profits than in a competitive market, even when efficiency, product quality, and output are lowered (Welch & Welch, 2010, pp. 386–390).

It should be noted on the side that the tendency of monopolies to reduce output at increased prices and thereby to reduce consumption has led to a debate on whether it is socially desirable for illegal markets to be monopolized (Buchanan, 1973; Hellman, 1980, p. 174; Reuter, 1994, p. 107).

The other basic form of centralized control over an illegal market, besides monopoly control by a single firm or a cartel, is ideal—typically represented by what Alan Block (1983) has called power syndicates. In these cases a power structure is superimposed on a competitive market populated by a number of illegal firms. These illegal firms run their businesses in essentially the same way they would otherwise. However, the firms are forced to share some of their profits with the power syndicate. Because ideally all illegal firms in a market under the control of a power syndicate are affected in the same way, this does not influence competition. The firms simply pass on the additional costs to consumers (Schelling, 1971, pp. 82–83).

There has been some controversy over the basis of power of power syndicates. According to one view, it is essentially a matter of the threat and use of violence. What power syndicates do is regarded as a form of extortion, even though subordinates may receive some benefits in return, for example, protection against predatory criminals and against law enforcement (Schelling, 1971). According to another view, power syndicates exploit the dependence of illegal enterprises on certain vital services. This view rests on two assumptions. One is that illegal enterprises involved in the provision of illegal goods and services—for example, illegal gambling—need certain resources themselves—namely, capital, immunity from law enforcement, and violence—in order to stay in business. The other assumption is that criminal groups gain control over illegal enterprises because they are able to monopolize the provision of these vital resources (Rubin, 1973; see also Reuter, 1983). To what extent power syndicates rely on force and to what extent they rely on the need of illegal enterprises for certain services appears to be largely an empirical question. There are examples supporting both views (see, e.g., Block, 1983; Gardiner, 1970).

MONOPOLIES IN ILLEGAL MARKETS

To clarify the distinction between illegal-market monopolies and quasi-governmental structures, both phenomena are discussed separately in this chapter. First, the nature, prevalence, and causes of monopolies in illegal markets will be examined.

Defining the Scope of Illegal Markets

The question of whether an illegal market is monopolized is directly tied to the question of how one defines an illegal market. Defined in abstract terms (see Chapter 4), an illegal market is an arena for the regular voluntary exchange of goods and services for money, where the goods and services themselves, their production, selling and/or consumption violate the law (Arlacchi, 1998, p. 203; Beckert & Wehinger, 2011, p. 2). This abstract definition, however, is not helpful when it comes to the question of monopoly control. In order to determine if a market is monopolized, it is important to clearly delineate the boundaries of that market. An example may clarify this point: If in a neighborhood there is only one illegal gambling casino, does it mean this casino holds a monopoly? What if there are many more casinos in nearby neighborhoods? What if this casino offers roulette, but illegal card games are held in the backrooms of many bars in the same neighborhood?

There are two parameters that define the boundaries of a market for the purpose of determining if a monopoly exists. In essence, firms "are in the same market when they sell similar products and compete with each other for the same buyers" (Welch & Welch, 2010, p. 366). This implies that a market can be delineated by the "product boundary" and the "geographic boundary" (Welch & Welch, 2010, p. 367).

The product boundary depends on the substitutability of a product. All commodities that buyers accept as equally suited to meet a specific demand define a single market. If buyers in the example given above look for any kind of illegal gambling, then there is one illegal gambling market. However, if buyers, even when given a choice, are only interested in one particular type of gambling (e.g. poker instead of roulette), then this specific type of gambling defines the market. The geographic boundary depends on the mobility of buyers and sellers and on the geographical distances across which they can come together. Accordingly, markets can be highly localized, they may be regional, national, or international. Both product boundary and geographic boundary define legal markets as well as illegal markets. What distinguishes both classes of markets is the level of transparency of sellers, buyers, commodities, and prices. The flow of information that is necessary to constitute a market in the sense of an arena for the exchange of goods and services is greatly restricted under conditions of illegality. Namely, illegal businesses cannot extensively advertise their goods and services (Reuter, 1983).

This means that illegal markets are largely closed markets where transactions depend on and are defined by the nature and reach of underlying social bonds. Buyers and sellers primarily meet within the confines of networks of criminally exploitable ties and have limited options in the choice of transaction partners (see Chapter 5). Reflecting these concerns, Martin Bouchard defines a market as "the network in which a set of buyers and sellers interact to exchange goods and services for money" (Bouchard, 2007, p. 328).

Given the reliance on social network ties, several illegal markets may coexist in the very same geographical location with little or no overlap (Dwyer & Moore, 2010, p. 87). At the same time, there are also illegal markets defined by far-reaching social networks that can cover enormous geographical distances. The case of the Larry Lavin drug enterprise, presented in Chapter 6, with its customers spread across the United States provides such an example. Reuter and Haaga (1989, p. 50), in discussing the geographical scope of drug markets in the United States, also found that while most drug dealers they interviewed operated exclusively in one metropolitan area, a significant minority "were able and willing to sell elsewhere if the opportunity arose, and others reported dealing with multicity suppliers." It is problematic, therefore, to define illegal markets in conventional geographical terms, perhaps with the exception of open markets characterized by the congregation of vendors within confined public spaces, such as street squares or inner-city parks (see, e.g., Antonopoulos, Hornsby, & Hobbs, 2011; Edmunds, Hough, & Urquia, 1996; Moeller, 2012).

Another aspect that needs to be considered in the analysis of illegal markets is that the degree of concentration, that is, the number of sellers, may vary across market levels. Typically one might expect a pyramidal structure with few sellers on the upper level, more sellers on the mid-level, and a large number of sellers on the retail level (Hellman, 1980, pp. 148–149). But other configurations, for example, a concentration on the middle-market level, also appears possible (see Pearson & Hobbs, 2001, p. 36). These caveats in the definition of illegal markets notwithstanding, the question remains to what extent and by what mechanisms illegal markets may be subject to monopolization.

Empirical Research on the Structure of Illegal Markets

It seems that most empirical research on the structure of illegal markets undermines the frequently held assumption that there is a tendency toward monopolization (Desroches, 2007). Peter Reuter, for example, in his examination of the bookmaking, numbers lottery, and loan-sharking markets in the Mafia stronghold New York City of the 1970s found that "the weight of evidence is against the claim that they are monopolized" (Reuter, 1983, p. 2). John Eck and Jeffrey Gersh came to a similar conclusion in their study of drug markets in the Washington-Baltimore area. According to their research, "the overwhelming majority of trafficking organizations have very small market shares for the areas they serve" (Eck & Gersh, 2000, p. 262), resembling a "cottage industry" rather than a market "controlled by a few highly organized groups" (Eck & Gersh, 2000, p. 244). Letizia Paoli (2003b), summarizing a number of studies, likewise found little evidence of concentrated drug markets in Germany, Italy, and Russia. She concluded that in most cases, drug enterprises are small scale and operate in a competitive environment. The only exception to the commonly observed pattern of decentralized, fragmented illegal markets, as Paoli (2003b) and others have pointed out, may be provided by highly localized illegal markets.

Conditions Conducive to
the Emergence of Illegal Market Monopolies

A monopoly, as indicated before, is characterized by a single firm or a cartel of several firms functioning as the only seller of a given commodity. The domination of a market by a monopolist firm or by a cartel can be the result of a number of factors. In legal markets, the following four factors are commonly identified, not counting illegitimate means employed by legal businesses (see Case & Fair, 1992, pp. 360–363; Welch & Welch, 2010, p. 386):

- State licensing
- Patents
- Exclusive control over scarce resources
- Economies of scale

State licenses grant the right to sell a commodity, while selling without a license would be illegal. Patents grant the exclusive right to sell a commodity produced or designed in an innovative way. In illegal markets, state licenses and patents cannot play any role because these legal guarantees do not apply to illegal contexts (Luksetich & White, 1982, p. 207). However, arrangements between governments and criminal enterprises may exist that effectively constitute licenses to operate with impunity. Depending on the circumstances, such a license, issued by corrupt officials, may grant a monopoly position to an illegal firm or to a cartel of illegal firms (see Chapter 11).

More relevant within the immediate context of an illegal market may be the exclusive control over scarce resources and economies of scale. In addition, there is a commonly held assumption that monopolies in illegal markets are established through the use of violence, by one firm eliminating all competition and keeping potential competitors out of the market through force or the threat of force.

Exclusive Control Over Scarce Resources

It is at least theoretically possible that a monopoly exists in an illegal market based on one illegal firm having sole access to a factor necessary for producing and procuring the commodity that defines the market. However, real-life examples are difficult to come by. One scenario described in the literature is that a monopolization on the lower levels, namely of drug markets, may occur as the result of exclusive access to supply channels (see Costa Storti & de Grauwe, 2009, p. 54). Frequently cited, especially in the popular literature, is the example of the heroin market in New York City up until the early 1970s. Reportedly, Italian American wholesale dealers belonging to various Cosa Nostra families took advantage of exclusive links to heroin refineries in Marseille, the famous French Connection, "to monopolize the heroin trade" and to control "an estimated 95 percent of all of the heroin entering New York City" (President' Commission on Organized Crime, 1986, p. 106). While this may be an exaggeration, there is indeed some evidence that drug dealers in New York had little choice but to procure drugs from a small number of Italo-American suppliers (see Ianni, 1974, p. 239). The situation changed with the disruption of the French Connection and the opening of new supply lines that connected the drug market in New York City with sources in Southeast Asia and Mexico and that proved impossible to be controlled by a single entity (Schneider, 2008, p. 183). In general it seems that monopolies in illegal markets, should they exist, are vulnerable given the principle ease with which new sellers can enter a market (Reuter, 1983), unless other factors come into play. One such factor that "naturally" leads to market concentration and may give particular market participants a competitive advantage is what economists call economies of scale.

Economies of Scale

Economies of scale are cost-reducing effects that favor large firms over small firms. In extreme cases, the most efficient way to run a business requires a scale that only allows one firm to exist in a market. This is what economists refer to as a natural monopoly. A traditional textbook example would be a local utility company (Carroll, 1983, p. 471).

Two types of economies of scale can be distinguished, technical economies of scale and financial economies of scale. *Technical economies of scale* allow reducing average costs through increasing output with the help of large equipment or staff. *Financial economies of scale* exist where substantial financial outlays help reduce average costs—for example, by procuring raw materials in bulk (Carroll, 1983, p. 248; Hellman, 1980, p. 173; Luksetich & White, 1982, pp. 213–214).

Financial Economies of Scale. A situation that seems to come close to a monopoly based on financial economies of scale in an illegal market has been reported by Gary Potter (1994). He studied the crime landscape in an industrial town in the northeastern United States and found that a "local drug network (was) able to set the retail price for heroin, methamphetamines, and even cocaine for an entire metropolitan area simply by operating a highly efficient and cost-effective importation network through Toronto" (Potter, 1994, p. 126). This means that competing drug dealers could have procured drugs from other sources, as opposed to the heroin market in New York City in the 1960s, but not at competitive prices (see Hellman, 1980, pp. 148, 173).

Another constellation in which financial economies of scale may lead to a concentration within an illegal market involves the payment of bribes to neutralize law enforcement. The assumption is that corruption may be necessary to operate an illegal business and that the payment of large bribes to high-ranking officials by a large criminal enterprise is more cost-effective than the payment of small bribes to low-ranking officials by a large number of small illegal enterprises (Luksetich & White, 1982, pp. 214–216). Note that where only a single illegal firm is able to buy protection from corrupt officials, this constellation resembles a monopoly based on state licensing. As will be discussed in Chapter 11, there are interesting variations in the prevalence of corruption of public officials and in the degree to which corruption is centralized both on the part of illegal businesses and on the part of corrupt public officials.

Technical Economies of Scale. An example for an illegal market monopoly based on technical economies of scale is perhaps provided by John Torrio, the mentor of Al Capone and a major player in the illegal alcohol market in Prohibition-era Chicago. Early on, Torrio had been able to bring a number of breweries and distilleries under his control, which allowed him to produce alcohol for the black market at an industrial scale (Allsop, 1968, pp. 47–48; Kobler, 1971, p. 104).

Theoretically, the ability to produce high volumes of alcohol at lower average costs could have put Torrio in a position to undercut prices and to push competitors out of the market to then charge higher prices. Indeed, according to Allsop (1968, p. 48), this is what happened. However, the available information on the development of prices on the illegal alcohol market are contradictory and do not fully support this claim (see Allsop, 1968, p. 34; Kobler, 1973, p. 223).

The example of Torrio is also problematic in the present context because there was a political dimension to his position in the illegal alcohol market. Torrio has been credited with brokering an agreement with competing gangs that granted each gang exclusive rights to sell alcohol to illegal bars (speakeasies) in their respective territory (Kobler, 1971, p. 105). If indeed at some point in time Torrio was able to increase prices without concern for competition, then it might have been because of this agreement, not because of his control of large production facilities and the resulting economies of scale.

The territorial agreement brokered by Torrio leads over to the question to what extent illegal markets can be monopolized by violent means. The fact that the leading gangs of Chicago were able to guarantee each other exclusive territories for the distribution of illegal alcohol suggests two things: that they had the means for keeping other competitors not party to the agreement out of the illegal alcohol market in the city altogether and that these means were first and foremost the threat and use of violence.

However, before moving on to discussing the monopolization of illegal markets through the violent elimination of competition, another possible link between violence and monopolization of illegal markets has to be considered: economies of scale in the crime-specific use of violence.

Economies of Scale in the Crime-Specific Use of Violence. It has been suggested that violence is an integral part of certain illegal activities and that economies of scale in the use of violence can lead to a concentration of the respective illegal markets. The prime example is the loan-sharking business.

The underlying assumption is twofold: (a) that a loan shark, someone who illegally lends money at usurious rates, has to rely on the threat or use of violence to collect outstanding debts because there is no recourse to the courts, and (b) that a large organization can acquire and maintain a potential for violence at lower average costs than an individual loan shark. Luksetich and White (1982, p. 214) have made this argument as follows: "As a group, the loan sharks would need to use violence less frequently than they would if they operated independently. The need for 'muscle' could be reduced by organization, thereby reducing costs and increasing profits."

The expected outcome would be that the loan-sharking business is characterized by a few suppliers or only a single supplier rather than by a large number of small firms and individual entrepreneurs. It is a matter of debate to what extent this assumption is accurate. At least in the United States, there is little empirical evidence for a monopolization of the loan-sharking business (Reuter, 1983, pp. 107–108; Seidl, 1968, p. 68). At the same time, research suggests that typically a long-term relationship connects loan sharks with their customers and that the desire to receive future loans provides a sufficient incentive for customers to repay loans. Accordingly, the ability to use violence may not be a prerequisite for success in the loan-sharking business (Ianni, 1974, p. 39; Reuter, 1983, p. 106; see also Seidl, 1968, p. 53).

Monopolization Through Violence

The discussion of illegal market monopolies typically centers on scenarios of violent competition for market shares. Many regard the monopolization of illegal markets through violence as a defining characteristic of organized crime (Abadinsky, 2013, p. 4; Albanese, 2011, p. 3; Ignjatovic, 1998, p. 25), and incidents of violence among criminals are quickly interpreted as being the result of clashes between competing illegal enterprises.

Illegal Markets and Violence

It is true that illegal markets can be linked to high levels of violence. However, not all illegal markets in all countries are equally violent and not all violence that occurs in the context of illegal markets is directed against competitors in an effort to increase market shares and eventually to achieve a monopoly position (Andreas & Wallman, 2009). Violent conflicts can also occur between suppliers and customers, within illegal enterprises, and in the form of predatory attacks on illegal market participants (Amir, 1995; Berg & Loeber, 2015; Wright & Decker, 1997).

Drug markets generally are considered to display higher levels of violence than other illegal markets, and among different drug markets the cocaine market, for example, has been found to be more violent than the marijuana market.

Image 8.2   The St. Valentine's Day massacre of 1929, according to one interpretation, was ordered by Al Capone to eliminate competition and to gain monopoly control over Chicago's illegal alcohol market. Seven members and associates of the rival Bugs Moran gang had been lined up in a garage and killed with shotguns and machine guns. According to more plausible explanations this still unsolved crime was committed in retaliation for the hijacking of illegal liquor shipments or, even less connected to the alcohol business, in revenge of another murder (Abadinsky, 2013, p. 67; Eig, 2010, p. 252).

Photo: ASSOCIATED PRESS/Uncredited

At the same time, cross-national differences exist where the same drug spurs high levels of violence in some countries but not in others (Naylor, 2009; Reuter, 2009). These variations cannot be explained by differences in the level and fierceness of competition alone. Research on the causes of violence in illegal markets suggests that competition over market shares accounts for only a rather small percentage of observable violent events and that most violence occurs within distribution networks rather than between competing criminal groups (see Hopkins, Tilley, & Gibson, 2013; Schlegel, 1987).

In a classical study drawing on police data, Paul Goldstein and colleagues examined drug-market-related homicides in New York City and compared what they called "territorial disputes between rival dealers" with other circumstances, such as robberies of drug dealers, assaults to collect debts, punishment of workers within illegal enterprises, and disputes over drug theft. They found that in connection with crack cocaine, 44 percent of homicides were tied to territorial disputes, while in the case of powder cocaine that share was only 22 percent and in the case of other drugs only 18 percent (Goldstein, Brownstein, Ryan, & Bellucci, 1989, p. 668).

In a more recent study based on field research in New York City, Angela Taylor investigated the background of 53 disputes involving 25 drug sellers, 35 disputes ending in violence and 18 having nonviolent outcomes. Only 11 of the 53 disputes involved competing drug dealers. The most common constellation, found in 20 cases, was disputes between sellers and buyers (Taylor, 2007, p. 55). Like Goldstein et al., Taylor notes the importance of territory for conflicts between drug dealers. This means that drug dealers, more specifically retail drug dealers, try to establish and maintain an exclusive area in which they sell drugs. This area can be small and may not extend beyond a single street corner or block. The exclusive control over territory and the resulting exclusive access to customers within this territory provide some guarantee for steady income. At the same time, it seems that the stakes are not exclusively economic in nature. There is also an element of status and respect that may motivate drug sellers to establish and protect their turf (Taylor, 2007, pp. 127–130).

Whereas in the academic literature conflicts between market competitors over territory are primarily discussed with regard to the street level of illegal markets, it should be noted that, in the case of the drug war in Mexico, higher market levels may be involved. Some of the violence that has erupted in Mexico since the mid-2000s has been linked to conflicts over the exclusive use of territory for trafficking drugs into the United States (Beittel, 2011, p. 5; see also Chapter 11).

The observation that competitive violence within illegal markets is primarily linked to disputes over territory is consistent with the research on the structure of illegal markets, which has found, as mentioned, that monopoly control is most likely to be observed in highly localized settings. This is also in line with the existing theorizing on the monopolization of illegal markets.

The Theory of Illegal Market Structures

The theoretical discussion of the question to what extent there is a tendency toward the violence-based monopolization of illegal markets has focused on two sets of factors: incentives and obstacles for establishing a monopoly.

Incentives for Establishing a Monopoly in an Illegal Market. The starting point for the debate is the widely shared assumption that violence, for various reasons, is far more prevalent in illegal markets than in legal markets (see Chapter 5). It also appears plausible to assume that illegal entrepreneurs, just as their legal counterparts, have an interest in eliminating competition in order to attain monopoly profits. Yet, it is problematic to infer that illegal entrepreneurs will regularly resort to violence against competitors. There are a number of theoretical arguments that suggest that monopolies in illegal markets are more the exception than the rule, that there is no ubiquitous trend toward monopolization, and that violence is only of limited value for establishing monopoly control.

The first argument is that the incentives to establish monopoly control are weaker for illegal businesses than for legal businesses. One explanation is that profit margins are believed to be generally higher for illegal goods and services than for legal goods and services. The reason given is that suppliers of illegal goods and services can charge a premium, the so-called the crime tariff, which compensates for the risks inherent in conducting an illegal business (Potter, 1994, pp. 125, 170; Wisotsky, 1990, pp. 34–35).

Another explanation for the lesser appeal of monopoly control in illegal markets is that illegal markets are believed to have a lower density than legal markets (see Chapter 6). Law enforcement culls out a certain number of illegal enterprises (Potter, 1994, p. 170), and illegality serves as a barrier of entry to the market for those not willing to take the risk of arrest and punishment, which is said to be true for suppliers much more than for customers (Wisotsky, 1990, p. 32). According to this line of reasoning, then, demand in illegal markets tends to exceed supply. As one illegal entrepreneur interviewed by Potter and Jenkins (1985, p. 59) put it, "there's plenty for everybody." Thus there would be no need to eliminate competitors through violence or any other means.

An exception to this rule can be found in cases where markets are linked to particular locations and exclusive control of territory is a prerequisite for economic success. This is commonly assumed to be the case namely in open drug markets where dealers seek to control lucrative vending places (Hellman, 1980, p. 149; Rengert, Chakravorty, Bole, & Henderson, 2000, p. 220; Reuter, 2009, p. 277). Once dealers have established territorial control, typically over a narrow space within a larger area where drug dealing is concentrated, they may not have an incentive to expand their domain further by eliminating surrounding competitors. Rather, individual drug sellers may profit from the presence of other nearby drug sellers because it increases protection from law enforcement similar to the protection a swarm offers for an individual fish. Perhaps more importantly, a large number of drug sellers concentrated in one area may also increase profits for the individual seller because more buyers are attracted to the area (Taniguchi, Rengert, & McCord, 2009).

Obstacles for the Monopolization of Illegal Markets. When drug sellers seek to establish control over a street corner, they do not face a problem other illegal entrepreneurs striving for monopoly control will typically face, the problem of identifying who the competition is that needs to be eliminated. In the case of open drug markets, whoever shows up to sell drugs in a particular place is obviously a competitor. Matters are less obvious in closed illegal markets where market participants are known to each other primarily through social network ties. It seems that most commonly illegal firms will not be fully aware of who else operates in a market unless the market is confined to a transparent local setting where everyone knows everyone else (Wilkins & Casswell, 2003, p. 766).

The embeddedness of illegal markets in social networks also creates problems once a competitor has been eliminated. It is not a given that the illegal firm that removes a competitor through violence or any other means for that matter can simply take his or her place. The firm that seeks to aggressively expand its market share would need to identify and win over the customers of the eliminated competitor. Once again this appears likely only in an illegal market that is highly transparent (von Lampe, 2003a, p. 19; see also Reuter, 1983, p. 140).

A further problem facing monopoly-seeking firms is that they need to grow organizationally in order to be able to keep up with the growth of their business. In this respect, they encounter the same challenges of monitoring staff and of avoiding law enforcement attention that large criminal organizations generally face (see Chapter 6). In fact, illegal-market monopolists may be preferred targets for law enforcement (Reuter, 1983, p. 134).

Finally, it should be noted that maintaining a monopoly position is possibly as difficult as attaining that position in the first place. This is true at least in those cases where no barriers for market entry exist except for the threat of violence from the monopolist. The monopolist firm would have to constantly monitor the market for new competitors that, especially in closed markets, would require effective intelligence-gathering capacities (Wilkins & Casswell, 2003, p. 770). Overall, in Peter Reuter's words, "violence-based monopolies are unlikely to be pervasive or enduring" (Reuter, 1983, p. 142).

Two other aspects could have been addressed here, the problem for a monopoly-seeking firm of acquiring a sufficiently large military potential and the problem of avoiding the long-term costs of maintaining military superiority over any potential future rivals. These aspects, however, are not unique to violence-based market monopolies. They are as relevant, perhaps even more relevant in practical terms, for the emergence and continued existence of power syndicates. That is why these issues will be addressed in the following section, which deals with quasi-governmental structures.

QUASI-GOVERNMENTAL STRUCTURES

The concept of quasi-governmental structures encompasses a broad range of phenomena, which have in common that they serve certain protective and regulatory functions among criminals that are similar to functions of the state, that is, government, within legitimate society. In fact, the emergence of quasi-governmental structures within the underworld has been compared to the historical process of state formation (Skaperdas & Syropoulos, 1995; see also Tilly, 1985). As already indicated, the power of quasi-governmental structures can extend into the upperworld. For example, criminal groups may provide protection to legitimate businesses and may assist in collecting debts and settling disputes (Volkov, 2002). As one of three basic types of criminal structures, however, it is first and foremost important to understand the function quasi-governmental structures play within the underworld.

The concept of quasi-governmental structures as used here is derived from Anneliese Anderson's analysis of the Cosa Nostra family in Philadelphia. She speaks of quasi-governmental functions performed by a "criminal government (or quasi-government)" (Anderson, 1979, pp. 2, 44). Other authors have used similar terminology for describing essentially the same phenomenon, for example, "governing authority in the underworld" (Schelling, 1971, p. 74), "extralegal governance" (Varese, 2011, p. 6), or "illegal governance" (Campana, 2011, p. 214; Campana, 2013, p. 318). Just like in previous chapters, the term structure is used as a generic term that encompasses different arrangements of relationships between criminals, ranging from formal organizations to informal, ephemeral alliances.

What Quasi-Governmental Structures Do

The common denominator in the discussion of quasi-governmental structures is the distinction between, on the one hand, criminal groups engaged in the provision of illegal goods and services, and those criminal groups that are engaged in activities that are political rather than economic in nature. The latter groups "provide public goods such as the protection of property rights and the enforcement of contracts" to subordinates, namely the criminals that populate a particular illegal market or territory (Fiorentini, 2000, p. 434). In essence, the existence of a quasi-governmental structure makes life safer and more predictable for criminals who would otherwise be left in a much more chaotic, anarchic, and violent world of crime (Dixit, 2004, pp. 1–2; Haller, 1992, p. 3; Skaperdas, 2001, p. 174).

Often subsumed to the generic term of protection, the functions of quasi-governmental structures can be grouped into four broad categories: (a) the regulation of behavior of subordinates, (b) the resolution of conflicts between subordinates, (c) the protection against external threats, and (d) the generation of revenues through some form of taxation. To what extent each of these functions is performed is a matter of the specific circumstances. In one extreme, illegal governance borders on mere extortion by a terror regime that coerces its subordinates into making tribute payments while giving little or nothing in return. In the other extreme, an underworld government provides fairly comprehensive protection against competitors, predatory criminals, and law enforcement.

Regulation

Quasi-governmental structures can be found to control *who* operates in a given territory or illegal market, *what* activities criminals engage in, and *how* these illegal activities are carried out. This may amount to a more or less dense regulatory framework consisting of rules that are either originally set by a quasi-governmental structure or have emerged as subcultural norms and that are claimed to be binding for all members of the underworld.

The Outfit control over illegal gambling in Chicago (see above) provides an example of a power syndicate that regulates *who* gets to engage in a particular kind of illegal activity. In effect, the Outfit has established a form of licensing system. Illegal enterprises, in exchange for paying a street tax, are given the right to operate (Gambetta, 1993, p. 31). This kind of control over a territory or market serves first and foremost the interests of the power syndicate. It can limit illegal enterprises to a number that makes it easy enough to monitor while yielding the highest possible tax revenues. Depending on the circumstances, a power syndicate may choose to allow only one enterprise to operate, which would then be granted a monopoly position (Reuter, 1983, p. 134).

The control of entry to a territory or market, however, does not only benefit the power syndicate. Imposing a street tax means establishing a barrier for entry for new enterprises so that, to some degree, the existing illegal enterprises are protected against additional competition (Gambetta, 1993, pp. 31–32). This has various implications. First, the existing enterprises do not have to give up market shares to new entrants to their illegal market. Second, for the existing enterprises the environment within which they operate remains fairly transparent and predictable over time. Third, the likelihood of violent confrontation between established and new illegal enterprises, a main reason for violence among criminals, is reduced, which in turn reduces the risk of attracting unwanted attention from law enforcement and the general public.

For the very same reason of avoiding attention, a power syndicate may determine *what* kind of illegal activities criminals are allowed to engage in. Rules may restrict or prohibit certain criminal activities that are likely to provoke public resentment and increased police scrutiny—for example, the sale of certain drugs, such as heroin, or certain modi operandi (the *how* of criminal activities), namely, the use of violence (Anderson, 1979, p. 44). One concrete example of such a rule setting and rule enforcement within the underworld has already been mentioned in Chapter 7: the prohibition of kidnapping imposed by the *commissione* of the Sicilian Mafia for the entire island of Sicily in 1975. The prohibition was not only enforced within the Mafia but also against non-affiliated criminals. Kidnappers were either killed or the police were tipped off (Gambetta, 1993, pp. 177–179). In this case, the Sicilian Mafia employed a functional equivalent of criminal justice by setting a rule (the ban on kidnapping) and enforcing this rule through (direct or indirect) punishment.

Quasi-governmental structures not only mimic the criminal justice system, they may also serve functions similar to the civil justice system. In contrast to criminal justice where the state metes out punishment in response to what are essentially seen as wrongs against the state and society as a whole, civil justice regulates relationships between private citizens to protect individual interests (Michalowski, 1985, pp. 138–139). This is also the case when quasi-governmental structures arbitrate disputes between criminals. These disputes typically emanate from interactions within existing criminal networks.

Conflict Resolution

Conflicts between criminals may arise from personal altercations or from business dealings. The latter may involve contractual agreements or property rights pertaining to illegal firms and illegal commodities and may pertain to market-based crimes as well as predatory crimes. Typical constellations include disputes among accomplices over the sharing of crime proceeds and between suppliers and customers of illegal goods and services over such issues as late payments, product quality, and the consequences of law enforcement intervention. For example, there may be disagreement on who has to incur the financial loss when a shipment of contraband is seized: the sender, the receiver, or both (see Marks, 1998, p. 160).

Compared to legitimate society, conflicts are more likely to arise under conditions of illegality because agreements between criminals rarely exist in unambiguous, written form. At the same time, criminals have no recourse to the legal system. In this situation, Peter Reuter argues, there are incentives for criminals to "seek nonviolent third-party dispute resolution" by a quasi-governmental structure like a Cosa Nostra family rather than resorting to violence (Reuter, 1984, p. 34). A violent confrontation, as Reuter points out, can be costly in terms of the material and personal resources needed to use violence effectively, it may attract unwanted attention, and it can be costly in terms of reputation (Reuter, 1984, pp. 34–36; see also Desroches, 2007, Desroches, 2005, p. 148). The underlying assumption is that illegal entrepreneurs, at least in certain markets, value a reputation of being a reasonable businessperson who prefers nonviolent conflict resolution over the use of force against business partners (Reuter, 1984, pp. 34–35).

Protection Against External Threats

Apart from conflicts within criminal networks, criminals arguably face two main threats: the threat of law enforcement and the threat of predatory criminals. Quasi-governmental structures may provide protection against both.

Protection against law enforcement can be achieved through corruption. Quasi-governmental structures, by pooling money for bribes or by virtue of privileged access to corrupt officials, may be in a position to neutralize law enforcement more effectively than individual illegal enterprises or individual criminals (Gardiner, 1970, p. 20). This and other constellations of corrupt ties between underworld and upperworld will be discussed in more detail in Chapter 11. Protection against predatory criminals is typically achieved through the threat or use of violence. Tipping off the police may also be used as a means to neutralize a particular predatory criminal. The Sicilian Mafia's campaign against kidnapping provides an example of how both methods are employed in an effort to provide security for those under the protection of a quasi-governmental structure (Gambetta, 1993, p. 178).

Taxation

The fourth main function typically performed by a quasi-governmental structure, apart from regulation, conflict resolution, and protection, is the taxation of illegal activities. This means that a share of illicit profits is extracted from the illegal enterprises under its control. As indicated, there is some controversy over the character of these payments. While Schelling (1971) sees quasi governments in the role of extortionists, Gambetta (1993) argues that illegal enterprises willingly pay because they receive valuable services in return. Of course, it is an empirical question if in a given case illegal enterprises do in fact benefit in any way from a gang that collects a street tax and what the quality of the services is that are actually provided. From criminological research and journalistic accounts no clear picture emerges (Anastasia, 1993; Anderson, 1979; Griffin, 2002; Lombardo, 2013; Reuter, 1983). It seems that how despotic or how service-oriented illegal governance is depends to some degree on individual styles of governing and the time horizon of those in power.

The Quality of Services Provided by Quasi-governmental Structures

Quasi-governmental structures are similar to governments not only with regard to the functions they serve, but they are also in a similar position in so far as they are not under a higher authority that could supervise the fair and universal performance of their functions. That is why it could be argued that quasi-governmental structures are not likely to provide their services based on considerations of justice or the common good and instead will tend to truly protect only "the highest bidder" (Gambetta, 1993, p. 33; Varese, 2010, p. 18). Protection, then, would just be another moneymaking scheme of criminal groups. However, this seems fully plausible only where the time horizon for protection is short. As Gambetta suggests, those capable of providing protection only in the short term will seek to "maximize present over future income," and customers "will be reluctant to buy protection" (Gambetta, 1993, p. 33). In the long run, it seems more likely that quasi-governmental structures will "attempt to legitimate authority" (Anderson, 1979, p. 45). Legitimacy is a central concept in political theory. It refers to the capacity of a system "to engender and maintain the belief that the existing political institutions are the most appropriate ones for the

Image 8.3 Members of a criminal gang overlooking a slum (favela) in Brazil. Since the 1980s, many urban slums in this country have come under the rule of criminal groups that control drug trafficking and other illegal activities as well as legal businesses. They also offer individual security and access to informal criminal justice to slum dwellers, for example by finding and punishing those responsible for crimes such as robbery and rape (Pedra & Dal Ri, 2011).

Photo: Lunae Parracho/Reuters/Corbis

society" (Lipset, 1963, p. 64; see also Weber, 1968, p. 31). The assumption is that over time a regime cannot persist without some level of consent of the governed (Bluhm, 1978, p. 117). In this light, quasi-governmental structures with a long lifespan, such as the Sicilian Mafia, can be expected to vie for the support of their subordinates by providing genuine services that "are often useful to and actively sought by customers" (Gambetta, 1993, pp. 33, 187).

One should also consider the motivation of criminals involved in illegal governance. It may be less about money and more about power and respect. As several observers have noted, the behavior of mafiosi can be explained by an eagerness "to control other criminals and to be in control of their activities, and to ensure that they have respect for the authority that is exercised over them" (Edelhertz & Overcast, 1993, p. 121; see also Gambetta, 2009, p. 50; Lombardo, 2013, p. 157). How successful quasi-governmental structures are in this endeavor and how effectively they exercise their power is a different matter. The cases of the Sicilian Mafia and the American Cosa Nostra and their failure to establish full control over the territories and markets they have laid claim on illustrate the imperfections even of relatively mature systems of illegal governance (Gambetta, 1993; Lupo, 2009; Reuter, 1983).

The Structure of Illegal Governance

The focus so far has been on mafia organizations. This should not obscure the fact that quasi-governmental structures can take on very different forms. In fact, in some cases quasi-governmental functions are performed by individuals. In the German underworld, for example, there is a long history of dispute settlement by individuals with high prestige in criminal circles. In the 19th century, older, experienced and well-known criminals reportedly held court in certain bars and offered their arbitration services to other criminals (Hartmann & von Lampe, 2008, p. 126). Similar mechanisms for conflict resolution still exist. Highly respected underworld figures or, confined to migrant communities, self-appointed magistrates arbitrate disputes among criminals and criminal groups on a case-by-case basis. They may charge for their services, and the judgments can take the form of civil law verdicts aiming at compensation, or they can take the form of criminal law verdicts aiming at retribution (Behr, 1987, pp. 105–107; Rebscher & Vahlenkamp, 1988, p. 46; Henninger, 2002).

Quasi-governmental structures also exist in the form of ad hoc arrangements between criminals that may or may not become institutionalized over time. Criminals with some status may convene to set and enforce rules or to adjudicate disputes (Volkov, 2002, pp. 81–82). An illustration of such an arrangement is provided by the above mentioned agreement John Torrio brokered between the leading gangs in Chicago in the early years of Prohibition. The agreement not only entailed the division of the city into exclusive zones of influence for each of the gangs, but the gangs also made a commitment to assist each other against outsiders, and they accepted Torrio as an arbitrator of disputes arising from transactions between the gangs (Kobler, 1971, p. 105).

Opposite such rudimentary regulatory frameworks, at the other end of the spectrum of quasi-governmental structures, are centralized, hierarchical organizations exemplified by the families of the Sicilian Mafia and the American Cosa Nostra. It has been argued that most quasi-governmental structures follow this latter pattern (Skaperdas, 2001, p. 184). According to Gambetta, quasi-governmental structures can be expected "to be military in nature, that is centralized and hierarchical" because of the need to efficiently deploy violence (Gambetta, 1993, p. 68).

Another salient feature of quasi-governmental structures emphasized in the academic literature is that, almost by definition, they hold a monopoly of violence. In other words, within their respective domain they are the only providers of illegal governance services. According to this view, legal governance and illegal governance have in common that they are not practical in the face of competition. Even the extortionist at the very least has to provide protection against rival extortionists (Fiorentini, 2000, p. 436; Gambetta, 1993, p. 31; Schelling, 1971, p. 74).

In comparison to the debate on illegal-market monopolies, therefore, the question with regard to illegal governance is not if there is a trend toward monopolization, but at what scale illegal monopolies of violence are likely to emerge. One could speculate that in a continuous power struggle ever more powerful gangs come to control ever larger territories, taking advantage of economies of scale in the use of violence. Once again, however, there are a number of theoretical considerations that lets this kind of scenario appear to be rather unlikely.

Gambetta has argued that where groups of roughly equal strength compete, agreements on exclusive territories or other forms of "jurisdictional sharing" are the most probable outcome in light of the enormous costs of a violent confrontation (Gambetta, 1993, p. 70–71; see also Schelling, 1971, p. 75). To the extent this is true, the territories individual gangs have under their control would tend to be rather small. The territorial agreements between the leading gangs in Chicago during the early years of Prohibition (mentioned above) provide one illustration. Another instructive example is that of two competing mafia groups in the Sicilian town of Gela. The warring groups, one of which belonging to the Cosa Nostra, eventually came to an agreement on exclusive territories. They also agreed to form extortion teams with members from both groups to jointly collect protection payments in order to guarantee that both sides would profit from extortion (Becucci, 2011, p. 8). These two examples not only illustrate how accommodation is chosen over continued confrontation but also how this accommodation can lead to the formation of overarching structures serving the enforcement of territorial agreements (Gambetta, 1993, p. 71). In such a case, there are two layers of illegal governance, the governance by each gang of its own exclusive territory and the governance of the overall system of jurisdictional sharing. In the absence of such an overarching structure, jurisdictional sharing amounts to nothing more than peaceful coexistence of independent, typically smaller gangs in control of limited territories (Gambetta, 1993, p. 165). It should be reemphasized at this point that large criminal organizations, such as the various mafia-type organizations in Italy, Chinese triads like the Sun Yee On, and organizations like the Solntsevskaya in Moscow, are not the monolithic entities the media sometimes purport them to be. As already indicated in this and the previous chapter, these criminal organizations can be seen as primarily umbrella structures for a number of semi-autonomous or even independent criminal groups.

Conditions Conducive to
the Emergence of Quasi-Governmental Structures

The expectation that quasi-governmental structures holding an illegal monopoly of violence are most likely at a small scale, confined to localized settings, is reaffirmed when considering the contingencies of illegal governance. A comprehensive understanding of the phenomenon of quasi-governmental structures needs to take into account the conditions that favor their emergence and the resources that are needed to take advantage of these conditions (Figure 8.2). The starting point for this discussion is the assumption that quasi-governmental structures emerge in areas that the state, that is, legitimate government, is unwilling or unable to control and to regulate and where self-regulation through trust-based relations is not viable (Fiorentini, 2000; Gambetta, 1993; Skaperdas, 2001; Skaperdas & Syropoulos, 1995).

Power Vacuum

Stergios Skaperdas identifies four constellations where the lack of presence of legitimate government creates a power vacuum that quasi-governmental structures may fill: prohibition of goods and services, geographic distance, major political change, and ethnic and social distance (Skaperdas, 2001, p. 184; see also Skaperdas & Syropoulos, 1995).

The first constellation pertains to the scenario that is at the center of the discussion on organized crime and illegal governance. The state is unwilling to provide governance for those engaged in illegal activities. Instead of protecting and regulating the behavior of criminals, legitimate government is intent on suppressing their activities (Gambetta, 1993, p. 42).

The other constellations involve scenarios of state weakness or state failure: the inability of a government to control remote areas within its territory, the inability to effectively function in times of regime change and civil war, or the inability to reach marginalized segments of society. In these latter cases, quasi-governmental structures tend to replace legitimate government rather than merely filling a limited void in governance. The clearest examples for the replacement of government by quasi-governmental structures are provided by insurgent groups such as the FARC guerilla organization in Colombia (Saab & Taylor, 2009) or the Jaish-Al-Mahdi militia in Iraq (Williams, 2009). A more in-depth discussion of these groups lies beyond the scope of this book. The focus here is on illegal governance in areas that legitimate government has principally no intention of regulating: the supply of illegal goods and services as well as predatory criminal activities.

Illegal Activities Most Vulnerable to and in Need of Illegal Governance

Even though the criminalization of any activity automatically leads to a void in governance, there is a consensus in the academic literature that certain areas of crime are more likely than others to see the emergence of quasi-governmental structures. These areas of crime are characterized by specific vulnerabilities to control and by specific demands for illegal governance.

Crimes Most Vulnerable to Control. The crimes believed most likely to come under the control of a quasi-governmental structure are those most visible, where the criminals committing these crimes are most easily located and identified. This is the case especially on the retail level of illegal markets characterized by frequent interactions between sellers and a large number of customers and where criminal activities are carried out on a regular basis at fixed locations (Schelling, 1971, p. 78). The bulkiness of the product may also play a role (Reuter, 1983, p. 134).

Figure 8.2   Factors Conducive to the Emergence of Quasi-Governmental Structures

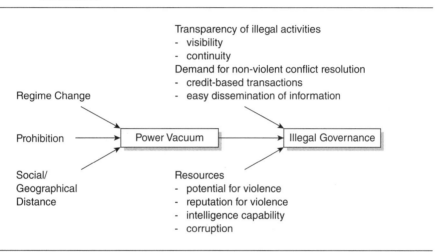

The graph highlights key factors identified in the academic literature as contributing to the emergence of quasi-governmental structures. At the center is a power vacuum created by prohibition or as a result of state weakness. Certain illegal activities are more prone to illegal governance than others, because of specific vulnerabilities to and demands for illegal governance. The resulting opportunities for establishing a quasi-governmental structure can be exploited only by those in command of certain resources, such as the potential and reputation for violence.

Source: Reuter (1983, 1984, 1994); Schelling (1971)

An additional vulnerability exists where not only the crimes as such are easily observable but also the volume of earnings. This facilitates determining the optimal amount of protection payments, while avoiding continuous conflicts over what a subordinate is able to pay (Fiorentini, 2000, p. 437). Typically, standardized percentages are used across the board, such as the 50 percent street tax levied on all gambling enterprises by the Outfit in Chicago (Lombardo, 1994, p. 303; Schelling, 1971, p. 79).

Crimes Creating the Highest Demand for Illegal Governance. As already indicated, criminals may have incentives to seek the protection and arbitration services offered by quasi-governmental structures. It can be costly for a criminal to use violence and to be known as someone who quickly resorts to violence when a dispute arises. Instead, it is advantageous to have an arbiter who can resolve conflicts peacefully and who can authoritatively determine that a particular conduct was honorable. The incentives to seek arbitration services, however, as Peter Reuter (1983; Reuter, 1984) argues, are unevenly distributed across criminal activities and illegal markets. He posits that the demand for illegal governance is strongest where the reputational costs of violence are the highest (Reuter, 1984, p. 35). This, Reuter assumes, depends on two factors. The first factor is the importance of a reputation for honorable conduct. The more market participants have to rely on mutual trust in the absence of safeguards against disloyal behavior, the more important such a reputation becomes. This depends in large part on the way a business is conducted. A reputation for honorable conduct is most valued where transactions are made on credit rather than on a cash basis and where the quality of a good or service cannot easily be tested on the spot (Reuter, 1984, pp. 35–36). The second factor determining the demand for illegal governance is the ease with which information can be credibly disseminated and, accordingly, how easy it is for a criminal's reputation to be shaped and tarnished. Reuter argues that this is primarily a matter of the intensity of law enforcement. Where penalties following arrest are slight, market participants can be expected to "readily exchange information with others about particular transactions and operators" (Reuter, 1984, p. 36). Both factors, the need for nonviolent conflict resolution and the ease of communication in criminal circles, Reuter assumes to be most salient in illegal sport betting, in contrast, for example, to illegal drug markets (Reuter, 1983, 1984).

Resources on Which Illegal Governance Is Based

The existence of conditions conducive to illegal governance does not automatically lead to the emergence of quasi-governmental structures. There must be someone present with the necessary resources to take advantage of these conditions. In a nutshell, illegal governance rests on the ability to enforce decisions. In some cases, the authority of an individual, based on charisma and high esteem, may be sufficient (Rebscher & Vahlenkamp, 1988, p. 46). In most cases, however, the ability, and the reputation for the effective use of violence appears to be necessary in combination with an intelligence capability for collecting information that indicates against whom the threat or use of violence needs to be directed (Gambetta, 1993, p. 59; Varese, 2010, pp. 14–15).

Violence. The ability to use violence is an individual skill as well as a collective resource. Quasi-governmental structures, as Peter Reuter (1983, pp. 133–136) has argued, will tend to command a military potential defined primarily by their strength in numbers. This, in turn, implies that a sufficient number of sufficiently skilled individuals is present or is available for recruitment. The key is to gain superiority over those to be governed individually and combined and over any potential rivals. Once a group has acquired this position, others are discouraged from investing in military resources (Fiorentini, 2000, p. 441; Gambetta, 1993, p. 40; Reuter, 1983, p. 136).

There are several possible scenarios for such a situation to emerge. One can think of a process starting with a state of anarchy where everyone is left to fend for him- or herself. Out of a constant struggle for survival, some can be expected to emerge as better skilled and better equipped for violent confrontation than others. Individuals and small groups may form alliances and band together and eventually the group with the greatest potential for violence will establish a permanent position of power (see Skaperdas & Syropoulos, 1995). The history of the Sicilian Mafia could be interpreted in this way. In other cases, the dominance of a given group may be short lived and the process is more one of periodical change, where the demise of one powerful group is followed by the ascent of another.

There are also cases of groups that command a potential for violence as a by-product of processes unrelated to any power struggles within the underworld. At some point in time, however, these groups may come to take advantage of their military potential. The history of the Hell's Angels and other outlaw motorcycle gangs as well as of the German Ringvereine suggests such a development (see Chapter 7). These organizations were originally created to serve the social needs of their members. Yet, because of their recruitment patterns they almost inevitably built up a military potential along the way. Outlaw motorcycle gangs have from the start attracted violence-prone individuals who do not shy away from a fight, and the German Ringvereine as self-help organizations of ex-convicts more or less by definition had a membership made up of professional criminals. Before long, these intimidating collectives began to exert influence within the underworld (see Barker, 2007; Hartmann & von Lampe, 2008).

Intelligence Capability. The second key resource for quasi-governmental structures mentioned in the literature, apart from a potential for violence, is the capacity to gather information about subordinates and potential rivals (Gambetta, 1993, pp. 37–38, 126; Varese, 2010, p. 15). In this respect a quasi-government faces challenges similar to those described earlier in this chapter with regard to the violent monopolization of illegal markets. Once again, no problems may arise in highly localized, transparent settings where everyone knows everyone else. Otherwise, however, a quasi-governmental structure will have to rely on what Gambetta (1993, p. 59) has called an "intelligence network" to identify those who defy and challenge its power, communications channels resting on social network ties, underworld business contacts, the underworld "grapevine system" and in some cases even a specialized staff of lookouts (Gambetta, 1993, pp. 37–38; Lombardo, 1994, p. 304).

In addition, a quasi-governmental structure needs mechanisms for processing and sharing information internally in order to be able to effectively coordinate its governance activities, thereby avoiding that its members come into conflict with each other (Reuter, 1983, p. 172). Both aspects, the gathering and the internal processing of information about subordinates and potential rivals, hint at possible limitations to the size of the territory and the range of illegal activities a quasi-governmental structure is realistically capable of controlling.

Reputation. The flow of information is relevant yet in another way, going in the opposite direction, from the quasi-governmental structure to its subordinates and to potential rivals. The underlying assumption is twofold: that quasi-governmental structures need to advertise their existence and their services and that they rely on the dissemination of information to build and maintain a reputation for the effective use of violence (Gambetta, 1993, p. 251).

The Nature and Origins of a Reputation for Violence. Reputation is considered the key resource for quasi-governmental structures. According to Gambetta, it "is nearly everything in the protection business" (Gambetta, 2009, p. 216). Reputation in this context is a combination of the *knowledge* that a quasi-governmental structure exists and the *belief* that it has the power to impose its will (Reuter, 1994, p. 111).

Reputation is deemed essential because of its cost-saving effects. Once established, it dramatically reduces the need for the actual use of violence (Gambetta, 2009, pp. 204–205), and a robust reputation even permits a cost-saving reduction in the military potential without loss of authority (Reuter, 1983, p. 135). In fact, since a reputation is the product of communication, it does not necessarily have to have a factual basis at all and may be a pure myth (Gambetta, 1993, p. 44; Reuter, 1994, p. 95). What should also be noted is that whereas under conditions of illegality information is normally spread through clandestine communication channels, the same does not apply here. In the case of a reputation for violence, the media can play a central role by turning the spotlight on particular individuals or gangs who are accurately or inaccurately portrayed as violent and powerful (Gambetta, 1993, p. 65).

Threats and Challenges to a Reputation for Violence. Direct challenges aside, which may come from rivals or recalcitrant subordinates, there are two possible threats to the reputation of a quasi-governmental structure. Both threats highlight that there has to be an identifiable and delineable group that serves as a clear reference point for the reputation for violence in order to be effective.

One threat stems from *imposters* misusing and thereby undermining the reputation of a criminal group. The other threat is linked to the problem of *succession* and the question to what extent reputation is attached to individuals or to an organizational entity. A group cannot function effectively as a quasi-governmental structure if its identity remains elusive and subordinates are unable to determine if someone who claims to act on its behalf is indeed authorized to do so.

Where the members belonging to a quasi-governmental structure are not known to subordinates in person, imposters can fairly easily "pose as an authentic mafioso and reap the benefits" (Gambetta, 1993, p. 45). For example, the Solntsevskaya, considered to be the most powerful racketeering organization in Moscow (see Chapter 7), has reportedly faced increasing problems with impersonators as a result of the practice to allow numerous small gangs to operate under its name (Serio, 2008, pp. 216–217). The effect is similar to a situation where rival groups compete for dominance: "the protector dislikes unfair competition and is eager to reassure customers that they are not paying the wrong person" (Gambetta, 1993, p. 124; see also Grayson, 2014, pp. 37–39).

The threat from imposters is reduced if all those belonging to a quasi-governmental structure are easily identifiable, namely, because they are ethnically distinct, as in the case of the American Cosa Nostra, or because they wear exclusive symbols such as the "colors" and tattoos of outlaw motorcycle gangs. This of course is not effective unless unauthorized use of these symbols is prevented. Accordingly, organizations that have distinctive symbols that can easily be counterfeited tend to use draconian measures against nonmembers who dare to display these symbols (Gambetta, 2009, p. 179). Outlaw biker gangs, for example, are reputed to go as far as removing a tattoo by cutting off the respective patch of skin (Marsden & Sher, 2007, p. 289).

The reputation of a quasi-governmental structure can also be undermined by a change in membership if the reputation is linked to individuals rather than to the structure itself. Arrests or deaths could then quickly lead to the demise of a once powerful gang (see, e.g., Kray & Kray, 1988). That is why there is an incentive for a quasi-governmental structure to develop a recognizable collective identity, which in turn requires the establishment of "clear and credible rules and practices" for the selection and conduct of members (Gambetta, 2009, pp. 205–206). As a result, the reputation of the quasi-governmental structure would no longer hinge on the individual reputation of members. Instead, the reputation would be an asset that members acquire through membership (Reuter, 1994, p. 103). It is against this backdrop that Diego Gambetta characterizes the Sicilian Mafia as a set of firms that share "a common asset of reputation, equivalent to a trademark: a guarantee of high-quality protection and effective intimidation. This reputation is distinct from that of each individual family or member, but each gains from it, and each has an interest in maintaining its distinctive features" (Gambetta, 1993, p. 245).

While reputation is a vital asset for quasi-governmental structures, it is a "two-edged sword" (Reuter, 1983, p. 142). A reputation can be a liability because it is likely to attract the attention of law enforcement and the general public (Reuter, 1983, p. 137). That is why Reuter and others have argued that a reputation for the effective use of violence alone may not be sufficient and that it needs to be supplemented by the ability of a quasi-governmental structure to neutralize law enforcement through corruption or by some other means (Reuter, 1994, p. 104). Another possible scenario is that a quasi-governmental structure is tolerated by the authorities because it is considered the lesser evil (Whyte, 1943/1981, pp. 138–139).

DELINEATING ILLEGAL-MARKET MONOPOLIES AND QUASI-GOVERNMENTAL STRUCTURES

As already indicated, quasi-governmental structures do not always appear in a pure form. There may be some overlap with entrepreneurial and especially with associational structures (see Chapter 7). Likewise, quasi-governmental structures and illegal-market monopolies may coincide. A careful analysis is necessary to determine the nature of the specific link between the two types of structures. In some instances, the two structures may be identical; in some instances they may partially overlap or coexist without any degree of organizational integration. The latter would be the case where a quasi government allows a single firm to operate in a given illegal market (see Reuter, 1983, p. 134).

A partial overlap of associational and quasi-governmental structures would exist where individual members of the quasi-governmental structure own and operate a monopoly firm. A complete overlap, finally, would exist where a quasi-governmental structure is identical to an illegal firm monopolizing an illegal market (see Anderson, 1979, p. 49). For example, a gang that is selling drugs in its neighborhood and is keeping competition away, thus holding an illegal-market monopoly, may at the same time regulate and tax other illegal activities in its territory, such as gambling and prostitution, thus also functioning as a quasi government. It is a question, however, to what extent quasi-governmental and entrepreneurial structures would indeed be one and the same. Even though the membership may be identical, the structures could still be fundamentally different because of the different organizational requirements of running a business versus running a government (Campana, 2011, p. 223; Densley, 2012). Providing an illegal good or service will tend to be a more time-consuming activity than regulating and taxing illegal behavior (see Chapter 5). Therefore, a gang may function as a quasi-governmental structure with a military-style hierarchy, and at the same time the gang members may operate a drug distribution enterprise on a partnership basis with decentralized authority to flexibly adapt to the intricacies of the drug business (see Chapters 5 and 6).

An analytical framework that accounts for these differentiations is not only necessary for adequately capturing the complexities and variability of criminal structures as such, but it is also important for anticipating the consequences of events, such as the arrest or elimination of individual criminals. The removal of the head of a quasi-governmental structure may undermine the ability to regulate a market and may lead to uncontrolled violence. In comparison, the removal of the head of an illegal firm might disrupt the operations of this firm, and in the case of a monopoly firm, could lead to the emergence of new competitors in the market while the governance structure may well remain unaffected.

ILLEGAL-MARKET MONOPOLIES AND
MONOPOLIES OF VIOLENCE: SUMMARY AND CONCLUSION

Following the discussion of entrepreneurial structures and associational structures in the two previous chapters, this chapter has examined two forms in which criminals can achieve dominance over other criminals: illegal-market monopolies and illegal monopolies of violence. The discussion of illegal-market monopolies is an extension of the examination of entrepreneurial structures, more specifically illegal firms, presented in Chapter 6. An illegal-market monopoly exists if there is only one firm or a cartel of firms selling an illegal good or service.

In the case of an illegal monopoly of violence, criminals form quasi-governmental structures. They do not act as an illegal firm engaged in economic activity but as a form of underworld government serving political functions. This entails controlling and regulating an illegal market or a territory functionally similar to the state in legitimate society. Under certain circumstances, the influence of a quasi-governmental structure can extend beyond the underworld into the upperworld. This will be explored in more detail in Chapter 11.

A central point of debate addressed in this chapter has been the question to what extent there is a tendency toward the monopolization of illegal markets. A review of the empirical and theoretical literature suggests that for a variety of reasons, illegal-market monopolies are a relatively rare occurrence, and where they emerge, they are typically confined to highly localized settings.

The question of a trend toward monopolization does not pose itself in the same way with regard to quasi-governmental structures. Illegal governance, just like legal governance, is not practical in the presence of competition. The question instead is under what circumstances and on what scale quasi-governmental structures holding an illegal monopoly of violence come into existence. This is first of all a matter of the power vacuum that legitimate government creates by prohibiting certain goods and services. This vacuum may be filled by criminals who are capable of providing governance services. Respected individuals may assume this role solely based on their social esteem, especially with respect to the arbitration of disputes. But typically the key resources required are the capacity and reputation for the effective use of violence. Just like in the case of illegal-market monopolies, this is most likely in highly localized, transparent settings that are easy to monitor and where a reputation linked to an identifiable and delineable quasi-governmental structure can most easily form. This suggests that on a grander scale the most likely scenario is the co-existence of numerous smaller gangs who each control a small territory based on some formal or informal jurisdictional sharing agreement with neighboring gangs, rather than a process toward an ever-expanding underworld government.

Discussion Questions

1. What is preferable from the perspective of criminals, to hold an illegal-market monopoly or to control an illegal market in the form of a quasi-governmental structure?

2. What is preferable from the perspective of legitimate society, to have an underworld under the control of a quasi-governmental structure or one with no such regulatory framework?

3. What would it take for a criminal gang to establish a monopoly in the cocaine market in your country?

Research Projects

1. Analyze the autobiographies of organized criminals with a view to failed and successful attempts of the monopolization and regulation of illegal markets.

2. Examine the changes in illegal drug prices for a particular area and see if sudden increases or decreases in prices occurred that could be an indicator for the creation, respectively breakdown of a market monopoly.

Further Reading

The Organization of Illegal Markets

Brownstein, H. H., Mulcahy, T. M., Fernandes-Huessey, J., Taylor, B. G., & Woods, D. (2012). The organization and operation of illicit retail methamphetamine markets. *Criminal Justice Policy Review, 23*(1), 67–89.

Hagedorn, J. (1994). Neighborhoods, markets, and gang drug organization. *Journal of Research in Crime and Delinquency, 31*(3), 264–294.

Jager, M. (2003). The market and criminal law: The case of corruption. In P. C. Van Duyne, Petrus C. K. von Lampe, & J. L. Newell (Eds.), *Criminal finances and organising crime in Europe* (pp. 153–173.). Nijmegen, the Netherlands: Wolf Legal.

Moeller, K., & Hesse, M. (2013). Drug market disruption and systemic violence: Cannabis markets in Copenhagen. *European Journal of Criminology, 10*(2), 206–221.

Conflict Resolution and Governance Under Conditions of Illegality

Jacques, S., & Wright, R. (2013). How victimized drug traders mobilize police. *Journal of Contemporary Ethnography, 42*(5), 545–575.

Liddick, D. (1999). *The Mob's daily number: Organized crime and the numbers gambling industry.* Lanham, MD: University Press of America.

Morselli, C., Tanguay, D., & Labalette, A.-M. (2008). Criminal conflicts and collective violence: Biker-related account settlements in Quebec. In D. Siegel & H. Nelen (Eds.), *Organized crime: Culture, markets and policies* (pp. 145–163). New York: Springer.

Varese, F. (2014). Protection and extortion. In L. Paoli (Ed.), *The Oxford handbook of organized crime* (pp. 343–358). Oxford: Oxford University Press.

PART III

Organized Crime and Society

The previous five chapters have examined the various activities and structures associated with organized crime. The umbrella term *organized crime* was broken down into smaller categories along the three basic dimensions of criminal activities, criminal structures, and illegal governance. Three basic types of "organized" criminal *activities* were discussed: market-based crimes, predatory crimes, and illegal governance crimes. Organized criminal *structures* were examined based on the distinction of entrepreneurial structures, associational structures, and quasi-governmental structures. Relatively little attention has been paid so far to the social context of all of these phenomena. The purpose of the following four chapters is to better understand the social position of organized crime. The discussion revolves around two questions. The first question refers to the location of organized crime in society: What segments of society are involved in and affected by organized crime? The second question pertains to the nature of the relationship between organized crime and society: Is organized crime a threat to society, a necessary evil, or an integral part of the social fabric?

The following three chapters will address the general social embeddedness of organized crime (Chapter 9), the link between organized crime and legal business (Chapter 10), and the link between organized crime and government (Chapter 11). In addition, one chapter (Chapter 12) will deal with organized crime on a transnational, global scale, including organized crime in cyberspace.

CHAPTER 9

The Social Embeddedness of Organized Crime

INTRODUCTION

This chapter explores in general terms what place organized crime occupies in society. The focus is on the social embeddedness of organized *crimes*, organized *criminals*, and organized criminal *structures*. The term *social embeddedness* refers, in the first instance, to underlying social relations that enable or at least facilitate the emergence of criminal networks, by providing participants with a common basis of trust (Kleemans & Van de Bunt, 1999; Morselli, 2001). As discussed in Chapter 5, familial, friendship, and community ties are commonly believed to provide the glue that holds criminal structures together, while other social groupings, such as business networks, may also be relevant for the formation of criminal relations.

In a more general sense, social embeddedness refers to the social environment within which organized criminals find themselves. How supportive is society of organized criminals with respect to what they are and what they do? Understood in this way, the starting point for the discussion of the social embeddedness of organized crime is a simple notion: Organized crime is not something that exists in a social or cultural vacuum (Van Duyne, 1996, p. 344; Woodiwiss, 1993, p. 28). In former times, there may have been autarkic, self-contained communities of pirates and highway robbers ("picaresque organizations" in McIntosh's (1975) terminology) that came into contact with the outside world only when they encountered their next victim. But overall it appears safe to say that organized criminals continuously operate within and interact with a social environment, a social microcosm (Chapter 4) that includes people who are *not* involved in criminal conduct themselves (Kleemans & Van de Bunt, 1999, p. 19). While this is almost a truism, there has been some controversy over the nature of the relationship between organized crime and society. At what level of the social hierarchy can organized criminals be found? Is organized crime something at the margins of society or rather something that is located in the midst of society or even at the top of society? And how hostile or amicable are the relations between organized crime and society; can the two be separated at all? The different viewpoints can be placed on a continuum ranging from *confrontation* to *accommodation* to *integration*.

When organized crime is framed in terms of delineable criminal organizations, such as the American Cosa Nostra, the relationship between organized crime and society tends to be depicted as adversarial, as a clash between two separate entities. Organized crime, according to this view, is something alien to society, "a malignant parasite" (New York State, 1966, p. 19) that undermines legitimate social institutions and constitutes a "growing threat to the global community" (Mallory, 2012, p. xix). The prototypical organized criminal, according to this perspective, is a foreigner or someone who for other reasons is at the margins of society. Another perspective holds that organized crime coexists with legitimate society. Some interaction and overlap between criminal and legal structures is believed to exist, characterized by "accommodation and compromise" (Smith, 1975, p. 18). A third view, finally, sees organized crime as an integral part of the fabric of society. Organized crime and society, it is argued, form a symbiotic rather than parasitical relationship (Ianni, 1974, pp. 330–331), and even more so, organized crime is seen to be "part and parcel of the overarching social system" (Potter, 1994, p. 183).

It is important to note that these different perspectives may reflect differences in the phenomena that are being observed. It may also play a role through what ideological lens observations are made. And sometimes the controversies seem to be more a struggle over words rather than disagreements in substance. It cannot be the purpose of this chapter to determine which view is the most accurate one. The real world of crime is simply too diverse and complex to be exhaustively addressed from a single vantage point. The purpose of this chapter, instead, is to highlight some of the dimensions across which the relationship between organized crime and society varies and to caution against simplistic conceptions.

The relationship between organized crime and society will be discussed with a view to two recurring themes in the literature. One contention is that the existence of organized crime depends on the public demand for illegal goods and services. The other contention is that organized criminals and criminal organizations are rooted in specific social milieus, subcultures, and local communities.

THE SOCIAL EMBEDDEDNESS OF ORGANIZED CRIME: ILLEGAL GOODS AND SERVICES

To the extent organized crime can be equated with the provision of illegal goods and services, it is easy to say that organized crime and society are inherently linked. One can argue that organized crime only exists because there is a public demand for such things as illegal drugs, illegal gambling, counterfeit designer clothes, smuggled cigarettes, or child pornography (Albini, 1971, p. 55; Block & Chambliss, 1981; Potter, 1994). While this link between the demand for and the supply of illegal goods and services is obvious, there are some complications that need to be considered. First, with the focus on illegal markets, predatory crimes are largely ignored. Second, it is taken for granted that illegal markets are demand driven. Block and Chambliss (1981, p. 32), for example, contend, "the iron law of capitalism is that where there is a demand there will be a supplier if the profit is high enough" (see also Rawlinson, 2002, p. 296). But this is not a given and does not explain why there are such great variations in the demand for illegal goods and services and why people are willing to pay for illegal goods and services in the first place.

Variations in the Prevalence of Illegal Markets

Illegal markets are not constant across space and time. The abstract statement, therefore, that organized crime exists because there is a demand for illegal goods and services does not explain that much. To begin with, certain illegal goods and services are very popular in some countries and almost unheard of in others. This may be linked to underlying sociocultural and economic differences. For example, the trafficking of children for camel jockeying is concentrated in the Middle East, while being virtually absent in other parts of the world, although other forms of child trafficking do exist elsewhere (Kooijmans & Van de Glind, 2010, pp. 30–32). Obviously, where there is no camel racing, there is no demand for child camel jockeys. However, even in the case of commodities that are omnipresent in the world and for which there is potentially a global illicit demand, there are dramatic differences in the extent of illegal markets. Cigarettes are a case in point.

It has been estimated in the late 2000s that 11.6 percent of the globally smoked cigarettes were illicit, which means they were sold without paying proper taxes, and sometimes they were also illegal because they were counterfeit-brand cigarettes. At the same time, the share of illegal cigarettes has been found to be as low as 1 percent of the overall cigarette market in some countries and as high as 80 percent in others (Joossens, Merriman, Ross, & Raw, 2009). These differences escape simple explanations. Surprisingly, they are not closely linked to different levels of taxation and different income levels. It would seem logical to assume that more smokers will turn to cheap illegal cigarettes where the legal prices (due to taxation) are high and smokers have little money to spend on cigarettes (Farrell & Fray, 2013). However, comparative research has shown that some high-tax countries have had less of a problem with illegal cigarettes than some low-tax countries. In contrast, other factors such as levels of corruption appear more relevant (Joossens & Raw, 1998, 2012).

Illegal drug markets provide another illustration of cross-national variations that are not easily explained. Overall, it is estimated that 4.5 percent of the global adult population use illegal drugs. There are great differences between countries, however, namely with regard to the popularity of particular drugs and the levels of consumption (Anderson, 2006; UNODC, 2014a). Globally the most widely used illicit drug is cannabis. In 2010, prior to the legalization of nonmedical marijuana in parts of the United States and in Uruguay (Pardo, 2014; Room, 2014), an estimated 119 to 224 million persons aged 15 to 64 years, equal to between 2.6 and 5.0 percent of the adult population, had used cannabis at least once. However, prevalence varied considerably. The highest levels of use were found in Australia and New Zealand (up to 14.6 percent of the adult population), followed by North America (10.8 percent) and Western and Central Europe (7.0 percent). In contrast, cannabis use in Asia was prevalent only among an estimated 1.0 to 3.4 percent of the adult population (UNODC, 2012, p. 8).

Similar discrepancies in the prevalence of consumption can also be shown with regard to other illegal drugs. Prevalence of cocaine use in 2010, for example, was estimated at 2.1 percent in Australia, 2.16 percent in the United States, and 2.2 percent in England and Wales, compared with much lower levels in such diverse countries as Norway (0.4 percent), Russia (0.23 percent), and South Korea (0.03 percent) (UNODC, 2012, Statistical Annex; see also UNODC, 2014a, Annex I, p. xii). One explanation that has been offered for these variations is that drugs are viewed differently in different cultures (Pakes & Silverstone, 2012).

A noteworthy example for cross-national variations is also provided by the synthetic drug methamphetamine, which has historically been very popular in just a few countries—namely, Japan, since World War II, and the Czech Republic (formerly a part of Czechoslovakia), since the 1970s (Hill, 2003; UNODC, 2014a; Zabransky, 2007). This is particularly puzzling because there is apparently no direct link between the Japanese and the Czech methamphetamine markets, and their respective neighboring countries show different patterns of drug use despite similar historical developments and socioeconomic conditions. This is especially true when one compares the Czech Republic to other former Soviet Bloc countries in central Europe, such as Poland and Hungary (see EMCDDA, 2002).

Interestingly, the prevalence of illegal markets also varies within individual countries. In the United States, for example, methamphetamine use has for many years been fairly widespread in the western states while being largely absent on the East Coast (Gonzales, Mooney, & Rawson, 2010, p. 388; Goode, 2005, p. 151). Similarly, the cigarette black market in—for example, England, Germany, and Poland—has been concentrated in certain parts of these countries (Calderoni, Favarin, Ingrasci, & Smit, 2013, p. 64; Ciecierski, 2007; von Lampe, 2005a, 2006a).

Variations in the consumption of illegal goods and services—namely, illicit drugs—can also be found by gender, age, social class, and ethnicity (EMCDDA, 2013; Smart, Adlaf, & Walsh, 1994; UNODC, 2014a, pp. 2–3; U.S. Department of Health and Human Services, 2014). In some cases, consumption is concentrated in particular subcultures. For example, the spread of cannabis in Europe has been closely connected to the "middle-class counter-cultures" of the 1960s and 1970s (Sandberg, 2012, p. 1145), and the spread of ecstasy in the 1980s and 1990s has been closely connected to the dance and techno-music scene (Antonopoulos, Papanicolaou, & Simpson, 2010; Gruppo Abele, 2003).

Finally, illegal markets change over time. A common pattern is that an illegal commodity gains popularity, marked by rapid increase in consumption, followed by a decline in use after a few years (EMCDDA, 2013; Goode, 2005). In the United States, for example, cocaine has gone through several fashion cycles. It was largely absent from the drug market in the wake of its criminalization by the Harrison Act of 1914 up until the mid-1960s. Through the early 1980s, cocaine use increased sharply. In the mid- to late-1980s, cocaine use decreased and, after a new increase during the 1990s, appears to have been in decline again since the early 2000s (Goode, 2005, p. 101; UNODC, 2014a, p. 35). In contrast, the prevalence of methamphetamine has substantially increased since the 1980s and 1990s (Shukla, Crump, & Chrisco, 2012).

The Relative Importance of Illegal Supply and Demand

The demand for illegal goods and services is a poorly understood phenomenon. Writing about drug use, Goode (2005, p. 54) notes that there is "an almost bewildering array of theories." Yet, the issue is even more complex. Some argue that supply rather than demand is the driving force behind the creation of illegal markets. So the bigger question is twofold: (a) what creates demand for illegal goods and services? And (b) are illegal markets shaped more by the demand for or more by the supply of illegal goods and services? The question of the relative importance of supply and demand for the shaping of illegal markets is not purely academic. There are obvious policy implications (Rydell & Everingham, 1994). Should resources primarily be deployed to tackle the production and smuggling of illicit goods (supply side)? Or instead, should resources be used to reduce the urge and willingness of consumers to buy illicit goods (demand side)? The question of the relative importance of supply and demand, therefore, deserves closer inspection, although a definitive answer cannot be given (Besozzi, 2001; Fuentes & Kelly, 1999).

Pat O'Malley and Stephen Mugford (1991), writing about drug use, have identified four *discourses* dealing with the consumption of illegal goods and services. This classification, which is still valid today, can help in better understanding the different views on why illegal markets exist and how they fit into society. O'Malley and Mugford (1991, p. 50) distinguish "discourses of pathology, profit, the state, and pleasure." These discourses point to various macro- and micro-level factors on the supply and demand side (Table 9.1).

Table 9.1 Factors Influencing the Emergence of Illegal Markets

		Factors	Examples
Macro Level		Political Decisions	Prohibitions defining certain goods and services as illegal
	Pathologies	Social Deficiencies	Poverty creating a demand for cheap illegal goods
		Individual Deficiencies	Genetic factors increasing the intoxicating and addictive effect of drugs
Micro Level	Individual Choices	Pleasure	Hedonistic lifestyle leading to recreational drug use
		Cost-Benefit Calculations	Cost savings from using illegal labor
		Power and Security	Illegal debt collection by criminal group
	Supply		Offering novel drug to potential consumers

Source: Integration of classifications from Besozzi (2001) and O'Malley and Mugford (1991).

Individual and Social Deficiencies as Drivers of Illegal Markets

The *pathology discourse* suggests that the use of illegal goods and services results from individual or social deficiencies. In other words, illegal markets are believed to be demand driven. Demand, in turn, is assumed to exist because there is something wrong with people or with society as a whole. A large body of academic literature falls into this category.

There is extensive research linking the demand for illegal goods and services, such as drugs, gambling, and prostitution, to a host of biological and psychiatric disorders. For example, biological and in particular genetic factors can account for variations in the intoxicating and addictive effects of illegal drugs on the individual. Biological predispositions toward compulsive behavior and addiction may also play a role with regard to illegal gambling (Ibáñez, Blanco, Perez de Castro, Fernandez-Piqueras, & Sáiz-Ruiz, 2003) and possibly illegal prostitution (Kafka, 2010). Psychiatric disorders such as schizophrenia, depression, and attention-deficit-hyperactivity disorder have likewise been linked to illicit demand, namely, for illegal drugs (Cami & Farre, 2003). And neurodevelopmental disorders, including head injuries in early childhood, have been discussed as potential causes of pedophilia. By extension, these factors may account in part for a demand for child pornography and child prostitutes (Seto, 2008, pp. 173–175). Other research has associated the demand for illegal goods and services with social problems, such as poverty and racial discrimination (Hunte & Barry, 2012; Shaw, Egan, & Gillespie, 2007). The very same problems may also account for the supply side of illegal markets, for example, in the case of child trafficking when parents sell their children out of financial despair (Shen, Antonopoulos, & Papanicolaou, 2013, pp. 34–35).

Supply-Driven Illegal Markets

The *profit discourse* focuses on the role of supply and on the profitability of illegal markets. Similar to the pathology discourse, demand for illegal goods and services is not seen as resulting from autonomous decisions of consumers, nor, however, is it linked to individual circumstances. Instead, demand appears as something that is purposefully created by aggressive entrepreneurs who exploit human weaknesses. For example, drug use is seen as the result of ruthless dealers enticing weak-minded consumers to use drugs. This view is reflected in drug policies that focus on supply-side interventions in the form of crop eradication, increased border controls, and aggressive policing against drug dealers.

Research findings on the importance of supply are mixed (MacCoun & Reuter, 2001, p. 77), while anecdotal evidence suggests that at least in some instances supply creates demand. The case of the Larry Lavin enterprise presented in Chapter 6, for example, is noteworthy in this context, because the shift from selling marijuana to selling cocaine was brought about by suppliers urging Lavin to introduce his customers to this drug (Bowden, 2001, pp. 56–57; Saline, 1989, p. 60). One dealer told Lavin, "You know how it works, Larry. If you start selling it, they'll start buying it" (Bowden, 2001, p. 65).

Another example for supply-side factors accounting for the emergence of an illegal market is provided by the case of methamphetamine in the Czech Republic. Until the 1970s, drug abuse in Czechoslovakia was largely confined to alcohol and prescription drugs. Then, a method to produce methamphet-amine from freely available pharmaceuticals was developed in the Czech drug scene, and subsequently methamphetamine use became widespread (Zabransky, 2007, pp. 157–159).

It should also be noted that an increase in the use of drugs can be observed along trafficking routes. This is likely the result of a spillover effect. Increased drug consumption may be attributed to the greater availability of drugs gener-ally and especially to the tendency of traffickers to pay for services not in cash but in the form of drugs (Besozzi, 2001, p. 27; Beyrer et al., 2000; Brouwer et al., 2006; Fenopetov, 2006). Likewise, drug consumption tends to be higher with proximity to source countries. This applies to geographical proximity as well as to social proximity resulting from colonialism or migration (Lenke, 2008). In other words, the greater the availability of drugs (supply), the greater the consumption (demand).

Illegal Markets as Products of Political Decisions

The *state discourse,* according to O'Malley and Mugford's (1991) typology, deals with the role of legal prohibitions for the creation of illegal markets. The underlying notion is that all illegal goods and services have initially been legal and unregulated and have been restricted and criminalized only at a later point in time.

In the state discourse, the use of illegal goods and services, namely drugs, is treated as a normal feature of society. However, demand is not a central issue in this discourse. The main focus is on the question why certain commodities are legal while others are illegal.

Spontaneously one might say that levels of harm are the main determinant. It lies in the very nature of criminal law that criminal offenses pertain to harmful conduct. Yet in some cases, namely drugs, harm is but one factor. Neither addic-tiveness nor dangerousness can explain where the line between legal and illegal substances is drawn. After all, addictive and harmful drugs such as nicotine and alcohol are not prohibited, at least as far as contemporary western industrial-ized countries are concerned.

Other explanations for what appear to be arbitrary decisions to criminalize certain substances point to political and economic interests (Michalowski, 1985). It has been argued, for example, that the criminalization of agriculturally based drugs such as cocaine, heroin, and marijuana serves to protect the pharmaceutical industry in First World countries against unwanted competition from the Third World. According to this view, cocaine, heroin, and marijuana share a market with pharmaceutical products such as antidepressants (Amendt, 1990, p. 54).

Illegal Markets as Products of Rational Consumer Choices

The fourth discourse identified by O'Malley and Mugford (1991), finally, is centered on demand for illegal goods and services as an expression of indepen-dent needs and desires of consumers. O'Malley and Mugford only consider pleasure as a driving motive. However, the underlying notion of an autono-mous role of demand in the creation of illegal markets can also be applied to other spheres.

The main point O'Malley and Mugford are trying to make is that drug use is an integral part of any culture, including that of modern capitalist societies. They note that in western societies drug use appears in two main forms, deficit use manifested in compulsive, harmful behavior and the much more frequent recreational use manifested in a hedonistic lifestyle. The latter, O'Malley and Mugford argue, is at the same time a natural counterpoint to the rigorous work culture of the capitalist economy and an expression of the consumer culture that emphasizes the "search for the new" (O'Malley & Mugford, 1991, p. 58).

There are other commodities besides drugs that may fit into the pleasure category, such as stolen art and antiquities (Bowman, 2008; Bowman Proulx, 2011; Lane, Bromley, Hicks & Mahoney, 2008; Massy, 2008) and endangered species or products from these species sought after for their exotic or assumed medicinal value (Moyle, 2009; Pires, 2012).

Beyond hedonistic lifestyles, the demand for illegal goods and services can be linked to independent consumer decisions that appear more calculating and rational overall. In other words, consumers are credited with having good reasons, at least within their own logic, for demanding illicit goods and services. Claudio Besozzi (2001) suggests that there are three main types of human needs that can be met by illegal goods and services: pleasure, economic benefits, and the need for power and security. This typology helps in broadening the scope of the analysis beyond drugs to a much wider range of illegal markets. It also

Image 9.1   In this November 2014 photo, Kumar Budathoki, a victim of organ trafficking, displays the surgery scars after he sold one of his kidneys in Nepal. Budathoki received only a fraction of the $5,000 a shady broker had promised him. Demand for trafficked organs is high because of a lack of legally donated organs.

Photo: AP Photo/Niranjan Shrestha

suggests that the demand for illegal goods and services, far from being something that is imposed on consumers, can be the result of rational choices based on the calculation of costs and benefits. Perhaps most dramatically, this applies to organ trafficking. A demand for trafficked human organs exists in the absence of a sufficient supply of donated (legal) organs available for transplantation (Ambagtsheer, Zaitch, & Weimar, 2013; Lundin, 2012; Mendoza, 2010). Opting for the illegal market for organ transplants will tend to be a matter of life and death. In other instances, demand for illegal goods and services is linked to the weighing of *monetary* costs and benefits. This is true for a number of illegal markets that are linked to economic activity, such as illegal labor, including slave labor, and illegal waste disposal. In these cases, legitimate businesses, by drawing on illegal services, are able to avoid certain costs that result from government regulations or labor agreements, for example, the obligation of employers to contribute to welfare funds (Van Duyne & Houtzager, 2005; Massari & Monzini, 2004).

Cost-saving motives likewise may explain, for example, the demand for stolen and pirated products (luxury goods, movies, software, etc.) and fiscal contraband (cigarettes, gasoline, etc.) (Farrell & Fry, 2013; Merriman, 2010; Rutter & Bryce, 2008). Quite simply, many illegal products are cheaper than their legal counterparts (Naylor, 2003).

An element of rationality, the weighing of costs and benefits, can also be seen in the case of loan sharking. Even though demand for usurious loans often stems from compulsory gambling, individuals and legal businesses may for other purposes find it preferable under certain circumstances to seek the services of a loan shark rather than a bank, if only to avoid lengthy credit checks (Jacobs, 1999, p. 21; Seidl, 1968).

Finally, as Besozzi has argued, the need for power and security can lead to a rational demand for illegal goods and services, namely, illegal firearms and extra-legal protection (Besozzi, 2001, p. 24). The demand for extra-legal protection—for example, in the form of illegal debt collection—is linked to the quasi-governmental functions criminal groups may play (see Chapter 8).

Clearly, the issue of demand is multifaceted and has political undertones. Depending on whether one favors a welfare approach or a repressive approach to illegal markets, one will emphasize the importance of either demand-side factors or supply-side factors (Reuband, 1998). It does not seem possible to draw any general conclusions about the relative importance of supply and demand that would apply to all illegal commodities under all circumstances. Accordingly, it would be an oversimplification to discuss the social embeddedness of illegal markets and, by extension, the social embeddedness of organized crime only in terms of either the demand for or the supply of illegal goods and services. At the same time, any analysis of illegal markets would fall short by simply stating the obvious, that there is no market without supply and demand.

THE SOCIAL EMBEDDEDNESS OF ORGANIZED CRIMINALS

The argument that organized crime is socially embedded because it provides illicit goods and services to meet a public demand tends to pertain to society at large. However, there is also a widespread notion that organized crime is intimately linked to very specific segments of society. The discussion of the social roots of organized crime refers less to criminal activities and more to the social background of organized *criminals* and to the social environment of organized criminal *structures*. Typically the focus is on the lower classes. Mainstream society and societal elites are much less often considered in this respect.

Inner-City Slums as "Breeding Grounds" of Organized Crime

A central theme, particularly in American criminology and urban sociology, has long been to draw a link between organized crime and marginalized inner-city areas populated by immigrants and other disadvantaged groups. These neighborhoods, it is assumed, function as a "breeding ground" for organized crime (see, e.g., Lupsha, 1983, p. 75). "The gangster," John Landesco noted in his classical study of organized crime in Chicago, "is a natural product of his environment—that is, of the slums of our large American cities" (Landesco, 1929, p. 1057).

In a similar vein, organized crime has been associated with areas populated by poor, deprived segments of society in countries other than the United States, for example "traditional working class communities" in the United Kingdom (Hobbs, 2001, p. 550), townships in South Africa (Standing, 2006), and the shanty towns of São Paolo and Rio de Janeiro in Brazil (Pedra & Dal Ri, 2011).

Deviant Subcultures and Recruitment

The scholarly literature offers a wide range of theoretical considerations that bolster these observations. Poverty and blocked upward mobility, it has been argued, may cause members of the lower classes and marginalized immigrant communities to experience strain that pushes them toward involvement in acquisitive criminal activities. They see crime, the argument goes, as an alternative route to economic success. Organized crime, then, becomes "a queer ladder of social mobility" (Bell, 1953, p. 133; see also Ianni, 1974, p. 324). At the same time, individuals may cope with strain by turning to illegal goods and services, such as illicit drugs and gambling (Cloward & Ohlin, 1960; Merton, 1968). These criminal activities take place in an environment marked by "suspicion of official institutions, and in particular a lack of trust in the police" (Hobbs, 2013, p. 60). This, it is assumed, provides a layer of protection for criminal activities. Similarly, cultural and language barriers between immigrant communities and mainstream society are believed to create "defense mechanisms" against law enforcement (Williams & Godson, 2002, p. 331).

Criminals operating in these marginalized communities may be further empowered by the existence of a "deviant subculture" that approves of and justifies criminal condut to the point that "prestige is allocated to those who achieve material gain and power through avenues defined as illegitimate by the larger society" (Cloward & Ohlin, 1960, p. 22). Far from being ostracized, then, successful criminals may become local heroes and role models for the young (Cloward & Ohlin, 1960, p. 23; Shaw & McKay, 1942, p. 167). Henry Hill, an associate of the New York Cosa Nostra, whose life story provided the basis for the movie *Goodfellas*, recalls:

At the age of twelve my ambition was to be a gangster. To be a wiseguy. To me being a wiseguy was better than being president of the United States. It meant power among people who had no power. It meant perks in a working-class neighborhood that had no power. To be a wiseguy was to own the World. I dreamed about being a wiseguy the way other kids dreamed about being doctors or movie stars or firemen or ballplayers. (Pileggi, 1985, p. 19)

A similar quote can be found in André Standing's study of crime in the townships of South Africa:

You grow up in the township, the first people you admire are gangsters, because of the way they dress, their beautiful clothing, the beautiful cars they drive, and very importantly, they get the best women. You say, damn it man, I must also go that route. (Standing, 2006, p. 201)

One important function, then, that marginalized communities are seen to perform is to continuously produce new recruits for illegal enterprises and criminal groups (Lombardo & Lurigio, 1995, p. 89).

Legitimacy Through Services to the Community

In turn, criminals may reinforce social support by providing services to the community. Iconic criminals have famously adopted the role of benefactor and social sponsor. Al Capone, for example, gave out free meals to the hungry in Depression-era Chicago (Bergreen, 1994, p. 400). John Gotti, a prominent New York mafioso, hosted barbecues and organized illegal firework displays on the Fourth of July in his Ozone Park neighborhood (Mustain & Capeci, 2002, p. 287), and Pablo Escobar, the notorious head of the Medellin Cartel, is credited with such deeds as donating money for the construction of a soccer stadium, financing the pavement of roads, and handing out cash to the poor (Canon, 1994, p. 75).

Beyond these charitable acts, criminals may create local dependencies through the sheer economic importance of their illegal activities, by providing investment capital and employment (Cloward & Ohlin, 1960, p. 197). One historical example is the illegal lottery business in the Bedford-Stuyvesant neighborhood of New York City, which around 1970 reportedly constituted the largest private employer in the community (Kenney & Finckenauer, 1995, p. 214).

Apart from cultural and economic bonds between organized crime and society, criminals may also try to gain legitimacy and community support by providing security and maintaining order (Grayson, 2010). As already discussed in Chapter 8, to the extent the state is unable to effectively control marginalized neighborhoods, a power vacuum is created that may be filled by criminals. In an interview with researcher Robert Lombardo, a resident of the Taylor Street neighborhood in Chicago explains the role of the Outfit, the Chicago branch of Cosa Nostra:

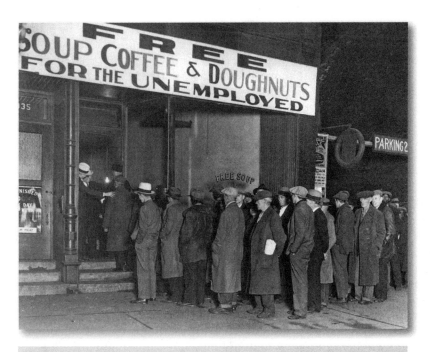

Image 9.2   Men waiting in line outside a soup kitchen set up by Al Capone that reportedly fed about 3,500 people daily in November 1930.

Photo: Bettmann/Corbis

The outfit guys never bothered anybody except their own. . . . If you'd cross them, they would take care of you. But as far as hurting innocent people, that just never happened. You could even say they protected the neighborhood. Nobody came on Taylor Street to do robberies or to break into houses—they'd be dead if they tried anything like that. We didn't have to lock our doors or windows; the outfit made us feel safe. And from Capone's days till now, you know, the syndicate has been known to help people out with hospital bills and whatnot. . . . It burns me up when I see police pickin' on them and letting the real crooks go free. (Lombardo & Lurigio, 1995, p. 106)

"Organized" and "Disorganized" Neighborhoods

Not all marginalized communities develop illegal markets and criminal structures to the same degree. There is no automatism between poverty, deprivation, and the emergence of organized crime. Cloward and Ohlin (1960), in their classic study of criminal opportunity structures, distinguish between organized neighborhoods and disorganized neighborhoods and mention primarily two factors that may account for the difference: (a) the sophistication of the slum population and (b) the nature of the local political system. Cloward and Ohlin argue that slums will remain disorganized if they are populated only by "failures in the conventional world" and "outcasts of the criminal world" who are unable to establish corrupt relations with police and politicians to obtain immunity from law enforcement (Cloward & Ohlin, 1960, p. 173). This, in turn, implies that in "disorganized" neighborhoods the local elites cannot draw any substantial benefits from colluding with criminals. In organized neighborhoods, on the other hand, criminals may play a role, for example, in the commission of voter fraud and voter intimidation and as a source of illegal campaign financing. This aspect will be examined further in the discussion of the relationship between organized crime and politics later in this book (Chapter 11).

It has also been suggested that the social fabric of a community influences the level of "organization" of crime. The underlying assumption is that where families are intact and adults have some authority over juveniles and adolescents, younger generations can grow into a more or less stable, established criminal subculture and into criminal organizations that are able to survive generational change (Cloward & Ohlin, 1960; Suttles, 1972).

Many of the neighborhoods have disappeared that sociologists and criminologists had in mind when they wrote about the link between organized crime and community. Namely, Italian immigrants in the United States have largely been assimilated into mainstream society and are no longer concentrated in inner-city areas like the Taylor Street neighborhood in Chicago (Lombardo, 2013, p. 172). Many tight-knit working-class communities in the United Kingdom have met a similar fate and disappeared in the course of deindustrialization and urban renewal (Hobbs, 2013). As a result, criminal structures that were once rooted in these kinds of communities have vanished or they have become physically, though perhaps not emotionally, detached from specific confined territories (Hobbs, 2001, 2013; Lombardo, 2013; Lombardo & Lurigio, 1995).

Organized Criminals Among the Middle and Upper Classes

It is somewhat problematic to focus so much attention on the link between organized crime and marginalized segments of society. In the end, it might suggest that organized crime is confined to these milieus and cannot be rooted elsewhere in society. Such a view would resonate with much of the public discourse on organized crime in the United States and other countries. The stereotypical imagery of organized criminals tends to be that of individuals who in terms of their ethnicity, culture, and social status stand outside of mainstream society (Kuschej & Pilgram, 1998; Smith, 1976; Woodiwiss & Hobbs, 2009).

Members of legitimate society, such as lawyers, bankers, accountants, and technician, appear in this imagery merely in the form of facilitators who provide "specialist support" to criminals (President's Commission on Organized Crime, 1986, Appendix A). These individual facilitators can indeed play a key role in the context of criminal endeavors and criminal networks and therefore deserve attention (Morselli & Giguere, 2006). Yet, in order to avoid stereotypical imagery, one needs to broaden the scope of analysis to also consider the embeddedness of organized crime in higher social strata (Van Duyne, 1997, p. 202).

Middle- and Upper-Class Consumption of Illegal Goods and Services

One way to gauge the extent to which organized crime is embedded in mainstream society is to determine whether or not members of the middle and upper classes consume illicit goods and services. That they do and that illegal markets can extend across all class divisions is famously illustrated by the case of Prohibition in the United States (Allsop, 1968; see also Rutter & Bryce, 2008). The illegal alcohol market during Prohibition (1920–1933), just like many illegal markets today, however, still seem to fit largely the stereotype of socially marginalized organized crime because the suppliers of illicit goods and services tend to come from the lower socioeconomic strata, while their customer base is more diverse (Hagedorn, 1994; Haller, 1985). In fact during Prohibition, alcohol consumption among the rich increased, while it appears to have substantially decreased among the lower classes (Cook, 2007, p. 26).

In an essay about drug policies in the United States, William Stuntz has argued that illegal markets tend to be segmented by class:

Upscale markets serve upscale customers. Downscale markets serve mostly (but, importantly, not only) downscale customers.... Though the crimes in these upscale and downscale markets are similar, lawmakers and especially law enforcers tend not to treat them the same.... A variety of factors push the system toward defining the relevant offenses more harshly and enforcing them more consistently against participants in lower-class markets than against their upscale counterparts. (Stuntz, 1998, p. 1799)

In other words, illegal goods and services are consumed across all segments of society while public and law enforcement attention is centered on the lower classes. These considerations notwithstanding, there are some illegal markets that support the view that organized crime can be socially embedded particularly in the higher socioeconomic strata.

In the illegal market for organ transplants, for example, members of the medical profession cater to well-to-do customers, although more stereotypical criminals may play a role as brokers and as procurers of organs (Scheper-Hughes, 2004). Likewise, the illegal market for antiquities and cultural artifacts encompasses "respectable" actors on both the supply and the demand side, while also incorporating some less respectable actors (Bowman Proulx, 2011).

Without downplaying these examples, the argument that organized crime can be embedded in higher social strata can perhaps best be made with reference to corporate crime.

Table 9.2 Similarities Between Lower-Class and Corporate Organized Crime

Similarities	Examples Lower-Class OC	Examples Corporate OC
Continuous criminal activities	Drug dealing	Price-fixing
Co-offending networks	Drug-dealing street gang	Price-fixing conspiracy
Criminogenic subcultures	Gangster as role model	Ruthless profit seeking

The Subcultural Embeddedness of Organized Corporate Crime

Corporate crime pertains to offenses committed within the framework of legal businesses by officials of these businesses (Coleman, 2002). Corporate crime falls into a larger category of *elite crime*, also called *power crime*. The distinctive feature is that these crimes are committed by exploiting opportunities that present themselves only to individuals who have gained status and respectability and a position of power within legitimate society. The power of the perpetrators may even go as far as being able to redefine their harmful behavior in a way that it is considered justified and legal (Ruggiero & Welch, 2009). This means there is corporate crime that constitutes crime in the narrow sense of the word, and then there is harmful, antisocial conduct in the form of "legal corporate crime" (Passas, 2005), which does not violate the letter of the law.

When one focuses narrowly on crime in the formal sense, corporate crime is for the most part predatory crime. The victims are employees, investors, the general public, or the environment. Corporate offenders may "pollute the environment, engage in financial frauds and manipulations, fix prices, create and maintain hazardous work conditions, knowingly produce unsafe products, and so forth" (Simpson, 2002, p. 7).

Corporate crime does not fit the stereotypical imagery of organized crime. Accordingly, the two tend to be treated as separate phenomena. Upon closer inspection, however, this distinction is rather artificial (Gerber, 2000; Pontell & Calavita, 1993; Sutherland, 1949).

A number of parallels can be drawn between the kind of lower-class crime commonly associated with organized crime and corporate crime. There are similarities in the systematic, continuous way in which criminal activities may be carried out. Price-fixing conspiracies, for example, can span many years. In these cases, businesses that sell the same product collude to keep prices above a certain level, thereby limiting market competition (Hay & Kelley, 1974). One of the most far-reaching conspiracies has involved pharmaceutical companies and the fixing of prices for vitamins. One such cartel in the global vitamin market was initiated in the mid-1980s and lasted until 1999, when it was exposed by antitrust authorities (Connor, 2007).

Similarities between lower-class crime and corporate crime also exist with regard to the patterns of cooperation among offenders. Corporate offenders may act collectively within businesses or within criminal networks that transcend corporate boundaries. Price-fixing conspiracies, for example, by definition involve networks of coconspirators. A typical pattern appears to be that of top executives and general managers of the colluding businesses establishing price-fixing policies, which are then implemented by lower-level managers. The conspiracies require regular or continuous interaction within the illegal network (Baker & Faulkner, 1993). Another illustration of corporate criminal networks is provided by accounting fraud committed by publicly traded companies. In these cases, false information is provided to financial analysts and investors in order to boost share prices. For this to happen, corporate executives typically collude with others inside their business as well as with coconspirators in auditing firms and law firms (Tillman, 2009).

Image 9.3   A man takes a yogurt pack from a refrigerator in a supermarket in Paris, March 2015. France's competition authority handed the country's top yogurt makers 192 million euro in fines for fixing prices over the course of several years, striking secret deals in hotel rooms and on special phone lines created to avoid detection. Penalties for price-fixing cartels such as this have been criticized for being too lenient to serve as a deterrent.

Photo: AP Photo/Michel Euler

A third similarity and perhaps the most striking one, between lower-class crime and corporate crime is that criminal activities and criminal structures can be found to be embedded in a subculture conducive to crime. Corporate crime has been attributed to the organizational culture of specific companies and more broadly to "deviant subcultures" that encompass business sectors and the entire capitalist market system. Research has found a cultural environment within companies that is fostered by the top management and which induces unethical and criminal behavior by employees. Rather than giving specific orders, the top management "signals" what kind of conduct is expected (Berger, 2011, p. 40). Law breaking then becomes "a routine and taken-for-granted part of everyday life in the organization" (Tillman, 2009, p. 270). These criminogenic cultures, in turn, are seen to be embedded in a broader cultural environment in which ruthless profit seeking, even if it involves law breaking, is condoned (Simon & Eitzen, 1982).

While the social and cultural embeddedness of collective, continuous crime can be found in cases of lower-class as well as corporate organized crime, there are also marked differences. Corporate organized crime tends to cause greater harm and produce greater profits than lower-class organized crime. At the same time, corporate and other elite offenders are less likely to be investigated and apprehended. And if they are brought to justice, sanctions tend to be less severe. In fact, it may be the case that fines are set so low that corporate crimes remain profitable even if they are detected (Coleman, 2002).

The financial harm caused by corporate crimes as well as the profits they produce can easily go into the billions of dollars (Tillman, 2009), and the physical harm caused by corporate environmental crimes and the organized violation of work-place and product safety standards may well dwarf the violence attributable to criminal gangs (Coleman, 2002; Tombs, 2007).

Contrary to the higher social costs of corporate crime, offenders appear to be more immune from law enforcement, and that is for various reasons. Corporate criminals, to begin with, simply do not fit the gangster stereotype. Police are less likely to keep potential corporate criminals under surveillance and less likely to use tools such as wiretaps, informants, and undercover agents in investigations of corporate crime. In the United States and presumably in many other countries, traditional investigative strategies and tools routinely applied in cases of lower-class organized crime have only fairly recently and cautiously been introduced to corporate crime investigations (Miller, 2013; Sheppard & Dougherty, 2012). Corporate crime also tends to be more complex and sophisticated and therefore more difficult and more time consuming for the government to pursue than typical organized crimes, such as drug trafficking (Coleman, 2002). The result is that corporate crime tends to be exposed in scandals rather than through continuous, systematic, proactive police work, which characterizes the control of criminal subcultures in lower-class and migrant communities (see Chapter 14). The exceptions are countries where normal entrepreneurial activity is criminalized. This is true for political systems with a state-planned economy instead of a free-market economy, for example, North Korea under the Kim regime or the Soviet Union. In these cases, a broad range of police tactics and tools are employed against economic crime under the banner of fighting "capitalist profiteering" and "speculation" (Lankov, 2009; Ledeneva, 1998).

THE SOCIAL EMBEDDEDNESS OF ORGANIZED CRIME: SUMMARY AND CONCLUSION

Organized crime is not something that exists in a social vacuum. Organized criminals, organized criminal activities, and organized criminal structures are in many ways linked up with and embedded in society. The social embeddedness of organized crime is commonly discussed with respect to two central themes: the provision of illegal goods and services to a demanding public and the rooting of organized criminals and criminal groups in marginalized segments of society. The main purpose of this chapter was to examine these two themes in detail and to highlight some complexities. These complexities call into question simplistic explanations of the relationship between organized crime and society.

When one equates organized crime with the provision of illegal goods and services, an obvious link to society exists: Organized crime and society are connected through voluntary transactions between suppliers and customers. In this respect, organized crime exists because it fulfills a function in society by addressing needs that are not met otherwise.

Some organized criminal activities, however, do not fit this mold. Predatory crimes, such as theft and fraud, are based on victimization rather than voluntary transactions. Only in a broader context can some predatory crimes be linked to illegal markets and a public demand. For example, there is a market for stolen goods sold at prices below those on the legal market.

It is also problematic to put so much emphasis on the provision of illegal goods and services without taking into account that illegal markets vary greatly across space and time. Substantial differences exist with regard to the types of illegal goods and services and with regard to the scale at which they are supplied. Accordingly, the social embeddedness of organized crime in terms of the provision of illegal goods and services can be quite limited in some instances and quite extensive in others.

In order to understand the prevalence of illegal markets, one needs to consider a broad range of factors. Illegal markets, just like all other markets, are the product of a convergence of supply and demand. However, there are no generally applicable explanations for the existence of supply and demand and for how the two come together. The emergence of illegal markets can be influenced by demand-side as well as supply-side factors and, inevitably, it is determined by political decisions to prohibit certain goods and services.

The demand for illegal goods and services is explained by "an almost bewildering array of theories" (Goode, 2005, p. 54). These include individual deficiencies, social conditions, pleasure seeking, cost-and-benefit calculations, and the need for security. It is a matter of controversy how far demand-side factors go in explaining illegal markets. Some argue that illegal markets exist because criminals respond to an existing demand. There are, however, also indications that supply may create demand. The extent of illegal markets also depends on where political decisions have drawn the line between legal and illegal goods and services. The weaker the legitimacy of prohibitions, the more embedded in society illegal markets will be.

The consumption of illegal goods and services may vary across a host of social categories, including age, gender, ethnicity, and socioeconomic status. Likewise, organized criminals and organized criminal structures may be rooted in particular segments of society. Typically, a connection is made between organized crime and immigrant and lower-class communities. However, by the same token organized crime can also be rooted in higher social strata. Criminal networks may develop out of social networks formed, for example, in ghetto neighborhoods or in business communities. In both cases, underlying social relations are important for providing a common basis of trust. The bonds between offenders as well as their motivation to commit crimes may be strengthened by criminogenic subcultures. Both in marginalized neighborhoods and in higher social strata, namely, in a corporate environment, subcultural norms and values may foster defiance of the law, although the specific justifications for illegal behavior may differ. Secluded subcultures, whether in the lower or upper classes, may also create protective mechanisms against law enforcement. In the case of marginalized communities, shared mistrust of authorities and cultural and language barriers may hamper the work of the police. In the case of elite-based subcultures, law enforcement tends to be sporadic rather than routine and tends to be hampered by a lack of resources to investigate what are usually rather complex criminal endeavors.

This chapter could examine the social embeddedness of organized crime only in fairly general terms. A more in-depth look will be taken in the following chapters, with a view to the link between organized crime and legal business and between organized crime and government.

Discussion Questions

1. What level of organized criminal activities in society is tolerable?

2. Is the provision of illegal goods and services victimless crime?

3. Are organized crimes more dangerous than "un-organized" crimes?

4. What are the similarities and differences between criminal subcultures embedded in lower classes and in upper classes?

5. Assume that smoking is made illegal in all countries, similar to cocaine or heroin. Will there be a black market? What would this black market look like in terms of suppliers, customers, and product?

Research Projects

1. Find out what illegal market is most prevalent in your area.

2. Pick a country for which data are available and investigate the development of the illegal market for cannabis (or cocaine or heroin or methamphetamine) over a period of several decades. Try to come up with explanations for any changes in trend that are discernible.

3. Examine a case of corporate crime with a view to whether offenders were influenced by a criminogenic subculture.

Further Reading

Supply and Demand in Illegal Markets

Ciccarone, D., Unick, G. J., & Kraus, A. (2009). Impact of South American heroin on the US heroin market 1993–2004. *International Journal of Drug Policy*, 20(5), 392–401.

Fitzgerald, J. (2005). Illegal drug markets in transitional economies. *Addiction Research and Theory*, 13(6), 563–577.

Paoli, L. (2002). The development of an illegal market: Drug consumption and trade in post-soviet Russia. *The British Journal of Criminology*, 42(1), 21–39.

Paoli, L., & Donati, A. (2014). *The sports doping market: Understanding supply and demand, and the challenges for their control.* New York: Springer.

Williams, P. (1999). Trafficking in women and children: A market perspective. In P. Williams (Ed.), *Illegal immigration and commercial sex: The new slave trade* (pp. 145–170). Abingdon, UK: Frank Cass.

Social Embeddedness of Organized
Criminals and Organized Criminal Structures

Corsino, L. (2013). They can't shoot everyone: Italians, social capital, and organized crime in the Chicago Outfit. *Journal of Contemporary Criminal Justice, 29*(2), 256–275.

Hales, G., & Hobbs, D. (2010). Drug markets in the community: A London borough case study. *Trends in Organized Crime, 13*(1), 13–30.

Lombardo, R. M. (2010). *The black hand: Terror by letter in Chicago*. Urbana, IL: University of Illinois Press.

Marshall, H. (2013). "Come heavy, or not at all": Defended neighborhoods, ethnic concentration, and Chicago robberies; examining the Italian American organized crime influence. *Journal of Contemporary Criminal Justice 29*(2), 276–295.

O'Kane, J. M. (1992). *The crooked ladder: Gangsters ethnicity and the American dream*. New Brunswick, NJ: Transaction.

Van de Bunt, H. G., Siegel, D., & Zaitch, D. (2014). The social embeddedness of organized crime. In L. Paoli (Ed.), *The Oxford handbook of organized crime* (pp. 321–339). Oxford, UK: Oxford University Press.

Whyte, W. F. (1981). *Street corner society: The social structure of an Italian slum* (3rd ed.). Chicago, IL: The University of Chicago Press. (Original work published in 1943)

CHAPTER 10

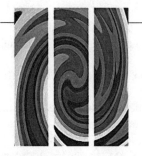

Organized Crime
and Legitimate Business

INTRODUCTION

This chapter examines the relationship between organized crime and legitimate business. The theme has already been touched upon in the previous chapter (Chapter 9), mainly with regard to corporate crime and criminogenic corporate subcultures. Corporate crime, however, is seldom mentioned in the debate on the link between organized crime and legitimate business. Rather than high-status criminals at the helm of corporations, the focus typically is on criminals from the margins of society who in one way or the other come to influence the legal economy from the outside. The discussion in this chapter will follow these more conventional conceptions of organized criminal involvement in the legal economy, without ignoring the limitations of such a narrow view.

Criminal involvement means more than simply benefiting from the legal economy. Of course, criminals are consumers of legal goods and service for their personal use and also for criminal purposes. For example, criminals use mobile phones to communicate, and they draw on hauling companies and parcel services to move drugs and other contraband. Of interest here is a higher level of involvement, one where criminals gain an influence over legal businesses and legal markets beyond the power they possess as consumers.

CONCEPTUALIZATIONS OF ORGANIZED CRIME AND LEGITIMATE BUSINESS ALONG THE DIMENSIONS OF ACTIVITIES, STRUCTURES, AND GOVERNANCE

The relationship between organized crime and legitimate business has been discussed in the academic literature from mainly two angles. One perspective is to examine similarities and differences between legal and illegal businesses on an analytical level (see, e.g., Levi & Naylor, 2000; Smith, 1975, pp. 335–347). Another perspective, focusing on the empirical level, is to explore the role of specific criminal organizations and their members in the legal economy (see, e.g., Anderson, 1979; Edelhertz & Overcast, 1993; Hill, 2003). The range of possibilities for addressing the relationship between organized crime and legitimate business, however, is much broader. In a comprehensive analysis one needs to consider the three basic dimensions of organized crime: activities, structures, and governance.

Organized Criminal Activities in Legitimate Business

When one equates organized crime with certain forms of illegal *activities*, the link between organized crime and legitimate business can be framed in terms of organized illegal business practices. The pervasiveness of such practices would determine the level of organized crime within the legal economy irrespective of the identity of the perpetrators. Those engaging in these illegal practices may be underworld figures who have moved into the realm of legal business, or the perpetrators may be outwardly legitimate businesspeople with no connection to the underworld. Businesses with no link whatsoever to stereotypical gangsters may, for example, use illegal labor, sell illegal goods, and systematically violate safety standards and evade taxes. At times both types of perpetrators may act independently, at times they may collude, and sometimes they may learn from each other (Ruggiero, 1996, p. 154).

Organized Criminal Structures in Legitimate Business

When one equates organized crime not with illegal activities but with illegal *structures*, then the focus is on criminal organizations, understood in a broad sense, that operate within the legal economy. Networks of corporate criminals that are rooted in the legal economy have already been mentioned (Chapter 9). The main emphasis in the organized-crime literature, in contrast, is on criminal organizations that cross the line from the underworld into the upperworld.

It is somewhat misleading in this context, however, to narrowly focus attention on criminal organizations in the sense of purposefully acting entities. Criminal organizations in the narrow sense of the word, be they illegal enterprises or criminal associations or illegal governance structures, will rarely be found to acquire and run legal businesses. First of all, in a legalistic sense it is not possible for an illegal organization to obtain an interest in or ownership of a legitimate business. Straw persons would have to be used by a criminal organization to acquire and operate a business on its behalf. Secondly, in discussions of the infiltration of the legal economy by crime syndicates, mafias or drug cartels, what is referred to, arguably, are in most cases individual criminals, the members and associates of organized criminal groups rather than the criminal groups themselves, who invest in and operate legal businesses (Edelhertz & Overcast, 1993, p. 63; see also Cressey, 1967a, p. 25).

Individual criminals may draw on the resources of the criminal organizations they belong to. For example, they may use funds generated by an illegal enterprise, and they may profit from the violent reputation of a mafia organization.

Yet it seems that they are commonly making their own independent decisions to pursue their own interests (Edelhertz & Overcast, 1993, p. 69).

There are two exceptions to this rule, one pertaining to illegal enterprises, the other to extortion gangs and quasi-governmental structures. The involvement in the legal economy can appropriately be framed as that of criminal organizations rather than of individual criminals, where the formation and operation of a legitimate business is an integral part of a crime scheme. For example, a drug trafficking group (= illegal enterprise) that uses overseas containers to transport drugs may set up businesses in different countries so that these businesses can show up on the freight papers as the official senders and receivers of shipments. Likewise, in the case of extortion and illegal governance (see below) it may be more appropriate to ascribe the influence on legitimate businesses to criminal groups instead of individual members of these groups. This is true at least where the collection of protection payments and other activities are closely coordinated by a criminal group.

Matters are far less clear in the much more common cases of investments in legal businesses and business activities in the legal economy made by individual organized criminals. It is not a given that their involvement automatically poses a threat to the integrity and functioning of the legal economy.

Illegal Governance in Legitimate Business

When one equates organized crime with illegal *governance*, then the focus of the debate on the link between organized crime and legitimate business is on the regulation of legal business activities by criminals. Just like criminal groups may perform quasi-governmental functions with regard to criminal milieus and illegal markets, they may also come to control segments of the legal economy. Control typically comes in one of three forms: extortion, protection, and cartel organization. In the case of extortion, businesses are forced to make "protection" payments to criminals while obtaining little or nothing in return, except perhaps protection from other extortionists. The targets of extortion can be individual businesses, businesses in a particular geographical area, businesses owned and operated by members of a particular ethnic group, or businesses of a particular type—for example, restaurants. The same is true where criminal control goes beyond extortion and criminals actually provide some level of protection to legal businesses—for example, against predatory criminals, competitors, delinquent debtors, recalcitrant workers, trade unions, or against government interference (Hill, 2003; Partridge, 2012; Volkov, 2000, 2002). The third form of criminal control over legitimate businesses involves the creation and management of cartels in particular legal markets. In these cases, criminal influence is aimed at suppressing market forces (Reuter, 1985, 1993). It should be noted, however, that typically cartels in the legal economy are established without the involvement of underworld elements. In any case, illegal governance in the legal economy can be observed at different levels: on the level of individual businesses, on the level of business communities defined by territory or ethnicity, and on the level of specific legal markets.

ORGANIZED CRIMINALS AND LEGITIMATE BUSINESS

From the foregoing discussion it should be clear that it depends very much on the perspective one adopts what the nature of the relationship between organized crime and legitimate business is. Organized crime in terms of illegal business conduct, corporate criminal networks, and business cartels is very much a facet and integral part of the legal economy. At the same time, the link between organized crime and the legal economy can also be construed as the contact between two separate spheres: underworld and upperworld. According to simplistic views, it does not matter much how exactly this contact manifests itself. Wherever contact is made, legal business is assumed to be tainted and prone to fall under complete criminal control. The reality is arguably much more complex.

There are variations in the criminal influence over the legal economy in at least two respects. First, the degree of involvement of organized criminals in legitimate businesses varies greatly, from marginal interaction to complete ownership control. Second, there are variations in the degree to which the integrity of the legal economy is compromised. In some cases, the presence of organized criminals has no direct impact. In other cases, the consequences can go as far as severely disrupting the functioning of legitimate businesses and of entire legal markets.

Variations in the Degree of Involvement of Organized Criminals in Legitimate Businesses

The simplest and most widespread form of criminal involvement in the legal economy is probably at the level of individual businesses. The implications of this involvement are not always the same. Much depends on the nature of the various roles that mafiosi, outlaw bikers, drug traffickers, and the like are playing.

Provision of Illegal Goods and Services to Legitimate Businesses

At one end of the spectrum (Figure 10.1), organized criminals and legal businesses enter into contractual relations. The criminals are merely providers of illegal goods and services to legitimate businesses. The effect in many cases is that legitimate businesses are able to cut costs. For example, construction firms may hire illegal laborers at low wages through illegal labor brokerages, or factories may dispose of hazardous waste cheaply with the help of criminals, or a store may stock up its inventory with stolen goods.

Criminals may also offer solutions to problems not directly linked to high costs. For example, criminal gangs may be hired to intimidate workers or to provide protection against predatory criminals, or smugglers may be employed to circumvent trade restrictions (see, e.g., Lee & Collin, 2006). In all of these cases criminals and businesspeople theoretically meet as independent partners in illegal market transactions.

Figure 10.1   Variations in the Degree of Involvement of Organized Criminals
in Legitimate Businesses

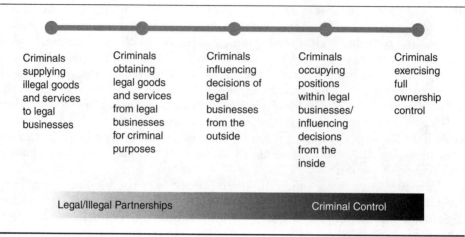

Provision of Legal Goods and Services to Criminals

Further toward criminal control over legitimate businesses go cases where legitimate businesses knowingly provide goods and services to criminals for criminal purposes. For example, a bank may help criminals to launder their illicit proceeds. The relationship is still one of (illegal) transactions between principally independent partners. However, the role of the legitimate businesses changes from that of consumer of illegal goods and services to accomplice and coconspirator in criminal endeavors carried out by members of the underworld.

Direct Influence on Business Decisions

The threshold of actual criminal control over a legitimate business is reached where criminals directly influence business decisions. In some cases, control is exerted from the outside and typically extends only to particular aspects of the business. In other cases, criminals occupy positions of influence within a business.

An example for external control over business decisions is provided in cases of extortion. In its simplest form, legitimate businesses are coerced into making payments to criminals (Partridge, 2012). In more sophisticated extortion schemes, criminals set up businesses of their own and provide goods or services to other businesses at inflated prices (Hill, 2003, p. 95). This means, criminals dictate for certain goods and services where and under what conditions a legitimate business has to get its supply from (Krevert, 1997).

In cases of internal control, a criminal group places members or associates inside a legitimate business, for example, as bookkeeper or as executive. This facilitates the monitoring of the business and helps, for example, in determining the optimal amount of money that can be extorted. At the same time, occupying positions within a legitimate business makes it possible for organized criminals to exert control more directly (Volkov, 2000, p. 46).

The end of the spectrum is reached where a legitimate business is fully owned and operated by organized criminals or by straw persons who own and operate businesses on behalf of organized criminals.

Means of Acquiring Control Over Legitimate Businesses

Control over a business can be obtained by various legal and illegal means. At one extreme a business is established or bought in the same way a legitimate businessperson would acquire a legitimate business. At the other extreme, control is acquired by brute force. A notorious example is that of South Boston gangster James "Whitey" Bulger, who at one point in time had the desire to own a liquor store. He reportedly went to the owners of the store that he liked to own and under threat of death forced the owners to sell their business and to accept a price far below market value. Bulger then used the store as his base of operation and to claim that he had a legitimate source of income (Lehr & O'Neill, 2001).

Between the two extremes of legal acquisition and violent take-over there are various shades of grey. Influence over a legitimate business may be obtained more or less directly as the result of illegal conduct. A typical scenario is the transformation of gambling debts into usurious loans for which, eventually, an interest in a legitimate business is accepted as payment (McKeon, 1971, p. 124).

The Consequences of the Involvement of Organized Criminals for the Integrity of Legitimate Businesses and Legal Markets

The presence of organized criminals in the legal economy has long been a central theme in the debate on organized crime, especially in countries like the United States, Italy, Russia, and Japan. The concern is that criminals gain increasing influence in the realm of legitimate business through the use of illegal profits, violence, coercion, and corruption. But what exactly are the implications of organized criminals gaining influence over legal businesses? Once again, as with all facets of the problem of organized crime, one needs to differentiate. The many ways in which the presence of organized criminals in legitimate business can manifest itself are at odds with simplistic notions of an infiltration or undermining of the legal economy by organized crime.

Following a typology suggested by Donald Cressey (1969, p. 100), four basic constellations can be distinguished with a view to the acquisition and operation of a legal business by organized criminals, where acquisition includes both building up a new firm as well as obtaining control over an existing firm. A business may be legally acquired and operated. A business may be legally acquired but operated in violation of the law. A business may be acquired through illegal means but operated legally. And a business may be acquired and operated illegally (Table 10.1).

Table 10.1   Cressey's Classification of Criminal Involvement in Legitimate Business

Acquisition	Operation	
	Legal	Illegal
Legal	Use of legal funds and legal means to establish/buy and operate a business	Use of legal funds and legal means to establish/buy a business Use of illegal means to operate the business
Illegal	Use of illegal funds and/or illegal means to establish/buy a business Use of legal means to operate the business	Use of illegal funds and means to establish/buy and to operate a business

Source: Adopted from Cressey (1969, p. 100).

These four constellations, as Cressey himself has emphasized, are not merely theoretical possibilities. Cressey noted with reference to the American Mafia that "Cosa Nostra members participate in all of them" (Cressey, 1969, p. 100; see also Anderson, 1979). This becomes plausible when one considers the different motives and incentives that organized criminals may have for getting involved in a legal business. In the literature, a long list of such motives and incentives can be found: profit, diversification of sources of income, enabling the legal transfer of funds, legitimizing income for tax purposes, providing legal employment, money laundering, providing fronts and logistical support for illegal activities, and attaining societal respectability (Anderson, 1979, pp. 79–80; Cressey, 1969, p. 107; Edelhertz & Overcast, 1993, pp. 67–69; Fiorentini, 2000, p. 448; Maltz, 1990, pp. 119–120; McKeon, 1971, pp. 123–124; Potter, 1994, pp. 136–137; Reuter, 1985, pp. 52–53). For some of these purposes it is necessary or at least wise for organized criminals to strictly abide by the law when acquiring and especially when they are operating a legal business. For other purposes, the mere appearance of legality in the acquisition and operation of a legal business is sufficient for minimizing the risk of detection, while the business is more or less at the center of criminal conduct (Figure 10.2).

Noncriminal Involvement in Legal Businesses

Organized criminals have the greatest incentives for a purely legal involvement in a legitimate business when their main concern is with securing and transferring assets. By nature, illegal enterprises and illegally obtained assets are only poorly protected. Property rights are constantly challenged in the underworld, and any assets that are tainted by illegal activity are under threat of seizure and forfeiture (see Chapter 14). In contrast, by legally acquiring and operating a legitimate business, these risks can be greatly reduced. A legal business legally acquired and operated provides some degree of financial security

Figure 10.2 Forms of Involvement in Legitimate Businesses

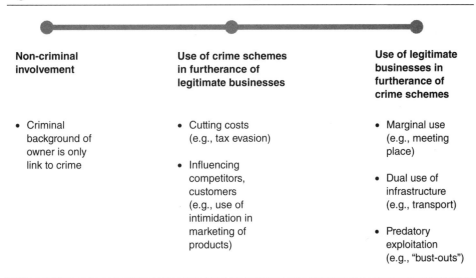

Non-criminal involvement	Use of crime schemes in furtherance of legitimate businesses	Use of legitimate businesses in furtherance of crime schemes
• Criminal background of owner is only link to crime	• Cutting costs (e.g., tax evasion) • Influencing competitors, customers (e.g., use of intimidation in marketing of products)	• Marginal use (e.g., meeting place) • Dual use of infrastructure (e.g., transport) • Predatory exploitation (e.g., "bust-outs")

for an organized criminal, and it can relatively safely be transferred to dependents in the event of death or incarceration (Anderson, 1979, pp. 79, 112). Of course, the acquisition of a legitimate business in strict accordance with the law is difficult for a criminal if only illicit funds are available. The use of illicit funds would constitute the offense of money laundering (see below). But there are enough criminals with legitimate sources of income—for example, from legal employment—so that the legal acquisition of a business by a criminal is not just a hypothetical category.

The use of illegal means is not only counterproductive when the aim is to secure and to transfer assets, but also, to some extent, the same applies when involvement in a legitimate business is intended to provide a legitimate facade for a lifestyle funded by crime. The cocaine dealer Larry Lavin, for example, found it easy to explain his wealth to friends and neighbors, with reference to a record company he co-owned and a gold record he put on display (Bowden, 2001, p. 163).

For organized criminals who come from the lower social strata, a legal business can also create an "aura of respectability" (Cressey, 1969, p. 107). Gaining status in legitimate society is a motivation often ascribed to organized criminals (Van Duyne, 1997, p. 211). They may seek the kind of recognition that possibly has been denied to them growing up in poverty, or they may try to attain "respectability because of a desire not to embarrass their children and grandchildren and thus jeopardize their chances for success in the legitimate world" (Rockaway, 1993, p. 246).

It should be noted, however, that involvement in legal business is not necessarily a phase late in an organized criminal's career, marked by a shift from illegal to legal entrepreneurship. Organized criminals may begin early on to operate parallel illegal and legal businesses (Ianni & Reuss-Ianni, 1972, p. 88). Likewise, a shift may occur from first being involved in strictly legal business activities to involvement in illegal business activities later in life. This has been observed, for example, in sectors such as banking and transport that are logistically valuable for profitable criminal activities, such as money laundering services and drug smuggling (Kleemans & de Poot, 2008).

In any case, there are constellations where criminal involvement does not translate into criminal conduct. In some instances, crime money may be used to buy entry into a life without crime. In some instances, where legally obtained funds are being used, the criminal background of the owner may be the only thing that links a legitimate business to crime. This may raise moral objections. But, as Levi and Naylor (2000, p. 8) argue, "there is not the slightest reason to suspect that in so doing the criminal will be controlling or corrupting legal markets."

Use of Crime in Furtherance of Legitimate Businesses

Legitimate businesses are an element in criminal conduct in essentially two ways. Crime may be used in furtherance of a legitimate business, and in the opposite direction, a legitimate business may be used in furtherance of crime.

When the main purpose is to promote a legitimate business, criminal conduct commonly serves either the cutting of costs or the influencing of employees, competitors, and customers. There are a number of criminal schemes with which to reduce the operating costs of a business. These schemes, however, such as tax evasion, the violation of safety standards, and the corruption of regulatory agencies, are not specific to the involvement of stereotypical organized criminals in the legal economy. They are, as already indicated, illicit business practices that also respectable businesspeople may engage in (Coleman, 2002).

More akin to stereotypical organized criminals than to respectable business-people is the threat and use of violence. Whereas violence is an essential component in the toolkit of the underworld, as discussed in previous chapters, violence is much less common in the legal economy. When scholars speak of *corporate violence*, they refer to the unintended harmful outcomes of reckless and illicit business practices. They do not have practices in mind such as arson, murder, or kidnapping (Clinard, 1990, p. 91; Friedrichs, 2010, p. 65).

How the threat and use of violence can be employed in furtherance of business interests is illustrated by the following example. A group of criminals connected to the 'Ndrangheta, the Calabrian mafia, started mozzarella production. In order to win customers, they simply went to all restaurants and grocery stores in the area and coerced them into buying their cheese (Ulrich, 2005, p. 83). There are limits to this kind of strategy, however, as is shown by a notorious case involving members of the American Cosa Nostra and a soap factory. In the mid-1960s, several New York area stores of the A&P supermarket chain were firebombed, and two store managers murdered in a failed attempt to force A&P to stock inferior soap produced by a company with mafia links. One can assume that it was not only bravery or stubbornness that made the A&P management stand up against mafia intimidation. Ultimately, they had to consider what soap consumers would be willing to buy. Interestingly, other stores had agreed to put the soap on their shelves, apparently under more subtle pressure involving mafia controlled labor unions (Demaris, 1986, pp. 80–81; Kwitny, 1979, pp. 274–276).

Anderson's (1979) study of the business activities of the Philadelphia branch of the Cosa Nostra suggests that violence and other illicit means are seldom used by criminals to distort competition or to otherwise gain an advantage within the legal economy. Anderson came across only one case where violence in connection with the operation of a legal business was merely contemplated but not actually used (Anderson, 1979, p. 37). Other criminal methods were employed only rarely and only sporadically (Anderson, 1979, pp. 103, 117, 123). She concludes that "aggressive effort to earn extraordinary profit in business or industries through illegal means does not explain the entry of members of the [Philadelphia Cosa Nostra] family into legitimate business" (Anderson, 1979, p. 103).

Use of Legitimate Businesses in Furtherance of Crime

Legitimate businesses can play a role in the commission of crime to different degrees. In some cases, illegal activities are carried out with little or no interference with the day-to-day affairs of the legal business. For example, a restaurant, apart from its normal operation, may serve as a place where criminals meet and exchange information (Edelhertz & Overcast, 1993, p. 63).

In other cases, illegal activities are intertwined with legal business processes. This means, the logistical infrastructure of a legitimate business is used for legal and criminal purposes. For example, a trucking firm engaged in legal commerce can at the same time transport contraband (Caulkins, Burnett, & Leslie, 2009, p. 79; Johansen, 2005, p. 195), or a gas station, in the course of normal business, may be used to sell illegal fuel in a tax-fraud scheme (Moore, 1995). The effect is that illegal activities are hidden behind legal activities or they are given the appearance of legitimate conduct. A legal business thus provides camouflage, which allows offenders "to hide in plain sight" (Felson, 2006a, p. 283).

There are variations in the degree to which legal and illegal activities are carried out side-by-side within the context of the same legitimate business. In one extreme, illegal activities are marginal occurrences; in the other extreme, a legal business is "no more than an empty front headed by a drunk as a strawman" (Van Duyne, 1993a, p. 114) with no legitimate dealings whatsoever. Still, all of these schemes have in common that they are not aimed against the legitimate business itself. There are other schemes, in contrast, that amount to predatory exploitation where the liquidation of the legitimate businesses is an accepted consequence of the criminal endeavor. The prime example for this category is planned bankruptcy fraud, also known as *long-firm fraud* or *bust-outs* (Edelhertz & Overcast, 1993; Levi, 2008). This is a crime that is not confined to stereotypical organized criminals. However, it can occur under organized crime specific circumstances. Long-firm fraud pertains to a business that orders substantial quantities of goods on credit without the intention to pay for them. The goods are sold through the business or are disposed of for a profit in other ways (Levi, 2008). Criminals may set up a business with the purpose of defrauding creditors, or they may attain control over an existing business and decide to use it to commit fraud. A typical constellation is the use of a business that has been taken over in payment of a gambling debt (Cressey, 1969, pp. 105–107). In these cases, there is a functional connection between long-firm fraud, illegal gambling, and loan sharking.

Image 10.1   The Bank of Credit and Commerce International (BCCI), one of the largest private banks in the world, was implicated in numerous illegal activities and the laundering of illicit proceeds during the 1970s through 1990s (Passas & Groskin, 2001).

Photo: Barry Iverson / Contributor

Money Laundering

A special case in the use of legal businesses for criminal purposes is the laundering of illicit proceeds. *Money laundering* (ML) constitutes a part of the overall "logistics of organized crime" (Sieber & Bögel, 1993; see Chapter 4). It is a process by which the criminal origin of assets is obscured and a perception is created that these assets are legitimately owned by the criminal (Buchanan, 2004; Levi, 2014).

Until fairly recently, the second half of the 1980s, money laundering itself was not a crime (Levi, 2002a), and the activities that are illegal today would have fallen under the category of noncriminal efforts to create and maintain an "aura of respectability." Offenders simply tried to avoid suspicion when investing and spending their illicit proceeds.

Money laundering is characterized by a broad range of schemes in ever changing variations (Kennedy, 2005; Reuter & Truman, 2004; Simser, 2013). It entails three main types of activities, usually framed as phases in a sequential process: (a) the conversion of cash into negotiable instruments or assets, commonly called *placement*, (b) the concealing of the source of the funds (*layering*), and (c) the *integration* of the funds into the legitimate economy. In all three phases, legitimate businesses can play a key role, either as facilitators providing money laundering services to criminals or as a tool directly used by criminals in the management of their crime money (Serio, 2004).

The placement of illicit proceeds is a challenge where criminal profits are generated in the form of cash, especially small denomination bills—for example, in the trafficking of drugs and other contraband. In contrast, cash is less common in cases of fraud (Levi, 2002a). The placement of illicit proceeds can fairly easily be accomplished with the help of cash-intensive businesses, such as restaurants or car dealerships (Edelhertz & Overcast, 1993, p. 61). By pretending that the cash comes from legitimate customers, illegal funds inserted into the cash flow of a legitimate business are immediately given the appearance of legal income. These funds can then be spent directly or introduced into the financial system under the guise of normal business activity.

Where a larger volume of cash is involved, namely at the higher levels of the illicit drug market, more elaborate and sophisticated schemes may come into play to convert cash and to disguise the illicit origin of the funds (Simser, 2013). The most direct way to insert crime money into the financial system is through banks. There is a long history of banks and of financial institutions, not just those based in off-shore tax havens, facilitating the laundering of illegal profits (Block & Griffin 1999; Paoli, 1995; Passas, 1993; Young, 2013). At the same time, criminals have acquired or created their own banks. For example, *vory v zakone* have established banks in Russia to manage their communal fund (*obshchak*) and to invest the money in commercial enterprises (Volkov, 2002, p. 62).

Once illicit proceeds are inserted into the financial system, real businesses or front companies that exist only on paper may be used in schemes designed to make it difficult or impossible to trace funds back to criminal activities. These layering schemes can be elaborate and transnational in scope, with funds being moved between bank accounts in various jurisdictions around the globe (Borlini, 2014).

Eventually, the laundered funds may be invested in the legal economy to create outwardly legitimate sources of income. For example, criminals may end up receiving a salary or a loan from a legitimate business they control and through which laundered funds are channeled (Kennedy, 2005; Serio, 2004).

The use of legitimate businesses in money laundering schemes serves first and foremost the purpose of securing illicit proceeds. But it may be beneficial for organized criminals also in other ways. At least theoretically, the influx of crime money gives a competitive advantage to businesses under the control of organized criminals. These businesses can be operated at costs much lower than those of a truly legitimate business, which has to rely on the capital market for financing. Even an utterly unprofitable business can be subsidized with crime money to the extent that it is not only able to survive but to outcompete any and all businesses with no access to illicit funds. Money laundering then becomes another scenario of organized criminals employing illegal means in the operation of legitimate businesses, with the effect that market forces are distorted. The consequences of criminal control, thus, are not limited to the affected business but extend to other businesses that find themselves faced with unfair competition. However, it is not clear how pervasive such elaborate money laundering schemes are. In contrast to controversial estimates that suggest illicit proceeds at a scale of hundreds of billions of dollars are laundered annually (e.g., UNODC, 2011a), some studies have found that even financially successful criminals make little efforts to launder their illicit proceeds through legitimate businesses or through the use of professional money launderers (Malm & Bichler, 2013; Soudijn, 2012; Van Duyne, 2003b).

RACKETEERING: CRIMINAL CONTROL OVER BUSINESS SECTORS

The most extreme forms of criminal influence on the legal economy are reached where entire markets and business sectors come under the control of organized criminals. In the United States, criminal influence at this level has historically been tied to two mechanisms: labor racketeering and business racketeering.

The term *racketeering* is derived from the term *racket*, the origin of which is obscure. Racket used to mean making a noise or making easy money (Albini, 1971, pp. 29–30). Today, in the context of organized crime, it is commonly used to denote predatory practices in the realm of legitimate business. The racketeer who runs a racket and engages in racketeering is a gangster and extortionist. Such a narrow meaning of the term, however, leaves out other forms of criminal involvement in the legal economy that the term racketeering originally has also referred to.

When the racketeering terminology first emerged in the mid-1920s, it pertained less to a confrontational and much more to a collusive relationship between upperworld and underworld (Smith, 1975, pp. 66–69). In the first treatise of the subject, rackets were defined as "criminal conspiracies of exploitation in which the conspiring factors are business men, certain types of labor union leaders, underworld forces, and politicians" (Hostetter & Beesley, 1929, p. 6). Understood in this way, racketeering is not just another criminal scheme to victimize legitimate businesses akin to long-firm fraud. It is "an outgrowth of business rather than crime" (Smith, 1975, p. 68).

Racketeering can be construed as an illicit approach to dealing with the uncertainties and challenges that businesses face in two respects: the organization of workers and the competition within unregulated markets. Arguably the key dimension along which cases of racketeering vary is the balance of power between upperworld and underworld. At one extreme, the racketeers are mere servants of business interests; at the other extreme, racketeering is a sophisticated form of extortion.

Labor Racketeering

The two types of racketeering, labor racketeering and business racketeering, have historically been closely connected. It may well be that in the combination of the two the highest level of criminal control over the legal economy is achieved. Yet, both phenomena need to be examined separately to understand their respective nature.

Concept and History of Labor Racketeering

Labor racketeering means the creation or infiltration of labor unions by criminals for criminal purposes. The involvement of criminals in labor unions in the

United States can be traced back to the *labor wars*, a period of violent confrontation between employers and workers that extended from the 1860s until the 1930s. Both sides drew on the aid of gangsters. In some cases, the gangsters gained a foothold in unions that they were able to consolidate through violence, intimidation, election fraud, and patronage (Jacobs, 2006, p. 24, 29–31; Jacobs & Peters, 2003, p. 232). "From policing strikes," Block (1983, p. 168) writes, "it was a short step to helping in organizing workers and to the domination of key locals."

The criminal infiltration of unions had broader ramifications. It meant a weakening of the radical elements of the labor movement who had formed the most forceful opposition against racketeers (Block, 1983; Block & Chambliss, 1981; Kimeldorf, 1988).

Labor racketeering can affect unions at all levels, from individual locals to entire international organizations. Four major North American labor unions in particular have come under the influence of criminals: the Hotel and Restaurant Employees International Union (HEREIU), the Laborers' International Union of America (LIUNA), the International Longshoremen's Association (ILA), and the International Brotherhood of Teamsters (IBT) (Jacobs, 2006, p. 42).

Implications of Labor Racketeering

Similar to the control of legitimate businesses, the control over labor unions can serve a number of purposes. First of all, racketeers are in a position to negotiate so-called "sweetheart contracts" between businesses and unions in exchange for kickbacks. Under-the-table payments are made for agreements that favor the interests of the employer over those of the employees (Block & Chambliss, 1981, p. 78). Holding elected offices or official positions within labor unions, just like owning a legitimate business can also create an aura of respectability for criminals.

Secondly, labor racketeering makes labor unions targets of crime other than the victimization through sweetheart contracts. Unions and their rank-and-file members have been exploited by the misuse and misappropriation of union funds. These schemes range from inflated salaries for union officials to the diversion of assets from health, welfare, and retirement funds. In one case, for example, criminals siphoned money from a LIUNA health fund through a dental plan, which allocated 68 percent of its budget to "administrative costs" (Jacobs, 2006, p. p. 48). Most famously, members of the Cosa Nostra received loans from a Teamsters pension fund to obtain interests in and then illegally skim profits from casinos in Las Vegas, Nevada (Jacobs, 1994).

Thirdly, in its most elaborate form, labor racketeering entails the instrumentalization of union power to influence legitimate businesses and entire business sectors. An example for this has already been given with the case of the low-quality soap that New York area mafiosi tried to market through the use of violence and intimidation. Representatives of two unions helped in the effort to convince stores to put the inferior product on their shelves. When A&P refused despite the murder of two of its managers, a butchers' union, backed by the Teamsters, threatened to go on strike. Interestingly, it was only then, according to one journalistic account, that A&P decided to seek help from the federal government (Demaris, 1986, p. 81).

In this case, criminals were able to distort competition in a legal market, the market for soap in the New York area. However, the influence fell short of a comprehensive control over this market. The targeted businesses were customers of the mafia-connected soap factory, not its competitors. No efforts were made to exert pressure on other producers of soap or directly on consumers. Labor unions were essentially used to extort individual stores and supermarket chains. Similar to many forms of extortion that rest on the threat or use of violence, the affected stores were forced to purchase a good or service they would otherwise not have acquired at all or not at the set price (Krevert, 1997).

There are other cases where the threat of labor action and other coercive means are not just used to influence individual businesses but to gain control over an entire legal market by systematically targeting all suppliers of a given good or service. These cases fall in the category of business racketeering.

Business Racketeering

Business racketeering is centered on the creation of cartels in legal markets. Racketeers organize legal businesses that operate in the same market with the aim of limiting competition. What distinguishes business racketeering from the kinds of price-fixing conspiracies among white-collar criminals discussed earlier is the involvement of underworld figures and the threat and use of violence.

The Case of the Long Island Waste Carting Industry

One of the most notorious examples of business racketeering is the case of the waste carting industry in Long Island, New York (Jacobs, 1999; Reuter, 1987, 1993). Beginning in the 1950s, criminals connected to the Cosa Nostra initiated the formation of carters' associations. These trade associations established what has been called a *property-rights system* or a *customer-allocation system*. Under this system, each garbage pickup location belonged to a particular member of the association to the exclusion of other (member or nonmember) carting businesses. As a result, carters in Long Island could charge exorbitant prices for low-quality service without fear that customers might switch to another provider. The system was enforced through various mechanisms. The trade association functioned as a court of arbitration. It would order a carter who had taken away a customer from another member to hand over a customer of equal or greater value, and in some instances, financial penalties were imposed. The decisions of the association were enforced with the help of a local of the Teamsters Union, which represented the drivers of the individual carting firms. The boss of the union local reportedly took direct orders from mafiosi, who oversaw the Long Island carting business. The union threatened carters stepping out of line with strikes or other job actions. In the case of one business that refused to participate in the property-rights system, drivers were beaten, trucks were destroyed, and finally the owner was murdered. With the support of carters and local politicians the system remained in place until the 1990s when, after a number of convictions, the entire Long Island waste-hauling industry was placed under monitorship by the federal government (Jacobs, 1999).

Image 10.2 National waste-hauling firms like Chicago-based Waste Management, Inc. (WM) and Houston-based Browning Ferris Industries (BFI) long stayed away from the waste carting business in the New York area because of the domination of Mafia-controlled business associations. Only after authorities launched systematic crackdowns against racketeering did WM and BFI begin to establish a presence in the region. Shortly after BFI began to collect refuse in New York City in 1992, at rates markedly lower than those charged by local firms, a company executive found the severed head of a German shepherd on his front lawn with a note that read "Welcome to New York" (Jacobs, 1999, p. 195).

Photo: AP Photo/Wayne Parry

Implications of Business Racketeering

Criminals can derive benefits from business racketeering in different ways. If they themselves are business owners, as was the case in the Long Island carting industry, they profit in the same way other complicit businesses do, perhaps even more so if they receive preferential treatment in the allocation of customers. To the extent criminals occupy official positions in the trade associations under their control, they are also able to draw salaries and to convey the impression of legitimate employment.

Business racketeering, as Peter Reuter (1985, pp. 58–59) has argued, can even be an inconspicuous way to generate monopoly profits in a legal market. In this scenario, the members of a trade association would have to adhere to uniformly set prices at inflated levels. The resulting profits would be siphoned off through membership dues to the trade association and would then be handed over to the racketeers in the form, for example, of salaries for association officials. Interestingly, despite their firm control over the carting industry in Long Island, mafiosi made no attempt in this direction. Rather than centrally setting prices for garbage collection, they left the decision what to charge customers to the individual carting businesses. This may be due to the difficulties of closely monitoring the conduct of individual businesses on a daily basis. Customer allocation schemes, in contrast, provide a simple, fairly easily enforceable rule (Gambetta & Reuter, 1995, pp. 121–125; Reuter, 1987, p. 7)

Just like in the relationship between criminals and individual businesses, the nature of the relationship between racketeers and the involved legal business can vary greatly. In one extreme, business racketeering is a form of extortion; in the other extreme, criminals are service providers welcomed by the business community (Block, 1983, p. 172; Chamberlin, 1932, p. 659; Landesco, 1929, p. 982; Reuter, 1987, p. 55). In Long Island, according to an investigation by the U.S. Senate, waste carters had initially "invited" a godson of mafia boss Albert Anastasia to organize their market (Investigation of Improp., 1957, pp. 6724, 6821).

BUSINESS SECTORS VULNERABLE TO CRIMINAL INFLUENCE

The influence of organized criminals over legitimate businesses does not seem to be evenly distributed across all business sectors. Some sectors are much more likely to see a presence of organized criminals than others. In addition, the kinds of individual businesses that are most at risk of coming under the control of organized criminals are not necessarily the same that are most vulnerable to labor racketeering and business racketeering.

Business Sectors Preferred by Organized Criminals

Limited systematic data exist on the kinds of businesses that have come under the influence of organized criminals. These data pertain primarily to members of Cosa Nostra and stem from the 1960s through the 1980s, when arguably the influence of mafiosi on the U.S. economy was at its peak (Marine, 2006). While it is difficult to compare the data because of different categorizations, they suggest that mostly small businesses in service-oriented sectors of the economy, especially bars and restaurants, have been affected.

Research on the Relative Importance of Particular Business Sectors

According to a 1968 analysis conducted by the Internal Revenue Service and cited by McKeon (1971, 120), 98 out of the 113 top organized crime figures in the United States had interests in 159 legitimate businesses, including the following:

Casinos and nightclubs	32
Land investment and real estate	17
Hotels and motels	11
Vending machine companies	10
Restaurants	8
Trucking and transportation	8
Manufacturing	8
Sports and entertainment	8
Wholesale food distribution	7
Money lending	6

Other businesses mentioned include funeral parlors, picnic groves, advertising companies, and florist shops.

Anderson (1979) in her study of the Philadelphia Cosa Nostra family found a similar pattern. She lists holdings by the 75 members and their 16 close associates in a total of 144 businesses. Most of these businesses fall into eight broad categories. Just like in the IRS analysis, bars and restaurants form the largest group (46 businesses), followed by other retail trade and services (25); finance, insurance, and real estate (18); vending machines and related businesses (13); casinos and related services (12); food and kindred products: manufacturing and wholesaling (11); trucking and transportation (7); and construction and building services (7) (Anderson, 1979, pp. 74–84).

Edelhertz and Overcast (1993) counted legal business activities in a database of 165 federal organized crime investigations that for the most part led to indictments in the years 1986 and 1987. Again, bars and restaurants, including adult entertainment, formed the largest category of legitimate businesses with organized crime involvement. Activities related to these businesses were mentioned 31 times. Retail and wholesale businesses were mentioned 19 times. Businesses from the financial sector, including banking, investment, and insurance, appear 18 times, followed by transportation (15) and construction (12). Less frequently mentioned were auto wrecking/parts (5) and waste disposal (3) as well as a variety of other service-oriented businesses. Interestingly, real estate and manufacturing, with only one mention, respectively, appear far less often in the Edelhertz and Overcast data set than in the IRS and Anderson studies (Edelhertz & Overcast, 1993, p. 57).

Explanations for the Targeting of Specific Kinds of Businesses

There are a number of factors that may account for the observed patterns of organized crime involvement (Edelhertz & Overcast, 1993; see also Albanese, 1987; Vander Beken & Van Daele, 2008). The preference for bars and restaurants as well as for retail stores and other small service-oriented businesses is perhaps best explained by the easy access organized criminals have to these sectors. Few if any technical or other skills are required for operating these kinds of businesses, and the need for investment capital tends to be limited. A key factor may also be familiarity. Organized criminals, irrespective of their social background, will be familiar with these businesses, at least from a customer perspective (Edelhertz & Overcast, 1993, p. 58).

Bars, restaurants, and other small service-oriented businesses are also attractive for organized criminals because of their logistical value for criminal activities. These businesses tend to be cash intensive and thereby they are particularly suitable for money laundering and, through skimming, for tax evasion.

The logistical value for criminal activities may also explain the involvement of organized criminals in other kinds of businesses. For example, vending machine companies can be a vehicle for illegal gambling operations. The servicing of the vending machines that are placed in bars and stores provides a convenient cover for collecting betting slips (Potter, 1994, p. 73). Other examples have already been mentioned before, such as the use of banks for the laundering and management of illicit funds and the use of transport companies for moving contraband. Profitability is a further, obvious reason for organized criminals to target specific businesses and business sectors. It is the "same reason that motivates legitimate entrepreneurs—the perception that there is money to be made" (Edelhertz & Overcast, 1993, p. 61). However, certain types of business are especially lucrative because they can be operated much more profitably by illegal than by legal means. Waste disposal services are a case in point. It has been estimated "that profits through illegal waste management are about three to four times higher than for legal activities" (Vander Beken & Van Daele, 2008, p. 746).

Variations in the degree to which businesses and business sectors come under the influence of organized criminals may also be due to variations in vulnerability. Businesses engaged in illicit practices will be less likely to seek help from law enforcement and from the public than businesses that strictly abide by the law. Likewise, businesses and business sectors with weak government oversight and little public scrutiny will be more prone to organized crime involvement (Edelhertz & Overcast, 1993, p. 65).

There may also be variations in the vulnerability stemming from the nature of legitimate business operations. For example, where the volume of business undergoes seasonal changes there may be an increased demand for loans to bridge periods of low turnover. In some cases, this demand may be met by loan sharks, which in turn may lead to an eventual take-over by organized criminals (Edelhertz & Overcast, 1993, p. 156; Jacobs, 1999, p. 21).

All of these considerations leave open the possibility that businesses are targets of opportunity unrelated to the characteristics of a particular business sector. The owner of any kind of business, for example, can run up illegal gambling debts to eventually be forced to turn over control of the business to organized criminals (Edelhertz & Overcast, 1993, p. 62).

Business Sectors Most Affected by Racketeering

Just like certain kinds of businesses are more prone to organized crime involvement than others, not all business sectors are equally at risk of coming under the influence of racketeers.

The experience with racketeering in the United States suggests that those sectors are most affected that are characterized by four factors: (a) the competition between numerous small firms, (b) the prevalence of entrepreneurs with a low-status social background, (c) a workforce made up of low-skilled workers, and (d) the vulnerability of businesses to short-term strikes (Reuter, 1985, 1987). Businesses operating in such an environment are easily replaceable and face the constant threat of being pushed out of the market by competitors. Therefore, they have strong incentives to form cartels in order to reduce competition. At the same time, it is difficult for the large number of firms in such a market to come to an agreement. Racketeers are a solution to this problem. With their reputation for the effective use of violence, racketeers can facilitate and enforce cartel agreements (Gambetta & Reuter, 1995).

A low social status of the entrepreneurs in a market means that contacts to racketeers who typically also have a low social status are fairly easy to establish. In addition, where the workforce is low skilled, racketeers find it easier to gain control over unions, which then can be used to apply pressure on businesses. Finally, even a short disruption of work as a result of a strike could be fatal to individual businesses in a fragmented market, because customers can readily switch to other businesses. Accordingly, businesses are easily brought in line under the threat of labor conflict (Reuter, 1987, pp. 6–7).

Within vulnerable business sectors, racketeers tend to concentrate on certain "choke points" (Edelhertz & Overcast, 1993, p. 65). For example, the control over trucking firms through a corrupt union local and a business association gave Cosa Nostra members control over the entire garment district in New York City. Clothing businesses heavily relied on the trucking firms for the timely transportation between designers and manufacturers based in different parts of Manhattan (Jacobs, 1999, p. 20).

Dynamics of the Infiltration of the Legal Economy

The notion of an "infiltration" of the legal economy by organized criminals conjures up images of underworld figures forcing their way into the realm of legitimate businesses in a quest for profit and power. The case mentioned above of the Boston gangster who acquired ownership of a liquor store by massive threats is just one small example illustrating that this is not only a hypothetical scenario. At the same time, it would be wrong to assume that the initiative is always on the part of the organized criminals who establish their presence in the legal economy.

As already indicated, organized criminals may be welcomed into a business or a business sector as investors, as providers of illegal goods and services, as protectors, or as cartel organizers (Hill, 2003, p. 184). Edelhertz and Overcast (1993, p. 151) note that a large part of organized crime involvement in the legal economy "does not involve victims, but rather the eagerness of business persons who see advantages in the collaborative contributions of organized crime figures."

The boundary between upperworld and underworld, then, is not necessarily a manifest barrier that is breached when organized criminals enter the legal economy. It may be more appropriate in many instances to speak of a grey zone where actors from both sides meet on common grounds. As Petrus van Duyne (1996, p. 371) has argued, there are actors in the underworld as well as in the upperworld who share two important traits that facilitate collusion: "lack of morals and an insatiable greed."

The receptiveness of legitimate businesses for organized crime involvement does not mean that the nature of the relationship and the balance of power remain the same over time. The relationship may shift—for example, from collusion to the predatory exploitation of businesses by organized criminals (Hill, 2003, p. 190). But the development may also go in the opposite direction. Vadim Volkov (2000), writing about the link between crime and business in Russia in the post-Communist transition period of the 1990s, describes a three-stage process of increasing integration of criminal and business structures. In the first stage, criminals provide protection in exchange for payments. In the second stage, criminals invest in the businesses they protect and become business partners. In the third stage, finally, criminals take over full control of a business. Volkov does not interpret this process as a criminalization of business. Instead, he sees criminals increasingly forced to adapt to the logic of the market and to the principles of business administration. This means they are forced to realize that the benefits of using violence in the legal economy are limited in the long run (Volkov, 2000, p. 54).

ORGANIZED CRIME AND LEGITIMATE BUSINESS: SUMMARY AND CONCLUSION

This chapter has examined the relationship between organized crime and legitimate business from a variety of angles. The main focus has been on the myriad ways in which the underworld can be involved in the legal economy. If only one conclusion can be drawn from this examination, it is that the presence of organized criminals in the legal economy does not follow a simple pattern. The nature and extent of criminal involvement in legitimate businesses varies, as do the implications of this involvement.

Some basic constellations can be distinguished with regard to the level at which criminal influence occurs: individual businesses, territories, and markets (Table 10.2). Criminal influence arguably occurs most often on the level of individual businesses. Legitimate businesses can be the target or the tool of illegal activities, and they may be a vehicle for securing or establishing a position in legitimate society for criminals and their dependents. The societal consequences in each separate case will tend to be rather limited. In some instances, where the objective of criminals is to secure assets and to transfer them to dependents in the event of incarceration or death, the acquisition and operation of legitimate businesses may well be kept within the limits of the law. In these cases, the criminal background of the owner would be the only link between the legitimate business and crime, provided no illicit proceeds were used in acquiring or establishing the business. In contrast, the most far-reaching impact can be expected where criminal involvement in an individual legitimate business leads to a distortion of competition. This is the case namely when the business is subsidized by crime money and when illegal means are employed against competitors and customers.

Individual businesses, it seems, tend to be affected by criminal influence in an opportunistic and sporadic fashion. But criminal influence can also be exerted systematically. Legitimate businesses in a particular territory or in a particular market may become the targets of organized criminals. The systematic influence on legitimate businesses within a territory is linked to the existence of criminal groups that claim control over a geographical area such as an inner-city neighborhood. The influence may be purely predatory. In the case of true protection, however, the criminal influence has broader ramifications. For example, protection may include protection against rival businesses, which, in turn, means that criminal influence leads to a limitation or distortion of competition in a legal market.

The most profound criminal influence on the legal economy exists in the case of labor and business racketeering, where criminals gain control over entire legal markets and business sectors. The typical scenario is that criminals use their power to organize cartels, thereby eliminating competition, and to engage in a variety of other illegal schemes at the expense of businesses, customers, and the general public.

According to conventional wisdom, the influence of organized crime over the legal economy is one-dimensional and goes in the direction of increasing criminal control. Arguably, the endpoint of this process is reached when criminals control individual businesses and at the same time manipulate markets in their favor through corrupt unions and business associations. The U.S. experience with labor racketeering and business racketeering shows that this is a real threat and that criminal involvement in the legal economy can have dramatic consequences. The same experience also shows, however, that this process is not inevitable and can be reversed. Racketeering was widespread only in certain business sectors and has been in decline since the 1980s, mainly as a result of rigorous enforcement efforts (see Chapter 14). There is also something else that this and other historical examples suggest. The dispositions of legitimate businesses

Table 10.2 Forms and Consequences of Criminal Involvement in the Legal Economy

Level of Involvement	Type of Involvement	Consequence
Individual Business	Noncriminal	Respectable social status in legitimate society
	Use of crime in furtherance of legitimate business	Distortion of competition
	Use of legitimate business in furtherance of crime	Facilitation of crime
Businesses in a Particular Territory	Extortion	Predatory exploitation
	Regulation of business activities	Distortion of competition (to the advantage of protected businesses)
Businesses in a Particular Legal Market	Racketeering	Cartel building (elimination of competition)

toward unethical and illegal practices have a major impact on whether or not organized criminals can establish a presence in the legal economy at all and what the nature and extent of this presence is. Even where criminals have great financial resources and the means and willingness to use violence, their ability to gain positions of power within the legal economy appears to be limited, unless there is some connivance on the part of legitimate businesses.

Discussion Questions

1. What is the primary motive for organized criminals to obtain control over a legitimate business?

2. What is the lesser evil: organized corporate crime or the infiltration of the legal economy by members of the underworld?

3. What is the worst-case scenario for the future development of criminal involvement in legitimate businesses?

4. What role does (or could) the threat and use of violence play in the legal economy?

5. What sectors of the economy in the digital age are prone to racketeering?

Research Projects

1. Analyze the autobiography of an organized criminal, with a view to the involvement in legitimate business.

2. Analyze a case of organized corporate crime and discuss what would have been different if underworld figures had been involved.

3. Find a well-documented case of money laundering and examine the use of legitimate businesses in the scheme.

Further Reading

Block A. A., & Scarpitti, F. R. (1985). *Poisoning for profit: The Mafia and toxic waste in America*. New York: William Morrow.

Kelly, R. J. (1999). *The upperworld and the underworld: Case studies of racketeering and business infiltrations in the United States*. New York: Kluwer Academic/Plenum.

Lippmann, W. (1931). The underworld: Our secret servant. *Forum, 55*(1), 1–4.

Riccardi, M. (2014). When criminals invest in businesses: Are we looking in the right direction? An exploratory analysis of companies controlled by mafias. In S. Canappele & F. Calderoni (Eds.), *Organized Crime, Corruption and Crime Prevention - Essays in Honor of Ernesto U. Savona* (197-206). Cham: Springer.

Szymkowiak, K. (2002). *Sokaiya: Extortion, protection, and the Japanese corporation*. Armonk, NY: M.E. Sharpe.

CHAPTER 11

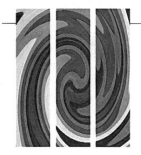

Organized Crime and Government

INTRODUCTION

The previous two chapters have examined the relationship between organized crime and society and specifically the relationship between organized crime and legitimate business. This chapter concludes the survey of the broader context of organized crime within society, with an examination of the relationship between organized crime and government. Government is understood here in a broad sense to encompass not only the executive branch but also the legislature and the judiciary, and it is meant to encompass not only national governments but governments on all levels, from village and town councils all the way to supranational structures, such as the European Union. Of interest is the state as an institution capable of purposeful action as well as the individuals and groups who hold positions within the state apparatus.

In the academic literature, the relationship between organized crime and government has been discussed from mainly two perspectives. One perspective is to highlight the functional similarities between criminal organizations and the state and to draw parallels between the historical process of state formation and the emergence of illegal governance (e.g., Skaperdas & Syropoulos, 1995; Tilly, 1985). Another perspective, characteristic of most of the public and academic debate, is centered on what has been called the *political-criminal nexus*, the link between "the legal, governmental and political establishment" and "the criminal underworld" (Godson, 2003b, p. 3). The typical scenario is that criminal organizations, such as the Sicilian Mafia or the Colombian and Mexican drug cartels, use bribes and intimidation to impose their will on public officials. The Cali Cartel in Colombia, for example, reportedly had a large percentage of the police and military on its payroll so that it could traffic drugs with impunity (Rempel, 2012, p. 111). But this extreme case of a powerful criminal organization influencing and undermining the state apparatus is just one of many possible constellations. The problem is much more complex. To begin with, one could argue that without the state, without criminal law enacted and enforced by government, there could be no organized crime (see O'Malley & Mugford, 1991; Chapter 9). Criminal law defines the kinds of behavior the state seeks to suppress. This implies an antagonistic, confrontational relationship between government and crime, and by extension, between government and organized *crimes*. At the same time, no government has ever been able to completely suppress the behavior that is defined as criminal, neither individual wrongdoing nor collective, organized law breaking in the form of, for example, gang crime or illegal markets. There is, therefore, always a more or less coherent sphere within society that is centered on criminal activities. This sphere of illegality is created and defined by criminal law.

The fundamental relationship between government and crime or organized crime is therefore contradictory. On the one hand, government is constitutive to the existence of organized crime in that it creates a sphere of illegality. On the other hand, government creates the main constraints for organized crime to develop. Government, through the enforcement of the law, bears the brunt of the burden of disrupting and suppressing organized criminal conduct, namely, by arresting and punishing offenders and by seizing the tools, products, and proceeds of illegal activities (see Chapter 14).

CONCEPTUALIZATIONS OF ORGANIZED CRIME AND GOVERNMENT: ACTIVITIES, STRUCTURES, AND GOVERNANCE

In order to understand the complexity of the links between underworld and upperworld in the sphere of government, it is important, once again, to consider the three basic dimensions of organized crime: activities, structures, and governance. Just like the relationship between organized crime and legitimate business does not only fit one mold, the relationship between organized crime and government takes on many different forms depending on how organized crime is conceptualized and depending on the specific circumstances.

Organized Criminal Activities and Government

The link between organized crime and government mirrors to some extent the relationship between organized crime and legitimate business. When one equates organized crime with illegal *activities*, it is the nature and prevalence of organized crimes that define the relationship. Who the organized *criminals* are, in contrast, is only of secondary importance from this perspective. There can be a host of illegal activities of an organized nature in the sphere of government without the involvement of stereotypical criminal organizations and underworld figures. Organized criminal conduct may be directed *against* government, it may take place *within* government, or organized criminal conduct may be carried out *by* government. There are numerous organized crimes involving the state, such as subsidy fraud or the selling of surplus military equipment in violation of arms embargos, where there is a great likelihood that these crimes are instigated and carried out by offenders rooted in the upperworld. The major players may be legitimate businesses and banks, public officials, government agencies, or the government as such (Arsovska & Kostakos, 2008; Passas & Nelken, 1993).

Organized Criminal Structures and Government

When one equates organized crime not with illegal activities but with illegal *structures*, then the focus is on how criminals and their organizations, understood in a broad sense, relate to government. Arguably, this is the main perspective from which the relationship between organized crime and government is discussed in public and academic discourse. At the center of attention are attempts by criminal organizations to influence government in an effort to reduce the risk of arrest and punishment. The question is if organized criminals also pursue other and more far-reaching goals. Ultimately, the question is whether organized criminals have a political agenda. Commonly, the lack of political goals is seen as a defining characteristic of organized crime that distinguishes it from ideologically and religiously motivated terrorist and insurgent groups (e.g., Abadinsky, 2013, p. 3). It is widely assumed that organized criminals do not seek to change the political order but simply wish "to be left alone and to carry on their crime-trade without interference" (Van Duyne, 1997, p. 213). On the other hand, many criminal organizations such as the Sicilian Mafia and Japanese yakuza groups have demonstrated an affinity to political groups, often, it seems, to those on the right and far right of the political spectrum (Hill, 2003; Paoli, 2003a; Schulte-Bockholt, 2001). Some also argue that there is a nexus between terrorism and organized crime. The claim is that terrorist groups have either assumed characteristics of criminal groups and engage in organized criminal activities or that terrorist groups have established collaborative relations with criminal groups (Makarenko, 2004; Mincheva & Gurr, 2010; Shelley, 2014).

Criminal structures that are separate from and in conflict with government are not the only phenomena being discussed in the debate on the relationship between organized crime and government. Some attention has also been paid to criminal structures that to different degrees are interwoven with and integrated into governmental structures. There are criminal structures that connect members of the underworld with state officials. The Sicilian Mafia, for example, historically has had a number of politicians within its ranks (Arlacchi, 1993; Paoli, 2003a). In other cases, criminals have attained formal positions within government through appointments and elections (Bezlov & Gounev, 2012, p. 99; Kupatadze, 2008, p. 289). A famous case is the election of Pablo Escobar, the leader of the so-called Medellin Cartel, to the Colombian parliament (Clawson & Lee, 1996, p. 48). Some criminal groups enter into alliances with power elites and the government—for example, to suppress opposition movements (Schulte-Bockholt, 2001). In other cases, criminals are believed to have a dominating influence on state institutions in a scenario that is called "state capture," where criminal groups are in a position to shape state policy in their own interest through illicit and non-transparent methods (Hellman & Schankerman, 2000, p. 546; Cornell, 2006, p. 39; Kupatadze, 2009, p. 152). Finally, some criminal structures exist within government without the involvement of underworld figures. For example, it is a rather frequently occurring pattern that groups of police officers extort criminals and legal businesses, deal in confiscated drugs, or engage in systematic theft (Bezlov & Gounev, 2012; Prenzler, 2009). In extreme cases the state apparatus or major elements of the state apparatus function as criminal organizations. These cases, where crimes are "committed by state officials in the pursuit of their job as representatives of the state," fall under the category of *"state-organized crime"* (Chambliss, 1989, p. 184).

Organized Crime and Governance

When one equates organized crime not with illegal activities or illegal structures but with illegal *governance*, then the focus is primarily on criminals playing a quasi-governmental role in place of legitimate government. Illegal governance challenges the claim of the state to "the monopoly of the legitimate use of physical force" (Weber, 1968, p. 54) within a given territory. Illegal governance, as elaborated in Chapter 8, emerges in spheres of society that the state is unwilling or unable to regulate. Criminals may fill this vacuum, for example, by providing protection, by enforcing rules, by arbitrating disputes, and in turn, by taxing licit and illicit businesses (see, e.g., Mannozzi, 2013; Wang, 2011). In this respect, the relationship between organized crime and legitimate government is one of mutual exclusion. The exercise of power by quasi-governmental criminal structures only works where the state does not exercise its power effectively. However, there have also been cases where underworld figures and government officials have jointly exercised power—for example, in the control over illegal markets (e.g., Chambliss, 1978). Finally, there are instances where criminals do not replace government but where government replaces criminals in the regulation of illegal activities. This means that in some instances, government officials have exercised control over illegal markets and, ironically, have functioned as a sort of underworld government (e.g., Albini, 1971, p. 74).

THE RELATIONSHIP BETWEEN ORGANIZED CRIME AND GOVERNMENT AS TWO SEPARATE ENTITIES

When one takes organized crime and government to constitute two separate entities, then the relationship can take on three ideal-typical forms: evasion, corruption, and confrontation (Bailey & Taylor, 2009; Table 11.1). Each of these types of relationships represents a particular strategy that criminals may pursue. Sometimes different strategies are pursued at the same time. *Evasion* means that criminals operate clandestinely in order to avoid detection by the authorities. *Corruption* means exerting illegal influence on government officials in furtherance of criminal interests. *Confrontation*, finally, means that criminals challenge the state as such, that they seek to force government into submission, by "directly targeting multiple symbols of state power" (Bailey & Taylor, 2009, p. 11).

Evasion as an Alternative to Corruption and Confrontation

According to a widely held view, organized crime is inherently connected to the corruption of public officials. The underlying rationale for making this

Table 11.1 Strategies Employed by Criminal Groups Vis-à-Vis the State

Strategies	Objectives	Forms of Criminal Conduct
Evasion	Criminals seek to avoid detection by government	Clandestine mode of operation
		Self-restriction to illegal activities with low law-enforcement priority
Corruption	Criminals seek	Bribery
	Protection	Intimidation
	Logistical support	Use of social network ties
Confrontation	Criminals seek to force the government into submission	Violence targeting law enforcement
		Violence targeting political figures
		Indiscriminate terror attacks

Source: Further elaboration of a typology proposed by Bailey & Taylor (2009).

connection is twofold. One assumption is that organized criminal activities by their very nature would not be possible without corruption. Activities such as illegal gambling and illegal prostitution, it is argued, are carried out on a regular basis and are highly visible and therefore would be easy targets for the police were it not for organized criminals neutralizing law enforcement through corruption (e.g., Hughes & Denisova, 2001, p. 57). The other assumption is that organized criminals have the necessary resources readily available to influence government in their favor. Organized criminals, it is assumed, generate sufficient illegal profits to easily bribe public officials, and where this is not successful, the threat and use of violence gives organized criminals the necessary leverage. Many examples of criminal influence at all levels of government in developed as well as in developing countries appear to support these assumptions (e.g., Block & Chambliss, 1981; Cornell, 2006; Giannakopoulos, 2001; Gounev & Ruggiero, 2012; Kukhianidze, 2009; Kupadaze, 2009; Lauchs & Staines, 2012). Cross-national comparative research likewise suggests that there is a correlation between corruption and organized crime (Sung, 2004; Van Dijk, 2007). However, micro-level research shows that corruption is not always a precondition for carrying out criminal activities in an organized way. Complex, well-planned, well-coordinated criminal endeavors that are pursued over long periods of time are sometimes possible without the neutralization of law enforcement. Various reasons can account for the nonenforcement of the law. For example, the authorities may not have the necessary resources to intervene, they may be inefficiently organized and staff may be inadequately trained, there may be competing priorities for selecting law enforcement targets, or the authorities may feel that there is insufficient support for enforcing certain laws (Morris, 2013, p. 199). Thus, organized criminals do not always have to depend on influencing or directly confronting government in order to carry out their criminal activities unimpeded. Edelhertz and Overcast (1993, p. 18), for example, in their analysis of 165 federal organized crime investigations in the United States, found only nine cases with any indication of public corruption. Likewise, Van Duyne examined the police and court files of 44 organized crime cases situated in the Netherlands or relating to the Netherlands, most of which concerned either drug trafficking or business fraud. He concluded that "many organized crime-entrepreneurs appear to have developed their prospering business without resorting to corruption" (Van Duyne, 1997, p. 205). Interview-based research has produced similar findings. Desroches, for example, summarizes his interviews with 70 Canadian drug traffickers with regard to the importance of corruption as follows:

> Many subjects in this study paid airline employees, truckers, and ordinary citizens to store, hide, transport, and courier drugs. Lawyers, bank employees, and accountants are also used to establish legitimate businesses, launder money, and facilitate foreign exchanges. Although this type of graft is common, few dealers corrupt public officials.

> Only one syndicate reported bribing a law enforcement employee—a secretary who worked in a police department and provided information on car registrations. Three drug-dealing syndicates reported bribing officials in source countries to assist them in exporting illicit drugs and/or avoid criminal prosecution. Apart from the police secretary, subjects made no attempt to bribe or corrupt public officials in Canada. Most believed that police and Customs officials were difficult and dangerous to bribe, and that their business could function without corrupt officials. (Desroches, 2005, pp. 131–132)

Johansen, in his interview-based research on the Norwegian illegal alcohol trade, has reached essentially the same conclusion:

> Corruption related to organised crime is not a big issue at the present time. It is quite possible to make large sums of money through smuggling without the need for bribes or corrupt protection. (Johansen, 2005, p. 201)

Given the empirical evidence from various countries, pertaining to different manifestations of organized crime, corruption cannot be viewed as an inherent, ubiquitous feature of organized crime. Instead, evasion of government, staying under the radar of law enforcement, appears to be a viable option in many instances. This does not mean, however, that corruption is entirely irrelevant for understanding organized crime.

Corruption

The concept of *corruption*, just like the concept of organized crime, is vague and ambiguous (Genaux, 2004). It encompasses "a mixture of bribery, self-enrichment, fraud, cronyism and mismanagement" (Van Duyne, 2001, p. 74). In a more narrow sense, the concept of corruption pertains to irregular influence on decision making in government (public-sector corruption) or in business (private-sector corruption). For the purpose of the present discussion of the link between organized crime and government, of course, it is only important to understand the scope of public-sector corruption. Corrupt influence can be exerted on all branches of government, namely in the form of police corruption, judicial corruption, and political corruption. Low-ranking, front-line officers (low-level corruption) may be targeted as well as high-ranking officials all the way to the heads of government (high-level corruption). In some cases, influence taking is sporadic and confined to just a few officials (individual corruption); in other cases influence taking is widespread and occurs on a regular basis (systemic corruption).

Modes of Criminal Influence Taking on Government

The concept of *criminal influence taking on government* as used here pertains to cases where the interaction between organized crime and government serves primarily the interest of criminals. But how exactly are criminals able to influence government, and for what specific purposes?

Bribery. Much of the criminal influence taking fits the mold of bribery. The typical scenario is that criminals pay public officials,—for example, police officers or prison guards, in exchange for favorable treatment. Apart from the stereotypical attaché case or brown bag filled with cash, bribes can come in a variety of forms. Take, for example, an illegal brothel that provides "free services" to police officers in exchange for protection (Gaines & Kappeler, 2004, p. 234).

A special kind of bargaining chip that socially well-entrenched organized criminals have used for gaining influence on government are electoral votes. The Sicilian Mafia, for example, has historically owed much of its power to the ability to control votes, mainly through a system of patronage, and to deliver these votes to those politicians who are most receptive to criminal interests (Catanzaro, 1992). Another example is Bulgaria. Bezlov and Gounev report that criminals on the local level, especially in close-knit minority communities, pressure voters into supporting a specific party. The politicians in Bulgaria, just like in Sicily, "ensure either protection from prosecution or access to government contracts" in exchange for the votes (Bezlov & Gounev, 2012, p. 98).

Coercion. Bribery is not the only form of criminal influence taking on government. Coercion can also come into play, namely in the form of blackmail, threats, and intimidation or open acts of violence against officials and their families (Ruggiero & Gounev, 2012). Korsell, Wallström, and Skinnari (2007, p. 336), in a study of unlawful influence on public officials in Sweden, provide one example of how rather subtle pressure can be exerted by criminals. They report that outlaw bikers have mapped the movements of police officers and their families and then arranged for this intimidating information to be found by the police in searches of biker premises.

At the other extreme are cases of direct, open and brute force displayed in the targeted killings of law enforcement officials. Infamous are the murders of the two prominent Sicilian anti-Mafia judges Giovanni Falcone and Paolo Borsellino. In 1992, in a phase when political support for the Mafia was fading, a roadside bomb killed Falcone along with his wife and three bodyguards. Two months later, Borsellino and five bodyguards also died in a bomb blast (Stille, 1996). These and other cases will be discussed more extensively further below in this chapter as examples of violent confrontations between organized crime and government.

Social Bonds. A third mechanism, apart from bribery and coercion, through which criminal influence may be exerted on government, is by way of social network ties that directly or indirectly connect criminals and public officials. Social bonds rooted, for example, in familial ties, childhood friendship, or relationships built in a leisure context can in many instances explain why public officials neglect or violate their duties in support of criminals (Ruggiero & Gounev, 2012, p. 25; Wang, 2014). A low-level police officer in the Chinese city of Fuzhou explained this scenario as follows:

> Not every police officer that is affiliated with a gangster does it just for money, free meals, or entertainment. Many police officers are associated with underworld figures because the two were classmates, neighbors, relatives, etc. Besides, these gangsters are not the monsters you imagine. They are usually very nice. (Chin and Godson, 2006, p. 26)

The motivation behind corruption, then, may not be monetary reward but rather a sense of moral or social obligation that public officials feel to, for example, warn friends of investigations or impending raids or arrests (Desroches, 2005, p. 132).

This is what saved Larry Lavin, the Philadelphia cocaine dealer described in Chapter 6, early in his career. A good friend and customer of Ken, Larry's business partner, had a wife who worked in the district attorney's office. This wife, in turn, had a colleague who was privy to a list of drug-raid targets that included someone from the dental school Ken, his friend, and Larry attended. As a friendly gesture the wife of Ken's friend was told by her colleague about the raid, just in case Ken's friend was involved. The information was then quickly passed on to Larry, who removed all the cocaine from his apartment, just barely in time before the police arrived (Saline, 1989, p. 100).

The example of Larry Lavin highlights the importance of social networks in connecting criminals and public officials. Criminal influence is not always exerted directly between the criminal who seeks favorable treatment and the public official in charge of making the decision. The connection may be established and mediated through a complex web of relations. Some relationships may be characterized by coercion, others by a sense of moral obligations, and yet others by a business-like give-and-take of favors.

Purposes of Criminal Influence Taking

Organized criminals seem to pursue at least one of two objectives when they exert influence on public officials. They seek to obtain protection and/or logistical support.

Protection. Neutralization of law enforcement is arguably the most important motivation behind criminal influence taking. Criminals seek protection against arrest, prosecution, conviction, and the seizure of assets. This is achieved primarily through police and judicial corruption.

In extreme cases, criminals may also seek to change the law in order to avoid prosecution. For example, in the early 1990s, Colombian drug traffickers campaigned for the inclusion of a ban on extraditions in the constitution of Colombia. The constitutional amendment, allegedly facilitated by corruption and intimidation, meant that the Colombian government could no longer extradite drug traffickers to the United States (Clawson & Lee, 1996).

A second motivation for police and judicial corruption is to increase law enforcement pressure on other criminals. In these cases the government is instrumentalized to eliminate competition or to resolve other kinds of conflicts within the underworld (Gardiner, 1970, p. 20; Lupo, 2009, p. 251).

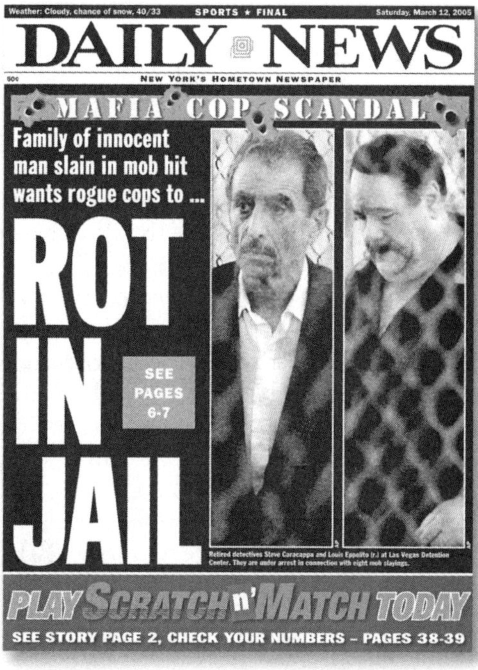
Weather: Cloudy, chance of snow, 40/33 SPORTS ★ FINAL Saturday, March 12, 2005
DAILY NEWS
60¢ NEW YORK'S HOMETOWN NEWSPAPER
MAFIA COP SCANDAL
Family of innocent man slain in mob hit wants rogue cops to ...
ROT IN JAIL
SEE PAGES 6-7
Retired detectives Steve Caracappa and Louis Eppolito (r.) at Las Vegas Detention Center. They are under arrest in connection with eight mob slayings.
PLAY SCRATCH n' MATCH TODAY
SEE STORY PAGE 2, CHECK YOUR NUMBERS – PAGES 38-39

Image 11.1 A front-page story of the New York tabloid *Daily News* blasts retired police detectives Steve Caracappa and Louis Eppolito following their arrest in 2005. Both were later found guilty of participation in several Mafia murders.

Photo: New York Daily News Archive/Contributor

Logistical Support. Apart from protection against law enforcement and against other criminals, corruption can also help in directly furthering and supporting criminal activities. Criminal influence can be exerted to create or maintain conditions conducive to crime. For example, Johansen (2005, p. 193) reports that Norwegian alcohol smugglers have donated some of their proceeds in support of temperance politics in order to keep the price of legal liquor high.

In other cases, criminal influence is used to recruit public officials for criminal endeavors. Corruption, then, becomes part of the logistics of crime. This is true where the government is the target, such as in subsidy frauds or in the smuggling of high-excise goods. In these cases the participation of corrupt public officials is either necessary or at least it greatly facilitates the commission of crime (Barone & Narciso, 2015; Van Duyne, 1996, p. 358; Van Duyne, 1997, p. 207).

In crime schemes not directed against government, corrupt officials may contribute their specific resources to the commission of crimes. For example, corrupt police officers have aided mafia groups in the United States in the extortion of illegal gambling businesses. The officers confiscated the books and records of these businesses and allowed mafiosi to review the documents. The mafiosi were then able to determine how much money they could extort from a particular illegal gambling business (Edelhertz & Overcast, 1993, p. 48).

Another example of police corruption in support of crime is the case of two New York City police detectives who worked for a leading member of the Cosa Nostra. In exchange for money the two detectives not only passed on classified information—the names of police informants—they also actively participated in several mafia murders, using police powers such as traffic stops and arrests to overwhelm victims (Lawson & Oldham, 2007).

The Balance of Power in Corrupt Relations Between Organized Crime and Government: Six Case Studies

Criminals are typically depicted as the driving force and the dominant element in corrupt relationships with government officials. However, state capture, corrupt relations that are initiated and shaped by the criminal side and serve primarily criminal interests, is just one scenario. Another scenario is that criminals and officials interact more or less as equals in the pursuit of corresponding or common interests. Adequate terms for this kind of relationship with a more or less even balance of power would be *illegal-legal partnerships*. A third scenario, finally, is that officials dominate corrupt relationships. This means that, for example, bribes paid to corrupt officials are more adequately classified as extortion payments or informal taxes levied on the operations of illicit businesses (Morris, 2013, p. 205; Wang, 2013). In these latter cases, one can speak of *police rackets* or *judicial rackets* or *political rackets*, or more generally of *state rackets* (see Ruggiero & Gounev, 2012). These three scenarios (state capture, illegal-legal partnerships, state rackets) are ideal types. In the real world, things tend to be more complex because the state and organized crime are not monolithic entities. Different kinds of relationships between underworld and upperworld tend to exist at the same time, some of them more one-sided in the interest of criminals, others more one-sided in the interest of government officials, and yet others where the interaction is mutually beneficial with no side clearly keeping the upper hand (Godson, 2003b; Kupatadze, 2009).

To understand the complexities and variations in corrupt relationships between underworld and upperworld, it is helpful to look at a number of case studies. The first case examined below pertains to the Cali Cartel, arguably one of the most extreme examples of criminal influence taking. This is followed by three case studies of local underworld-upperworld alliances in different parts of the United States. They have been selected from a larger number of roughly similar studies (see Chin, 1990; Potter & Gaines, 1995; Whyte, 1943/1981). The last two cases, finally, involve systems of underworld-upperworld alliances on a national scale, one in Russia and the other in Mexico.

The Influence of the Cali Cartel on the Government in Colombia

When one looks for extreme cases of criminal influence on government, it is difficult to ignore the so-called Cali Cartel. The Cali Cartel, as mentioned in Chapter 6, was a Colombian cocaine trafficking enterprise headed by brothers

Gilberto and Miguel Rodriguez Orejuela and their childhood friend Jose Santacruz Londono. The Cali Cartel is an example of the systematic corruption of public officials to attain immunity from law enforcement. It also shows how illicit proceeds can be used in ways other than traditional corruption to influence government.

The Cali Cartel is credited with having been one of the major suppliers of cocaine to markets in North America and Europe in the 1980s and 1990s (Chepesiuk, 2005, p. 251). The leaders of the Cali Cartel pursued three inter-locking strategies to reduce the risk of prosecution. One strategy was to invest heavily in legitimate businesses to give themselves an aura of respectability and to form ties with influential members of the political, social, and business elites (Chepesiuk, 2005, p. 118). For example, Gilberto Rodriguez Orejuela became chairmen of the board of directors of a bank that was not only used to launder drug proceeds but also to forge a relationship with a powerful senator who likewise served on the bank's board of directors (Chepesiuk, 2005, p. 69).

The second strategy was to use bribes to form a vast network of Cartel supporters in key upperworld positions. According to a document seized by authorities in 1995, shortly before the Cali Cartel was dismantled, 2,800 individuals—politicians, police, journalists, congress members, state governors, and military personnel—received monthly payments totalling nearly $5.6 million (Chepesiuk, 2005, p. 221).

The third strategy, finally, was to employ modern information technology for counterintelligence. With the help of a highly placed source within Colombia's national telephone company, for example, it became possible for the Cali Cartel to monitor phone calls. When the police created a hotline for information on the Cali Cartel, calls were intercepted and some tipsters died before their tips could be investigated (Rempel, 2012, p. 199). In addition, listening devices were planted in the offices of the commander of the joint police-military task force charged with investigating the Cali Cartel. Periodic electronic sweeps ordered by the commander brought no results because the technicians tasked with the sweeps were the same who had planted the bugs in the first place (Rempel, 2012, pp. 101, 144).

The web of paid insiders combined with electronic surveillance ensured that the Cali Cartel was warned early of any hostile government activities and that it could respond quickly. For example, in the case of impending charges, corrupt prosecutors not only notified the Cali Cartel but also took steps to disrupt the proceedings (Kenney, 1999a, p. 134). In two instances, the Cali Cartel exerted influence on the highest levels of government. Bribes were reportedly paid to several members of the Constitutional Assembly in support of the ban on the extradition of Colombian citizens (Kenney, 1999a, p. 129), and significant contributions were made to a presidential election campaign (Kenney, 1999a, pp. 131–132). These efforts were successful in the short run but not in the long run. The extradition ban was included in the constitution in 1991, thereby nullifying an existing extradition treaty between Colombia and the United States. Likewise, the presidential election of 1994 was narrowly won by the candidate secretly supported by the Cali Cartel. However, after the campaign contributions were publicly exposed, the newly elected president found himself under pressure to move against the Cali Cartel (Rempel, 2012, p. 159).

Image 11.2   Ernesto Samper celebrates his victory in Colombia's 1994 presidential election. Two years later his campaign manager declared that Samper had knowingly accepted large financial contributions from the Cali Cartel.

Photo: ASSOCIATED PRESS/Joe Zelsky

One year later, the Rodriguez brothers were arrested and eventually convicted in Colombia. Then, after the signing of a new extradition treaty and allegations of continued drug trafficking, Colombia extradited the two leaders of the Cali Cartel to the United States, where they were sentenced to long prison terms in the year 2006 (Rempel, 2012, p. 316).

The Cali Cartel matches in many ways the cliché imagery of a criminal organization that thanks to huge illicit profits can infiltrate legitimate society and buy itself immunity from law enforcement. Yet, the example also shows that there are limits to the influence such an organization can exert on government. Not all public officials could be bribed, even in a country as ripe with corruption as Colombia in the 1980s and 1990s (Zaitch, 2002, p. 36). The commander of the joint police-military task force, for example, rejected a $300,000 bribe offer (Rempel, 2012, p. 143). And public scrutiny as well as international pressure did their parts in derailing the efforts of the Cali Cartel to bring the Colombian government under its control.

Gardiner: Wincanton

A classic example of an alliance between underworld and upperworld in the United States is the case of Reading, an industrial town in Pennsylvania. John A. Gardiner has given a detailed account in his book *The Politics of Corruption: Organized Crime in an American City* (Gardiner, 1970). Gardiner did not refer to Reading by its real name but used the pseudonym "Wincanton."

Wincanton, according to Gardiner, had the reputation of a sin city. In the mid-1950s, all gambling and prostitution came under the control of a criminal organization led by "Irv Stern," a Russian immigrant. Stern's illegal activities centered on an illegal lottery. He was also a partner in a large illegal dice game and an illegal distillery. Other illegal businesses in Wincanton operated under Stern's protection. For a fee, he guaranteed security from police intervention.

His influence over the police resulted from close ties to local politicians. Stern contributed to primary and general election campaigns and made weekly payments "to the mayor, police chief, and other city and county officials" (Gardiner, 1970, p. 24).

The local police not only tolerated the illegal businesses under Stern's direct or indirect control, through arrests they helped maintain discipline within the Stern syndicate and harassed gamblers who refused to pay tribute. In return, Stern facilitated the "corrupt enterprises" of city officials. Gardiner explains below:

> Some local officials were not satisfied with their legal salaries from the city and their illegal salaries from Stern, and decided to demand payments from prostitutes, kickbacks from salesmen, etc. Stern, while seldom receiving any money from these transactions, became a broker, bringing politicians into contact with salesmen, merchants, and lawyers willing to offer bribes to get city business, setting up "middlemen" who could handle the money without jeopardizing the officials' reputations, and providing enforcers who could bring delinquents into line. (Gardiner, 1970, p. 25)

In Wincanton, in other words, criminals and corrupt officials provided mutual support for their respective illegal endeavors. The situation only changed after the election of a reform mayor (Gardiner, 1970, p. 36).

Chambliss: Seattle, Washington

A scenario that is somewhat similar to the case of Wincanton has been described by William Chambliss in his book *On the Take: From Petty Crooks to Presidents*, which deals with organized crime and corruption in the city of Seattle, Washington, during the 1960s and early 1970s (Chambliss, 1978).

After several years of field research, Chambliss concluded that gambling and prostitution were controlled by "a coalition of businessmen, politicians, law enforcers and racketeers" (Chambliss, 1978, p. 73). This coalition had a common interest in guaranteeing the smooth and profitable operation of the local vice industry. Illegal and semi-legal businesses that were part of the system could operate more or less unmolested by the police and other agencies and also enjoyed some level of protection against unwanted competition. In exchange, government officials, politicians, and businessmen who belonged to the coalition received payments and other benefits, such as "liquor, parties and women" and the opportunity to invest in lucrative illegal deals (Chambliss, 1978, p. 65).

Within the heterogeneous network of criminal and social elites that Chambliss discovered, he did not see any underworld figure in a powerful position similar to that occupied by Irv Stern in Wincanton. Rather, the most influential network members came from the public and business spheres, including a prosecutor, a city council president, an assistant chief of police, city police captains, a sheriff, a county jail chief, undersheriffs, the president of an association representing pinball machine businesses, a police major, and an official of the Teamsters Union (Chambliss, 1978, p. 62).

Potter: Morrisburg

A more recent study by Gary Potter (1994) of the industrial town of "Morrisburg," a pseudonym, also found ties between underworld and upper-world embedded in a system of pervasive local corruption. During the 1970s and 1980s, the underworld of Morrisburg was dominated by three criminal groups who owed their position to economic success as well as to political connections. The relationships among the three groups were characterized by personal and business links. In part they also used the same channels to political circles and to law enforcement agencies (Potter, 1994, pp. 47–50). Payments were made to police and in the form of (legal or illegal) campaign contributions to both major parties. One of the criminal groups also offered investment opportunities to political and government figures (Potter, 1994, pp. 103–104). In exchange, the existing criminal structures remained unchallenged as long as their illegal activities did not overstep certain boundaries. For example, the police would act against drug dealing and prostitution on the street but would not violate the "sanctity" of bars and clubs (Potter, 1994, p. 103).

The three major criminal groups were not the only ones who corrupted public officials. Just like in Wincanton, corruption was widespread. Prostitutes, pimps, and drug dealers as well as respectable citizens and businessmen paid bribes to avoid arrest and prosecution (Potter, 1994, pp. 104–105).

The Krysha System in Transition-Era Russia

Another interesting case study of alliances between underworld and upperworld is provided by Russia in the 1980s and 1990s during the period of transition from a communist to a free-market system. The case of Russia is remarkable for the scale of crime and corruption and the pervasiveness of partially interlocking and partially competing criminal and governmental structures. The crime landscape in transition-era Russia was shaped by essentially three types of actors: (a) corrupt government officials, (b) shady businessmen, and (c) members of criminal gangs headed by so-called authorities (*avtoritety*) and loosely tied to each other through the criminal fraternity of Vory v Zakone.

Alliances between these actors had first emerged in the Soviet Union during the 1960s, when government and Communist Party bureaucrats, participants of the shadow economy, and professional criminals began to establish a corrupt system of mutually beneficial relations (Finckenauer & Voronin, 2001). These alliances took on new forms with the advent of capitalism. On the one hand, collusion occurred in the process of the privatization and subsequent exploitation of formerly state-owned industries. Huge fortunes were amassed from the mostly illicit export of strategic raw materials such as non-ferrous and rare metals, jewels, timber, and various products of the military-industrial complex (Finckenauer & Voronin, 2001; Glinkina, 1994; Varese, 2001). On the other hand, alliances between underworld and upperworld emerged to bring some level of order to a largely unregulated market economy. In the absence of effective business law and civil courts, a system of private protection came into being, consisting of criminal groups, elements of the state apparatus, and private security companies. Many of these security companies, in turn, were owned and operated by criminals and current and former government officials (Varese, 2001; Volkov, 2002).

Most of the private businesses that were established in Russia since the late 1980s operated under some form of what has been called a protective roof or

Image 11.3   An armed guard secures a Rolls Royce showroom in downtown Moscow in 1993.

Photo: ASSOCIATED PRESS/Alexander Zemlianichenko

krysha. In its crudest form, the *krysha* is an extortion gang, and the only protection provided is that against other extortionists. More sophisticated forms of *krysha* provide a wide range of services, including physical protection against predatory criminals, the collection of debts, the settling of business-related disputes, and assistance in dealings with state authorities—for example, to obtain licenses or tax exemptions (Volkov, 2002, p. 140).

The effectiveness of a particular roof depended on its power relative to other roofs. Much of the operation of protective roofs consisted of negotiating with other roofs on behalf of their respective clients (Volkov, 2002, p. 90). For example, the collection of a debt would typically have involved a sit-down (*strelka*) with the roof of the debtor. The power of a criminal group providing protection was a function of its size and military strength but also of its relationship to other criminal groups and to the state. Less powerful criminal groups would seek to align themselves with more powerful criminal groups, who in turn were likely to obtain their own *krysha* from corrupt government officials (Finckenauer & Voronin, 2001, p. 8; Galeotti, 1998, pp. 424–425; Varese, 2001, p. 174). The result was a multilayered system of protective roofs that connected various players from the underworld and upperworld. Initially, the protection of newly established private businesses was the domain of criminal groups. Later, private security companies and branches of government moved into the protection market. For example, to secure government protection, private businesses would hire an acting or retired high-ranking officer of the FSB (formerly KGB) as a manager or consultant (Volkov, 2002, p. 145). This led to a situation where a multitude of criminal, private-sector, and public-sector roofs competed for clients and found themselves pitted against each other in cases of conflict between their clients.

How the ensuing confrontations played out provides an indication of where power ultimately resided. Generally speaking, efforts were made by those providing protection to avoid violent clashes and to resolve conflicts peacefully. Violence, Volkov (2002, p. 93) observes, echoing other analyses of organized crime (see Chapter 8), "is the ultimate and most costly method of dispute settlement." In addition, conflicts involving criminal and public-sector roofs appear to have been resolved in favor of the public-sector roof. A typical scenario of such a conflict is described by Joseph Serio as follows:

> In the case of an extortion attempt or the offer of ongoing "protection"; such as a *krysha* (roof), a "mafia" sit-down would be arranged: the underworld "mafia" on one side of the table and the state "mafia" on the other side. Once it was explained by, for example, a KGB colonel that he was already providing protection to the target company, invariably the traditional gangsters would apologize and leave. Period. End of story. (Serio, 2008, p. 248)

Conflicts *within* government, in turn, where different branches of the state apparatus found themselves on opposite sides of the negotiating table, ended to the advantage of the clients whose roof was higher up in the state hierarchy. For example, in a conflict involving the automobile consortium LogoVaz, the federal counter-intelligence service FSK prevailed over the local Moscow antiorganized crime unit RUOP (Varese, 2001, p. 67).

There is some indication that since the 2000s the *krysha* system has come more completely under the purview of the state apparatus. Building on their relative superiority vis-à-vis underworld roofs that could be observed in the 1990s, corrupt elements within the security and law enforcement branches of government have taken over the protection racket. "We have now Russian police (militia) as an organized criminal group," Yakov Gilinskiy, one of the country's leading organized-crime scholars, concluded from interviews conducted with various law enforcement officials in the mid-2000s (Gilinskiy, 2012, p. 176). While the police extracts protection payments from legitimate businesses, the criminal "authorities," under the continued protection of corrupt officials, appear to have moved on to other illegal activities (Serio, 2008, p. 266).

Narco-Corruption in Mexico in the 1960s Through 1990s

Mexico is another country where underworld-upperworld alliances have historically existed on a national scale. However, there are significant differences to the case of transition-era Russia. For more than seven decades, since the late 1920s, Mexico was under a one-party rule by the Partido Revolucionario Institucional (PRI). From the president down to the local level, a system of patron-client relationships permeated the country (Pimentel, 1999, p. 11). Under the protective umbrella of the PRI, alliances developed between politically influential elite families, public officials, and drug traffickers (Bunker, 2013; Flores Perez, 2014; Lupsha, 1991; Shelley, 2001).

Mexico has a long tradition of drug trafficking as a source and transit country for opium, marijuana, and cocaine (Astorga, 1999; McIllwain, 2001),

Image 11.4   Juan Nepomuceno Guerra (left) and his nephew Juan Garcia Abrego (top right) are considered the founders of the Gulf Cartel based in the Mexican state of Tamaulipas across the border from Texas. Protected by close ties to influential members of the political elite, the Gulf Cartel is said to have begun smuggling drugs into the United States in the 1970s (Flores Perez, 2014).

Photo: ASSOCIATED PRESS/REFORMA

and more recently of methamphetamine (Brouwer et al., 2006). Peter Lupsha (1991, p. 42) has described the protection of the illegal drug trade during the PRI era as a multi-tiered system. On the lowest level, ad hoc protection was provided by low-ranking officials to drug mules and user dealers. On a higher level, drug dealers received continuous protection from local and state officials or local offices of the federal police. Up to this level, the drug traffickers, according to Lupsha, tended "to be outside the legitimate political upperworld of Mexican elite life and national politics" (Lupsha, 1991, p. 43). Further up in the system, traffickers were well connected to state and national politics and operated under the protection of the federal police, customs, or the military. On the highest level, finally, internationally connected drug traffickers were protected by the top tiers of the political hierarchy.

A central element of Mexican narco-corruption has been "La Plaza," a synonym for the licensing of drug traffickers by the most influential members of the local power elite. A particular drug trafficker was granted the exclusive right to operate in a given territory by corrupt officials who would pass some of the

protection payments up within the patron-client system of the PRI. More notorious drug traffickers who attracted the attention of state and federal agencies
had to purchase additional protection (Lupsha, 1991, p. 44; Poppa, 1998, p. 44).
However, if a trafficker gained too much notoriety or provoked international
pressure, protection was withdrawn. "It was a system," journalist Terrence Poppa
(1998, p. 45) explains, "that enabled the Mexican political and police structures
to keep a lid on drugs and profit handsomely from it at the same time."

The system of centralized narco-corruption weakened as the PRI started to lose
its monopoly of political power beginning in the mid-1980s (Snyder & Duran-
Martinez, 2001, p. 263), and it was nearing its collapse with the election of the
opposition candidate Vincente Fox as president in the year 2000 (Beittel, 2011,
p. 4). What consequences these developments had on the relationship between
drug traffickers and the Mexican state will be discussed further below as an example
of the open confrontation between organized crime and government.

The trend of a weakening system of state-sponsored protection is in marked
contrast to the trajectory of the developments in Russia where the *krysha* system
seems to have increasingly merged with a consolidated state apparatus.

The cases of PRI-era Mexico and transition-era Russia also differ insofar as
the PRI established a centralized system of protection while in post-Soviet
Russia different branches and levels of government competed against each other.
On the other hand, perhaps the most striking similarity between PRI-era Mexico
and transition-era Russia is that in the relationship between organized crime
and government, corrupt officials appear to have wielded power superior to that
of their respective criminal counterparts. Insofar, the Russian and Mexican cases
mirror the situation in Seattle and Morrisburg while contrasting the situation in
Cali and Wincanton.

General Patterns of Underworld-Upperworld Alliances

It is difficult to discern general patterns of underworld-upperworld alliances
from the available research. A key question is what factors influence the balance
of power between criminals and corrupt government officials. From the cases
examined here, only the situations in Cali and Wincanton come close to cliché
imagery of state capture where powerful gangster bosses have the government
in their pocket.

One possibility is that the balance of power in underworld-upperworld
alliances varies with the relative cohesiveness of political and bureaucratic
elites on one side and criminal elites on the other (Kupatadze, 2009; von
Lampe, 1999). Gardiner (1970, p. 12) has emphasized the fragmented nature
of the political system in Wincanton. The Stern syndicate, in contrast, had a
hierarchical structure that facilitated coordinated action. This might explain
why Stern could amass the influence he apparently held over the local government. A similar observation can be made with respect to the systematic way in
which the Cali Cartel corrupted key players in a rather fragmented and volatile
political landscape in Colombia.

In the Seattle described by Chambliss (1978), the social elites seem to have
been bound by a strong sense of common interests. In comparison, the underworld was apparently much less cohesive and more conflict prone. From this

angle, it is not surprising to see the criminal element in a subservient role within the network that controlled the vice industry in Seattle. A similar picture emerges in PRI-era Mexico, where competing drug traffickers were confronted with a centralized power structure capable of selectively enforcing the law. Corrupt officials appeared to be in control of the illegal drug trade as long as the PRI held its political monopoly.

In the case of Morrisburg, Potter's (1994) account suggests that both political and criminal elites lacked coherence and where not able, respectively, to speak with one voice. However, it also appears that the three main criminal groups had to rely on the general willingness of corrupt officials to tolerate a certain level of illegal activities.

The case of transition-era Russia, finally, indicates that even in a time of turmoil and state weakness, the resources the government has at its disposal provide corrupt officials with enough leverage to advance their own interests in corrupt relations with criminals. From reading the scholarly literature on organized crime in Russia, one gets the impression that despite widespread corruption, law enforcement intervention still posed a constant threat to criminal groups, even in the most tumultuous times of the 1980s and 1990s (Rawlinson, 2010, p. 108).

Confrontation Between Organized Crime and Government

The relationship between organized crime and government seems to be characterized for the most part by arrangements that are geared toward conflict avoidance. Criminals either try to evade government scrutiny or they seek to neutralize the state through corruption. In contrast, the use of violence against representatives of the state is an exception rather than the rule. There may be isolated incidents of violence, for example, when criminals resist arrest or settle a score with an individual corrupt official. Otherwise, the notion that a direct and open confrontation with the government is futile appears to prevail at least among organized criminals in the western world. Violence, whether directed against other criminals or against the public, is simply "bad for business." A historical anecdote from the New York underworld of the 1930s can illustrate this point. According to legend, one of the most prominent gangster bosses of the time, Dutch Schultz, allegedly moved to assassinate then special anti-organized crime prosecutor Thomas E. Dewey. But instead, Dutch Schultz himself was killed at the hand of his underworld allies who feared that the murder of Dewey "might bring down upon the house of crime the combined law enforcement forces of the city, state, and federal governments" (Sann, 1971, p. 279). This and other examples notwithstanding, incidents of the systematic use of criminal violence against the state do exist. In these cases, the relationship between organized crime and government is marked by confrontation rather than evasion or corruption.

Three examples can serve as illustrations of a violent confrontation of organized crime and the state: (a) the campaign of violence of the Sicilian Mafia against representatives of the Italian state in the 1970s, 1980s, and early 1990s, (b) the campaign of "narco-terrorism" waged by Pablo Escobar and his followers against the Colombian state in the 1980s and early 1990s, and (c) the violence against public officials committed by the so-called Mexican drug cartels during the presidency of Felipe Calderon between 2006 and 2012.

The Mafia Campaign of Violence
Against the Italian State 1971 Through 1993

The Sicilian Mafia's campaign of violence is situated in a broader historical era of deteriorating relations between mafiosi and representatives of the Italian state. Following a time of oppression and persecution during Mussolini's fascist rule, the Sicilian Mafia had reemerged in the 1940s as a politically well-entrenched criminal fraternity. Mafiosi had established close ties to politicians on the local and national levels, especially to the conservative Christian Democratic Party, which from 1948 onward dominated Italian politics (Jamieson, 1994; Lupo, 2009).

The close alliance of Mafia and politics deteriorated markedly since the 1960s and eventually turned into open confrontation. The process culminated in the year 1992, when mafiosi not only murdered the two prominent anti-Mafia magistrates Giovanni Falcone and Paolo Borsellino but also the main middlemen between the Sicilian Mafia and the political establishment in Rome, Salvatore Lima and Ignazio Salvo. Lima, a former mayor of Palermo, had served as Prime Minister Giulio Andreotti's top aide in Sicily and Salvo, an influential businessman with longstanding Mafia links, had likewise belonged to Andreotti's faction within the Christian Democratic Party (Lupo, 2009, p. 257; Paoli, 2003a, p. 202; Stille, 1996, p. 420).

The violent campaign against the state had no precedent in Mafia history. The only assassination of a public official ascribed to the Mafia in the first one hundred or so years of its existence had occurred in 1893 (Lupo, 2009, p. 95). Against this background it is not surprising to see that the first representatives of the state to be killed at the hand of the Mafia in the 20th century were the unintended victims of an internal conflict within the Mafia. In 1963 seven policemen were killed by a car bomb aimed at a mafioso in a dispute between two mafia groups over a botched heroin deal (Catanzaro, 1992, pp. 173–176). What became known as the Ciaculli massacre triggered a massive response by the government and for the first time since World War II exposed mafiosi to significant law enforcement pressure. Numerous mafiosi were arrested and put on trial or went into hiding, even forcing the Mafia's coordinating body, the *commissione* to be temporarily dissolved (Lupo, 2009, p. 229).

The first mafia murder since 1893 that was intentionally directed against a representative of the state took place in 1971 with the killing of the attorney general in Palermo, Pietro Scaglione. This event marks the starting point of the Mafia's campaign of violence against the Italian state. However, the murder of Scaglione, just like the Ciaculli massacre in 1963 and the subsequent murder of a carabinieri colonel, Giuseppe Russo, in 1977, can be traced back to internecine conflicts. In the 1970s two warring factions had formed within the Sicilian Mafia. One side, led by the family from Corleone, allegedly committed the murders of Scaglione and Russo to cast suspicions on their internal rivals (Catanzaro, 1992, pp. 186–187). It was only later that the killing of public officials took on the character of a direct, straightforward confrontation between Mafia and

Image 11.5   The armored car of Paolo Borsellino destroyed in a bomb blast that killed the anti-Mafia judge and five police escorts and injured 20 others in downtown Palermo, Sicily, on July 19, 1992. Eight weeks earlier a bomb had killed judge Giovanni Falcone, Falcone's wife, and three bodyguards.

Photo: ASSOCIATED PRESS/AP

government. For example, in 1979 a police inspector was murdered who had launched investigations into the banking channels through which illicit proceeds were laundered. A year later, the president of the Sicilian regional government fell victim to Mafia violence after he had begun to review the assignment of public works contracts, an important source of revenue for mafiosi (Catanzaro, 1992, p. 187). The year 1982 marked another decisive year in the confrontation between Mafia and the state. Pio La Torre, leader of the Communist party in Sicily and anti-Mafia activist, and General Carlo Dalla Chiesa, the new prefect of Palermo, were assassinated. In the wake of these two murders, the legislature in Rome passed sweeping laws that made it a crime to be a member of the Mafia and also gave authorities the power to seize property from mafiosi (Paoli, 2003a, p. 204; see Chapter 14). The new laws paved the way for the indictment and ultimate conviction of large numbers of Mafiosi in a series of so-called maxi-trials. The first maxi-trial ended in 1987 with the conviction of 342 out of 474 accused, including 18 bosses, who received life sentences (Dickie, 2004, pp. 397–398). During the appeals process, more acts of violence against the state were committed, costing the lives of a Palermo Appeals Court judge and a prosecutor of the Court of Cassation. In 1992 the defendants of the first maxi-trial had exhausted all possibilities of appeal. The Supreme Court confirmed most convictions. Shortly thereafter, Lima and Salvo as well as Falcone and Borsellino were killed (Jamieson, 2005, p. 170; Paoli, 2003a, pp. 203–204).

In the following year, the Mafia began "a full scale terrorist bombing campaign on the Italian mainland" (Dickie, 2004, p. 409). A car bomb intended to kill a TV journalist exploded in Rome, another bomb damaged the Uffizi museum and killed five persons in Florence, and three bombs set off almost simultaneously exploded in Rome and Milan, killing six and wounding many others as well as damaging two sacred buildings (Paoli, 2003a, p. 207).

Once again, the state responded to the escalating violence with renewed resolve. The military was sent to Sicily to free up resources within the police, and new laws were passed to further facilitate the fight against the Mafia. Numerous mafiosi turned themselves in, and Toto Riina, the head of the Corleone faction who had been implicated by turncoats as the mastermind behind the Mafia's terror campaign, was arrested after having spent some twenty years in hiding (Dickie, 2004, pp. 411–413; Jamieson, 2005, p. 170).

While there seems to be a consensus that the strategy of directly and openly confronting the state backfired and proved counterproductive from the point of view of the Mafia, there is no consensus on the reasons why the Mafia chose to use violence against representatives of the state. One explanation, that the initial attacks were rooted in internecine conflicts within the Mafia, has already been mentioned. Closely linked to this train of thought is the notion that the violence was meant by Mafia bosses to be a show of strength in an effort to bolster internal support (Catanzaro, 1992, p. 188). Another explanation, especially for the violence between 1979 and 1992 is that "it was a campaign of scorn." The Mafia, according to this viewpoint, was emboldened by the wealth derived from heroin trafficking and felt it could impose its will on a weak government (Dickie, 2004, p. 385; Jamieson, 2005, p. 168). And when corrupt officials failed to keep up their end of the bargain, for example suppressing criminal investigations, the Mafia acted out of "revenge" (Paoli, 2003a, p. 202). With less emphasis on emotions, the campaign of violence appears as a calculated attempt to specifically target the most capable representatives of the state, those that posed the greatest threat to Mafia interests (Jamieson, 2005, p. 168; Lupo, 2009, p. 243). There are also allegations that some of the violence has been falsely ascribed to the Mafia and that in the case of other violence, the Mafia acted on the behest of interest groups within politics and the security apparatus keen on destabilizing the political system in Italy (Jamieson, 1994). This, of course, would make it difficult to speak of a confrontation between Mafia and the state.

Narco-Terrorism in Colombia in the 1980s and 1990s

During the same historical period that saw the Sicilian Mafia launch violent attacks against representatives of the Italian state, the so-called Medellin Cartel, a coalition of drug traffickers under the leadership of Pablo Escobar, employed similar tactics in Colombia.

Escobar was arguably the most important and most powerful Colombian drug trafficker of his time. His fortunes were in large part built on his ability to smuggle cocaine in bulk into the United States. He offered transport services to other drug traffickers and for a fee guaranteed compensation in case a shipment got lost (Clawson & Lee, 1996, p. 38). At first he was on friendly terms with the other major drug traffickers, including the leaders of the Cali Cartel, and he sought a place for himself in the political arena. In the early 1980s, Escobar formed a political movement and managed to be elected, in 1982, to the Colombian Congress as an alternate deputy (Clawson & Lee, 1996, p. 48). His political career, however, was short lived. The government and the media exposed Escobar's involvement in the drug trade and in 1984 a warrant was issued for his arrest (Clawson & Lee, 1996, p. 50). From then on, Escobar's political strategy seems to have shifted from integration to confrontation.

The greatest threat Escobar as well as the other drug traffickers faced stemmed from the extradition treaty Colombia had signed with the United States in 1979. Partly in collaboration with each other, partly in separate campaigns, the Colombian drug traffickers attempted to nullify the extradition treaty and to come to an agreement with the government that would allow them to retire from the drug trade with little or no punishment. While the Cali Cartel, as described earlier in this chapter, pursued this aim through systematic corruption, the Medellin Cartel opted for a strategy of violence and intimidation. The Medellin Cartel allegedly maintained a standing army of 3,000 hired killers and drew on additional expert help from an array

Image 11.6 Bogota's secret police headquarters in 1989 destroyed by a bomb that also killed some 100 people. The attack was reportedly ordered by Pablo Escobar, the head of the Medellin Cartel.

Photo: EDUARDO SOTOMAYOR/Staff

of Colombian guerilleros and international mercenaries (Clawson & Lee, 1996, p. 53). "Almost 500 policemen and 40 judges," Clawson and Lee (1996, p. 51) report, "were killed during the 1980s and early 1990s." In the year 1990 alone, some 200 police officers were murdered after Escobar had offered a $4,000 reward for every one killed (Jamieson, 2005, p. 168). A minister of justice, a Supreme Court justice, a governor, an attorney general, and the leading contestant in the 1990 presidential elections were also reportedly killed by the Medellin Cartel (Clawson & Lee, 1996, p. 51).

In 1989, Escobar and his followers escalated their campaign of violence further by switching from the targeted killing of individual officials "to indiscriminate terror attacks against the Colombian state and the society in general" (Clawson & Lee, 1996, p. 52). According to Luis Canon's (1994, p. 178) interpretation of events, Escobar was confident that he could impose his will on the government. And when the government increased the pressure on Escobar, he responded with more violence. One bomb attack on a government building in the capital city of Bogota in December 1989 killed some 100 people and seriously injured 250 more (Canon, 1994, p. 181).

The campaign of violence achieved two of its main objectives insofar as the U.S.-Colombian extradition treaty was nullified by the constitutional amendment mentioned earlier, the same amendment that the Cali Cartel had promoted through bribery, and the Colombian government entered into negotiations with the drug traffickers, including Escobar. Pablo Escobar did indeed surrender to authorities in 1991 following the constitutional ban on extraditions. However, a year later, after it had become apparent that Escobar continued his drug trafficking operations from inside prison, he escaped and resumed his terrorist campaign (Canon, 1994, pp. 351–352). Eventually, late in 1993, Escobar was hunted down by the authorities and killed in a shoot-out.

Just as in the case of the Sicilian Mafia, there appears to be a broad consensus that in the end the campaign of violence unleashed by Pablo Escobar and his followers backfired. Despite the intimidating effect the terrorist strategy had in the short run, in the long run, it isolated the Medellin Cartel and made it the prime target of law enforcement (Clawson & Lee, 1996, p. 54).

One explanation for the escalation of violence against the state, particularly since 1989, is that Escobar saw himself confronted not only by the state but by an alliance of the Colombian government and the Cali Cartel. In the mid-1980s, a violent struggle had flared up between the drug traffickers from Cali and from Medellin over the control of the cocaine market in New York City, originally a domain of the Cali Cartel (Clawson & Lee, 1996, p. 46). In 1988 this conflict had escalated into open war, waged with a series of bombings and assassinations (Rempel, 2012, p. 22). With some justification, Escobar accused the Cali Cartel of aiding the government in its investigations against the Medellin Cartel (Rempel, 2012, p. 75). The bomb that claimed 100 lives in Bogota in December 1989, for example, was aimed at a police general who Escobar had suspected of colluding with the Rodriguez Orejuela brothers from Cali (Canon, 1994, pp. 220–221). In a sense, therefore, Escobar's violent campaign against the state evolved within the logic of the violent underworld conflict that had engulfed the Medellin Cartel and the Cali Cartel. Accordingly, it is difficult in this case to speak of a clear-cut confrontation between organized crime and government. The same blurring of frontlines can be found in the case of Mexico, which arguably presents the most notorious case of criminal violence directed against the state since the mid-2000s.

The Violent Confrontation Between Mexican Drug Cartels and the Mexican State During the Presidency of Felipe Calderon

In Mexico during the presidency of Felipe Calderon (2006–2012), the confrontation between so-called drug-trafficking organizations (DTOs) and the state reached unprecedented levels. Amidst a general increase in drug-related violence, public officials became the target of attacks at a scale and with a degree of cruelty not witnessed before in Mexico or, arguably, in any other country in the world. In 2001, around 1,000 drug-related killings were counted in Mexico. By the end of the decade, in 2009, the annual count had increased to between 6,000 and 8,000, and it increased further to around 12,000 in the year 2010 (International Crisis Group, 2013, p. 47; Shirk, 2010, p. 4). At the same time, the violence spread from a few hot spots to large portions of the country (Shirk, 2010). While most of the victims were believed to be members of rivalling drug-trafficking organizations, public officials were also among the victims. Between 2006 and 2010, drug-trafficking organizations allegedly killed more than 2,500 officials, including some 2,200 police officers and 200 soldiers as well as judges, mayors, a leading gubernatorial candidate, the leader of a state legislature, and dozens of federal officials (Grillo, 2011, p. 11; see also Flanigan, 2012, p. 288). Some of the attacks on public officials took on the form of terrorist and paramilitary operations. "Mexican thugs," journalist Iaon Grillo (2011, p. 11) observed, "regularly shower police stations with bullets and rocket-propelled grenades, they carry out mass kidnappings of officers and leave their mutilated bodies on public display; and they even kidnapped one mayor, tied him up, and stoned him to death on a main street" (see also Longmire & Longmire, 2008, p. 48).

Image 11.7   The decapitated bodies of nine men are lined up in a morgue in Chilpancingo in southern Mexico in December 2008. Some of the victims were identified as soldiers.

Photo: ASSOCIATED PRESS/AP

In certain limited geographic areas, drug-trafficking organizations have prevailed in their confrontation with the authorities to the extent that they were able to establish operational control in place of legitimate government (Shirk, 2011, p. 3). According to one 2010 study commissioned by the Mexican Senate, 195 Mexican municipalities (8% of the total) were "completely under control of organized crime" and another 1,536 (63% of the total) reportedly were "infiltrated" by organized crime (as cited in Beittel, 2011, p. 26).

This has prompted some commentators in the United States, especially those with links to the military, to suggest that the drug-related violence in Mexico no longer merely constituted a traditional organized crime problem but that it had developed into a "criminal insurgency," an organized movement aimed at overthrowing the constitutional government through the use of subversion and armed conflict (Bunker, 2013; Longmire & Longmire, 2008). While there is a broad consensus that the goals of drug-trafficking organizations remained economical rather than political, it has been argued that with the creation of "areas of impunity," which are free from state influence, the cartels had become "de facto politicized" (Bunker, 2013, p. 132).

Numerous attempts have been made to explain the escalation of drug-related violence and open confrontation between criminals and the state in Mexico. A common theme is to trace the development back to the 1980s, when the centralized control of drug trafficking under the one-party rule of the PRI began to crumble. Corrupt officials lost their ability to guarantee protection against law enforcement and rival drug traffickers. Even more so, the Mexican government, under pressure from the United States, began to effectively target leading drug traffickers. The perceived result has been a fragmentation of the narco-underworld into a large number of smaller groups of drug traffickers that coalesce in ever-shifting alliances or cartels (Rios, 2013, p. 141; Shirk, 2010, p. 9).

These processes within Mexico since the 1980s have coincided with a major shift in drug trafficking between Latin America and the United States. Increased enforcement efforts against the smuggling of drugs to the United States through the Caribbean led to a displacement of trafficking routes to Mexico (Corcoran, 2013). At first, Colombian traffickers hired Mexicans to deliver cocaine to Colombian distributors in the United States. Before long, however, especially after the dismantling of the Medellin Cartel and the Cali Cartel in 1993 and 1995, Mexican drug trafficking organizations assumed a more independent role and eventually replaced Colombians as the most important suppliers of drugs in the United States (Shirk, 2011, p. 7). This means that as corruption and drug trafficking structures fragmented, the stakes for the drug trafficking groups that vied for a share of the drug trade in Mexico dramatically increased (Beittel, 2011, p. 5).

Two events in the mid-2000s added fuel to the emerging violent conflicts. In 2004, the legislative ban on assault weapons in the United States expired, which gave criminals in Mexico easy access to military-grade arms (Dube, Dube, & Garcia-Ponce, 2013). And in 2006, the newly elected president Felipe Calderon deployed large military contingents in a campaign that specifically targeted the most prominent drug traffickers (Flannery, 2013).

All of these developments since the 1980s provide explanations, first of all, for the violent conflicts within and between drug-trafficking organizations, conflicts that, as indicated, accounted for the largest share of drug-related violence. But these developments have also served to explain the violent confrontation between drug-trafficking organizations and the state. According to one widely held view, violent attacks against government officials were a functional equivalent to corruption. Officials were given a choice of *plomo o plata* (the bullet or the bribe) (Morris, 2013, p. 204; see also Dulin & Patino, 2014). Violence and intimidation, just like bribes, were used by drug traffickers in an effort to safeguard trafficking operations against law enforcement intervention and competition from other trafficking groups. Violence targeted uncooperative officials, including officials suspected of colluding with rival drug-trafficking organizations. Insofar, the violence against public officials followed the logic of intercartel violence (Beittel, 2011, pp. 10–12; Grayson, 2010, p. 63; Morris, 2013, p. 214). In fact, the arrests and killings of leading drug traffickers by the authorities are considered to be a crucial factor in the triggering and fueling of drug-related violence (Dickenson, 2014; Rios, 2013). The power vacuum resulting from the arrest of drug kingpins, it has been argued, ignited conflicts within and between drug-trafficking organizations, and when the opposing sides enlisted the support of corrupt officials, these officials became targets in the violent struggle (Morris, 2013, p. 214).

Some violent attacks, however, appear to have been acts of revenge, carried out in direct retaliation of government conduct (Dulin & Patino, 2014, p. 277; Kan, 2012, p. 50). For example, when prison guards refused to smuggle luxuries to some inmates belonging to Los Zetas, a particularly violence-prone cartel, the guards were abducted, killed, and left by the prison gates (Grillo, 2011, pp. 102–103). In another case, also involving Los Zetas, members of the grieving family of a slain special forces soldier were shot in their home hours after the funeral. The soldier had been involved in the killing of a drug kingpin (Kellner & Pipitone, 2010, p. 33). Another cartel known in the late 2000s for extreme violence is La Familia Michoacana (LFM). When the authorities arrested one of its leading members in 2009, LFM reportedly launched simultaneous attacks on a dozen police facilities claiming the lives of fifteen officers (Grillo, 2011, p. 196). Brazen acts of violence like these are believed to have served the additional purpose of communicating "a lack of fear of the government" (Beittel, 2011, p. 15) and to aim at undermining public support for a state that appears weak in the face of violent opposition (Flanigan, 2012, p. 290). However, the use of violence by drug-trafficking organizations can also be taken as a sign of their own weakness. According to this view, drug traffickers resorted to violence because they were unable to influence government through corruption and because measures against drug trafficking proved to be effective (Morris, 2013, p. 213). Calderon's efforts were indeed successful in the sense that more than half of the "drug capos" that had operated in Mexico in 2008 were captured, resulting in a further splintering of drug-trafficking organizations (Robles, Calderon, & Magaloni, 2013, pp. 3–4).

If there is a trend, then, in the open confrontation between organized crime and government in Mexico between 2006 and 2012, it is an accentuation of the embeddedness of the violence against the state in violent conflicts between increasingly fragmented rival crime groups (Bailey & Taylor, 2009, p. 24).

ORGANIZED CRIME WITHIN GOVERNMENT

The main focus so far in this chapter has been on the relationship between organized crime and government in terms of the interaction of separate entities. Three strategies that criminals pursue in this relationship vis-à-vis the state have been highlighted: evasion, corruption, and confrontation. To complete the analysis, a brief glance at manifestations of organized crime *within* government is necessary.

Academic interest in these phenomena is largely driven by a desire to contrast the mainstream notions of organized crime as being rooted in marginalized segments of society (see Chapter 9) with a counter-narrative of organized criminals holding the reins of power. Similar to Edwin Sutherland's (1949) concept of white-collar crime, which attempted to direct the attention of criminologists to high-status criminals in the realm of business, the concern here is with high-status criminals in the realm of politics and public office (Chambliss, 1989; Pearce, 1976; Woodiwiss, 2001).

The phenomena that fall into this category range from criminal activities and criminal structures *inside* the state apparatus to organized crime *by* the state. The limited room given here to the examination of organized crime in the governmental sphere is a reflection of the less than central role it plays in the mainstream debate on organized crime, not a judgment of its relative importance. In fact, organized crime within government is arguably far more dramatic in its scope than any of the forms of organized crime ordinarily addressed in the public and scholarly debates (Friedrichs, 2010, p. 131).

Organized Crime Inside the State Apparatus

Organized crime inside the state apparatus pertains to illegal activities and criminal structures linked to officials and politicians who seek direct personal benefit, either financial gain or the extension or maintenance of power (Friedrich, 2010, p. 128). Some examples have already been mentioned earlier in this chapter, namely groups of police officers who extort criminals and legal businesses, deal in confiscated drugs, or engage in systematic theft. One such case involved the Special Operations Section (SOS), an elite unit of the Chicago Police Department. In 2006, ten members of the unit were indicted for aggravated kidnapping, theft, burglary, home invasion, armed violence, and false arrest. In one scheme, the officers allegedly misused police powers to stop motorists, take their keys, and then burglarize their homes. In five separate episodes in 2004 and 2005, the group reportedly stole some $600,000 (Hagedorn et al., 2013, pp. 12–13; Punch, 2009, pp. 75–76).

Organized Crime by the State

Organized crime *by* the state or state-organized crime involves public officials who engage in criminal conduct not for personal benefit but on behalf of the state or of some state agency (Chambliss, 1989, p. 184; Friedrichs, 2010, pp. 127, 141).

State-Sponsored Organized Crime

Chambliss, in his discussion of state-organized crime, focuses largely on state-sponsored crime, criminal activities that are supported by a government for political purposes. For example, Chambliss points out that many pirates between the sixteenth and nineteenth century operated with the support and under the protection of major powers of the time, including France, England, and Holland (Chambliss, 1989, pp. 185–186). A more recent example mentioned by Chambliss is the logistical support provided by the CIA to drug traffickers during the Vietnam War. The CIA-owned airline Air America transported opium from remote villages to heroin refineries within Laos, all in an effort to maintain local tribes as allies in the fight against Vietnamese communists (McCoy, 2003, pp. 288–290).

State-Organized Crime in the Narrow Sense

State-organized crime, in the narrow sense of the word, goes beyond the sponsoring of criminal activities conducted by non-state actors. It pertains to cases where state agencies or the state as such operates as criminal organizations. The most obvious example is the Holocaust, the systematic expropriation and annihilation of the Jewish population in German-controlled Europe during World War II. A long list of other international crimes, including genocides, crimes against humanity, war crimes, and crimes of aggression, fall into the same category (Friedrichs, 2010, pp. 133–136).

Image 11.8 A group of prisoners arrives in the Auschwitz concentration camp, victims to the ultimate state-organized crime, the Holocaust.

Photo: ASSOCIATED PRESS/dpa/picture-alliance/dpa/AP Images

These crimes, of course, are far removed from the types of criminal activities ordinarily associated with the concept of organized crime, namely, the supply of illegal goods and services. However, there are also cases where governments have been implicated as the instigators and perpetrators of these kinds of more common organized crimes. Perhaps the most notorious example is North Korea under the leadership of Kim Jong-Il. Allegedly, the North Korean regime has been engaged in the production and international distribution of counterfeit currency, counterfeit cigarettes as well as heroin and methamphetamine (Chestnut Greitens, 2014; Kan, Bechtol, & Collins, 2010; Perl, 2007; Perl & Nanto, 2007). These activities are believed to be organized by a branch of the government structure, the so-called Central Committee Bureau 39 of the ruling Korean Workers' Party. It had been formed in 1974 "for the explicit purpose of running illegal activities to generate currency for the North Korean government" and had been under the supervision of Kim Jong-Il from the beginning, even before he succeeded his father Kim Il-sung as dictator in the year 1994 (Kan et al., 2010, p. 4).

It is important to emphasize that the North Korean case is different from most other cases of government involvement in organized crime. It is not a matter of the state sponsoring the activities of non-state actors. In the case of North Korea, illegal activities are believed to be directly carried out by the government itself, drawing on state resources and taking advantage of state sovereignty and diplomatic immunity (Kan et al., 2010, pp. 2–3).

THE RELATIONSHIP BETWEEN ORGANIZED CRIME AND GOVERNMENT: SUMMARY AND CONCLUSION

This chapter and the previous two chapters have examined how organized crime relates to the broader society within which it manifests itself. In Chapter 9 it was argued that organized crime does not exist in a social vacuum and that criminal activities and criminal structures are in many ways shaped by society. It was also argued in Chapter 9 that the relationship between organized crime and society does not lend itself to simplistic characterizations. Depending on the circumstances, the relationship varies greatly across a spectrum from confrontation to accommodation to integration. These themes were reiterated in Chapter 10 with regard to the relationship between organized crime and legitimate business and in this chapter with regard to the relationship between organized crime and government.

According to stereotypical imagery, organized crime is something that develops at the margins of society but has the power to undermine, infiltrate, and eventually to control, legitimate business, and the state.

This stereotype suggests that wherever organized criminal activities are carried out and criminal organizations exist, the government will be corrupted and law enforcement will be neutralized through bribes and intimidation. However, the reality of crime is more complicated. Evading the state rather than corrupting the state appears to be a viable option for many organized criminals. And where corrupt ties to government do exist, organized criminals are not necessarily the dominating part in the relationship. There are cases that at first glance resemble the scenario of organized crime controlling government, but upon closer inspection it turns out that corrupt public officials control organized crime and extract protection payments from organized criminals.

Whether or not there is a link between organized crime and government and what the nature of this link is if it exists appears to depend on a number of factors, such as the conspicuousness or inconspicuousness of illegal activities and the relative cohesiveness of social and criminal elites. Where cohesive social elites meet a fragmented underworld, there is reason to believe that the balance of power will be in favor of corrupt public officials rather than the criminals who operate under their protection. Where powerful criminal organizations emerge, as in the case of the Cali Cartel, criminal influence on government can be pervasive and can lead to the neutralization of law enforcement. However, there appear to be clear limits to the ability even of the most powerful criminal organizations to sustain this influence over extended periods of time. From the cases that have been examined in this chapter, it seems that even relatively weak states, such as those that could be found in certain historical periods in countries like Colombia, Mexico, and Russia, can muster sufficient resources to prevail in the long run. This is particularly true where organized criminals have opted for an open confrontation with government. Campaigns of violence against the state can spread fear and can undermine the functioning of the government, but in the absence of a "revolutionary" agenda on the part of criminal organizations, government as such is not in jeopardy. Criminal organizations, even those that provide illegal governance, have neither the ambition nor the ability, it seems, to replace government. While the use of violence can be seen as an extension of corrupt influence on government, it appears to be a sign of weakness and irrationality and, historically, the use of violence against the state results in the fragmentation and destruction of criminal structures.

The highest forms of a penetration of government by organized crime are arguably those where criminal structures evolve within the realm of politics and where illegal activities are carried out under the sponsorship of or directly by government. State-sponsored organized crime, such as the drug trafficking in Mexico from the 1940s through the 1980s under the centralized control of a one-party system, or the state-organized crime ascribed to the Kim regime in North Korea are not crime problems as much as they are political problems.

Discussion Questions

1. What is the primary motive for organized criminals to influence government?

2. What is the primary motive for organized criminals to openly and violently confront the state?

3. What is the lesser evil: state-organized crime or the infiltration of government by the underworld?

4. What is the worst-case scenario for the future development of criminal involvement in government?

5. What is the worst-case scenario for the future development of violent confrontations between criminal organizations and the state?

Research Projects

1. Analyze the autobiography of an organized criminal with a view to criminal influence taking on government.

2. Find media reports on incidents of the corruption of public officials by criminals in a particular country, and try to find out what kind of underlying social relationship, if any, existed between them.

3. Find media reports on incidents of criminal violence against public officials in a particular country, and try to find out what the underlying rationale for the use of violence has been.

Further Reading

Godson, R. (Ed.). (2003). *Menace to society: Political-criminal collaboration around the world*. New Brunswick, NJ: Transaction Publishers.

Holzlehner, T. (2007). "The harder the rain, the tighter the roof": Evolution of organized crime networks in the Russian Far East. *Sibirica, 6*(2), 51–86.

Karstedt, S. (2014). Organizing crime: The state as agent. In L. Paoli (Ed.), *The Oxford handbook of organized crime*, (pp. 302–320). Oxford, England: Oxford University Press.

Kupatadze, A. (2012). *Organized crime, political transition and state formation in post-Soviet Eurasia*. New York, NY: Palgrave MacMillan.

Marat, E. (2006). *The state-crime nexus in Central Asia: State weakness, organized crime, and corruption in Kyrgyzstan and Tajikistan*. Washington, DC: Johns Hopkins University.

CHAPTER 12

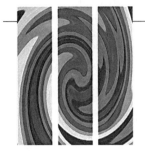

Transnational
Organized Crime

The previous three chapters have examined how organized crime relates to the broader social context within individual countries, either on the national or on the local level. This chapter examines the international ramifications of organized crime and explores how illegal activities and criminal structures extend across borders. What is excluded from this analysis is the special case of maritime piracy, where criminals cross national maritime borders onto the high seas (Bueger, 2014; Twyman-Ghoshal & Pierce, 2014).

Since around the 1980s, the focus of the traditional debate on organized crime has shifted from a local and national to an international frame of reference, with an emphasis on what is commonly called *transnational organized crime* (von Lampe, 2001a, 2011c). After the end of the cold war, transnational organized crime even advanced to the status of a major security threat and partly replaced the perceived threat of military conflict (Edwards & Gill, 2002; Felsen & Kalaitzidis, 2005; Paoli & Fijnaut, 2004; Mitsilegas, 2003).

The concept of transnational organized crime, broadly speaking, refers to crime that somehow transcends national borders. It is framed in the context of globalization, where national borders have supposedly become less of an obstacle for offenders and "criminogenic asymmetries" (Passas, 1998) between rich and poor countries have become more virulent. Against this backcloth, different images and perceptions of transnational organized crime have emerged in public and academic discourse.

What is meant when people speak about transnational organized crime? Some rhetoric lets transnational organized crime appear as if it was something that existed in a quasi-metaphysical sphere with no roots in any particular location and touching ground only in the moment when a crime is committed. A more concrete notion is that mobile, rationally acting offenders operate on an international scale, searching for the most lucrative markets for illegal goods and services and the most suitable targets for predatory crime and taking advantage

293

of cross-border mobility to evade prosecution (Mittelman and Johnston, 1999). Another widely held view associates transnational organized crime with the discrepancies between East and West and North and South. Developing countries and countries in transition with a weak or corrupt law enforcement system are believed to serve as safe havens for internationally operating offenders (Shelley, 1999a; Wagley, 2006; Williams, 1999a). Yet another image of transnational organized crime is that of locally based offenders establishing transnational links to other offenders (Hobbs & Dunnighan, 1998; Hobbs, 1998). In this view, not the transnational movement of criminals but the cross-border networking and cooperation between locally based criminals is the main feature of transnational organized crime (see also Adamoli, Di Nicola, & Savona, 1998; Castells, quoted in Sheptycki, 2003). In many ways, the concept of transnational organized crime simply adds the notion of transnationality to fuzzy and ambiguous conceptions of organized crime (Van Duyne & Nelemans, 2012).

Some of the conceptual confusion can be overcome by once again organizing the discussion along the three basic dimensions of organized crime: activities, structures, and illegal governance. Accordingly, *transnational* organized crime can be conceptualized in terms of the following three categories:

- *Illegal activities* that cross international borders
- *Criminal organizations* that are either transnationally mobile—or have a presence in more than one country
- *Illegal governance* that extends across international borders

Although empirically these three categories may overlap, in the interest of clarity it is important to examine each category separately. It is also important to start with an examination of transnational criminal activities, because without an understanding of the patterns of transnational crimes it is difficult to understand the organization of transnational criminals.

TRANSNATIONAL CRIMINAL ACTIVITIES

By stating that transnational crimes are characterized by somehow transcending international borders, a rough distinction can be made to ordinary, domestic criminal activities. But it says fairly little about the nature of transnational crimes. In fact, transnational criminal activities are highly diverse, and the form and the degree of their "transnationality" vary greatly. This complexity is ignored in the often simplistic depictions of transnational crime.

Patterns of Cross-Border Movement in Transnational Crime

Variations in transnational criminal activities can be observed, first and foremost, in the patterns of cross-border movement. Two key dimensions defining a transnational crime are (a) the nature of what actually crosses the border and (b) the directionality of the cross-border movement (von Lampe, 2011c, p. 4).

What Crosses Borders?

Transnational crime involves the cross-border movement of one or more of the following:

- Persons
- Goods
- Information

It has been argued that much of transnational organized crime (and, in fact, much of organized crime) is essentially some variation of the smuggling of illicit goods (Kleemans & Van de Bunt, 1999, p. 23; Kleemans & de Poot, 2008, p. 75; Van Duyne, 1996, p. 346). For the most part this means that prohibited, controlled, or highly taxed goods are illegally transported across borders—for example, child pornography, stolen motor vehicles, pirated textiles, counterfeit medicine and counterfeit currency, protected wildlife, illegally logged timber, protected cultural artifacts, arms, drugs, embargoed technology, hazardous waste, gasoline, liquor, or cigarettes.

In the case of human trafficking and human smuggling, persons instead of objects are brought across the border. Whether offenders accompany the smuggled goods or persons is a question of the specific modus operandi. However, criminals do cross borders as an essential characteristic of some transnational crimes, namely, cross-border predatory crimes. For example, gangs engaged in serial burglary or serial robbery in one country may operate from home bases in another country, so that they cross the border whenever they go on a burglary or robbery spree (Weenink, Huisman, & Van der Laan, 2004).

Another type of transnational predatory crime may merely involve the cross-border movement of information—for example, certain cases of so-called 419 frauds. With a ruse like the promise of a lottery win or high profits from a business deal, victims are enticed to transfer money to recipients abroad solely based on communication with perpetrators by email, phone, or fax (Ampratwum, 2009).

Table 12.1 How Borders Are Crossed in Transnational Crime Schemes

Pattern of Cross-border Movement	Examples
→ Unidirectional	Drug smuggling
↺ Bi-directional	Cross-border burglary from home base
↻ Multidirectional (circular)	Carousel VAT-fraud within the European Union

The Directionality of Cross-Border Movement

The directionality of cross-border movement likewise varies by type of crime. Directionality as understood here refers to patterns in which borders are traversed in the course of a crime (von Lampe, 2011c). Three types of directionality can be distinguished (Table 12.1): (a) unidirectional movement, (b) bi-directional movement, and (c) multidirectional, circular movement.

Smuggling is commonly a unidirectional activity of transporting contraband from source to destination country, perhaps via one or more transit countries. Payment for contraband goods, however, will go in the opposite direction, potentially posing a separate and possibly a bigger problem of moving large amounts of cash across borders (Reuter & Truman, 2004, p. 28; Chapter 10). In the case of the illegal export of hazardous waste, the cross-border movement appears to be more clearly unidirectional (Massari & Monzini, 2004).

Other transnational crime schemes are bi-directional, for example, in the case of serial burglars operating from safe home bases. Here, each criminal endeavor is completed only after a border has been crossed once in each direction between the home and the target country (Weenink et al., 2004). Certain cigarette-smuggling schemes also involve such a *U*-shaped pattern of movement, namely when untaxed cigarettes are officially procured for export to a third country only to be smuggled back to the country of origin for distribution on the black market (von Lampe, 2006a). "Carousel fraud" schemes targeting the system of value-added tax reimbursement within the EU may even develop, as the term indicates, a circular pattern linking a number of fraudulent firms in different countries in repeated rounds of cross-border transactions (Pashev, 2008; Van Duyne, 1999). Finally, there are crime schemes with complex transnational ramifications. The illicit production of synthetic drugs in the Netherlands provides one such example. Dutch ecstasy producers may procure precursor chemicals from suppliers in Eastern Europe and East Asia. The ecstasy is then produced in the Netherlands or Belgium to be smuggled through and into yet other countries for retail distribution (Blickman, Korf, Siegel, & Zaitch, 2003).

Table 12.2   Smuggling Schemes

Scheme	Where is the border crossed?	What is concealed?	Volume of contraband
Green/Blue Border	Outside of regular border crossings	Any cross-border movement	Low to high
Noncommercial Traffic	Regular border crossings for tourist travel	Cross-border transportation of goods	Low to medium
International Trade	Regular border crossings for commercial goods	Cross-border transportation of illegal goods	High
Mail and Parcel Service	Regular border crossings for commercial goods/mail	Cross-border transportation of goods/cross-border transportation of illegal goods	Low

Modes of Smuggling

Smuggling, the illegal movement of tangible objects or persons across borders, constitutes the core of most kinds of transnational crime. This is not to say that smuggling ventures are confined to the crossing of borders. Smuggling schemes may involve elaborate preparatory work, such as the concealing of contraband within means of transportation, elaborate activities at transshipment points, such as reloading, repackaging, relabeling, and temporary storage of contraband, and finally, elaborate activities in the destination country, such as the clearing of cover loads with customs after crossing the border and retrieval of contraband concealed inside containers and vehicles used for transportation (see, e.g., Decker & Townsend Chapman, 2008). Still, at the center of any analysis of smuggling must be an examination of the ways in which contraband is brought across the border.

The smuggling of goods occurs in essentially four different forms by land, air, or sea (Table 12.2):

- Cross-border transportation outside of regular border crossings
- Cross-border transportation under the guise of noncommercial cross-border traffic
- Cross-border transportation under the guise of international trade
- Cross-border transportation by mail or parcel services

Image 12.1 A 600-meter drug-smuggling tunnel unearthed by Mexican authorities in November 2011 that connects the state of Baja California with San Diego on the U.S. side of the border.

Photo: AFP/Stringer

Each mode of smuggling entails specific logistical requirements with regard to the means and forms of transportation, the routes taken, and the volume of contraband moved in a single shipment.

Smuggling Outside of Regular Border Crossings

When smugglers cross the border outside of regular border crossings, they seek to hide from authorities the fact that there is any cross-border movement at all. The objective is to completely evade official scrutiny. In the case of smuggling over land, smugglers typically select a stretch of border (the "green border") that is remote, poorly monitored, or difficult to monitor. And they will use means of transportation suitable for the terrain. For example, in mountainous border regions, such as those between Iran and Iraq, smugglers travel on foot or use mules (Murphy, 2002). Smugglers crossing from Egypt into Israel through the Negev desert travel on foot or use camels or off-road vehicles and take advantage of caves along the way to avoid detection (Siegel, 2009). In more densely monitored stretches of the border, smugglers may dig tunnels to cross the border undetected underground (Almog, 2004).

Smuggling across the green border by air involves the use of aircraft flying under the radar and either landing on irregular strips or staying airborne and dropping packages of contraband in prearranged drop zones (Decker & Townsend Chapman, 2008, pp. 80–83).

For smugglers moving by sea (the "blue border"), boats, sometimes launched from larger vessels, come ashore at remote stretches of the coastline to evade detection. In the smuggling across the blue border the counterpart to tunnels are submarines and semisubmersible vessels. Speedboats are an alternative means of transportation on water where offenders try to evade official scrutiny by reducing the time of exposure to border surveillance or by simply outpacing border patrols (Decker & Townsend Chapman, 2008, pp. 69–70).

Smuggling Under the Guise of Noncommercial Cross-Border Traffic

In contrast to smuggling across the green border or the blue border, smuggling schemes using regular border crossing points are not designed to conceal the cross-border movement as such. The border is crossed openly in the regular flow of noncommercial traffic. What is concealed is the fact that goods are being transported across the border.

Smuggling embedded in licit cross-border traffic can take many different forms depending on the mode of transportation and the level of concealment. Some variation also exists with regard to the type of contraband. For example, gold (Naylor, 2002) requires different modes of transportation than living, protected birds (Wyatt, 2009).

Perhaps the most common form of smuggling in terms of the number of incidents is smuggling by individuals who cross the border on foot, by bicycle, motorcycle, car, train, plane, ship, or ferry embedded in international tourist travel. The contraband may be hidden inside the body, under or inside clothing, or inside personal luggage. By swallowing the contraband, usually drugs, gold, or diamonds, the highest level of concealment is achieved because the contraband cannot be detected by a normal, nonintrusive search of the person (Cawich, Valentine, Evans, Harding, & Crandon, 2009; Traub, Hoffman, & Nelson, 2003). Similarly, the detection of contraband hidden, for example, in false bottoms of suitcases or sewn into stuffed toys, may require the use of some form of technology such as Xray scanners and may entail damaging or destroying the objects within which the contraband is hidden.

Personal vehicles, including bicycles, motorcycles, cars, vans, campers, and vessels like fishing boats, sailing boats, and motor yachts, provide numerous opportunities for concealing contraband in secret compartments. These compartments exist by design—for example, underneath the dashboard of a car—or are created specifically to hide contraband—for example, by dividing the gas tank of a car or motorboat. Creating these compartments, hiding the contraband, and retrieving the contraband after the border has been successfully crossed can be elaborate operations in their own right, at times requiring a high level of expertise and technical

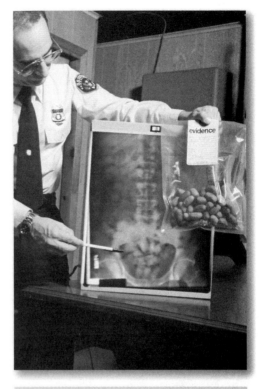

Image 12.2 A customs officer showing the drugs a smuggler had tried to bring into the United States hidden inside the stomach.

Photo: Jacques M. Chenet/CORBIS

skills on the part of transnational offenders (Decker & Townsend Chapman, 2008, pp. 75–78; Desroches, 2005, pp. 97–98).

Reducing the likelihood of inspections can further increase the chances of successful smuggling runs. One method is bypassing controls altogether, for example, with the help of complicit baggage handlers at airports (Kleemans & Van de Bunt, 2008, p. 193) or with the help of diplomats whose official luggage is not subject to customs inspection (Naylor, 2002, pp. 149–150). Diplomatic bags (also called diplomatic pouches) used for the confidential conveyance of official correspondence between a government and its diplomatic missions abroad are considered as inviolable under international law as the premises of a diplomatic mission. Diplomatic bags are not necessarily bags in the literal sense. They can be as large as trucks or overseas containers (Zabyelina, 2013).

Another method to avoid inspection is the use of people who because of their (apparent) age, gender, religion, or social status may be unlikely to raise the suspicion of customs and border patrol officers, such as women with small children, older women, catholic priests, orthodox Jews, or celebrities (Campbell, 2008; Kostakos & Antonopoulos, 2010; Naylor, 2002).

Smuggling Under the Guise of International Trade

Arguably the most inconspicuous way to move contraband across the border, at least in larger volume, is the integration of smuggling into legal cross-border trade.

Just like smuggling embedded in tourist travel, no effort is made to conceal cross-border movement as such. In addition, no effort is made to conceal the fact that goods are being transported across the border. The smuggling virtually takes place under the nose of customs officers who may or may not be bribed. What is concealed from authorities is the true nature of the goods crossing the border. This is achieved by either hiding contraband among legal goods or by falsely declaring the contraband as legal goods. For example, the shipping papers may state that a container holds a consignment of plastic shopping bags while in reality the container is filled with counterfeit cigarettes. As long as the container is not scanned or physically inspected, the contraband remains undetected.

Smuggling under the guise of legal cross-border trade requires offenders to behave like any legitimate commercial business and to have a more or less continuous transnational presence. Shipments have to be cleared with customs, and taxes and duties have to be paid on the declared goods. The kind of documents required for the cross-border movement of goods varies depending, for example, on the means of transportation and the kind of cargo, but in general the sender, the carrier, and the recipient of the goods have to be disclosed. This means that a business sending the shipment from one country and a business receiving the shipment in another country have to at least exist on paper, and someone acting on behalf of one of these businesses has to interact with customs directly or indirectly through a dispatch forwarding agent. The integration into legal cross-border commerce can go so far that the entire smuggling operation, including transportation, customs clearance, and delivery, is outsourced to legitimate businesses while the criminals remain in the background (Caulkins et al., 2009, p. 80; von Lampe, 2007).

Image 12.3 Customs agents at the port of Hamburg, Germany, confiscate 53 million contraband cigarettes hidden behind loads of towels in six 40 ft freight containers in July 2013.

Photo: Marcus Brandt/dpa/Corbis

Smuggling by Mail and Parcel Services

A fourth smuggling scheme in addition to smuggling outside of regular crossing points and smuggling embedded in flows of legitimate cross-border travel and trade is sending contraband by mail or parcel service. This method is closely linked to the marketing of illicit goods over the Internet, such as cigarettes (von Lampe, 2006a, p. 242) and counterfeit medicine (World Health Organization, 2010), but it is also used as an alternative means of smuggling other items, for example drugs (Caulkins et al., 2009, p. 83) and endangered species (Warchol, Zupan, & Clack, 2003, p. 23). Similar to the use of commercial transportation, smuggling by mail and parcel service requires an infrastructure for receiving shipments in the destination country.

Strategic Choices Made by Smugglers

There is another aspect to smuggling that is important to understand: the choices that smugglers make in the constant game of cat and mouse they play with customs. One kind of choice smugglers make pertains to the profiling by customs. While customs agencies try to establish patterns in smuggling activities and devise new techniques and introduce new technologies to make borders less easily penetrable, smugglers try to avoid detection by becoming less predictable, increasing their level of sophistication, changing their modus operandi, switching their means of transportation, and shifting their smuggling routes (Decker & Townsend Chapman, 2008, p. 161; Desroches, 2005, pp. 97–98).

Smugglers may also respond to interdiction efforts by changing the scale of smuggling operations. One basic decision smugglers have to make is whether to move contraband in bulk or to break it down into a number of smaller shipments to spread the risk. In drug smuggling, for example, a consignment may be divided among a group of couriers (*mules*) with the expectation that only some of them will be caught, leaving the overall operation profitable. In fact, some smuggling enterprises intentionally give up some mules as bait in order to divert the attention of customs away from the other mules (Caulkins et al., 2009, p. 74; Van Duyne, 1993b, p. 11). What may be celebrated by customs as a success against smuggling may in fact be a victory for the smugglers.

The size of contraband shipments is closely linked to the mode of smuggling. Generally speaking, embedding contraband in legal cross-border trade permits the largest smuggling loads. This can be illustrated using cigarette smuggling as an example (von Lampe, 2007): An individual smuggler or mule, can carry up to about 3,000 cigarettes, weighing about 4.5 kilograms, strapped to the body and hidden under clothes. About 50,000 cigarettes, weighing about 75 kilograms, fit into the trunk of a car. In contrast, a standard 40 ft freight container can hold about 10 million cigarettes, weighing about 15,000 kilograms.

The Geography of Transnational Criminal Activities

Cross-border crime does not occur at random (Hall, 2012). There are certain patterns discernible in which cross-border predatory criminals operate and in which contraband is smuggled. Countries and world regions are affected by transnational criminal activities in different ways and to different degrees. In previous chapters, it has already been noted that some countries show markedly higher levels of organized criminal activities than others—for example, with regard to illegal drugs (UNODC, 2014a) or illegal cigarettes (Joossens et al., 2009, p. 10). Apart from these quantitative differences, there are also functional differences in the roles countries and regions play in transnational criminal activities. In the area of transnational *predatory* crimes, the main distinction is between countries that serve as home bases for criminal groups (home-base countries) and countries where predatory crimes such as theft, burglary, and fraud are being committed (countries of operation). In the area of transnational *market-based* crimes, the main distinction is between source, transit, and destination countries for contraband.

Home-Base Countries and Countries of Operation in Transnational Predatory Crimes

Transnational predatory crime is characterized by offenders based in one jurisdiction committing crimes in another jurisdiction. If for no other reason, this modus operandi makes sense from the point of view of the offender in so far as the risk of apprehension and conviction is potentially reduced. Successful law enforcement in these cases tends to require cross-border cooperation between law enforcement agencies, and even where collaboration functions well it places an additional burden on criminal investigations (Casey, 2010, p. 136).

In home-base countries, offenders are recruited and trained and criminal endeavors are prepared that are then carried out in the countries of operation. The stereotypical geographical pattern of transnational predatory crime is that offenders based in poor Third World or transition countries seek their victims in rich, affluent countries of the First World. Certain countries are more notorious as home bases for predatory criminals than others. For example, transnational theft and burglary in North America and Western Europe have been linked to such Eastern and Southeast European countries as Lithuania, Poland, Romania, and the former Yugoslavia (Korsell & Larsson, 2011; Lindberg, Petrenko, Gladden, & Johnson, 1998; Weenink et al., 2004); and 419 frauds against victims in North America, Europe, and elsewhere have been linked to Nigeria (Ampratwum, 2009). Many cybercrimes, to give another example, have been traced to the Russian Federation, again with the victims primarily located in North America and in Western Europe (Holt, 2013).

The picture that emerges is that of a few countries that form hubs for transnational predatory crime from which victims in a large number of other countries are targeted. This picture, however, is not fully accurate. First, it would be an oversimplification to link transnational predatory crime to just a handful of countries. Probably no international border in the world is immune from cross-border predatory crime. Second, the roles that countries play are not fixed. In some cases, for example, transnational predatory offenders have moved their bases of operation closer to the countries of operation. An illustration of these dynamics is provided by Nigerian 419 fraudsters who have relocated to operate from the Netherlands (Oboh & Schoenmakers, 2010). And in some cases, transnational predatory criminals are based in first-world countries from the start. For example, there is a long tradition of cross-border investment fraudsters based in North America and Western Europe enticing victims to invest their money in worthless ventures (Van Duyne, 1993b, pp. 25–26).

Source, Transit, and Destination Countries in Smuggling Schemes

The geographical patterns of *market-based* transnational crimes are somewhat different from the geographical patterns of transnational predatory crimes. The movement of contraband, it seems, tends to be concentrated along so-called trafficking routes. These are transportation channels that connect major source, transit, and destination countries by land, sea, or air, sometimes over great distances.

The stereotypical pattern is that illegal commodities are moved from poorer to richer countries, similar to the general movement of cross-border predatory criminals. The main destination countries are commonly believed to be in North America and Western Europe, while the main source countries vary with the type of illegal commodity, and they also vary over time.

Historically, illegal drugs marketed in North America and Western Europe originated from a rather small number of countries in specific world regions. The main source countries for cocaine have been Bolivia, Peru, and especially Colombia (Wisotsky, 1990). The main supply of heroin has come from Southeast Asia and the Middle East. One center of opium poppy cultivation and heroin production, especially during the 1960s and 1970s, has been the so-called Golden Triangle, encompassing Birma, Thailand, and Laos. In the Middle East, the so-called Golden Crescent encompassing Iran, Afghanistan, and Pakistan has been the main source for heroin, especially since the 1970s. Previously, Turkey had played an important role as a producer of heroin in the region (Paoli, Greenfield, & Reuter, 2009; Windle, 2014). The traditional supplier of marijuana to North America has been Mexico, while most of the cannabis products smuggled to Western Europe have come from Morocco (Leggett & Pietschmann, 2008).

The image of a general movement of illegal goods from poorer to richer countries is incomplete, as there is also significant movement in the opposite direction. For example, synthetic drugs have traditionally been produced in industrialized countries. Europe has been the world's main producer of amphetamine (EMCDDA & Europol, 2011) and has also been an important source for ecstasy (MDMA) marketed overseas (UNODC, 2014a). It should also be noted at this point that domestic production of cannabis in North America and Europe likewise has accounted for a significant share of the market (Leggett & Pietschmann, 2008).

To add to the complexity, certain countries play important roles as source as well as destination countries. The United States, for example, is not only the main country of destination for illegal drugs from Mexico. At the same time, the United States is the main source of weapons being smuggled to Mexico as well as to Canada (Cook, Cukier, & Krause, 2009). China is another major source and destination country for illegal goods. It is considered the main producer of counterfeit goods (Lin, 2011), and it is also considered to be a major consumer of trafficked wildlife products, such as ivory and tiger skin and tiger bones (Moyle, 2009; Stiles, 2004).

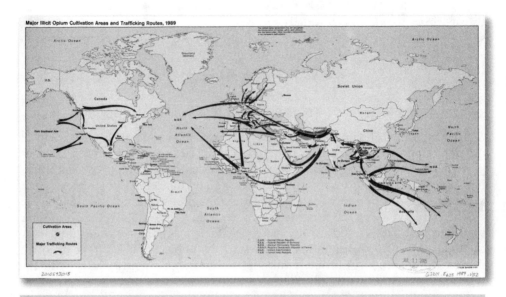

Image 12.4   A world map showing the major global trafficking routes for opium in 1989, the year that marked the end of the Cold War. How similar or different are the trafficking routes today?

Photo: Library of Congress, Geography and Map Division

Trafficking Routes

The trafficking routes along which contraband is smuggled do not necessarily mark the shortest distance between source and destination country. Trafficking routes are also not static; they may change over time more or less abruptly. The trafficking of cocaine provides a good illustration. In the 1980s and early 1990s, cocaine was primarily moved from Colombia to the United States by air or sea through the Caribbean. Then in response to intensified interdiction efforts, the trafficking route shifted to Mexico (Corcoran, 2013). At the same time, a new major trafficking route opened up to Europe via West Africa (Ellis, 2009).

Along the trafficking routes, there can be ports, cities, and entire countries that serve as transshipment centers. In these places, contraband may be repackaged and reloaded from one means of transportation to the other. For example, drugs may be transported by air or sea from Colombia to Mexico from where they are smuggled into the United States by land. This may be done to adapt to differences in the transportation infrastructure or to reduce the risk of detection.

Transshipment centers can have a central importance for the trafficking of illegal goods to the point that contraband en route to these transshipment centers is moved through later destination countries. Amsterdam is a case in point. The Dutch city is arguable the main transshipment center for drugs in Europe. Cocaine arrives through nearby ports, such as Rotterdam (The Netherlands) and Antwerp (Belgium) or from much farther away. Cannabis comes by land from Morocco through Spain and France just as heroin is traditionally shipped along the so-called Balkan route that connects the Golden Crescent through

Turkey, Bulgaria, and former Yugoslavia with Western Europe. It is quite common that drugs first pass through countries like France and Germany and then are sold in bulk in Amsterdam only to be smuggled back to these previous transit countries for retail distribution (see Huisman, Huikeshoven, & Van de Bunt, 2003; Zaitch, 2002). Miami, Florida, has played a similar role as a transshipment center for Colombian cocaine going to the domestic U.S. market and to Canada. Even cocaine flown via the Bahamas to North Carolina was first shipped back south to Miami before it was transported northward again for distribution in places like New York City (see Porter, 1993, p. 140).

Table 12.3 Factors Assumed to Shape the Geography of Transnational Organized Crime

Factor	Meaning	Example
Criminogenic Asymmetries	Cross-national differences creating incentives and opportunities for cross-border crime	Income inequalities between Eastern and Western Europe fostering cross-border predatory crime like serial burglary
Geographical Proximity	Crime opportunities presenting themselves to criminals in one country because of the short distance to another country	Iran functioning as a transshipment country for heroin from neighboring Afghanistan and Pakistan
Social Proximity	Crime opportunities presenting themselves to criminals in one country because of social ties to another country	Heroin smuggling by members of the same family that is spread across Turkey and Western Europe as a result of labor migration
Legal Flows of Goods and Persons	Trafficking routes mirroring legal-trade routes and/or routes of tourist travel	Drug trafficking between West Africa and China following West African traders coming to China to purchase consumer goods
Weak Controls	Transnational criminals preferring to operate where border controls and law enforcement are weakest	Drug trafficking from Latin America to Western Europe through corruption-ridden Guinea-Bissau

Explaining the Geography of Transnational Crime

The discernible geographical patterns of transnational criminal activities have been explained by reference to a number of factors (Table 12.3). Some of these factors pertain to the relationship between countries and some factors to conditions within particular countries.

Criminogenic Asymmetries. Perhaps the most general approach is Nikos Passas' notion of *criminogenic asymmetries*. In essence, Passas contends that transnational crime is driven by differences between countries, "structural disjunctions, mismatches and inequalities in the spheres of politics, culture, the economy and the law" (Passas, 2002, p. 26). Crime is assumed to be attracted by these differences just like water flows to the lowest point. Transnational income inequalities, for example, have been identified as a major driver for the illegal cross-border movement of people, either in the form of illegal migration or in the form of human trafficking, where the desire to find a better life elsewhere is exploited by traffickers (Aronowitz, 2001).

Cultural and legal differences can also promote transnational crime. For example, the absence of effective enforcement of laws against the sexual exploitation of children and public tolerance for child prostitution has attracted sex tourists to certain countries, such as in South East Asia, where they (individually or collectively) engage in child abuse (Lau, 2008). Likewise, cross-border illegal waste disposal is driven in part by different standards in environmental protection (Baird, Curry, & Cruz, 2014).

Another criminogenic asymmetry can be found in differential levels of taxes and customs duties. In a typical pattern, goods such as cigarettes, alcohol, gasoline, and precious metals are smuggled from low-tax to high-tax jurisdictions (see, e.g., Yürekli & Sayginsoy, 2010).

Other criminogenic asymmetries have less to do with man-made circumstances and more with natural conditions. Many trafficking routes that span the globe reflect climatic, geological, and ecological differences. For example, certain regions are more suitable than others for the cultivation of coca, poppy, or cannabis plants (Casale & Klein, 1993; Morrison, 1997; Paoli et al., 2009, p. 53). Similarly, certain protected wildlife—such as certain kinds of parrots in demand by collectors or sturgeon, the source of caviar—is confined to limited areas from where, then, trafficking routes extend to consumer countries (Pires, 2012; Zabyelina, 2014).

Geographical and Social Proximity. The notion of criminogenic asymmetries highlights fundamental, underlying conditions that explain the occurrence of transnational crime in broad strokes. But it does not always explain specific geographical patterns, for example, why certain trafficking routes constitute a detour between source and destination countries and why certain countries are more affected by transnational crime than others.

One explanation is that countries differ in what is called *social proximity*, as opposed to *geographical proximity*. Countries that may be far apart geographically can still be closely connected because of a shared language and culture and because of existing social ties. This is especially true between former colonial powers and their former colonies and between source and destination countries of migration. Social proximity can explain, for example, drug trafficking routes between the Dutch Antilles and the Netherlands and between Turkey, a major source country of labor migrants, and Northwestern Europa, historically a major area of destination for Turkish labor migrants (Paoli & Reuter, 2008; Van Duyne, 1996).

This does not mean, however, that geographical proximity is an entirely irrelevant factor. The importance of Iran as a key transit country for heroin, for example, is easily explained by the fact that it neighbors two major source countries for heroin, Afghanistan and Pakistan, with which it shares porous borders characterized by mountainous and desert terrain (Sabatelle, 2011). Likewise, Mexico's role in the international drug trade is explained to no small degree by the fact that it neighbors the largest consumer market for illegal drugs, the United States. More generally, geographical proximity is an important factor where transnational crime is narrowly confined to cross-border crime connecting neighboring countries (see, e.g., Junninen & Aromaa, 1999). Sometimes these criminal activities are concentrated along the border affecting the border regions more than the rest of the country (Ceccato, 2007).

Legal Flows of Goods and Persons. Apart from social and geographical proximity, trafficking routes have been explained by reference to the legal transnational movement of goods and persons. The contention is that "most smuggling parallels the methods and routes of legal commerce" (Andreas, 1999, p. 89; see also Zaitch, 2002, p. 101). This means that the emergence of trade routes is followed by the emergence of trafficking routes. For example, exploring African traders who are bringing consumer goods from China to their home countries "have figured out that a quick and convenient way to acquire hard currency is through drug trafficking" (Chin & Zhang, 2007, p. 39).

The link between legal and illegal trade routes also means that the larger the flow of legal goods, the greater the volume of illegal goods that are moved through the same channels. By embedding contraband in the large flow of legal cross-border movement, it is argued, smugglers take advantage of lower costs and the decreased likelihood of detection (Russo, 2010).

Weak Controls. The notions of social and geographical proximity and of criminogenic asymmetries allude to the relation between two or more countries. Another frequently proposed explanation for transnational crime patterns pertains to conditions within individual countries, specifically those that lack the capacity to enforce laws and protect their borders. These countries are classified as "weak states" or "failed states" and are believed to be used by transnational criminals as safe havens and as passageways for the transportation of contraband (Williams & Godson, 2002). A classic example is Guinea-Bissau. Located at the southwestern most tip of West Africa between Senegal and Guinea with a population of 1.6 million, the former Portuguese colony is ranked as one of the poorest and most underdeveloped countries in the world. In the mid-2000s, Guinea-Bissau is alleged to have become an important transshipment center for Latin American cocaine en route to Western Europe, following efforts by European law enforcement agencies to curb the influx of cocaine through direct air and maritime routes (Ellis, 2009; UNODC, 2008; Van Riper, 2014). Guinea-Bissau is considered attractive for drug traffickers for mainly two reasons. It is within range of small airplanes that can make the roughly 2,500 km trip from Latin America with a sizeable load of cocaine, and it suffers from a chronic weakness of state institutions. Since its independence in 1974, the country has experienced a series of coup attempts and successful coups that have left power largely in the hands of military leaders alleged to collude with drug traffickers.

Image 12.5 People gather around a speedboat of a type believed to be used by drug traffickers, as it unloads cargo at a quay in Bissau, Guinea-Bissau, in July 2007.

Photo: ASSOCIATED PRESS/AP

Military units have reportedly provided logistical support for the transportation and storage of cocaine, including the building of landing strips, in return for bribe payments. While the police have made some sizeable seizures of cocaine, they suffer from a lack of resources in comparison to corrupt branches of the government. In one notorious incident in 2006, three Colombian drug traffickers arrested by the Judiciary Police were liberated by heavily armed Interior Ministry Police, who also forced the surrender of the 674 kg of cocaine that had been confiscated (Nossiter, 2012, 2013; Traub, 2010).

CROSS-BORDER MOBILITY AND CROSS-BORDER NETWORKING OF CRIMINALS

The patterns of transnational criminal activities that have been discussed in the previous section reflect crime opportunities that present themselves to those who are willing and able to overcome borders in one way or the other. The next section will examine how offenders organize around these transnational crime opportunities. First, however, two underlying aspects need to be examined that form the basis for the emergence and functioning of any kind of transnational criminal structures: the cross-border mobility and the cross-border networking of criminals. Both are closely linked. The cross-border mobility of criminals can promote cross-border criminal networking, just like the cross-border networking of criminals can increase their cross-border mobility. Finally, cross-border networking can be a functional alternative to cross-border mobility. Put in another way, criminals who have accomplices on the other side of the border have fewer reasons to cross the border themselves. This is important, as there can be substantial barriers to cross-border mobility.

Cross-Border Mobility

According to a widely held view, globalization has greatly facilitated not only the general cross-border movement of goods and people but also the cross-border movement of contraband and criminals (Shelley, 2011; Williams & Godson, 2002). Some borders may be porous because of natural conditions or a lack of state resources (Townsend, 2006), others have become more permeable as a result of political changes, namely the fall of the Iron Curtain with the demise of the Soviet Bloc, and some borders, like those within Western Europe, have ceased to exist in the traditional way (Faure Atger, 2008). Still, even in the era of globalization, crossing borders can pose a major obstacle for criminals. Considerable advances in international law enforcement cooperation have gone hand in hand with technological innovations to greatly facilitate the identification and monitoring of (potential) transnational offenders, while international borders have gained renewed importance since September 11, 2001 (Franko Aas, 2013).

Borders as Obstacles for Transnational Crime

Efforts to curtail international terrorism and irregular migration have resulted in tightened border control regimes between, for example, the United States and Mexico and between the European Union and its neighbors to the East and South (Baldaccini, 2008; Shamir, 2005).

At the same time, traditional border controls have been scaled down or removed along certain borders, namely, within Europe's Schengen area. But this does not mean that borders are being abolished. Rather, the monitoring and control of cross-border movement becomes "dispersed in a complex fashion across space and time" (Jamieson, South, & Taylor, 1998, p. 308; see also Wonders, 2007). As Petrus van Duyne has argued, the borders of modern states generally extend into a dense web of information and control within a country, leaving little moving space for those trying to evade detection except at the margins of society (Van Duyne, 1998, pp. 259–260; see also Broeders, 2007; Loftus, 2015).

Ironically, crime control efforts can sometimes facilitate the crossing of borders by criminals and the expansion of transnational criminal networks. This is the case when migrants are deported because of crimes they have committed in their country of residence. For example, it has been argued that the deportation of criminals from the United States has fostered drugs and arms trafficking between the United States and countries in Central America and in the Caribbean (Dudley, 2010; Williams & Roth, 2011).

Image 12.6   Technological advances like surveillance drones similar to the one shown taking off on a U.S. Customs Border Patrol mission from Fort Huachuca, Arizona, in October 2007, have made borders less penetrable for transnational criminals.

Photo: ASSOCIATED PRESS/AP

Operating in an Alien Environment

The crossing of borders as such is not the only challenge that transnational criminals face. Once in a foreign country, they have to cope with an unfamiliar environment. Legal, cultural, and language barriers may prevent them from taking full advantage of the legitimate infrastructure, for example, to set up a business or open a bank account. Of course, these problems are greatly reduced when migrants operate in their own country of origin (see, e.g., Soudijn & Kleemans, 2009, p. 467) or when transnational criminals take advantage of similarities in language, culture, and the legal system between former colonial powers and their former colonies (Zaitch, 2002, p. 89). Still, being an outsider in the country of operation will tend to increase the risk of detection. Behaving in an unconventional way, for example, can draw unwanted attention and may raise suspicion. This is why the Cali Cartel reportedly instructed U.S.-based operatives who managed stash houses to blend into their social environment by doing such things as regularly cutting the lawn and going to the movies every Thursday night (Kenney, 1999b, p. 106).

Familiarity with the respective legal system also seems important. Decker and Townsend Chapman (2008, p. 140), for example, found that many of the incarcerated drug traffickers they interviewed had been ignorant of crucial aspects of the substantive and procedural criminal law in the United States, thereby becoming more vulnerable to arrest and lengthy prison sentences.

There is a plausible assumption that offenders operating in a foreign country as outsiders tend to be limited in the types of crime they can commit (Massari, 2003, p. 65). It is probably no coincidence that criminals without social support within the country of operation tend to specialize in overt "hit-and-run" crimes like serial robbery and serial burglary that do not require blending into conventional patterns of behavior (Felson, 2006a, p. 254; von Lampe, 2008b, p. 15).

Given these constraints, transnational offenders may be confined to "niches of familiarity" (von Lampe, 2011c, p. 6) that migrant communities provide. These subcultural enclaves are often highlighted as an important support infrastructure for transnational offenders, even providing some level of protection against law enforcement because of the shielding effects of cultural and language differences to the host society (Kleemans & Van de Bunt, 1999, p. 25; Paoli & Reuter, 2008, p. 24; Shelley, 2001, p. 4; Williams & Godson, 2002, pp. 330–331).

Some obstacles can also be overcome, if only gradually, by taking up permanent residence in a foreign country. There is some evidence that this has happened, especially in the area of drug trafficking. Colombian drug traffickers are said to have relocated to important transshipment centers in Mexico, the Netherlands, and West Africa, namely Guinea-Bissau, where they may work for one or for several drug trafficking groups, or they may try to organize smuggling operations on their own (Ellis, 2009, p. 172; Kenney, 1999a, p. 127; Zaitch, 2002, pp. 160–161). African traffickers, in turn, have reportedly taken residence in Pakistan and India, at times registering as students to procure drugs for drug entrepreneurs based in Europe (Ruggiero & Khan, 2006, p. 481; Van Duyne, 1993b, p. 14). Likewise, British drug traffickers have set up residence in the Netherlands and in Spain, which is also the permanent residence of some Dutch traffickers (Soudijn & Huisman, 2011).

However, from the available evidence it seems that transnational offenders relocating to another country for the purpose of facilitating and committing crimes is more the exception than the rule. More commonly, it seems, links are established or activated to individuals already present and well entrenched in the country of operation. Depending on the circumstances, these may be individuals sharing the same ethnic background as the transnational offenders, members of other migrant communities, or individuals indigenous to the country of operation (Gounev & Bezlov, 2008, p. 424; Lee, 1999, p. 15; McIllwain, 2001, p. 47; Sieber & Bögel, 1993, p. 80; Van Daele & Vander Beken, 2009, p. 57; von Lampe, 2009c).

Awareness Space

Limitations in cross-border mobility not only affect the ability to engage in cross-border crime, they reduce the likelihood that criminals become aware of transnational crime opportunities in the first place.

Offenders are generally limited to opportunities within their respective "awareness space," mainly shaped in time and physical space by past activities (Brantingham & Brantingham, 1993, p. 269). An offender "commits crime in the areas he knows" (Felson, 2006a, p. 234). This implies that cross-border mobility of some form is not only an inherent characteristic of transnational crime but a precondition.

Image 12.7   Africans and Chinese stand outside a clothing wholesale market in Guangzhou, China, a city with a large community of traders from West Africa. Expatriate communities like these can provide "niches of familiarity" for transnational criminals who explore and exploit crime opportunities in an otherwise foreign environment.

Photo: David Hogsholt/Contributor

However, this cross-border mobility does not have to be linked to criminal conduct. In fact, opportunities encountered in the course of legal cross-border movement, such as tourist travel, business travel, migration, study, or military deployment abroad, have been at the root of many transnational criminal ventures. For example, there are indications that a direct link exists between the presence of American troops in Indochina in the 1960s and 1970s and the emergence of heroin trafficking routes between Southeast Asia and the United States (McCoy, 2003, p. 258). Likewise, it seems that tourists discovering cross-border price discrepancies in the legal cigarette market contributed significantly to the emergence of major cigarette black markets in Germany and the United Kingdom (Hornsby & Hobbs, 2007; von Lampe, 2002b). Of course, media reports, the Internet, and person-to-person communication, such as within diaspora networks, may also alert potential offenders to the existence of transnational crime opportunities (Chin & Zhang, 2007, p. 37; Clarke & Brown, 2003, p. 209; Decker & Townsend Chapman, 2008, p. 119; Gounev & Bezlov, 2008, p. 425).

Criminal Foraging

Apart from the coincidental discovery of crime opportunities, transnational criminals may actively and purposefully seek out opportunities for crime. This kind of behavior is what Marcus Felson (2006a, p. 241) has termed "criminal foraging." Exploring opportunities is typical for a wide range of crime. However, offenders generally "tend to forage near their homes and other places they already know" (Felson, 2006a, p. 263). At least some transnational criminals appear to be more exploratory and more daring than that. In one extreme case "drug traffickers from Latin America smuggled several kilos of cocaine into China to test the market and see if they can find a local buyer" (Chin & Zhang, 2007, p. 40). Not surprisingly it was a Chinese police official who had this story to tell.

But there is also evidence that transnational criminals do indeed fit the mold of sophisticated, organized offenders who are capable of taking the initiative and of seeking out and creating crime opportunities (Ekblom, 2003, p. 252). This is illustrated by an analysis of transnational criminals from Eastern Europe committing serious property offenses in Belgium. Van Daele, Vander Beken, and Bruinsma (2012) found that these transnational offenders travelled greater distances and where more flexible in their movements within Belgium than comparable domestic Belgian offenders. Human traffickers, likewise, "are said to undertake informal market surveys to identify the most advantageous market, calculating costs, risks and benefits" (Surtees, 2008, p. 48). In a similar vein, Michael Kenney has described Colombian drug trafficking organizations as "learning organizations" that conduct research on crime opportunities by "gathering information about alternative routes and transshipment methods, experimenting with certain alternatives that proved capable of transporting large quantities" (Kenney, 1999a, p. 110).

Overall, it seems that discovering transnational crime opportunities may for the most part be linked to routine, licit cross-border mobility of persons and information, but some adventurous offenders may go beyond these established paths.

Cross-Border Networking

Transnational crime does not necessarily require the organization of criminals. Just like crime that occurs within a single country, the spectrum ranges from individual, lone offenders to complex criminal organizations (Gamella & Jimenez Rodrigo, 2008, pp. 286–287). And just like criminal structures in general, where transnational criminal structures do exist, at their core they constitute networks of criminally exploitable ties (see Chapter 5).

The Need for Cross-Border Networking

As has already been indicated, the importance of cross-border networking varies by crime type. Cross-border networking is inherent in the functioning of transnational illegal markets. Inevitably, suppliers and customers from different countries have to be somehow connected across borders (Kleemans & de Poot, 2008, p. 75). In contrast, cross-border predatory criminals do not depend on contacts in the country of operation, although in practice they may receive local support (Sieber & Bögel, 1993, p. 80; Van Daele & Vander Beken, 2009, p. 57; Weenink et al., 2004).

The need for cross-border networking also seems to be dependent in part on the scale of a criminal venture. Research on cannabis and cigarette smuggling operations shows a positive correlation between the size of contraband shipments and the size and diversity of the entrepreneurial structures handling these shipments (Gamella & Jimenez Rodrigo, 2008; von Lampe, 2007).

Cross-border networking can enable or facilitate crime, and in various ways it can reduce risks inherent in transnational crime (McIllwain, 2001). For example, where in the eyes of law enforcement a specific nationality or ethnicity is linked to certain criminal activity, such as Colombians in drug trafficking, transnational offenders may transfer certain tasks to local criminals in order to reduce visibility (Decker & Townsend Chapman, 2008, p. 71; Zaitch, 2002, p. 167). Establishing relationships with local criminals may also be necessary to avoid conflicts, namely, where criminal groups exert territorial control. These groups, in addition, may be in a position to provide access to resources, such as logistical support and protection from law enforcement (Arlacchi, 1986, pp. 151–153).

Another facet of the networking of transnational criminals is the recruitment of individuals positioned within the sphere of legal business. For example, smuggling enterprises transporting contraband by air can link up with airline staff, airplane cleaners, and luggage handlers at airports to bypass customs controls (Caulkins et al., 2009, p. 82; Kleemans & Van de Bunt, 2008, pp. 192–193). Similarly, smuggling enterprises using transport by land and sea will seek the cooperation of individuals with a background in boating, fishing, import and export, and transportation (Decker & Townsend Chapman, 2008, p. 101; Desroches, 2005, p. 45; Kostakos & Antonopoulos, 2010, p. 53; Soudijn & Kleemans, 2009, p. 464). Establishing relationships with corrupt officials to gain immunity from law enforcement and to facilitate smuggling operations can also be advantageous, although, as already indicated, corruption is not always necessary for successfully committing transnational crimes (Chapter 11).

The Formation of Transnational Criminal Links

In Chapter 5, the formation of criminal networks was explained as the result of essentially two mechanisms, the activation of preexisting social ties for criminal purposes and the establishment of contacts between criminals who meet at offender convergence settings. Both mechanisms are also relevant for the formation of transnational criminal networks.

A recurring theme in the literature on transnational organized crime is how criminal networks are embedded in webs of social relations that provide a basis of trust (see von Lampe & Johansen, 2004b). Ethnicity is often mentioned in this respect, although only rarely is the explicit claim made that it is shared ethnicity rather than underlying social ties that bring coconspirators together (Decker & Townsend Chapman, 2008, p. 96; see also Desroches, 2005, p. 63). In most cases, it seems, ethnic homogeneity is a superficial characteristic of criminal networks based on family, friendship, or local community ties (see Chapter 5). As a result of migration, these close social ties may span great geographical distances. For example, heroin trafficking from production in Eastern Turkey to sale in Western Europe may be handled by members of the same family (Bruinsma & Bernasco, 2004, p. 87). Ritual kinship ties created by fraternal associations with branches in different countries, namely, the major outlaw motorcycle gangs and mafia associations like Camorra, Cosa Nostra, and 'Ndrangheta, are even more likely to foster the cross-border networking of criminals (Barker, 2011; Varese, 2011; Chapter 7).

Yet, close bonds of that nature are not necessarily a precondition for the emergence of transnational criminal networks. As anecdotal evidence suggests, relatively weak social ties can be sufficient grounds for transnational criminal cooperation (Antonopoulos, 2008a, p. 277; Chin & Zhang, 2007, pp. 37–38; Desroches, 2005, pp. 65–66; von Lampe, 2009c, pp. 26–34). Even indirect contacts and a reputation for trustworthiness and reliability gained within (legitimate or illegitimate) milieus have been found to provide a basis for the formation and expansion of transnational criminal networks (Decker & Townsend Chapman, 2008, p. 96; Kleemans & de Poot, 2008, pp. 90–91).

Networking across borders is also facilitated by international offender convergence settings. These are places where criminals from different countries come together and establish working relationships without preexisting ties. Miami has been dubbed a "perfect melting pot for gangsters" (Robinson, 2000, p. 214) as it attracts criminals from Latin America, North America, and Europe. Amsterdam has been identified as a similarly important meeting place in Europe, especially for drug traffickers (Caulkins et al., 2009, p. 68; Huisman et al., 2003; Junninen, 2006, p. 157; Ruggiero & Khan, 2006, p. 479; Ruggiero & Khan, 2007, p. 170; Zaitch, 2002, p. 106).

An illustrative example of a less prominent convergence setting, Puerto Vallarta in Mexico, is provided by Bruce Porter in his biography of legendary American drug smuggler George Jung (Porter, 1993). In the late 1960s, long before coming into contact with the Medellin Cartel, Jung distributed Mexican marijuana obtained from a local source in Southern California. At some point in time, he decided to buy the drugs for a better price directly in Mexico. Jung and two accomplices flew to Puerto Vallarta because it was rumored to be "the place to get marijuana in large quantities." Although they knew little Spanish, possessed no knowledge about Puerto Vallarta, and had no initial contact to start with, Jung and his accomplices eventually did succeed in finding a supplier. After three weeks of fruitless socializing, they were contacted by a local drug trafficker who had observed them for some time "and wanted to see if they could do business" (Porter, 1993, pp. 69–71).

A second crucial convergence setting for transnational criminals are prisons. It was in a U.S. penitentiary where George Jung met Carlos Lehder, an ally of Pablo Escobar. Subsequently Jung, through Lehder, advanced to become a key associate of the Medellin Cartel (Porter, 1993). Another illustrative example of the importance of prisons as incubators of transnational criminal networks is provided by the case of Ronald Miehling, who went from pimp and small-time criminal to one of Germany's major drug traffickers. Miehling met a cocaine dealer from the Dutch Antilles in a German prison who invited him to a Christmas party in Amsterdam. There, Miehling was introduced to a drug trafficker from New York City who eventually brought him in direct contact with cocaine suppliers in Colombia (Miehling & Timmerberg, 2004). The case of Miehling and similar examples show that, despite the barriers that political, legal, and cultural borders create, it is possible for some criminals to form viable transnational structures.

The case of Miehling is also instructive in that it shows the variety of constellations in which transnational criminal networks can develop, including "routine activities of everyday life," such as going to a party or going on a vacation (Decker & Townsend Chapman, 2008, p. 108). While certain patterns in the organization of transnational offenders exist, reflecting, for example, flows of migration and the direction of trafficking routes, the multiplicity of factors that are at work almost inevitably combine to form a diffuse patchwork of activities and actors.

TRANSNATIONAL CRIMINAL STRUCTURES

In previous chapters, particularly in Chapters 5 through 8, criminal structures have already been discussed at great length. Everything that has been said in general terms about the various types of illegal structures, how they emerge and how they are shaped, also applies to the transnational sphere. In this chapter, the focus is on how specifically the general patterns identified in Chapters 5 through 8 manifest themselves in a transnational context. The discussion follows the distinction of entrepreneurial structures, associational structures, and quasi-governmental structures.

Transnational Illegal Entrepreneurial Structures

Illegal entrepreneurial structures have been defined in Chapter 5 as criminal structures that are geared toward generating financial or other material benefits. This broad concept encompasses three ideal-typical forms: markets, (entrepreneurial) networks, and hierarchies (illegal firms).

Transnational Illegal Markets

Transnational illegal markets, just like illegal and legal markets in general, can be examined from two perspectives. One perspective is to see markets as an ideal-typical mode of organization distinct from networks and hierarchies (Chapter 5). Another perspective is to view markets as an institution that, through the free competition of numerous sellers and buyers, determines the price and production volume of a product. It is with regard to this second perspective that the transnational dimension deserves added attention.

In order for the market mechanism to function, potential buyers have to be aware of potential sellers and have to be able to opt for the best offer (Carroll, 1983, p. 331). This level of transparency, of course, is not a given under conditions of illegality because the flow of information is greatly restricted (Chapter 8). Transparency among potential sellers and buyers of illegal goods and services appears even less likely across borders and across language and cultural differences. The question is, accordingly, to what extent transnational illegal markets, in the sense of arenas for the exchange of illegal commodities, do exist at all. While frequently used terms like *global drug market* suggest that illegal markets do extend across international borders, little research has been done that would support this notion. One exception is a study by Claudia Costa Storti and Paul De Grauwe (2009) on international trends in cocaine and heroin prices. They explain the substantial decreases, 50% to 80%, in the retail prices for cocaine and heroin in the United States and Europe between 1990 and the mid-2000s with the reduced ability of wholesale and retail dealers to mark up their prices. Costa Storti and De Grauwe argue that this is to a large part the result of increased competition on a global scale, similar to price declines in legal consumer markets. This would suggest that there are indeed markets in the sense of price-setting institutions for cocaine and heroin on an international scale.

Transnational Entrepreneurial Networks and Transnational Illegal Firms

Determining the transnational nature of illegal markets is relatively straightforward. It can be observed by looking at the exchange of illegal goods and services across borders and by establishing the degree to which prices follow uniform trends.

The transnational nature of other, more integrated structures is at least as much a conceptual question as an empirical question. What exactly makes a group of criminals who cooperate in the commission of crimes transnational? The question pertains to illegal entrepreneurial networks as well as to delineable organizational entities in the form of illegal firms (Chapter 6). Six possible scenarios can be distinguished:

- *Travelling criminal group.* A criminal group that is continuously moving from one country of operation to another without a home base. The members of the group have no permanent residency in any country.
- *Cross-border mobile criminal group.* A criminal group is based in one country and operates in another country. Members of the group cross borders for the commission of crimes.
- *Migrating criminal group.* A criminal group is migrating from one country to another. The members of the group permanently relocate to the new country.
- *Multinational criminal group.* A criminal group based in one country establishes bases in other countries. Some of its members permanently relocate to the other countries, or new members are recruited there.
- *Transnational merger or joint venture.* A criminal group from one country enters into a collaborative relationship with a criminal group from another country.
- *Emergent transnational criminal group.* Individuals from different countries come together to cooperate in the commission of crimes on a permanent basis, thereby forming a new (transnational) criminal structure.

Some of these scenarios appear to be more common than others.

Travelling Criminal Groups. Criminal groups consisting of members with no permanent residence who travel from place to place and from one country to another appear to be primarily a phenomenon of historical significance. Bands of travelling criminals are a prominent theme in crime reports in Europe in the 15th through 19th century (Danker, 1988; Radbruch & Gwinner, 1991).

Cross-Border Mobile Criminal Groups. Criminal groups that operate across borders from a home-base country are more typical in the present day. They are commonly engaged in predatory crimes. One example is the so-called Koszalin gang (also known as "Hammer gang" and "Rolex gang"), named after a town in Northwestern Poland. The gang comprised about 200 members and existed over a time span of about 10 years until it was dismantled in 2004. It engaged in robberies of jewelry stores in Western European countries, using either stolen cars to gain entry into stores by brute force or entering stores during business hours to then, within minutes, smash show cases with sledgehammers and remove high-value merchandise, such as luxury watches. Gang members were typically recruited for the execution of these crimes from among unemployed men in their mid-20s to mid-30s. They operated in teams under the direction of group leaders who cooperated with residents in the target areas and reported to the gang leadership in Koszalin (Rieger, 2006).

Migrating Criminal Groups and Multinational Criminal Groups. It is difficult to find examples of migrating illegal enterprises that have moved entirely from one country to another. More common are entrepreneurial criminal structures that expand across borders by establishing branches in other countries without giving up their original home base. In its simplest form, all it takes is one group member who has a permanent presence in another country. In other cases, elaborate structures exist in two or more countries. One example, the Cali Cartel, has already been mentioned in Chapter 6 and in Chapter 11. The Cali Cartel had operatives stationed in several source and transit countries and in the United States as the main destination country for cocaine (Chepesiuk, 2005; Rempel, 2012).

Another example of a complex transnational criminal firm is a criminal organization that was involved in the trafficking in stolen motor vehicles between Western Europe and Lithuania in the early 2000s. The organization has been described by one of the German police investigators working on the case (von der Lage, 2003). The organization had its home base in Lithuania from where several subunits were directed that operated within Germany and other Western European countries. The subunits in Germany stole cars on order. The cars were later shipped to Lithuania in whole or in parts. Most members were Lithuanian citizens who, since 1999, no longer required a visa to travel to Germany. The Lithuanian members of the organization were in charge of stealing the cars and altering their appearance or taking them apart. For some technically sophisticated tasks, specialists were hired or "borrowed" from other organizations. The few German members of the organization fulfilled such tasks as registering vehicles, renting warehouses, or driving stolen cars to Lithuania. The operatives in Germany received fixed amounts of money for each car from headquarters in Lithuania. The funds were divided among members after covering costs. The subunits could also sell cars in Germany or in the Netherlands to cover their operating costs. The leadership in Lithuania exercised control over the subunits through a middleman. Members were promoted or demoted based on merit (von der Lage, 2003, p. 360).

Transnational Mergers and Joint Ventures. Illegal entrepreneurial structures that come into existence as the result of a merger of previously independent criminal groups have been mentioned in the literature, but concrete, well-documented examples are hard to come by (Williams, 2002, p. 69). What perhaps comes closest to this scenario is the kind of strategic partnership or joint venture that Colombian drug traffickers and Mexican criminal groups had formed in the 1980s and 1990s to smuggle cocaine into the United States. Some of the cocaine went to California for distribution by Mexican dealers, while the rest was distributed elsewhere in the United States by Colombian traffickers. In this case, the two sides combined complementary resources to mutual advantage, one side with access to cocaine and the other with expertise in smuggling drugs across the U.S. Mexico border (Williams, 1995, pp. 64–65).

More generally, illegal firms along transnational supply chains can be seen to cooperate on a regular basis. These patterns have variously been observed along trafficking routes, not only in the area of drug trafficking but also, for example, in the areas of human smuggling and the trafficking in stolen motor vehicles. The picture that emerges is that of small groups of criminals, each handling in sequence a small portion of the overall process of transnational crime (Bruinsma & Bernasco, 2004, p. 89; Icduygu & Toktas, 2002, p. 46; Kaizen & Nonneman, 2007, p. 127; Soudijn, 2006, pp. 87-89). Icduygu and Toktas give an example of a case of illegal migration:

> Illegal migrants are taken from city to city or from country to country via the "hand-to-hand" or "smuggler-to-smuggler" approach. The migrant who illegally crosses the border is handed over to another smuggler in the country of arrival and continues on his route. (2002, p. 46)

The illegal firms that directly cooperate with each other along the chain may establish close relationships, although generally the assumption seems to be that they "carry out their activities not as members of a large, central organization for illegal migration, but as independent pieces, which form only a small part of the larger chain" (Icduygu & Toktas, 2002, p. 47; see also Kaizen & Nonneman, 2007, p. 128).

Emergent Transnational Criminal Groups. Emergent transnational entrepreneurial structures may well be the most common of the five identified scenarios. They take shape in the continued cross-border interaction between criminals who exploit a particular crime opportunity.

The career of legendary Welsh smuggler Howard Marks ("Mr. Nice") provides several examples for emergent transnational structures in the illegal cannabis trade. His contacts to various individuals and groups in a number of different countries in Europe and Asia as well as in the United States led to the formation of several—though rather ephemeral—smuggling operations (Marks, 1998; see also Morselli, 2001).

Transnational Illegal Associational Structures

Associational criminal structures are a prominent reference point in the public debate on transnational organized crime. The international presence of members of organizations such as the Italian mafia associations, the post-Soviet Vory v Zakone, the Chinese triads, and the Japanese yakuza groups have served as a key facet in the narrative of a global spread of organized crime.

Apart from the cross-border mobility of individual members, a major concern is the spread of these associations as such. The major international outlaw motorcycle gangs provide clear evidence that such an expansion across borders has taken place. Outlaw motorcycle gangs like the Hell's Angels and Bandidos have official chapters in many parts of the world (see Chapter 7). It is not readily apparent, however, what this transnational presence implies.

Implications of the International Presence of Members of Criminal Associations

When individual members of criminal associations travel or relocate to another country, it may not mean much. Associational structures are primarily inwardly oriented. As has been pointed out in Chapter 7, their four main functions are to (a) create and reinforce social bonds between members, to (b) facilitate communication among members, to (c) promote mutual aid, and to (d) establish and enforce internal codes of conduct. For individual members who are geographically separated from other members, belonging to a criminal association may for all practical purposes be irrelevant. They may not be able to draw on the support of their brethren, and they may not be able to draw on the reputation and status that comes with membership in their country of origin. This is especially true, of course, for criminal associations that are secret societies. By nature, their members are not recognizable to outsiders, and a member of an organization such as the Sicilian Mafia, for instance, is not allowed to disclose his membership status to others (Chapter 7).

The presence of one individual member of a criminal association abroad will in all likelihood be primarily of importance for the other members. Their network of criminally exploitable ties is being expanded internationally, which, in turn, may create new opportunities for crime. For example, members abroad may assist in laundering illegal profits, give shelter to fugitives, or provide logistical support for the commission of crimes (Campana, 2011).

Cross-Border Expansion of Associational Criminal Structures

Beyond the cross-border mobility of individual members, criminal associations can expand internationally as structural entities in a variety of ways. One scenario is that several members relocate to another country and their number reaches a critical mass to form a satellite branch. Some examples are the new units of Italian mafia organizations, namely of the Cosa Nostra and 'Ndrangheta, that have sprung up within migrant communities in various European countries as well as in North and South America and Australia (Paoli, 2003a, p. 32; Sciarrone & Storti, 2014; Sergi, 2014). International expansion also occurs when an association recruits new members in another country or when associations of criminals from different countries merge. Examples for these two scenarios are provided by the international expansion strategies pursued by outlaw motorcycle gangs. Organizations like the Hell's Angels and Bandidos have established their international presence by creating new chapters or by "patching over" local outlaw motorcycle gangs. Patching over means that the members of an existing gang are collectively granted membership status in an international biker organization (Barker, 2007).

There is some variation in the degree of cohesion between the associational structures in the country of origin and in the countries into which an association expands. In one extreme, the members in the new country are merely an outpost with no authority of their own to accept new members (Sciarrone & Storti, 2014; Varese, 2011). In the other extreme, new associational structures come into being that keep few if any ties to the original association. In the case of the mafiosi who migrated to the United States in the early part of the 20th century and became involved in the formation of the American Cosa Nostra, effectively a new, autonomous organization was created. By the 1930s, membership in the Sicilian Mafia no longer constituted a sufficient qualification for membership in its American counterpart (Critchley, 2009, p. 70). Another example is provided by Chinese triad members who migrated to the United States and created new triad-inspired organizations in the form of so-called tongs. While belonging to one triad subculture, these uniquely American associations were independent from any Chinese triad (Chin, 1990; McIllwain, 2004).

Transnational Quasi-Governmental Structures

The international expansion of organizations, such as the Italian mafia associations, has not only raised concern because of their sinister, secretive nature as criminal fraternities but also because they might be able to establish the same kind of territorial control in other countries and, indeed, on an international scale that they have exercised in their country of origin. In this respect, mafia organizations are not addressed as associational structures but as quasi-governmental structures. The controversial question is to what extent these structures, which historically are local and at best national in nature, can replicate their position of power in a transnational context.

Mafia Transplantation

Fears that Italian mafia-type organizations, such as the Sicilian Mafia, the Neapolitan Camorra, and the Calabrian 'Ndrangheta, or Russian Criminal groups, such as the Moscow-based Solntsevskaya (see Chapter 7), might colonize other countries have been a recurring theme for decades (see von Lampe, 2013). These fears are fueled by the historical precedent of the American Cosa Nostra. While not a transplantation in the narrow sense of the word, because the American Cosa Nostra is not simply an offspring of the Sicilian Mafia, the case of the American Cosa Nostra shows how migrating criminals with a background in illegal governance can replicate the kind of territorial control they had previously exercised in their country of origin (Critchley, 2009; Varese, 2011).

According to one view, quasi-governmental structures are unlikely to expand their territorial control across borders because of the specific sociopolitical context within which they have emerged (Gambetta, 1993, p. 251). According to another view, Federico Varese's property-right theory of mafia emergence, mafias are able to establish themselves in new territories provided two conditions coincide: (a) there is a demand for criminal protection as a result of the inability of the state to regulate newly emerging (legal or illegal) markets and (b) this demand for protection is not met by any domestic criminal organization (Varese, 2011). From the available evidence, it seems that the kind of mafia transplantation discussed by Varese is an exception and that quasi-governmental structures for the most part are unable to replicate themselves in other countries (Sciarrone & Storti, 2014).

One case study shedding light on this issue is an analysis of a Camorra clan that included some members who had relocated to Scotland and the Netherlands. Campana (2011) found that, while the clan provided illegal protection services at its home base in Italy in the form of, for example, protection against competitors and thieves, dispute settlement, and debt collection, there was no evidence that any such activities were carried out abroad.

In a related study, Varese (2011) investigated the presence of members and associates of the Solntsevskaya in Italy and Hungary. In the case of Italy, Varese found a picture similar to that described by Campana. Russian mafiosi residing in Italy aided members of Solntsevskaya in the laundering of money, but they made no attempt to establish any form of territorial control or to engage in any form of criminal protection in Italy (Varese, 2011, p. 81). In contrast, Varese argues that a successful transplantation of Solntsevskaya had taken place in Hungary in the 1990s, citing evidence that a group led by a Ukrainian-born businessman with "solid connections with the Solntsevskaya's leaders" extracted protection payments from criminals and owners of legitimate businesses (Varese, 2011, p. 92). From the evidence presented by Varese, however, it is not clear whether this can be attributed to Solntsevaskaya as an organizational entity or whether it is more appropriately interpreted as the work of individuals and groups operating within the context of Hungary's transition economy. In the latter case, the example of criminals from the former Soviet Union operating in Hungary would better fit a more general pattern of multiethnic underworlds that appear to be characteristic of most if not all European countries. Criminals of particular ethnic and national backgrounds may achieve prominence in certain localities and certain illegal markets for certain periods of time independent from the migration or transplantation of criminal organizations.

Transnational Mafia Alliances

The notion of mafia transplantation (Varese, 2011) has to do with the replication of power structures on a local level. There is also concern that criminal organizations may expand their influence on a much grander, truly international scale. The scenario most often envisioned is that of a few powerful criminal organizations from different countries coming together to divide the world into exclusive spheres of interest, reminiscent of the power play of nation-states.

Famously, U.S. journalist Claire Sterling claimed that "a planetwide criminal consortium" consisting of "the Sicilian and American mafia, the Turkish arms-drugs mafia, the Russian mafia, the Chinese Triads, and the Japanese Yakuza" had declared a "pax mafiosa—an agreement to avoid conflict, devise common strategy, and work the planet peaceably together" (Sterling, 1994, pp. 14, 22–23). While Sterling did not go so far as to claim that representatives from all of these countries had actually come together at the same place at the same time (Sterling, 1994, p. 36), there are reports of meetings that have brought together criminals from different parts of the world. In early 1990, members of the Sicilian Mafia, the Camorra, the 'Ndrangheta, and criminals from Russia, Poland, and Colombia are said to have convened on the outskirts of Vienna, Austria, "to get to know another and to explore the feasibility of strategic alliances" (Robinson, 2000, p. 11). A meeting "on a yacht off Monte Carlo in July 1993" is said to have brought together Colombian, Russian, and Italian criminals with "Chinese Triad members, American La Cosa Nostra (LCN), and Israeli criminals" (Lupsha, 1996, p. 25). In November 1994, representatives of the New Yorker Gambino family of Cosa Nostra, of the Sun Yee On triad from Hong Kong, of Japanese yakuza groups, and of drug trafficking organizations from Medellin reportedly met in Beaune, France, to define territories for specific illegal activities and to accept Russian criminals into "the club" (Williams, 2002, p. 77; see also Robinson, 2000, p. 171). According to other sources, "the first known summit of Eastern and Western mafias" was held in Warsaw in March 1991 followed by a meeting in Prague in October 1992 and possibly another meeting in 1993 in Moscow (Freemantle, 1996, p. 50) or in Berlin (Jamieson, 2001, p. 381).

The vague and contradictory nature of the accounts about these alleged "mafia summits" does not necessarily mean that such meetings have not taken place. What is doubtful, however, is that any authoritative agreements could have been reached. As Williams (2002, p. 77) argues, "the participants are very unlikely to have the authority to speak for all Russian, Chinese, or even Italian organized crime." Robinson (2000, p. 170) seems to agree. If criminals should draw up a map of spheres of influence, he notes, "as soon as it's drawn, the map will be obsolete."

THE CYBERIZATION OF ORGANIZED CRIME AND THE ORGANIZATION OF CYBERCRIME

Any discussion of transnational crime would be incomplete without a discussion of cybercrime. The global networking of computers and other electronic devices has led to new ways in which cross-border crime is carried out and in which transnational criminal structures are formed and shaped. This does not mean that cybercrime is always and inevitably transnational in nature. Many cyber-criminal endeavors are confined to a national or even local context. Still, there is a unique quality in which borders are transcended by crime within cyberspace that requires particular attention. Cybercrime also needs to be considered in a more general sense in a discussion of organized crime. There is a debate on whether there is a trend toward a "cyberization" of organized crime and an increasing "organization" of cybercrime. These issues will also be briefly addressed in this section.

The Concept of Cybercrime

Cybercrime is a term that is about as vague and contested as the concept of organized crime. It refers to criminal activities in connection with information technology infrastructures, namely, the Internet (Finklea & Theohary, 2013, p. 6).

Cybercrimes encompass diverse types of criminal behavior, namely, attacks on the integrity and availability of information technology that in turn may be used for various predatory crimes, such as fraud, forgery, theft, and extortion. Cyberspace is also a market place for all kinds of illegal commodities, such as drugs or pirated videos (see Broadhurst et al., 2013, p. 8; Finklea & Theohary, 2013, p. 15).

A differentiation is commonly made between offenses *enabled* by information technology and offences *enhanced* by information technology (Choo, 2008, p. 283). This distinction pertains, on the one hand, to cybercrimes that are specific to cyberspace, such as the theft of electronic currency, and on the other hand, traditional crimes that are merely facilitated by the use of modern information technology, such as the distribution of child pornography over the Internet (Broadhurst et al., 2013, p. 25; Finklea & Theohary, 2013, p. 1).

A distinction is also often made with respect to role technology plays in the commission of crime. In some instances, information technology is the *target* of crime, while in others information technology is the *means* by which crimes are committed (Broadhurst et al., 2013, p. 8; Choo, 2008, p. 283; Finklea & Theohary, 2013, p. 3; McGuire, 2012, p. 12).

Finally, there is variation in the degree to which a crime involves online and offline activity. In one extreme, the entire crime takes place in cyberspace—for example, when hackers obtain passwords to online games and steal virtual valuables, such as gold, weapons, and armor that they then resell through online auction sites (McGuire, 2012, p. 31). In the other extreme, information technology is incidentally used in furtherance of criminal events in the real world (Broadhurst et al., 2013, p. 8). For example, illegal goods such as drugs may be marketed through the Internet and through the so-called Dark Net, a part of the Internet based on encryption that enables communication and web browsing without revealing the identity and physical location of the users (Martin, 2014a; Martin, 2014b; Phelps & Watt, 2014).

The Organization of Cybercriminals

Cyberspace is believed to be attractive for criminals because of the perceived anonymity and the borderless nature of the Internet, enabling them to exploit crime opportunities across great geographical distances in relative safety from law-enforcement intervention (Finklea & Theohary, 2013, p. 1).

Whereas originally cybercrime was believed to be the domain of technically highly skilled offenders, more recently a "deskilling process" (McGuire, 2012, p. 21) has been observed. Tools have become available that enable criminals with little to no IT skills to commit cybercrimes (Samani & Paget, 2013).

Classifications of Criminal Structures in Cyberspace

Cybercrime is not necessarily organized in the sense that it involves the collaboration of several offenders. In fact, research drawing on law-enforcement data tends to show a majority of cases involving individual, independently acting criminals; although there is some doubt that these data provide an accurate picture of the actual situation (Broadhurst et al., 2013, p. 19; Lu, Jen, Chang, Weiping, & Chou, 2006, p. 3; see also Hutchings, 2014).

While cybercrime can be the work of lone offenders, criminal structures do a role in cyberspace. Just like cybercrime as an activity, criminal structures involved in cybercrime vary by the degree to which they are rooted and present in cyberspace. Some criminal structures are centered on activities and interactions in cyberspace—for example, criminal groups exclusively engaged in online fraud, such as the sale of nonexistent goods. For other criminal structures, the use of cyberspace is only rather marginal—for example, when Mexican criminal gangs like Los Zetas post video messages on the Internet (Corcoran, 2013, p. 322).

McGuire (2012, pp. 21–23) distinguishes three basic types of criminal groups with a presence in cyberspace:

- Type I groups that operate essentially online
- Type II groups that combine online and offline offending
- Type III groups that operate mainly offline but use online technology to facilitate their offline activities

There are also differences in the way cyberspace is used. Some criminal structures use information technology in furtherance of criminal endeavors; others use information technology, namely, digital encryption, for the purpose of internal communication.

Finally, an important distinction has to be made between criminal structures that originate in real life versus those criminal structures that emerge in cyberspace, involving individuals who may never have met face-to-face in the real world. There has been some debate about the extent to which existing criminal organizations have moved into cybercrime and to what extent criminal structures in cyberspace resemble criminal structures in the real world. Much of this debate is highly speculative and suffers from conceptual confusion (McCusker, 2006). A main problem is that the crucial analytical distinction between entrepreneurial, associational, and quasi-governmental structures is seldom made.

Entrepreneurial Criminal Structures in Cyberspace

Entrepreneurial criminal structures are patterns of relationships centered on obtaining financial or other material benefits either through market-based crime or through predatory crime (Chapter 6). In cyberspace just as in the real world, entrepreneurial criminal structures can exist in the form of markets, networks, or organizations (illegal firms).

Illegal firms active in cyberspace, from what is known, tend to exist in the form of individual entrepreneurs, partnerships, and small groups, with a low degree of vertical and horizontal integration (Holt, 2013, p. 156). Insofar, there do not seem to be any fundamental differences to the nature of illegal enterprises in the real world—for example, in the areas of drug trafficking or human trafficking (Chapter 6).

Image 12.8   In this sketch, a courtroom deputy reads the jury's verdict against Ross William Ulbricht, far left, on February 4, 2015, in New York. Ulbricht was convicted on charges he created the multimillion-dollar Silk Road marketplace for illegal drugs and other contraband on the Internet by adopting the alias Dread Pirate Roberts and promising buyers and sellers anonymity through use of encryption and bitcoins.

Photo: ASSOCIATED PRESS/Elizabeth Williams

What appears to be the main difference between cyberspace and the real world with respect to the organization of crime is how these individual criminals and criminal groups are connected. In the real world, individuals and smaller organizational units tend to be embedded in larger networks of criminally exploitable ties, where interacting criminals are linked to each other by underlying bonds of trust. In cyberspace, not networks but markets appear to be the predominant coordinating mechanism. This is true in particular in the core area of cybercrime where vulnerabilities of the information technology infrastructure are exploited for profit (Holt, 2013; Holt & Lampke, 2010;

Samani & Paget, 2013). Instead of cooperating with trusted accomplices in the commission of crime, highly specialized criminals offer their products or services essentially to anyone willing to pay the requested price. A common mode of payment is through the peer-to-peer currency Bitcoin (Phelps & Watt, 2014, p. 236). Items on sale online include all the separate components that make up complex cybercriminal endeavors—for example, stolen credit card data and malware, such as viruses and trojans. Certain products can also be rented, for example, botnets (networks of infected, remotely controlled computers) for the purpose of distributing phishing mails (Broadhurst et al., 2013, p. 41). Services offered online also include the so-called "bulletproof" hosting of illegal websites or the withdrawal of funds from compromised bank accounts (Holt, 2013; Samani & Paget, 2013).

The prototypical criminal endeavor in cyberspace involves independently operating criminals who perform interlocking tasks but who are coordinated by no other mechanism than one-off Internet-based exchanges between buyers and sellers of goods or services. For example, a programmer may sell malware that is used to create botnets. One of the botnets set up with the purchased malware, in turn, may be rented out to someone sending phishing mails that direct victims to fraudulent websites hosted by a complicit bulletproof hosting provider. The websites may entice victims to disclose their online banking information. This information is then sold individually or in bulk to buyers, who may draw on the services of yet others to withdraw and transfer funds from the compromised bank accounts. Cybercrime that at first glance looks like the work of a well-functioning complex criminal organization of global expansion is in all likelihood the outcome of the interplay of numerous criminals linked through contractual relations and with no mutual commitment beyond specific transactions (Holt, 2013, p. 156).

Trust only plays a role from the perspective of buyers who are at risk of paying for goods and services they never receive or that are of inferior quality. This risk is minimized by the ability of buyers to publically share their experiences, either through online postings or through online rating systems, and by the use of escrow services. In contrast, sellers of illegal goods and services in cyberspace seem to have little concern for the trustworthiness of their customers, given that they can wait with the delivery of the product until the customer has paid (Martin, 2014a).

What enables the effective coordinated interaction of numerous cybercriminals, even on a global scale, are online forums that function as offender convergence settings (Soudijn & Zegers, 2012; Chapter 5). Online forums are websites where individuals can post messages to advertise goods and services and to exchange information and opinions (Holt & Lampke, 2010, p. 35). Negotiations between seller and buyer and actual transactions, for example, of stolen credit card data, typically take place via private messaging systems (Holt, 2013, p. 156).

Some forums require users to first create a user account with username and password. This does not restrict access, but it makes the forum more difficult for the general public to identify, because search engines cannot log or index the content. Some forums are accessible by invitation only so that the general public is effectively excluded (Holt, 2013, p. 159).

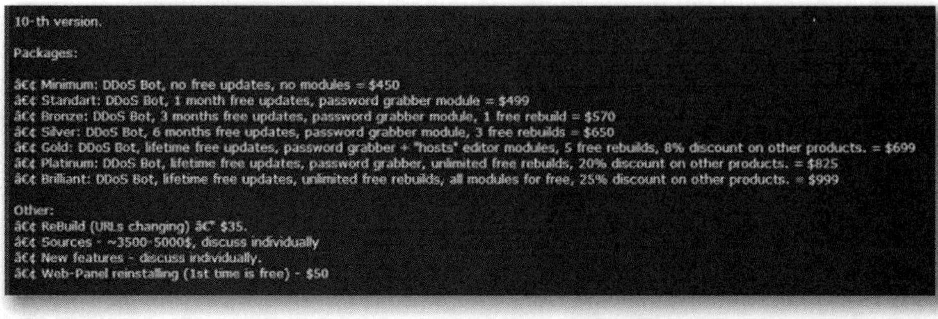

```
10-th version.

Packages:

•  Minimum: DDoS Bot, no free updates, no modules = $450
•  Standart: DDoS Bot, 1 month free updates, password grabber module = $499
•  Bronze: DDoS Bot, 3 months free updates, password grabber module, 1 free rebuild = $570
•  Silver: DDoS Bot, 6 months free updates, password grabber module, 3 free rebuilds = $650
•  Gold: DDoS Bot, lifetime free updates, password grabber + "hosts" editor modules, 5 free rebuilds, 8% discount on other products. = $699
•  Platinum: DDoS Bot, lifetime free updates, password grabber, unlimited free rebuilds, 20% discount on other products. = $825
•  Brilliant: DDoS Bot, lifetime free updates, unlimited free rebuilds, all modules for free, 25% discount on other products. = $999

Other:
•  ReBuild (URLs changing) – $35.
•  Sources - ~3500-5000$, discuss individually
•  New features - discuss individually.
•  Web-Panel reinstalling (1st time is free) - $50
```

Image 12.9 An online offer for various botnet services documented in Samani and Paget (2013, p. 11). The authors note that this example "illustrates the cost of renting a botnet and the flexible options available . . . to suit any budget."

Photo: Samani & Paget

Associational Criminal Structures in Cyberspace

Online forums serve economic functions as marketplaces for the exchange of illegal goods and services. But they also serve important noneconomic, social functions. Online forums are a key mechanism by which associational criminal structures develop in cyberspace.

As pointed out in Chapter 7, associational criminal structures facilitate contacts between criminals; they give status, reinforce deviant values, and provide an arena for the exchange of criminally relevant information. In online discussions, feedback posts and forum-based rating systems, users of online forums collectively establish and reinforce subcultural norms and values that define how cybercriminals generally or in specific areas of crime should behave (Holt et al., 2010, p. 4). For example, in forums for the exchange of stolen banking data, emphasis is placed on such things as timely delivery and quick response to customer complaints (Holt & Lampke, 2010, p. 44).

Online forums also lead to a differentiation in the status of individual cybercriminals. Their reputation and standing is influenced by the feedback they receive on past transactions or, for example, by the number of posts they have created in a forum (Holt, 2013, p. 166). Invitation-only forums resemble clearly delineable criminal associations through formal membership. They may also be selective in the recruitment of new members. Insofar, they show similarities to criminal associations such as the Sicilian Mafia. However, while Mafiosi engage in a broad range of criminal activities, online forums tend to confine their membership to offenders specializing in a narrow area of crime. The website Dark Market, for example, through which stolen bank account and credit card information was sold, had more than 2,500 members who had to prove their ability to provide usable credit card information and had to go through a nomination and vetting process (Broadhurst et al., 2013, p. 40). In the case of the Wonderland site for the distribution of child pornography, prospective members had to be willing and able to share at least 10,000 images, they had to be sponsored by an existing member, and they had to be vetted by a membership committee (Broadhurst et al., 2013, p. 39).

Quasi-Governmental Structures in Cyberspace

Among criminals in the physical world, there is a tendency for quasi-governmental structures to emerge. A criminal group such as a Cosa Nostra family establishes itself as an underworld government and sets and enforces rules, which creates some sense of order. In cyberspace there are also some forms of self-regulation and governance among criminals. However, an important element is missing in cyberspace. Underworld governments in the real world rely to some extent on the threat and use of violence (Chapter 8). This is an option cybercriminals simply do not have, because in most cases they do not know the true identity and physical whereabouts of other cyber-criminals (Lusthaus, 2013).

Illegal governance in cyberspace is confined to online forums, more specifically the regulation of activities within a particular forum. The governance function is performed by individuals called administrators or moderators who have the power to change and remove content and to ban users from a forum. Forum administrators may regulate market transactions as well as the communication between forum users (Holt, 2013; Holt & Lampke, 2010).

Market regulation can extend to a number of different aspects of illegal online trading within a forum, namely the following three:

- Market entry
- Range of products
- Modes of transaction

Administrators can make decisions on who may sell or buy goods and services in a given forum. This is obvious in invitation-only forums, but administrators can also remove users from open forums and forums that are open to registered users. A typical scenario is the ban of sellers who "rip off" customers (Holt, 2013, p. 156). Forum administrators may also regulate the types of goods and services that can be offered in a forum. The administrators of the Dark Market website, for example, did not tolerate any activity relating to drugs and child pornography (Broadhurst et al., 2013, p. 40). Finally, the way products are advertised and sold may be regulated by forum administrators. In one forum, for example, sellers had to post complete lists of their goods and prices, and vendors were not allowed to use intermediaries (Holt, 2013, p. 165). Administrators may also guarantee transactions and provide escrow services to prevent fraud among users, or they may offer dispute resolution services (Broadhurst et al., 2013, p. 40; Lusthaus, 2013, p. 55). Interestingly, the governance function appears to be performed by less than a handful of administrators per forum (Holt, 2013). The Dark Market website with its some 2,500 users was reportedly run by a maximum of four administrators at any time (Broadhurst et al., 2013, p. 40).

Entry of Traditional Organized Crime Groups Into Cyberspace

According to a frequently made claim, there is a trend toward an increasing use of cyberspace by conventional criminal groups (see Broadhurst et al., 2013, p. 19). From what is known, however, it seems that the realms of organized crime in the real world and of crime in cyberspace are largely two separate spheres. It also seems that the cyberization of real-world organized crime is limited and lags behind the cyberization of society at large. This should not come as a surprise, given the fundamental differences between offline and online environments in terms of human interaction and the importance of physical violence.

There also appears to be a general reluctance on the part of conventional criminals to embrace new technological developments that hold the potential for more extensive and more effective police surveillance, such as smartphones and the Internet (McGuire, 2012, p. 37). Otherwise there would have to be more convincing examples of conventional criminal groups involved in cybercrime than the few that have appeared in the pertinent literature. One case described by Leukfeldt (2014) in some detail involves a group engaged in phishing attacks against customers of two Dutch banks. The group members came from the same immigrant neighborhood in Amsterdam, all had prior criminal records, and according to police sources, they also "were likely to be acquainted within the criminal underworld of Amsterdam" (Leukfeldt, 2014, p. 236). However, it is not clear if these individuals moved into phishing as a group or only formed a group in the process of committing cybercrimes.

There are also reports of conventional criminal groups extorting gambling and pornography websites by the threat of denial-of-service attacks (Choo, 2008, p. 275), and there are reports of members of the American Cosa Nostra using offshore gambling websites as logistical components of illegal gambling operations within the United States (Broadhurst et al., 2013, p. 26; McGuire, 2012, p. 57). A widely repeated claim, originally made in 2006, that criminal organizations have recruited IT specialists, has not been corroborated in more recent research (McGuire, 2012, p. 20). The only such case that has been publicized is that of a young computer programmer who, in 2010, was allegedly coerced to work for Mexican drug traffickers (McGuire, 2012, p. 57).

TRANSNATIONAL ORGANIZED CRIME AND ORGANIZED CYBERCRIME: SUMMARY AND CONCLUSION

This chapter has examined the international ramifications of organized crime in the sense of criminal activities, criminal structures, and illegal governance that transcend international borders. Transnational criminal activities are shaped by the opportunities and constraints that are constituted by international borders, by differences between countries, and by the special links that connect certain countries. Borders themselves can create opportunities for transnational crime in that the need for cross-border law enforcement cooperation may hamper criminal investigations. At the same time, borders continue to constitute a significant obstacle for transnational crime. Globalization notwithstanding, there seems to be a tendency to reinforce borders to make them less penetrable for illegal migrants, terrorists, and transnational criminals. It is problematic, therefore, to speak of an increasingly "borderless world."

Cross-national differences, "criminogenic asymmetries" (Passas, 1998), create opportunities and incentives for transnational crime. For example, differences in the legality or the price of commodities can fuel smuggling, and socioeconomic differences may be at the root of such phenomena as cross-border predatory crimes, human smuggling, and human trafficking. Differences in the intensity of law enforcement between strong states and weak states can also account for variations in the prevalence of transnational crime. At the same time, cultural and language differences between countries can limit the ability of criminals to exploit transnational crime opportunities.

Much depends on the cross-border mobility and cross-border networking of criminals that can be enhanced by three types of links between countries: geographical proximity, social proximity, and the legal flow of goods and persons. Geographical proximity means that criminals have to cover only short distances, namely, between neighboring countries, to exploit transnational opportunities for crime. Social proximity exists where great geographical distances are bridged by close social ties that criminals can use to their advantage. Transnational crime is also facilitated where it can be embedded in established routes of legal trade and tourist travel. All of these factors need to be considered in the analysis of the diverse patterns of transnational criminal activities.

The criminals who exploit transnational crime opportunities may act individually or as part of transnational criminal structures. There are many ways in which a criminal structure can be transnational. The stereotypical imagery is that of criminal organizations that operate transnationally or expand across borders by establishing branches in other countries. Some examples of these kinds of transnational illegal firms have been highlighted, namely, the Cali Cartel and the so-called Koszalin gang. In the grand picture of transnational crime, however, these integrated structures seem to be exceptions to the rule of smaller, less integrated enterprises. More typical appear to be locally based individuals and small groups that cooperate with each other across international borders within broader transnational networks of criminally exploitable ties.

Associational criminal structures can play a role in providing a basis of trust between transnationally operating criminals. Italian mafia organizations, Chinese triads, and outlaw motorcycle gangs are examples of criminals associations with members and even entire organizational units based in different countries. However, it seems safe to assume that these criminal fraternities account for only a relatively small share of the transnational networking of criminals. Social network ties that stretch across borders as a consequence of migration or relations established in the context of international tourism and trade are in all likelihood far more important for the formation of criminally exploitable ties on an international scale than all criminal associations combined.

Similarly, there are only very few cases of a transnational expansion of quasi-governmental structures. And international alliances between powerful criminal organizations appear to have been short-lived, if they have ever existed to begin with.

Overall, transnational organized crime seems to be driven far more by the transnational mobility and networking of individual criminals and small groups than by criminal organizations that purposefully expand their areas of operation and spheres of influence.

The Internet and other transnational IT infrastructures have created a new sphere for the commission of cross-border crimes and the formation of criminal structures across borders. Cyberspace has become the arena for a broad range of criminal activities, some of which are merely digital versions of conventional crimes, such as 419 frauds; others exploit opportunities specific to cyberspace. These cybercrimes in the narrow sense of the word can be complex, involving numerous interlocking schemes. In contrast, the degree of organization of cybercriminals appears to be rather low. Independently operating criminals and small criminal groups that specialize, respectively, in the supply of a particular tool or service contribute to complex criminal schemes without belonging to overarching criminal organizations. Instead, the participants interact as partners of market-based transactions with online forums serving as virtual market places. Illegal online markets enable a broad range of criminals to commit cybercrimes, even if they do not have sophisticated technical skills. This is a potential entry gate for conventional criminals who may lack technical skills and may also be adverse to the use of technology that may well increase the capacity of the police to detect and monitor criminal conduct. Conventional criminals as customers of cybercriminals appear to be the most likely scenario for a cyberization of organized crime. In contrast, the violent skills of conventional criminals have no value in a cyber environment.

Illegal power structures in cyberspace follow a different logic. They are technology based and confined to the regulation and policing of individual forums by the respective forum administrators. While in the international sphere and in cyberspace, criminals address the same functional needs as criminals on a local or national level, the resulting structures (entrepreneurial, associational, and quasi-governmental structures) take on specific forms and differ in their relative importance. Entrepreneurial structures that center on profit-making criminal activities are the most pervasive form of criminal organization. Associational criminal structures extend from the local to the international level and take on unique forms in cyberspace with the emergence of online subcultures and communities of cybercriminals.

Quasi-governmental structures are largely local in nature, with little impact on transnational crime. In cyberspace, illegal governance exists confined to individual online forums, exercised by small numbers of forum administrators.

Overall, it is important to recognize the similarities as well as the differences between the various spheres within which the organization of crimes and criminals takes place: local settings, nation-states, the international arena, the real world, and cyberspace; each context has its own dynamics and contingencies in shaping the incentives and opportunities for criminals to engage in illegal activities, to form criminal structures, and to exercise illegal governance.

Discussion Questions

1. What is the primary motive for organized criminals to cross international borders?

2. Assuming that organized criminals move into cyberspace, what is their primary motive for doing so?

3. What is the lesser evil: crime being dominated by domestic criminals or by transnational criminals?

4. What is the worst-case scenario for the future development of transnational organized crime?

Research Projects

1. Analyze the autobiography of an organized criminal with a view to international ramifications.

2. Find media reports of a case of transnational organized crime and find out what kind of cross-border movement has taken place (persons, goods, information)?

Further Reading

Albanese, J., & Reichel, P. (Eds.). (2014). *Transnational organized crime: An overview from six continents*. Thousand Oaks, CA: Sage.

Allum, F., & Gilmour, S. (Eds.). (2012). *Routledge handbook of transnational organized crime*. London, UK: Routledge.

Andreas, P. (2013). *Smuggler nation: How illicit trade made America*. New York: Oxford University Press.

Arsovska, J. (2015). *Decoding Albanian organized crime: Culture, politics, and globalization*. Oakland: University of California Press.

Beare, M. (Ed.). (2003). *Critical reflections on transnational organized crime, money laundering and corruption*. Toronto, Ontario, Canada: University of Toronto Press.

Coho, K.-K. R., & Grabosky, P. (2014). Cybercrime. In L. Paoli (Ed.), *The Oxford handbook of organized crime* (pp. 482–499). Oxford, UK: Oxford University Press.

Karras, A. L. (2010). *Smuggling: Contraband and corruption in world history*. Lanham, MD: Rowman & Littlefield.

Miklaucic, M., & Brewer, J. (Eds.). (2013). *Convergence: Illicit networks and national security in the age of globalization*. Washington, DC: National Defense University Press.

Nordstrom, C. (2007). *Global outlaws: Crime, money and power in the contemporary world*. Berkeley: University of California Press.

Wright, G. (2011). Conceptualising and combating transnational environmental crime. *Trends in Organized Crime, 14*(4), 332–346.

NOTE

Parts of this chapter have been adopted from the following publications: Klaus von Lampe (2011c). Re-conceptualizing transnational organized crime: Offenders as problem solvers. *International Journal of Security and Terrorism, 2*(1), 1–23; Klaus von Lampe (2012a). The practice of transnational organized crime. In F. Allum & S. Gilmour (Eds.), *Routledge handbook of transnational organized crime* (pp. 186–200). London, UK: Routledge; Klaus von Lampe (2014). Transnational organized crime in Europe. In J. Albanese & P. Reichel (Eds.), *Transnational organized crime: An overview from six continents* (pp. 75–92). Thousand Oaks, CA: Sage.

PART IV

The Big Picture
and the Arsenal
of Countermeasures

INTRODUCTION TO PART IV

The previous four chapters have dealt with the broader context and the international ramifications of organized crime. In this last part of the book, the subject of organized crime will be addressed comprehensively. Chapter 13 integrates the various facets of the organized crime problem into an overall comprehensive framework and explores to what extent these facets are indeed interconnected. Chapter 14 provides a systematic overview of the countermeasures that have been devised to respond to the phenomena that are variously labelled organized crime.

CHAPTER 13

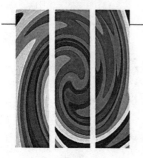

The Big Picture of Organized Crime

INTRODUCTION

The purpose of this chapter is twofold. First the various elements of the elusive concept of organized crime that have been separately addressed in the previous chapters will be brought together into one big picture, although this big picture inevitably has to remain vague, fragmentary, and somewhat contradictory. Second, a few details will be added to aspects that have received only scant attention so far, namely, individual characteristics of organized criminals.

What is the big picture of organized crime? This book rests on the notion that organized crime is not a clearly delineable, coherent phenomenon. While the phenomena that are variously labeled organized crime are quite real, some exaggerations, mystifications, and distortions notwithstanding, organized crime *as such* is not something that is tangible, nothing that could be observed or measured. Organized crime is a construct, an umbrella term for various facets of the reality of crime. Painting the big picture of organized crime, therefore, does not mean a summary description in the form of a situation report that enumerates certain crimes, criminal groups, and the like. The big picture of organized crime has to be analytical rather than descriptive and abstract rather than concrete. Painting the big picture of organized crime along these lines means demarcating in general terms the range of the kinds of phenomena that fall under the umbrella term of organized crime, highlighting their variations and pondering to what extent they are inherently connected.

THE RANGE OF PHENOMENA THAT FALL UNDER THE UMBRELLA CONCEPT OF ORGANIZED CRIME

The different conceptions of organized crime, as has been emphasized throughout this book are, for the most part, centered on three basic dimensions: the organization of crime, the organization of criminals, and the exercise of illegal governance. When organized crime is conceptualized as crime that is organized,

336

then organized crime falls somewhere on a continuum between simple, spontaneous, impulsive crimes on one side and complex, continuous, well-planned criminal operations on the other. When organized crime is equated with the organization of criminals, then organized crime is located somewhere on a continuum from lone, socially isolated offenders to large, complex criminal organizations. When organized crime, finally, is equated with illegal governance, then organized crime is positioned somewhere on a continuum between a situation where criminals and criminal groups are anarchically going about committing crimes in pursuit of their own interests and a situation where the conduct of criminals in a given territory is regulated, with rules being set and enforced by a criminal organization that functions as an underworld government.

There are other dimensions along which conceptions of organized crime vary, namely, with respect to the social embeddedness of organized crime and with respect to the nexus between illegal and legal structures. The social embeddedness of organized crime is sometimes seen as a matter of criminal groups rooted in marginalized subcultures or based in foreign countries, and sometimes organized crime is seen as an integral facet of the social fabric and encompassing all layers of society. Viewed as a matter of the nexus between legal and illegal spheres, organized crime manifests itself on a continuum from a situation where criminals stay below the radar of law enforcement and invest all efforts into avoiding public attention to a situation where criminals have entered into alliances with political, business, and social elites, where criminal organizations replace legitimate government, or where government itself functions as a criminal organization.

Another dimension of the concept of organized crime that may well be of crucial importance but has received only little attention in this book and in the academic literature in general is the individual organized criminal (Aniskiewicz, 2012; von Lampe, 2006c). Approaches aiming at explaining organized crime by the structure of criminal organizations, be they networks or organizations in the narrow sense of the word, tend to underestimate the importance of individual skills and characteristics for the creation and shaping of criminal structures. To paraphrase a popular motto (see Coles, 2001), it may not be who you are but who you know that counts in organized crime; but who you know may depend to a considerable degree on who you are and what social skills you have. It is who you are that may decide whether or not you get to know the people you need to know to be a successful, networked criminal (von Lampe, 2008c, p. 23; see also Morselli & Tremblay, 2004; Robins, 2009). In the absence of systematic research on the individual characteristics of organized criminals, conceptions of organized crime currently tend to vary along a continuum from "ordinary" offenders that do not stand out in any way from mainstream society to stereotypical gangsters that are ruthless, violence-prone individuals from the marginalized segments of society.

Narrow Conceptions of Organized Crime

A lot of energy has been devoted to debating which dimensions (activity, structure, governance, illegal-legal nexus, individual) are defining features of organized crime and where exactly the line has to be drawn between organized crime and non-organized crime. This "endless scholarly debate about the essence of organized crime," Petrus van Duyne has noted, "resembles the hairsplitting of learned monks, disputing the pure idea of 'horseness,' 'greenness,' or 'virtue'" (van Duyne, 2003, p. 24).

Focus on Partial Aspects

Some have argued that attention should be focused on one particular aspect— for example, on the entrepreneurial activities of criminals as part of an overall "criminal trade" (Van Duyne, 2003, p. 43) or on illegal governance—the supply of protection (Varese, 2011). The advantage of narrowing down the scope of analysis in such a way is that a clear and coherent conceptual framework can be applied to precisely definable phenomena. At the same time, however, other aspects that have raised concerns under the rubric of organized crime would have to be neglected. For example, viewing organized crime solely through the lens of illegal governance means that most criminal activities with their dynamics and logistics, including such high profile crimes as drug trafficking and human trafficking, are effectively ignored. The exclusive focus on illegal governance also means that illegal associational structures receive attention only if they are also performing quasi-governmental functions.

Focus on Extreme Cases

Another way of narrowing down the scope of the concept of organized crime has been to confine organized crime to extreme cases positioned at the far end of the continuum across all dimensions (see Figure 13.1a). According to this view, organized crime is synonymous with complex criminal organizations that employ violence and corruption and are three things at once: criminal enterprises engaged in a host of profit-making crimes; criminal associations with formal, restricted membership; and underworld governments (see Abadinsky, 2013; Cressey, 1969; Finckenauer, 2005; Hagan, 2006). This view is heavily fixated on specific historical cases that are deemed to be quintessential representations of organized crime, namely the American and Sicilian Mafia. There are two problems with this perspective, however. The first problem is that it rests on a somewhat oversimplified perception of mafia organizations. Characterizing them as simultaneously being illegal enterprises, criminal associations, and underworld governments makes sense only if the criminal endeavors of individual members are conflated with what mafia organizations as organizational entities do, given that mafia organizations typically are not criminal enterprises that carry out profit-making crimes. The only crime a mafia organization as such, with its hierarchical, formalized structure, is normally engaged in on a continuous basis is the illegal supply of protection (Gambetta, 1993).

The second problem with equating organized crime with extreme, more or less hypothetical cases of criminal organizations is that it rests on a static, one-dimensional conception of the pertinent phenomena. The implicit or explicit assumption is that there is little variation among cases of organized crime and that there is only one trajectory in the development from non-organized crime

Figure 13.1a   Narrow Conceptualizations of Organized Crime

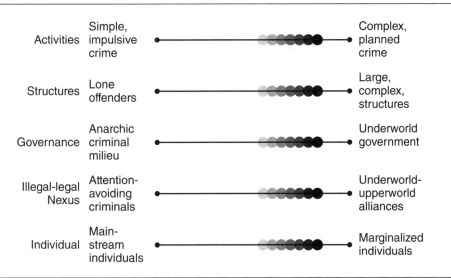

Conceptualizations of organized crime vary with respect to the dimensions
that are encompassed and with respect to where along these dimensions the
dividing line between organized crime and non-organized crime is drawn.
Narrow conceptions position organized crime at the extreme ends, especially
of the dimensions of activities, structures, governance, and illegal-legal nexus.

to organized crime with an organization like the American or Sicilian Mafia
constituting the natural endpoint in the process of the organization of crime and
criminals. This view neglects other constellations and developmental dynamics
without involvement of mafia-like organizations, for example, cases where
illegal markets flourish without a formalized illegal governance structure and
without criminals being connected through membership in criminal fraternities
(see Figure 13.1b). There are several reasons why these latter constellations
should not be ignored in the study of organized crime. First, these constellations
without mafia involvement are often subsumed to organized crime, especially in
countries with no indigenous mafia problem. Second, these constellations that
do not fit the imagery of stereotypical criminal organizations may well pose
similar or even more substantial threats to society than, for example, the Sicilian
Mafia. Third and most importantly, narrowing down attention to particular
historical cases not only means that other phenomena are arbitrarily excluded
from the big picture of organized crime, but it also means that efforts to better
understand how and why crimes and criminals are organized are severely hampered.

The Analytical Approach to Conceptualizing Organized Crime

Progress in the social sciences relies a lot on the comparison of cases that vary
across key dimensions. Limiting observation to a few extreme cases that are
highly similar would be counterproductive. Instead it is much more fruitful from

Figure 13.1b   Constellations Not Captured by Narrow Conceptions of Organized Crime

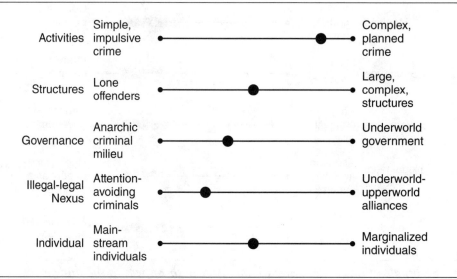

Narrow conceptions of organized crime as depicted in Figure 13.1a do not capture numerous constellations that according to other, broader conceptions fall squarely within the scope of organized crime. Figure 13.1b depicts a constellation that can be considered typical for the situation in Western Europe where complex criminal endeavors are carried out by individuals, partnerships, and small groups in shifting alliances within larger networks of criminally exploitable ties and little influence on legitimate government (von Lampe, 2008c).

an analytical perspective to place the emphasis on the fluidity and diversity of the constellations in which the various attributes commonly ascribed to organized crime manifest themselves and to see what patterns exist (see Figure 13.1c). For example, it is important to know under what circumstances the coordination of criminals occurs in a market setting between autonomous actors, as in the case of some cybercrime, in a network setting, which seems to be the normal case in most areas of crime, or within integrated criminal organizations, such as in the cases of the Larry Lavin enterprise or the Cali Cartel. Translated to the five dimensions mentioned above, the task is to examine, for example, what positions along the continuum from lone offender to criminal organization correspond to what kinds of activities, illegal governance, illegal-legal nexus, and individuals. The underlying rationale is the assumption that there is not one evolutionary path for organized crime but different evolutionary paths depending on the circumstances. Each path could be thought of as the best adaptation to a particular setting defined by crime opportunities, available resources for exploiting these opportunities, such as individual skills of offenders, and restraints, such as the direction and intensity of law enforcement pressure (Ekblom, 2003; Smith, 1994; Southerland & Potter, 1993). The diversity of phenomena and scenarios that are addressed in the debate on organized crime and that have been reviewed in this book may, in fact, not be so much a matter

Figure 13.1c Focus on the Interdependencies of Factors

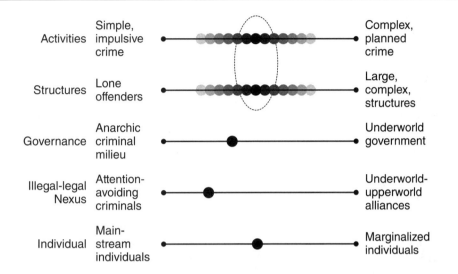

A broader conceptual frame of reference shifts the focus from the question, is it organized crime? to the question, what patterns in the organization of crime and criminals exist and what interdependencies and causal relations (e.g., between the nature of a crime and the nature of the criminal structures committing the crime) account for the emergence and the change of these patterns?

of conceptual ambiguity and confusion but a reflection of the various directions the organization of crimes and criminals can take.

In order to capture these complexities, it is necessary to first go back to the basic dimensions of organized crime and to recapitulate for each dimension the range and variations of phenomena that may come into play and to highlight from different vantage points the interdependencies that appear to exist.

Variations in the Organization of Crime and Their Influence on Other Aspects of Organized Crime

For those who equate organized crime with crime that is organized, criminal activities are part of the big picture to the extent they are organized as opposed to disorganized. Criminal activities are organized to different degrees. They vary in terms of duration, complexity, and rationality. Some crimes are impulsive, on-the-spot acts that are committed in the heat of passion. Some crimes are likewise one-off endeavors, but they are the result of careful planning, falling into the category of project crimes (McIntosh, 1975), such as the 2003 Antwerp Diamond Heist that after years of preparation netted an estimated 100 to 400 million Euros worth of diamonds, jewelry, and gold (Selby & Campbell, 2010). Other criminal activities, such as illegal gambling, drug trafficking, or serial burglary, are carried out on a continuous basis. Some continuous criminal activities are simple in nature, others more sophisticated, well planned, and combining different tasks with different skill requirements, similar to one-off project crimes.

When one defines organized crime in terms of the organization of crime, it is difficult to fit all types of criminal activities into the big picture of organized crime, because some crimes simply are not organized by any measure. When, however, organized crime is linked to the organization of criminals, even the most impulsive spur-of-the moment crimes have their place in the big picture of organized crime, provided they are committed by members of criminal organizations. And this is not an uncommon occurrence. Criminal associations such as the American Cosa Nostra, Sicilian Mafia, Chinese triads, or Japanese yakuza groups, through their selective recruitment practices, may tend to attract the more level-headed, sober-minded criminals, and their rules and procedures for nonviolent conflict resolution may reduce the likelihood of spontaneous outbreaks of violence. Yet, the big picture would be incomplete without all the disorganized violent and nonviolent, serious and petty crimes committed by the members of these criminal organizations (see, e.g., Pistone, 1989).

Direct Links Between the Nature of Criminal Activities and the Nature of Criminal Structures. From an analytical perspective, it is important to consider the full range of criminal activities and to include all variations of criminal activities because they may matter in the complex interplay of crimes, criminals, criminal structures, and society. For example, there are at least three direct links discernible between the nature of criminal activities and the emergence and nature of criminal structures. There is the apparent correlation between the scale of a criminal activity—for example, the volume of contraband in a smuggling scheme—and the size and diversity of co-offending structures. Simply put, the more there is to do, the more co-offenders are involved; and the larger the number of co-offenders, the less likely it is that they can all be recruited from the same homogeneous, close-knit pool of people.

There are also indications that with the increasing complexity of a criminal activity, the likelihood increases that this activity will be carried out by complex offender structures, characterized by a division of labor between different criminals with different skills and by some coordination mechanism such as a centralized chain of command (Cornish & Clarke, 2002, p. 54). In a classical numbers lottery operation, for example, there is a hierarchy of authority and a division of labor between those collecting the bets, which primarily requires social skills, those processing the bets and computing the payouts, which primarily requires book-keeping skills, and those financing the operation and bearing overall responsibility, which requires entrepreneurial resources including capital.

The third salient link between the nature of criminal activities and the nature of offender structures exists with respect to the degree of interdependence between different steps in a crime script. The different phases in the production of cocaine, for example, are largely independent from each other. How coca is cultivated has little impact on the way the coca leaves are processed, and the method chosen for producing coca paste (acid extraction or solvent extraction technique) has no influence on the way coca paste is turned into cocaine base and, in turn, cocaine base is turned into cocaine hydrochloride. Accordingly, the process of producing cocaine does not require the coordination of tasks within an all-encompassing vertically integrated firm. Each intermediate product, from coca leaves to coca base, can be produced by independent actors and put on the market for sale to anyone specializing in the respective next step in the production process. In contrast, in the case of stolen motor vehicles, the phases in the typical crime script are *inter*dependent to a relatively high degree. The type of car that is stolen and the method of stealing influence what kind of techniques and what kind of resources are needed to alter the identity of the car. For example, if the car is stolen by breaking a window and destroying the steering-wheel lock, then these parts have to be replaced with parts that fit the particular make and model of the stolen car. Likewise, the choice of car that is stolen is influenced by consumer preferences. This means that overall efficiency can be increased when the phases of theft, alteration of identity, and marketing of a car are all coordinated by one vertically integrated firm specializing in certain makes and models. The case described in Chapter 12 of the complex transnational criminal organization involved in the trafficking of stolen motor vehicles between Western Europe and Lithuania (von der Lage, 2003) is one example for such an integrated illegal enterprise.

Indirect Links Between the Nature of Criminal Activities and the Nature of Criminal Structures. There are also some indirect channels through which the nature of criminal activities influences the organization of criminals. One mediating factor is the intensity of law enforcement. For a variety of reasons, the risk of apprehension, conviction, and the confiscation of assets is believed to work against the formation of enduring, complex structures. For example, the risk of betrayal increases with every additional co-offender (Reuter, 1983). At the same time, law enforcement pressure may work in the opposite direction, enticing criminals to improve security by increasing the size and complexity of criminal structures. For example, criminals may try to insulate themselves from arrest by hiring staff to carry out the most exposed and risky tasks, or criminals may hire staff to serve as look-outs, or an illegal enterprise may duplicate its structures so that the arrest of some participants would not disrupt operations overall.

Under what circumstances law enforcement pressure leads to small, simply structured offender groups and under what circumstances it leads to large, complex structures is an open research question. It could be a matter, for example, of the criminal activities in question, a matter of organizational talent and management styles, or a matter of the availability of trusted accomplices (see, e.g., Morselli, Giguere, & Petit, 2007). Irrespective of these considerations about how law enforcement pressure shapes the organization of criminals, it seems fairly safe to say that the nature of criminal activities can have an influence on the intensity of law enforcement. As a rule of thumb, the greater the perceived harm and the lower the public tolerance for a particular kind of crime—for example, child prostitution compared to the illegal sale of marijuana—the greater the intensity of law enforcement. This means that as the nature of an illegal activity influences the intensity of law enforcement, it also indirectly influences how criminals involved in this activity organize themselves (Southerland & Potter, 1993, p. 260).

A similar interconnectedness has also been suggested to exist between the nature of criminal activities and the emergence of illegal governance. Certain crimes, namely, those that are committed openly and continuously at fixed locations, such

Image 13.1   Street vendors of illegal cigarettes in Berlin, Germany, shown in a January 1995 photo, were forced to make regular protection payments to extortion gangs. The high visibility and regularity of the selling activity made it easy for extortionists to control the retail end of the cigarette black market (von Lampe, 2002b).

Photo: ASSOCIATED PRESS/Paulus Ponizak

as certain forms of illegal gambling or prostitution, are more prone to extortion and regulation than criminal activities that are more difficult to monitor (Schelling, 1971). In turn, under the protection of an underworld government, illegal enterprises may be able to develop more elaborate and stable organizational structures than illegal enterprises that are under constant threat from law enforcement, predatory criminals, or competing illegal enterprises.

The direct and indirect links between the nature of criminal activities and the nature of offender structures is most obvious with respect to illegal entrepreneurial structures. But somewhat the same also applies to associational and to quasi-governmental structures. All three types of criminal structures (entrepreneurial, associational, and quasi governmental) can vary greatly, from small groups with no formalization and role differentiation to complex organizations. Yet, associational and quasi-governmental structures are much more likely than entrepreneurial structures to develop a hierarchy of authority with a clear line of command. Clearly defined leadership structures facilitate the coordination and monitoring of large numbers of participants. This can be beneficial for an illegal business as well as for a fraternal association of criminals or an underworld government. However, a hierarchical structure of an illegal business means that there is frequent and continuous communication between management and staff. This greatly increases the risk of the communication being detected and intercepted by law enforcement. In the case of associational and quasi-governmental structures, there is little need for communication on a daily basis, except perhaps in times of crisis, so that over-all the risk of detection and interception is much lower compared to illegal entre-preneurial structures.

Variations in the Organization of Criminals and the Interplay With Other Aspects of Organized Crime

When one considers the many ways in which the nature of criminal activities influences the nature of offender structures, it appears as if the organization of criminals is solely determined by the kinds of illegal activities the respective criminals are involved in. While this is a compelling assumption, cause-and-effect relations may also exist in the opposite direction: If and how criminal activities are carried out may depend on the existence and nature of offender structures.

Main Kinds of Organizational Structures Among Criminals. The kinds of orga-nizational structures that have to be considered in the big picture of organized crime are manifold. There is, first of all, the network of criminally exploitable ties that determines to what extent an individual criminal can draw on other crimi-nals. Secondly, there are the structures that emerge from networks of criminally exploitable ties: entrepreneurial structures, associational structures, and quasi-governmental structures. These criminal structures vary in size and complexity and the level of integration. Some structures consist of atomized, autonomous offenders that interact in one-off exchanges. The main example for structures with a low level of integration is a pure-market setting for the exchange of illegal goods and services, but noneconomic (associational and quasi-governmental) structures may also show a low level of integration. For example, one can think of a criminal subculture where members share a sense of belonging and adhere to certain norms that are enforced on an ad hoc basis by whoever becomes aware of a transgression, without any overarching quasi-governmental organization.

Networks are arguably the most common organizing scheme among criminals. Networks connect offenders who act autonomously but have longer-term commitments to each other, which give patterns of relations some degree of permanency. Apart from pure networks there are criminal organizations in the narrow sense of the word that integrate offenders so that their actions are coordinated under the direction of a common management. If and how criminals are organized depends in part on the logistical requirements of their criminal activities, but at the same time, criminal structures also influence the nature and prevalence of criminal activities. Many if not most crimes can be committed by lone offenders, and in some respects it may be safer to act autonomously rather than in collusion with others. However, in many instances it is the interaction with other criminals that makes a criminal endeavor possible, more efficient, or less risky.

How Criminal Structures May Influence Criminal Activities. Criminal activities can be thought of as the result of motivated offenders finding and exploiting opportunities for crime (Cohen & Felson, 1979). In every respect, the interaction between criminals can play a role. To begin with, the motivation to commit crimes can be fostered and reinforced by other criminals. For example, associational structures, by giving criminals a sense of belonging in the company of other criminals and by advocating a criminal ideology and a criminal lifestyle, will make it more likely that an individual opts for committing a crime.

Membership in a criminal association may also entail the obligation to commit a crime. A typical scenario is that of a mafioso who is ordered to kill another mafioso for cooperating with the police. Interaction between criminals will also make it more likely that opportunities for crime become known to motivated offenders. This may in one extreme be a matter of underworld gossip that makes the rounds in criminal circles, and in the other extreme, it may be a matter of a criminal group systematically scouting crime settings and crime targets.

In the actual commission of a crime, including the safeguarding and the use of the proceeds of crime, success and failure may depend on the pooling of resources, namely, manpower, skills, knowhow, tools, and capital. It is important to reemphasize, however, that the benefits that individual criminals can derive from the interaction with other criminals are not necessarily dependent on the existence of integrated criminal structures. The dark web forums where large numbers of cybercriminals connect and coordinate their activities in a market setting is a case in point. Another example are the individual organized criminals who skillfully navigate the underworld and activate their criminally exploitable ties in varying combinations as needs and opportunities arise (Rebscher & Vahlenkamp, 1988). It is those individualistic organized criminals, as Block (1983, p. 256) notes, that may be the most efficient ones. The focus on delineable organizational entities, be they illegal firms, criminal associations, or criminal organizations that exercise illegal governance, are therefore somewhat misleading.

Variations in Illegal Governance and Interdependencies With Other Aspects of Organized Crime

The fixation on formal organizations also obfuscates the reality of illegal governance. The phenomenon of illegal governance can be approached from two directions. On one hand, there is the need of criminals for protection and predictability in an environment that is unregulated by legitimate government, and there are the various informal practices and mechanisms that help criminals to cope with the uncertainties of a life of crime. On the other hand, there are the criminals who for various reasons have the resources to exercise power over other criminals and who use this power in the pursuit of their own or of common interests.

To understand the variations in illegal governance, it is important to understand both aspects, the need for order and the ability to establish order, and it is important to understand how they play out under different circumstances. Establishing and maintaining order, historically speaking, is not dependent on an institution holding a monopoly of violence. Pre-state societies have been able to regulate themselves through norms and belief systems and collective responses to wrongdoing (Michalowski, 1985). In a similar way, criminal milieus tend to have some kind of order. There are norms, such as the rule of not cooperating with authorities and the rule not to cheat other criminals, which are widely accepted as binding. Even though these rules may be broken on occasion, they still appear to have a restraining effect on the individual behavior of criminals. There are also mechanisms through which underworld rules are enforced, even in the absence of an underworld government. The mere "reaction of disapproval" (Weber, 1968, p. 34) by other criminals resulting in a loss of status within the underworld, may be a sufficient deterrent. There is no incentive, for example, in being called a "rat," a "snitch," or a "grasser." Underworld norms may also provide for punishment meted out by individuals or by ad hoc tribunals that assume quasi-governmental powers in a transient fashion. Violent retribution, for example, may be an accepted response against a wrongdoer (he had it coming) who in turn is not allowed to seek revenge. Otherwise there would be the risk of an uncontrollable escalation of violence.

Informal status hierarchies that evolve within criminal milieus just as in other social contexts predispose certain individuals to carry out quasi-governmental functions, namely, those individuals that hold the highest social prestige (Rebscher & Vahlenkamp, 1988, p. 46). Even the role of members of mafia organizations can be viewed in this light (Albini, 1971; Hess, 1996). Individual mafiosi rather than the mafia organization as such, it seems, are typically sought out as arbiter and protector, even though, of course, their reputation as mafiosi may add significantly to their status (Gambetta, 1993). In turn, the ability of mafia organizations to direct and coordinate these individual mafiosi appears to be limited. In his analysis of the Cosa Nostra in New York, for example, Peter Reuter found little evidence that the provision of protection was managed by the five Cosa Nostra families beyond making sure that only members provided protection and that these members did not compete against each other (Reuter, 1983).

Only within a limited geographical area is it likely to see a criminal organization—for example, an individual Mafia family—effectively coordinating and managing its members to function as a cohesive underworld government. Viewed in this light, mafia organizations can be found toward one extreme in a broad range of structural patterns that serve the regulation and self-governance of criminals. But there is illegal governance even in the absence of mafia organizations when one understands illegal governance in a broad sense, in terms of practices and mechanisms that create order in criminal milieus.

When one approaches the phenomenon of illegal governance from the perspective of emerging or existing criminal groups that exercise power over other criminals, the most salient variations are in the range of activities that are controlled and in the degree to which genuine quasi-governmental services are provided as opposed to mere extortion. In its ideal-typical form, illegal governance encompasses all illegal activities and all illegal-market levels in a given territory and provides protection against other criminals and, through corruption, against law enforcement. Normally, however, illegal governance is confined to just a few crimes and to the lower levels of illegal markets.

These variations in the nature and extent of illegal governance likely have a profound influence on the organization of crime and criminals. The more effective and comprehensive illegal governance is exercised, the lower the risk of conflict and disruption that criminals face. It becomes easier to carry out illegal activities on a continuous basis and to form durable, efficient organizational structures. This is first of all a direct result of the predictability and security that illegal governance provides. But there is also an indirect influence. To the extent illegal governance entails the systematic reduction of violence and other criminal behavior that is likely to draw media and police attention, the risk of law enforcement intervention is reduced, irrespective of whether or not corruption is at play.

Variations in the Illegal-Legal Nexus and Interdependencies With Other Aspects of Organized Crime

The nature of criminal activities, criminal structures, and illegal governance as well as the various interdependencies between them are themselves influenced by the broader social context. To begin with, the basic parameters of crime are set by the reach of the criminal law. Put in simple terms, the more prohibitions there are the more crimes there are to commit. In a country that criminalizes gambling, drugs, and prostitution, all else being equal, criminals have more options to engage in crime than in a country where these activities are decriminalized or outright legal. Apart from this fundamental link, there are three main paths of influence between the legal and illegal spheres of society that have to do with law enforcement, crime opportunities, and motivations to engage in crime.

Important variations exist with respect to the enforcement of the law. Generally speaking, law enforcement sets a major constraint for the organization of crime and criminals, but the intensity and direction of law enforcement can vary greatly for a number of reasons. The presence or absence of corruption is the most commonly addressed factor. But variations in law enforcement exist also with respect to the resources available to law enforcement agencies and the priorities set by the political level or the police leadership. What relevance these differences have can be observed where radical shifts in anticrime policies take place. For example, in Italy in 1982 sweeping legislation that, among other things, outlawed membership in mafia-type organizations led to a substantial weakening of the Sicilian Mafia when hundreds of mafiosi were convicted in the so-called maxi-trials (Chapter 11). Variations in the nature of law enforcement also exist with respect to the legitimacy of the police and the criminal justice system. Poor police performance, abuse of power, systemic corruption, and a general weakness of the rule of law undermine community support for the authorities, even where honest efforts are made to curb crime (Van Dijk, 2007).

The second major path of influence between the legal spheres of society and organized crime, apart from the enforcement of the law, pertains to crime opportunities. Opportunities for market-based crimes are linked to the demand for illegal goods and services. Opportunities for predatory crimes emerge from the vulnerabilities of potential victims. And opportunities for illegal governance emerge in areas that legitimate government is unwilling or unable to effectively regulate. All of these opportunities are highly variable across social settings—for example, when one compares affluent and stable Scandinavian welfare states, authoritarian and corruption-prone post-Soviet regimes in Eurasia, and weak states in Africa.

The same variability can be observed in the presence or absence of motivated offenders willing and able to exploit these opportunities, the third major path of influence between legal and illegal spheres of society. It is not a given that there is a criminal for every crime opportunity and that for every crime opportunity that requires the cooperation of several criminals, offenders with the necessary resources come together. There are variations in the number of motivated offenders willing to engage in organized crimes and to join criminal organizations, and there are variations in the skillfulness and sophistication of these offenders. These variations can have a number of different reasons. The spread of extortion and criminal protection in post-Soviet societies in the 1990s, for example, has been explained in part by the restructuring of the government apparatus after the fall of Communism. As a result of the scaling-down of the security services, the military, and state-sponsored athletics, especially martial arts, large numbers of men skilled in the efficient use of violence found themselves on the street with hardly any options for legal employment (Tzvetkova, 2008; Volkov, 2002). Another example, showing the opposite effect, is the demise of the American Cosa Nostra, which has been ascribed in part to recruitment problems. Young Italian-Americans, it is said, now have much better legitimate career opportunities than in the 1940s and 1950s when discrimination against Italians was common (Paoli, 2003a, p. 11; Reuter, 1995, p. 96; see also Raab, 2005, p. 424).

Variations in Individual Offender Characteristics and Interdependencies With Other Aspects of Organized Crime

The skillfulness and sophistication of recruits of criminal associations is one of the recurring themes in the debate on organized crime that pertain to the individual characteristics of organized criminals. Individual capabilities are commonly addressed as crime-specific prerequisites that limit the pool of potential offenders for certain crimes (Cornish & Clarke, 2002, p. 55). Other individual characteristics are mentioned that are believed to set organized criminals apart from ordinary criminals or leading underworld figures apart from lower-ranking organized criminals. For example, it has been suggested that organized criminals, or at least leading organized criminals, stand out because of a higher intelligence and a lower impulsiveness compared to other criminals (Bovenkerk, 2000; Gilbert, 2007, p. 418; Kelland, 1987, p. 356; Lichtenwald, 2004). There is no coherent debate and no systematic research on these aspects, however. The only individual-level variables that have received some attention with respect to organized criminals are age and gender.

The Age-Range of Organized Criminals. It is commonly assumed that involvement in conventional crime is concentrated in late adolescence and early adulthood, while involvement in organized crime tends to be a life-long commitment (Kleemans & de Poot, 2008). Some differentiations have to be made, however, between the involvement in organized criminal activities on the one hand and the involvement in criminal organizations, namely mafia-type associations, on the other.

The onset of organized crime commission can be very early in life. Apart from the phenomenon that juveniles show higher rates of co-offending than older criminals (Van Mastrigt & Farrington, 2009), even children can be part of criminal firms in the narrow sense of the word. Namely, children are recruited into pick-pocketing and serial burglary gangs where their size but also their relative immunity from punishment is exploited. Of course, in these cases, the children are not only perpetrators but also victims. In other areas of crime, namely, transnational crimes and especially in smuggling operations, a late onset of criminal careers and a predominance of older offenders have been observed. This can be explained in part by logistical needs, such as access to the international transportation, trading, and banking infrastructures that only individuals established in legitimate careers tend to have who then become involved in criminal activities (Desroches, 2005; Kleemans & de Poot, 2008; Van Dijk, 2007; Van Koppen, de Poot, Kleemans & Nieuwbeerta, 2009).

Criminal associations, be they mafia-type organizations or outlaw motorcycle gangs, tend to be restricted to adults, and in most cases membership tends to be for life. However, the option of retirement from an association does exist in some cases—for example, retirement from yakuza organizations and leaving an outlaw motorcycle gang "in good standing" (Hill, 2003; Barker, 2007)—a notion that is completely alien to organizations such as the Sicilian Mafia (Paoli, 2003a). Accordingly, members in criminal associations tend to have a rather high average age and older members tend to occupy the leadership positions. Anderson, for example, noted in her study of the Philadelphia Cosa Nostra, that half of the members were over 60 years of age (Anderson, 1979, p. 3).

Organized Criminals and Gender. The common perception of organized crime is that it is largely a men's world. Conventional wisdom is summed up in the following quote from a book on international crime published in 1955:

> In the International Underworld, women's role is quiet and unobtrusive. There are exceptions, of course. Hot, noisy, emotional exceptions. But in the main, without over-straining some attempt at generalisation, it may be said that women lack not simply sufficient physical powers to wage crime on a grand scale, but a sufficient taste for dramatic action to hanker after this indulgence. (Forrest, 1955, p. 192)

The secondary role ascribed to women pertains in the first instance to criminal associations that commonly do not accept women as members. There are only a few exceptions to this rule, including some Chinese triads (Chapter 7) and (historically) some Yakuza groups (Otomo, 2007, p. 211) who reportedly have given full membership status to women. Even without formal membership status, however, some women have played an active role in criminal associations, typically as aides to husbands and male relatives—for example, in a capacity as messengers. In some cases, women have even (informally) attained leading roles, typically to take the place of husbands and male relatives in case of death or arrest (Siegel, 2014, p. 60).

The involvement of women in criminal *enterprises* is much more prominent than in criminal *associations*, and the history of crime knows quite a few prominent females in areas such as human trafficking, illegal gambling, trafficking in stolen goods, and drug trafficking (Carey, 2014; O'Kane, 1992). Still, female offenders remain underrepresented in illegal entrepreneurial structures and are

Image 13.2   Griselda Blanco (1943–2012), the "Queen of Cocaine," was a leading figure in the cocaine business and known for her penchant for violence.

Photo: ASSOCIATED PRESS/REDACCIÓN MEDELLÍN

mostly found in subordinate positions. For example, among the 220 suspects charged between 1997 and 2004 with participation in a criminal organization engaged in a profit-making crime under the Canadian Criminal Code, only 4 (1.8%) were women (Beare, 2010, p. 32). An analysis of organized crime cases in the Netherlands found that in most cases (102 out of 150 or 68%) there was at least one female suspect. Yet overall, the number of female suspects was limited to 247 for a share of only 11 percent of the total of 2,295 suspects; and only in 8 out of the 150 selected cases did women occupy a leading role (Kleemans, Kruisbergen, & Kouwenberg, 2014, p. 21, 24).

The involvement of women in illegal enterprises appears to vary across countries and areas of crime. Particularly large shares of female offenders with women playing leading roles in illegal enterprises have been observed in the areas of human smuggling and human trafficking for sexual exploitation (UNODC, 2010, p. 47) and especially among Chinese and Nigerian criminal networks (Lo Iacono, 2014; Mancuso, 2014; Zhang, Chin, & Miller, 2007).

The debate on women and organized crime is centered on the various ways in which the status of women in society may impact on their absence or presence and their rank in criminal networks (Arsovska & Allum, 2014; Beare, 2010; Siegel, 2014; Van San, 2011). For example, the phenomenon of Nigerian "madams" who organize prostitution has been explained by the cultural acceptance of independent businesswomen in Nigeria (Arsovska & Begum, 2014).

Relatively little has been said in the academic literature about the consequences of female involvement in organized crime. The implication, however, seems to be that with larger shares of women in the underworld, the importance of violence and intimidation would decrease. For example, Zhang et al. (2007, p. 723) allude to "the construction of the basic masculine identity around interpersonal violence" and the concern to establish and protect turf as significant features of male-dominated areas of organized crime (see also Schoenmakers, Bremmers, & Kleemans, 2013, p. 329). There is no reason to believe, however, that female offenders are entirely adverse to violence. In a study of female drug traffickers in Melbourne, Australia, for example, Denton and O'Malley (1999) found that violence and intimidation were used on occasion when deemed necessary to stay in business. And then there is the case of infamous drug trafficker Griselda Blanco. She was at the helm of a network of men and women who distributed cocaine for the Medellin Cartel in Miami and New York in the 1970s and early 1980s. Reportedly Blanco relied heavily on the use of violence to achieve and maintain her status in the underworld and is said to have contributed directly to more than two hundred murders (Carey, 2014, pp. 177–193).

MODELING ORGANIZED CRIME

The many interdependencies that appear to exist between the various facets of organized crime beg the question if it is possible to capture them within one comprehensive model. Ideally, one would want to simulate how the interdependencies between the nature of criminal activities, criminal structures, illegal governance, and other factors play out under different conditions.

Given the fragmentary nature of current knowledge about these interdependencies, however, such a simulation model is firmly out of reach. What appears feasible is to use a model as a heuristic device to clarify what kinds of tentative insights the study of organized crime has produced and where further research is needed.

Descriptive Models of Organized Crime

Models are representations of reality, though on a lower level of complexity. They are sometimes treated as synonymous with theory, sometimes they are seen as necessary precursors to theories, and sometimes they are seen as tools to test and apply theories (Morrison & Morgan, 1999). In the organized crime literature, in contrast, the term *model* has been used more in the sense of perspectives or descriptive concepts.

The notion of models of organized crime has in the past been most closely linked to a threefold classification proposed by Jay Albanese (1989; 1994; 2011), who distinguishes a hierarchical model, a patron-client model, and an enterprise model. All three models originally referred to the American Cosa Nostra. The hierarchical model pertains to the official view that emerged during the 1950s and 1960s and framed organized crime, synonymous with Cosa Nostra, in terms of a nationwide bureaucratic organizational entity (Cressey, 1969). The patron-client model refers to the works of Joe Albini (1971) and Francis Ianni and Elizabeth Reuss-Ianni (1972), who reconceptualized the associations of Italian American criminals as webs of asymmetric ties (patron-client relationships) embedded in local or ethnic networks. The enterprise model, finally, is associated with Dwight C. Smith's (1975; Smith, 1980) spectrum-based theory of enterprise, which centers on economic activities and the primacy of market forces over group structures. As Jay Albanese himself has emphasized, these models really represent different ways of looking at organized crime, different paradigms in Albanese's wording, which he believes can fruitfully be combined to get a more complete picture (Albanese, 1994, 2011).

In a similar vein, Dickie and Wilson (1993) have distinguished two major theoretical models of organized crime: a mafia or evolution-centralist model and a social systems model. The mafia model is understood in roughly the same way as Albanese's hierarchical model, in that it refers to a view that associates organized crime with ethnically homogeneous bureaucratic criminal organizations. The social systems perspective, on the other hand, is similar to Albanese's patron-client model of criminal associations based on kinship ties or patron-client relationships (see also Abadinsky, 2013). Frank Hagan, finally, has integrated the various perspectives in his continuum or ordinal model of organized crime (Hagan, 1983, p. 54; see also Hagan, 2006). This model is designed to help determine how closely a criminal group and its activities resemble the ideal-typical imagery of a bureaucratic mafia organization.

Explanatory Models of Organized Crime

Some authors have gone beyond an understanding of models of organized crime as devices primarily for classifying manifestations of organized crime on the descriptive level. Boronia Halstead (1998), for example, has added an explanatory dimension to the notion of models of organized crime. She distinguishes different models not only by the underlying conception of the nature of organized crime but also by specific social conditions that are assumed to be responsible for the emergence of one or the other manifestation of organized crime. In one model, Halstead discusses how illegal enterprises can be perceived as organizations influenced by internal and external stakeholders that include offenders, customers of illegal goods and services, law enforcement, and policymakers (Halstead, 1998, p. 8).

Phil Williams and Roy Godson (2002) have taken the discussion yet another step further by linking certain social conditions with certain manifestations of organized crime and these, in turn, with certain social consequences or impacts. In their discussion of a methodology for anticipating "the further evolution of organized crime," they distinguish several potentially predictive models that emphasize causal relations between certain environmental conditions, certain manifestations of organized crime, and certain outcomes (Williams & Godson, 2002, p. 315; see also Morrison, 2002). Political models, according to Williams and Godson, can explain the increase in particular types of crime and the emergence of criminal structures as the result of a weak state, an authoritarian form of government, and a low degree of the institutionalization of the rule of law. Economic models include those approaches that attempt to predict organized criminal behavior with a view to the dynamics of supply and demand and the levels of control of illegal goods and services. Social models emphasize the cultural basis for organized crime, the idea of criminal networks as a social system, and the importance of trust and bonding mechanisms for the organization of criminals. The strategic or risk management model conceptualizes the activities of criminal enterprises, for example, the corruption of public officials or the exploitation of safe havens, as means to minimize the risks of operating in a hostile environment. Finally, Williams and Godson include hybrid or composite models that variously combine political, economic, social, and strategy factors to predict, for example, that in certain states characterized by weak government, economic dislocation, and social upheaval, transnational criminal organizations will take control of much of the domestic economy to use it as a basis for operating in host states where lucrative markets and supporting ethnic networks exist (Williams & Godson, 2002, pp. 315–347).

Comprehensive Analytical Models of Organized Crime

What the models identified by Albanese, Dickie and Wilson, Hagan, Halstead, and Williams and Godson have in common is a strong orientation toward concrete events and settings. The models are largely constructed with notorious manifestations of organized crime in mind that have emerged under specific historical circumstances. This limits their broader applicability. Even the composite models proposed by Williams and Godson (2002) still fall short of an overall framework designed to consistently capture, analyse, and compare phenomena across historical and cultural settings. The models arrange and link phenomena more or less as if the only possible constellations are those defined by specific historical cases.

In contrast, there are also attempts to design models that seek to capture how the phenomena that fall under the umbrella concept of organized crime manifest themselves in any conceivable constellation, regardless of whether or not these constellations resemble commonly known events or stereotypical imagery.

One such model has been proposed by Shona Morrison (2002, p. 2; see Figure 13.2), although it lacks detailed elaboration. It is essentially organized around the two dimensions of criminal structures (Groups) and criminal activities (Processes) and depicts how the social environment shapes criminal structures and criminal activities and how these structures and activities in turn impact on this environment.

Another model at a similar level of abstraction is shown in Figure 13.3. The model of the contextuality of organized crime (von Lampe, 2004a, p. 232) comprises four elements: criminal networks and their task environment as well as the social context and the institutional context. This model is based on the assumption that criminal networks face a particular task environment that offers specific opportunities for crime (Smith, 1978). These opportunities are shaped by the social environment, for example, by the demand for illegal goods and services and by the institutional context, namely, by the definition and enforcement of criminal law. Likewise, the model takes into account that criminal networks are shaped by the social and institutional environment. Socioeconomic conditions like unemployment and the discrimination of minorities influence the recruitment base of criminal networks, while law enforcement sets constraints

Figure 13.2   Shona Morrison's Representation of the Interrelated Aspects of
Organised Crime (2002)

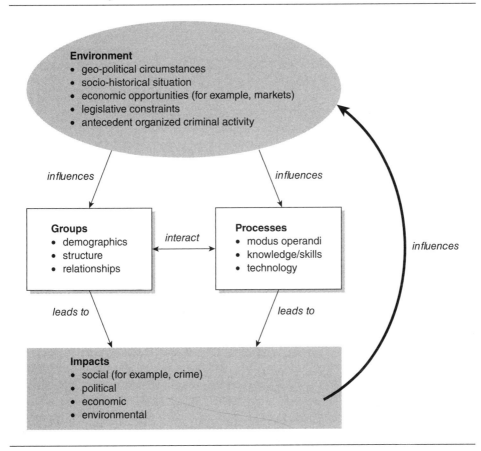

Source: Australian Institute of Criminology/Morrison (2002).

for the formation and operation of criminal networks. At the same time, criminal
networks are understood to influence their environment. They not only inflict
social harm through the crimes they commit but they may also interfere with the
functioning of social institutions, namely, government but also business and
media. Another important feature of the model is that it highlights the relation
between the social and institutional context. The degree of legitimacy of social
institutions, for example, has an impact on the relationship between criminal
networks and their social environment: The more unpopular prohibitions of
goods and services are, the greater the support for criminal groups that provide
these goods and services; and the weaker the government, the greater the support
for criminal groups that establish order through illegal governance.

Although the model consists of only four elements and conflates criminal
structures, criminal activities, and illegal governance into one element (Criminal
Networks), numerous facets of the debate on organized crime can be highlighted

Figure 13.3   Model of the Contextuality of Organized Crime

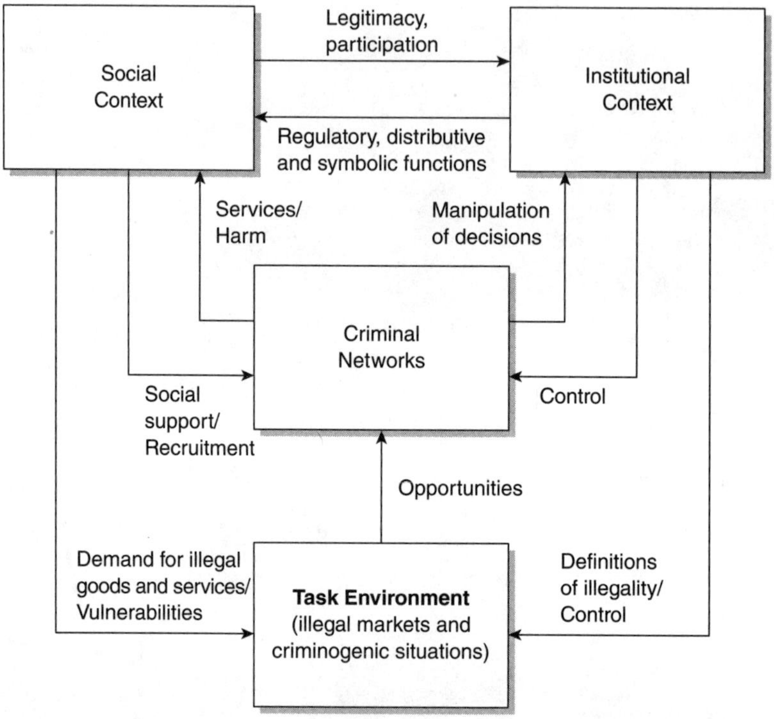

Source: Revised version of the model presented in von Lampe (2004a, p. 232).

and captured in a systematic way. At the same time, the limits of modeling organized crime are obvious. Many details are inevitably lost because of the small number of model elements that can be meaningfully displayed in a two-dimensional graph. But even if a more detailed graphical representation were feasible, efforts to construct a more refined model would soon hit a wall. Current knowledge is simply too fragmented to understand the complex interplay of the phenomena that fall under the umbrella concept of organized crime (von Lampe, 1999; von Lampe, 2011d). It is not possible to predict with any degree of certainty, for example, how a change in criminal law such as the prohibition of cigarettes would affect the structure of illegal enterprises or the extent of corruption. While the modeling of such dynamics does not seem feasible, what can be done is to see how the dynamics of organized crime play out and manifest themselves in certain constellations.

TYPOLOGIES OF ORGANIZED CRIME

The phenomena that fall under the umbrella concept of organized crime vary greatly across numerous dimensions. This has been emphasized throughout this book. At the same time, there are interdependencies that connect these phenomena, and there seem to be recurring patterns in the way certain forms of criminal activities, criminal structures, and illegal governance coincide with certain social and institutional contexts. These recurring patterns can be captured in typologies of typical constellations or scenarios of organized crime. The models of organized crime presented by Williams and Godson (2002) constitute one such typology.

Another typology is presented in Figure 13.4. Like the model in Figure 13.3, this typology is centered on the concept of criminal networks that in the interest of simplicity encompasses here the organization of criminals as well as the illegal activities these criminals are engaged in, including profit-oriented and illegal-governance crimes.

The typology likewise adopts a simplified view of society. Society is divided into three layers: a lower class with marginalized subcultures, a middle class representing the mainstream of society, and an upper class comprising the social elites. The typology is premised on two assumptions. The first assumption is that criminal networks tend to be homogeneous with members sharing the same social background according to the old adage, "birds of a feather flock together." The second assumption is that there is a positive correlation between the social position of criminals and the lucrativeness of crime opportunities. The higher the social position of an offender, the greater the rewards and the impact of the crime and the lower the risk of apprehension and conviction. For example, a welfare recipient who robs a bank may get a few thousand dollars and is likely to get arrested, if only because of the footage from a surveillance camera. The director of the same bank who embezzles funds or defrauds customers in phony investment deals may obtain millions of dollars while facing a much smaller risk. To begin with, one would assume that there are no surveillance cameras mounted above the desks of bank directors, and as the embezzlement or fraud

Figure 13.4 Typical Constellations of Organized Crime

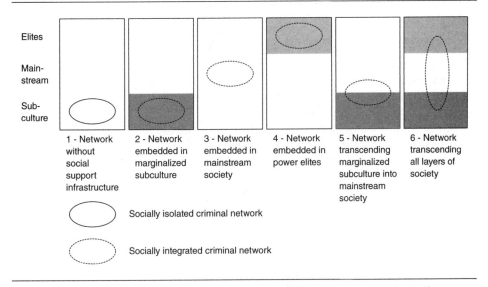

Source: Further elaboration of previous versions in von Lampe (2001b; 2004a; 2005b; 2008b).

takes place, the behavior on display is not different from what a bank director normally does. Finally, even if the bank director is caught in the act, it will be by internal or external auditors who may not even report the crime, because a criminal investigation might tarnish the reputation of the bank. The bank director then will be out of work but not in jail.

The six constellations that are distinguished in the typology presented in Figure 13.4 are ideal types that may only rarely if ever exist in their purest form. The first constellation (*networks without social support infrastructure*) is that of criminal groups operating in social isolation without drawing on their social environment in any way. The prime examples for these cases are Eastern European predatory criminal gangs that burglarize apartments or rob jewelry stores in Western Europe. While they are socially embedded at their home bases, these criminal groups may not have a support infrastructure in the countries where they commit their crimes. They do not register businesses or recruit accomplices, and in some cases, they do not even rent apartments or stay in hotels but camp out in the woods in order to avoid any contact with the local population. Correspondingly, they have no access to officials that they could bribe or otherwise influence. Their security strategy is to avoid and evade attention. That these groups engage in predatory crimes in a hit-and-run fashion is in line with their isolated position in the countries of operation. Market-based crimes, such as drug trafficking, in contrast, would require some interaction with suppliers and customers.

The second constellation (*networks embedded in marginalized subcultures*) is typified by immigrant and lower-class communities at the margins of society where criminal structures emerge around predatory and market-based crimes as well as around illegal governance. In comparison to isolated criminal networks, criminals in marginalized subcultures can rely on social support beyond the circle of their immediate accomplices, but they are largely confined to a community that is set apart from mainstream society and its institutions. The seclusion of marginalized subcultures can shield and foster organized crime. Drug trafficking, illegal gambling, and extortion are typical illegal activities in such an environment, and quasi-governmental structures are likely to gain control over these activities as well as over local legitimate businesses. At the same time, criminals from these communities are more likely to attract attention and to draw the interest of law enforcement agencies, especially once they venture outside their own turf. After all, they perfectly fit the organized criminal stereotype. Accordingly, these criminals have limited access to the legal social infrastructure, if not because of legal, cultural, educational, or language barriers then because of prejudice and discrimination; and they tend to lack the connections to public officials that could facilitate criminal endeavors and provide immunity from law enforcement, at least in comparison to middle and upper class criminals.

The third constellation (*criminal networks embedded in mainstream society*) pertains to outwardly law-abiding members of the middle class who engage in such crimes as investment fraud, health care fraud, or drug trafficking. They are not restricted by any practical, cultural, or legal obstacles in taking advantage of the legitimate social infrastructure. They can do such things as open bank accounts, transfer large amounts of cash, register businesses, and travel in furtherance of their criminal endeavors without having to be overly concerned about raising suspicions. In comparison to criminals from marginalized subcultures, criminals from mainstream society also have the strategic advantage of having natural interactions with public officials, be it in the course of business or on the tennis court. These relations to officials may easily translate into crime opportunities or reduced risks of law enforcement interference. Even in the absence of outright corruptive relations, police or prosecutors may be reluctant to start investigations against such well-respected and well-connected members of society.

The fourth constellation (*criminal networks embedded in power elites*) pertains to situations of state-organized crime where criminals have direct access to government decision-making. Here the issue of corruption does not present itself as a problem of corrupt relations between criminals and office holders because the office holders themselves are the criminals. Criminal networks embedded in the power elites can also extend beyond government to include leaders of business and the media. Examples are provided by a long series of scandals on the local, state, national, and supranational levels, involving the abuse or misuse of power for personal gain, for example in connection with public contracts, the rezoning of real estate, or the trade in embargoed goods.

The situations captured by constellations five and six deviate from the previous four scenarios in that criminal networks transcend the stratifications of society. The fifth constellation (*criminal networks that transcend marginalized subcultures into mainstream society*) are hybrids of the second and third constellations in that they combine members with different social backgrounds, some from the lower and some from the middle class. These networks combine important resources, for example the ability and willingness to use violence and access to source countries of illegal drugs with access to logistically valuable sectors such as transportation and banking. These networks may emerge as the result of targeted recruitment, for example when a drug trafficking group based in an immigrant community links up with businesspeople in the transport and finance sectors to facilitate the smuggling of drugs and the laundering of illicit proceeds. Another possibility is that some members of a criminal network that is rooted in a marginalized community gain respectability and a place in mainstream society without giving up their criminal activities. Hybrid networks can also emerge from social networks that extend across social strata, for example social networks that have formed in school or in the military.

The sixth constellation, finally, is that of criminal networks that transcend all layers of society from marginalized communities to the power elites. The Sicilian Mafia represents such a network as its membership and its circle of allies has traditionally encompassed individuals from the lower, middle, and upper classes, including businesspeople, politicians, and members of the clergy. The balance of power may shift between the underworld and upperworld elements, but essentially there seems to be a congruence of interests. Political leaders, for example, may be willing to use violent criminal groups in furtherance of their interests while in exchange they grant these groups immunity from prosecution in other illegal activities. Members of the social elites may also take direct advantage of these illegal activities, for example as investment opportunities or as sources of funding for political campaigns and political endeavors that could not be financed out of official budgets.

The main difference between the crimes of the powerful captured in the fourth constellation and the underworld-upperworld alliances captured in the sixth constellation is that in the former case legitimate institutions are instrumentalized for criminal purposes without recourse to the underworld. The range of crimes of the powerful will also be narrower than the range of criminal activities that are carried out by and under the protection of underworld-upperworld alliances. The question is if this makes crimes of the powerful a lesser evil compared to underworld-upperworld alliances. One could also argue that powerful criminals at the helm of society who do not need to take recourse to and seek alliances with the underworld constitute a more potent threat to the integrity and welfare of society. Another question is to what extent the six scenarios presented in Figure 13.4 are endpoints of developmental paths or, instead, represent different phases in a grander process of the organization of crime and criminals.

TRAJECTORIES IN THE DEVELOPMENT OF ORGANIZED CRIME

A number of propositions have been made about the developmental dynamics of organized crime. Typically, one-dimensional pathways from one state of affairs to another are described. Sometimes, these developments are seen as irreversible although they may be slowed or halted by certain factors, and sometimes the possibility of a regression to an earlier developmental state is taken into account. Only rarely are developmental pathways considered that are characterized by turning points and crossroads from where the process can go in different directions. What unites all authors who have contributed to this debate, however, is that organized crime is dynamic and not static, subject to constant (minor or major) changes. These changes pertain to individual criminal groups, criminal milieus, illegal markets, or the illegal-legal nexus.

Three main trajectories are described in the literature, each linked to a particular classification of organized crime phenomena. In one scenario, different kinds of structural arrangements, from loose networks to tightly knit organizations, are seen as natural phases in the development of organized crime. In another scenario, criminal associations, illegal enterprises, and quasi-governmental structures mark different developmental stages. In a third scenario, the development of organized crime is marked by changes in the relationship between criminal groups and government and, more generally, between underworld and upperworld.

Growth and Structural Sophistication of Individual Criminal Groups

According to a commonly held assumption, criminal structures progress along a pathway from "individuals to groups" (Shaw, 2006, p. 195), and from "co-offending [that] is low-level and unstable" to "full formal organization for crime" (Felson, 2009, pp. 161, 163; see also Best & Luckenbill, 1994; Cressey, 1972). This notion, which is most salient in the literature on street gangs, can be found as early as in Frederic Thrasher's classic study on Chicago gangs. He noted that under favorable conditions, "the gang tends to undergo a sort of natural evolution from a diffuse and loosely organized group into the solidified unit which represents the matured gang" (Thrasher, 1927/1963, p. 47). The implication is that criminal structures, if they progress, become larger, more cohesive and more formalized (Lamm Weisel, 2002, p. 29).

A number of factors come into play that may account for this development. Felson, for example, suggests with reference to Max Weber that the growth of criminal structures is driven by patrimony, "a form of personal and direct domination" of a patron over a number of clients who themselves lack an independent power base. The power of the patron, in turn, to which clients flock, "relies on one person's force of personality, often called charismatic authority, enabling him to secure cooperation from others" (Felson, 2009, p. 163). Another driver of growth and also increased structural sophistication is seen in conflicts with other criminal groups and from law enforcement pressure. In the face of adversity, it is assumed, criminal groups may develop self-awareness, become more integrated and cohesive, and larger entities may form as the result of a merging of smaller groups (Ayling, 2011b, p. 18; Densley, 2014, p. 519; Lamm Weisel, 2002, pp. 48, 55; Thrasher, 1927/1963, p. 45). This trend is not considered inevitable. Larger groups, to the extent they form at all, may splinter and fragment, and more sophisticated structures may regress to simpler forms (Ayling, 2011b, p. 10; Lamm Weisel, 2002, pp. 50–51).

Transformations in the Function of Criminal Groups

Apart from growth and structural sophistication there is also the notion that criminal groups may undergo a metamorphosis in the functions they serve. One transformation that is mentioned in the literature is that from delinquent groups engaged in random crime into specialized criminal enterprises (Ayling, 2011b, p. 12), and the transformation from criminal groups engaged in crime for profit into quasi-governmental structures exercising illegal governance (Reuter, 1994). James Densley (2014, p. 521) has even argued that there is a pathway encompassing associational, entrepreneurial as well as quasi-governmental structures, a "natural progression of gangs from recreational neighborhood groups to delinquent collectives to full-scale criminal enterprises to systems of extralegal governance." The assumption is that groups, as they develop, acquire the reputation and the means to use violence effectively.

Another scenario has been proposed by Skaperdas and Syropoulos (1995), who explain the emergence of quasi-governmental structures as a process that coincides with the initial formation of criminal groups in an anarchic underworld. They argue that from the start, criminals have to decide whether they invest their resources in "productive" activities, such as drug dealing, or "appropriative" activities such as the extortion of drug dealers. Very soon, they argue, "those who have the comparative advantage in the use of force and are thus less productive in useful activities tend to prevail" (Skaperdas & Syropoulos, 1995, p. 63).

Developmental Pathways in
the Relation Between Underworld and Upperworld

The third major frame of reference for the discussion of developmental pathways of organized crime is the relationship between underworld and upperworld. When one goes back to the typology of typical constellations of organized crime presented in Figure 13.4, then the pathway most discussed is the development of criminal networks in marginalized subcultures (Type 2) to hybrid networks of lower- and middle-class criminals (Type 5) and finally to criminal networks that transcend all layers of society (Type 6).

Donald Cressey, for example, argued with reference to the American Cosa Nostra that the demand for illegal goods and services nurtured the emergence of an ever more centralized and ever more powerful criminal organization which eventually succeeds in neutralizing law enforcement through corruption and destroying "the economic and political procedures designed to insure that American citizens need not pay tributes to criminals in order to conduct a legitimate business, to engage in a profession, to hold a job, or even to function as a consumer" (Cressey, 1972, p. 26; Cressey, 1969, pp. 73–74).

A somewhat different process of increased involvement of criminal organizations in the legal spheres of society has been described as a sequence of three phases by R. T. Naylor (1993) and Peter Lupsha (1996). They both distinguish a "predatory," a "parasitical," and a "symbiotic" stage while deviating in the exact description of each of these stages.

According to Naylor (1993, p. 20), the first, "predatory" stage, is characterized by loose associations of criminals, such as urban street gangs, that operate on a local level under constant threat from law enforcement. Their criminal activities "are essentially predatory with respect to formal society," namely, "hijacking, bank robbery and ransom kidnapping." During the second, parasitical stage, criminal activities become regional or even national in scope, and they may no longer be purely predatory. There is "a better supporting infrastructure" and although criminal activities "impose an on-going, long-term drain on formal society" there may be some demand for these activities, namely, illegal gambling and drug dealing. Embezzlement and protection rackets, the other two types of crime mentioned by Naylor, are clearly more predatory in comparison. The final, symbiotic stage, is marked by criminal activities that may extend to the international level and are closely linked to the legal spheres of society. Activities may involve "the provision of goods and services which may even be legal themselves, but are illegal in terms of the methods with which they are produced and distributed," for example, gambling casinos that are used for skimming profits and money laundering. Activities may also include illegal services "to otherwise legitimate corporations . . . varying from unionbusting to illegal waste-disposal" (Naylor, 1993, p. 20).

In the six-fold typology of typical constellations of organized crime (Figure 13.4) the symbiotic stage described by Naylor is a case primarily of Type 5, hybrid, lower-, and middle-class criminal networks. Lupsha, in contrast, describes all three stages as resembling Type 6, criminal networks that transcend all layers of society.

According to Lupsha (1996, p. 31), the initial, predatory stage is defined by gangs that have acquired dominant positions within the underworld and have already established links to "legitimate power brokers, local political notables and economic influentials who can use the gangs' organization and skills at impersonal violence for their own ends, such as debt collection, turning out the vote, or eliminating political rivals or economic competitors." What defines the predatory stage according to this interpretation is that "the criminal gang is the servant of the political and economic sectors and can easily be disciplined by them and their agencies of law and order" (Lupsha, 1996, p. 31). In the parasitical stage, according to Lupsha, the links between underworld and upperworld develop further in the direction of criminal organizations becoming "an equal of, rather than a servant to, the state" (Lupsha, 1996, p. 32). In the symbiotic stage, the merging of organized crime and the state is complete as "the legitimate political and economic sectors now become dependent upon the parasite." The endpoint is reached when "organized crime has become a part of the state; a state within the state" (Lupsha, 1996, p. 32).

Alfried Schulte-Bockholt (2001) has drawn on the same conception of a three-stage development to argue that criminal organizations, as they mature, may develop a political agenda: "While OC groups initially emerge as organization of the excluded and exploited, established criminal societies strive to become included" (Schulte-Bockholt, 2001, p. 237). Criminals may seek to integrate themselves "into existing structures of domination," typically in times of rapid socioeconomic change when the ruling elites feel threatened by counter-hegemonic movements and are receptive to assistance from criminal elements (Schulte-Bockholt, 2001, p. 226). As an illustration, Schulte-Bockholt cites the role of the Shanghai Green Gang in establishing the dictatorship of Chiang Kai-shek and the Kuomintang (KMT) in China in the year 1927. "In return for their help in the elimination of Communists and unions in Shanghai," Schulte-Bockholt (2001, p. 231) explains, "the new leader gave the Green Gang and its most prominent leader, Du Yue-sheng, free reign in that city's underworld and the narcotics trade."

Schulte-Bockholt argues that the entrenchment of criminals in positions of power is not irreversible. Citing the example of the Medellin Cartel, he notes that if the services of the criminal element "are no longer required, or if perceived as a threat, elites can and do turn against organized crime using the power of the state" (Schulte-Bockholt, 2001, p. 238).

The symbiosis of legitimate and criminal structures is one of three possible endpoints in the development that Schulte-Bockholt envisions. Another endpoint is the suppression of organized crime by a totalitarian regime, which itself is criminal and uses criminal methods, such as Fascist Italy and Nazi Germany. In the six-fold typology presented in Figure 13.4, these would be extreme cases of Type 4, elite-based criminal networks. The third-end scenario outlined by Schulte-Bockholt is "the control of the state by organized crime . . . a criminal elite bent on enriching itself, with the power of the state at its disposal" (Schulte-Bockholt, 2001, p. 236). Lupsha describes a similar worst-case scenario of criminals taking over the state, though in much more colorful detail:

In the long term the destabilizing effects of transnational organized crime can lead to delegitimization of the regime and the opening of Pandora's box of evils. Penetration of the legal system and legitimate sectors by organized crime tilts the scales of justice, unbalances the economy, eliminates the rule of fairness, and tilts the playing field against ordinary citizens. In the long term, criminal impunity creates political immunity that leads to fear, intimidation, oppression, violence and tyranny as the state becomes criminal and delegitimate. The end result is the rupture of civil society and community. (Lupsha, 1996, pp. 43–44)

The case of Colombia served Lupsha as a blueprint for this admonition. In hindsight it may serve better to stress the argument that the developmental pathways of organized crime are not one-way streets and that countermeasures can be successful, at least to some extent (see Chapter 14).

THE BIG PICTURE OF
ORGANIZED CRIME: SUMMARY AND CONCLUSION

This chapter has attempted to sketch the big picture of organized crime by bringing together the various facets of this elusive concept within one conceptual framework. What had to be done first is to reemphasize how greatly the phenomena vary that fall under the umbrella concept of organized crime. These variations have been highlighted across five key dimensions: activities, structures, and governance, as well as the illegal-legal nexus and the individual organized criminal. At the same time, numerous interdependencies could be pointed out between the nature of illegal activities, the nature of criminal structures, the nature of illegal governance, the social context, and the personal characteristics of criminals.

The second step in sketching the big picture of organized crime has been to review models that systematize these variations and interdependencies. Given the fragmented nature of current knowledge about organized crime, however, these models cannot go beyond an abstract representation of very general statements about the organization of crime and criminals. They fall far short of coherent theoretical models with which one could explain and simulate the complex mechanisms that produce and shape concrete organized crime phenomena.

The third step in sketching the big picture has been to systematize typical constellations in which organized crime phenomena manifest themselves. This has been done first in a static way with a six-fold typology that identifies different scenarios dependent on the social position of criminal networks. Finally, typical constellations of organized crime have been discussed in a dynamic way as stages in developmental processes. These developmental processes are described in the literature as processes of structural growth, consolidation, and sophistication, and as processes of approximation between underworld and upperworld.

The most likely worst-case scenario, it seems, is an alliance between political, business, and criminal elites. In this scenario, upperworld elites draw on criminal elements as soon and as long as it is necessary for them to maintain their own power. All cases of underworld-upperworld alliances discussed in this book, for example, the cases of the Cali Cartel, of the Sicilian Mafia, and of the Stern Syndicate in Wincanton (see Chapter 11) seem to fall into this category. These cases arguably are the result of a failure of law enforcement and of civil society as well as a result of the corruptness of upperworld elites.

Totalitarian regimes like that of Fascist Italy and Nazi Germany represent historical examples of criminal rule that does not rely on underworld support but rather on the support of upperworld elites and the resources of the state, while the underworld is ruthlessly suppressed. Such criminal regimes are attributable to a failure of civil society rather than to a failure of law enforcement, and they are a product of the corruptness of upperworld elites. The third worst-case scenario, the domination of society by the underworld, best fits the situation in so-called failed states where a functioning state apparatus does not exist and where crime may well be the most important sector of the economy.

For most of the world, it seems safe to assume, the problem of organized crime is primarily a matter of the consolidation and sophistication of criminal structures and of the formation of alliances of convenience between underworld and upperworld, where the criminal element remains in a subservient role. These processes are not deterministic. There are different pathways along which the organization of crime and criminals can develop, and the development can halt at some point and regress. In fact, rather than a development from bad to worse, the most typical trajectory of organized crime over the long run appears to be the waxing and waning of consolidated, powerful criminal structures. Some of the factors that influence the development are intrinsic, such as the individual capabilities and ambitions of organized criminals. Other factors are the social, political, and economic conditions that create crime opportunities and produce a pool of motivated criminals. But there is no scenario where it would not matter how government and civil society respond to the organization of crime and criminals. Any modeling of organized crime without taking the effectiveness of policing and civil vigilance into account would be incomplete. This will be the subject of the next and last chapter in this book, Chapter 14, which discusses countermeasures against organized crime.

Discussion Questions

1. What would organized crime be like if it were dominated by women?

2. What is the most common constellation in which organized crime phenomena manifest themselves?

3. Pick a country and discuss the most likely future development of organized crime?

Research Projects

1. Analyze the autobiography of an organized criminal with a view to the importance of individual characteristics.

2. Analyze the autobiography of an organized criminal with a view to the development of organized crime phenomena over time.

Further Reading

Comprehensive Discussions of Organized Crime

Albini, J. L., & McIllwain, J. S. (2012). *Deconstructing organized crime: An historical and theoretical study.* Jefferson, NC: McFarland.

Homer, F. D. (1974). *Guns and garlic: Myths and realities of organized crime.* West Lafayette, IN: Purdue University Press.

Levi, M. (2012). The organization of serious crime for gain. In R. Morgan, M. Maguire, & R. Reiner (Eds.), *The Oxford handbook of criminology* (5th ed., pp. 595–622). Oxford, UK: Oxford University Press.

Liddick, D. (1999b). *An empirical, theoretical, and historical overview of organized crime.* Lewiston, NY: Edwin Mellen Press.

Paoli, L. (Ed.). (2014). *The Oxford handbook of organized crime.* Oxford: Oxford University Press.

Gender and Organized Crime

Fiandaca, G. (Ed.). (2015). *Women and the Mafia: Female Roles in Organized Crime Structures.* New York: Springer.

Mullins, C.W., & Cherbonneau, M.G. (2011). Establishing Connections: Gender, motor vehicle theft, and disposal networks. *Justice Quarterly, 28*(2), 278–302.

Siegel, D., & de Blank, S. (2010). Women who traffic women: the role of women in human trafficking networks - Dutch cases. *Global Crime, 11*(4), 436–447.

Van den Eynde, J., & Veno, A. (2007). Depicting outlaw motorcycle club women using anchored and unanchored research methodologies. *The Australian Community Psychologist, 19*(1), 96–111.

CHAPTER 14

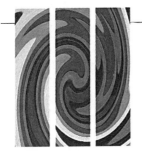

Countermeasures Against Organized Crime

INTRODUCTION

This chapter provides a systematic overview of what is being done about the phenomena that are variously labeled organized crime and that have been discussed at length in the previous chapters. The different types of countermeasures will be examined with two questions in mind:

1. What is the nature of the measure?

2. How are criminal activities, criminal structures, and illegal governance affected by the measure?

Given the social embeddedness of criminal activities and criminal structures (Chapter 9), a broad range of socioeconomic policies could qualify as measures against organized crime (Bjørgo, in press). For example, programs to reduce poverty, unemployment, and discrimination may reduce the appeal that joining a criminal organization has for young people (see Reuter, 1995, p. 96). It is beyond the scope of this book to comprehensively discuss the effects of general socioeconomic policies on organized crime. The same applies to the controversial debate on the actual and potential effects of the decriminalization of illegal goods and services on organized crime (see, e.g., Demleitner, 1994; Dombrink, 1981; Huisman & Kleemans, 2014; Spapens, 2013; Watt & Zepeda, 2015; Weatherburn, 2014; Wodak, 2014). Instead the focus here is on measures that explicitly and specifically target organized crime phenomena.

Most countermeasures fall in the category of criminal justice responses to organized crime. Within this broad category some measures pertain to *substantive criminal law* and have to do with broadening the scope and severity of punishments for organized crime related conduct. Other criminal justice measures pertain to *procedural criminal law* and to policing and have to do with increasing the likelihood that organized criminals are brought to justice, namely, by facilitating the collection of evidence.

Under the banner of combating organized crime, there have also been significant changes in the organization of law enforcement. Specialized units have been formed within police and prosecutorial agencies, and entirely new organizations devoted to the fight against organized crime have come into existence—for example, the police agency of the European Union, Europol. These organizational changes have gone hand-in-hand with the creation and networking of specialized databases for the processing and analysis of information relating to organized crime.

Criminal justice responses to organized crime, generally speaking, increase the risks for organized criminals both in terms of increasing the *likelihood* of arrest and conviction and in terms of increasing the *severity of the consequences* of arrest and conviction, for example, in the form of long prison sentences and the forfeiture of criminal assets. Beyond these straightforward effects, criminal justice measures can have other more or less direct consequences. They can make it more difficult in practical terms to carry out illegal activities. For example, laws that restrict access to precursor chemicals for the production of methamphetamine and that make the unauthorized handling of these chemicals a crime have forced illegal producers to go through additional efforts, such as producing precursor chemicals themselves (Shukla et al., 2012, p. 430). Criminal justice measures can also hamper the formation, maintenance, and expansion of criminal networks. For example, the use of electronic surveillance limits the ability of criminals to safely communicate with other criminals, and the use of informants and undercover agents forces criminals to invest more time and energy into screening potential accomplices.

Aside from the criminal justice system, governments have adopted administrative measures to curb organized crime. For example, licenses for operating a business may be revoked if it becomes apparent that the business is used for illegal purposes, or such licenses may be denied in the first place if the applicant is believed to have links to organized crime.

Arguably, governments bear the main burden in combating organized crime. However, private citizens, businesses, the media, and civil society as a whole can play an important role in setting limits to the organization of crime and criminals as well. Many nongovernmental initiatives to combat organized crime center on raising awareness—for example, by publicly exposing criminals and their links to politics and business. Where criminals have acquired positions of power, strategies of civil unrest and civil disobedience may be adopted by citizens in resemblance to political protest movements.

SUBSTANTIVE CRIMINAL LAW AS AN INSTRUMENT AGAINST ORGANIZED CRIME

It has long been lamented that traditional approaches to crime control are not effective against organized crime. Prosecuting individual organized criminals for committing individual crimes is considered difficult for a number of reasons. First, the clandestine nature of organized criminal activity and the absence of direct victims in many cases tend to leave crimes undetected. Second, individual responsibility is hard to establish where numerous coconspirators and co-offenders participate in a criminal endeavor. This is especially true for bosses, kingpins, and financiers who stay in the background and are not involved in the actual commission of crimes. Finally, at least the stereotypical organized criminals use violence, intimidation, and corruption to discourage witnesses from testifying or to derail the criminal justice process in other ways. And even if individual organized criminals are convicted on traditional charges, such as drug trafficking, illegal gambling, extortion, or murder, the assumption has been that this does not get at the root of the problem. Arresting and convicting an organized criminal here and there still leaves the underlying criminal structures intact. Organized criminals may continue to operate illegal enterprises from within prison, where often enough they only have to serve short sentences; or an incarcerated organized criminal may easily be replaced by another who moves up the ranks. One solution to these problems has been to make substantive criminal law a more potent weapon against organized crime by using existing criminal law more effectively and by amending and adding to existing criminal law.

Innovative Use of Conventional Criminal Law

Very early on, attempts have been made to use conventional criminal law in innovative ways to go after organized criminals. Famously, tax laws were applied in the United States against Prohibition Era gangsters who were charged with evading taxes by not declaring their illegal income from selling alcohol (Funderburg, 2014, pp. 121–122). In the 1960s, the U.S. Department of Justice launched a campaign against organized criminals that entailed detecting any wrongdoing, no matter how trivial or unrelated to organized criminal activity, to obtain convictions. In one case, the search of the home of a Chicago gangster resulted in charges of violating the Migratory Bird Act because 563 mourning doves had been found in a freezer, far above the legal limit of 24 (Goldfarb, 1995, p. 62). Apart from these efforts to make more exhaustive use of existing criminal law, the focus has been on increasing the severity of sanctions imposed on organized criminals and on creating new offenses that better capture what organized criminals do.

Expanding Criminal Penalties for Organized Criminals: Criminal Forfeiture

In accordance with the notion that organized crime is more serious than non-organized crime, a straightforward criminal law response to organized crime is to institute more severe penalties for the types of crimes that organized criminals are believed to commit, such as drug trafficking, human trafficking, and illegal gambling. This means, first of all, that higher mandatory (minimum) prison sentences and higher maximum prison sentences are implemented and that the portion of prison sentences that has to be served before a convicted organized criminal becomes eligible for parole is extended (Campbell, 2013).

In addition to increasing conventional penalties, namely prison sentences and fines, there have been attempts to introduce new forms of punishment that are believed to have a disruptive effect on criminal activities and criminal structures. Perhaps the best examples of new forms of punishment are laws that allow for the *forfeiture of criminal assets*. Forfeiture means that the government gains ownership of private property. Under criminal forfeiture laws, the government assumes ownership of property as an incident of conviction for a crime. Property is typically subject to criminal forfeiture if it has been employed as an instrument to commit the crime or if it is derived, directly or indirectly, from the crime.

Criminal forfeiture has to be distinguished from *civil and administrative forfeiture*. In these cases, the government gains ownership of criminal assets independent of a criminal conviction. For example, smuggled goods that are confiscated by customs are subject to forfeiture irrespective of whether or not the smugglers are identified and convicted. All varieties of forfeiture are broadly similar in their impact on criminals and criminal structures. "Tainted" assets are permanently taken out of the hands of criminals. Forfeiture deprives criminals of material resources for committing future crimes and denies them the material benefits from past crimes (Cassella, 2007).

Expanding the Scope of Criminal Law: The Case of Money Laundering

More far-reaching legislative strategies beyond simply increasing the severity of punishment entail the creation of new criminal offenses. These laws criminalize conduct that is believed to be characteristic of organized crime but that does not fit any offense category in existing criminal law. Two strategies are particularly noteworthy, the criminalization of money laundering and the criminalization of involvement in criminal organizations. Making money laundering a crime is arguably the best example for how the reach of substantive criminal law has been extended in the fight against organized crime. Another example would be the criminalization of the unauthorized handling of certain precursor chemicals needed for the production of illegal drugs (O'Connor, Chriqui, & McBride, 2006).

Core Money-Laundering Offenses

The concept of money laundering, as noted in Chapter 10, pertains to a broad range of schemes through which the criminal origin of assets is obscured and a perception is created that these assets are legitimately at the disposal of a given criminal. Until 1986, when the U.S. Money Laundering Control Act was passed, money laundering itself was not a crime anywhere in the world (Levi, 2002a), and the activities that are illegal today would have constituted noncriminal efforts to create and maintain an aura of respectability and to avoid suspicion when investing and spending illicit proceeds.

The criminalization of money laundering encompasses a number of offenses. The core offense of money laundering, as defined in UN conventions, such as the Palermo Convention of 2000, involves three different acts, each constituting a separate crime:

- The *conversion or transfer* of proceeds from a crime for the purpose of concealing or disguising their criminal origin
- The actual *concealment or disguise* of crime proceeds, for example, by obscuring ownership
- The *acquisition, possession, or use* of crime proceeds with knowledge of their criminal origin

(Luban, O'Sullivan, & Stewart, 2010, p. 583).

How exactly money laundering is defined in particular penal codes varies across countries. There are also variations in the kinds of predicate offenses from which the proceeds have to originate. For example, in many countries only the handling of proceeds from *serious* crimes constitutes money laundering (Walters, Budd, Smith, Choo, McCusker, & Rees, 2011).

Ancillary Money-Laundering Offenses

The criminalization of money laundering is flanked by two important mechanisms. One mechanism is the recovery of criminal assets through *seizure and forfeiture* in criminal or civil proceedings. This entails investigative techniques that enable law enforcement agencies to "follow the money" and, for example, to trace financial transactions through banks. This has become much easier as bank secrecy is no longer a fundamental obstacle for criminal investigations (Mühl, 2013; Van Duyne, Pheijffer, Kuijl, Van Dijk, & Bakker, 2001). The other mechanism is a complex regulatory framework for the continuous *monitoring* of financial transactions (Reuter & Truman, 2004). This regulatory framework contains criminal sanctions in addition to the core offense of money laundering, namely sanctions for violating recordkeeping and reporting requirements relating to transactions that potentially involve proceeds of crime. In many jurisdictions, there is an obligation for disclosing the movement of funds across the border if they exceed certain threshold levels. In the United States, for example, individuals have to file a report if they bring funds of more than $10,000 into or out of the country. Failure to report these funds can result in forfeiture and a prison sentence (see 31 U.S. Code §§ 5316, 5332).

A similar kind of obligation exists for businesses that typically handle large cash transactions. These businesses—namely banks but also such businesses as jewelry stores and casinos—may have to report transactions that exceed certain threshold levels, for example $10,000 in the United States. Another obligation for businesses that are prone to be used in money-laundering schemes is to report those transactions that are suspected of involving proceeds of crime (Walters et al., 2011). For example, a U.S. bank has to report cash deposits exceeding $10,000 or cash deposits below this threshold if the amounts appear to be disproportionately high for the assumed income of the depositor. In addition, acts with which individuals attempt to circumvent these anti-money-laundering controls have been criminalized as well. For example, under U.S. federal law it is a separate criminal offense to break one transaction of more than $10,000 into several smaller transactions in order to avoid triggering the reporting requirement of a bank or other business obliged to report transactions above $10,000 (Doyle, 2012, p. 34).

The Global Anti-Money-Laundering Regime and Its Consequences for Organized Criminals

Since 1970, when the U.S. Bank Secrecy Act for the first time introduced reporting requirements for financial transactions, an anti-money-laundering regime of global proportions has come into being. At the helm is the *Financial Action Task Force* (FATF), an international organization created in 1989 and based in Paris, France, that through its "Recommendations" has guided efforts against illicit finance (Roberge, 2011). On the national level, *Financial Intelligence Units* (FIUs) collect and process for each country the suspicious transaction reports that are generated by banks and other businesses. The FIUs are organized informally in a network called the *Egmont Group* that was established in 1995 with support from the FATF (Buchanan, 2004). From the level of international and national agencies, the anti-money-laundering regime extends into the private sector, where an entire "compliance industry" helps individual businesses to minimize the regulatory and reputational risks of exposure to illicit finances (Verhage, 2009).

The global anti-money-laundering regime is far from being a comprehensive and airtight control system (Harvey, 2011; Reuter & Truman, 2004; Sharman, 2011; Vesterhav, 2010). Yet, the criminalization of money laundering and the accompanying regulatory framework have had a profound impact on how criminals manage their finances. The broadened scope of criminal law means that more aspects of what organized criminals do constitute a criminal activity. Accordingly, the risk of arrest and conviction and the risk of loss of assets through forfeiture increase. There has also been the expectation that by seizing illegal assets, illegal enterprises could be disrupted because money supposedly is the "life blood of organized crime" (President's Commission on Organized Crime, 1984). This view, however, underestimates the ability of crime entrepreneurs to obtain illegal goods—namely, drugs—on credit, so that the seizing of assets does not necessarily force an illegal enterpreneur out of business (see Desroches, 2005). What has changed for organized criminals is that money management has become more cumbersome. A drug dealer or illegal gambling operator can no longer simply deposit large amounts of crumpled small denomination bills in a bank account and then transfer these funds to a foreign country or use these funds to buy property or to invest in a legal business. One effect ascribed to the reduced accessibility of the financial system for criminals is an increase in cash smuggling (Reuter & Truman, 2004, p. 28; Smith & Walker, 2010). Apparently, drug traffickers and other transnational criminals have been forced to physically transport money across borders, even though this may be far more arduous than the underlying crime. In the case of heroin, for example, according to a calculation from the 1990s, 10 kilograms of the drug generate about 116 kilograms of cash in $5, $10, and $20 bills (as cited in Luban, et al., 2010, p. 579).

Overall, the anti-money-laundering regime has had an effect on the social microcosm of illegal entrepreneurs as far as the use of illicit assets is concerned.

Those individuals that illegal entrepreneurs encounter when using their illicit funds potentially face criminal liability on money-laundering charges, be it the clerk in the bank, the salesperson at the luxury car dealership, the jeweler selling expensive watches, the cashier at a resort casino, or the girlfriend accepting a diamond ring (Soudijn, 2010). This means, all of these individuals have a strong legal incentive not to get involved in any monetary transactions with a criminal, and even more so, they may be inclined to cooperate with authorities. Put in another way, the criminalization of money laundering forces criminals to extend their networks of criminally exploitable ties to the individuals they need for handling their illicit funds. This may entail, for example, building up a relationship of trust to a bank clerk, which may be difficult to do, especially where this relationship would have to bridge differences in language, culture, and social status.

Expanding the Scope of Criminal Law: Criminalizing Involvement in a Criminal Group

The criminalization of money laundering typically pertains to the latter phases in a criminal endeavour, when the core crime has been committed and offenders want to reap the benefits from that crime. In contrast, laws that criminalize involvement in a criminal organization extend criminal liability to the very early stages of the crime process. Sometimes these laws criminalize conduct that takes place even before a concrete criminal endeavor has entered the stages of planning and preparation, namely setting up a criminal organization as such. This is what has been called the *anticipating function* of organization-related offenses (Calderoni, 2010, p. 56). Laws that criminalize involvement in a criminal organization tend to serve other functions as well. They lead law enforcement agencies to focus on collective criminal structures rather than on individual offenders (*strategic function*); they can expand individual criminal liability to the general activities of a group (*generalization function*); they can institute more severe penalties for group members compared to lone offenders and sometimes more severe penalties for group leaders compared to lower-ranking members (*aggravating function*); and they can provide the basis for the use of special investigative tools and techniques that are not permissible in investigations of other kinds of crimes (*procedural function*) (Calderoni, 2010, pp. 55–56).

The criminal offense that is defined by these laws is to somehow belong to an identifiable collective of criminals, either through the status of being a member or through acts that are committed in connection with this collective. How exactly these offenses are designed varies greatly across jurisdictions and legislative approaches. Andreas Schloenhardt (2012, p. 141) has usefully distinguished four main approaches to the criminalization of involvement in criminal organizations:

- The conspiracy model
- The participation model
- The enterprise model
- The labelling/registration model

These four models encompass older as well as more recent legislative developments around the world.

The Conspiracy Model: The Common Law Offense of Conspiracy

The *conspiracy model* is arguably the first legal response to the organization of criminals and predates the notion of organized crime. This approach is centered on the common law offense of conspiracy. The common law legal tradition has its origins in medieval England and has influenced criminal law all over the former British Empire, including the United States.

Conspiracy is defined differently across jurisdictions, but in essence it consists of "an agreement between two or more persons to accomplish a criminal or unlawful purpose, or some purpose, not in itself criminal or unlawful, by criminal or unlawful means" (Pollock, 2009, p. 133). The offense of conspiracy establishes far-reaching criminal liability. Conspiracy is an offense separate from the underlying crime. A conspirator can be punished both for agreeing to commit a crime and for committing the crime. In addition, in some jurisdictions the members of a conspiracy are held accountable for any crime committed by a coconspirator as long as the crime falls naturally and foreseeably within the scope of the conspiracy (so-called Pinkerton Rule). It is not necessary that the member of the conspiracy participated in or even knew of the specific crimes (Strader, 2002, pp. 33–34).

Conspiracy laws apply to more or less integrated entrepreneurial and quasi-governmental structures. Conspiracy is less easily charged in cases of criminal associations, because by definition they are not based on an agreement to engage in particular crimes (Chapter 7).

Criminal firms in the form of partnerships and groups of criminals as well as gangs exercising illegal governance can readily be construed as conspiracies because they are delineable entities organized around a common purpose of jointly carrying out particular criminal activities.

It is less obvious that criminal networks without an overarching organizational structure can also come under the purview of conspiracy laws, even if network members do not know each other and only collaborate indirectly (Desroches, 2013, p. 408). Two forms of such conspiracies are commonly distinguished: wheel conspiracies and chain conspiracies. In a *wheel conspiracy*, one or more central players interact with a number of peripheral individuals. For example, a drug dealer may use several individuals to store drugs in their respective homes. In a *chain conspiracy*, criminals cooperate in a sequential order, namely, along the supply chain of illegal goods. For example, the individuals involved in the distribution of a particular batch of illegal drugs, from manufacturer, smuggler, wholesale dealer, all the way down to the street seller, can be part of one conspiracy (Lee, 2005, pp. 6, 29). In both cases (wheel and chain conspiracies) the participants do not have to know of the other participants as long as they are aware of the broader scheme (Strader, 2002, p. 50).

Conspiracy continues to be a frequently charged offense in organized crime cases in at least some common law countries, for example, in Canada (Desroches, 2013). Conspiracy law has a potential deterrent effect against criminal cooperation and the formation of criminal (entrepreneurial and quasi-governmental) structures, as it significantly increases the risk of arrest and punishment for criminals who interact with other criminals. It provides a strong incentive for more peripheral members of criminal structures to inform on the more central members. As a result, conspiracy law may undermine trust and cohesion within criminal networks (Katyal, 2003).

The Participation Model: Criminalizing Participation in Criminal Organizations

In contrast to conspiracy laws that criminalize *agreements* to commit specific crimes, the *participation model* is centered on *conduct* relating to delineable structural entities. These entities do not have to specialize in any particular type of crime. They may well be linked to various kinds of criminal activity. Early examples of this approach, their origins going back to the 19th century, can be found in a number of continental European countries. These include the offense of participation in an *association de malfeiteurs* (association of wrongdoers) in the French Penal Code (Article 450-1), the offense of promoting, constituting, or organizing an *associazione per delinquere* (association for delinquency) in the Italian Penal Code (art. 416), or the offense of setting up, joining, recruiting for, or otherwise supporting a *kriminelle Vereinigung* (criminal association) in the German Penal Code (§ 129) (Wise, 2000).

More recently, efforts to criminalize involvement in criminal groups have been inspired by initiatives within the European Union and by the UN Convention Against Transnational Organized Crime (Palermo Convention) of 2000 (Calderoni, 2010; Campbell, 2013). Article 5 of the Palermo Convention mandates that signatory states have to criminalize participation in an organized criminal group in one of several ways. One proposed offense is that of taking an active part in the activities of an organized criminal group, another is that of "organizing, directing, aiding, abetting, facilitating or counselling the commission of serious crime involving an organized criminal group."

In cross-national comparison, there is no uniformity in what constitutes participation in a criminal organization. In some cases, for example art. 416 Italian Penal Code, membership *per se*, that is, belonging to a criminal organization as such, establishes criminal liability (Paoli, 2004, p. 265; see also Broadhurst, 2013, p. 99). In most cases, participation requires that an individual has to at least *facilitate* the activities of a criminal organization (Campbell, 2013, p. 25; Schloenhardt, 2012, p. 144). In a few cases, for example, Russia, the participation offense is limited to those who are *actively involved* in the activities of a criminal organization (Orlova, 2008, p. 109).

There are also variations in the way the purpose, size, and structure of criminal organizations are defined. A rather narrow definition is contained in article 416*bis* of the Italian Penal Code, a law that specifically targets mafia-type associations and amends the above mentioned general offense of involvement in an association for delinquency (art. 416). Article 416*bis* applies to groups that command "intimidating power" and exploit "resulting conditions of submission and silence" (Calderoni, 2010, p. 88). Interestingly, by definition it does not take more than three individuals to form a mafia-like association. Likewise, the association does not have to engage in illegal activities. It is sufficient that members take advantage of the intimidation power for the management or control of legal economic activities (Calderoni, 2010, p. 81–83; Scotti, 2002, p. 160). This is not unusual for participation offenses. While the idea is to target criminal structures, in some jurisdictions the commission of crime does not have to be the sole purpose of an organization. In some cases it is sufficient that an organization has as one of its main purposes the *facilitation* rather than the *commission* of crimes. This is noteworthy, because as a result these offenses become applicable to associations of criminals, such as outlaw motorcycle gangs, and to legitimate organizations, namely, businesses (Orlova, 2008; Schloenhardt, 2012).

Broad applicability is also ensured by limiting the structural requirements for the existence of a criminal organization. Participation offenses tend to take into account the often ephemeral and flexible nature of offender structures by setting low standards with regard to the vertical and horizontal differentiation and the formalization of organizational structures (see Chapter 5 and Chapter 6). Typically, all that is required for the existence of a criminal organization is some cohesion and functional connection between three or more individuals (Schloenhardt, 2012, p. 153). Some legal definitions of organized crime set the minimum number of participants lower (at least two individuals) or higher (more than three individuals) (Broadhurst, 2012, p. 163; Calderoni, 2010, pp. 68–71; Schloenhardt, 2012, p. 154).

The Irish Criminal Justice Act of 2009 is a good example for a modern participation offence. Inspired by the Palermo Convention, it requires conduct relating to "a structured group, however organised" as opposed to groups that are "randomly formed for the immediate commission of a single offence." The law clarifies that no elaborate structure is required and that a structured group exists even without "formal rules or formal membership," without "hierarchical or leadership structures" and without "continuity of involvement by persons in the group" (Part 2, 3.(1)(b) (a)-(c) Irish Criminal Justice (Amendment) Act 2009; see also Campbell, 2013, p. 24). Some countries have established stricter structural requirements, such as formalization, hierarchy, and division of labor. In these cases, the restrictions are not necessarily stated explicitly in a statute and instead may have emerged in case law (court rulings) only (Calderoni, 2010, p. 72; Schloenhardt, 2012, p. 153)

The Enterprise Model: RICO

Under the *enterprise model*, it is a criminal offense to engage in certain conduct in connection with an "enterprise." *Enterprise crimes* can be similar to participation offenses that criminalize involvement in the activities of a criminal organization. However, the enterprise model provides for a more varied and more complex combination of activities and structures to establish criminal liability. The enterprise model is primarily associated with the Racketeer Influenced and Corrupt Organizations (RICO) statute that came into force as part of the U.S. Organized Crime Control Act of 1970. Subsequently, most U.S. states have adopted their own variants of RICO.

The RICO statute combines criminal and civil provisions. It contains four criminal offenses with heavy sentences and provisions for the mandatory forfeiture of criminal assets. In addition, victims can sue perpetrators for treble damages, and the government can seek court orders to prevent future racketeering crimes (Jacobs & Cooperman, 2011, pp. 23–24). Because of this combination of complementary legal tools, the RICO statute is considered the most comprehensive and most potent instrument in the United States for dismantling criminal structures (Albanese, 2011, p. 299), even though some of the tools—namely, criminal forfeiture and civil action for treble damages—have only rarely if ever been used in cases involving members of Cosa Nostra (James B. Jacobs, personal communication, December, 24, 2014).

The success of the RICO statute is also linked to a number of advantages it brings especially for federal prosecutors in the United States. For example, the federal RICO statute allows prosecuting violations of state criminal law that would otherwise fall in the exclusive jurisdiction of individual states; it allows combining in a single trial a large number of defendants and crimes; and it allows introducing evidence that might otherwise be deemed prejudicial, for example, evidence on the relationships between defendants (Jacobs & Dondlinger Wyman, 2014, pp. 537–538).

RICO encompasses three separate substantive criminal offenses and in addition the offense of conspiracy to commit any of these three substantive crimes (Figure 14.1). All three substantive RICO offenses are centered on certain kinds of criminal conduct, either "pattern of racketeering activity" or the "collection of an unlawful debt," that has to relate in particular ways to an enterprise (Marine, 2009; Mercone, Shapiro, & Martin, 2006).

RICO Activities: Collection of Unlawful Debt, and Pattern of Racketeering Activities. The meaning of collecting unlawful debt is fairly straightforward. The legislative intention was to target the common practice of Cosa Nostra members to use gambling and loan-sharking debts to gain control over legitimate businesses (see Chapter 10). Compared to the element of pattern of racketeering activity the element of collection of unlawful debt is of relatively little practical relevance and can therefore be neglected in the discussion of the RICO statute.

The concept of *pattern of racketeering activity* has no counterpart in pre-RICO law (Blakey, 2006). It is defined as two or more criminal acts that are committed within a prescribed time period. In the case of the federal RICO statute, the two acts have to be committed within a period of ten years. However, according to the U.S. Supreme Court, a pattern requires more than that. There must be some continuity in the criminal conduct and there must be some relationship between the individual criminal acts (Marine, 2009, p. 90).

What is not required is that these criminal acts are of the same kind. The list of predicate offenses is long, and in the case of the federal RICO statute it comprises a broad range of federal criminal offenses, including those related to terrorism and illegal immigration as well as a long list of crimes under state law (18 U.S. Code § 1961 (1)). A pattern can exist even if a perpetrator never commits the same type of crime twice, as long as these crimes are related, namely, because they are committed in connection with the same criminal organization or enterprise (Marine, 2009, p. 96).

Figure 14.1 The Four RICO Offenses

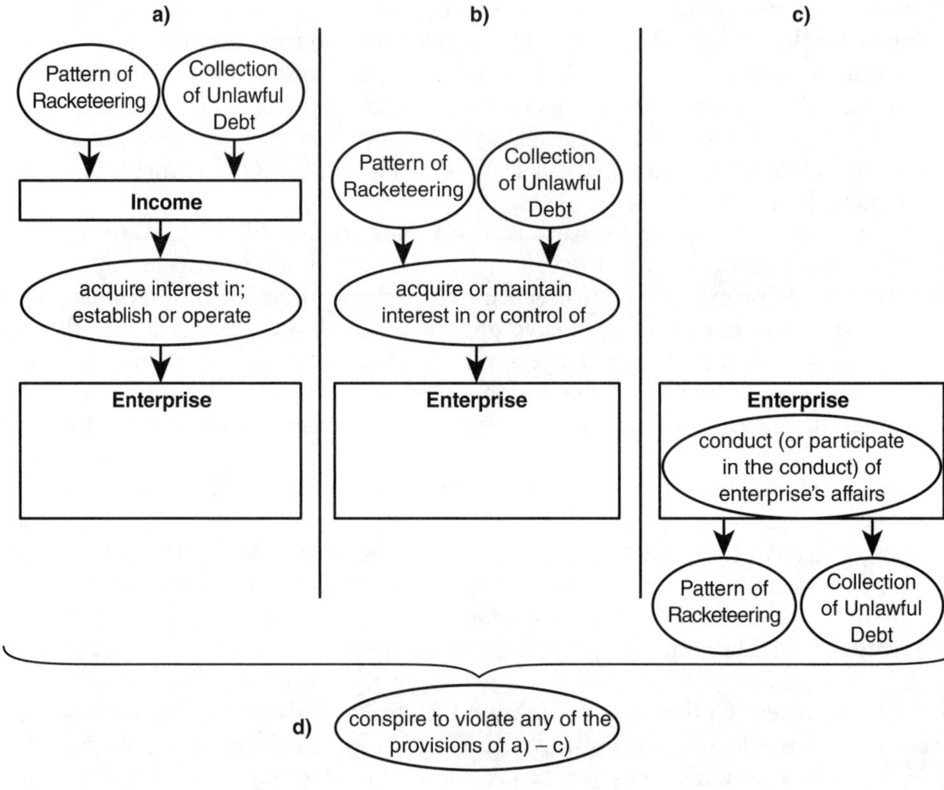

This graph depicts the three substantive RICO offenses (18 U.S. Code § 1962 (a–c)) and the offense of RICO conspiracy (d) as combinations of RICO conduct (pattern of racketeering, collection of debt) and RICO enterprise.

RICO Enterprise. The concept of *enterprise* in the RICO statute is extremely broad. It pertains first and foremost to legitimate businesses as well as to labor unions. It was the declared purpose of the law to prevent the infiltration of the legal economy by organized criminals (Geary, 2000, p. 346). However, a RICO enterprise can also be an entity that has hardly any resemblance to a legitimate business. The law explicitly states that a "group of individuals associated in fact although not a legal entity" can be an enterprise (18 U.S. Code § 1961 (4)). Subsequently, the U.S. Supreme Court has clarified that the term enterprise may also apply to wholly criminal entities (Marine, 2009, p. 52), including criminal organizations that are *not* primarily motivated by profit (Marine, 2009, p. 81).

The Three Substantive RICO Offenses. Three different constellations are captured by the three substantive RICO offenses. In two constellations, the enterprise is the *victim.* In one constellation the enterprise is the *vehicle* of criminal conduct. In the first constellation (§ 1962 (a)), *income derived from* pattern of racketeering activity or from the collection of unlawful debt is used to establish or to gain control over an enterprise, typically a legitimate business or a labor union.

In the second constellation (§ 1962 (b)), control over an enterprise, again typically a legitimate business or a labor union, is attained *through* either a pattern of racketeering activity or the collection of unlawful debt. In both cases (a and b) perpetrators do not have to act collaboratively. A lone offender who gains control over an enterprise can just as well be found guilty of these RICO violations.

The third constellation (§ 1962 (c)) likewise encompasses the acts of lone as well as of collective offenders. At the same time, it establishes an offense of participating in a criminal organization in that § 1962 (c) criminalizes the *operation* of an enterprise *through* a pattern of racketeering activity or through the collection of unlawful debt. This covers, first of all, those cases where a legitimate business or a labor union is used as a vehicle for criminal conduct by one or more offenders. It also covers criminal conduct and criminal networks within government. Entire governmental units such as police departments and sheriff's offices have been found to constitute RICO enterprises (Marine, 2009, pp. 55–57). Most importantly for the present purpose, however, § 1962 (c) covers cases where the enterprise is a wholly criminal organization.

The Offense of Participating in a Criminal Organization Encapsulated in § 1962 (c). The offense of participating in a criminal organization that is encapsulated in § 1962 (c) has two main elements: (a) a person has to be associated with an enterprise, and (b) that person has to be involved in the affairs of the enterprise (conduct or participate, directly or indirectly, in the conduct of such enterprise's affairs) through either a pattern of racketeering activity or through the collection of unlawful debt.

As indicated, the structural requirements for an enterprise, and by extension for a criminal organization under RICO, are low. It can be an informal association in fact. According to the U.S. Supreme Court, there must be "relationships among" the persons who are "associated in fact," they must have a common purpose, and there must be "longevity sufficient to permit these associates to pursue the enterprise's purpose" (as cited in Marine, 2009, p. 78). These structural requirements can be satisfied by an entrepreneurial criminal structure that manifests itself only in the actual commission of criminal acts. It is not necessary that there is an organizational structure distinct from the structure that is inherent in the criminal conduct (Marine, 2009, p. 70). Accordingly, co-offending criminals quickly run the risk of forming a RICO enterprise and of becoming liable under § 1962 (c). Each co-offender more or less automatically is associated with the enterprise and conducts the "enterprise's affairs through a pattern of racketeering activity," provided the enterprise is organized around the continuous commission of RICO predicate offenses. Even marginal co-offenders can be held liable. They do not have to participate or know about all activities of an enterprise as long as they are aware of its general nature (Marine, 2009, p. 64). As one court ruling put it, "the RICO net is woven tightly to trap even the smallest fish, those peripherally involved with the enterprise" (cit. in Marine, 2009, p. 122).

Apart from involvement in co-offending structures, the participation offense encapsulated in § 1962 (c) also encompasses scenarios where an organization exists distinct from any particular criminal conduct, namely, in the form of associational structures such as the Cosa Nostra or an outlaw motorcycle gang. Importantly, these noneconomic criminal structures can readily be designated RICO enterprises in the absence of a requirement that a RICO enterprise has to be profit seeking (Marine, 2009, p. 81).

Participation in the affairs of a criminal association can take on different forms. Even though criminal associations, by definition, support criminal endeavors only indirectly, there are crimes that can be committed on behalf of a criminal association—for example, murders to maintain internal discipline in a Cosa Nostra family. But the connection between criminal conduct (pattern of racketeering activity) and criminal association (enterprise) can also be much weaker so that, for example, the criminal activities carried out by an individual Cosa Nostra member can count as participation in the affairs of the respective Cosa Nostra family. In one court case, a sufficient nexus between the drug dealing activities of a Cosa Nostra member and his Cosa Nostra family was found to exist because he supplied drugs to other members of the family and, most importantly, because he used the names of two senior members of the family "to collect money for cocaine distribution." In the opinion of the court, this showed that membership in the Cosa Nostra family facilitated the drug trafficking (Marine, 2009, p. 132). The court spelled out the underlying principle as follows:

> A sufficient nexus or relationship exists between the racketeering acts and the enterprise if the defendant was able to commit the predicate acts by means of, by consequences of, by reason of, by the agency of, or by the instrumentality of his association with the enterprise. (as cited in Marine, 2009, p. 131)

This is somewhat reminiscent of the use of the "intimidating power" of a mafia-type association under art. 416*bis* of the Italian Penal Code (see above). However, the RICO statute (§ 1962 (c)) considers the benefits of belonging to a mafia-type association in a much broader sense, making it easier to connect, in a legal sense, individual activities and criminal association. In fact, it appears as if the criminal activities of individual mafiosi almost by default constitute RICO violations and that it is possible "to convict individuals for being active members of an LCN crime family" (Jacobs & Dondlinger Wyman, 2014, p. 537).

RICO Conspiracy (§ 1962 (d)). The scope of criminal liability under RICO is broadened even further with the offense of RICO conspiracy. The RICO conspiracy offense makes it a crime to conspire to violate any of the three substantive RICO offenses (§ 1962 (a), (b), (c)). An individual has to either agree to engage in a pattern of racketeering activity or agree to participate in the conduct of an enterprise with the knowledge and intent that other members of the conspiracy will engage in a pattern of racketeering activity in furtherance of the enterprise (Marine, 2009, p. 135). By this token, the leaders of a criminal organization can be found guilty of RICO conspiracy even if they are not directly involved in the commission of any crimes (Ickler, 1983, p. 605).

Because of the diverse ways in which a substantive RICO crime can be committed, a RICO conspiracy is more comprehensive than a common law conspiracy. Rather than being confined to agreements to commit a single or a few specific crimes, a RICO conspiracy can relate to the (intended) commission of highly diverse criminal acts (Marine, 2009, p. 148). Since coconspirators do not have to engage in a pattern of racketeering activity themselves and do not have to participate in the operation or management of the enterprise (Marine, 2009, p. 141), the RICO conspiracy provision comes close to criminalizing the mere membership in a criminal association (Wise, 2000).

The Labeling/Registration Model

Participation offenses, including the RICO statute, have been challenged for being too vague. It is a basic principle of due process that substantive criminal law is written in a language so clear and precise that ordinary people can understand what kind of conduct is prohibited (Pollock, 2009, pp. 13–14). While challenges of participation offenses on the grounds of vagueness have had little success (Marine, 2009, pp. 303–305; Schloenhardt, 2012, p. 160), certain jurisdictions have avoided some of these challenges by opting for the *labelling/registration model* of criminalizing involvement in a criminal organization.

Under the labelling/registration model, a two-tier system is established where first organizations are identified and individually given the status of criminal organizations and, second, certain links to these organizations are criminalized (Schloenhardt, 2012, pp. 148–149).

In one variant of the model, criminal organizations are labelled as such. For example, in Australia there are various laws aiming primarily at outlaw motorcycle gangs that allow the police to apply to a court for an organization to be declared a criminal organization. The declaration is made if a significant number of members of the organization associate for the purpose of organizing, planning, facilitating, supporting, or engaging in serious criminal activity and if the organization presents a risk to public safety and order (Ayling, 2011a, p. 156; Ayling, 2011c, p. 255; Rule of Law Institute of Australia, 2014). The declaration itself has no prohibitive force. Rather, it allows the police to request courts to impose so-called control orders with respect to individual members of a declared organization. For example, a person can be ordered not to communicate with specified other persons, not to approach certain premises, or not to undertake certain occupations. The orders can amount to the prohibition of all the conduct that defines being the member of the declared organization, namely, communicating and meeting with other members and participating in group activities. Defiance of these orders constitutes a criminal offense that carries a penalty of several years of imprisonment (Ayling, 2011c, p. 256).

A different approach has been taken in, for example, Hong Kong. Its Societies Ordinance requires all organizations to register and deems all unregistered organizations to be illegal. At the same time, certain organizations, those that pose a threat to public safety, are barred from registration (Schloenhardt, 2012, p. 149). Belonging to and providing support for an illegal organization constitute criminal offenses, whereby the highest penalties are reserved for triad societies (Kwok & Lo, 2013, p. 77; Schloenhardt, 2012, p. 150). The registration approach creates some of the same problems as the participation model because it is not necessarily clear what entities are required to register, what entities are

Image 14.1 Members of 14 New South Wales outlaw motorcycle gangs, including Hell's Angels and Bandidos, unite in June 2009 in Sydney, Australia, to protest against new legislation that gives government the power to declare an outlaw motorcycle gang a criminal organization.

Photo: © DEAN LEWINS/epa/Corbis

barred from registration, and what constitutes membership in an unlawful organization (Kwok & Lo, 2013). Like all other substantive criminal law prohibiting involvement in criminal collectives, however, it establishes criminal liability in some form or other for offenders to interact, cooperate, and associate with other offenders.

INVESTIGATIVE TOOLS AND INSTITUTIONAL INNOVATIONS AS INSTRUMENTS AGAINST ORGANIZED CRIME

Whereas many anti-organized crime measures have focused on increasing the criminal liability for conduct related to organized crime, efforts have also been made to increase the likelihood that organized criminals are brought to justice under existing criminal law. A central element in this strategy has been to improve the capacity of law enforcement agencies to collect information on organized criminals, for example, by systematically monitoring their communication and movement. Other elements of the strategy to make investigations and prosecutions in the area of organized crime more effective include measures to increase the willingness of witnesses to testify against organized criminals and to improve the collaboration of law enforcement agencies. Many of these measures have required changes in law, namely, the law of criminal procedure, but also changes in law enforcement policy, organization, and training, as well as changes in the use of technology.

Collection of Information: Intelligence and Criminal Investigation

Law enforcement agencies collect and process information on organized criminals for essentially two purposes, intelligence and criminal investigation (Lyman, 2005, p. 132). *Intelligence* means the collection and analysis of data independent of specific criminal proceedings (cases). In some jurisdictions, it is not even permissible to introduce intelligence as evidence in court (Campbell, 2013). However, the idea is that intelligence informs and guides criminal investigations (*intelligence-led policing*; see Congram, Bell, & Lauchs, 2013, p. 106). In the course of criminal investigations, information is collected in response to a specific criminal act. This information can become intelligence when it is of relevance beyond a single case, but the primary purpose of a criminal investigation is to support indictments and convictions. Despite their different purposes, both intelligence collection and criminal investigation in the area of organized crime are centered on the same phenomena, namely, criminal activities and criminal structures, and they are faced with problems that do not commonly emerge in normal police work. Typically, law enforcement agencies are prompted to investigate crimes by reports from victims and witnesses. In contrast, in the area of organized crime, inquiries tend to be launched proactively on the initiative of law enforcement agencies. In many instances there are no victims or witnesses to organized criminal activity that could alert the police to the fact that a crime has been committed; namely, in those cases where offenders operate clandestinely and where there are no direct victims because the criminal activity consists of illegal transactions between consenting participants. In instances where victims and witnesses exist, these may not be willing to report crimes to the police because of fear of retaliation or because they feel a sense of allegiance to the offenders. In addition, organized crime phenomena, unlike conventional crimes, do not tend to converge in time and space. There is typically not just one scene of crime to which perpetrators, victims, witnesses, and physical evidence are connected (see Chapter 4). In the area of organized crime, criminal events tend to extend across time and space. Bits and pieces of information about individuals and activities that at first glance may appear inconspicuous and unrelated have to be brought together into a coherent picture.

Conventional investigative techniques, such as witness interviews, fingerprint, and DNA analysis or the analysis of security camera footage, can play an important role in the area of organized crime. The same is true for financial investigations that involve the analysis of bank records and money flows through the financial system. However, some investigative techniques are more characteristically used in organized crime cases than in the investigation of ordinary crimes.

Two main forms of information gathering in the area of organized crime can be distinguished:

- Surveillance of the conduct and communication of organized criminals
- Infiltration of criminal structures by informants and undercover agents

Surveillance

Surveillance can be defined as "the surreptitious observation of persons, places, objects, or conveyances for the purpose of determining criminal involvement" (Lyman, 2007, p. 109). Some surveillance is *overt*, so that the targets are aware of the fact that they are being observed. For example, the police may openly record the license plates of those attending the funeral of a mafioso to establish associational patterns. In such cases, secrecy is not a necessity, and the overt surveillance may serve the additional purpose of increasing the stress level of organized criminals. However, it seems safe to say that most surveillance in the area of organized crime is *covert*. The aim is to monitor incriminating behavior and communication of organized criminals that they will tend to engage in only under the assumption that no law enforcement agency is watching or listening.

Traditionally, police surveillance is *physical*, which means that law enforcement officers directly observe their targets, for example, by tailing a drug courier to see where the drugs are delivered. For obvious reasons, the usefulness of *physical surveillance* is limited. Much of organized crime-related conduct occurs outside of public view, and even where organized criminals communicate and operate in public places or semi-public places, such as restaurants and bars, police officers can find it difficult to blend into the environment without raising suspicion.

Today, law enforcement agencies have a wide array of surveillance technology at their disposal that reduces the need for physical surveillance. *Technical* or *electronic surveillance* makes it possible in various ways to unobtrusively monitor places, movement, and communication as well as activity on the Internet.

Video- and audio-recording devices can be placed, for example, in a car or inside a building to record and transmit conversations and transactions. The challenge here is to install these devices without being detected by the targeted individuals. The movement of a vehicle or an object such as a cargo container can be monitored with the help of a *GPS (Global Positioning System) tracker* or a similar transmitter. These small devices are affixed to the target object and send signals to satellites in regular intervals. On this basis, the geographical location of the target object anywhere on the globe can be computed with a margin of error of just a few meters (Becker & Dutelle, 2013, p. 57; Lyman, 2005, p. 163; Roedl, Elmes, & Conley, 2014, p. 41). Telecommunication via phone lines, mobile phones, or the Internet can be intercepted in a variety of ways, typically with direct assistance of service providers as mandated by law (see, e.g., Dantos & Mason, 2009, p. 34/4). The surveillance may extend to the content of the communication or, in a less intrusive way, may be confined to recording connection data, for example, the numbers that are called from a monitored phone (*pen register*) or the numbers of incoming calls (*trap and trace*) (Mallory, 2012, p. 238). In addition, communication via the Internet and behavior on the Internet more generally can be monitored with the help of spy software that law enforcement agencies install on a targeted computer (Albanese, 2011, pp. 264–265). A special form of surveillance that has been applied in areas such as organized crime and terrorism is the systematic analysis of trash, also called a *trash cover*. The police sift through the garbage at a residence or business in an effort to find incriminating material, such as written notes (Bonanno, 1983, p. 356; Dyson, 2012, pp. 203–204). Surveillance measures can constitute an extreme invasion of privacy, especially when audio and video recording devices are placed in private homes. In one case, for example, the FBI listened in on the intimate encounters a Cosa Nostra boss had with his mistress inside his own home. Not only were conversations overheard that revolved around problems the boss had with impotence, the transcripts from the recorded conversations eventually made it to the public (O'Brien & Kurins, 1993, p. 163). Because of concerns over the protection of privacy, many countries have only reluctantly given their law enforcement agencies the authority to use surveillance measures such as *bugging* (microphones placed in homes and business) and *wiretapping* (interception of phone calls). The most intrusive forms of surveillance tend to be permissible only under strict legal limitations and only with prior court approval. Even if there were fewer legal restrictions, however, the number of surveillance operations may not necessarily increase, because they tend to be extremely costly and time consuming (Swanson, Chamelin, Territo, & Taylor, 2009, p. 656). It may well be that not the actual surveillance operations but the mere threat of coming under police surveillance has the greatest impact on organized criminals. Depending on how risk averse they are, organized criminals need to adapt their behavior to the possibility that they are being observed. This is not only true for surveillance but also for the use of informants and undercover agents.

Infiltration of Criminal Structures Through Informants and Undercover Agents

Similar to surveillance, informants and undercover agents are means to collect information. Their use, however, has a different quality. Whereas law enforcement agencies are largely passive, external observers when they conduct surveillance operations, informants and undercover agents permit law enforcement agencies to infiltrate criminal structures, to deceive organized criminals, and to actively influence their behavior.

Informants. An informant, broadly understood, is any person who provides information to a law enforcement agency on an occasional or regular basis. It can be a law-abiding citizen or an individual who is more or less directly involved in crime. In the area of organized crime, informants are widely used and they are generally considered a valuable investigative tool. The most highly valued but also the rarest types of informants are those who occupy central positions within criminal structures (Fitzgerald, 2007; Lyman, 2007, p. 88).

Informants supply information, and they may also be given certain tasks, such as introducing an undercover agent to a target person. The use of informants can be problematic because of conflicting interests, especially when the informant is a criminal (Swanson et al., 2009, p. 653). For example, by informing on rivals, informants may seek to exact revenge or eliminate competition within the underworld. If the law enforcement agency handling the informant follows up on these leads, it runs the risk of becoming a tool in the hands of a criminal. A related problem is that criminals may volunteer to be informants in order to learn about undercover tactics, ongoing investigations, or the identity of undercover agents and informants. There is also the problem that criminal activities of informants might be tolerated or even protected. For example, lower-level drug dealers may be allowed to continue dealing drugs in order to gain access to their suppliers (Lyman, 2005, p. 146). In one notorious case, FBI agents protected two leading figures of the Boston underworld in exchange for their assistance in the surveillance of the local Cosa Nostra boss. The FBI agents developed close personal ties to their informants and on various occasions shielded them from prosecution by sabotaging criminal investigations (Lehr & O'Neill, 2001). In such extreme cases, the question is whether the authorities run the informers or vice versa (Kruisbergen, de Jong, & Kleemans, 2011, p. 398).

A special category are *arrested informants* (Lyman, 2007, p. 89) who face criminal charges and agree to cooperate with law enforcement agencies in return for a reduced sentence. In the United States, this is the most frequently used technique to recruit informants (Fitzgerald, 2007, p. 45). Cooperating with authorities in exchange for leniency has become an increasingly lucrative option with the introduction of new and more severe penalties for organized criminals (see above). Even high-ranking Cosa Nostra members have worn a "wire," a hidden microphone, to covertly record incriminating conversations with fellow organized criminals (see, e.g., DeStefano, 2007).

Undercover Agents. Undercover agents, in contrast to informants, are law enforcement officers. They assume a fictitious identity in order to gain access to criminals. Most undercover operations are short term and may not involve more than a one-off encounter or transaction. For example, in a so-called buy-bust an undercover agent purchases drugs from a dealer who is then immediately arrested (Payne & Gainey, 2005, p. 84). Long-term, *deep cover* operations require an undercover agent to assume a different identity and lifestyle over an extended period of time with little direct supervision. Such assignments are generally considered dangerous, and they may expose the officer to enticements to break the law (Lyman, 2005, pp. 147–148).

Image 14.2 Joseph Pistone shown in a 2005 photo. Pistone, under the name Donnie Brasco, infiltrated the New York Cosa Nostra as a deep undercover agent for the FBI from 1976 until 1981.

Photo: Frederick M. Brown/Stringer

There are cross-national variations in the legal framework for undercover operations and specifically in the degree to which the involvement of undercover agents in criminal activities is tolerated. Generally speaking, undercover agents, just like informants, do not have a license to randomly engage in criminal activity. However, they can be participants in criminal conduct, for example, when they act as buyer or seller in a drug transaction. This means that "governments at least temporarily tolerate and even encourage crimes that they ultimately hope to suppress" (Ross, 2007, p. 497). In the United States, a public authority defense exempts undercover agents and informants from criminal liability for offenses committed undercover provided they have received prior approval from their supervisors within the police. In other parts of the world, namely in Europe, the matter is more controversial, and legal limits for undercover work tend to be stricter (Ross, 2007; Ross, 2008; see also Campbell, 2013, pp. 96–97; Nadelmann, 1997, pp. 227–229).

Undercover operations have been criticized not only for involving law enforcement officers in criminal activity but also for enticing target persons into committing crimes. When undercover agents (or informants) entice someone into committing a crime, it is called *entrapment* and is generally considered an illegal practice. In the United States, for example, undercover operatives are permitted to create *opportunities* for a suspect to commit a crime, but they may not *induce* the suspect to commit a crime (Lyman, 2005, p. 145).

Undercover operations are not only ethically problematic and dangerous but also time-consuming and costly, and it is not clear how effective they are (Albanese, 2011, p. 275). In a study of undercover operations by the Dutch police, Kruisbergen et al. (2011) found that most operations produced no results. The analysis encompassed all 34 undercover operations undertaken in the Netherlands during the year 2004. These included operations for the purpose of systematic intelligence collection as well as undercover buys of illegal goods. No infiltrations of criminal structures, the third type of undercover operation distinguished by Dutch law, were conducted in 2004. Seven of the 34 operations produced evidence that could be used in court, four operations led to the target person being excluded from further investigation because suspicions were not confirmed, and in one case the undercover operation did not produce clear indications of guilt or innocence but facilitated the use of other investigative methods. The remaining 22 operations did not produce any results, because no contact with the target person was made or because the contact did not lead to any relevant information (Kruisbergen et al., 2011, p. 401; see also Kruisbergen, Kleemans, & De Jong, 2012).

Undercover operations, similar to electronic surveillance, influence criminal activities and criminal structures beyond a specific case. Organized criminals tend to adapt in one way or the other to the possibility that they are the target of an undercover operation and that the persons they deal with are either informants or undercover agents (Johnson & Natarajan, 1995). In general, undercover policing contributes to an atmosphere of mistrust and paranoia within the underworld. It increases the stress level of organized criminals and forces them to invest time and effort in the screening and testing of potential accomplices in criminal endeavors and of potential business partners (suppliers and customers) in illegal transactions (Gambetta, 2009).

Witness Protection. Closely related to the use of informants are measures to increase the willingness of individuals to work as informants and to testify against organized criminals in court. The United States has pioneered such measures, consisting mainly of two components: granting cooperating witnesses who are involved in criminal activities immunity from prosecution or a reduction in sentences and protecting witnesses from potential reprisals. The Organized Crime Control Act of 1970, the same law that also comprised the RICO statute, gave prosecutors the authority to grant witnesses immunity from prosecution in exchange for testimony and laid the legal foundation for the federal *Witness Security Program* (WITSEC), which was introduced in 1971. WITSEC is operated by the U.S. Marshals Service and provides security and material support to witnesses and their immediate families, typically by relocating them under a new identity, making payments to cover basic living expenses, and assisting in obtaining legal employment (Fitzgerald, 2007, p. 262). A witness is eligible for WITSEC if his or her testimony is significant and essential to the prosecution of a serious crime, the testimony is credible and certain in coming, and there is a potential danger that the witness will be harmed (Fitzgerald, 2007, pp. 264–265).

WITSEC is a controversial institution, especially since many protected witnesses are themselves serious criminals. At the same time, the protection of witnesses appears to have facilitated the conviction of organized criminals (Albanese, 2011, pp. 295–296). As such it is an important component in a comprehensive law enforcement strategy against organized crime.

Following the example set by the United States, the protection of vulnerable witnesses, especially in cases of organized crime and terrorism, has become a major ethical and legal concern for criminal justice systems around the globe. Namely the UN Convention against Transnational Organized Crime mandates the adoption of appropriate measures to protect witnesses from intimidation and retaliation through such measures as physical protection, relocation, and the concealment of identities (Ram, 2001, p. 143; see also La Spina, 2008, p. 201; Vermeulen, 2005).

Institutional Innovations in the Fight Against Organized Crime

The introduction and development of law enforcement tools against organized crime have been closely linked to the formation of specialized organizational entities within the law enforcement apparatus. These entities tend to concentrate staff with expertise on organized crime phenomena and the know-how and authorization to use such investigative tools as electronic surveillance and undercover policing (Pütter, 1998). These specialized organizational entities can be found on all levels (local, national, and supranational). In many cases, specialized units are integral parts of law enforcement agencies or prosecutorial services, while in some cases separate organizations have been created, typically by drawing on experts from different existing agencies. Europol, for example, which supports and coordinates investigations against organized crime in Europe and facilitates the exchange of information between national law enforcement agencies, has been created for the expressed purpose of combating organized crime (Gerspacher & Lemieux, 2010). Other examples include the Organized Crime Strike Forces in the United States, which had been formed beginning in the late 1960s to combat specific Cosa Nostra families (Ryan, 1994), the *Direzione Investigativa Antimafia* (DIA) and the *Direzione Nazionale Antimafia* (DNA), which combine police and prosecutorial efforts against mafia-type organizations on the national level in Italy (Jamieson, 1999; La Spina, 2004; 2014), the Serious and Organised Crime Agency (SOCA) in the United Kingdom, which was later reorganized into the National Crime Agency

(NCA) (Sproat, 2012; Sproat, 2014), and the Directorate of Special Operations (DSO) in South Africa (Redpath, 2004).

NON-CRIMINAL JUSTICE APPROACHES TO COMBATING ORGANIZED CRIME

Effective law enforcement is a key factor in setting limits to the organization of crime and criminals. Not only the arrest and conviction of organized criminals and the forfeiture of their assets have a disruptive effect. It is also the mere threat of law enforcement intervention that makes it more difficult for criminals to organize and to operate. Still, even where law enforcement is effective—which, of course, is not the norm in many parts of the world—there appears to be a broad consensus that combating organized crime requires a more holistic response beyond the criminal justice system.

Two non-criminal justice approaches have received the most attention, the so-called *administrative approach to organized crime* and the *situational prevention of organized crime*. Both approaches overlap in theory and practice but they differ in at least two respects. The administrative approach focuses primarily on removing *known* organized criminals from the legal economy, while situational prevention aims at broadly reducing crime *opportunities*, irrespective of who the potential perpetrators might be. A further difference between the two approaches is that the administrative approach is largely confined to government action, although sometimes in collaboration with partners from the private sector. In contrast, situational crime prevention encompasses all sectors of society, including government, business, and private citizens.

Administrative Measures Against Organized Crime

The term administrative approach to organized crime is mostly associated with policies that have been adopted in the United States, Italy, and the Netherlands, where the government systematically uses means other than traditional law enforcement tools against organized criminals (Huisman & Nelen, 2007, p. 90).

Regulatory Systems to Eliminate Cosa Nostra Influence on Legitimate Businesses in the United States

An early example of administrative measures to combat organized crime is the regulation of casino gambling in the United States beginning in the 1950s. The state of Nevada, where casinos had been legal since 1931, established a regulatory framework with the aim of removing criminal influence, namely, the influence of Cosa Nostra members, from the industry. Applicants for gaming licenses had to undergo background checks, and individuals listed in a "Black Book" were explicitly barred from any involvement in the casinos (Bybee, 2013). An even more comprehensive licensing system was successfully established along with the legalization of casino gambling in Atlantic City, New Jersey, in 1977 (O'Brien & Flaherty, 1985).

Similar regulatory systems involving licensing and background checks were adopted in New York City during the 1990s, for business sectors infiltrated and controlled by members and associates of the Cosa Nostra. This included the Fulton Fish Market, the waste-hauling business, and the construction industry. In some cases, businesses have been obliged to hire a so-called Independent Private Sector Inspector General (IPSIG) as a precondition for obtaining a license or bidding for a public contract. IPSIGs are private firms, commonly run and staffed by individuals with a law enforcement background that monitor the conduct of their clients and report to the top management and to the authorities (Jacobs, 1999).

The Use of Civil RICO against Cosa Nostra Influence on Businesses and Labor Unions

The regulatory efforts undertaken in New York City in the 1990s were closely related to the use of civil RICO by the U.S. government to remove Cosa Nostra influence from the legal economy. As indicated before, the RICO statute does not only contain criminal provisions but also civil provisions that allow the government to seek court injunctions with the aim of preventing the future commission of RICO offenses. With the help of civil RICO proceedings, organized criminals have been removed from positions of influence in labor unions, and some labor unions have been placed under court-appointed trusteeship (Jacobs, 1999, 2006; Jacobs & Cooperman, 2011).

Forced Resettlement: The Italian Soggiorno Obbligato

Italy has experimented with a different administrative approach to controlling organized crime dating back to 1956. In that year, Italy implemented a law that provided for procedures to place dangerous individuals under "special surveillance" or under house arrest or to send them into internal exile (L. 27-12-1956 n. 1423). This law was later expanded to explicitly apply to members of mafia-like associations (L. 31-3-1965 n. 575; Manna, 1997, p. 249).

The law has been widely used for the forced relocation (soggiorno obbligato) of mafiosi from the south to the north of the country. However, contrary to expectations "that away from their home base and immersed in the civic, law-abiding culture of the north, mafiosi from the south would abandon their old ways," the soggiorno obligato had more of the opposite effect by leading to a geographical expansion of criminal networks (Varese, 2011, p. 16).

Other, more recent administrative measures adopted in Italy include awareness campaigns in schools and in the public and the financial compensation of businesses that refuse to make "protection" payments to mafia groups. In addition, efforts have been made to improve communication between administrative agencies and law enforcement agencies to prevent mafia influence on public contracts (La Spina, 2008).

The Administrative Approach to Organized Crime in Amsterdam

A similarly recent undertaking, inspired by the example of New York City, is the administrative approach of the city of Amsterdam in the Netherlands

(Fijnaut, 2002). Here, the term administrative approach stands for a multifaceted program to prevent and to reduce the influence of organized criminals on municipal government and the local economy, especially the construction industry and Amsterdam's red light district. At the core of the program, which was implemented for the most part in the early 2000s, is a system for the sharing and collation of information, including classified information, from municipal, law enforcement, and tax authorities. On the basis of this information, licenses and permits are refused or withdrawn and certain establishments are closed when it is apparent that they serve to launder illicit proceeds or otherwise facilitate criminal activity (Huisman & Nelen, 2007). In addition, the city government, in cooperation with third parties, has acquired real estate property in the inner city to end undesirable usage of buildings and to prevent leading figures of the red light district to gain a position of power within the legal spheres of society by buying up real estate (Ayling, 2014, p. 94; Köbben, 2002, pp. 82–85; Huisman & Nelen, 2007).

The administrative approach not only constrains the activities of organized criminals who have been identified as such, but also the systems of screening and monitoring that are set up under this approach apparently make it more difficult for any criminal to obtain public contracts, invest illicit proceeds in real estate or legitimate businesses, or to use legitimate businesses as cover for illegal activities. This became evident when at one point in time it was announced that the administrative approach would be extended to bars and catering businesses in a certain neighborhood of Amsterdam. As Huisman and Nelen (2007, p. 101) note, in response to the announcement "25 establishments immediately folded." In this respect, the administrative approach serves to reduce crime opportunities more generally. It is therefore not just a tool for the suppression but also for the prevention of organized crime.

The Situational Prevention of Organized Crime

The idea that organized crime should not only be addressed reactively by criminal justice or administrative means but also proactively, in a preventive way, has slowly gained ground since the 1990s, following a general trend in criminal policy toward a stronger emphasis on crime prevention. Crime prevention is a very broad notion encompassing "any activity, by an individual or group, public or private, that precludes the incidence of one or more criminal acts" (Brantingham & Faust, 1976, p. 284; Bjørgo, in press). Crime prevention ranges from long-term strategies to remove social and economic "root causes" of crime all the way to short-term opportunity-reducing measures that are subsumed under the concept of situational crime prevention.

Situational Crime Prevention

Situational crime prevention is a pragmatic approach to reducing crime. It has been successfully applied in dealing with a wide range of ordinary, non-organized offenses, such as theft and burglary (Guerette & Bowers, 2009; Poyner, 1993; Welch & Farrington, 1999). This has given rise to the question to what extent similar successes could be claimed against organized crime (Bullock, Clarke, & Tilley, 2010; Kleemans, Soudijn, & Weenink, 2012; Van de Bunt & Van der Schoot, 2003; Van der Schoot, 2006).

Situational crime prevention is inspired by routine activity theory and rational choice theory and rests on the assumption that crime is the result of the convergence in time and space of three factors: a motivated *offender*, a suitable *target*, and the absence of persons (*guardians*) who are in a position to intervene, directly or indirectly, with the criminal event (Clarke & Eck, 2005; Cohen & Felson, 1979). The motivated offender in this "crime triangle" is considered to be a "reasoning criminal" (Cornish & Clarke, 1986) who, while encountering crime opportunities in the course of day-to-day (routine) activities, takes into account the specifics of a given situation and makes decisions on whether or not to actually commit a crime based on a cost-benefit analysis. By changing the concrete situational circumstances in a way that the costs of crime increase and the benefits from crime decrease it is possible, the assumption goes, to influence the criminal decision-making process and to prevent crime (Clarke, 1997; Cornish & Clarke, 1986).

Five broad categories of opportunity reducing techniques have been distinguished:

- Increase the effort of crime
- Increase the risks of being apprehended
- Reduce the rewards
- Reduce provocations
- Remove excuses

(Clarke & Eck, 2005, p. 75).

These techniques have to be tailored to the concrete circumstances and to the specific nature of the crime that is supposed to be prevented. Textbook examples of situational prevention techniques include target hardening, such as the installation of steering-wheel locks in cars, and the increase of guardianship through trimming hedges so that passersby have an unobstructed view to a private home and are able to spot a burglary in progress.

The Applicability of Situational Crime Prevention to Organized Crime

The proponents of situational crime prevention have argued that the situational perspective is particularly fitting for organized crime because it "is rational crime par excellence" (Cornish & Clarke, 2002, p. 41; see also Felson & Clarke, 2012). Others have been more skeptical. For example, Edwards and Levi (2008) have advocated an extension and reformulation of the framework of situational crime prevention to include political, economic, and cultural contingencies of crime situations. Other concerns pertain to the question of how well organized crime phenomena fit the model of the crime triangle. Irrespective of crime-specific details, several caveats exist (von Lampe, 2010, 2011a).

First, organized crime is not commonly associated with one-off crime events in a specific location but with continuous criminal activity that, as in the case of intercontinental trafficking, may be dispersed across great geographical distances. In the course of the commission of such crimes, offenders may be faced with varying situational contexts. For example, in a typical car trafficking scheme, the theft of a car from a parking lot or the street poses challenges for offenders that are fundamentally different from altering the identity of the car inside a garage, transporting the car overseas inside a container under the guise of legal commerce, or selling the car fraudulently to an unwitting buyer through a posting on the Internet. The implication is that from one phase to the next in a crime script, the nature of the target and the presence of capable guardians may fundamentally change (von Lampe, 2011a). Accordingly, prevention measures need to target multiple situations or the one or two situations where the logistics of a criminal endeavor can be most effectively disrupted.

Second, it has been argued that organized criminals, through cooperation, tend to be more resourceful than ordinary criminals. They do not necessarily encounter lucrative crime situations in the course of routine activities. Instead they may well be able to methodically seek out or even engineer opportunities and circumvent and neutralize obstacles, for example, by corrupting officials (Ekblom, 2003, pp. 248–252, 257). This means that in the case of organized crime, situational crime prevention measures have to account for greater flexibility and adaptability on the part of potential offenders.

A third caveat in the applicability of situational crime prevention is that the mechanisms assumed to be at work in a normal crime setting may not work in the same way with respect to organized crime. The expectation underlying situational crime prevention is that the mere presence of third persons is usually sufficient to discourage crime, because potential offenders have to fear that these guardians would directly intervene or at least alert the police and eventually testify in court (Miethe & Meier, 1994, p. 90). However, as Marcus Felson (2006a, p. 91) and Edwards and Levi (2008, pp. 375, 377) have pointed out, the opposite can be true in areas dominated by criminal groups. In an atmosphere marked by fear and intimidation or by a profound distrust in government, bystanders are unlikely to intervene with criminal activity and may in fact be more likely to obstruct law enforcement efforts. For example, in a survey of small independent businesses in three neighborhoods in England "believed by the police to have been the site of significant organized criminal activity," Tilley and Hopkins (2008) found that offers of counterfeit, stolen, or smuggled goods were frequently received but rarely reported. The study concluded that businesses and local residents in general might see themselves as beneficiaries of crimes, such as the sale of illicit goods (Tilley & Hopkins, 2008, p. 452). The consequence is that in an area dominated by criminals the main emphasis may have to be placed on situational prevention techniques that do not rely on the guardianship of private citizens.

A further difference between normal crime and organized crime with respect to the applicability of situational crime prevention is the greater relevance of offender networking relative to the mere commission of criminal acts. Marcus Felson (2006b) has highlighted this aspect with his concept of offender convergence settings (see Chapter 5). He argues that illegal activities involving more than one offender are not only dependent on opportunities for crime but also on opportunities for meeting and associating with other offenders. This implies that situational prevention techniques should be implemented not only to reduce opportunities for criminal activity but also to undermine the formation of criminal networks.

Situational Prevention Strategies Aiming at Organized Crime

Much of the discussion on the situational prevention of organized crime is theoretical, contemplating possible applications and necessary reformulations of the situational crime prevention framework (Bullock et al., 2010; Lemieux, 2014). To date it does not seem that a holistic program for the prevention of organized crime has been designed and implemented that would comprehensively target illegal activities and criminal structures in a particular geographical area or in the context of a particular illegal market.

Examples of the situational prevention of organized crime typically pertain to measures that do not specifically target organized criminal activities but rather have a spillover effect on organized crime (Bouloukos, Farrell, & Laycock, 2003, p. 187; Hicks, 1998). For instance, the various measures of target hardening to prevent car theft, such as steering-wheel locks and electronic immobilizers, affect the theft of cars generally, not just in the case of the trafficking of stolen motor vehicles. Likewise, alarm and surveillance systems in private homes and businesses aim at discouraging burglary gangs and individual burglars alike. However, there is also a discussion to what extent such preventive measures and countermeasures in general contribute to a selection process that favors the emergence and predominance of more sophisticated and more resilient criminal structures.

Some efforts, namely, the administrative approach in Amsterdam, have retrospectively been interpreted as representing manifestations of situational crime prevention (Ayling, 2014; Nelen, 2010). Likewise, policing strategies have been recast in the mold of situational prevention (Kirby & Nailer, 2013). Along these lines, the anti-money-laundering regime is perhaps the most comprehensive program specifically aiming at the prevention of organized crime. After all, it mainly targets the economically more successful criminals—apart from terrorists and those who evade taxes on legal income—and it follows some of the core principles of situational crime prevention. For instance, a key component of the anti-money-laundering regime, as mentioned before, is the obligation of banks and other businesses to document and report financial transactions. In the terminology of situational crime prevention, these are measures to "extend guardianship" in order to "increase the risks of crime" (Clarke & Eck, 2005, p. 78). Many other measures aiming at organized crime could likewise be recast in the framework of situational crime prevention, such as the control orders issued under the Australian laws against criminal organizations or the systematic surveillance carried out in undercover policing operations. This highlights the "hybridity" (Ayling, 2014, p. 87) of modern anti-organized crime strategies where repressive (criminal justice) and preventive measures are combined and overlap in various ways.

Civil Society in the Fight Against Organized Crime

The countermeasures against organized crime that have been discussed in this chapter, with the exception of situational crime prevention, fall largely within the domain of government. What is left to address is the role that civil society plays in combating organized crime. *Civil society* is a contested concept that broadly pertains to the social sphere between the individual and the state. Important institutions of civil society are nongovernmental organizations (NGOs), grassroots initiatives, protest movements, and independent media (Edwards, 2009, 2011). The role that journalists play in exposing organized crime has already been alluded to in Chapter 3. The fact that many journalists have been harassed, assaulted, and killed because of their reporting is a clear indication of how sensitive organized criminals and their allies are to public exposure.

Image 14.3 Demonstrators in Palermo, Sicily, show their support for prosecutor Nino di Matteo after incarcerated Mafia boss Toto Riina had issued death threats against him.

Photo: Antonio Melita/Demotix/Corbis

Civic engagement against organized crime can take on various forms. An example for actions akin to political protest movements is provided by events that took place in the town of Galeana in the Mexican state of Chihuahua in 2009. After a string of kidnappings, the brother of the latest victim led a crowd to the central town square. Several thousand people occupied the square throughout the night, declaring that they would not pay ransom money. A few days later, the kidnapping victim was released without any money being paid. However, two months later the victim's brother who had initiated the protest was taken from his home and murdered (Kellner & Pipitone, 2010, p. 35).

The antimafia movement in Sicily provides an example for a more sustained campaign against organized crime. Initially, in the years after World War II, civil society's struggle with the Mafia was largely a matter of communist-led peasants fighting for land reform against an alliance of landowners, politicians, and mafiosi (Schneider & Schneider, 2001, p. 429). Then, as mafia violence against representatives of the state escalated, the social base of the antimafia movement widened considerably. Key events that aroused antimafia sentiments were the murders of Pio La Torre and Carlo Dalla Chiesa in 1982 and the murders of Giovanni Falcone and Paolo Borsellino in 1992 (see Chapter 11). One visible sign of success of the movement was the election of Leoluca Orlando, a pronounced opponent of the Mafia, as mayor of Palermo in 1985 and again in 1993, this time as the candidate of a newly formed single-issue antimafia party (Schneider & Schneider, 2001, p. 439).

Since the early 1980s, a number of organizations and grassroots-level initiatives have sprung up to attack the Mafia and the culture within which it is embedded. For example, on the night of Falcone's funeral, three sisters and their daughters, later dubbed the Committee of the Sheets (*Comitato dei Lenzuoli*), hung sheets with antimafia slogans from their balconies in Palermo and later distributed a pamphlet entitled *Nine Uncomfortable Guidelines for the Citizen Who Wants to Confront the Mafia*. In this pamphlet, the "committee" called on citizens to report corruption, extortion, and favoritism and to educate their children in a spirit of civic engagement (Jamieson, 1999, p. 131; Schneider & Schneider, 2001, p. 440).

Another example of a grassroots initiative against the Mafia is *Addiopizzo*, a community of consumers and businesses seeking to reduce the prevalence of protection payments (Partridge, 2012). Beginning in the mid-2000s, *Addiopizzo* has been publishing lists of businesses that publically declare not to pay protection money to the Mafia and lists of consumers who pledge to shop in stores that openly denounce Mafia protection (La Spina, 2008; Partridge, 2012). The initiative seems to have had a deterrent effect insofar as collectors of protection money, according to one mafia turncoat, stay away from businesses that belong to *Addiopizzo* (Partridge, 2012, p. 348). On the other hand, the reach of *Addiopizzo* has remained limited. Member businesses tend to be prevalent only in the better-off parts of Palermo, and consumer activists typically come from the younger, well-educated segments of society (Partridge, 2012, pp. 357–358).

This hints at a general problem of civic and political movements against organized crime. It is difficult to eradicate criminal practices and criminal structures that are deeply entrenched in the social, political, economic, and cultural fabric of society. This is especially true where people find their livelihood depending on organized crime, as in the case of business owners who profit from criminal protection or in the case of individuals who derive an income from illicit activities. Measures against organized crime, in order to be successful in the long run, need to secure sustained public support. For this to happen, countermeasures need to include functional alternatives to the benefits that especially the disadvantaged segments of society derive from the existence of illegal markets and illegal governance (Abadinsky, 2013, p. 35; Partridge, 2012; Schneider & Schneider, 2001).

COMBATING ORGANIZED CRIME: SUMMARY AND CONCLUSION

This chapter has attempted to provide a systematic, though not exhaustive, overview of what is being done to counter organized crime. The main emphasis has been on the role of government and in particular the criminal justice system. Other responses to organized crime that have been discussed include administrative approaches, namely the use of licensing systems, to reduce the influence of organized criminals, and situational approaches to reduce opportunities for criminal activities and offender networking. Finally, the role of civil society in the fight against organized crime has been discussed, focusing primarily on grassroots initiatives against the Sicilian Mafia as an illustrative example.

Because of the multifaceted nature of the phenomena that are subsumed under the term organized crime, there cannot be one universal remedy. The various countermeasures that have been devised and implemented address different components of the overall picture of organized crime (Chapter 13). Some measures aim at the social embeddedness and the social support base of criminal activities, criminal structures, and illegal governance. One example is provided by the *Addiopizzo* campaigns against Mafia protection. Other measures likewise seek to create a less compliant and more hostile environment for organized criminals. The anti-money-laundering regime, for example, has made it difficult for organized criminals to enlist the help of banks and other businesses in managing and protecting illegal funds.

The formation and maintenance of criminal structures is hampered by a variety of measures. Laws that criminalize involvement in criminal organizations increase the stakes of co-offending and criminal association. Investigative techniques, such as the use of informants and undercover agents, sow distrust and suspicion among criminals; and witness protection programs increase the likelihood of defection from criminal collectives. Criminal collaboration is further hampered by the continuously improving ability of law enforcement agencies to monitor the communication and movement of criminals. These investigative tools increase the risk of detection and conviction for a criminal as a direct result of the interaction with other criminals. Some measures even have an immediate effect on the networking of offenders, such as court orders under Australia's laws against criminal organizations. These orders can, for example, prohibit any contact among the members of an outlaw motorcycle gang.

Organized criminal activities are affected by situational prevention measures that reduce crime opportunities. Administrative measures that deny organized criminals business licenses and access to public contracts can have a similar opportunity-reducing effect. The actual operation of criminal enterprises and the functioning of illegal markets as well as the exercise of illegal governance are vulnerable to surveillance and undercover policing, just like the networking and interaction of organized criminals more generally.

How effective these measures are and to what extent their negative side effects, for example, in terms of the impact on privacy and civil liberties, outweigh their benefits is difficult to say. What seems certain, however, is that a functioning criminal justice system as part of a government that enjoys a high degree of legitimacy in combination with a vigilant civil society leave little breathing room for organized crime.

Discussion Questions

1. What type of countermeasure is most effective against organized crime?
2. Should informants and undercover agents be allowed to commit crimes?
3. Are witness protection programs similar to WITSEC feasible in all countries?
4. Can investigative tools such as electronic surveillance and undercover agents be used as effectively against organized corporate criminals as against drug trafficking or the Mafia?

Research Projects

1. Analyze the autobiography of an organized criminal with a view to personal experiences of the effect of countermeasures against organized crime.
2. Explore the existence of special units against organized crime in a particular police agency.
3. Select a local organized crime problem and devise a comprehensive prevention strategy.

Further Reading

Combating and Preventing Organized Crime

Beare, M. E., & Woodiwiss, M. (2014). U.S. organized crime control policies exported abroad. In L. Paoli (Ed.), *The Oxford handbook of organized crime* (pp. 545–571). Oxford, England:: Oxford University Press.

Broadhurst, R., & Farrelly, N. (2014). Organized crime "control" in Asia: Experiences from India, China, and the Golden Triangle. In L. Paoli (Ed.), *The Oxford handbook of organized crime* (pp. 634–654). Oxford, England: Oxford University Press.

Fijnaut, C. (2014). European Union organized crime control policies. In L. Paoli (Ed.), *The Oxford handbook of organized crime* (pp. 572–592). Oxford, England: Oxford University Press

Hartfield, C. (2008). The organization of "organized crime policing" and its international context. *Criminology and Criminal Justice*, 8(4), 483–507.

Kilchling, M. (2014). Finance-oriented strategies of organized crime control. In L. Paoli (Ed.), *The Oxford handbook of organized crime* (pp. 655–673). Oxford, England: Oxford University Press.

Levi, M., & Maguire, M. (2004). Reducing and preventing organised crime: An evidence-based critique, *Crime, Law and Social Change*, 41(5), 397–469.

Marx, G. T. (1988). *Undercover: Police surveillance in America*. Berkeley, CA: University of California Press.

Orlando, L. (2001). *Fighting the Mafia and renewing Sicilian culture*. San Francisco, CA: Encounter.

Paoli, L., & Fijnaut, C. (2008). Organised crime and its control policies. *European Journal of Crime, Criminal Law and Criminal Justice*, 14(3), 307–327.

Yordanova, M., & Markov, D. (2012). *Countering oganised crime in Bulgaria: Study on the legal framework*. Sofia, Bulgaria: Center for the Study of Democracy (CSD).

Investigating Organized Crime

Bonavolonta, J., & Duffy, B. (1996). *The good guys: How we turned the FBI 'round- and finally broke the mob.* New York, NY: Simon Schuster.

Dobyns, J., & Johnson-Shelton, N. (2009). *No angel: My harrowing undercover journey to the inner circle of the Hells Angels.* New York, NY: Crown.

Griffin, J. (2002). *Mob nemesis: How the FBI crippled organized crime.* New York, NY: Prometheus.

Lavigne, Y. (1997). *Hells Angels: Into the abyss.* New York, NY: Harper.

McClintick, D. (1993). *Swordfish: A true story of ambition, savagery, and betrayal.* New York, NY: Pantheon.

Pistone, J. D. (1987). *Donnie Brasco: My undercover life in the Mafia.* New York, NY: New American Library.

Queen, W. (2006). *Under and alone: The true story of the undercover agent who infiltrated America's most violent outlaw motorcycle gang.* New York, NY: Fawcett Books.

Roemer, W. F. (1989). *Roemer: Man against the mob.* New York, NY: Donald I. Fine.

Salerno, J., & Rivele, S., J. (1990). *The plumber: The true story of how one good man helped destroy the entire Philadelphia Mafia.* New York, NY: Knightsbridge.

Speziale, J. (2004). *Without a badge: Undercover in the world's deadliest criminal organization.* New York, NY: Pinnacle Books.

Verhoeven, M., & Van Gestel, B. (2011). Human trafficking and criminal investigation strategies in the Amsterdam Red Light District. *Trends in Organized Crime, 14*(2–3), 148–164.

Vizzini, S. (1972). *Vizzini: The secret lives of America's most successful undercover agent.* New York, NY: Arbor House.

Bibliography

Abadinsky, H. (1981). *The Mafia in America: An oral history.* New York, NY: Praeger.

Abadinsky, H. (2013). *Organized crime* (10th ed.). Belmont, CA: Wadsworth.

Adamoli, S., Di Nicola, A., & Savona, E. U. (1998). *Organised crime around the world.* Helsinki, Finland: European Institute for Crime Prevention and Control.

Adler, P. A. (1985). *Wheeling and dealing: An ethnography of an upper-level drug dealing and smuggling community.* New York, NY: Columbia University Press.

Ahrne, G. (1990). *Agency and organization: Towards an organizational theory of society.* London, England: Sage.

Ahrne, G. (1994). *Social organizations: Interaction inside, outside and between organizations.* London, England: Sage.

Albanese, J. S. (1987). Predicting the incidence of organized crime: A preliminary model. In T. S. Bynum (Ed.), *Organized crime in America: Concepts and controversies* (pp. 103–114). Monsey, NY: Criminal Justice Press.

Albanese, J. S. (1988). Government perceptions of organized crime: The presidential commissions 1967 and 1987. *Federal Probation, 52*(1), 58–63.

Albanese, J. S. (1989). *Organized crime in America* (2nd ed.). Cincinnati, OH: Anderson.

Albanese, J. S. (1994). Models of organized crime. In R. J. Kelly, K.-L. Chin, & R. Schatzberg (Eds.), *Handbook of organized crime in the United States* (pp. 77–89). Westport, CT: Greenwood.

Albanese, J. S. (2011). *Organized crime in our times* (6th ed.). Burlington, MA: Anderson.

Albanese, J. S., & Reichel, P. (Eds.). (2014). *Transnational organized crime: An overview from six continents.* Thousand Oaks, CA: Sage.

Albini, J. (1971). *The American Mafia: Genesis of a legend.* New York, NY: Meredith Corporation.

Albini, J. L. (1988). Donald Cressey's contributions to the study of organized crime: An evaluation. *Crime and Delinquency, 34*(3), 338–354.

Allsop, K. (1968). *The bootleggers: The story of Chicago's Prohibition Era.* New Rochelle, NY: Arlington House.

Allum, F., & Gilmour, S. (Eds.). (2012). *Routledge handbook of transnational organized crime.* London, England: Routledge.

Almog, D. (2004). Tunnel-vision in Gaza. *Middle East Quarterly, 11*(3), 1–8.

Ambagtsheer, F., Zaitch, D., & Weimar, W. (2013). The battle for human organs: Organ trafficking and transplant tourism in a global context. *Global Crime, 14*(1), 1–26.

Amendt, G. (1990). *Sucht, profit, sucht.* Reinbek, Germany: Rowohlt Taschenbuch.

Amir, M. (1995). Organized crime and violence, *Studies on Crime and Crime Prevention, 4*(1), 86–104.

Ampratwum, E. F. (2009). Advance fee fraud "419" and investor confidence in the economies of sub-Saharan African (SSA). *Journal of Financial Crime, 16*(1), 67–79.

Anastasia, G. (1993). *Blood and honor.* New York, NY: Zebra Books.

Anderson, A. G. (1979). *The business of organized crime: A Cosa Nostra family.* Stanford, CA: Hoover Institution Press.

Anderson, P. (2006). Global use of alcohol, drugs and tobacco. *Drug and Alcohol Review, 25*(6), 489–502.

Andersson, H. (2003). Illegal entrepreneurs: A comparative study of the liquor trade in Stockholm and New Orleans 1920–1940. *Journal of Scandinavian Studies in Criminology and Crime Prevention, 3*(2), 114–134.

Andreas, P. (1999). Smuggling wars: Law enforcement and law evasion in a changing world. In T. Farer (Ed.), *Transnational crime in the Americas: An inter-American dialogue book* (pp. 85–98). New York, NY: Routledge.

Andreas, P. (2013). *Smuggler nation: How illicit trade made America.* New York: Oxford University Press.

Andreas, P., & Wallman, J. (2009). Illicit markets and violence: What is the relationship? *Crime, Law and Social Change, 52*(3), 225–229.

Aniskiewicz, R. (2012). "Portraits" in the world of organized crime. In E. W. Plywaczewski (Ed.), *Current problems of the penal law and criminology* (pp.19–31). Warsaw, Poland: Wolters Kluwer Polska.

Antonopoulos, G. A. (2008a). The Greek connection(s): The social organization of the cigarette-smuggling business in Greece. *European Journal of Criminology, 5*(3), 263–288.

Antonopoulos, G. A. (2008b). Interviewing retired cigarette smugglers. *Trends in Organized Crime, 11*(1), 70–81.

Antonopoulos, G. A., Hornsby, R., & Hobbs, D. (2011). Sound and vision: Nigerian street entrepreneurs in Greece. In G. Antonopoulos, M. Groenhuijsen, J. Harvey, T. Kooijmans, A. Maljevic, & K. von Lampe (Eds.), *Usual and unusual organising criminals in Europe and beyond: Profitable crimes, from underworld to upper world—Liber Amicorum Petrus van Duyne* (pp. 804–822). Apeldoorn, the Netherlands: Maklu.

Antonopoulos, G. A., & Papanicolaou, G. (2009). "Gone in 50 seconds" The social organisation and political economy of the stolen cars market in Greece. In P. C. van Duyne, S. Donati, J. Harvey, A. Maljevic, & K. von Lampe (Eds.), *Crime, money and criminal mobility in Europe* (141–174). Nijmegen, the Netherlands: Wolf Legal Publishers.

Antonopoulos, G. A., Papanicolaou, G., & Simpson, M. (2010). Entertainment starts with an E: The ecstasy market in Greece. *Trends in Organized Crime, 13*(1), 31–45.

Appleton, G. W. (1868). The "Camorra" of Naples, *The Galaxy, 5*, 641–644.

Arlacchi, P. (1986). *Mafia business: The Mafia ethic and the spirit of capitalism.* London, England: Verso.

Arlacchi, P. (1993). *Men of dishonor: Inside the Sicilian Mafia.* New York, NY: William Morrow.

Arlacchi, P. (1998). Some observations on illegal markets. In V. Ruggiero, N. South, & I. Taylor (Eds.), *The new European criminology: Crime and social order in Europe* (pp. 203–215). London, England: Routledge.

Arnold, E. (1862). *The Marquis of Dalhousie's administration of British India.* London, England: Saunders, Otley, and Co.

Aronowitz, A. A. (2001). Smuggling and trafficking in human beings: The phenomenon, the markets that drive it and the organisations that promote it. *European Journal on Criminal Policy and Research, 9*(2), 163–195.

Arsovska, J. (2008). Interviewing serious offenders: Ms. Egghead meets Mr. Gumshoe. *Trends in Organized Crime, 11*(1), 42–58.

Arsovska, J. (2012). Researching difficult populations: Interviewing techniques and methodological issues in face-to-face interviews in the study of organized crime. In L. Gideon (Ed.), *Handbook of survey methodology for the social sciences* (pp. 397–415). New York: Springer.

Arsovska, J. (2015). *Decoding Albanian organized crime: Culture, politics, and globalization.* Oakland, CA: University of California Press.

Arsovska, J., & Allum, F. (2014). Introduction: Women and transnational organized crime. *Trends in Organized Crime, 17*(1–2), 1–15.

Arsovska, J., & Begum, P. (2014). From West Africa to the Balkans: Exploring women's roles in transnational organized crime. *Trends in Organized Crime, 17*(1–2), 89–109.

Arsovska, J., & Kostakos, P. A. (2008). Illicit arms trafficking and the limits of rational choice theory: The case of the Balkans. *Trends in Organized Crime, 11*(4), 352–378.

Asbury, H. (1927). *The gangs of New York: An informal history of the underworld.* New York, NY: Alfred A. Knopf.

Asbury, H. (1933). *The Barbary coast: An informal history of the San Francisco underworld.* Garden City, NY: Alfred A. Knopf.

Asbury, H. (1942). *Gem of the prairie: An informal history of the Chicago underworld.* Garden City, NY: Alfred A. Knopf.

Astorga, L. (1999). *Drug trafficking in Mexico: A first general assessment.* Paris, France: UNESCO.

Attacks on Gaynor at Whitman dinner. (1912, November 23). *New York Times.*

Atteslander, P. (2003). *Methoden der empirischen sozialforschung* (10th ed.). Berlin, Germany: de Gruyter.

Australian Crime Commission (2011). *Organised crime in Australia.* Retrieved from https://www.crimecommission.gov.au/sites/default/files/oca2011.pdf

Ayling, J. (2009). Criminal organizations and resilience. *International Journal of Law, Crime and Justice, 37*(4), 182–196.

Ayling, J. (2011a). Criminalizing organizations: Towards deliberative lawmaking. *Law and Policy, 33*(2), 149–178.

Ayling, J. (2011b). Gang change and evolutionary theory. *Crime, Law and Social Change, 56*(1), 1–26.

Ayling, J. (2011c). Pre-emptive strike: How Australia is tackling outlaw motorcycle gangs. *American Journal of Criminal Justice, 36*(3), 250–264.

Ayling, J. (2014). "Going Dutch"? Comparing approaches to preventing organised crime in Australia and the Netherlands. *European Review of Organised Crime, 1*(1), 78–107.

Bailey, J., & Taylor, M. M. (2009). Evade, corrupt or confront? Organized crime and the state in Brazil and Mexico. *Journal of Politics in Latin America, 1*(2), 3–29.

Baird, J., Curry, R., & Cruz, P. (2014). An overview of waste crime, its characteristics, and the vulnerability of the EU waste sector. *Waste Management and Research, 32*(2), 97–105.

Baker, W. E., & Faulkner, R. R. (1993). The social organization of conspiracy: Illegal networks in the heavy electrical equipment industry. *American Sociological Review, 58*(6), 837–860.

Baldaccini, A. (2008). Counter-terrorism and the EU strategy for border security: Framing suspects with biometric documents and databases. *European Journal of Migration and Law, 10*(1), 31–49.

Barger, R. "Sonny" (2001). *Hell's Angel: The life and times of Sonny Barger and the Hell's Angels motorcycle club,* London: Fourth Estate.

Barker, T. (2007). *Biker gangs and organized crime.* Newark, NJ: Matthew Bender.

Barker, T. (2011). American based biker gangs: International organized crime. *American Journal of Criminal Justice, 36*(3), 207–215.

Barker, T., & Human, K. M. (2009). Crimes of the big four motorcycle gangs. *Journal of Criminal Justice, 37*(2), 174–179.

Barone, G., & Narciso, G. (2015). Organized crime and business subsidies: Where does the money go? *Journal of Urban Economics, 86,* 98–110.

Beare, M. E. (1996). *Criminal conspiracies: Organized crime in Canada.* Scarborough, Ontario, Canada: Nelson.

Beare, M. E. (Ed.). (2003a). *Critical reflections on transnational organized crime, money laundering and corruption.* Toronto: University of Toronto Press.

Beare, M. E. (2003b). Purposeful misconceptions: Organized crime and the state. In E. C. Viano, J. Magallanes, & L. Bridel (Eds.), *Transnational organized crime: Myth, power, and profit* (pp. 157–168). Durham, NC: Carolina Academic Press.

Beare, M. E. (2010). Women and organized crime, Report No. 013, Department of Public Safety. Canada. Retrieved from http://publications.gc.ca/collections/collection_2012/sp-ps/PS4–106–2010-eng.pdf

Becker, R. F., & Dutelle, A. W. (2013). *Criminal investigation* (4th ed.). Burlington, MA: Jones & Bartlett.

Beckert, J., & Wehinger, F. (2011, November 9). *In the shadow: Illegal markets and economic sociology.* Max Planck Institute for the Study of Societies, MPIfG Discussion Paper.

Becucci, S. (2011). Criminal infiltration and social mobilisation against the Mafia. Gela: A city between tradition and modernity. *Global Crime, 12*(1), 1–18. doi: 10.1080/17440572.2022.548961.

Bedeian, A. G., & Zammuto, R. F. (1991). *Organizations: Theory and design.* Hinsdale, IL: Dryden.

Beech, A. R., Elliott, I. A., Birgden, A., & Findlater, D. (2008). The Internet and child sexual offending: A criminological review. *Aggression and Violent Behavior, 13*(3), 216–228.

Behr, H.-G. (1987). *Organisiertes verbrechen.* Frankfurt am Main, Germany: Ullstein.

Beittel, J. S. (2011). *Mexico's drug trafficking organizations: Source and scope of the rising violence.* Washington, DC: Congressional Research Service.

Bell, D. (1953). Crime as an American way of life. *The Antioch Review, 13*(2), 131–145.

Berg, M., & Loeber, R. (2015). Violent conduct and victimization risk in the urban illicit drug economy: A prospective examination. *Justice Quarterly, 32*(1), 32–55. doi: 10.108017418825.2012.724079.

Berger, P. L., & Luckmann, T. (1966). *The social construction of reality: A treatise in the sociology of knowledge.* New York, NY: Doubleday.

Berger, R. J. (2011). *White-collar crime: The abuse of corporate and government power.* Boulder, CO: Lynne Rienner.

Bergreen, L. (1994). *Capone: The man and the era.* New York, NY: Simon & Schuster.

Bernstein, L. (2002). *The greatest menace: Organized crime in cold war America.* Amherst, MA: University of Massachusetts Press.

Bersten, M. (1990). Defining organised crime in Australia and the USA. *Australian and New Zealand Journal of Criminology, 23*(1), 39–59.

Besozzi, C. (2001). *Illegal, legal—egal? Zur Entstehung, Struktur und Auswirkungen illegaler Märkte.* Bern, Germany: Haupt.

Best, J., & Luckenbill, D. F. (1994). *Organizing deviance.* Englewood Cliffs, NJ: Prentice Hall.

Beyrer, C., Razak, M. H., Lisam, K., Chen, J., Lui, W., & Yu, X.-F. (2000). Overland heroin trafficking routes and HIV-1 spread in south and south-east Asia. *AIDS, 14*(1), 75–83.

Bezlov, T., & Gounev, P. (2012). Bulgaria: Corruption and organised crime in flux. In P. Gounev & V. Ruggiero (Eds.), *Corruption and organized crime in Europe: Illegal partnerships* (pp. 95–107). London, England: Routledge.

Bisschop, L. (2012). Is it all going to waste? Illegal transports of e-waste in a European trade hub. Crime, Law and Social Change, 58(3), 221–249.

Bjørgo, T. (in press). *Preventing crime: A holistic approach.* Houndsmill, England: Palgrave Macmillan.

Blakey, G. R. (2006). RICO: The genesis of an idea. *Trends in Organized Crime, 9*(4), 8–34.

Blickman, T., Korf, D. J., Siegel, D., & Zaitch, D. (2003). Synthetic drug trafficking in Amsterdam. In G. Abele (Ed.), *Synthetic drugs trafficking in three European cities: Major trends and the involvement of organized crime* (19–94). Turin, Italy: Gruppo Abele.

Black, C., Vander Beken, T., Frans, B., & Paternotte, M. (2000). *Reporting on organised crime: A shift from description to explanation in the Belgian annual report on organised crime.* Antwerp, Belgium: Maklu.

Block, A. A. (1980). The Organized Crime Control Act 1970: Historical issues and public policy. *Public Historian, 2*(2), 39–59.

Block, A. A. (1983). *East side, west side: Organizing crime in New York 1930–1950.* New Brunswick, NJ: Transaction Publishers.

Block, A. A., & Chambliss, W. J. (1981). *Organizing crime.* New York, NY: Elsevier.

Block, A. A., & Griffin, S. P. (1999). Build it, and they will come: Narcotics and money laundering in the leeward islands. *Journal of Contemporary Criminal Justice, 15*(4), 397–420.

Block A. A., & Scarpitti, F. R. (1985). *Poisoning for profit: The mafia and toxic waste in America.* New York, NY: William Morrow and Co.

Blok, A. (1974). *The Mafia of a Sicilian village 1860—1960: A study of violent peasant entrepreneurs.* Oxford, England: Basil Blackwell.

Bluhm, W. T. (1978). *Theories of the political system: Classics of political thought and modern political analysis* (3rd ed.). Englewood Cliffs, NJ: Prentice Hall.

Boissevain, J. (1974). *Friends of friends: Networks manipulators and coalitions.* Oxford, England: Basil Blackwell.

Bonanno, J. (1983). *A man of honor.* New York, NY: Simon & Schuster.

Borlini, L. (2014). The economics of money laundering. In P. Reichel & J. S. Albanese (Eds.), *Handbook of transnational crime and justice* (2nd ed., pp. 227–242). Thousand Oaks, CA: Sage.

Bouchard, M. (2007). On the resilience of illegal drug markets. *Global Crime, 8*(4), 325–344.

Bouchard, M., & Morselli, C. (2014). Opportunistic structures of organized crime. In L. Paoli (Ed.), *The Oxford handbook of organized crime* (pp. 288–302). Oxford, England: Oxford University Press.

Bouchard, M., & Ouellet, F. (2011). Is small beautiful? The link between risks and size in illegal markets. *Global Crime, 12*(1), 70–86.

Bouchard, M., & Wilkins, C. (Eds.). (2010). *Illegal markets and the economics of organized crime.* London, England: Routledge.

Bouloukos, A. C., Farrell, G., & Laycock, G. (2003). Transnational organised crime in Europe and North America: Towards a framework for prevention. In K. Aromaa & M. Heiskanen (Eds.), *Crime and criminal justice in Europe and North America 1995–1997: Report on the sixth United Nations survey on crime trends and criminal justice systems* (pp. 176–192). Helsinki, Finland: HEUNI.

Boutwell, G. S. (1865, July 30). The reconstruction question. *The New York Times.*

Bovenkerk, F. (2000). Wanted: "Mafia boss"—Essay on the personology of organized crime. *Crime, Law and Social Change, 33*(3), 225–242.

Bovenkerk, F., Siegel, D., & Zaitch, D. (2003). Organized crime and ethnic reputation manipulation, *Crime, Law and Social Change, 39*(1), 23–38.

Bowden, M. (2001). *Doctor dealer: The rise and fall of an all-American boy and his multimillion-dollar cocaine empire.* New York, NY: Grove Press.

Bowman, B. A. (2008). Transnational crimes against culture: Looting at archaeological sites and the "grey" market in antiquities. *Journal of Contemporary Criminal Justice, 24*(3), 225–242.

Bowman Proulx, B. (2011). Organized criminal involvement in the illicit antiquities trade. *Trends in Organized Crime, 14*(1), 1–29.

Brantingham, P. J., & Faust, F. L. (1976). A conceptual model of crime prevention. *Crime and Delinquency, 22*(3), 284–296.

Brantingham, P. L., & Brantingham, P. J. (1993). Environment, routine, and situation: Toward a pattern theory of crime. In R. V. Clarke & M. Felson (Eds.), *Routine activity and rational choice* (pp. 259–294). New Brunswick, NJ: Transaction.

Brayley, H., Cockbain, E., & Laycock, G. (2011). The value of crime scripting: Deconstructing internal child sex trafficking. *Policing, 5*(2), 132–143.

Bright, D.A., Delaney, J.J. (2013). Evolution of a drug trafficking network: Mapping changes in network structure and function across time. *Global Crime, 14*(2-3), 238–260.

Bright, D. A., Hughes, C. E., & Chalmers, J. (2012). Illuminating dark networks: A social network analysis of an Australian trafficking syndicate. *Crime, Law and Social Change, 57*(2), 151–176.

Broadhurst, R. (2012). Black societies and triad-like organized crime in China. In F. Allum & S. Gilmour (Eds.), *Routledge handbook of transnational organized crime* (pp. 157–170). London, England: Routledge.

Broadhurst, R. (2013). The suppression of black societies in China. *Trends in Organized Crime, 16*(1), 95–113.

Broadhurst, R., Grabosky, P., Alazab, M., Bouhours, B., Chon, S., & Da, C. (2013). *Crime in cyberspace: Offenders and the role of organized crime groups.* Canberra: Australian National University Cybercrime Observatory.

Broeders, D. (2007). The new digital borders of Europe: EU databases and the surveillance of irregular migrants. *International Sociology, 22*(1), 71–92.

Brouwer, K., Case, P., Ramos, R., Magis-Rodríguez, C., Bucardo, J., Patterson, T., & Strathdee, S. (2006). Trends in production, trafficking, and consumption of methamphetamine and cocaine in Mexico. *Substance Use & Misuse, 41*(5), 707–727.

Brown, M. (2002). Crime, governance and the company Raj: The discovery of Thuggee. *British Journal of Criminology, 42*(1), 77–95.

Brownstein, H. H., Mulcahy, T. M., Fernandes-Huessey, J., Taylor, B. G., & Woods, D. (2012). The organization and operation of illicit retail methamphetamine markets. *Criminal Justice Policy Review, 23*(1), 67–89.

Bruinsma, G., & Bernasco, W. (2004). Criminal groups and transnational illegal markets: A more detailed examination on the basis of social network theory. *Crime, Law and Social Change, 41*(1), 79–94.

Brymer, R. A. (1991). The emergence and maintenance of a deviant sub-culture: The case of hunting/poaching sub-culture. *Anthropologica, 33*(1–2), 177–194.

Buchanan, B. (2004). Money laundering—a global obstacle. *Research in International Business and Finance, 18* 115–127.

Buchanan, J. M. (1973). A defense of organized crime? In S. Rottenberg (Ed.), *The economics of crime and punishment* (pp. 119–132). Washington, DC: American Enterprise Institute for Public Policy Research.

Bueger, C. (2014). Piracy studies: Academic responses to the return of an ancient menace. *Cooperation and Conflict, 49*(3), 406–416.

Bullock, K., Clarke, R. V., & Tilley, N. (2010). Introduction. In K. Bullock, R. V. Clarke, & N. Tilley (Eds.), *Situational prevention of organised crimes* (pp. 1–16). Cullompton, UK: Willan.

Bunker, R. (2013). Introduction: The Mexican cartels—organized crime vs. criminal insurgency. *Trends in Organized Crime, 16*(2), 129–137.

Bybee, S. (2013). History, development, and legislation of Las Vegas casino gaming. In C. H. C. Hsu (Ed.), *Legalized casino gaming in the United States: The economic and social impact* (pp. 3–24). New York, NY: Routledge.

Calderoni, F. (2010). *Organized crime legislation in the European Union: Harmonization and approximation of criminal law, national legislations and the EU framework decision on the fight against organized crime.* Berlin, Germany: Springer.

Calderoni, F., Favarin, S., Ingrasci, O., & Smit, A. (2013). *The factbook on the illicit trade in tobacco products: Issue 1 United Kingdom.* Trento, Italy: Transcrime.

California Bureau of Organized Crime and Criminal Intelligence (1979). *Organized crime in California. 1978: Part 2, Prison Gangs, Outlaw Motorcycle Gangs.* Sacramento, CA: Bureau of Organized Crime and Criminal Intelligence.

Cami, J., & Farre, M. (2003). Drug addiction. *New England Journal of Medicine, 349*(10), 975–986.

Campana, P. (2011). Eavesdropping on the Mob: The functional diversification of Mafia activities across territories. *European Journal of Criminology, 8*(3), 213–228.

Campana, P., & Varese, F. (2013). Cooperation in criminal organizations: Kinship and violence as credible commitments. *Rationality and Society, 25*(3), 263–289.

Campbell, H. (2008). Female drug smugglers on the U.S.-Mexico border: Gender, crime, and empowerment. *Anthropological Quarterly, 81*(1), 233–267.

Campbell, L. (2013). *Organised crime and the law: A comparative analysis.* Oxford, England: Hart.

Canon, L. (1994). *Pablo Escobar: Leben und plötzlicher tod des kokainkönigs.* Berlin, Germany: Aufbau-Verlag.

Carey, E. (2014). *Women drug traffickers: Mules, bosses, and organized crime.* Albuquerque: University of New Mexico Press.

Carroll, T. M. (1983). *Microeconomic theory: Concepts and applications.* New York, NY: St. Martin's Press.

Casale, J. F., & Klein, R. F. X. (1993). Illicit production of cocaine. *Forensic Science Review, 5*(2), 95–107.

Case, K. E., & Fair, R. C. (1992). *Principles of macroeconomics* (2nd ed.). Englewood Cliffs, NJ: Prentice Hall.

Casey, J. (2010). *Policing the world: The practice of international and transnational policing.* Durham, NC: Carolina Academic Press.

Cassella, S. D. (2007). *Assess forfeiture law in the United States* (2nd ed.). Huntington, NY: Juris Net.

Catanzaro, R. (1992). *Men of respect: A social history of the Sicilian Mafia.* New York, NY: Free Press.

Caulkins, J. P., Burnett, H., & Leslie, E. (2009). How illegal drugs enter an island country: Insights from interviews with incarcerated smugglers. *Global Crime, 10*(1&2), 66–93.

Cawich, S. O., Valentine, C., Evans, N. R., Harding, H. E., & Crandon, I. W. (2009). The changing demographics of cocaine body packers in Jamaica. *Internet Journal of Forensic Science, 3*(2).

Ceccato, V. (2007). Crime dynamics at Lithuanian borders. *European Journal of Criminology, 4*(2), 131–160.

Chamberlin, H. B. (1919, October 1). *Crime as a business in Chicago* (Bulletin No. 6). Chicago Crime Commission.1–6.

Chamberlin, H. B. (1920). The Chicago Crime Commission—How the businessmen of Chicago are fighting crime. *Journal of the American Institute of Criminal Law and Criminology, 11*(3), 386–397.

Chamberlin, H. B. (1921, January 19). *Report of the operating director* (Bulletin N0.10). Chicago Crime Commission. 6–7.

Chamberlin, H. B. (1932). Some observations concerning organized crime. *Journal of Criminal Law and Criminology, 22*(5), 652–670.

Chambliss, W. J. (1975). On the paucity of original research on organized crime: A footnote to Galliher and Cain. *American Sociologist, 10*(1), 36–39.

Chambliss, W. J. (1978). *On the take: From petty crooks to presidents.* Bloomington: Indiana University Press.

Chambliss, W. J. (1989). State-organized crime: The American Society of Criminology 1988 presidential address. *Criminology, 27*(2), 183–208.

Cheloukhine, S. (2008). The roots of Russian organized crime: From old-fashioned professionals to the organized criminal groups of today. *Crime, Law and Social Change, 50*(4–5), 353–374.

Cheloukhine, S. (2012). Transnational organized crime in Russia. In F. Allum & S. Gilmour (Eds.), *Routledge handbook of transnational organized crime* (pp. 111–126). London: Routledge.

Cheloukhine, S., & Haberfeld, M. R. (2011). *Russian organized corruption networks and their international trajectories.* New York: Springer.

Chepesiuk, R. (2005). *Drug lords: The rise and fall of the Cali Cartel, the world's richest crime syndicate.* Wrea Green, England: Milo Books.

Chestnut Greitens, S. (2014). Illicit: North Korea's evolving operations to earn hard currency. Washington, DC: The Committee for Human Rights in North Korea. Retrieved from www.hrnk.org.

Chibelushi, C., Sharp, B., & Shah, H. (2006). ASKARI: A crime text mining approach. In P. Kanellis, E. Kiountouzis, N. Kolokotronics, & D. Martakos (Eds.), *Digital crime and forensic science in cyberspace* (pp. 155–174). Hershey, PA: Idea Group.

Chin, K.-L. (1990). *Chinese subculture and criminality: Non-traditional crime groups in America.* New York, NY: Greenwood Press.

Chin, K.-L. (1996). *Chinatown gangs: Extortion, enterprise, and ethnicity.* New York, NY: Oxford University Press.

Chin, K.-L., & Godson, R. (2006). Organized crime and the political-criminal nexus in China. *Trends in Organized Crime, 9*(3), 5–44.

Chin, K.-L., & Zhang, S. X. (2007). *The Chinese connection: Cross-border drug trafficking between Myanmar and China, final report.* Newark, NJ: Rutgers University.

Chiu, Y.-N., Leclerc, B., & Tinsley, M. (2011). Crime script analysis of drug manufacturing in clandestine laboratories. *British Journal of Criminology, 51*(2), 355–374.

Choo, K.-K. R. (2008). Organised crime groups in cyberspace: A typology: *Trends in Organized Crime, 11*(3), 270–295.

Chu, Y. K. (2000). *The triads as business.* London, England: Routledge.

Ciccarone, D., Unick, G. J., & Kraus, A. (2009). Impact of South American heroin on the US heroin market 1993–2004. *International Journal of Drug Policy, 20*(5), 392–401.

Ciecierski, C. (2007). The market for legal and illegal cigarettes in Poland: A closer look at demand and supply-side characteristics. (IDRC Working Paper Series/ITEN Working Paper Series N0.1.)

Clark, M. (2005). Organised crime: Redefined for social policy. *International Journal of Police Science & Management, 7*(2), 96–109.

Clarke, R. V. (1997). Introduction. In R. V. Clarke (Ed.), *Situational crime prevention: Successful case studies* (pp. 1–43). Guilderland, NY: Harrow & Heston.

Clarke, R. V., & Brown, R. (2003). International trafficking in stolen vehicles. In M. Tonry (Ed.), *Crime and justice: A review of research* (pp. 197–227). Chicago: The University of Chicago Press.

Clarke, R. V., & Eck, J. E. (2005). *Crime analysis for problem solvers: In 60 small steps.* Washington, DC: US Department of Justice.

Clawson, P. L., & Lee, Rensselaer W. III. (1996). *The Andean cocaine industry.* New York: St. Martin's.

Clinard, M. B. (1990). *Corporate corruption: The abuse of power.* New York, NY: Praeger.

Cloward, R. A., & Ohlin, L. (1960). *Delinquency and opportunity: A theory of delinquent gangs.* New York, NY: Free Press.

Cohen, A. K. (1977). The concept of criminal organisation. *British Journal of Criminology, 17*(2), 97–111.

Cohen, L. E., & Felson, M. (1979). Social change and crime rate trends: A routine activity approach. *American Sociological Review, 44*(4), 588–608.

Coleman, J. W. (2002). *The criminal elite: Understanding white-collar crime* (5th ed.). New York, NY: Worth.

Coles, N. (2001). It's not what you know—It's who you know that counts. Analysing serious crime groups as social networks. *The British Journal of Criminology, 41*(4), 580–594.

Conboy, M. (1929). Organized crime as a business and its bearing upon the administration of criminal law. *New York University Law Quarterly Review, 7*(2), 339–351.

Congram, M., Bell, P., & Lauchs, M. (2013). *Policing transnational organized crime and corruption: Exploring the role of communication interception technology.* Houndsmill, England: Palgrave Macmillan.

Conklin, J. E. (2010). Criminology (10th ed.). Boston, MA: Pearson.

Connor, J. M. (2007). *Global pricefixing.* Berlin, Germany: Springer.

Cook, C. W. (1987). *The automobile theft investigator: A learning and reference text for the automobile theft investigator, the police supervisor, and the student.* Springfield, IL: Charles C Thomas.

Cook, P. J. (2007). *Paying the tab: The costs and benefits of alcohol control*. Princeton, NJ: Princeton University Press.

Cook, P. J., Cukier, W., & Krause, K. (2009). The illicit firearms trade in North America. *Criminology and Criminal Justice, 9*(3), 265–286.

Copes, H., & Cherbonneau, M. (2006). The key to auto theft: Emerging methods of auto theft from the offenders' perspective. *British Journal of Criminology, 46*(5), 917–934.

Corcoran, P. (2013). Mexico's shifting criminal landscape: Changes in gang operation and structure during the past century. *Trends in Organized Crime, 16*(3), 306–328.

Cornell, S. E. (2006). The narcotics threat in greater Central Asia: From crime-terror nexus to state infiltration? *China and Eurasia Forum Quarterly, 4*(1), 37–67.

Cornish, D. B. (1994). The procedural analysis of offending and its relevance for situational prevention. In R. V. Clarke (Ed.), *Crime prevention studies* (Vol. 3. pp. 151–196). Monsey, NY: Criminal Justice Press.

Cornish, D. B., & Clarke, R. V. (1986). Introduction. In D. B. Cornish & R. V. Clarke (Eds.), *The reasoning criminal* (pp. 2–16). New York, NY: Springer.

Cornish, D. B., & Clarke, R. V. (2002). Analyzing organized crimes. In A. R. Piquero &, S. G. Tibbetts (Eds.), *Rational choice and criminal behavior: Recent research and future challenges* (pp. 41–62). New York, NY: Routledge.

Costa Storti, C. & De Grauwe, P. (2009). Globalization and the price decline of illicit drugs. *International Journal of Drug Policy, 20*(1), 48–61.

Cressey, D. R. (1967a). The functions and structure of criminal syndicates. In task force on organized crime (Ed.), *Task force report: Organized crime, annotations and consultant's papers* (pp. 25–60). Washington, DC: Government Printing Office, Appendix A.

Cressey, D. R. (1967b). Methodological problems in the study of organized crime as a social problem. *Annals of the American Academy of Political and Social Science, 374*(1), 101–112.

Cressey, D. R. (1969). *Theft of the nation: The structure and operations of organized crime in America*. New York, NY: Harper & Row.

Cressey, D. R. (1972). *Criminal organization: Its elementary forms*. New York, NY: Harper & Row.

Critchley, D. (2009). *The origin of organized crime in America: The New York City Mafia, 1891–1931*. New York: Routledge.

Cruz, J. M. (2010). Central American maras: From youth street gangs to transnational protection rackets. *Global Crime, 11*(4), 379–398.

CSD. (2007). *Organized crime in Bulgaria: Markets and trends*. Sofia: Center for the Study of Democracy. Retrieved from http://www.csd.bg/fileSrc.php?id=2394

Cunningham, J. K., Liu, L.-M., & Callaghan, R. (2009). Impact of US and Canadian precursor regulation on methamphetamine purity in the United States. *Addiction, 104*(3), 441–453.

Curtis, R., & Wendel, T. (2000). Toward the development of a typology of illegal drug markets. In M. Natarajan & M. Hough (Eds.), *Illegal drug markets* (pp. 121–152). Monsey, NY: Criminal Justice Press.

Danker, U. (1988). *Räuberbanden im Alten Reich um 1700: Ein beitrag zur geschichte von herrschaft und kriminalität in der Frühen Neuzeit*. Frankfurt am Main, Germany: Suhrkamp.

Dantos, C., & Mason, J. (2009). Securing VoIP. In S. Bosworth, M. E. Kabay, & E. Whyne (Eds.), *Computer security handbook* (5th ed., pp. 34/1–16). Hoboken, NJ: John Wiley & Sons.

Dash, M. (2009). *The first family: Terror, extortion, revenge, murder, and the birth of the American Mafia.* New York, NY: Random House.

Dean, G., Fahsing, I., & Gottschalk, P. (2010). *Organized crime: Policing illegal business entrepreneurialism.* Oxford, England: Oxford University Press.

Decker, S. H., Bynum, T., & Weisel, D. (1998). A tale of two cities: Gangs as organized crime groups. *Justice Quarterly, 15*(3), 395–425.

Decker, S. H., & Townsend Chapman, M. (2008). *Drug smugglers on drug smuggling: Lessons from the inside.* Philadelphia, PA: Temple University Press.

Demaris, O. (1986). *The boardwalk jungle.* New York, NY: Bantam Books.

Demleitner, N. V. (1994). Organized crime and prohibition: What difference does legalization make? *Whittier Law Review, 15*(3), 613–646.

Densley, J. A. (2012). The organisation of London's street gangs. *Global Crime, 13*(1), 42–64.

Densley, J. A. (2014). It's gang life, but not as we know it: The evolution of gang business. *Crime & Delinquency, 60*(4), 517–546.

Denton, B. (2001). *Dealing: Women in the drug economy.* Sydney, Australia: University of New South Wales.

Denton, B., & O'Malley, P. (1999). Gender, trust and business: Women drug dealers in the illicit economy. *British Journal of Criminology, 39*(4), 513–530.

Desroches, F. J. (2005). *The crime that pays: Drug trafficking and organized crime in Canada.* Toronto, Ontario, Canada: Canadian Scholars' Press.

Desroches, F. (2007). Research on upper level drug trafficking: A review. *Journal of Drug Issues, 37*(4), 827–844.

Desroches, F. (2013). The use of organized crime and conspiracy laws in the investigation and prosecution of criminal organizations. *Policing, 7*(4), 401–410.

DeStefano, A. M. (2007). *King of godfathers.* New York, NY: Pinnacle.

Detrois, U. (2012). *Höllenritt: Ein deutscher Hells Angel packt aus* (5th ed.). Berlin, Germany: Ullstein.

Dick, A. R. (1995). When does organized crime pay? A transaction analysis. *International Review of Law and Economics, 15*(1), 25–46.

Dickenson, M. (2014). The impact of leadership removal on Mexican drug trafficking organizations. *Journal of Quantitative Criminology, 30*(4), 651–676.

Dickie, J. (2004). *Cosa Nostra: A history of the Sicilian Mafia.* London, England: Hodder & Stoughton.

Dickie, P., & Wilson, P. (1993). Defining organised crime: An operational perspective. *Current Issues in Criminal Justice, 4*(3), 215–224.

Dickson-Gilmore, J., & Woodiwiss, M. (2008). The history of Native Americans and the misdirected study of organised crime. *Global Crime, 9*(1&2), 66–83.

Dixit, A. K. (2004). *Lawlessness and economics: Alternative modes of governance.* Princeton, NJ: Princeton University Press.

Dobyns, J., & Johnson-Shelton, N. (2009). *No angel: My harrowing undercover journey to the inner circle of the Hells Angels.* New York, NY: Crown.

Dombrink, J. D. (1981). *Outlaw businessmen: Organized crime and the legalization of casino gambling* (PhD thesis). University of California, Berkeley.

Dorn, N., Levi, M., & King, L. (2005). *Literature review on upper level drug trafficking.* London, England: Home Office.

Dorn, N., Murji, K., & South, N. (1992). *Traffickers: Drugs markets and law enforcement.* London, England: Routledge.

Dorn, N., Oette, L., & White, S. (1998). Drugs importation and the bifurcation of risk: Capitalization cut outs and organized crime. *British Journal of Criminology, 38*(4), 537–560.

Doyle, C. (2012). *Money laundering: An overview of 18 U.S.C. 1956 and related federal criminal law.* Washington, DC: Congressional Research Service.

Dube, A., Dube, O., & Garcia-Ponce, O. (2013). Cross-border spillover: U.S. gun laws and violence in Mexico. *American Political Science Review, 107*(3), 397–417.

Dudley, S. S. (2010). *Drug trafficking organizations in Central America: Transportistas, Mexican cartels and maras.* Washington, DC: Woodrow Wilson Institute.

Dulin, A. L., & Patino, J. (2014). The logic of cartel car bombings in Mexico. *Trends in Organized Crime, 17*(4), 271–289.

Durkheim, E. (1964). *The rules of sociological method.* New York, NY: The Free Press. (Original work published in 1895).

Duterte, M., Jacinto, C., Sales, P., & Murphy, S. (2009). What's in a label? Ecstasy sellers' perceptions of pill brands. *Journal of Psychoactive Drugs, 41*(1), 27–37.

Dwyer, R., & Moore, D. (2010). Understanding illicit drug markets in Australia: Notes towards a critical reconceptualization. *British Journal of Criminology, 50*(1), 82–101.

Dyson, W. E. (2012). *Terrorism: An investigator's handbook* (4th ed.). Waltham, MA: Anderson.

Eck, J. E., & Gersh, J. S. (2000). Drug trafficking as a cottage industry. In M. Natarajan & M. Hough (Eds.), *Illegal drug markets* (pp. 241–271). Monsey, NY: Criminal Justice Press.

Edelhertz, H., & Overcast, T. D. (1993). *The business of organized crime: An assessment of organized crime business-type activities and their implications for law enforcement.* Loomis, CA: The Palmer Press.

Edmunds, M., Hough, M., & Urquia, N. (1996). *Tackling local drug markets.* London, England: Home Office.

Edwards, M. (2009). *Civil society* (2nd ed.). Cambridge, England: Polity Press.

Edwards, M. (2011). Introduction. In M. Edwards (Ed.), *The Oxford handbook of civil society* (pp. 3–14). New York, NY: Oxford University Press.

Edwards, A., & Gill, P. (2002). The politics of transnational organized crime: Discourse reflexivity and the narration of threat. *British Journal of Politics and International Relations, 4*(2), 245–270.

Edwards, A., & Levi, M. (2008). Researching the organization of serious crimes. *Criminology and Criminal Justice, 8*(4), 363–388.

Egmond, F. (1993). *Underworlds: Organised crime in the Netherlands 1650–1800.* Cambridge, England: Polity Press.

Eig, J. (2010). *Get Capone: The secret plot that captured America's most wanted gangster.* New York, NY: Simon & Schuster.

Eisenberg, U., & Ohder, C. (1990). Über organisiertes verbrechen. *Juristenzeitung, 45*(12), 574–579.

Ekblom, P. (2003). Organised crime and the conjunction of criminal opportunity framework. In A. Edwards & P. Gill (Eds.), *Transnational organised crime* (pp. 241–263). London, England: Routledge.

Ellis, S. (2009). West Africa's international drug trade. *African Affairs, 108*(431), 171–196.

EMCDDA. (2002). *Report on the drug situation in the candidate CEECs.* Lisbon, Portugal: European Monitoring Centre for Drugs and Drug Addiction.

EMCDDA. (2013). *European drug report: Trends and developments.* Lisbon, Portugal: European Monitoring Centre for Drugs and Drug Addiction.

EMCDDA & Europol. (2011). *Amphetamine: A European Union perspective in the global context.* Luxembourg: Publications Office of the European Union.

Englund, C. (2008). *The organisation of human trafficking: A study of criminal involvement in sexual exploitation in Sweden, Finland and Estonia.* Stockholm: Swedish National Council for Crime Prevention.

Europol. (2002). *2002 EU organised crime report* (nonclassified version). The Hague, the Netherlands: Europol.

Europol. (2006). *OCTA: EU organised crime threat assessment.* The Hague, the Netherlands: Europol.

Farrell, L., & Fry, T. R. L. (2013). Is illicit tobacco demand sensitive to relative price? *Economic Papers, 32*(1), 1–9.

Faure Atger, A. (2008). *The abolition of internal border checks in an enlarged Schengen area: Freedom of movement or a web of scattered security checks?* (CEPS Research Paper No. 8.). Retrieved from http://aei.pitt.edu/9405/2/9405.pdf

Federal Bureau of Investigation. (n.d.). *Glossary of terms.* http://www.fbi.gov/about-us/investigate/organizedcrime/glossary

Felsen, D., & Kalaitzidis, A. (2005). A historical overview of transnational crime. In P. Reichel (Ed.), *Handbook of transnational crime & justice* (pp. 3–20). Thousand Oaks, CA: Sage.

Felson, M. (2003). The process of co-offending. In M. J. Smith & D. B. Cornish (Eds.), *Crime Prevention Studies* (Vol. 16, pp. 149–167). Monsey, NY: Criminal Justice Press.

Felson, M. (2006a). *Crime and nature.* Thousand Oaks, CA: Sage.

Felson, M. (2006b). *The ecosystem for organized crime.* Helsinki, Finland: HEUNI.

Felson, M. (2009). The natural history of extended co-offending. *Trends in Organized Crime, 12*(2), 159–165.

Felson, M., & Clarke, R.V. (2012). Comments on the special issue. *Trends in organized crime, 15*(2–3), 215–221.

Fenopetov, V. (2006). The drug crime threat to countries located on the "Silk Road." *China and Eurasia Forum Quarterly, 4*(1), 5–13.

Fiandaca, G. (Ed.). (2015). Women and the Mafia: *Female Roles in Organized Crime Structures.* New York: Springer.

Fijnaut, C. (1990a). Organized crime: A comparison between the United States and Western Europe. *British Journal of Criminology, 30*(3), 321–340.

Fijnaut, C. (1990b). Researching organised crime. In R. Morgan (Ed.), *Policing organised crime and crime prevention* (pp. 75–86). Bristol, England: Bristol and Bath Centre for Criminal Justice.

Fijnaut, C. (2002). Introduction. In C. Fijnaut (Ed.), *The administrative approach to (organised) crime in Amsterdam* (pp. 11–30). Amsterdam, the Netherlands: City of Amsterdam.

Fijnaut, C. (2014a). European Union organized crime control policies. In L. Paoli (Ed.), *The Oxford handbook of organized crime* (pp. 572–592), Oxford, England: Oxford University Press.

Fijnaut, C. (2014b). Searching for organized crime in history. In L. Paoli (Ed.), *The Oxford handbook of organized crime* (pp. 53–95). Oxford, England: Oxford University Press.

Fijnaut, C., Bovenkerk, F., Bruinsma, G., & Van de Bunt, H. (1998). *Organized crime in the Netherlands.* The Hague the Netherlands: Kluwer Law International.

Finckenauer, J. O. (2005). Problems of definition: What is organized crime? *Trends in Organized Crime, 8*(3), 63–83.

Finckenauer, J. O., & Voronin, Y. A. (2001). *The threat of Russian organized crime.* Washington, DC: U.S. National Institute of Justice.

Finckenauer, J. O., & Waring, E. J. (1998). *Russian Mafia in America: Immigration, culture and crime.* Boston, MA: Northeastern University Press.

Finklea, K. M., & Theohary, C. A. (2013). *Cybercrime: Conceptual issues for Congress and U.S. law enforcement.* Washington, DC: Congressional Research Service.

Fiorentini, G. (2000). Organized crime and illegal markets. In B. Bouckaert & G. De Geest (Eds.), *Encyclopedia of law and economics: The economics of crime and litigation* (Vol. V., pp. 434–459). Cheltenham, England: Edward Elgar.

Fitzgerald, D. G. (2007). *Informants and undercover investigations: A practical guide to law, policy and procedure.* Boca Raton, FL: CRC.

Fitzgerald, J. (2005). Illegal drug markets in transitional economies. *Addiction Research and Theory, 13*(6), 563–577.

Flanigan, S. T. (2012). Terrorists next door? A comparison of Mexican drug cartels and Middle Eastern terrorist organizations. *Terrorism and Political Violence, 24*(2), 279–294.

Flannery, N. P. (2013). Calderon's war. *Journal of International Affairs, 66*(2), 181–196.

Flap, H. (2002). No man is an island: The research programme of a social capital theory. In O. Favereau & E. Lazega (Eds.), *Conventions and structures in economic organization: Markets, networks, and hierarchies* (pp. 29–59). Glos, England: Edward Elgar.

Flores Perez, C. A. (2014). Political protection and the origins of the Gulf Cartel. *Crime, Law and Social Change, 61*(5), 517–539.

Fordham, P. (1972). *Inside the underworld.* London, England: George Allen & Unwin.

Forrest, A.J. (1955). *Interpol.* London, England: Allan Wingate.

Fortin, F. (2014). Usenet newsgroups, child pornography, and the role of participants. In C. Morselli (Ed.), *Crime and networks* (pp. 231–246). New York, NY: Routledge.

Franko Aas, K. (2013). *Globalization & crime (2nd ed.).* London, England: Sage.

Freemantle, B. (1996). *The octopus: Europe in the grip of organized crime.* London, England: Orion.

Freye, E., & Levy, J. V. (2009). *Pharmacology and abuse of cocaine, amphetamines, ecstasy and related designer drugs: A comprehensive review on their mode of action, treatment of abuse and intoxication.* Dordrecht, Germany: Springer.

Friedrichs, D. O. (2010). *Trusted criminals: White collar crime in contemporary society* (4th ed.). Belmont, CA: Wadsworth.

Fuentes, J. R., & Kelly, R. J. (1999). Drug supply and demand: The dynamics of the American drug market and some aspects of Colombian and Mexican drug trafficking. *Journal of Contemporary Criminal Justice, 15*(4), 328–351.

Funderburg, J. A. (2014). *Bootleggers and beer barons of the Prohibition Era.* Jefferson, NC: McFarland & Co.

Gaines, L. K., & Kappeler V. E. (2011). *Policing in America* (7th ed.). Waltham, MD: Anderson.

Galeotti, M. (1998). The Mafiya and the new Russia. *Australian Journal of Politics and History, 44*(3), 415–429.

Galeotti, M. (2004). The Russian "Mafiya": Consolidation and globalisation. *Global Crime, 6*(1), 54–69.

Gambetta, D. (1993). *The Sicilian Mafia: The business of private protection.* Cambridge, MA: Harvard University Press.

Gambetta, D. (2009). *Codes of the underworld: How criminals communicate.* Princeton, NJ: Princeton University Press.

Gambetta, D., & Reuter, P. (1995). Conspiracy among the many: The mafia in legitimate industries. In G. Fiorentini & S. Peltzman (Eds.), *The economics of organised crime* (pp. 116–136). Cambridge: Cambridge University Press.

Gambino, R. (1994). Italian Americans, Today's immigrants. *Italian Americana, 12*(2), 226–234.

Gamella, J. F., & Jimenez Rodrigo, M. L. (2008). Multinational export-import ventures: Moroccan hashish into Europe through Spain. In S. Rödner Sznitman, B. Olsson, & R. Room (Eds.), *A cannabis reader: Global issues and local experiences: Perspectives on cannabis controversies, treatment and regulation in Europe* (pp. 263–289). Lisbon, Portugal: EMCDDA.

Gardiner, J. A. (1970). *The politics of corruption: Organized crime in an American city.* New York, NY: Russell Sage Foundation.

Geary, W. R. (2000). The creation of RICO: Law as a knowledge diffusion process. *Crime, Law and Social Change, 33*(4), 329–367.

Geis, G. (1963). Violence and organized crime. *Annals of the American Academy of Political and Social Science, 365*(1), 86–95.

Genaux, M. (2004). Social sciences and the evolving concept of corruption. *Crime, Law and Social Change, 42*(1), 13–24.

Gerber, J. (2000). On the relationship between organized and white-collar crime: Government business and criminal enterprise in post-communist Russia. *European Journal of Crime Criminal Law and Criminal Justice, 8*(4), 327–342.

Gerber, J., & Killias, M. (2003). The transnationalization of historically local crime: Auto theft in Western Europe and Russia Markets. *European Journal of Crime Criminal Law and Criminal Justice, 11*(2), 215–226.

Germans lost Riga to Bolshevist lure. (1919, March 30). *New York Times.*

Gerspacher, N., & Lemieux, F. (2010). A market-oriented explanation of the expansion of the role of Europol: Filling the demand for criminal intelligence through entrepreneurial initiatives. In F. Lemieux (Ed.), *International police cooperation: Emerging issues, theory and practice* (pp. 62–78). Cullompton, England: Willan.

Giannakopoulos, N. (2001). *Criminalité organisée et corruption en Suisse.* Bern, Germany: Haupt.

Giddens, A. (1990). *The consequences of modernity.* Cambridge, England: Polity Press.

Gilbert, J. N. (2007). *Criminal investigation* (7th ed.). Upper Saddle River, NJ: Pearson Prentice Hall.

Gilinskiy, Y. (2012). Organized crime in contemporary Russia. In E. W. Plywaczewski (Ed.), *Current problems of the penal law and criminology* (pp. 167–181). Warsaw, Poland: Wolters Kluwer Polska.

Gilinskiy, Y., & Kostjukovsky, Y. (2004). From thievish artel to criminal corporation: The history of organised crime in Russia. In C. Fijnaut & L. Paoli (Eds.), *Organised crime in Europe: Concepts, patterns and control policies in the European Union and beyond* (pp. 181–202). Dordrecht, Germany: Springer.

Glinkina, S. P. (1994). Privatizatsiya and kriminalizatsiya: How organized crime is hijacking privatization. *Demokratizatsiya, 2*(3), 385–391.

Godson, R. (2003a). The political-criminal nexus and global security. In R. Godson (Ed.), *Menace to society: Political-criminal collaboration around the world* (pp. 1–26). New Brunswick, NJ: Transaction Publishers.

Godson, R. (Ed.). (2003b). *Menace to society: Political-criminal collaboration around the world*. New Brunswick, NJ: Transaction Publishers.

Godson, R. (2003c). Transnational crime, corruption, and security. In M. E. Brown (Ed.), *Grave new world: Security challenges in the 21st century* (pp. 259–278). Washington, DC: Georgetown University Press.

Goldfarb, R. (1995). *Perfect villains, imperfect heroes: Robert Kennedy's war against organized crime*. New York, NY: Random House.

Goldstein, P. J., Brownstein, H. H., Ryan, P. J., & Bellucci, P. A. (1989). Crack and homicide in New York, NY City, 1988: A conceptually based event analysis. *Contemporary Drug Problems, 16*(4), 651–687.

Gonzales, R., Mooney, L., & Rawson, R. A. (2010). The methamphetamine problem in the United States. *Annual Review of Public Health, 31*(1), 385–398.

Goode, E. (2005). *Drugs in American society*. New York: McGraw-Hill.

Gounev, P., & Bezlov, T. (2008). From the economy of deficit to the black-market: Car theft and trafficking in Bulgaria. *Trends in Organized Crime, 11*(4), 410–429.

Gounev, P., & Ruggiero, V. (2012). Corruption and the disappearance of the victim. In P. Gounev & V. Ruggiero (Eds.), *Corruption and organized crime in Europe: Illegal partnerships* (pp. 15–31). London, England: Routledge.

Governor's Organized Crime Prevention Commission. (1973). *The beginning of the task*. Santa Fe, NM: GOCPC.

Granovetter, M. (1992). Problems of explanation in economic sociology. In N. Nohria & R. G. Eccles (Eds.), *Networks and organizations: Structure, form, and action* (pp. 25–56). Cambridge, MA: Harvard Business School Press.

Grayson, G. W. (2014). *The evolution of Los Zetas in Mexico and Central America: Sadism as an instrument of cartel warfare*. Carlisle, PA: United States War College Press.

Griffin, J. (2002). *Mob nemesis: How the FBI crippled organized crime*. New York, NY: Prometheus.

Griffin, S. P. (2003). Philadelphia's "Black Mafia": A social and political history. Dordrecht, Germany: Kluwer Academic.

Grillo, I. (2011). *El Narco: Inside Mexico's criminal insurgency*. New York, NY: Bloomsbury.

Gruppo Abele (2003). *Synthetic drugs trafficking in three European cities: Major trends and the involvement of organized crime*. Turin, Italy: Gruppo Abele.

Gruter, P., & Van de Mheen, D. (2005). Dutch cocaine trade: The perspective of Rotterdam cocaine retail dealers. *Crime, Law and Social Change, 44*(1), 19–33.

Gudehus, T., & Kotzub, H. (2012). *Comprehensive logistics* (2nd ed.). Berlin, Germany: Springer.

Guerette, R. T., & Bowers, K. J. (2009). Assessing the extent of crime displacement and diffusion of benefits: A review of situational crime prevention evaluations. *Criminology, 47*(4), 1331–1368.

Hagan, F. E. (1983). The organized crime continuum: A further specification of a new conceptual model. *Criminal Justice Review, 8*(2), 52–57.

Hagan, F. E. (2006). "Crime" and "organized crime": Indeterminate problems of definition. *Trends in Organized Crime, 9*(4), 127–137.

Hagedorn, J. (1994). Neighborhoods, markets, and gang drug organization. *Journal of Research in Crime and Delinquency, 31*(3), 264–294.

Hagedorn, J., Kmiecik, B., Simpson, D., Gradel, T. J., Zmuda, M. M., & Sterrett, D. (2013). *Crime, corruption and cover-ups in the Chicago police Department*

(Anti-Corruption Report No. 7). Chicago: University of Illinois at Chicago. Retrieved from http://www.uic.edu/depts/pols/ChicagoPolitics/policecorruption.pdf

Hales, G., & Hobbs, D. (2010). Drug markets in the community: A London borough case study. *Trends in Organized Crime, 13*(1), 13–30.

Hall, R. H. (1982). *Organizations: Structure and process* (3rd ed.). Englewood Cliffs, NJ: Prentice Hall.

Hall, T. (2012). The geography of transnational organized crime: Spaces, networks and flows. In F. Allum & S. Gilmour (Eds.), *Routledge handbook of transnational organized crime* (pp. 173–185). London, England: Routledge.

Haller, M. H. (1985). Bootleggers as businessmen: From city slums to city builders. In D. E. Kyvig (Ed.), *Law alcohol and order: Perspectives on national prohibition* (pp. 139–157). Westport, CT: Greenwood.

Haller, M. H. (1990). Illegal enterprise: A theoretical and historical interpretation. *Criminology, 28*(2), 207–235.

Haller, M. H. (1991). *Life under Bruno: The economics of an organized crime family*. Conshohocken, PA: Pennsylvania Crime Commission.

Haller, M. H. (1992). Bureaucracy and the Mafia: An alternative view. *Journal of Contemporary Criminal Justice, 8*(1), 1–10.

Halstead, B. (1998). The use of models in the analysis of organized crime and development of policy. *Transnational Organized Crime, 4*(1), 1–24.

Hancock, G., & Laycock, G. (2010). Organised crime and crime scripts: Prospects for disruption. In K. Bullock, R. V. Clarke, & N. Tilley (Eds.), *Situational prevention of organised crimes* (pp. 172–192). Cullompton, England: Willan.

Hartfield, C. (2008). The organization of "organized crime policing" and its international context. *Criminology and Criminal Justice, 8*(4), 483–507.

Hartmann, A., & von Lampe, K. (2008). The German underworld and the Ringvereine from the 1890s through the 1950s. *Global Crime, 9*(1&2), 108–135.

Harvey, J. (2011). Money laundering: Phantoms, imagery and facts. In G. Antonopoulos, M. Groenhuijsen, J. Harvey, T. Kooijmans, A. Maljevic, & K. von Lampe (Eds.), *Usual and unusual organising criminals in Europe and beyond: Profitable crimes, from underworld to upper world—Liber Amicorum Petrus van Duyne* (pp. 81–97), Apeldoorn, the Netherlands: Maklu.

Hawaii Crime Commission. (1978). *Organized crime in Hawaii* (Vol. 1). Honolulu: HCC.

Hay, G. A., & Kelley, D. (1974). An empirical survey of price fixing conspiracies. *Journal of Law and Economics, 17*(1), 13–38.

Heber, A. (2009a). The networks of drug offenders. *Trends in Organized Crime, 12*(1), 1–20.

Heber, A. (2009b). Networks of organised black market labour in the building trade. *Trends in Organized Crime, 12*(2), 122–144.

Heitmann, J. A., & Morales, R. H. (2014). *Stealing cars: Technology and society from the Model T to the Grand Torino*. Baltimore, MD: Johns Hopkins University Press.

Hellman, D. A. (1980). *The economics of crime*. New York, NY: St. Martin's Press.

Hellman, J., & Schankerman, M. (2000). Intervention, corruption and capture: The nexus between enterprises and the state. *Economics of Transition, 8*(3), 545–799.

Henninger, M. (2002). 'Importierte Kriminalität' und deren Etablierung. *Kriminalistik, 56*(12), 714–729.

Hepburn, S., & Simon, R. J. (2013). *Human trafficking around the world: Hidden in plain sight*. New York: Columbia University Press. (2011).

Hervieu, B. (2011). *Organized crime muscling in on the media*. Paris, France: Reporters Without Borders. Retrieved from http://en.rsf.org/IMG/pdf/organized_crime.pdf.

Hess, H. (1970). *Mafia: Zentrale Herrschaft und lokale Gegenmacht.* Tübingen, Germany: J.C.B. Mohr.

Hess H. (1996). *Mafia & Mafiosi: Origin power and myth.* New York: New York, NY University Press.

Hicks, David C. (1998). Thinking about organized crime prevention. *Journal of Contemporary Criminal Justice, 14*(4), 325–350.

Hill, P. B. E. (2003). *The Japanese Mafia: Yakuza, law, and the state.* New York: Oxford University Press.

Hill, T. (1980). Outlaw motorcycle gangs: A look at a new form of organized crime. *Canadian Criminology Forum, 3*(1), 26–36.

Hindelang, M. J., Gottfredson, M. R., & Garofalo, J. (1978). *Victims of personal crime: An empirical foundation for a theory of personal victimization.* Cambridge, MA: Ballinger.

Hobbs, D. (1998). Going down the glocal: The local context of organised crime. *Howard Journal, 37*(4), 407–422.

Hobbs, D. (2001). The firm: Organizational logic and criminal culture on a shifting terrain. *British Journal of Criminology, 41*(4), 549–560.

Hobbs, D. (2013). *Lush life: Constructing organized crime in the UK.* Oxford, England: Oxford University Press.

Hobbs, D., & Antonopoulus, G. A. (2013). 'Endemic to the species': Ordering the 'other' via organised crime. *Global Crime, 14*(1), 27–51.

Hobbs, D., & Dunnighan, C. (1998). Glocal organised crime: Context and pretext. In V. Ruggiero, N. South, & I. Taylor (Eds.), *The New European criminology: Crime and social order in Europe* (pp. 289–302). London, England: Routledge.

Hoffman, D. E. (1993). *Scarface Al and the crime crusaders.* Carbondale: Southern Illinois University Press.

Holden, C. R. (1920, January 19). *Report of the committee on origin of crime* (Bulletin No. 10). Chicago Crime Commission. 12–13.

Holt, T. J. (2013). Exploring the social organisation and structure of stolen data markets. *Global Crime, 14*(2–3), 155–174.

Holt, T. J., Blevins, K. R., & Burkert, N. (2010). Considering the pedophile subculture online. *Sexual Abuse, 22*(1), 3–24.

Holt, T. J., & Lampke, E. (2010). Exploring stolen data markets online: Products and market forces. *Criminal Justice Studies, 23*(1), 33–50.

Holzlehner, T. (2007). "The harder the rain, the tighter the roof": Evolution of organized crime networks in the Russian Far East. *Sibirica, 6*(2), 51–86.

Homer, F. D. (1974). *Guns and garlic: Myths and realities of organized crime.* West Lafayette, IN: Purdue University Press.

Hoover, J. E. (1933). Organized protection against organized predatory crimes: White slave traffic. *Journal of Criminal Law and Criminology, 24*(2), 475–482.

Hopkins, M., Tilley, N., & Gibson, K. (2013). Homicide and organized crime in England. *Homicide Studies, 17*(3), 291–313.

Hornsby, R., & Hobbs, D. (2007). A zone of ambiguity: The political economy of cigarette bootlegging. *British Journal of Criminology, 47*(4), 551–571.

Hostetter, G. L., & Beesley, T. Q. (1929). *It's a racket.* Chicago, IL: Les Quin.

Hughes, D. M., & Denisova, T. A. (2001). The transnational political criminal nexus of trafficking in women from Ukraine. *Trends in Organized Crime, 6*(3&4), 43–67.

Huisman, W., Huikeshoven, M., & Van de Bunt, H. G. (2003). *Markplaats Amsterdam: Op zoek naar de zwakste schakel in de logistiek van criminele processen aan de hand van Amsterdamse rechercheonderzoeken.* The Hague, the Netherlands: Boom Juridische uitgevers.

Huisman, S., & Jansen, F. (2012). Willing offenders outwitting capable guardians. *Trends in Organized Crime, 15*(2–3), 93–110.

Huisman, W., & Kleemans, E. R. (2014). The challenges of fighting sex trafficking in the legalized prostitution market of the Netherlands. *Crime, Law and Social Change, 61*(2), 215–228.

Huisman, W., & Nelen, H. (2007). Gotham unbound Dutch style: The administrative approach to organized crime in Amsterdam. *Crime, Law and Social Change, 48*(3–5), 87–103.

Hunte, H. E. R., & Barry, A. E. (2012). Perceived discrimination and DSM-IV-based alcohol and illicit drug use disorders. *American Journal of Public Health, 102*(12), e111.

Hutchings, A. (2014). Crime from the keyboard: Organised cybercrime, co-offending, initiation and knowledge transmission. *Crime, Law and Social Change, 62*(1), 1–20.

Hutchinson, G. (1870). The present state of the prison question in British India. In *Twenty-fifth annual report of the executive committee of the prison association of New York, and accompanying documents,* for the year 1869 (pp. 394–434). Albany, NY: The Argus Company.

Ianni, F. A. J. (1974). *Black mafia: Ethnic succession in organized crime.* New York, NY: Simon & Schuster.

Ianni, F. A. J., Fisher, S., & Lewis, J. (1973). *Ethnic succession and network formation in organized crime.* New York, NY: Columbia University.

Ianni, F. A. J., & Reuss-Ianni, E. (1972). *A family business: Kinship and social control in organized crime.* New York, NY: Russell Sage Foundation.

Ianni, F. A., & Reuss-Ianni, E. (1976). *The crime society: Organized crime and corruption in America.* New York, NY: New American Library.

Iannuzzi, J. (1995). *Joe Dogs: The life & crimes of a mobster.* New York, NY: Pocket Books.

Ibáñez, A., Blanco, C., Perez de Castro, I., Fernandez-Piqueras, J., & Sáiz-Ruiz, J. (2003). Genetics of pathological gambling. *Journal of Gambling Studies, 19*(1), 11–22.

Icduygu, A., & Toktas, S. (2002). How do smuggling and trafficking operate via irregular border crossings in the Middle East? Evidence from fieldwork in Turkey. *International Migration, 40*(6), 25–52.

Ickler, N. L. (1983). Conspiracy to violate RICO: Expanding traditional conspiracy law. *Notre Dame Law Review, 58*(3), 587–615.

Ignjatovic, Đ. (1998). *Organizovani Kriminalitet, drugi deo, Kriminoloshka analiza stanya u svetu.* Belgrade, Serbia: Politsiska Akademiya.

International Crisis Group. (2013). *Pena Nieto's challenge: Criminal cartels and rule of law in Mexico* (Latin America Report No. 48), Brussels: International Crisis Group. Retrieved from http://www.crisisgroup.org/~/media/Files/latin-america/mexico/048-pena-nietos-challenge-criminal-cartels-and-rule-of-law-in-mexico.pdf

Investigation of improper activities in the labor or management field. Hearings before the Select Committee on Improper Activities in the Labor or Management Field, U.S. Senate, 85th Cong., 1st Session, Part 17.

Ip, P. F. P. (1999). *Organized crime in Hong Kong.* Hong Kong: Centre for Criminology. Retrieved from http://www.crime.hku.hk/organizecrime.htm

Jacques, S., & Bernasco, W. (2013). Drug dealing: Amsterdam's red light district. In B. Leclerc & R. Wortley (Eds.), *Cognition and crime: Offender decision making and script analyses* (120–139). Milton Park, England: Routledge.

Jacques, S., & Wright, R. (2008). Intimacy with outlaws: The role of relational distance in recruiting, paying, and interviewing underworld research participants. *Journal of Research in Crime and Delinquency, 45*(1), 22–38.

Jacobs, J. B. (1994). *Busting the mob: United States v. Cosa Nostra.* New York: New York University Press.

Jacobs, J. B. (1999). *Gotham unbound: How New York City was liberated from the grip of organized crime.* New York: New York University Press.

Jacobs, J. B. (2006). *Mobsters, unions, and feds: The Mafia and the American labor movement.* New York: New York University Press.

Jacobs, J. B., & Cooperman, K. T. (2011). *Breaking the devil's pact: The battle to free the teamsters from the Mob.* New York: New York University Press.

Jacobs, J. B., & Dondlinger Wyman, E. (2014). Organized crime control in the United States of America. In L. Paoli (Ed.), *The Oxford handbook of organized crime* (pp. 529–544). Oxford, England: Oxford University Press.

Jacobs, J. B., & Peters, E. (2003). Labor racketeering: The Mafia and the unions. In M. Tonry (Ed.), *Crime and justice: A review of research* (pp. 229–282). Chicago, IL: The University of Chicago Press.

Jacques, S., & Wright, R. (2008). Intimacy with outlaws: The role of relational distance in recruiting, paying, and interviewing underworld research participants. *Journal of Research in Crime and Delinquency, 45*(1), 22–38.

Jacques, S., & Wright, R. (2013). How victimized drug traders mobilize police. *Journal of Contemporary Ethnography, 42*(5), 545–575.

Jager, M. (2003). The market and criminal law: The case of corruption. In P. C. van Duyne, K. von Lampe, & J. L. Newell (Eds.), *Criminal finances and organising crime in Europe* (pp. 153–173). Nijmegen, the Netherlands: Wolf Legal Publishers.

Jamieson, A. (1994). Mafia and institutional power in Italy. *International Relations, 12*(1), 1–24.

Jamieson, A. (1999). *The Antimafia: Italy's fight against organized crime.* Houndsmills, England: Macmillan.

Jamieson, A. (2001). Transnational organized crime: A European perspective. *Studies in Conflict and Terrorism, 24*(5), 377–387.

Jamieson, A. (2005). The use of terrorism by organized crime: An Italian case study. In T. Bjorgo (Ed.), *Root causes of terrorism: Myths, reality and ways forward* (pp. 164–177). London: Routledge.

Jamieson, R., South, N., & Taylor, I. (1998). Economic liberalization and cross-border crime: The North American free trade area and Canada's border with the U.S.A. Part II. *International Journal of the Sociology of Law, 26*(3), 285–319.

Jenkins, P. (2001). *Beyond tolerance: Child pornography on the Internet.* New York: New York University Press.

Jenkins, P., & Potter, G. (1987). The politics and mythology of organized crime: A Philadelphia case-study. *Journal of Criminal Justice, 15*(6), 473–484.

Johansen, P. O. (2005). Organised crime, Norwegian style. In P. C. van Duyne, K. von Lampe, M. van Dijck, & J. L. Newell (Eds.), *The organised crime economy: Managing crime markets in Europe* (pp. 189–208). Nijmegen, the Netherlands: Wolf Legal Publishers.

Johansen, P. O. (2008). Never a final design: Interviewing Norwegian alcohol smugglers. *Trends in Organized Crime, 11*(1), 5–11.

Johnson, B. D., & Natarajan, M. (1995). Strategies to avoid arrest: Crack sellers' response to intensified policing. *American Journal of Police, 14*(3–4), 49–69.

Joossens, L., Merriman, D., Ross, H., & Raw, M. (2009). *How eliminating the global illicit cigarette trade would increase tax revenue and save lives.* Paris, France: International Union Against Tuberculosis and Lung Disease.

Joossens, L., & Raw, M. (1998). Cigarette smuggling in Europe: Who really benefits? *Tobacco Control, 7*(1), 66–71.

Joossens, L., & Raw, M. (2012). From cigarette smuggling to illicit tobacco trade. *Tobacco Control, 21*(2), 230–234.

Junninen, M. (2006). *Adventurers and risk-takers: Finnish professional criminals and their organisations in the 1990s cross-border criminality.* Helsinki, Finland: HEUNI.

Junninen, M., & Aromaa, K, (1999). *Crime across the border: Finnish professional criminals and Estonian crime opportunities.* Helsinki, Helsinki: National Research Institute of Legal Policy.

Kafka, M. (2010). Hypersexual disorder: A proposed diagnosis for DSM-V. *Archives of Sexual Behavior, 39*(2), 377–400.

Kaizen, J., & Nonneman, W. (2007). Irregular migration in Belgium and organized crime: An overview. *International Migration, 45*(2), 121–146.

Kan, P. R. (2012). *Cartels at war: Mexico's drug-fueled violence and the threat to U.S. national security.* Dulles, VA: Potomac Books.

Kan, P. R., Bechtol, B. E., & Collins, R. M. (2010). *Criminal sovereignty: Understanding North Korea's illicit international activities.* Carlisle, PA: Strategic Studies Institute.

Karras, A. L. (2010). *Smuggling: Contraband and corruption in world history.* Lanham, MD: Rowman & Littlefield.

Karremann, M. (2007). *Es geschieht am hellichten Tag: Die verborgene Welt der Pädophilen und wie wir unsere Kinder vor Missbrauch schützen.* Cologne, Germany: DuMont.

Katyal, N. K. (2003). Conspiracy theory. *Yale Law Journal, 112*(6), 1307–1398.

Kelland, G. (1987). *Crime in London: From postwar Soho to present-day "supergrasses."* London, England: Grafton.

Kellner, T., & Pipitone, F. (2010). Inside Mexico's Drug War. *World Policy Journal, 27*(1), 29–37.

Kelly, R. J. (1978). *Organized crime: A study in the production of knowledge by law enforcement specialists.* (PhD thesis). City University of New York.

Kelly, R. J. (1986). Criminal underworlds: Looking down on society from below. In R. J. Kelly (Ed.), *Organized crime: Cross-cultural studies* (pp. 10–31). Totowa, NJ: Rowman & Littlefield.

Kelly, R. J. (1999). *The upperworld and the underworld: Case studies of racketeering and business infiltrations in the United States.* New York, NY: Kluwer Academic/ Plenum.

Kennedy, A. (2005). Dead fish across the trail: Illustrations of money laundering methods. *Journal of Money Laundering Control, 8*(4), 305–319.

Kenney, D. J., & Finckenauer, J. O. (1995). *Organized crime in America.* Belmont, CA: Wadsworth.

Kenney, M. (1999a). Summary of Guillermo Pallomari's testimony in the 1997 Operation Cornerstone trial of Michael Abbell and William Moran. *Transnational Organized Crime, 5*(1), 120–138.

Kenney, M. (1999b). When criminals out-smart the state: Understanding the learning capacity of Colombian drug trafficking organizations. *Transnational Organized Crime, 5*(1), 97–119.

Kenney, M. (2007). The architecture of drug trafficking: Network forms of organisation in the Colombian cocaine trade. *Global Crime, 8*(3), 233–259.

Kerner, H.-J. (1973). *Professionelles und organisiertes Verbrechen: Versuch einer Bestandsaufnahme und Bericht über neuere Entwicklungstendenzen in der Bundesrepublik Deutschland und in den Niederlanden.* Wiesbaden, GER: Bundeskriminalamt.

K. H. R. (1835, May). Passages in the life of a hunchback. *The Ladie's Companion,* 154–160.

Kimeldorf, H. (1988). *Reds or rackets? The making of radical and conservative unions on the waterfront.* Berkeley: University of California Press.

Kinzig, J. (2004). *Die rechtliche Bewältigung von Erscheinungsformen organisierter Kriminalität.* Berlin, Germany: Duncker & Humblot.

Kirby, S., & Nailer, L. (2013). Reducing the offending of a UK organized crime group using an opportunity-reducing framework—a three year case study. *Trends in Organized Crime, 16*(4), 397–412.

Kirby, S., & Penna, S. (2010). Policing mobile criminality: Towards a situational crime prevention approach to organised crime. In K. Bullock, R. V. Clarke, & N. Tilley (Eds.), *Situational prevention of organised crimes* (pp. 193–212). Cullompton, England: Willan.

Kleemans, E. R. (2013), Organized crime and the visible hand: A theoretical critique on the economic analysis of organized crime. *Criminology and Criminal Justice, 13*(5), 615–629.

Kleemans, E. R., & de Poot, C. J. (2008). Criminal careers in organized crime and social opportunity structure. *European Journal of Criminology, 5*(1), 69–98.

Kleemans, E. R., Kruisbergen, E.W., & Kouwenberg, R. F. (2014). Women, brokerage and transnational organized crime: Empirical results from the Dutch Organized Crime Monitor. *Trends in Organized Crime, 17*(1–2), 16–30.

Kleemans, E. R., Soudijn, M. R. J., & Weenink, A. W. (2012). Organized crime, situational crime prevention and routine activity theory. *Trends in Organized Crime, 15*(2–3), 87–92.

Kleemans, E. R., & Van de Bunt, H. G. (1999). The social embeddedness of organized crime. *Transnational Organized Crime, 5*(1), 19–36.

Kleemans, E. R., & Van de Bunt, H. G. (2008). Organised crime, occupations and opportunity. *Global Crime, 9*(3), 185–197.

Knoke, D., & Kuklinski, J. H. (1982). *Network analysis.* Newbury Park, CA: Sage.

Kobler, J. (1971). *Capone: The life and world of Al Capone.* Greenwich, CT: Fawcett Crest.

Kobler, J. (1973). *Ardent spirits: The rise and fall of prohibition.* New York, NY: G. P. Putnam's Sons.

Koehler, R. (2000). The organizational structure and function of La Nuestra Familia within Colorado state correctional facilities. *Deviant Behavior, 21*(2), 155–179.

Köbben, A.-C. (2002). The Wallen project. In C. Fijnaut (Ed.), *The administrative approach to (organised) crime in Amsterdam* (pp. 73–95). Amsterdam, the Netherlands: City of Amsterdam.

Kollmar, H. (1974). Organisierte Kriminalität: Begriff oder Bezeichnung eines Phänomens? *Kriminalistik, 28*(1), 1–7.

Kooijmans, J., & Van de Glind, H. (2010). Child slavery today. In G. Craig (Ed.), *Child slavery now: A contemporary reader* (pp. 21–41). Bristol, England: Policy Press.

Korsell, L., & Larsson, P. (2011). Organized crime the Nordic way. In M. Tonry (Ed.), *Crime and justice: A review of research* (pp. 519–554). Chicago, IL: The University of Chicago Press.

Korsell, L., Vesterhav, D., & Skinnari, J. (2011). Human trafficking and drug distribution in Sweden from a market perspective—similarities and differences. *Trends in Organized Crime, 14*(2–3), 100–124.

Korsell, L., Wallström, K., & Skinnari, J. (2007). Unlawful influence directed at public servants: From harassment, threats and violence to corruption. *European Journal of Crime, Criminal Law and Criminal Justice, 15*(3–4), 335–358.

Kostakos, P. A., & Antonopoulos, G. A. (2010). The "good," the "bad" and the "Charlie": The business of cocaine smuggling in Greece. *Global Crime, 11*(1), 34–57.

Kray, R., & Kray, R. (1989). *Our story.* London: Pan.

Krevert, P. (1997). *Schutzgelderpressung: Das große Geschäft mit der Angst.* Lübeck, Germany: Schmidt Römhild.

Kruisbergen, E. W., de Jong, D., & Kleemans, E. R. (2011). Undercover policing: Assumptions and empirical evidence. *British Journal of Criminology, 51*(2), 394–412.

Kruisbergen, E. W., Kleemans, E. R., & de Jong, D. (2012). Controlling criminal investigations: The case of undercover operations. *Policing, 6*(4), 398–407.

Kube, E. (1990). Organisierte Kriminalität: Die Logistik als Präventionsansatz. *Kriminalistik, 44*(12), 629–634.

Kukhianidze, A. (2009). Corruption and organized crime in Georgia before and after the "Rose Revolution." *Central Asian Survey, 28*(2), 215–234.

Kukhianidze, A., Kupatadze, A., & Gotsiridze, R. (2004). *Smuggling through Abkhazia and Tskhinvali Region of Georgia.* Tbilisi, Georgia: TraCCC Georgia Office.

Kupatadze, A. (2008). Organized crime before and after the Tulip Revolution: The changing dynamics of upperworld-underworld networks. *Central Asian Survey, 27*(3–4), 279–299.

Kuschej, H., & Pilgram, A. (1998). *Fremdenfeindlichkeit im diskurs über "Organisierte Kriminalität."* Vienna, Austria: Institut für Rechts- und Kriminalsoziologie.

Kwitny, J. (1979). *Vicious circles: The Mafia in the marketplace.* New York, NY: W.W. Norton.

Kwok, S. I., & Lo, T. Wing. (2013). Anti-triad legislations in Hong Kong: Issues, problems and development. *Trends in Organized Crime, 16*(1), 74–94.

Lacey, R. (1991). *Little man: Meyer Lansky and the gangster life.* Boston, MA: Little, Brown and Company.

Lait, J., & Mortimer, L. (1950). *Chicago confidential.* New York, NY: Dell.

Lamm Weisel, D. (2002). The evolution of street gangs: An examination of form and variation. In W. L. Reed & S. H. Decker (Eds.), *Responding to gangs: Evaluation and research* (pp. 26–65). Washington, DC: National Institute of Justice.

Landesco, J. (1929). Organized crime in Chicago. In Illinois Association for Criminal Justice (Ed.), *The Illinois crime survey* (pp. 823–1087). Chicago: Illinois Association for Criminal Justice.

Lane, D. C., Bromley, D. G., Hicks, R. D., & Mahoney, J. S. (2008). Time crime: The transnational organization of art and antiquities theft. *Journal of Contemporary Criminal Justice, 24*(3), 243–262.

Lankov, A. (2009). Pyongyang strikes back: North Korean policies of 2002–08 and attempts to reverse "De-Stalinization from below." *Asia Policy, 8*(July), 47–71.

Larsson, P. (2009). Up in smoke! Hash smuggling the Norwegian way. In K. Ingvaldsen & V. L. Sørli (Eds.), *Organised crime: Norms, markets, regulation and research* (pp. 63–82). Oslo, Norway: Unipub.

Lashly, A. V. (1930). The Illinois crime survey. *Journal of the American Institute of Criminal Law and Criminology, 20*(4), 588–605.

La Spina, A. (2004). The paradox of effectiveness: Growth, institutionalisation and evaluation of Anti-Mafia policies in Italy. In C. Fijnaut & L. Paoli (Eds.), *Organised crime in Europe: Concepts, patterns and control policies in the European Union and beyond* (pp. 641–676). Dordrecht, Germany: Springer.

La Spina, A. (2008). Recent anti-Mafia strategies: The Italian experience. In D. Siegel & H. Nelen (Eds.), *Organized crime: Culture, markets and policies*. New York, NY: Springer.

La Spina, A. (2014). The fight against the Italian Mafia. In L. Paoli (Ed.), *The Oxford handbook of organized crime* (pp. 593–611). Oxford, England: Oxford University Press.

Lau, C. (2008). Child prostitution in Thailand. *Journal of Child Health Care, 12*(2), 144–155.

Laub, J. H. (1983). *Criminology in the making: An oral history*. Boston, MA: Northeastern University Press.

Lauchs, M., & Staines, Z. (2012). Career path of a corruption entrepreneur. *Global Crime, 13*(2), 109–129.

Lavigne, Y. (1997). *Hells Angels: Into the abyss*. New York, NY: Harper.

Lavigne, Y. (1989). *Hell's Angels: "Three can keep a secret if two are dead."* New York, NY: Lyle Stuart.

Lavorgna, A. (2014). Internet-mediated drug trafficking: Towards a better understanding of new criminal dynamics. *Trends in Organized Crime, 17*(4), 250–270.

Lawson, G., & Oldham, W. (2007). The brotherhoods: The true story of two cops who murdered for the Mafia. New York, NY: Pocket Books.

Lebeya, S. G. (2007). *Organised crime in the Southern African development community with specific reference to motor vehicle theft* (LLM dissertation). University of South Africa.

Lebeya, S. G. (2012). Defining organised crime: A comparative analysis (Doctoral dissertation). University of South Africa. Retrieved from http://uir.unisa.ac.za/bitstream/handle/10500/6547/thesis_lebeya_sg.pdf?sequence=1

Ledeneva, A. V. (1998). *Russia's economy of favours: Blat, networking and informal exchange*. Cambridge, England: Cambridge University Press.

Lee, G. D. (2005). *Conspiracy investigations: Terrorism, drugs and gangs*. Upper Saddle River, NJ: Pearson Prentice Hall.

Lee, K., & Collin, J. (2006). "Key to the Future": British American Tobacco and cigarette smuggling in China. *PLoS Medicine, 3*(7), 1081–1089.

Lee, R. W. (1999). "Transnational Organized Crime: An Overview." In T. Farer (Ed.), *Transnational crime in the Americas: An inter-American dialogue book* (pp. 1–30). New York, NY: Routledge.

Leggett, T., & Pietschmann, T. (2008). Global cannabis cultivation and trafficking. In S. R. Sznitman, B. Olsson, & R. Room (Eds.), *A cannabis reader: Global issues and local experiences* (pp. 187–198). Lisbon, Portugal: European Monitoring Centre for Drugs and Drug Addiction.

Lehr, D., & O'Neill, G. (2001). *Black mass: The true story of an unholy alliance between the FBI and the Irish Mob*. New York, NY: Perennial.

Leman, J., & Janssens, S. (2008). The Albanian and post-Soviet business of trafficking women for prostitution: Structural developments and financial modus operandi. *European Journal of Criminology, 5*(4), 433–451.

Lemieux, A. M. (Ed.). (2014). *Situational prevention of poaching*. New York, NY: Routledge.

Lemieux, A. M., & Clarke, R. V. (2009). The international ban on ivory sales and its effects on elephant poaching in Africa. *British Journal of Criminology, 49*(4), 451–471.

Lemieux, V. (2003). *Criminal networks.* Ottawa, Ontario: Royal Canadian Mounted Police. Retrieved from http://cpc.phippsinc.com/cpclib/pdf/56312e.pdf

Lenke, L. (2008). An analysis of the significance of supply and market factors for variations in European cannabis use. In S. R. Sznitman, B. Olsson, & R. Room (Eds.), *A cannabis reader: Global issues and local experiences* (pp. 293–297). Lisbon, Portugal: European Monitoring Centre for Drugs and Drug Addiction.

Leukfeldt, E. R. (2014). Cybercrime and social ties: Phishing in Amsterdam. *Trends in Organized Crime, 17*(4), 231–249.

Levi, M. (1998a). Organising plastic fraud: Enterprise criminals and the side-stepping of fraud prevention. *The Howard Journal of Criminal Justice, 37*(4), 423–438.

Levi, M. (1998b). Reflections on organized crime: Patterns and control. The *Howard Journal of Criminal Justice, 37*(4), 335–438.

Levi, M. (2002a). Money laundering and its regulation. *Annals of the American Academy of Political and Social Science, 582*(1), 181–194.

Levi, M. (2002b). The organisation of serious crimes. In M. Maguire, R. Morgan, & R. Reiner (Eds.), *The Oxford handbook of criminology* (3rd ed. pp. 878–913). Oxford, England: Oxford University Press.

Levi, M. (2008). Organized fraud and organizing frauds: Unpacking research on networks and organization. *Criminology and Criminal Justice, 8*(4), 389–419.

Levi, M. (2012). The organization of serious crime for gain. In R. Morgan, M. Maguire, & R. Reiner (Eds.), *The Oxford handbook of criminology* (5th ed. pp. 595–622). Oxford: Oxford University Press.

Levi, M. (2014). Money laundering. In L. Paoli (Ed.), *The Oxford handbook of organized crime* (pp. 419–443). Oxford, England: Oxford University Press.

Levi, M., Innes, M., Reuter, P., & Gundur, R. V. (2013). *The economic, financial and social impacts of organised crime in the EU.* Brussels, Belgium: European Parliament. http://www.europarl.europa.eu/RegData/etudes/etudes/join/2013/493018/IPOL-JOIN_ET%282013%29493018_EN.pdf

Levi, M., & Maguire, M. (2004). Reducing and preventing organised crime: An evidence-based critique. *Crime, Law and Social Change, 41*(5), 397–469.

Levi, M., & Naylor, R. T. (2000). *Organised crime, the organisation of crime, and the organisation of business.* Unpublished manuscript.

Levine, M. (1999). Rethinking bystander nonintervention: Social categorization and the evidence of witnesses at the James Bulger murder trial. *Human Relations, 52*(9), 1133–1155.

Levitt, S. D., & Venkatesh, S. A. (2000). An economic analysis of a drug-selling gang's finances. *Quarterly Journal of Economics, 115*(3), 755–789.

Lewis, G. C. (1836). *Local disturbances in Ireland.* London, England: B. Fellowes.

Lichtenwald, T. G. (2004, Spring). Drug smuggling behavior: A developmental smuggling model (Part 2, pp. 14–22). *Forensic Examiner.*

Liddick, D. (1999a). *The Mob's daily number: Organized crime and the numbers gambling industry.* Lanham, MD: University Press of America.

Liddick, D. (1999b). *An empirical, theoretical, and historical overview of organized crime.* Lewiston, NY: Edwin Mellen.

Lin, Y.-C. J. (2011). *Fake stuff: China and the rise of counterfeit goods.* New York: Routledge.

Lindberg, K., Petrenko, J., Gladden, J., & Johnson, W. A. (1998). Emerging organized crime in Chicago. *International Review of Law Computers & Technology, 12*(2), 219–256.

Lippmann, W. (1931). The underworld: Our secret servant. *Forum, 55*(1), 1–4.

Lipset, S. M. (1963). *Political man: The social bases of politics*. Garden City, NY: Doubleday.

Lo, T. W. (2010). Beyond social capital: Triad organized crime in Hong Kong and China. *British Journal of Criminology, 50*(5), 851–872.

Loftus, B. (2015). Border regimes and the sociology of policing. *Policing and Society: An International Journal of Research and Policy, 25*(1), 115–125.

Lo Iacono, E. (2014). Victims, sex workers and perpetrators: Gray areas in the trafficking of Nigerian women. *Trends in Organized Crime, 17*(1–2), 110–128.

Lombardo, R. M. (1994). The social organization of organized crime in Chicago. *Journal of Contemporary Criminal Justice, 10*(4), 290–313.

Lombardo, R. M. (2010). *The black hand: Terror by letter in Chicago*. Urbana: University of Illinois Press.

Lombardo, R. M. (2013). *Organized crime in Chicago: Beyond the Mafia*. Urbana: University of Illinois Press.

Lombardo, R. M., & Lurigio, A. J. (1995). The neighborhood's role in recruiting and perpetuating membership in street crews: The case of the Chicago outfit. In J. S. Albanese (Ed.), *Contemporary issues in organized crime* (pp. 87–110). Monsey, NY: Criminal Justice Press.

Longman, M. (2006). The problem of auto theft. In E. Stauffer & M. S. Bonfanti (Eds.), *Forensic investigation of stolen-recovered and other crime-related vehicles* (pp. 1–21). Burlington, MA: Academic Press.

Longmire, S. M., & Longmire, J. P. (2008). Redefining terrorism: Why Mexican drug trafficking is more than just organized crime. *Journal of Strategic Security, 1*(1), 35–52.

Lu, C., Jen, W., Chang, W., & Chou, S. (2006). Cybercrime & cybercriminals: An overview of the Taiwan experience. *Journal of Computers, 1*(6), 11–18.

Luban, D., O'Sullivan, J. R., & Stewart, D. P. (2010). *International and transnational criminal law*. Austin, TX: Wolters Kluwer Law and Business.

Luhmann, N. (1988). Familiarity, confidence, trust: Problems and alternatives. In D. Gambetta (Ed.), *Trust: Making and breaking cooperative relations* (pp. 94–107). Oxford, England: Basil Blackwell.

Luk, R., Cohen, J. E., Ferrence, R., & McDonald, P. W. (2009). Prevalence and correlates of purchasing contraband cigarettes on First Nations reserves in Ontario, Canada. *Addiction, 104*(3), 488–495.

Luksetich, W. A., & White, M. D. (1982). *Crime and public policy: An economic approach*. Boston, MA: Little, Brown and Company.

Lundin, S. (2012). Organ economy: Organ trafficking in Moldova and Israel. *Public Understanding of Science, 21*(2), 226–241.

Lupo, S. (2009). *History of the Mafia*. New York, NY: Columbia University Press.

Lupsha, P. A. (1983). Networks versus networking: Analysis of an organized crime group. In G. P. Waldo (Ed.), *Career criminals* (pp. 59–87). Beverly Hills, CA: Sage.

Lupsha, P. A. (1986). Organized crime in the United States. In R. J. Kelly (Ed.), *Organized crime: Cross-cultural studies* (pp. 32–57). Totowa, NJ: Rowman & Littlefield.

Lupsha, P. A. (1988). Rational choice not ethnic group behavior: A macro perspective. *Law enforcement intelligence analysis digest, 3*(2), 1–8.

Lupsha, P. A. (1991). Drug lords and narco-corruption: The players change but the game continues. *Crime, Law and Social Change, 16*(1), 41–58.

Lupsha, P. A. (1996). Transnational organized crime versus the nation-state. *Transnational Organized Crime, 2*(1), 21–48.

Lusthaus, J. (2012). Trust in the world of cybercrime. *Global Crime, 13*(2), 71–94.

Lusthaus, J. (2013). How organised is organised cybercrime? *Global Crime, 14*(1), 52–60.

Lyman, M. D. (2005). *Criminal investigation: The art and the science* (4th ed.). Upper Saddle River, NJ: Pearson Prentice Hall.

Lyman, M. D. (2007). *Practical drug enforcement* (3rd ed.). Boca Raton, FL: CRC Press.

Lyman, M. D., & Potter, G. W. (2011). *Organized crime* (5th ed.). Upper Saddle River, NJ: Prentice Hall.

Maas, P. (1997). *Underboss: Sammy the Bull Gravano's life in the Mafia.* New York, NY: HarperCollins.

MacCoun, R. J., & Reuter, P. (2001). *Drug war heresies: Learning from other vices times and places.* Cambridge, England: Cambridge University Press.

Mack, J. A., & Kerner, H.-J. (1975). *The crime industry.* Westmead, England: Saxon House.

The Mafia in the United States. (1890, October 24). *New York Times.*

Makarenko, T. (2004). The crime-terror continuum: Tracing the interplay between transnational organised crime and terrorism. *Global Crime, 6*(1), 129–145.

Mallory, S. L. (2012). *Understanding organized crime* (2nd ed.). Sudbury, MA: Jones and Bartlett.

Malm, A., & Bichler, G. (2011). Networks of collaborating criminals: Assessing the structural vulnerability of drug markets. *Journal of Research in Crime and Delinquency, 48*(2), 271–297.

Malm, A., & Bichler, G. (2013). Using friends for money: the positional importance of money-launderers in organized crime. *Trends in Organized Crime, 16*(4), 365–381.

Maltz, M. D. (1990). *Measuring the effectiveness of organized crime control efforts.* Chicago, IL: Office of International Criminal Justice.

Maltz, M. D. (1994). Defining organized crime. In R. J. Kelly, K.-L. Chin, & R. Schatzberg (Eds.), *Handbook of organized crime in the United States* (pp. 21–37). Westport, CT: Greenwood.

Mancuso, M. (2014). Not all madams have a central role: Analysis of a Nigerian sex trafficking network. *Trends in Organized Crime, 17*(1–2), 66–88.

Mangine, R. F. (2006). Anti-theft systems. In E. Stauffer & M. S. Bonfanti (Eds.), *Forensic investigation of stolen-recovered and other crime-related vehicles* (pp. 207–226). Burlington, MA: Academic Press.

Manna, A. (1997). Measures of prevention: Dogmatic-exegetic aspects and prospects of reform. *European Journal of Crime, Criminal Law and Criminal Justice, 5*(3), 248–255.

Mannozzi, G. (2013). Victim-offender mediation in areas characterized by high levels of organized crime. *European Journal of Criminology, 10*(2), 187–205.

Mansour, W. (2008). "Ali Baba and the forty thieves": An allusion to Abbasid organised crime. *Global Crime, 9*(1&2), 8–19.

Marat, E. (2006). *The state-crime nexus in Central Asia: State weakness, organized crime, and corruption in Kyrgyzstan and Tajikistan,* Washington, DC: Johns Hopkins University.

Marine, F. J. (2006). The effects of organized crime on legitimate businesses. *Journal of Financial Crime, 13*(2), 214–234.

Marine, F. J. (2009). *Criminal RICO: 18 U.S.C. §§ 1961–1968—a manual for federal prosecutors*(5th ed.). Washington, DC: U.S. Department of Justice. Retrieved from http://www.justice.gov/usao/eousa/foia_reading_room/usam/title9/rico.pdf

Marks, H. (1998). *Mr. nice.* London, England: Vintage.

Marsden, W., & Sher, J. (2007). *Angels of death: Inside the bikers' empire of crime.* Toronto, Ontario: Vintage Canada.

Marshall, H. (2013). "Come heavy, or not at all": Defended neighborhoods, ethnic concentration, and Chicago robberies; examining the Italian American organized crime influence. *Journal of Contemporary Criminal Justice, 29*(2), 276–295.

Martin, J. (2014a). *Drugs on the dark net: How cryptomarkets are transforming the global trade in illicit drugs.* New York, NY: Palgrave Macmillan.

Martin, J. (2014b). Lost on the silk road: Online drug distribution and the "cryptomarket." *Criminology and Criminal Justice, 14*(3), 351–367.

Marx, G. T. (1988). *Undercover: Police surveillance in America,* Berkeley: University of California Press.

Massari, M. (2003). Transnational organized crime between myth and reality: The social construction of a threat. In F. Allum & R. Siebert (Eds.), *Organized crime and the challenge to democracy* (pp. 55–69). London, England: Routledge.

Massari, M., & Monzini, P. (2004). Dirty businesses in Italy: A case-study of illegal trafficking in hazardous waste. *Global Crime, 6*(3&4), 285–304.

Massari, M., & Motta, C. (2007). Women in the Sacra Corona Unita. In G. Fiandaca (Ed.), *Women and the Mafia: Female roles in organized crime structures* (pp. 53–66). New York, NY: Springer.

Massy, L. (2008). The antiquity art market: Between legality and illegality. *International Journal of Social Economics, 35*(10), 729–738.

Matrix Knowledge Group. (2007). *The illicit drug trade in the United Kingdom.* London, England: Home Office.

McCarthy, B., & Hagan, J. (2001). When crime pays: Capital, competence, and criminal success. *Social Forces, 79*(3), 1035–1060.

McClintick, D. (1993). *Swordfish: A true story of ambition, savagery, and betrayal.* New York, NY: Pantheon.

McCoy, A. W. (2003). *The politics of heroin: CIA complicity in the global drug trade.* Chicago, IL: Lawrence Hill.

McCusker, R. (2006). Transnational organised cyber crime: Distinguishing threat from reality. *Crime, Law and Social Change, 46*(4), 257–273.

McGuire, M. R. (2012). *Organised crime in the digital age.* London, England: John Grieve Centre for Policing and Security.

McKeon, T. J. (1971). The incursion by organized crime into legitimate business. *Journal of Public Law, 20*(1), 117–141.

McIllwain, J. S. (2001). An equal opportunity employer: Opium smuggling networks in and around San Diego during the early twentieth century. *Transnational Organized Crime, 4*(2), 31–54.

McIllwain, J. S. (2004). *Organizing crime in Chinatown: Race and racketeering in New York City, 1890–1910.* Jefferson, NC: McFarland.

McIntosh, M. (1975). *The organisation of crime.* London, England: MacMillan.

McKetin, R., McLaren, J., Kelly, E., & Chalmers, J. (2009). The market for crystalline methamphetamine in Sydney, Australia. *Global Crime, 10*(1&2), 113–123.

Mercone, J. M., Shapiro, J. B., & Martin, T. B. (2006). Racketeer influenced and corrupt organizations. *American Criminal Law Review, 43*(2), 869–919.

Mejia, D., & Posada, C. E. (2008). *Cocaine production and trafficking: What do we know?* (World Bank Policy Research Working Paper No. 4618). Retrieved from http://www-wds.worldbank.org/external/default/WDSContentServer/IW3P/IB/2008/05/13/000158349_20080513084308/Rendered/PDF/wps4618.pdf

Mendoza, R. L. (2010). Kidney black markets and legal transplants: Are they opposite sides of the same coin? *Health Policy, 94*(3), 255–265.

Merriman, D. (2010). The micro-geography of tax avoidance: Evidence from littered ciga-rette packs in Chicago. *American Economic Journal: Economic Policy, 2*(2), 61–84.

Merton, R. K. (1968). *Social theory and social structure.* New York, NY: Free Press.

Michalowski, R. (1985). *Order, law and crime.* New York, NY: Random House.

Miehling, R., & Timmerberg, H. (2004). *Schneekönig: Mein Leben als Drogenbos.* Reinbek, Germany: Rowohlt Taschenbuch Verlag.

Miethe, T. D., & Meier, R. F. (1994). *Crime and its social context: Toward an integrated theory of offenders, victims, and situations.* Albany, NY: State University of New York Press.

Miller, S. (2013). Drawing the line. *Journal of Technology, Law & Policy, 13*(2), 2013, 1–14.

Mincheva, G. L., & Gurr, R. T. (2010). Unholy alliances: Evidence of the linkages between trans-state terrorism and crime networks: The case of Bosnia. In B. Wolfgang, C. Daase, V. Dimitrijevic, & P. Van Duyne (Eds.), *Transnational terror-ism, organized crime and peace-building* (pp. 265–286). London, England: Palgrave.

Missouri Task Force on Organized Crime. (n.d.). *Report.*

Misztal, B. A. (1996). *Trust in modern societies: The search for the bases of social order.* Cambridge, England: Polity Press.

Mitsilegas, V. (2003). From national to global from empirical to legal: The ambivalent concept of transnational organized crime. In M. E. Beare (Ed.), *Critical reflections on transnational organized crime money laundering and corruption* (pp. 55–87). Toronto, Ontario, Canada: University of Toronto Press.

Mittelman, J. H., & Johnston, R. (1999). The globalization of organized crime, the courte-san state, and the corruption of civil society. *Global Governance, 5*(1), 103–126.

Moeller, K. (2012). Costs and revenues in street-level cannabis dealing. *Trends in Organized Crime, 15*(1), 31–46.

Molano, A. (2004). *Loyal soldiers in the cocaine kingdom: Tales of drugs, mules, and gunmen.* New York, NY: Columbia University Press.

Mooney, M. (1935). *Crime incorporated.* New York, NY: Whittlesey House.

Moore, M. H. (1986). Drug policy and organized crime. In President's Commission on Organized Crime (Ed.), *America's habit* (Appendix G). Washington, DC: Government Printing Office.

Moore, R. H. (1995). Motor fuel tax fraud and organized crime: The Russians and the Italian-American Mafia. In J. S. Albanese (Ed.), *Contemporary issues in organized crime* (pp. 189–200). Monsey, NY: Criminal Justice Press.

Moore, W. H. (1974). *The Kefauver committee and the politics of crime 1950–1952.* Columbia, MO: University of Missouri Press.

Moreto, W. D., & Clarke, R. V. (2013). Script analysis of the transnational illegal market in endangered species: Dream and reality. In B. Leclerc & R. Wortley (Eds.), *Cognition and crime: Offender decision making and script analyses* (pp. 209–220). Milton Park, England: Routledge.

Morris, N., & Hawkins, G. (1970). *The honest politician's guide to crime control.* Chicago, IL: University of Chicago Press.

Morris, S. D. (2013). Drug trafficking, corruption, and violence in Mexico: Mapping the linkages. *Trends in Organized Crime, 16*(2), 195–220.

Morrison, S. (1997). The dynamics of illicit drugs production: Future sources and threats. *Crime, Law and Social Change, 27*(2), 121–138.

Morrison, S. (2002, July). Approaching organised crime: Where are we now and where are we going? *Trends and Issues in Crime and Criminal Justice* (No. 231). Canberra, Australia: Australian Institute of Criminology.

Morrison, M., & Morgan, M. S. (1999). Models as mediating instruments. In M. S. Morgan & M. Morrison (Eds.), *Models as mediators: Perspectives on natural and social sciences* (pp. 10–37). Cambridge, England: Cambridge University Press.

Morselli, C. (2001). Structuring Mr. Nice: Entrepreneurial opportunities and brokerage positioning in the cannabis trade. *Crime, Law and Social Change, 35*(3), 203–244.

Morselli, C. (2003). Career opportunities and network-based privileges in the Cosa Nostra. *Crime, Law and Social Change, 39*(4), 383–418.

Morselli, C. (2005). *Contacts, opportunities, and criminal enterprise.* Toronto, Ontario, Canada: University of Toronto Press.

Morselli, C. (2009a). Hells Angels in springtime. *Trends in Organized Crime, 12*(2), 145–158.

Morselli, C. (2009b). *Inside criminal networks.* New York, NY: Springer.

Morselli, C., & Giguere, C. (2006). Legitimate strengths in criminal networks. *Crime, Law and Social Change, 45*(3), 185–200.

Morselli, C., Giguere, C., & Petit, K. (2007). The efficiency/security trade-off in criminal networks. *Social Networks, 29*(1), 143–153.

Morselli, C., & Petit, K. (2007). Law-enforcement disruption of a drug importation network. *Global Crime, 8*(2), 109–130.

Morselli, C., & Roy, J. (2008). Brokerage qualifications in ringing operations. *Criminology, 46*(1), 71–98.

Morselli, C., & Tremblay, P. (2004). Criminal achievement, offender networks and the benefits of low self-control. *Criminology, 42*(3), 773–804.

Morselli, C., & Savoie-Gargiso, I. (2014). Coercion, control, and cooperation in a prostitution ring. *The ANNALS of the American Academy of Political and Social Science, 653*(1), 247–265.

Morselli, C., Tanguay, D., & Labalette, A.-M. (2008). Criminal conflicts and collective violence: Biker-related account settlements in Quebec, 1994–2001. In D. Siegel & H. Nelen (Eds.), *Organized crime: Culture, markets and policies* (pp. 145–163). New York, NY: Springer.

Morton, J. (1992). *Gangland: London's underworld.* London, England: Little, Brown and Company.

Moyle, B. (2009). The black market in China for tiger products. *Global Crime, 10*(1&2), 124–143.

Mühl, B. (2013). Access by law enforcement agencies to financial data. In B. Unger & D. van der Linde (Eds.), *Research handbook on money laundering* (pp. 452–459). Cheltenham, England: Edward Elgar.

Mullins, C.W., & Cherbonneau, M.G. (2011). Establishing Connections: Gender, motor vehicle theft, and disposal networks. *Justice Quarterly, 28*(2), 278–302.

Mulrooney wants criminals exiled. (1933, August 15). *New York Times.*

Murphy, S. (2002, March 24). Smugglers' route. *New York Times Magazine,* p. 72.

Mustain, G., & Capeci, J. (2002). *Mob star: The story of John Gotti.* Indianapolis. In Alpha.

Nadelmann, E. A. (1997). *Cops across borders: The internationalization of U.S. criminal law enforcement.* University Park, PA: Pennsylvania State University Press.

Natarajan, M. (2000). Understanding the structure of a drug trafficking organization: A conversational analysis. In M. Natarajan & M. Hough (Eds.), *Illegal drug markets* (pp. 273–298). Monsey, NY: Criminal Justice Press.

Natarajan, M. (2006). Understanding the structure of a large heroin distribution network: A quantitative analysis of qualitative data. *Journal of Quantitative Criminology, 22*(2), 171–192.

National Advisory Committee on Criminal Justice Standards and Goals. (1976). *Organized crime—Report of the task force on organized crime*. Washington, DC: Government Printing Office.

Naylor, R. T. (1993). The insurgent economy: Black market operations of guerilla organizations. *Crime, Law and Social Change, 20*(1), 13–51.

Naylor, R. T. (2002). *Wages of crime: Black markets, illegal finance, and the underworld economy*. Ithaca, NY: Cornell University Press.

Naylor, R. T. (2003). Towards a general theory of profit-driven crimes. *British Journal of Criminology, 43*(1), 81–101.

Naylor, R. T. (2009). Violence and illegal economic activity: A deconstruction. *Crime, Law and Social Change, 52*(3), 231–242.

Nelen, H. (2010). Situational organised crime prevention in Amsterdam: The administrative approach. In K. Bullock, R. V. Clarke, & N. Tilley (Eds.), *Situational prevention of organised crimes* (pp. 93–110). Cullompton, England: Willan.

Nelli, H. S. (1976). *The business of crime: Italians and syndicate crime in the United States*. New York, NY: Oxford University Press.

New York State. (1966). *Combating organized crime: A report of the 1965 Oyster Bay, New York, conferences on combating organized crime*. Albany, NY: Office of the Counsel to the Governor.

Newton, M. (2011). *Chronology of organized crime worldwide, 6000 B.C.E. to 2010*. Jefferson, NC: McFarland.

Nohria, N. (1992). Introduction: Is a network perspective a useful way of studying organizations? In N. Nohria & R. G. Eccles (Eds.), *Networks and organizations: Structure, form, and action* (pp. 1–22). Cambridge, MA: Harvard Business School Press.

Nossiter, A. (2012, November 2). Leader ousted, nation is now a drug haven. *New York Times*.

Nossiter, A. (2013, April 16). U.S. sting that snared African ex-admiral shines a light on the drug trade. *New York Times*.

Oboh, J., & Schoenmakers, Y. (2010). Nigerian advance fee fraud in transnational perspective. *Cahiers Politiestudies, 2*(15), 235–254.

O'Brien, J. F., & Kurins, A. (1993). *Boss of bosses: The fall of the godfather—The FBI and Paul Castellano*. New York, NY: Pocket Books.

O'Brien, T. R., & Flaherty, M. J. (1985). Regulation of the Atlantic City casino industry and attempts to control its infiltration by organized crime. *Rutgers Law Journal, 16*(3–4), 721–758.

O'Connor, J. C., Chriqui, J. F., & McBride, D. C. (2006). Developing lasting legal solutions to the dual epidemics of methamphetamine production and use. *North Dakota Law Review, 82*(4), 1165–1194.

O'Kane, J. M. (1992). *The crooked ladder: Gangsters ethnicity and the American dream*. New Brunswick, NJ: Transaction.

O'Malley, P., & Mugford, S. (1991). The demand for intoxicating commodities: Implications for the "War on Drugs." *Social Justice, 18*(4), 49–75.

Orlova, A. V. (2008). A comparison of the Russian and Canadian experiences with defining "organized crime." *Trends in Organized Crime, 11*(2), 99–134.

Otis sees Gompers's fall. (1912, December 31). *New York Times*.

Orlando, L. (2001). *Fighting the Mafia and renewing Sicilian culture*. San Francisco, CA: Encounter.

Otomo, R. (2007). Women in organized crime in Japan. In G. Fiandaca (Ed.), *Women and the Mafia: Female roles in organized crime structures* (pp. 205–217). New York, NY: Springer.

Packer, H. L. (1964). The crime tariff. *The American Scholar, 33*(4), 551–557.

Pakes, F., & Silverstone, D. (2012). Cannabis in the global market: A comparison between the UK and the Netherlands. *International Journal of Law, Crime and Justice, 40*(1), 20–30.

Paoli, L. (1995). The Banco Ambrosiano case: An investigation into the underestimation of the relations between organized and economic crime. *Crime, Law and Social Change, 23*(4), 345–365.

Paoli, L. (2002). The development of an illegal market: Drug consumption and trade in post-Soviet Russia. *The British Journal of Criminology, 42*(1), 21–39.

Paoli, L. (2003a). *Mafia brotherhoods: Organized crime, Italian style.* New York, NY: Oxford University Press.

Paoli, L. (2003b). The "invisible hand of the market": The illegal drugs trade in Germany, Italy, and Russia. In P. C. Van Duyne, K. von Lampe, & J. L. Newell (Eds.), *Criminal finances and organising crime in Europe* (pp. 20–43.). Nijmegen, the Netherlands: Wolf Legal.

Paoli, L. (2004). Organised crime in Italy: Mafia and illegal markets—Exception and normality. In C. Fijnaut & L. Paoli (Eds.), *Organised crime in Europe: Concepts, patterns and control policies in the European Union and beyond* (pp. 263–303). Dordrecht, Germany: Springer.

Paoli, L. (Ed.). (2014). *The Oxford handbook of organized crime.* Oxford, England: Oxford University Press.

Paoli, L., & Donati, A. (2014). *The sports doping market: Understanding supply and demand, and the challenges for their control.* New York, NY: Springer.

Paoli, L., & Fijnaut, C. (2004). Introduction to Part I: The history of the concept. In C. Fijnaut & L. Paoli (Eds.), *Organised crime in Europe: Concepts, patterns and control policies in the European Union and beyond* (pp. 21–46). Dordrecht, Germany: Springer.

Paoli, L., & Fijnaut, C. (2008). Organised crime and its control policies. *European Journal of Crime, Criminal Law and Criminal Justice, 14*(3), 307–327.

Paoli, L., Greenfield, V. A., & Reuter, P. (2009). *The world heroin market: Can supply be Cut?* Oxford, England: Oxford University Press.

Paoli, L., Greenfield, V. A., & Zoutendijk, A. (2013). The harms of cocaine trafficking: Applying a new framework for assessment. *Journal of Drug Issues, 43*(4), 407–436.

Paoli, L., & Reuter, P. (2008). Drug trafficking and ethnic minorities in Western Europe. *European Journal of Criminology, 5*(1), 13–37.

Papachristos, A. V., & Smith, C. M. (2014). The embedded and multiplex nature of Al Capone. In C. Morselli (Ed.), *Crime and networks* (pp. 97–115). New York, NY: Routledge.

Pardo, B. (2014). Cannabis policy reforms in the Americas: A comparative analysis of Colorado, Washington, and Uruguay. *International Journal of Drug Policy, 25*(4), 727–735.

Partridge, H. (2012). The determinants of and barriers to critical consumption: A study of Addiopizzo. *Modern Italy, 17*(3), 343–363.

Pashev, K. (2008). Cross-border VAT fraud in an enlarged Europe. In P. C. van Duyne, J. Harvey, A. Maljevic, M. Scheinost, & K. von Lampe (Eds.), *European crime-markets at crossroads: Extended and extending criminal Europe* (pp. 237–259). Nijmegen, the Nethelands: Wolf Legal Publishers.

Passas, N. (1993). Structural sources of international crime: Policy lessons from the BCCI Affair. *Crime, Law and Social Change, 20*(4), 293–309.

Passas, N. (1998). A structural analysis of corruption: The role of criminogenic asymmetries. *Transnational Organized Crime, 4*(1), 42–55.

Passas, N. (2002). Cross-border crime and the interface between legal and illegal actors. In P. C. van Duyne, K. von Lampe, & N. Passas (Eds.), *Upperworld and underworld in cross-border crime* (pp. 11–41). Nijmegen, the Netherlands: Wolf Legal Publishers.

Passas, N. (2005). Lawful but awful: "Legal corporate crimes." *Journal of Socio-Economics, 34*(6), 771–786.

Passas, N., & Groskin, R. (2001). Overseeing and overlooking: The US federal authorities' response to money laundering and other misconduct at BCCI. *Crime, Law and Social Change, 35*(1–2), 141–175.

Passas, N., & Nelken, D. (1993). The thin line between legitimate and criminal enterprises: Subsidy frauds in the European community. *Crime, Law and Social Change, 19*(3), 223–243.

Payne, B. K., & Gainey, R. R. (2005). *Drugs and policing: A scientific perspective.* Springfield, IL: Charles C Thomas.

Pearce, F. (1976). *Crimes of the powerful: Marxism, crime and deviance.* London, England: Pluto Press.

Pearson, G., & Hobbs, D. (2001). *Middle market drug distribution.* London, England: Home Office.

Pedra, A., & Dal Ri, A. (2011). The role of organized crime in informal justice systems: The Brazilian case. *International Journal of Security and Terrorism, 2*(1), 59–80.

Pennington, J. R., Ball, A. D., Hampton, R. D., & Soulakova, J. N. (2009). The Cross-national market in human beings. *Journal of Macromarketing, 29*(2), 119–134.

Perl, R. F. (2007). *Drug trafficking and North Korea: Issues for U.S. policy.* Washington, DC: Congressional Research Service.

Perl, R., & Nanto, D. K. (2007). *North Korean crime-for-profit activities.* Washington, DC: Congressional Research Service.

Pershing asks repeal of prohibition law. (1932, May 20). *New York Times.*

Phelps, A., & Watt, A. (2014). I shop online—recreationally! Internet anonymity and Silk Road enabling drug use in Australia. *Digital Investigation, 11*(4), 261–272.

Pietschmann, T. (2004). Price-setting behaviour in the heroin market. *Bulletin on Narcotics, 56*(1&2), 105–139.

Pileggi, N. (1985). *Wiseguy: Life in a Mafia family.* New York: Simon & Schuster.

Pimentel, S. A. (1999). The nexus of organized crime and politics in Mexico. *Trends in Organized Crime, 4*(3), 9–28.

Piracy and terrorism. (2004, April 10). *New York Times.*

Pires, S. F. (2012). The illegal parrot trade: A literature review. *Global Crime, 13*(3), 176–190.

Pistone, J. D. (1989). *Donnie Brasco: My undercover life in the Mafia,* New York, NY: Signet.

Pitkin, T. M., & Cordasco, F. (1977). *The black hand: A chapter in ethnic crime.* Totowa, NJ: Littlefield, Adams.

Pollock, J. M. (2009). *Criminal Law* (9th ed.). Newark, NJ: Matthew Bender.

Pontell, H. N., & Calavita, K. (1993). White-collar crime in the savings and loan scandal. *Annals of the American Academy of Political and Social Science, 525*(1), 31–45.

Poppa, T. E. (1998). *Drug lord: The life and death of a Mexican kingpin.* Seattle, WA: Demand.

Porter, B. (1993). *Blow: How a small-town boy made $100 million with the Medellin cocaine cartel and lost it all.* New York, NY: HarperCollins.

Potter, G. W. (1994). *Criminal organizations: Vice racketeering and politics in an American city.* Prospect Heights, IL: Waveland Press.

Potter, G., & Gaines, L. (1995). Organizing crime in Copperhead County: An ethnographic look at rural crime networks. In J. S. Albanese (Ed.), *Contemporary issues in organized crime* (pp. 61–86). Monsey, NY: Criminal Justice Press.

Potter, G. W., & Jenkins, P. (1985). *The city and the syndicate: Organizing crime in Philadelphia.* Lexington, MA: Ginn Custom Publishing.

Powers, R. G., (1987). *Secrecy and power: The life of J. Edgar Hoover.* New York, NY: The Free Press.

Porteous, S. D. (1998). *Organized crime impact study: Highlights.* Ottawa, Ontario: Public Works and Government Services of Canada.

Powell, W. W. (1990). Neither market nor hierarchy: Network forms of organization. *Research in Organizational Behavior, 12*(1), 295–336.

Poyner, B. (1993). What works in crime prevention: An overview of evaluations. In R. V. Clarke (Ed.), *Crime prevention studies* (Vol. 1, pp. 7–34). Monsey, NY: Criminal Justice Press.

Prenzler, T. (2009). *Police corruption: Preventing misconduct and maintaining integrity.* Boca Raton, FL: CRC Press.

President's Commission on Organized Crime. (1983, November 29). *Organized crime: Federal law enforcement perspective.* Record of Hearing I. Washington, DC: Government Printing Office.

President's Commission on Organized Crime. (1984). *The cash connection: Organized crime, financial institutions, and money laundering.* Interim Report to the President and the Attorney General, Washington, DC: Government Printing Office.

President's Commission on Organized Crime. (1986). *America's habit: Drug abuse, drug trafficking, and organized crime.* Washington, DC: Government Printing Office.

Pütter, N. (1998). *Der OK-Komplex: Organisierte Kriminalität und ihre Folgen für die Polizei in Deutschland,* Münster, Germany: Westfälisches Dampfboot.

Pullat, R. (2009). *Organized crime related drug trafficking in the Baltic Sea region: Police point of view.* Tallinn: Estonian Police Board.

Punch, M. (2009). *Police corruption: Deviance, accountability and reform in policing.* Cullompton, England: Willan.

Queen, W. (2006). *Under and alone: The true story of the undercover agent who infiltrated America's most violent outlaw motorcycle gang.* New York, NY: Fawcett Books.

Quinn, J., & Koch, D. S. (2003). The nature of criminality within one-percent motorcycle clubs. *Deviant Behavior, 24*(3), 281–305.

Raab, S. (2005). *Five families: The rise, decline, and resurgence of America's most powerful Mafia empires.* New York, NY: St. Martin's Press.

Radbruch, G., & Gewinner, H. (1991). *Geschichte des Verbrechens: Versuch einer historischen Kriminologie.* Frankfurt am Main, Germany: Eichborn.

Ram, C. (2001). The United Nations convention against transnational organized crime and its protocols. *Forum on Crime and Society, 1*(2), 135–145.

Ratzel, M.-P., & Lippert, F. (2001). International organisierte Kraftfahrzeugkriminalität. *Kriminalistik, 55*(11), 705–713.

Rawlinson, P. (2002). Capitalists, criminals and oligarchs—Sutherland and the new "robber barons." *Crime, Law and Social Change, 37*(3), 293–307.

Rawlinson, P. (2008). Look who's talking: Interviewing Russian criminals. *Trends in Organized Crime, 11*(1), 12–20.

Rawlinson, P. (2010). *From fear to fraternity: A Russian tale of crime, economy and modernity.* London, England: Pluto.

Rebscher, E., & Vahlenkamp, W. (1988). *Organisierte kriminalität in der Bundesrepublik Deutschland: Bestandsaufnahme, entwicklungstendenzen und bekämpfung aus sicht der polizeipraxis.* Wiesbaden, Germany: Bundeskriminalamt.

Redpath, J. (2004). *The scorpions: Analysing the directorate of special operations.* Pretoria, Republic of South Africa: Institute for Security Studies.

Reid, E. (1952). *Mafia.* New York, NY: Random House.

Rempel, W. C. (2012). *At the devil's table: The man who took down the world's biggest crime syndicate.* London, England: Arrow Books.

Rengert, G., Chakravorty, S., Bole, T., & Henderson, K. (2000). A geographic analysis of illegal drug markets. In M. Natarajan & M. Hough (Eds.), *Illegal drug markets* (pp. 219–239). Monsey, NY: Criminal Justice Press.

Reuband, K.-H. (1998). Drug policies and drug prevalence: The role of demand and supply. *European Journal on Criminal Policy and Research, 6*(3), 321–336.

Reuter, P. (1983). *Disorganized crime: The economics of the visible hand.* Cambridge, MA: MIT Press.

Reuter, P. (1985). Racketeers as cartel organizers. In H. E. Alexander & G. E. Caiden (Eds.), *The politics and economics of organized crime* (pp. 49–65). Lexington, MA: D.C. Heath.

Reuter, P. (1987). *Racketeering in legitimate industries: A study in the economics of intimidation.* Santa Monica, CA: Rand.

Reuter, P. (1993). The cartage industry in New York. In M. Tonry & A. J. J. Reiss (Eds.), *Beyond the law: Crime in complex organizations* (pp. 149–202), Chicago, IL: University of Chicago Press.

Reuter, P. (1994). Research on American organized crime. In R. J. Kelly, K.-L. Chin, & R. Schatzberg (Eds.), *Handbook of organized crime in the United States* (pp. 91–120). Westport, CT: Greenwood.

Reuter, P. (1995). The decline of the American Mafia. *Public Interest, 120,* 89–99.

Reuter, P. (2009). Systemic violence in drug markets. *Crime, Law and Social Change, 52*(3), 275–284.

Reuter, P., & Haaga, J. (1989). *The organization of high-level drug markets: An exploratory study.* Santa Monica, CA: Rand Corporation.

Reuter, P., & Truman, E. M. (2004). *Chasing dirty money: Progress on anti-money laundering,* Washington, DC: Institute for International Economics.

Reynolds, M. (1995). *From gangs to gangsters: How American sociology organized crime 1918 to 1994.* Guilderland, NY: Harrow and Heston.

Rhodes, R. P. (1984). *Organized crime: Crime control vs. civil liberties.* New York, NY: Random House.

Riccardi, Michele (2014). When criminals invest in businesses: Are we looking in the right direction? An exploratory analysis of companies controlled by mafias. In S. Canappele & F. Calderoni (Eds.), *Organized Crime, Corruption and Crime Prevention - Essays in Honor of Ernesto U. Savona* (197–206). Cham: Springer.

Rieger, S. (2006, July). *Der Rolex-Banden fall.* (Seminar paper). Fachhochschule Villingen-Schwenningen, Germany, Seminar Berühmte Kriminalfälle Deutschlands in strafrechtlicher und kriminalistisch-kriminologischer Analyse.

Rios, V. (2013). Why did Mexico become so violent? A self-reinforcing violent equilibrium caused by competition and enforcement. *Trends in Organized Crime, 16*(2), 138–155.

Ritter, A. (2006). Studying illicit drug markets: Disciplinary contributions. *International Journal of Drug Policy, 17*(6), 453–463.

Roberge, I. (2011). Financial action task force. In T. Hale & D. Held (Eds.), *Handbook of transnational governance: Institutions and innovations* (pp. 45–49). Cambridge, England: Polity Press.

Robins, G. (2009). Understanding individual behaviors within covert networks: The interplay of individual qualities, psychological predispositions, and network effects. *Trends in Organized Crime, 12*(2), 166–187.

Robinson, J. (2000). *The merger: The conglomeration of international organized crime.* Woodstock, NY: The Overlook Press.

Robles, G., Calderon, G., & Magaloni, B. (2013). *The economic consequences of drug trafficking violence in Mexico.* Stanford, CA: Stanford University. Retrieved from http://fsi.stanford.edu/sites/default/files/RoblesCalderonMagaloni_EconCosts5.pdf

Rockaway, R. A. (1993). *But he was good to this mother: The lives and crimes of Jewish gangsters.* Jerusalem, Israel: Gefen Publishing House.

Roedl, G., Elmes, G. A., & Conley, J. (2014). Spatial tracking applications. In G. A. Elmes, G. Roedl, & J. Conley (Eds.), *Forensic GIS: The role of geospatial technologies for investigating crime and providing evidence* (pp. 39–51). Dordrecht, Germany: Springer.

Roemer, W. F. (1989). *Roemer: Man against the mob.* New York, NY: Donald I. Fine.

Roemer, W. F. (1989). *Roemer: Man against the Mob.* New York, NY: Donald I. Fine.

Rogovin, C. H., & Martens, F. T. (1992). The evil that men do. *Journal of Contemporary Criminal Justice, 8*(1–2), 62–79.

Room, R. (2014). Legalizing a market for cannabis for pleasure: Colorado, Washington, Uruguay and beyond. *Addiction, 109*(3), 345–351.

Roth, M. P. (2010). *Organized crime.* Upper Saddle River, NJ: Prentice Hall.

Rottman, A. (1997, December 9). *Erythroxylum: The coca plant* (Ethnobotanical Leaflets). Southern Illinois University, Carbondale. Retrieved from http://www.ethnoleaflets.com/leaflets/coca.htm

Ross, J. E. (2007). The place of covert surveillance in democratic societies: A comparative study of the United States and Germany. *The American Journal of Comparative Law, 55*(3), 493–579.

Ross, J. E. (2008). Undercover policing and the shifting terms of scholarly debate: The United States and Europe in counterpoint. *Annual Review of Law and Social Science, 4*(1), 239–273.

Rubin, P. (1973). The economic theory of the criminal firm. In S. Rottenberg (Ed.), *The economics of crime and punishment* (pp. 155–166). Washington, DC: American Enterprise Institute for Public Policy Research.

Rudolph, R. (1992). *The boys from New Jersey: How the mob beat the Feds.* New York, NY: William Morrow.

Ruggiero, V. (1996). *Organized and corporate crime in Europe: Offers that can't be refused.* Aldershot, England: Dartmouth.

Ruggiero, V., & Khan, K. (2006). British South Asian communities and drug supply networks in the UK: A qualitative study. *International Journal of Drug Policy, 17*(6), 473–483.

Ruggiero, V., & Khan, K. (2007). The organisation of drug supply: South Asian criminal enterprise in the UK. *Asian Journal of Criminology, 2*(2), 163–177.

Ruggiero, V., & South, N. (1995). *Eurodrugs: Drug use markets and trafficking in Europe*. London, England: UCL Press.

Ruggiero, V., & Welch, M. (2009). Power crime. *Crime, Law and Social Change, 51*(3–4), 297–301.

Rule of Law Institute of Australia. (2014). Criminal organisation control legislation and cases 2008–2013. Retrieved from http://www.ruleoflaw.org.au/wp-content/uploads/2012/07/Rule-of-Law-Institute-Summary-of-Control-Order-Legislation-and-Cases1.pdf

Russo, F. F. (2010). *Cocaine: The complementarity between legal and illegal trade* (Working Paper No. 253). Naples, Italy: Centre for Studies in Economics and Finance.

Rutter, J., & Bryce, J. (2008). The consumption of counterfeit goods. *Sociology, 42*(6), 1146–1164.

Rydell, C. P., & Everingham, S. S. (1994). *Controlling cocaine: Supply versus demand programs*. Santa Monica, CA: RAND.

Ryan, P. J. (1994). A history of organized crime control: Federal strike forces. In R. J. Kelly, K.-L. Chin, & R. Schatzberg (Eds.), *Handbook of organized crime in the United States* (pp. 333–358). Westport, CT: Greenwood.

Saab, B. Y., & Taylor, A. W. (2009). Criminality and armed groups: A comparative study of FARC and paramilitary groups in Colombia. *Studies in Conflict and Terrorism, 32*(6), 455–475.

Sabatelle, D. R. (2011). The scourge of opiates: The illicit narcotics trade in the Islamic Republic of Iran. *Trends in Organized Crime, 14*(4), 314–331

Salerno, J., & Rivele, S. J. (1990). *The plumber: The true story of how one good man helped destroy the entire Philadelphia Mafia*. New York, NY: Knightsbridge.

Saline, C. (1989). *Dr. Snow: How the FBI nailed an Ivy League coke king*. New York, NY: Signet.

Samani, R., & Paget, F. (2013). *Cybercrime exposed: Cybercrime-as-a-service*. Santa Clara, CA: McAfee. Retrieved form: http://www.mcafee.com/us/resources/white-papers/wp-cybercrime-exposed.pdf

Sandberg, S. (2012). The importance of culture for cannabis markets: Towards an economic sociology of illegal drug markets. *British Journal of Criminology, 52*(6), 1133–1151.

Sandberg, S., & Copes, H. (2013), Speaking with ethnographers: The challenges of researching drug dealers and offenders. *Journal of Drug Issues, 43*(2), 176–197.

Sann, P. (1971). *Kill the Dutchman: The story of Dutch Schultz*. New Rochelle, NY: Arlington House.

Savona, E. U., & Giommoni, L. (2013). Human trafficking for sexual exploitation in Italy. In B. Leclerc & R. Wortley (Eds.), *Cognition and crime: Offender decision making and script analyses* (pp. 140–163). Milton Park, England: Routledge.

Schelling, T. C. (1971). What is the business of organized crime? *The Journal of Public Law, 20*(1), 69–82.

Scheper-Hughes, N. (2004). Parts unknown: Undercover ethnography of the organs-trafficking underworld. *Ethnography, 5*(1), 29–73.

Schlegel, K. (1987). Violence in organized crime: A content analysis of the De Cavalcante and De Carlo transcripts. In T. S. Bynum (Ed.), *Organized crime in America: Concepts and controversies* (pp. 55–70). Monsey, NY: Criminal Justice Press.

Schloenhardt, A. (2012). Fighting organized crime in the Asia Pacific region: New weapons, lost wars. *Asian Journal of International Law, 2*(1), 137–167.

Schmelz, G. (2010). Tätowierungen und kriminalität [Tattoos and Crime]. *Kriminalistik,* *64*(2), 102–110.

Schneider, E. C. (2008). *Smack: Heroin and the American city.* Philadelphia: University of Pennsylvania Press.

Schneider, H. J. (1993). *Einführung in die kriminologie* [Introduction to Criminology] (3rd ed.). Berlin, Germany: De Gruyter.

Schneider, J., & Schneider, P. (2001). Civil society versus organized crime: Local and global perspectives. *Critique of Anthropology, 21*(4), 427–446.

Schoenmakers, Y. M. M., Bremmers, B., & Kleemans, E. R. (2013). Strategic versus emergent crime groups: The case of Vietnamese cannabis cultivation in the Netherlands. *Global Crime, 14*(4), 321–340.

Schulte-Bockholt, A. (2001). A Neo-Marxist explanation of organized crime. *Critical Criminology, 10*(3), 225–242.

Schwartz, D. M., & Rousselle, T. (2009). Using social network analysis to target criminal networks. *Trends in Organized Crime, 12*(2), 188–207.

Sciarrone, R., & Storti, L. (2014). The territorial expansion of mafia-type organized crime: The case of the Italian mafia in Germany. *Crime, Law and Social Change, 61*(1), 37–60.

Scott, J. (2000). *Social network analysis: A handbook* (2nd ed.). London, England: Sage.

Scott, W. R. (1981). *Organizations: Rational, natural, and open systems.* Englewood Cliffs, NJ: Prentice Hall.

Scotti, B. (2002). RICO vs. 416-bis: A comparison of U.S. and Italian anti-organized crime legislation. *Loyola of Los Angeles International and Comparative Law Review, 25*(1), 143–164.

Seidl, J. M. (1968). Upon the hip: A study of the criminal loan-shark industry (PhD thesis). Harvard University.

Selby, S. A., & Campbell, G. (2010). *Flawless: Inside the largest diamond heist in history.* New York, NY: Union Square Press.

Seligman, A. B. (1997). *The problem of trust.* Princeton, NJ: Princeton University Press.

Sellin, T. (1963). Organized crime as a business enterprise. *Annals of the American Academy of Political and Social Science, 347*(1), 12–19.

Senator Morton's committee. (1871, January 26). *The New York Times.*

Sergi, A. (2014). The evolution of the Australian 'ndrangheta: An historical perspective. *Australian and New Zealand Journal of Criminology.* Advance online publication. doi: 10.1177/0004865814554305

Serio, J. D. (2004). Fueling global crime: The mechanics of money laundering. *International Review of Law, Computers & Technology, 18*(3), 435–444.

Serio, J. D. (2008). *Investigating the Russian Mafia.* Durham, NC: Carolina Academic Press.

Serio, J. D., & Razinkin, V. (1995). Thieves professing the code: The traditional role of "Vory v Zakone" in Russia's criminal world. *Low Intensity Conflict and Law Enforcement, 4*(1), 72–88.

Seto, M. C. (2008). Pedophelia: Psychopathology and theory. In D. R. Laws & W. T. O'Donohue (Eds.), *Sexual deviance: Theory, assessment, and treatment* (pp. 164–182). New York, NY: Guilford Press.

Shamir, R. (2005). Without borders? Notes on globalization as a mobility regime. *Sociological Theory, 23*(2), 197–217.

Sharman, J. C. (2011). *The money laundry: Regulating criminal finance in the global economy.* Ithaca, NY: Cornell University Press

Sharpe, J. A. (1984). *Crime in early modern England 1550–1750.* Burnt Mill, England: Longman.

Shaw, C. R., & McKay, H. D. (1942). *Juvenile delinquency and urban Areas: A study of rates of delinquents in relation to differential characteristics of local communities in American cities.* Chicago, IL: University of Chicago Press.

Shaw, A., Egan, J., & Gillespie, M. (2007). *Drugs and poverty: A literature review.* Glasgow: Scottish Drugs Forum. Retrieved from http://www.sdf.org.uk/index.php/download_file/view/271/167/

Shaw, M. (2006). Drug trafficking and the development of organized crime in post-Taliban Afghanistan. In D. Buddenberg & W. A. Byrd (Eds.), *Afghanistan's drug industry: Structure, functioning, dynamics, and implications for counter-narcotics policy* (pp. 189–214). Vienna, Austria: United Nations Office on Drugs and Crime.

Sheldon Z., & Ko-lin, C. (2002). *Characteristics of Chinese human smugglers: A cross-national study.* San Diego, CA: San Diego State University.

Shelley, L. (1999a). Identifying, counting and categorizing transnational criminal organizations. *Transnational Organized Crime, 5*(1), 1–18.

Shelley, L. I. (1999b). Transnational organized crime: The new authoritarianism. In R. H. Friman & P. Andreas (Eds.), *The illicit global economy and state power* (pp. 25–51). Lanham, MD: Rowman & Littlefield.

Shelley, L. (2001). Corruption and organized crime in Mexico in the post-PRI transition. *Journal of Contemporary Criminal Justice, 17*(3), 213–231.

Shelley, L. (2010). *Human trafficking: A global perspective.* Cambridge, England: Cambridge University Press.

Shelley, L. (2011). The globalization of crime. In M. Natarajan (Ed.), *International crime and justice* (pp. 3–10). Cambridge, England: Cambridge University Press.

Shelley, L. (2014). *Dirty entanglements: Corruption, crime, and terrorism.* New York: Cambridge University Press.

Shen, A., Antonopoulos, G. A., & von Lampe, K. (2010). "The dragon breathes smoke": Cigarette counterfeiting in the People's Republic of China. *British Journal of Criminology, 50*(2), 239–258.

Sheppard, M. B., & Dougherty, E. C. (2012). Tapping into Wall Street: The government employs tougher tactics against money crimes. *Criminal Justice, 26*(4), 20–29.

Sheptycki, J. (2003). Against transnational organized crime. In M. E. Beare (Ed.), *Critical reflections on transnational organized crime money laundering and corruption* (pp. 120–144). Toronto, Ontario, Canada: University of Toronto Press.

Shirk, D. (2010). *Drug violence in Mexico: Data and analysis from 2001–2009.* San Diego, CA: Trans-Border Institute. Retrieved from http://www.justiceinmexico.org/resources/pdf/drug_violence.pdf

Shirk, D. (2011). *The drug war in Mexico: Confronting a shared threat.* New York, NY: Council on Foreign Relations.

Shukla, R. K., Crump, J. L., & Chrisco, E. S. (2012). An evolving problem: Methamphetamine production and trafficking in the United States. *International Journal of Drug Policy, 23*(6), 426–435.

Siddharth, K. (2010). *Sex trafficking: Inside the business of modern slavery.* New York, NY: Columbia University Press.

Sieber, U. (1995). Logistik der Organisierten Kriminalität in der Bundesrepublik Deutschland—Ergebnisse eines neuen Forschungsansatzes. *Juristenzeitung, 49*(15–16), 758–768.

Sieber, U., & Bögel, M. (1993). *Logistik der organisierten Kriminalität.* Wiesbaden, Germany: Bundeskriminalamt.

Siegel, D. (2008). Conversations with Russian mafiosi. *Trends in Organized Crime, 11*(1), 21–29.

Siegel, D. (2009). Hot sands or the "romantics" of the desert: Women smuggling from Egypt to Israel. In P. C. van Duyne, S. Donati, J. Harvey, A. Maljevic, & K. von Lampe (Eds.), *Crime, money and criminal mobility in Europe* (pp. 97–115). Nijmegen the Netherlands: Wolf Legal Publishers.

Siegel, D. (2012). Vory v zakone: Russian organized crime. In D. Siegel & H. van de Bunt (Eds.), *Traditional organized crime in the modern world* (pp. 27–47). New York, NY: Springer.

Siegel, D. (2014). Women in transnational organized crime. *Trends in Organized Crime, 17*(1–2), 52–65.

Siegel, D., & de Blank, S. (2010). Women who traffic women: the role of women in human trafficking networks - Dutch cases. *Global Crime, 11*(4), 436–447.

Simpson, S. S. (2002). *Corporate crime, law, and social control.* New York, NY: Cambridge University Press.

Simon, D. R., & Eitzen, D. S. (1982). *Elite deviance.* Boston, MA: Allyn and Bacon.

Sims, E. W. (1920). Fighting crime in Chicago: The Crime Commission. *Journal of the American Institute of Criminal Law and Criminology, 11*(1), 21–28.

Simser, J. (2013). Money laundering: Emerging threats and trends. *Journal of Money Laundering Control, 16*(1), 41–54.

Skaperdas, S. (2001). The political economy of organized crime: Providing protection when the state does not. *Economics of Governance, 2*(3), 173–202.

Skaperdas, S., & Syropoulos, C. (1995). Gangs as primitive states. In G. Fiorentini & S. Peltzman (Eds.), *The economics of organised crime* (pp. 61–82). Cambridge, England: Cambridge University Press.

Skarbek, D. (2014). *The social order of the underworld: How prison gangs govern the American penal system.* Oxford, England: Oxford University Press.

Skoblikov, P. A. (2007, September/October). Russian shadow justice: Its assumptions, nature, and essence. *Crime & Justice, 23,* 39–44.

Smart, R. G., Adlaf, E. M., & Walsh, G. W. (1994). Neighborhood socio-economic factors in relation to student drug use and programs. *Journal of Child and Adolescent Substance Abuse, 3*(1), 37–46.

Smith, D. C. (1971). Some things that may be more important to understand about organized crime than Cosa Nostra. *University of Florida Law Review, 24*(1), 1–30.

Smith, D. C. (1975). *The Mafia mystique.* New York, NY: Lanham.

Smith, D. C. (1976). Mafia: The prototypical alien conspiracy. *The Annals of The American Academy of Political and Social Science, 423*(1), 75–88.

Smith, D. C. (1978). Organized crime and entrepreneurship. *International Journal of Criminology and Penology, 6*(2), 161–177.

Smith, D. C. (1980). Paragons, pariahs and pirates: A spectrum-based theory of enterprise. *Crime and Delinquency, 26*(3), 358–386.

Smith, D. C. (1982). White-collar crime, organized crime and the business establishment: Resolving a crisis in criminological theory. In P. Wickman & T. Dailey (Eds.), *White-collar and economic crime* (pp. 23–38). Lexington, MA: Lexington Books.

Smith, D. C. (1991). Wickersham to Sutherland to Katzenbach: Evolving an official definition for organized crime. *Crime, Law and Social Change, 16*(2), 135–154.

Smith, D. C. (1994). Illicit enterprise: An organized crime paradigm for the nineties. In R. J. Kelly, K.-L. Chin, & R. Schatzberg (Eds.), *Handbook of organized crime in the United States* (pp. 121–150). Westport, CT: Greenwood.

Smith, E. H. (1926, September 5). Crime has now evolved as a big business. *The New York Times,* VIII, 4–5.

Smith, R. G., & Walker, J. (2010, October). The illegal movement of cash and bearer negotiable instruments: Typologies and regulatory responses. *Trends and Issues in Crime and Criminal Justice* (No. 402). Canberra, Australia: Australian Institute of Criminology.

Snyder, R., & Duran-Martinez, A. (2009). Does illegality breed violence? Drug trafficking and state-sponsored protection rackets. *Crime, Law and Social Change, 52*(3), 253–273.

Sobolev, V. A., Rushchenko, I. P., & Volobuev, A. F. (2002). *Organized criminal groups in Ukraine: Traditional and typical (sociological essay).* Kharkov, Ukraine: National University of Internal Affairs.

Soudijn, M. R. J. (2006). *Chinese human smuggling in transit.* The Hague, the Netherlands: Boom.

Soudijn, M. R. J. (2010). Wives, girlfriends and money laundering. *Journal of Money Laundering Control, 13*(4), 405–416.

Soudijn, M., & Huisman, S. (2011). Criminal expatriates: British criminals in the Netherlands and Dutch criminals in Spain. In G. Antonopoulos, M. Groenhuijsen, J. Harvey, T. Kooijmans, A. Maljevic, & K. von Lampe (Eds.), *Usual and unusual organising criminals in Europe and beyond: Profitable crimes, from underworld to upper world—Liber Amicorum Petrus van Duyne* (pp. 233–246). Apeldoorn, the Netherlands: Maklu.

Soudijn, M. R. J., & Kleemans, E. R. (2009). Chinese organized crime and situational context: Comparing human smuggling and synthetic drugs trafficking. *Crime, Law and Social Change, 52*(5), 457–474.

Soudijn, M. R. J., & Zegers, B. C. H. T. (2012). Cybercrime and virtual offender convergence settings. *Trends in Organized Crime, 15*(2–3), 111–129.

Soudijn, M. R. J., & Zhang, S. (2013). Taking loan sharking into account: A case study of Chinese vest-pocket lenders in Holland. *Trends in Organized Crime, 16*(1), 13–30.

Southerland, M., & Potter, G. W. (1993). Applying organization theory to organized crime. *Journal of Contemporary Criminal Justice, 9*(3), 251–267.

Spapens, T. (2010). Macro networks, collectives, and business processes: An integrated approach to organized crime. *European Journal of Crime, Criminal Law and Criminal Justice, 18*(2), 185–215.

Spapens, T. (2013). *Decriminalization as regulation: The gambling and cannabis markets in the Netherlands* (Research Paper Series No. 05/2013). Tilburg Law School Legal Studies.

Special Crime Study Commission on Organized Crime (1953). *Final Report.* Sacramento, CA: SCSCOC.

Spencer, H. (1881, November). The industrial type of society. *Popular Science, 20,* 1–29.

Speziale, J. (2004). *Without a badge: Undercover in the world's deadliest criminal organization.* New York, NY: Pinnacle Books.

Sproat, P. (2012). Phoney war or appeasement? The policing of organised crime in the UK. *Trends in Organized Crime, 15*(4), 313–330.

Sproat, P. (2014). Landscaping the policing of organised crime: Some designs and reflections. In J. M. Brown (Ed.), *The future of policing* (pp. 252–268). Milton Park, England: Routledge.

S. Rep. No. 307 (1951). *Third interim report of the special committee to investigate organized crime in interstate commerce pursuant to S. Res. 202. 81st Cong., 82nd Cong., 1st Session.*

Standing, A. (2006). *Organised crime: A study from the Cape Flats*. Pretoria, Republic of South Africa: Institute for Security Studies.

Sterling, C. (1994). *Thieves' world: The threat of the new global network of organized crime*. New York, NY: Simon & Schuster.

Stiles, D. (2004). The ivory trade in elephant conservation. *Environmental Conservation, 31*(4), 309–321.

Stille, A. (1996). *Excellent cadavers: The Mafia and the death of the first Italian republic*. New York, NY: Vintage.

St. John, H. (1852). *History of the British conquests*. London, England: Colburn and Co.

Stolberg, M. M. (1995). *Fighting organized crime: Politics, justice and the legacy of Thomas E. Dewey*. Boston, MA: Northeastern University Press.

Strader, J. K. (2002). *Understanding white collar crime*. Newark, NJ: Matthew Bender.

Stuntz, W. J. (1998). Race, class, and drugs. *Columbia Law Review, 98*(7), 1795–1842.

Sundberg, R. (1999). *Mc-brott*. Rapport 6. Stockholm, Sweden: Brottsförebyggande rådet.

Sung, H.-E. (2004). State failure, economic failure and predatory organized crime: A comparative analysis. *Journal of Research on Crime and Delinquency, 41*(2), 111–129.

Surtees, R. (2008). Traffickers and trafficking in Southern and Eastern Europe: Considering the other side of human trafficking. *European Journal of Criminology, 5*(1), 39–68.

Sutherland, E. H. (1937). *The professional thief: By a professional thief*. Chicago, IL: The University of Chicago Press.

Sutherland, E. H. (1949). *White-collar crime*. New York, NY: Dryden.

Suttles, G. D. (1972). *The social construction of communities*. Chicago, IL: The University of Chicago Press.

Swain, T. (2009). *Organized crime*. New York, NY: Jax Desmond Worldwide.

Swanson, C. R., Chamelin, N. C., Territo, L., & Taylor, R. W. (2009). *Criminal investigation* (10th ed.). New York, NY: McGraw-Hill.

Sykes, G. M., & Matza, D. (1957). Techniques of neutralization: A theory of delinquency. *American Sociological Review, 22*(6), 664–670.

Symeonidou-Kastanidou, E. (2007). Towards a new definition of organised crime in the European Union. *European Journal of Crime, Criminal Law and Criminal Justice, 15*(1), 83–103.

Taniguchi, T. A., Rengert, G. F., & McCord, E. S. (2009). Where size matters: Agglomeration economies of illegal drug markets in Philadelphia. *Justice Quarterly, 26*(4), 670–694.

Tannenbaum, F. (1951). *Crime and the community*. New York, NY: Columbia University Press.

Taylor, A. (2007). *How drug dealers settle disputes: Violent and nonviolent outcomes*. Monsey, NY: Criminal Justice Press.

Taylor, L. (1984). *In the Underworld*. Oxford, England: Basil Blackwell.

Tenti, V., & Morselli, C. (2014). Group co-offending networks in Italy's illegal drug trade. *Crime, Law and Social Change, 62*(1), 21–44.

Terp, G. (2006). Vehicle tracking. In E. Stauffer & M. S. Bonfanti (Eds.), *Forensic investigation of stolen-recovered and other crime-related vehicles* (pp. 505–520). Burlington, MA: Academic Press.

Thompson, J. D. (1967). *Organizations in action*. New York, NY: McGraw-Hill.

Tompson, L., & Chainey, S. (2011). Profiling illegal waste activity: Using crime scripts as a data collection and analytical strategy. *European Journal on Criminal Policy and Research, 17*(3), 179–201.

Thrasher, F. M. (1963). *The gang: A study of 1313 gangs in Chicago* (Abridged edition). Chicago, IL: University of Chicago Press. (Original work published in 1927)

Tilley, N., & Hopkins, M. (2008). Organized crime and local businesses. *Criminology and Criminal Justice, 8*(4), 443–459.

Tillman, R. (2009). Reputations and corporate malfeasance: Collusive networks in financial statement fraud. *Crime, Law and Social Change, 51*(3–4), 365–382.

Tilly, C. (1985). War making and state making as organized crime. In P. B. Evans, D. Rueschemeyer, & T. Skocpol (Eds.), *Bringing the state back* (pp. 169–191). Cambridge, England: Cambridge University Press.

Todd, J. (1837). *The Sabbath school teacher.* Northhampton, MA: J.H. Butler.

Tombs, S. (2007). "Violence," Safety Crimes and Criminology. *British Journal of Criminology, 47*(4), 531–550.

Tompson, L., & Chainey, S. (2011). Profiling illegal waste activity: Using crime scripts as a data collection and analytical strategy. *European Journal on Criminal Policy and Research, 17*(3), 179–201.

Topics of the *Times.* (1906, December 21). *New York Times.*

Townsend, J. (2006). The logistics of opiate trafficking in Tajikistan, Kyrgyzstan and Kazakhstan. *China and Eurasia Forum Quarterly, 4*(1), 69–91.

Traub, J. (2010, April 11). Africa's drug problem. *New York Times Magazine.*

Traub, S. J., Hoffman, R. S., & Nelson, L. S. (2003). Body packing: The internal concealment of illicit drugs. *New England Journal of Medicine, 349*(26), 2519–2526.

Tremblay, P. (1993). Searching for suitable co-offenders. In R. V. Clarke & M. Felson (Eds.), *Advances in criminological theory: Vol. 5. Routine activity and rational choice* (pp. 17–36). New Brunswick, NJ: Transaction.

Tremblay, P. (2002). *Social interactions among paedophiles.* Unpublished paper. Retrieved from http://www.childtrafficking.com/Docs/trembaly_2002__social_inter.pdf

Tremblay, P., Talon, B., & Hurley, D. (2001). Body switching and related adaptations in the resale of stolen vehicles: Script elaborations and aggregate crime learning curves. *British Journal of Criminology, 41*(4), 561–579.

Troshynski, E. I., & Blank, J. K. (2008). Sex trafficking: An exploratory study interviewing traffickers. *Trends in Organized Crime, 11*(1), 30–41.

Turvey, B. E. (2011). *Criminal profiling: An introduction to behavioral evidence analysis* (3rd ed.). Burlington, MA: Academic Press.

Tusikov, N. (2012). Measuring organised crime-related harms: Exploring five policing methods. *Crime, Law and Social Change, 57*(1), 99–115.

Twyman-Ghoshal, A., & Pierce, G. (2014). The changing nature of contemporary maritime piracy: Results from the contemporary maritime piracy database 2001–10. *British Journal of Criminology, 54*(4), 652–672.

Tzvetkova, M. (2008). Aspects of the evolution of extra-legal protection in Bulgaria (1989–1999). *Trends in Organized Crime, 11*(4), 326–351.

Ulrich, A. (2005). *Das Engelsgesicht: Die Geschichte eines Mafia-Killers aus Deutschland,* München, Germany: Deutsche Verlags-Anstalt.

Undesirable citizens. (1907, April 25). *New York Times.*

UNODC. (2002). *Results of a pilot survey of forty selected organized criminal groups in sixteen countries.* Vienna, Austria: United Nations Office on Drugs and Crime.

UNODC. (2008). *Drug trafficking as a security threat in West Africa.* Vienna, Austria: United Nations Office on Drugs and Crime. Retrieved from https://www.unodc.org/documents/data-and-analysis/Studies/Drug-Trafficking-WestAfrica-English.pdf

UNODC. (2009). *Addiction, crime and insurgency: The transnational threat of Afghan opium*. Vienna, Austria: United Nations Office on Drugs and Crime. Retrieved from http://www.unodc.org/documents/data-and-analysis/Afghanistan/Afghan_Opium_Trade_2009_web.pdf

UNODC. (2010). *The globalization of crime: A transnational organized crime threat assessment*. Vienna, Austria: United Nations Office on Drugs and Crime. Retrieved from http://www.unodc.org/documents/data-and-analysis/tocta/TOCTA_Report_2010_low_res.pdf

UNODC. (2011a). *Estimating illicit financial flows resulting from drug trafficking and other transnational organized crimes*. Vienna, Austria: UNODC. Retrieved from http://www.unodc.org/documents/data-and-analysis/Studies/Illicit_financial_flows_2011_web.pdf

UNODC. (2011b). *World drug report 2011*. Vienna, Austria: United Nations Office on Drugs and Crime. Retrieved from http://www.unodc.org/documents/data-and-analysis/WDR2011/World_Drug_Report_2011_ebook.pdf

UNODC. (2012). *World drug report 2012*. Vienna, Austria: United Nations Office on Drugs and Crime. Retrieved from http://www.unodc.org/documents/data-and-analysis/WDR2012/WDR_2012_web_small.pdf

UNODC. (2014a). *Global synthetic drugs assessment*. Vienna, Austria: United Nations Office on Drugs and Crime. Retrieved from http://www.unodc.org/documents/scientific/2014_Global_Synthetic_Drugs_Assessment_web.pdf

UNODC. (2014b). *World drug report 2014*. Vienna, Austria: United Nations Office on Drugs and Crime. Retrieved from https://www.unodc.org/documents/wdr2014/World_Drug_Report_2014_web.pdf

Uslaner, E. M. (2002, September 20). *The moral foundations of trust*. Paper prepared for the Symposium Trust in the Knowledge Society. University of Jyväskyla, Finland. Retrieved from http://www.bsos.umd.edu/gvpt/uslaner/working.htm

U.S. Comptroller General. (1977). *War on organized crime faltering: Federal strike forces not getting the job done*. Washington, DC: GAO.

U.S. Department of Health and Human Services. (2014). Results from the 2013 National Survey on Drug Use and Health: Summary of Findings. Rockville, MD: Substance Abuse and Mental Health Services Administration. Retrieved from http://www.samhsa.gov/data/sites/default/files/NSDUHresultsPDFWHTML2013/Web/NSDUHresults2013.pdf

U.S. Senate (1983). *Organized crime in America* (Report by the Committee on the Judiciary). Washington, DC: Government Printing Office.

Valencic, B., & Mozetic, P. (2006). Slovenia. In T. Vander Beken (Ed.), *European organised crime scenarios for 2015* (pp. 95–135). Antwerp, Belgium: Maklu.

Van Daele, S., & Vander Beken, T. (2009). Out of step? Mobility of "itinerant crime groups." In P. C. van Duyne, S. Donati, J. Harvey, A. Maljevic, & K. von Lampe (Eds.), *Crime, money and criminal mobility in Europe* (pp. 43–70). Nijmegen, the Netherlands: Wolf Legal Publishers.

Van Daele, S., Vander Beken, T., & Bruinsma, G. J. N. (2012). Does the mobility of foreign offenders fit the general pattern of mobility? *European Journal of Criminology, 9*(3), 290–308.

Van de Bunt, Henk G., & Van der Schoot, C. (2003). *Prevention of organised crime: A situational approach*, The Hague, The Netherlands: WODC.

Van den Eynde, J., & Veno, A. (2007). Depicting outlaw motorcycle club women using anchored and unanchored research methodologies. *The Australian Community Psychologist, 19*(1), 96–111.

Vander Beken, T., Defruytier, M., Bucquoye, A., & Verpoest, K. (2005). Road map for vulnerability studies. In T. Vander Beken (Ed.), *Organised crime and vulnerability of economic sectors: The European transport and music sector* (pp. 7–56). Antwerp, Belgium: Maklu.

Vander Beken, T., & Van Daele, S. (2008). Legitimate businesses and crime vulnerabilities, *International Journal of Social Economics, 35*(10), 739–750.

Van der Hulst, R. C. (2009). Introduction to social network analysis (SNA) as an investigative tool. *Trends in Organized Crime, 12*(2), 101–121.

Van der Schoot, C. R. A. (2006). *Organised crime prevention in the Netherlands: Exposing the effectiveness of preventive measures.* The Hague, the Netherlands: Boom Juridische uitgevers.

Van Dijk, J. (2007). Mafia markers: Assessing organized crime and its impact upon societies. *Trends in Organized Crime, 10*(4), 39–56.

Van Dijk, J. (2011). Highlights of the International Crime Victims Survey. In M. Natarajan (Ed.), *International crime and justice* (pp. 462–470). Cambridge, England: Cambridge University Press.

Van Duyne, P. C. (1993a). Organized crime and business crime-enterprises in the Netherlands. *Crime, Law and Social Change, 19*(2), 103–142.

Van Duyne, P. C. (1993b). Organized crime markets in a turbulent Europe. *European Journal on Criminal Policy and Research, 1*(3), 10–30.

Van Duyne, P. C. (1996). The phantom and threat of organized crime. *Crime, Law and Social Change, 24*(4), 341–377.

Van Duyne, P. C. (1997). Organized crime, corruption and power. *Crime, Law and Social Change, 26*(3), 201–238.

Van Duyne, P. C. (1998). Die Organisation der grenzüberschreitenden Kriminalität in Europa. In G. Wolf (Ed.), *Kriminalität im Grenzgebiet 2: Wissenschaftliche Analysen* (pp. 259–283). Berlin, Germany: Springer.

Van Duyne, P. C. (1999). VAT fraud and the policy of global ignorance. *European Journal of Law Reform, 1*(4), 425–443.

Van Duyne, P. C. (2000). Mobsters are human too: Behavioral science and organized crime investigation. *Crime, Law and Social Change, 34*(4), 369–390.

Van Duyne, P. C. (2001). Will "Caligula" go transparent? Corruption in acts and attitudes. *Forum on Crime and Society, 1*(2), 73–98.

Van Duyne, P. C. (2003). Medieval thinking and organized crime economy. In E. C. Viano, J. Magallanes, & L. Bridel (Eds.), *Transnational organized crime: Myth power and profit* (pp. 23–44). Durham, NC: Carolina Academic Press.

Van Duyne, P. C. (2004). The creation of a threat image: Media policy making and organised crime. In P. C. van Duyne, M. Jager, K. von Lampe, & J. L. Newell (Eds.), *Threats and phantoms of organised crime corruption and terrorism* (pp. 21–50). Nijmegen, the Netherlands: Wolf Legal Publishers.

Van Duyne, P. C. (2006). The organisation of business crime. In P. C. van Duyne, A. Maljevic, M. van Dijck, K. von Lampe, & J. Newell (Eds.), *The organisation of crime for profit* (pp. 177–205). Nijmegen, the Netherlands: Wolf Legal.

Van Duyne, P. C., & Houtzager, M. J. (2005). Criminal sub-contracting in the Netherlands: The Dutch "koppelbaas" as crime entrepreneur. In P. C. van Duyne, K. von Lampe, M. van Dijck, & J. L. Newell (Eds.), *The organised crime economy: Managing crime markets in Europe* (pp. 163–188). Nijmegen, the Netherlands: Wolf Legal Publishers.

Van Duyne, P. C., & Nelemans, M. D. H. (2012). Transnational organized crime: Thinking in and out of Plato's Cave. In F. Allum & S. Gilmour (Eds.), *Routledge handbook of transnational organized crime* (pp. 36–51). London, England: Routledge.

Van Duyne, P. C., Pheijffer, M., Kuijl, H. G., van Dijk, A. T. H. & & Bakker, G. J. C. M. (2001). *Financial investigation of crime: A tool of the integral law enforcement approach*. The Hague, the Netherlands: Koninklijke Vermande.

Van Gestel, B. (2010). Mortgage fraud and facilitating circumstances. In K. Bullock, R. V. Clarke, & N. Tilley (Eds.), *Situational prevention of organised crimes* (pp. 111–129). Cullompton, England: Willan.

Van Koppen, M. V., de Poot, C. J., Kleemans, E. R., & Nieuwbeerta, P. (2009). Criminal trajectories in organized crime. *British Journal of Criminology, 50*(1), 102–123.

Van Mastrigt, S. B., & Farrington, D. P. (2009). Co-offending, age, gender and crime type: Implications for criminal justice policy. *British Journal of Criminology, 49*(4), 552–573.

Van Riper, S. K. (2014). *Tackling Africa's first narco state: Guinea-Bissau in West Africa*. Carlisle, PA: United States Army War College Press.

Van San, M. (2011). The appeal of "dangerous" men: On the role of women in organized crime. *Trends in Organized Crime, 14*(4), 281–297.

Van Wees, H. (1998). The Mafia of early Greece: Violent exploitation in the seventh and sixth centuries B.C. In K. Hopwood (Ed.), *Organised crime in antiquity* (pp. 1–51). London, England: Duckworth.

Varese, F. (2001). *The Russian Mafia: Private protection in a new market economy*. Oxford, England: Oxford University Press.

Varese, F. (2010). What is organized crime? In F. Varese (Ed.), *Organized crime: Critical concepts in criminology* (Vol. I, pp. 1–33). London, England: Routledge.

Varese, F. (2011). *Mafias on the move: How organized crime conquers new territories*. Princeton, NJ: Princeton University Press.

Venkatesh, S. (2008). *Gang leader for a day: A rogue sociologist takes to the streets*. New York, NY: Penguin Press.

Veno, A. (2009). *The brotherhoods: Inside the outlaw motorcycle clubs*. Crows Nest, Australia: Allen & Unwin.

Verhage, A. (2009). Between the hammer and anvil? The anti-money laundering complex and its interactions with the compliance industry. *Crime, Law and Social Change, 52*(1), 9–32.

Vermeulen, G. (Ed.). (2005). EU standards in witness protection and collaboration with justice. Antwerp, the Netherlands: Maklu.

Vesterhav, D. (2010). Measures against money laundering in Sweden: The role of the private sector. In P. C. van Duyne, G. A. Antonopoulos, J. Harvey, A. Maljevic, T. Vander Beken, & K. von Lampe (Eds.), *Cross-border crime inroads on integrity in Europe* (169–188). Nijmegen, the Netherlands: Wolf Legal.

Viuhko, M. (2010). Human trafficking for sexual exploitation and organized procuring in Finland. *European Journal of Criminology, 7*(1), 61–75.

Vizzini, S. (1972). *Vizzini: The secret lives of Americas most successful undercover agent*. New York, NY: Arbor House.

Volkov, V. (2000). Organized violence, market building, and state formation in post-Communist Russia. In A. V. Ledeneva & M. Kurkchiyan (Eds.), *Economic crime in Russia* (pp. 43–61). The Hague, the Netherlands: Kluwer Law International.

Volkov, V. (2002). *Violent entrepreneurs: The use of force in the making of Russian capitalism*. Ithaca, NY: Cornell University Press.

von der Lage, R. (2003). Litauische Kfz-Banden in der Bundesrepublik Deutschland. *Kriminalistik, 57*(6), 357–363.

von Lampe, K. (1999). *Organized crime: Begriff und theorie organisierter Kriminalität in den USA.* Frankfurt am Main, Germany: Lang, Frankfurter kriminalwissenschaftliche Studien 67.

von Lampe, K. (2001a). Not a process of enlightenment: The conceptual history of organized crime in Germany and the United States of America. *Forum on Crime and Society, 1*(2), 99–116.

von Lampe, K. (2001b). Organisierte Kriminalität unter der Lupe: Netzwerke kriminell nutzbarer Kontakte als konzeptueller Zugang zur OK-Problematik, *Kriminalistik, 55*(7), 465–471.

von Lampe, K. (2002a). Organized crime research in perspective. In P. C. van Duyne, K. von Lampe, & N. Passas (Eds.), *Upperworld and underworld in cross-border crime* (pp. 189–198). Nijmegen, the Netherlands: Wolf Legal Publishers.

von Lampe, K. (2002b). The trafficking in untaxed cigarettes in Germany: A case study of the social embeddedness of illegal markets. In P. C. van Duyne, K. von Lampe, & N. Passas (Eds.), *Upperworld and underworld in cross-border crime* (pp. 141–161). Nijmegen, the Netherlands: Wolf Legal Publishers.

von Lampe, K. (2003a). Criminally exploitable ties: A network approach to organized crime. In E. C. Viano, J. Magallanes, & L. Bidel (Eds.), *Transnational organized crime: Myth, power and profit* (pp. 9–22). Durham, NC: Carolina Academic Press.

von Lampe, K. (2003b). Organising the nicotine racket: Patterns of criminal cooperation in the cigarette black market in Germany. In P. C. van Duyne, K. von Lampe, & J. L. Newell (Eds.), *Criminal finances and organising crime in Europe* (pp. 41–64). Nijmegen, the Netherlands: Wolf Legal Publishers.

von Lampe, K. (2004a). Making the second step before the first: Assessing organized crime—the case of Germany. *Crime, Law & Social Change, 42*(4–5), 227–259.

von Lampe, K. (2004b). Measuring organised crime: A critique of current approaches. In P. C. van Duyne, M. Jager, K. von Lampe, & J. L. Newell (Eds.), *Threats and phantoms of organised crime, corruption and terrorism: Critical European perspectives* (pp. 85–116). Nijmegen, the Netherlands: Wolf Legal Publishers.

von Lampe, K. (2005a). Explaining the emergence of the cigarette black market in Germany. In P. C. van Duyne, K. von Lampe, M. van Dijck, & J. L. Newell (Eds.), *The organised crime economy: Managing crime markets in Europe* (pp. 209–229). Nijmegen, the Netherlands: Wolf Legal Publishers.

von Lampe, K. (2005b). Organized crime in Europe. In P. Reichel (Ed.), *Handbook of transnational crime & justice* (pp. 403–424). Thousand Oaks, CA: Sage.

von Lampe, K. (2006a). The cigarette black market in Germany and in the United Kingdom, *Journal of Financial Crime, 13*(2), 235–254.

von Lampe, K. (2006b). Gewaltandrohung und Gewaltanwendung im Kontext organisierter Kriminalität (The use and threat of violence in the context of organized crime). In W. Heitmeyer & M. Schröttle (Eds.), *Gewalt* (pp. 412–421). Bonn, Germany: Bundeszentrale für Politische Bildung.

von Lampe, K. (2006c). The interdisciplinary dimensions of the study of organized crime. *Trends in Organized Crime, 9*(3), 2006, 77–95.

von Lampe, K. (2007). Criminals are not alone: Some observations on the social microcosm of illegal entrepreneurs. In P. C. van Duyne, A. Maljevic, M. van Dijck, K. von Lampe, & J. H. (Eds.), *Crime business and crime money in Europe: The dirty linen of illicit enterprise* (pp. 131–155). Nijmegen, the Netherlands: Wolf Legal Publishers.

von Lampe, K. (2008a). Introduction to the special issue on interviewing "organized criminals," *Trends in Organized Crime, 11*(1), 1–4.

von Lampe, K. (2008b). Organized crime in Europe: Conceptions and realities. *Policing, 2*(1), 7–17.

von Lampe, K. (2008c). Organised crime research in Europe: Development and stagnation. In P. C. van Duyne, J. Harvey, A. Maljevic, M. Scheinost, & K. von Lampe (Eds.), *European crime-markets at cross-roads: Extended and extending criminal Europe* (pp. 17–41). Nijmegen, the Netherlands: Wolf Legal Publishers.

von Lampe, K. (2009a). Human capital and social capital in criminal networks: Introduction to the special issue on the 7th Blankensee Colloquium. *Trends in Organized Crime, 12*(2), 93–100.

von Lampe, K. (2009b). The study of organised crime: An assessment of the state of affairs. In K. Ingvaldsen & V. Lundgren Sørli (Eds.), *Organised crime: Norms, markets, regulation and research* (pp. 165–211). Oslo, Norway: Unipub.

von Lampe, K. (2009c). Transnational organised crime connecting Eastern and Western Europe: Three case studies. In P. C. van Duyne, S. Donati, J. Harvey, A. Maljevic, & K. von Lampe (Eds.), *Crime, money and criminal mobility in Europe* (pp. 19–42). Nijmegen, the Netherlands: Wolf Legal Publishers.

von Lampe, K. (2010). Preventing organized crime: The case of contraband cigarettes. In K. Bullock, R. V. Clarke, & N. Tilley (Eds.), *Situational prevention of organised crimes* (pp. 35–57). Cullompton, England: Willan Publishing.

von Lampe, K. (2011a). The application of the framework of situational crime prevention to "Organized Crime." *Criminology & Criminal Justice, 11*(2), 149–168.

von Lampe, K. (2011b). The illegal cigarette trade. In M. Natarajan (Ed.), *International crime and justice* (pp. 148–154). New York, NJ: Cambridge University Press.

von Lampe, K. (2011c). Re-conceptualizing transnational organized crime: Offenders as problem solvers. *International Journal of Security and Terrorism, 2*(1), 1–23.

von Lampe, K. (2011d). The use of models in the study of organised crime. In G. Antonopoulos, M. Groenhuijsen, J. Harvey, T. Kooijmans, A. Maljevic, & K. von Lampe (Eds.), *Usual and unusual organising criminals in Europe and beyond: Profitable crimes, from underworld to upper world—Liber Amicorum Petrus van Duyne* (pp. 291–306). Apeldoorn, the Netherlands: Maklu.

von Lampe, K. (2012a). The practice of transnational organised crime. In F. Allum & S. Gilmour (Eds.), *Routledge handbook of transnational organised crime* (pp. 186–200). London, England: Routledge.

von Lampe, K. (2012b). Transnational organized crime challenges for future research. *Crime, Law and Social Change, 58*(2), 179–194.

von Lampe, K. (2013). Fears and forecasts: Notions about future trends in the early phases of the German debate on organised crime revisited. In P. C. van Duyne, J. Harvey, G. A. Antonopoulos, K. von Lampe, A. Maljevic, & J. Spencer (Eds.), *Human dimensions in organised crime, money laundering and corruption* (pp. 25–49). Nijmegen, the Netherlands: Wolf Legal Publishers.

von Lampe, K. (2014). Transnational organized crime in Europe. In P. Reichel & J. Albanese (Eds.), *Transnational organized crime: An overview from six continents* (pp. 75–92). Thousand Oaks, CA: Sage.

von Lampe, K. (2015). *Definitions of organized crime.* http://www.organized-crime.de/organizedcrimedefinitions.htm

von Lampe, K., & Per Ole Johansen, P. O. (2004a). Criminal networks and trust: On the importance of the expectation of loyal behavior in criminal relations. In S. Nevala

& K. Aromaa (Eds.), *Organised crime, trafficking, drugs: Selected papers presented at the annual conference of the European Society of Criminology in Helsinki, 2003* (102–113). Helsinki, Finland: HEUNI.

von Lampe, K., & Johansen, P. O. (2004b). Organised crime and trust: On the conceptualization and empirical relevance of trust in the context of criminal networks. *Global Crime, 6*(2), 2004, 159–184.

von Lampe, K., Kurti, M., & Bae, J. (2014). Land of opportunities: The illicit trade in cigarettes in the United States. In P. C. van Duyne, J. Harvey, G. A. Antonopoulos, K. von Lampe, A. Maljevic, & A. Markovska (Eds.), *Corruption, greed and crime money: Sleaze and shady economy in Europe and beyond* (pp. 267–289). Nijmegen, the Netherlands: Wolf Legal Publishers.

von Lampe, K., Kurti, M., Shen, A., & Antonopoulos, G. (2012). The changing role of China in the global illegal cigarette trade. *International Criminal Justice Review, 22*(1), 43–67.

von Lampe, K., van Dijck, M., Hornsby, R., Markina, A., & Verpoest, K. (2006). *Organised crime is. . . . Findings from a cross-national review of literature.* In P.C. van Duyne, A. Maljevic, M. van Dijck, K. von Lampe, & J. Newell (Eds.), *The organisation of crime for profit* (pp. 17–42). Nijmegen, the Netherlands: Wolf Legal Publishers.

Wagley, J. R. (2006). *Transnational organized crime: Principal threats and U.S. responses.* Washington, DC: Congressional Research Service.

Walters, J., Budd, C., Smith, R. G., Choo, K.-K. R., McCusker, R., & Rees, D. (2011). *Anti-money laundering and counter-terrorism financing across the globe: A comparative study of regulatory action.* Canberra: Australian Institute of Criminology. Retrieved from http://www.aic.gov.au/documents/4/E/E/%7B4EE0EECA-9079–45DB-80A1–743CFCE5D58E%7Drpp113.pdf

Wang, P. (2011). The Chinese mafia: private protection in a socialist market economy. *Global Crime, 12*(4), 290–311.

Wang, P. (2013). The rise of the Red Mafia in China: a case study of organised crime and corruption in Chongqing. *Trends in Organized Crime, 16*(1), 49–73.

Wang, P. (2014). Extra-legal protection in China: how quanxi distorts China's legal system and facilitates the rise of unlawful protectors. *British Journal of Criminology, 54*(5), 809–830.

Warchol, G. L., Zupan, L. L. & Clack, W. (2003). Transnational criminality: An analysis of the illegal wildlife market in Southern Africa. *International Criminal Justice Review, 13*(1), 1–27.

Waring, E. J. (1993). *Co-offending in white collar crime: A network approach* (PhD thesis). Yale.

Watt, P., & Zepeda, Roberto (2015). Perspectives of decriminalization and legalization of illicit drugs. In R. Zepeda & J. D. Rosen (Eds.), *Cooperation and drug policies in the Americas: Trends in the twenty-first century* (pp. 223–232). Lanham, MD: Lexington.

Weatherburn, D. (2014). The pros and cons of prohibiting drugs. *Australian and New Zealand Journal of Criminology, 47*(2), 176–189.

Weber, M. (1968). *Economy and society: An outline of interpretive sociology.* New York, NY: Bedminster.

Weenink, A. W., Huisman, S., & Van der Laan, F. J. (2004). *Crime without frontiers: Crime pattern analysis Eastern Europe 2002–2003.* Driebergen Netherlands: Korps Landelijke Politiediensten.

Weenink, A., & Van der Laan, F. (2006). The search for the Russian Mafia: Central and Eastern European criminals in the Netherlands, 1989–2005. *Trends in Organized Crime, 10*(4), 57–76.

Weerman, F. M. (2003). Co-offending as social exchange. Explaining characteristics of co-offending. *British Journal of Criminology, 43*(2), 398–416.

Welch, B. C., & Farrington, D. P. (1999). Value for money? A review of the costs and benefits of situational crime prevention. *British Journal of Criminology, 39*(3), 345–368.

Welch, P. J., & Welch, G. F. (2010). *Economics: Theory and practice* (9th ed.). Hoboken, NJ: Wiley.

White, S., Garton, S., Robertson, S., & White, G. (2010). *Playing the numbers: Gambling in Harlem between the wars.* Cambridge, MA: Harvard University Press.

Whyte, W. F. (1981). *Street corner society: The social structure of an Italian slum.* Chicago, IL: The University of Chicago Press. (Original work published in 1943)

Wilkins, C., & Casswell, S. (2003). Organized crime in cannabis cultivation in New Zealand: An economic analysis. *Contemporary Drug Problems, 30*(4), 757–778.

Williams, C., & Roth, M. P. (2011). The importation and re-exportation of organized crime: Explaining the rise and fall of the Jamaican posses in the United States. *Trends in Organized Crime, 14*(4), 298–313.

Williams, P. (1995). Transnational criminal organizations: strategic alliances. *Washington Quarterly, 18*(1), 57–72.

Williams, P. (1999a). Getting rich and getting even: Transnational threats in the twenty-first century. In S. Einstein & M. Amir (1999), *Organized crime: Uncertainties and dilemmas* (pp. 19–63). Chicago, IL: Office of International Criminal Justice.

Williams, P. (1999b). Trafficking in women and children: A market perspective. In P. Williams (Ed.), *Illegal immigration and commercial sex: The new slave trade* (pp. 145–170). Abingdon, England: Frank Cass.

Williams, P. (2001). Transnational criminal networks. In J. Arquilla & D. F. Ronfeldt (Eds.), *Networks and netwars: The future of terror, crime, and militancy* (pp. 61–97). Santa Monica, CA: RAND.

Williams, P. (2002). Cooperation among criminal organizations. In M. Berdal & M. Serrano (Eds.), *Transnational organized crime and international security: Business as usual* (pp. 67–80). Boulder, CO: Lynne Rienner.

Williams, P. (2009). *Criminals, militias, and insurgents: Organized crime in Iraq.* Carlisle, PA: Strategic Studies Institute.

Williams, P., & Godson, R.(2002). Anticipating organized and transnational crime. *Crime, Law & Social Change, 37*(4), 311–355.

Williamson, O. E. (1975). *Markets and hierarchies: Analysis and antitrust implications.* New York, NY: Free Press.

Williamson, O. E. (1985). *The economic institutions of capitalism.* New York, NY: Free Press.

Williamson, O. E. (1989). Transaction cost economics. In R. Schmalensee & R. D. Willig (Ed.), *Handbook of industrial organization* (Vol. I, pp. 135–182). Amsterdam, the Netherlands: North-Holland.

Windle, J. (2014). A very gradual suppression: A history of Turkish opium controls. 1933–1974. *European Journal of Criminology, 11*(2), 195–212.

Winslow, R. W., & Zhang, S. X. (2008), *Criminology: A global perspective*. Upper Saddle River, NJ: Pearson Prentice Hall.

Wise, E. M. (2000). RICO and its analogues: Some comparative considerations. *Syracuse Journal of International Law and Commerce, 27*(1), 303–324.

Wisotsky, S. (1990). *Beyond the war on drugs: Overcoming a failed public policy*. Buffalo, NY: Prometheus Books.

Wodak, Alex (2014). The abject failure of drug prohibition. *Australian and New Zealand Journal of Criminology, 47*(2), 190–201.

Wolff, K. (Ed.). (1950). The sociology of Georg Simmel (K. Wolff, Trans.). Glencoe, IL: The Free Press.

A woman's dread of the effect of war upon the living. (1915, August 28). *New York Times*.

Wonders, N. A. (2007). Globalization, border reconstruction projects, and transnational crime. *Social Justice, 34*(2), 33–46.

Woodiwiss, M. (1990). *Organized crime USA: Changing perceptions from Prohibition to the present day*. Brighton, England: British Association for American Studies.

Woodiwiss, M. (1993). Crime's global reach. In F. Pearce & M. Woodiwiss (Eds.), *Global crime connections: Dynamics and control* (pp. 11–24). Houndsmills, England: Macmillan.

Woodiwiss, M. (2001). *Organized crime and American power: A history*. Toronto, Ontario, Canada: University of Toronto Press.

Woodiwiss, M. (2003). Transnational organized crime: The strange career of an American concept. In M. E. Beare (Ed.), *Critical reflections on transnational organized crime money laundering and corruption* (pp. 3–34). Toronto, Ontario, Canada: University of Toronto Press.

Woodiwiss, M., & Hobbs, D. (2009). Organized evil and the Atlantic Alliance: Moral panics and the rhetoric of organized crime policing in America and Britain. *British Journal of Criminology, 49*(1), 106–128.

World Health Organization. (2010). *Medicines: Counterfeit medicines* (Fact sheet No. 275). Geneva: WHO.

Wright, A. (2006). *Organised crime*. Cullompton, England: Willan.

Wright, R. T., & Decker, S. H. (1997). Armed robbers in action: Stickups and street culture. Boston, MA: Northeastern University Press.

Wyatt, T. (2009). Exploring the organization of Russia Far East's illegal wildlife trade: Two case studies of the illegal fur and illegal falcon trades. *Global Crime, 10*(1&2), 144–154.

Yordanova, M., & Markov, D. (2012). *Countering organised crime in Bulgaria: Study on the legal framework*. Sofia, Bulgaria: Center for the Study of Democracy (CSD).

Young, M. A. (2013). The exploitation of offshore financial centres: Banking confidentiality and money laundering. *Journal of Money Laundering Control, 16*(3), 198–208.

Yürekli, A., & Sayginsoy, Ö. (2010). Worldwide organized cigarette smuggling: An empirical analysis. *Applied Economics, 42*(5), 545–561.

Zabludoff, S. J. (1997). Colombian narcotics organizations as business enterprises. *Transnational Organized Crime, 3*(2), 20–49.

Zabransky, T. (2007). Methamphetamine in the Czech Republic. *Journal of Drug Issues, 37*(1), 155–180.

Zabyelina, Y. G. (2013). The untouchables: Transnational organized crime behind diplomatic privileges and immunities. *Trends in Organized Crime, 16*(3), 343–357.

Zabyelina, Y. G. (2014). The "fishy" business: A qualitative analysis of the illicit market in black caviar. *Trends in Organized Crime, 17*(3), 181–198.

Zaitch, D. (2002). *Trafficking cocaine: Colombian drug entrepreneurs in the Netherlands,* The Hague, the Netherlands: Kluwer Law International.

Zhang, S., & Chin, K.-L. (2002). *Characteristics of Chinese human smugglers: A cross-national study.* San Diego, CA: San Diego State University.

Zhang, S., & Chin, K.-L. (2004). *Characteristics of Chinese human smugglers.* Washington, DC: National Institute of Justice.

Zhang, S. X., Chin, K.-L., & Miller, J. (2007). Women's participation in Chinese transnational human smuggling: A gendered market perspective. *Criminology, 45*(3), 699–733.

Index